ABOU
CHILE EX

This guide is written in the spirit of exploration and adventure.

In the course of writing it, we've been forced (like many travelers) into consideration of what these terms actually mean in the modern era. Is there really any exploration left to be done by common folk on this shrinking planet? Can adventure be televised or transformed into a sporting event? Might not the term 'adventure travel' itself be an oxymoron? What about 'soft adventure'? What exactly are we talking about here?

Over time, we've come to the conclusion that exploration and adventure are alive and well, though perhaps not as we always conceived of them: these concepts are personal and unique to each of us. As children, we explore our backyards, our neighborhoods. As our zones of comfort and knowledge expand, our explorations, too, lead us further afield. For some, the path of exploration is a physical one leading into the mountains, or out to sea, or to a foreign country. Others find their quotient of novelty and challenge in learning a new language or a new flower, in investigating the dynamics of the changing earth or the mysteries of a past civilization. Wherever your explorations lead you, the spirit is the same.

If your explorations lead you to Chile, you're in good company. In great measure, this guide is inspired by the exploratory spirit of past ages, and by the long and distinguished line of explorers who have stamped their impression on this long, narrow strip of land between the mountains and the sea.

Chile's exploratory history dates from long before recorded history. In a sense, it begins over 12,000 years ago, when the first bands of nomadic hunter-gatherers wandered down out of the Andes into this paradise of rich soils, endless coastlines, and wildly diverse forests. If nothing else, the ongoing study of these 'first Americans' has made it clear that the urge to explore is not exclusively a modern one, and that the term 'discovery' is always relative; it could be argued that mankind's greatest age of exploration came to an end over 8,000 years ago, when a group of Amerindians crossed a slowly disappearing land bridge onto the island of Tierra del Fuego – and thus completed the greatest human migration the world has ever witnessed.

The next paradigm-changing epoch of exploration was a long time coming, and its motivations were at once very ordinary and very peculiar. In a word, Europe's 'discovery' of America had its roots in something very common to our daily lives: spices.

Middle Age Europe was a strange and provincial place – no less strange than the as yet 'undiscovered' continents to the south and the west. With the fall of the Romans, the old knowledge had been lost, and the old roads had fallen into disrepair; the days in which travelers' and geographers' reports were systematically collected were long past. Geographers' image of the world had reverted to the authority of Alexandrian scholar Ptolomeo, who envisioned Africa as a vast *tierra australis*, with the Sahara Desert extending infinitely to the south. Of the ocean west, who could say?

The route linking Europe with India and the Spice Islands was a harrowing and costly one. For a sack of spice to reach the courts of medieval Europe, it had to be shipped across the Indian Ocean to Egypt or Syria, then packed across the desert by the camels of Arabia, and shipped again to Venice. From here, the precious cargo – its price now grossly inflated by the taxes levied along the route – could finally be lugged over

HUASO, WATERCOLOR BY A. GIAST

the mountains and into the eager hands of kings and nobles. Spices became at once so highly coveted and so absurdly expensive that a man's worth was commonly measured in sacks of pepper.

History's stage was set for the entrance of a visionary, and that visionary turned out to be Portuguese prince Dom Enrique, better known as Henry the Navigator. For centuries, Portugal had considered itself doomed by geography, cut off from direct access to the Mediterranean and the vast riches of the Orient. Yet in the course of a lifetime, Henry transformed Portugal into Europe's great naval power. His ships ranged ever further south, returning with new maps and transforming Ptolomeo's *tierra australis* into a real geography, with real names – Guinea, Cape Branco, Cape Verde – and real riches. Such was their dominion over the southern oceans that the Pope, in 1476, granted Portugal dominion over all lands south of the Canary Islands, with the stipulation that they see to the evangelization of the 'heathens' living there. By 1486,

THE FIRST VOYAGE AROUND THE GLOBE, BY PIGAFETTA

Portuguese mariner Bartolome Diáz had already rounded the Cape of Good Hope, paving the way for Vasco de Gama's first historic voyage around the Cape to India, in 1498.

Meanwhile, another visionary had entered the scene, this one an Italian from Genova. Improbable as it may have seemed, Columbus' proposal to sail west to the Indies was a justifiable risk; the Spanish were missing out of the Portuguese bounty, and even if only one out of four ships returned, you could still turn a profit in the spice game.

The gamble paid off, changing the course of history forever. In the wake of Co-

lumbus' 'discovery,' Spain petitioned the Church for ownership of the lands to the west, and after negotiations with the Portuguese, the 1494 treaty of Tordesillas granted the Castillians dominion over all the lands west of a line drawn '300 leagues west of the Cape Green islands.' In other words, everything west of Brazil was theirs.

Meanwhile, a general frenzy had seized Europe, with expeditions shipping out in all directions. In this epoch we see Pinzon and Cabral sailing along the Brazilian coast, staring into the Amazon; we see Cabot in Labrador, Américo Vespucio off Argentina, Ponce de Lyon in Florida, Balboa gazing upon the Pacific from the Darien Gap. We see the rapid evolution of maps, which were jealously guarded, feverishly updated, elegantly illustrated and, whenever possible, copied or stolen. Finally, we see a unique class of scholars known as *cronistas* accompanying each journey, immortalizing the deeds of the great navigators and fascinating their European audiences with tales of far-off lands, wild beasts and pagan cultures.

Imagine how Europe's image of the world changed from one trip to the next. In 1520, Ferdinand Magellan discovered the entrance to the tempestuous Strait that now bears his name, and sailed triumphantly into the Pacific Ocean. Continuing on to the west, his expedition was the first to circumnavigate the world. *Around the globe* – finally it could be said with certainty!

As the blank spaces on the map were slowly filled in, the land called Chile began to acquire a certain status, somewhere between myth and reality: a land of fierce and noble natives, of unequalled fertility side by side with desolate wastelands, a land of extremity and wilderness. Describing the land and its creatures was the task of a new class of explorers, bent not on conquest and territory, but on knowledge.

JUAN IGNACIO MOLINA

Chile's unusual flora and fauna was first described by native-born naturalist Juan Ignacio Molina, who published his Compendium of the Geographic, Natural, and Civil History of the Kingdom of Chile in 1776 in Bologne. Molina's work piqued the interest of European colleagues such as German naturalist Alexander Humboldt, who visited Chile during a five-year voyage throughout South America, collecting specimens and making careful notes for the 30 volumes of his Travels to the (Equinoxiales) Regions of the New World, published in Paris from 1807-1834.

CHARLES DARWIN

On the heels of these pioneers came other naturalists and scientists from around the world, including Charles Darwin, who visited during his four-year stint as resident naturalist aboard the *HMS Beagle*. However, while we tend to envision a young Darwin puzzling over his theories in long solitary hours, the truth is that 19th century Chile was a veritable academy for naturalists. Darwin would have found ample partners for conversation and speculation – many of these with far greater experience in the local material than himself.

'Chile fairly swarms with collectors; there are more naturalists in the country, than Carpenters or Shoemakers or any other honest trade.'

– Charles Darwin, in a letter to Cambridge professor John Stevens Henslow.

For while Darwin may be the most famous and emblematic of the explorers to have passed through Chile, his achievements here pale besides those of a select few who returned again and again, drawn to the wild and unknown fringes of their respective fields. For French illustrator and naturalist Claudio Gay, Antarctic explorer Ernest Shackleton, archaeologists Junius Bird and Thor Heyerdahl, anthropologists such as Martín Gusinde and great mountaineers such as Eric Shipton and Alberto de Agostini, this part of the world has had a singularly irresistible appeal – and one which they have repaid in kind, leaving us all the richer for their passing.

We believe that the exploratory spirit that motivated these legendary individuals is the same as that which motivates us today as travelers, and we recognize that no guidebook can replace the open, inquisitive mind that is the hallmark of the engaged traveler. With this in mind, we envision the present work as a point of departure, a framework to guide your own personal exploration. We invite you to lose yourself in your travels, to seek the beautiful and the unknown, and to share this perspective with the travelers and locals you meet along the way.

With any luck, we'll see you out there. As we say in Chile, *que te vaya bien*.

TRAVEL GUIDE
CHILE®
experience

EDITOR
©Turismo y Comunicaciones S.A.,
TURISCOM
Phone: 56-2-3658800
Fax: 56-2-3658805
www.turistel.cl
info@turistel.cl

LEGAL REPRESENTATIVE
Rubén Caro

CHIEF & EDITORIAL MANAGER
Tomás Sánchez

AUTHOR
Josh Howell

COPY EDITOR
Greg Toledo

SENIOR DESIGNER
Miguel Angel González

LAYOUT
Patricia Figueroa

DIGITAL CARTOGRAPHY
Edmundo Ross

ILUSTRATIONS
Ana García

ADVERTISING
Ernesto Amaya
Claudia Avendaño
Sandra Pizarro

PRE-PRESS
Tecnología Uno
Megagráfica

PRINTED BY
Quebecor World S.A.
Santiago, Chile

ISBN 956-7264-79-1
21 August 2001

MAPAS Y CARTAS GEOGRAFICAS
«Autorizada su circulación en cuanto a los límites y fronteras actuales de Chile, por Resolución N° 270 del 31 de Julio de 2001 de la Dirección Nacional de Fronteras y Límites del Estado».
La edición y circulación de mapas, cartas geográficas u otros impresos y documentos que se refieran o relacionen con los límites y fronteras de Chile no comprometen, en modo alguno, al Estado de Chile, de acuerdo con el Art. 2° letra g del DFL N° 83 de 1979, del Ministerio de Relaciones Exteriores.

MAPS AND CARTOGRAPHIC CHARTS WHOSE
The publication and distribution of maps, geographical charts or other printed matter and documents that refer to or have to do with Chile's borders and frontiers, under no circumstances, obligate the Chilean State.

Sponsored by:

 CPT
Chilean Tourism
Promotion Corporation

 SERNATUR
National Tourism
Board

 PROCHILE

 CONAF
Corporación
Nacional Forestal

About the Author

Josh Howell grew up in Maine, was educated in Colorado, and was first drawn to the South American continent on a 1996 kayaking trip. Though he's been a writer, photographer, and outdoor junkie for years, it wasn't until he landed in Chile that the creative and exploratory urge really kicked into high gear, and by all accounts it appears to have ruined him. Four years in the making, Chile Experience is his first book. You can contact Josh directly at jhowell@andeantravel.com.

Acknowledgements

This guide is first and foremost a collaborative effort, and mentioning all those who have contributed would be frankly impossible. So in addition to the friends, colleagues, and organizations appearing below, we'd like to extend our gratitude to all those who have helped out in one way or another, knowingly or otherwise. All photos have been reproduced with the consent of the copyright holder.

ORGANIZATIONS

Special thanks to Conaf, Sernatur, the Corporación de Promoción Turística, CATA, Fundación Claudio Gay, Dirección de Fronteras y Límites, Colegio de Ecólogos Paisajistas, Unión de Ornitólogos de Chile.

INDIVIDUALS

Special thanks to Lila Musser, Alan Coar, Marta Barra, Britt and Graham Lewis, Carlos Whiting, Arnt Stormyhr and Andrea Torres, Yerko Ivelic, Cristian 'Tordillo' Duran, Paola Minetto, Rick Bravo, Pamela Yolito, Bárbara Knapton, Jorge Sánchez Reyes, Bill and Sally Howell, Augusto Dominguez, Mario Monteverde, Juan Lecaros and Fernanda Chacón.

FIELD GUIDES

Nature

Special thanks to Adrianna Hoffmann and the Fundación Claudio Gay for the use of drawings of Chilean flora.
Special thanks to Eduardo Pavez and Claudio Bedoya of BioAmerica for general information on flora and fauna, and to Jorge Mella for information on Chilean reptiles.

Culture

Special thanks to Miguel Cervantes from the Museo de Atacama, Café Etniko in San Pedro de Atacama, and Elizabeth Briones of AndeanHands.com.

ACTIVE AND ADVENTURE TRAVEL CONSULTANTS

Overland

Special thanks to Patricio Ríos of Track Aventura

Mountain Biking

Special thanks to Pablo Sepúlveda of Pared Sur Expediciones, Javier Valdivia C. of Pangea Expediciones and Travelart.

Mountaineering

Special thanks to Carlos Whiting, Javier Pinto Duk, Hans Gapp of Trawen Outdoor Center, and the late Sergio Zárate.

Rock and Ice Climbing

Special thanks to www.escalando.cl and Juan Pablo Vásquez of Suramérica Expediciones.

Canyoning

Special thanks to Bruno Veerhoven and Barbara Winter.

Skiing

Special thanks to the Portillo, La Parva, Valle Nevado, Lagunillas, Chapa Verde, Villarrica-Pucón, and Antillanca ski resorts.

Paragliding

Special thanks to Philip Maltry of Altazor Skysports and Jens Tannen of Sky Adventure.

Sea Kayaking

Special thanks to Francisco Valle of Altué Expediciones.

Whitewater Rafting and Kayaking

Special thanks to Josh Lowry, Robby Dastin, Jonathan Leidich of Patagonia Adventure Expeditions, Mauricio Gonzalez, Marco Zúñiga, and the late John Foss. Photo: Xavier the Belgian; Colin the Scot.

Surfing

Special thanks to Carlos Lara and Revista Marejada.

Windsurfing

Special thanks to Pablo Valenzuela of Windsurfing Chile

Scuba Diving and Snorkeling

Special thanks to Daniel Súnico, Pedro Niada of Endémica Expediciones, and Michel Garcia of Centro de Buceo ORCA.

Fishing

Special thanks to Jim Repine of Futaleufú Lodge, Pablo Negri of Andean Rivers and Trails, Adrian Dufflocq of Cumilahue Lodge, and Hernán Barrientos of Gray Fly Fishing.

Photography Credits

 When more than one photograph appears on page, credits are listed from left to right, top to bottom, as shown in the drawing.

Across Chile, photos pg: 150a-247c-232b-233b.
Aerotec, photos pg: 91b,c,d.
Alejandro Moreno, photos pg: 358a-365b.
Alerce Mountain Lodge, photo pg: 182d.
Alex Huber, photo pg: 206b.
Alfredo Escobar, www.a_escobar.com, photos pg: 108a,b-110.
Altazor, Philip Maltry. Cover, small photo b. Photos pg: 93-288.
Angel Cabeza, photos pg: 50c-200b-201b-207c-559.
Archivo del Consejo de Monumentos Nacionales, photos pg: 234a-235a-289.
Austral Adventures, photo pg: 96a.
Bioamérica, photo pg: 159b.
Bruce Ashley, photo pg: 125.
Cámara de Turismo de Isla de Pascua, photos pg: 75c-117b-199b-252c,d-255c-582b-583b,c-585-587a.
Camel Trophy, photos pg: 498a,d.
Carlos Whiting. Cover, large bottom photo. Photos pg: 91a-260g-261d-331.
Carolina Fritz, photos pg: 92a,b-369.
Cliff Buckton, photos pg: 174g-190a-191c.
Colin the Scot, photo pg: 107b.
Corporación Tierras Desconocidas, photos pg: 268c.
Club Deportivo Colo Colo, photo pg: 257b,c.
Corporación Nacional Forestal (CONAF). Back cover, small photos d and_e. Photos pg: 49a-134b-152a-157f-158e-161b-173g-174a,f-176a-180d,g,h-181c,d- 183e-190d,e-191a,d-193a-206a-228b-278-282-283-427-570-587b-594.
Cruce de Lagos, photo pg: 14.
Cruceros Australis, photos pg: 24b-97a,b,c.
Desert Adventure , photos pg: 155-164a.
Edmundo Ross, photos pg: 19-25-24e-27-216a-355-357a,d-364b-253b.
Eduardo Morales, photo pg: 273b.
Eduardo Pavez, photo pg: 174d.
Emma Elgueta, photos pg: 192c-193b.
Enrique Couve, photos pg: 187a,d-188a.
Escalando.cl, photo pg: 85a.
Ernesto Amaya, photos pg: 138-241.

European Southern Observatory Education and Public Relations Department (ESO ERP), photos pg: 169a,b-170-171.
Explora, photo pg: 118.
Federación del Rodeo Chileno, photos pg: 254b-256a.
Fernándo Gómez, photos pg: 357b-358c-363a-364a.
Felipe Riquelme, Cover, small photo a._Photos pg: 54-55a,b-66-222-260b-261a-263a-498e-522.
Fundación Pablo Neruda, photo pg: 359a.
Gabriel Pérez, photos pg: 192a,b-193f-576-578a.
Geoinformación, photos pg: 150c-313.
Hacienda Los Lingues, photos pg: 215a,b.
Harald Kockch, photos pg: 157b-160e-161a-166a-173c-185d-330b.
Hilda López, photo pg: 204a.
Hotel Petrohué, photo pg: 50a.
Hotelsa. Cover, small photo e. Photos pg: 122-123-184-185a-511-541.
Hotel Portillo, photo pg: 383.
Ilustre Municipalidad de Andacollo, photo pg: 226c.
Instituto Antártico Chileno, photos pg: 50d-194b-195a,b,f-602a.
Ivan Irsara, photos pg: 39a,b,c,d,e,f-40-78a,c-79-80b-84a-8b,c.
Jorge Mella, photos pg: 152-159c,d,f-161d-176b,c,d,e,g,i.
Jorge Sánchez R. Back cover, small photo_a. Photos pg: 136c-156c-157c-173d,e-207a,b-217b-218b-219a-228e-253e-255d-264b,d-295-311-315-327-334a-392-393-395b-409-411-419-473-479-491-551-562.
José Soffia, photo pg: 50b-562.
Josh Howell. Cover, small photos d y f._Photos pg: 28c49b-52-53a-56-64-68a,b-69-70-74b-76-86-88a,d-94b-96b-98-100-101-102-103-104a,b-106a,b-120-121a-124- 154-160a,c-162b-163b-164c-165e-166f,g-172a-173b-174e-178b-179-181h-182d-187b-189e-204b-211a-239b-252a-261b- 334b-359b-499c-512.
Juan Pablo Mena, photos pg: 73-273c-362e.
Kenneth Lein, Southern Cross Adventure, photo pg: 80a.
Lincoyán Parada, photo pg: 199c.
Manuel Gedda, photos pg: 156b-157a,e-196f-208a-264c.
Mario Monteverde, photos pg: 32-216c-362c.
Miguel A. González, photos pg: 18-29c-30c-31b,c-33-42a,b-77-136a,b-147a,c-149c-167-178a-196c-198a-214-216b-225b,c,d,e,f-227a,c-232c-233a,c-234c-235c-238a,e-239b-242a,b- 244c,d-246a,b,c,d-251a,c-252b-253a,b-257d-263c-273a-333-340- 341a,b,c- 435- 438-500-505-582a.

6

Ilustrations

Contribute to the next

Your opinion is important to us, and important to your fellow travelers. Please help us improve the next edition of Chile Experience, by submitting your comments, corrections, criticisms, updates, recommendations, and any other information you might think relevant. Send emails to **chileexperience@turistel.cl**, and letters to Chile Experience Editor, Turiscom S.A., Av. Santa Maria 0120, Providencia, Santiago de Chile. Remember to include your name, address and country of residence, date and area of your visit, and where you got your copy of Chile Experience. Thanks!

HOW TO USE THIS GUIDE

This guidebook is designed to be of use to travelers with diverse interests, from the initial stages of trip planning through journey's end. Spending a bit of time acquainting yourself with the structure of the guide will allow you to take fuller advantage of the information contained within.

Generally speaking, the guide may be divided into four main sections: introductory chapters (including practical and background information), activity chapters, field guides to nature and culture, and regional chapters with specific information on cities, national parks, excursions and other local details. Services (including a listing of tour operators) are located at the back of the guide together with a road atlas.

PRACTICAL INFORMATION

Illustrated reference with essential information on documentation, currency, transportation, safety and health, lodging, food and drink, and communication. Includes a select glossary, specific information on equipment and preparation for active and wilderness travel, and a bibliography for further research.

ACTIVE AND ADVENTURE TRAVEL

Here you'll find information on fourteen separate sporting and active travel options, intended for both independent travelers and those hoping to book an organized tour. In most cases, information is segmented by region, and accompanied by a georeferenced list of excursions described in regional chapters.

BACKGROUND INFORMATION

Contains contextual information on the land and its people, focusing on geology and topography, climate, environment, history and present economy. Preceding each regional chapter you'll find similar texts providing more specific contextual information in a highly readable illustrated format

FIELD GUIDES

The Field Guides section is in reality part encyclopedia and part field guide. In the chapter entitled 'Natural Attractions,' you'll find detailed information on ten distinct Chilean ecosystems, with descriptions, drawing and photos of especially noteworthy flora and

Also located in the services section, this list provides contact Chilean tour operators and outfitters, most with a specific focus on adventure or special interest travel. Companies are listed alphabetically and assigned a number which is used throughout the guide to indicate the excursions and services offered by each.

ROAD ATLAS

22 pages of road maps, organized from north to

REGIONAL CHAPTERS

This is the core of the guide. Here you'll find detailed information on cities, national parks and other highlights, specific descriptions of selected excursions, and dozens of maps and photos. Information is organized as follows:

1) Major city

2) Major geographic highlight or area

3) Minor geographic highlight

4) Services / practical information

5) Numbers refer to hotels and restaurants in city maps

6) Local telephone area code

7) Activity title and icon These are also listed in Activities sections, and may appear in local relief maps. Several similar excursions may be listed together for compara tive purposes

8) Activity symbols (details are given in Activities sections)

9) Activity abreviaturas
 h = hour / hours
 d = day / days
 w = week / weeks
 rt = round trip
 ow = one way
 NA = not available

10) Activity text
 Operators: 33 - 151 (Numbers refer to operator list).

More detailed information appears in preceding text.

More detailed information appears in following text.

More detailed information in Field Guides: Natural Attractions.

More detailed information in Field Guides: Cultural Attractions.

More detailed information in Active and Adventure Travel section.

More detailed information in Practical Information.

---

① Curicó   Pop. 77,733 (⌚ city code 75)

al Valley, Curicó is a service cen-
d vineyards, and doesn't hold a
sightseeing. One of the town's
ra de Armas, southeast of
ing of legendary Mapuche toqui
t is Cerro Carlos Condell, with a
ews ⑤ nsor the city. Each year the
during the third week in March.

2 Residencial Rahue **$**, Peña 410.
  ☎ 312194.
3 Hotel Turismo **$$**, Carmen 727.
  ☎ 310823.
More info at www.turistel.cl

BUS STATION AND/OR OFFICES
Most companies at Av. Camilo
Henríquez and Membrillar. Buses Lit
and Tur-Bus are southeast of
downtown, near the intersection of
Manso de Velasco and the Panamerican.
or buses to Lago Vichuquén, Molina
and Radal / Siete Tazas, the Terminal de
buses Rurales is at the west end of Prat.

RAIN STATION
stación de Ferrocarriles is at the west
nd of Prat. ☎ 310028.

② round Curicó

aro are
Miguel
on the
while
an on
ercity

**Reserva Nacional
Radal Siete Tazas**
The entrance to the park at Radal is
50km SE of Curicó, via the town of Molina.
See 🛈 for details.

**Lago Vichuquén and Reserva
Nacional Laguna Torca**
Vichuquén is 110km from Curicó, trans-
port by regular bus. See 🛈.

east
t and
nd a
oth-
bus.

Río Lontué

🕐**4h**
The Lontué is a favorite with
boaters from Santiago, as this is the first clearwater
river on the way south – an indication of the lower
elevations (and fewer g...) of this section of
the Andes. In order to ... the put-in, you must
ask permission from the ...os on either side of
the valley. Beginning at the confluence of the Río
de los Palos and the Río Colorado, starts as a
beautiful, continuous Class III-IV that soon mellows
to Class II-III.
  Operators: 214

412

607

www.elcoloradoski.cl

25128, 325211

ir and Yagán (I)
os Álamos

ampuchilena.com

33587

**SAN CARLOS
DE BARILOCHE**

1 2339768

vutue.com

a.co.cl

colorado@intemet.cl

FROM LLANQUIHUE TO CHAITÉN

---

fauna. 'Cultural Attractions' highlights some of Chile's most unusual or otherwise outstanding cultural phenomenon and artifacts. This section is organized by topic rather than geographically, allowing users to zero in specific interests such as archaeology or architecture.

TABLE OF CONTENTS

PRACTICAL
INFORMATION

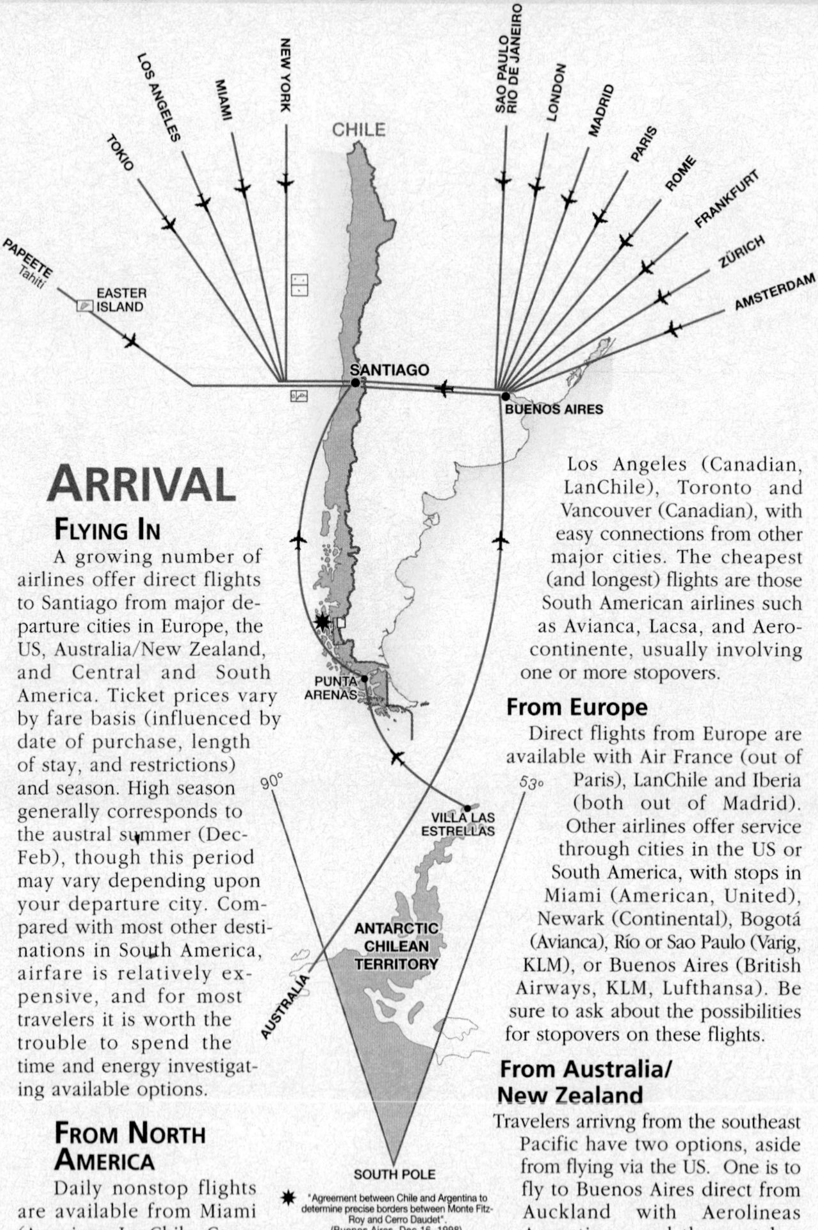

LOS ANGELES

MIAMI

NEW YORK

TOKIO

SAO PAULO
RIO DE JANEIRO

LONDON

MADRID

PARIS

ROME

FRANKFURT

ZÜRICH

AMSTERDAM

CHILE

PAPEETE
Tahiti

EASTER
ISLAND

SANTIAGO

BUENOS AIRES

PUNTA
ARENAS

90°

53°

VILLA LAS
ESTRELLAS

ANTARCTIC
CHILEAN
TERRITORY

AUSTRALIA

SOUTH POLE

*Agreement between Chile and Argentina to
determine precise borders between Monte Fitz-
Roy and Cerro Daudet".
(Buenos Aires, Dec 16, 1998).*

ARRIVAL

FLYING IN

A growing number of airlines offer direct flights to Santiago from major departure cities in Europe, the US, Australia/New Zealand, and Central and South America. Ticket prices vary by fare basis (influenced by date of purchase, length of stay, and restrictions) and season. High season generally corresponds to the austral summer (Dec-Feb), though this period may vary depending upon your departure city. Compared with most other destinations in South America, airfare is relatively expensive, and for most travelers it is worth the trouble to spend the time and energy investigating available options.

FROM NORTH AMERICA

Daily nonstop flights are available from Miami (American, LanChile, Canadian, United), New York (Continental), and Dallas/Fort Worth (American). There are also daily flights with brief stopovers from Los Angeles (Canadian, LanChile), Toronto and Vancouver (Canadian), with easy connections from other major cities. The cheapest (and longest) flights are those South American airlines such as Avianca, Lacsa, and Aerocontinente, usually involving one or more stopovers.

From Europe

Direct flights from Europe are available with Air France (out of Paris), LanChile and Iberia (both out of Madrid). Other airlines offer service through cities in the US or South America, with stops in Miami (American, United), Newark (Continental), Bogotá (Avianca), Río or Sao Paulo (Varig), or Buenos Aires (British Airways, KLM, Lufthansa). Be sure to ask about the possibilities for stopovers on these flights.

From Australia/ New Zealand

Travelers arriving from the southeast Pacific have two options, aside from flying via the US. One is to fly to Buenos Aires direct from Auckland with Aerolineas Argentinas, and then catch a short flight across the Andes to Chile. The other is to fly to Tahiti and connect with a LanChile flight to Santiago.

INTERNATIONAL PASSES

Discount Tickets

Discounted tickets come in many different forms, each with its own particular inconveniences. The cheapest and most restrictive option is to fly as a courier, which basically means filling a seat booked by an international courier company. Luggage restrictions make this an unattractive to all but the most spartan and flexible of travelers.

Student tickets are an excellent option for those planning to stay longer than one month. Students and those 25 years or younger who register with the ISIC (see 🔲) are eligible for student fares on 3-month, 5-month, and year-long return tickets. Savings are substantial, and these tickets are often free of restrictions, allowing date changes for no fee.

The best way to be sure that you're getting the best available price is to browse one of the many websites dedicated to discount travel. Be aware, however, that the cheapest tickets are almost always loaded down with restrictions and usually involve several stops, making a long trip even longer.

Arrival from Neighboring Countries

By Air

In the north, frequent flights link La Paz to Arica or Iquique. In the Lake Region, flights leave Neuquén and Bariloche (Arg.) bound for Concepción, Temuco, or Puerto Montt. In Patagonia, you can fly from Ushuaia or Puerto Stanley (Falkland Islands) to Punta Arenas.

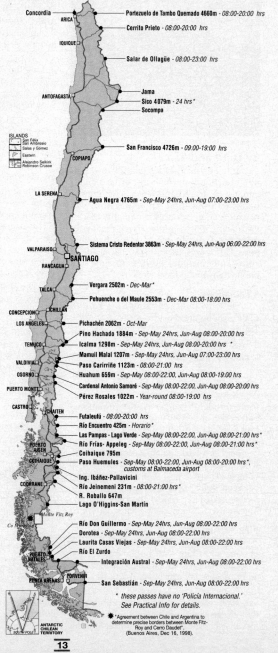

Portezuelo de Tambo Quemado 4660m - *08:00-20:00 hrs*
Cerrito Prieto - *08:00-20:00 hrs*
Salar de Ollagüe - *08:00-23:00 hrs*
Jama
Sico 4079m - *24 hrs**
Socompa
San Francisco 4726m - *09:00-19:00 hrs*
Agua Negra 4765m - *Sep-May 24hrs, Jun-Aug 07:00-23:00 hrs*
Sistema Cristo Redentor 3863m - *Sep-May 24hrs, Jun-Aug 06:00-22:00 hrs*
Vergara 2502m - *Dec-Mar**
Pehuenche o del Maule 2553m - *Dec-Mar 08:00-18:00 hrs*
Pichachén 2062m - *Oct-Mar*
Pino Hachado 1884m - *Sep-May 24hrs, Jun-Aug 08:00-20:00 hrs*
Icalma 1298m - *Sep-May 24hrs, Jun-Aug 08:00-20:00 hrs **
Mamuil Malal 1207m - *Sep-May 24hrs, Jun-Aug 07:00-23:00 hrs*
Paso Carirriñe 1123m - *08:00-21:00 hrs*
Huahum 659m - *Sep-May 08:00-22:00, Jun-Aug 08:00-19:00 hrs*
Cardenal Antonio Samoré - *Sep-May 08:00-22:00, Jun-Aug 08:00-20:00 hrs*
Pérez Rosales 1022m - *Year-round 08:00-19:00 hrs*
Futaleufú - *08:00-20:00 hrs*
Río Encuentro 425m - *Horario**
Las Pampas - Lago Verde - *Sep-May 08:00-22:00, Jun-Aug 08:00-21:00 hrs**
Río Frías- Appeleg - *Sep-May 08:00-22:00, Jun-Aug 08:00-21:00 hrs**
Coihaique 795m
Paso Huemules - *Sep-May 08:00-22:00, Jun-Aug 08:00-20:00 hrs*, customs at Balmaceda airport*
Ing. Ibáñez-Pallavicini
Río Jeinemeni 231m - *08:00-21:00 hrs**
R. Roballo 647m
Lago O'Higgins-San Martín
Río Don Guillermo - *Sep-May 24hrs, Jun-Aug 08:00-22:00 hrs*
Dorotea - *Sep-May 24hrs, Jun-Aug 08:00-22:00 hrs*
Laurita Casas Viejas - *Sep-May 08:00-22:00, Jun-Aug 08:00-22:00 hrs*
Río El Zurdo
Integración Austral - *Sep-May 24hrs, Jun-Aug 08:00-22:00 hrs*
San Sebastián - *Sep-May 24hrs, Jun-Aug 08:00-22:00 hrs*

* these passes have no 'Policía Internacional.' See Practical Info for details.

✱ **Agreement between Chile and Argentina to determine precise borders between Monte Fitz-Roy and Cerro Daudet" (Buenos Aires, Dec 16, 1998).*

CRUCE DE LAGOS, LAGO TODOS LOS SANTOS

By Land and Sea

Although many roads link Chile with its neighboring countries, not all are maintained year-round and fewer have regular public transportation. Those traveling with private vehicles – and especially 4WD – have many more options, though many remote crossings do not have resident customs staff (see Customs, ⬇). The diagram above only includes border crossing with public transportation services.

• FROM PERU

The only direct crossing from Perú to Chile is along the coast from Tacna to Arica. Trains, buses, and taxi *colectivos* (see ⬇) are all abundantly available.

• FROM BOLIVIA

There are two bus routes between La Paz and Arica: a paved highway through Lauca National Park and a longer, slower route through Visviri, near the tri-national border of Chile, Perú, and Bolivia. Passenger train service between La Paz and Arica is no longer available.

Further south, a painfully slow but worthwhile train connects Uyuni (Bolivia) with Calama. There is no other public transport between Bolivia and Chile, although highly recommended jeep trips connect San Pedro de Atacama with Uyuni via the Salar de Uyuni.

• FROM ARGENTINA

The northernmost crossing between Argentina and Chile with public transport is Paso Libertadores, which connects Mendoza and Santiago. Regular buses run year-round.

Further south, it is possible to cross from San Rafael to Talca via Paso Pehuenche, though bus service is limited to the summer months. The same is true of buses linking Zapala and Temuco via Paso Pino Hachado, as well as those linking San Martín de los Andes and Pucón via Paso Mamuil Malal, though these last will likely increase in the coming years.

At present, the only paved highway linking the Chilean and Argentine lake districts is that linking San Carlos de Bariloche with Osorno via Paso Cardenal Antonio Samoré. Regular buses run year-round.

One of the most spectacular ways to cross into Chile is via the Cruce de Lagos, a series of buses and ferries connecting Bariloche with Puerto Varas and Puerto Montt. Transportation services decline during the winter months.

Though you can easily hitch from Esquel into Futaleufú, the northernmost crossing in Patagonia with public transport is that connecting Comodoro Rivadavia (on Argentina's Atlantic coast) with the city of Coihaique. It is also possible to cross by bus from Perito Moreno to Chile Chico via Paso Jeinimeni.

The Magallanes Region in Southern Patagonia is more closely integrated with Argentina than any other region in the country. Frequent buses connect Puerto Natales with El Turbio, with connections to Calafate and Río Gallegos. Río Gallegos also connects with Punta Arenas via Paso Integración Austral.

In Tierra del Fuego, the Chilean Port of Porvenir has bi-weekly bus service to Río Grande and Ushuaia, Argentina. Ferries occasionally operate between Ushuaia and Puerto Williams, Chile's southernmost town, on Isla Navarino. Puerto Williams is more easily reached directly from Punta Arenas.

TRAVEL INSURANCE

Some homeowner's insurance, credit cards, and health insurance policies actually offer some measure of travel insurance, so be sure to verify this before spending a lot of money on a travel insurance policy. If you do wind up taking out travel insurance, ask carefully about what is covered, and in what situations. In any case you'll have to notify local police in case of theft or loss in order to be covered at all. Most companies will only reimburse you upon your return to your home country. A good bet for travel insurance is the Student Travel Association, ⬇.

DOCUMENTATION AND OTHER RED TAPE

Entry Requirements

Passports are required of all foreign visitors to Chile, except those from Argentina, Brazil, Colombia, Paraguay, and Uruguay, who only need present a national identity card. Visas are required only for citizens of New Zealand, Guyana, Kuwait, Haiti, African countries, Cuba and some East European countries. An onward ticket and proof of sufficient funds are technically required, though these details are seldom asked for.

Upon arrival, visitors' passports will be stamped and they will be issued a tourist card, valid for 90 days. This card will be asked for upon departure, so it is important that it not be lost. Upon arrival, a one-time 'reciprocity fee' is charged to citizens of the US (US$45), Canada (US$50) and Australia (US$20).

Visitors wishing to stay longer than the allotted 90 days have two options. One is to solicit a 90-day extension, which costs US$100 and is available from the Extranjería in Santiago (corner of Teatinos and Balmaceda, arrive early) and at the *Intendencia* in most major cities. The other option is simply to cross the border into a neighboring country and return again, at which point you will be issued a new tourist card and another 90 days. Some travelers have repeated this process for years on end, though it should be noted that officials at Paso Libertadores are liable to suspect foreigners of working illegally.

Technically, you are not allowed to work on a standard tourist visa. See the Working section below for details.

Foreign Embassies in Santiago

Argentina
Miraflores 285, ☎ 6331076

Australia
Av. Gertrudis Echeñique 429, ☎ 2885065

Austria
Barros Errázuriz 1968, 3rd floor, ☎ 2334774

Belgium
Av. Providencia 2653, 11th floor, ☎ 2321071

Brasil
Alonso Ovalle 1665, ☎ 6982486

Britain
Av. El Bosque Norte 0125, 3rd floor, ☎ 2313737

Canada
Nueva Tajamar 481 Torre Norte 12th floor, ☎ 3629660

Columbia
Av. Presidente Errázuriz 3843, ☎ 2061999

Denmark
Jacques Cazotte 5531, ☎ 2185949

Ecuador
Av. Providencia 1979, 5th floor, ☎ 2315073

France
Av. Condell 65, ☎ 2251030

Germany
Augustinas 785, 8th floor, ☎ 6335785

Holland
Las Violetas 2368, ☎ 2336825

Israel
San Sebastián 2812, 5th floor, ☎ 2461570

Japan
Av. Ricardo Lyon 520, 1st floor, ☎ 2321807

Mexico
Félix de Amesti 128, ☎ 2066133

New Zealand
Av. Isidora Goyenechea 3516, ☎ 2314204

Norway
San Sebastián 2839 of. 509, ☎ 2342888

Paraguay
Huérfanos 886, of. 514, ☎ 6394640

Peru
Av. Andrés Bello 1751, ☎ 2352356

South Africa
Av. 11 de Septiembre 2353, 16th floor, ☎ 2312862

Spain
Av. Andrés Bello 1895, ☎ 2352755

Sweden
Av. 11 de Septiembre 2353, 4th floor, ☎ 2312733

Switzerland
Av. Amerigo Vespucio Sur 100, 14th floor, ☎ 2634211

United States
Av. Andrés Bello 2800, ☎ 2322600

Uruguay
Av. Pedro de Valdivia 711, ☎ 2744066

Venezuela
Bustos 2021, ☎ 2250021

OTHER DOCUMENTS

Students traveling or studying in Chile should consider signing up for an international student card, which will help you get discounts on a limited variety of services, airfare being the most significant. Travelers of up to 25 years of age can sign up for the ISIC's 'GO 25' card, which entitles the holder to similar benefits. A Hostelling International card is good for discounts at member hostels.

Hostelling International
www.iyhf.org

www.isic.org

CUSTOMS

All visitors arriving in Chile may be subject to routine checks, and customs officials may require that serial numbers of expensive items, such as video cameras and laptop computers, be noted on tourist cards to assure that they not be sold in the country.

In order to protect Chile's remarkable pest-free agriculture, it is illegal to bring any fruit, vegetables, or other products of vegetal or animal origin into the country.

Duty-free allowances include 500 cigarettes or 50 cigars, 2.5 liters of alcohol, and perfume for personal use only. Visitors leaving duty-free areas (*zona franca*) in Región I (Tarapacá) or XII (Magallanes) may be subject to additional searches.

As a general rule, border crossings are fairly relaxed and moderately efficient, though visitors travelling with a private or rented vehicle are subject to greater delays and paperwork. Some rural border crossings do not have their own *Policía Internacional*, which means that you must get your paperwork taken care of at the nearest major town before arriving at the border.

TOURIST INFORMATION

Chile's national tourist bureau is Sernatur, the Servicio Nacional de Turismo (Av. Providencia 1550, ☎ (2)7318322. They have offices in all major towns, where you can pick up hotel listings and an overview of general interest attractions. Many towns also have their own municipal tourist offices, which provide similar services.

Spanish speakers – especially those with their own transportation – are encouraged to check out Turiscom's flagship *Turistel* series, which provides in-depth region by region coverage of Chile (3 volumes) and Argentina (6 volumes). *Camping* is primarily of interest for those traveling by car.

For information on topographical maps and nautical charts, see the Preparing for the Outdoors section, below.

Local currency is the Chilean peso ($), which at the time of writing hovered around 620 to the dollar. In this book, prices are listed in Chilean pesos ($) and in some cases in US dollars (US$).

The simplest and most efficient way to carry and change money is with a debit or ATM card. Most often identified as 'Redbanc,' these ATM machines normally give better rates than banks or money changers, charge no commission, and are compatible with most major networks. All major cities and many smaller towns with a significant tourist economy have one or more ATMs. Some banks, however, charge rather exorbitant fees for international withdrawals, and per-day withdrawal limits are usually around US$300.

Cash (in US dollars) gets the next best rates and may be exchanged almost anywhere, though with obvious risks. Only clean, new bills should be used, as most changers will closely examine all foreign bills and will reject anything that looks remotely suspicious. It is usually unnecessary to pay a commission on cash exchanges.

Many hotels and tour agencies accept US dollars. Foreign travelers who pay in dollars are exempted from paying the 18% IVA tax.

Travelers' checks are the least widely accepted and fetch the lowest exchange rates, although they may be exchanged directly for cash at the issuing agency's main offices in Santiago. Although it may be a good idea to bring a few travelers' checks as backup funds, they are not recommended as a primary source.

Credit cards, including Mastercard, Visa, American Express, and Diners' Club, are sporadically accepted throughout the country, though visitors should not count on being able to use their card in rural areas. Store owners will sometimes charge more for purchases made with a credit card. Lost cards may be reported using the following numbers:

Visa / Mastercard ☎(2)6317003

Diners' Club ☎(2)2320000

American Express ☎ 800201022

Money transfers may be made in one of two ways. Western Union (*Chile Express* locally) is the simplest, fastest, and most expensive: fees for international wires are assigned according to a sliding scale, ranging from about 25% for minor amounts to about 5% on a US$4000 wire. Bank-to-bank transfers are considerably cheaper but more complicated, as access to a local account is necessary in order to receive funds. The local bank's routing number, name of account holder, account number and branch office are necessary for wire transfers. Funds are normally available within 48 hours.

Those planning on buying a car or who for other reasons need to bring large amounts of money may consider bringing a cashier's check, drawn upon a major bank. These may be exchanged (with some delay) for cash exchange rates, without commission, and without the risks associated with cash. Money changers will often raise their exchange rates a peso or two for large transactions.

Cost of living in Chile depends greatly upon style of travel. Food – especially fruits, vegetables, and other basics – are very reasonable. Cheap fixed lunches (*menú*) cost from US$2-6, and budget lodging starts at about US$8, while higher-end meals and lodging are only slightly less expensive than in the US or Europe. Most travelers will spend at least $200/week.

SAFETY AND HEALTH

Chile is a remarkably safe country for travelers. Low crime rates prevail throughout the country, especially in non-urban areas. Tropical diseases, poisonous snakes and insects, and other commonly perceived dangers of Latin American travel are simply not present here.

PHARMACIES

Farmacias are everywhere in Chile. Many drugs that are available only by prescription in North America or Europe are available over the counter, although most are domestically produced and thus cannot be identified by brand names. Keep a list of the active ingredients for any drugs you may need. Antibiotics are no longer available over the counter.

Homeopathic pharmacies are fairly common in major cities.

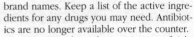

HOSPITALS

Nearly every town has a rural hospital post of some sort of another, but definitive care is usually available only in major towns and cities. The finest hospitals (and the dearest) are private clinics like the *Clínica Alemana* and the *Clínica Indisa* in Santiago. See regional chapters for hospital listings.

HEALTH CONCERNS

Almost none of the tropical diseases common in other Latin American destinations – such as malaria, typhoid, and yellow fever – are a concern in Chile. Most health problems may be avoided by observing a few routine precautions.

Tap water throughout the country is generally safe to drink, though visitors should exercise caution in rural areas and in the desert north. This means that raw fruit and vegetables – considered off-limits in many tropical countries – may be safely consumed as long as they are properly washed.

Shellfish is a trickier issue, and travelers must use their personal judgement. Chileans are great fans of raw shellfish, and many visitors partake without any adverse effects. The greatest risk is of red tide (*marea roja*), a toxic algae bloom, but markets and restaurants are carefully monitored. You only need to be concerned about red tide if you plan on collecting your own shellfish.

Travelers' diarrhea is a fairly common occurrence, resulting from changes in everyday microbes present in all food. Usually this passes quickly, the best treatment being to drink plenty of liquids and eat simple foods. Random cases of cholera are still occasionally reported, so if your problem persists, see a doctor.

The pan-American *hantavirus* is a dangerous but easily avoided concern. First identified in the US in 1993, hanta is carried by long-tailed rats, and is generally only a concern in rural areas in the south. The best recommendations to avoid hanta when camping are to avoid probable rat habitat such as downed logs, dense underbrush, and strewn rubbish; use a sealed, floored tent; and do not leave food or unwashed dishes about. Abandoned cabins and shacks are especially dangerous, and should be aired out for several hours before using, especially if you notice rat feces inside. Fresh air and sunlight generally eliminate the virus, but if in doubt you can wipe down surfaces with a chlorine solution.

Other health concerns for travelers include altitude sickness, dehydration, sunstroke and hypothermia. See the Preparing for the Outdoors section for tips on how to avoid these conditions.

HOSPITAL

VACCINATIONS

No vaccinations are required to enter Chile. For a list of recommended vaccinations for travel in Latin America, visit the Center for Disease Control and Prevention at www.cdc.gov

HYGIENE

Travelers should be aware that public toilets in Chile generally are not equipped with toilet paper, so it is a good idea to have a roll of your own. Furthermore, a small fee (usually $100) is charged for the use of toilets in bus terminals and other public buildings. In most areas, toilet paper is deposited in a wastecan rather than in the toilet itself, in order to reduce stress on inadequate waste treatment systems.

CRIME

Violent crime is a topic of minimal concern in Chile. Most travelers need worry only about petty theft, pickpockets, and the like, and even these can be easily avoided with a bit of common sense. Widely available money belts, worn beneath the clothes, are a good place to keep your passport, money, and other documents.

Bus stations are probably the most common sites for petty robberies. Keep your bag close by, but don't let it make you paranoid. Many travelers are more worried about theft than is really necessary. Just stay alert!

Most travelers, women included, will experience no troubles traveling alone. Though foreign women often attract attention from Chilean men, including whistles and occasional unwanted contact, a firm response is usually respected. All travelers should learn to recognize and avoid dangerous situations – the outskirts of large cities (and downtown at night) generally pose the greatest dangers.

CARABINEROS (POLICE)

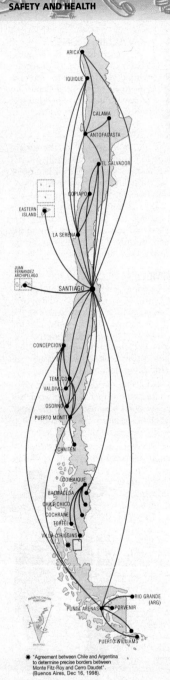

LAW ENFORCEMENT

Chile's primary police force is the *Carabineros*, who technically are considered part of the armed forces. *Carabineros* are typically very friendly and helpful towards foreign travelers, but they do stick to the word of the law. Keep your documents in order and do not attempt to bribe them, but feel free to ask for directions or other help. In some border areas or near posts, photography is prohibited. Arbitrary road blocks are fairly common, but pose no problem as long as all documents are up to date.

A plainclothes police force, *Investigaciones*, is responsible for curbing drug traffic, controlling border crossings, and other non-routine activities. Most major border crossings are staffed by *Investigaciones*.

DOMESTIC AIRLINES	☎	
Lan Chile	600 600 4000	www.lanchile.cl
Ladeco	600 601 3000	
Aerocontinente	600 209 2358	

REGIONAL AIRLINES	☎		
Flights to Robinson Crusoe Island: (Juan Fernández Archipelago)	SAE	LASSA	R.CRUSOE
Santiago	2112443	2735209	5313772

Flights Between Concepción and Chaitén	AEROMET
Puerto Montt	295105
Chaitén	731340
Temuco	232326
Concepción	215556

Flights in Palena and Aisén	DON CARLOS	AEROSUR
Cochrane	522150	
Coihaique	231981	
Chaitén		731228
Chile Chico	411490	
Futaleufú		258633 anexo 268
Palena		258623 anexo 275
Puerto Montt		252523
Puerto Aisén	332918	

Flights From Punta Arenas	DAP
Porvenir	580089
Puerto Williams	621051
Punta Arenas	223340
Rio Grande (Arg)	(54-964) 30700

✱ "Agreement between Chile and Argentina to determine precise borders between Monte Fitz-Roy and Cerro Daudet". (Buenos Aires, Dec 16, 1998).

GETTING AROUND

INTER-CITY TRAVEL

Traveling in Chile is fast, inexpensive, safe and easy. Both within and between cities, an abundance of public transportation makes getting around a snap, though the situation is a little more complicated when you wish to access national parks and other remote areas.

Air

A couple of major national airlines connect major cities throughout the length of the country, and are an excellent option for those traveling on a limited time budget or wishing to avoid backtracking. Prices are very reasonable and the quality of these airlines (especially Ladeco, the domestic subsidiary of LanChile) is excellent. In Patagonia, a number of smaller airlines connect regional destinations via flights whose scenic value alone makes them worthwhile.

Air passes

An excellent alternative for those planning on making multiple flights within the country is LanChile's Visit Chile Pass. If purchased abroad, the pass costs US$250 and is good for three flights within the country in the span of a month's time. Passes purchased within Chile cost US$400 and are good for four flights.

Rail

Aside from international rail service in the north (Arica – Tacna and Calama – Uyuni), rail travel is only an option for north-south travel between Santiago and Temuco.

As buses are faster, cheaper, and serve more destinations, most rail travelers will have motives beyond the purely practical. For this reason, tourist class, with its hard, upright seats, is probably not worthwhile; it's well worth the extra money to travel salon class. Bunks (*literas* or *clase cama*) and cabins (*departamentos*) in antique German sleeper cars are an elegant and relaxing option for overnight travel.

During the summer high season, private vehicles may be shipped south aboard the *Autotren*. Call for fare information and departures times.

TRAIN SERVICE SOUTH OF SANTIAGO

① **Frequency**: 3 departures daily.
② **Frequency**: 1 daily overnight express.
③ **Frequency**: 1 daily overnight express.

Average Duration: (in hours from Santiago) Chillán 4:55, Concepción 8:30, Temuco 11:30.

Reservations

Concepción	☎ (41) 226925	San Fernando	☎ (72) 711087
Curicó	☎ (75) 310028	Santiago	☎ (2) 3768500
Chillán	☎ (42) 222424	-Escuela Militar	☎ (2) 2282983
Laja	☎ (43) 461187	-Est. Alameda	☎ (2) 6883284
Lautaro	☎ (45) 531173	-San Bernardo	☎ (2) 8591977
Linares	☎ (73) 216352	Talca	☎ (71) 226254
Parral	☎ (73) 462734	Temuco	☎ (45) 233416
Rancagua	☎ (72) 230361	Victoria	☎ (45) 842397
San Carlos	☎ (42) 411300	Viña del Mar	☎ (32) 680501

Indicates Stops
for each service

BUSES

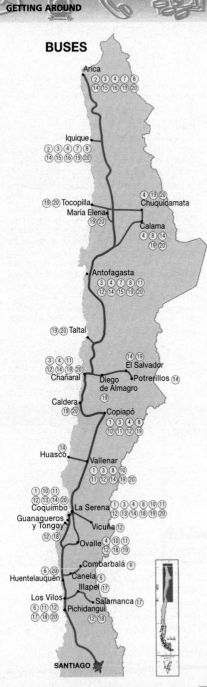

North of Santiago

Numbers ((1), (5)) indicate bus companies serving each destination.

TERMINAL NORTE
San Borja 184/Est Central

(1)	AMB	☎7787360
(2)	Buses Carmelita	☎6985615
(3)	Buses Evans	☎6985953
(4)	Buses Géminis	☎6972132
(5)	Buses Ligua	☎6987339
(6)	Combarbalá	☎7787362
(7)	Fenix	☎7787074
(8)	Flota Barrios	☎7787076
(10)	Libac	☎7787071
(11)	Los Corsarios	☎7787086
(12)	Los Diamantes de Elqui	☎7787073
(13)	LIT	☎5212712
(14)	Pullman Bus	☎7787086
(15)	Ramos Cholele	☎7787566
(16)	San Andrés	☎7787586
(17)	Tacc Vía Choapa	☎7787570
(18)	Tas Choapa	☎7786827
(19)	Tramaca	☎7787555

TERMINAL LOS HEROES
Tucapel Jiménez 21

(7)	Fénix	☎6969089
(8)	Flota Barrios	☎6969311
(9)	Lasval	☎6724904
(10)	Libac	☎6985974
(12)	Los Diamantes de Elqui	☎6969321
(18)	Tas Choapa	☎6969326
(19)	Tramaca	☎6969839

TORRES DEL TAJAMAR
Av Providencia 1072

(10)	Libac	☎ 2352520
(12)	Los Diamantes de Elqui	☎2359707
(14)	Pullman Bus	☎2358142
(18)	Tas Choapa	☎2352405
(7)	Fenix	☎2359707
(11)	Los Corsarios	☎2354810
(19)	Tramaca	☎2351695

TERMINAL ALAMEDA
Av Lib. Bdo. O'Higgins 3750

(20)	Tur Bus	☎ 2707500
	Cargos	☎2707300

Buses

Bus travel in Chile is inexpensive, punctual, and surprisingly comfortable. Major companies offer frequent service between all major destinations, while smaller towns off the Panamerican are generally served by local buses. Some of these local services decline in frequency during the off-season.

South of Santiago

Numbers (①,②) indicate bus companies serving each destination.

TERMINAL ALAMEDA
Av Lib Bdo O'Higgins 3750

①	Tur Bus	☎ 2707500
	Cargo	☎ 2707300

TERMINAL LOS HEROES
Tucapel Jiménez 21

②	Cruz del Sur	☎ 6969324-5
③	Fenix	☎ 6969089

TERMINAL SANTIAGO
Av Lib Bdo O'Higgins 3848

②	Cruz del Sur	☎ 7790607
④	Buses Al Sur	☎ 7792305
⑤	Bus Norte	☎ 7795433
⑦	Igi Llaima	☎ 7791751
⑧	JAC	☎ 7761582
⑩	Lit	☎ 7795710
⑫	Pangui Sur	☎ 7796282
⑬	Turibus	☎ 7791377
⑭	Unión del Sur	☎ 7764111
⑮	Via Tur	☎ 7793839
⑯	Andimar	☎ 7793810
⑱	Colchagua	☎ 7793852
⑲	Panorama	☎ 7764197
⑳	Tacoha	☎ 7799412

TORRES DE TAJAMAR
Av Providencia 1072

⑧	JAC	☎ 2352484
㉑	Varmontt	☎ 2313505
		☎ 6324742
		☎ 5550593
㉒	Turimontt	☎ 2512703

Many cities have a single bus station (*Terminal de Buses*) for all destinations, while others may have one for inter-city travel and another for local departures. Still others have no bus station at all – buses depart directly from their respective company offices. See individual city listings for bus terminal information.

Destinations, departure times, and prices are usually displayed prominently. During high season is a good idea to purchase tickets in advance, as most Chileans travel by bus.

BUSES

Most long-distance buses travel overnight, allowing budget travelers to save money on lodging and avoid losing travel days. When traveling long distance, consider upgrading to *Ejecutivo* (also known as *Semi-Cama*), which provides comfortable calf supports and fully reclining seats. Traveling *Salón Cama* basically allows you to sleep in a bed while you travel. Some long distance companies include meals as part of the fare, either to be served on the bus or (less often) involving a brief stop at roadside restaurant.

Luggage restrictions vary by company, though for most travelers luggage will never be an issue. Those traveling with bikes, kayaks, or other bulky items should consult with individual companies. Bus freight service (*encomiendas*) is an inexpensive option for those wishing to lighten their load: most bus companies will hold packages free of charge for up to a month.

Boat
The numerous options for boat travel in the Lake Region, Chiloé, and Patagonia are described in detail in the appropriate regional chapters under Navigation. Information on boats to the Juan Fernández Archipelago is provided in the Pacific Islands chapter.

INTRA-CITY TRAVEL

Taxi
In most cities, cabs are metered; in Santiago, they charge an initial $150 (US$.33) for passenger pickup, followed by and additional $70-80 per 100 meters. Cabs in some other cities may not be metered at all, so you must agree on a fare before departing. Fares are typically displayed in yellow on the windshield. Tipping is not necessary.

Radio Taxis
Radio taxis are an excellent option for airport transport or in lieu of a regular taxi. In most cities they charge a flat rate to the airport that may actually be less than a regular cab on the street would charge, plus you get picked up right at your hotel. Again, agree on your fare before departing.

Taxi Colectivos
Taxi *colectivos* run a fixed route similar to a local bus, but once they have filled up they do not have to stop for passengers, making them much faster and more comfortable. Unlike regular taxis, *colectivos* are all black and carry a banner on their roof advertising their route. They are slightly more expensive than buses, cheaper than taxis. Fares are more expensive on weekends, holidays, and at night.

Metro
Santiago's *Metro* is the country's only subway system. A commuter rail also links the cities of Viña del Mar and Valparaíso. See individual city listings for detailed information.

Micros

City buses in Chile are called *micros*. In most cities, they are fairly simple to understand: placards in the windshield announce fares and the sequence of streets to be followed. If you're not sure if a given *micro* will be passing your destination, simply ask the driver (*'Pasa por ___?'*).

The same system applies in Santiago, but the sheer number of buses and routes is rather overwhelming. See the Santiago listing for details.

HITCHHIKING

As anywhere in the world, hitchhiking in Chile can be a great success or a greater test of patience. Along the Panamericana and in the densely populated central region, the sheer volume of traffic can make for fairly reliable hitching, but only outside of urban areas. In the north and in Patagonia, traffic is so sparse that long waits should be expected, though the proportion of cars that will actually stop is probably greater.

You're likely to have the best luck hitchhiking in La Araucanía, the Lake Region, and Chiloé, where traffic is moderate and a pleasant community spirit prevails. In the summer months, however, hordes of Chilean youths from the capital descend upon the south, making competition for rides rather fierce. You are almost always better off when you can establish personal contact with drivers: an excellent tactic in many areas is to wait at a service station and solicit rides from truck drivers.

Generally speaking, hitchhiking in Chile is probably safer than in the US and many parts of Europe. Nonetheless, women should exercise caution, and should hitch in pairs or with male companions.

DRIVING

See Ⓐ Overlands.

COURTESY / BEHAVIOR

SOCIAL NORMS

As a rule, Chileans are very appearance-conscious, and dress sharply. Foreign visitors who don't wish to stand out should follow suit, but in truth there are very few social prohibitions regarding clothing. Nudity is not permitted at beaches, and is rare even at remote hotsprings.

Men and women, and women and women, typically greet and take leave of each other by exchanging a quick kiss on the right cheek. Men simply shake hands.

TIPPING

10% is a normal and much-appreciated restaurant tip. Bell hops and other service workers should also be tipped, usually with change – though there is no reason not to reward excellent service. Tipping is not necessary in taxis.

BARGAINING

Bargaining is not nearly as common as in the Andean nations to the north. Prices for lodging and tours are usually not open to discussion, and even many handicraft markets are relatively closed to bargaining, especially for single items. Haggling over minuscule amounts can be construed as a lack of respect.

BUSINESS HOURS

Business hours vary by region and sector of the economy. Banks are open Monday-Friday, 9 – 1400. Most stores are open by 1000 and stay open until 2000; some, but by no means all, close from 13-1500 or 14-1600 in the afternoon. Museums and some restaurants are closed on Mondays, while liquor stores usually stay open until late at night (though new ordinances now require them to close at midnight in several townships within Santiago). If you need to go to the bank or deal with any paperwork (known collectively as *trámites*), you are advised to arrive as early as possible, or else risk spending hours waiting on line.

CHILEAN HOLIDAYS

JANUARY	FEBRUARY	MARCH	APRIL
1 New Year		Holy Week*	

Holidays marked with an asterisk may be celebrated on dates other than those indicated, depending upon the day of the week on which they occur each year. For more information on religious festivities in Chile, see **c**.

MAY	JUNE	JULY	AUGUST
1 Labor Day	**2** Corpus Christi*		**15** Assumption
21 Naval Battle of Iquique	**29** St. Peter and St. Paul*		

SEPTEMBER	OCTOBER	NOVEMBER	DECEMBER
11 *Reconciliación Nacional**	**12** Columbus Day*	**1** All Saint' Day	**8** Immaculate Conception
18 Independence Day			**24** Christmas
19 Armed Forces Day			

Summer Hollidays

LODGING

Lodging in Chile falls under a variety of different categories, with a wide range of prices and levels of comfort. Visitors should feel free to inspect lodging carefully before committing to stay. Note that not all the places to stay recommended in this guide have been personally inspected, and third-party recommendations have been considered an acceptable basis for inclusion. Our criteria for the selection of budget lodging includes a predisposition for ample outdoor spaces and patios, and for added services such as laundry and kitchen use. For more upscale lodging, we try to include a selection of unique local options and standard, no-surprises hotel chains. You can find more lodging information at www.turistel.cl. Value is an important criteria across the board.

> Prices in this guide are indicated using the following symbology. Room prices are based on double occupancy:
> $ US$20/night or less per room, US$15 or less pp
> $$ US$20-75 per room
> $$$ US$75-150 per room
> $$$$ US$150 and above per room (Santiago only)

Hotels in Chile are classified by the familiar system of 1-5 stars, though this rating is not always so dependable. Hotels typically provide services similar to those in North America or Europe – telephone, private bath, television, etc.

Apart-hotels are hotel rooms with kitchenettes and other added amenities, ideal for families.

Cabañas or cabins are an excellent option for families or groups, typically providing beds for 4-8 people. Another option for stays of a week or more is to rent a home or apartment. Families in the south often rent their homes out during the summer high season; look in the *Mercurio* and other newspapers for listings.

Hosterías are home-style lodges, usually with a restaurant and frequently providing other tourist services. These can be among the most charming and most comfortable of all lodging options, combining local flavor with modern amenities.

Hospedajes, Residenciales and Pensiones are all budget lodging options, and the differences between them are not always clear. Rooms most often hold two or more beds, though single travelers usually will not have to share with strangers. Baths are usually shared, and breakfast is often included. Ask about access to kitchen and laundry facilities.

Campgrounds can be a great value and lots of fun, often providing the same services as a hospedaje (showers, access to kitchen and laundry, etc) at a considerably lower price. National park campgrounds typically provide fewer services, at a higher cost, but the setting usually makes up for it. Travelers are recommended to purchase all camping equipment before arrival.

Refugios are wilderness huts, ranging from staffed shelters with restaurants and hot showers (as is the case in Torres del Paine) to simple hovels in the mountains, providing only the most basic of shelter. If backpacking in remote areas, you should almost always carry a tent, even if a *refugio* appears on your route. Rangers and local inhabitants can often provide updated information on the current condition of backcountry *refugios*.

'Wild' camping is the term we use for camping in non-designated sites. In the desert north and in many parts of Patagonia, there are plenty of spots to camp for free, though visitors should respect private property; it may be best to offer to pay local landowners to camp on their land. In central Chile and the Lake Region, free roadside camping is hard to come by, though there are countless spots to camp on beaches, in national parks, and in other wilderness or near-wilderness areas in the Andes. Those traveling in a private vehicle will find it much easier to find sites than those using public transport.

FOOD AND DRINK

The strength of Chilean cuisine lies in raw ingredients and locally produced specialties. Though culinary diversity in restaurants is rather limited, the available products – pomegranate to goat cheese, spiny lobster to apple cider – vary entirely by region and often by season. Sampling these products is a great way to make contact with local people and discover new favorite foods while saving a bundle on what you'd spend at a restaurant. Municipal and country markets (*mercados* and *ferias*, respectively) are often a highlight of local culture. Buying produce from street vendors is also an option; just wash your produce well, as you always should, especially with low-lying items such as lettuce and strawberries. See Regional Specialties in C for suggestions on locally produced and seasonal items.

Fruits and Vegetables

Chile is a produce paradise, and you can count on finding at least some fresh fruits and vegetables no matter where you happen to be. In general, produce shifts from tropical and subtropical products in the north, to colder-climate crops such as potatoes in the south. The central region combines characteristics of both extremes and produces the majority of Chile's considerable fruit exports.

The potato is an extremely important element in Chilean cuisine, served mashed (*puré*), broiled (*papas doradas*), as french fries (*papas fritas*) and as potato salad (*papas mayo*), as well as in countless local versions. This is especially true in Chiloé,

COUNTRY MARKET IN QUILPUE

where potatoes (like the *Solanum tuberosum*) are one of few crops that can be produced in the poor, rocky soil.

Corn is prepared in a number of tasty and imaginative dishes dating back to the Precolumbian era. These include *humitas*, in which ground corn is steamed in husk wrappers, creating a sort of tamale, and *pastel de choclo*, a cornmeal-based casserole with onion, chicken, ground beef, and a single olive, all baked in an earthenware dish.

Tomatoes are excellent and very nearly unavoidable. *Ensalada chilena* is *the* classic Chilean salad, composed very simply of diced tomatoes, onions, lemon juice and oil.

Avocado (*palta*) is another cheap, delicious, and abundant staple. Add a piece of bread, a slice of cheese and a tomato and you have a never-fail lunch that has faithfully fed generations of budget travelers.

CALDILLO DE CONGRIO
(conger eel chowder)
serves 6-8

- 1 cup white wine
- 3 tomatoes, peeled, seeded and sliced
- Salt and pepper
- 2 medium onions, peeled and juli enned
- 3 tablespoons grated Parmesan cheese
- 2 tablespoons olive oil
- 1 teaspoon paprika
- 1 bay leaf ● 1 cup water
- 3 pounds black conger eel (or salmon), skinned and cut into 2-inch steaks ● 1 egg yolk ● ½ cup milk ● Lemon slices.

In a soup pan sauté the onion in oil and paprika. Add the tomatoes, bay leaf, parsley, wine, salt and pepper; slowly cook for 15 minutes. Add water, milk and conger steaks, and slowly simmer for 20 minutes or until the conger is tender.

Just before serving beat the egg yolk with some milk; pour over the fish and stir. Sprinkle with Parmesan cheese. Serve in soup bowls with a lemon slice as garnish.

CHARQUICÁN
(dry beef and vegetable stew)
serves 6

- 1 pound round beef rump, ground
- 3 tablespoon oil
- 1 tablespoon paprika
- 1 cup pumpkin, diced
- 2 cups beef broth
- Salt and pepper
- 4 medium potatoes, peeled and diced ● 1 medium onion, chopped
- 10 ounces fresh or frozen corn kernels
- Tabasco sauce ● 1 pinch cumin ● 1 cup carrots, peeled and diced ● 10 ounces fresh or frozen sweet peas ● pickled onions.

In a large skillet sauté the meat in the oil and paprika; add the onion and corn and sauté for few minutes. Season with Tabasco sauce, cumin, salt and pepper, and set aside.

In a large saucepan add the broth, pumpkin, carrots, sweet peas and potatoes, and cook over low heat 30 minutes until the vegetables are soft. With a fork or wooden spoon mash the vegetables and season with salt and pepper. Add the reserved meat mixture and cook over low heat another 20 minutes. Serve hot with pickled onions.

MEAT

Meat plays a indispensable role in Chilean cuisine, to the point that in many rural areas vegetarians may have trouble finding satisfying restaurant meals. Those who do eat meat are in luck, as Chilean and Argentine beef is of excellent quality and quite inexpensive, and it is the rare visitor who is not invited to a traditional *asado* or barbecue. In the south and Patagonia, lamb and goat are common additions to the grill. Many restaurants specialize in *parrilladas*, a somewhat intimidating mixed grill, usually for two people or more.

Chicken is commonly served stewed as *cazuela* or *pollo arvejado*, in sandwiches, or – for fast food junkies – roasted or fried with a heaping side of french fries.

Pork is served as the unavoidable *completo* (hot dog), in pork chops, and in distinct varieties of sausages.

SEAFOOD

Chile's seafood is unparalleled in variety and quality. Hundreds of fishing villages (*caletas pesqueras*) dot this shoreline, and fishermen typically set out in the wee hours of the morning, returning by nine or ten to sell their catch locally or for national distribution, usually selling out by early to mid-afternoon. The freshest seafood, therefore, is to be had in these small coastal towns, where you can be sure what you buy was caught that morning.

The best variety of seafood, however, is to be had at seafood markets in major cities or in coastal resort towns. Check the fish's gills to be sure that they are bright red, a good sign of freshness. If you're not sure what to buy, ask the fishmongers what is freshest, how to cook it, and so on.

Chile's finest restaurants are often those that specialize in seafood. Reliable restau-

FRESH SALMON IN ANGELMO

rant choices include *paila marina*, a catch-all seafood stew, or a *mariscal*, with similar ingredients but served raw with lemon, much like *ceviche*. In Puerto Montt and on the island of Chiloé, the traditional *curanto* should not be missed.

BREAD AND BAKED GOODS

Bread is excellent in Chile and is likely to form a great part of the budget traveler's diet. Bakeries (*panaderías*) and pastry shops (*pastelerías*) are present in even the smallest towns. Common bread varieties include individual-sized white loaves like *marraqueta* and *hallulla*, sliced bread (*pan de molde*), whole wheat (*pan integral*), and homemade *pan amasado*. In restaurants, bread is often accompanied by a spicy salsa known as *pebre*, consisting of tomato, onion, hot pepper (*ají*), and cilantro.

DAIRY PRODUCTS

Milk and cheese are widely produced in the Lake Region, and are available throughout the country. Visitors may be surprised to notice that milk (and eggs) are not refrigerated in supermarkets. Yogurt is available nearly everywhere. Drinkable yogurt is called *leche cultivada*.

Cheese is also produced on a local scale throughout central and southern Chile, and sold in waxed wheels in supermarkets and *ferias*. Excellent goat cheese (*queso de cabra*) is produced by local farmers in the *Norte Chico* during late winter and early spring.

SNACKS AND DESSERTS

Chile's most popular and patriotic snack is the ubiquitous *empanada*: a baked (*al horno*) or fried (*frita*) turnover, filled with ground beef (*pino*), cheese, or shellfish.

Those who like sweets will be delighted with *dulce de leche* or *manjar*, a coffee-colored paste made of caramelized condensed milk. Manjar is an essential ingredient in cakes, *pasteles*, and *alfajor* cookies, and is also sold in its pure form in markets everywhere.

Some excellent chocolate is produced here. *Sahne Nuss* is a big favorite, though better still are

---

HUMITAS
(chilean tamales)   serves 10

- 12 ears fresh yellow corn
- Large and tender corn leaves
- 1 medium onion, chopped
- 3 tablespoons oil
- 1 tablespoon paprika
- Fresh basil leaves chopped
- 4 tomatoes, peeled, seeded and finely chopped
- $1/2$-1 cup milk • Salt.

Grate the corn with a hand grater and set aside.

In a large saucepan sauté the onion and tomatoes in the oil and paprika. Remove from the heat and add the grated corn, salt, basil and add a little milk until the mixture is thick but not dry.

To assemble the humitas, place two corn leaves together, overlapping the wide ends and leaving the tips facing out. Put 2 tablespoons of the corn mixture in the middle of the leaves. Fold the sides to the middle overlapping them in the center by about 2 inches. Fold one end over, stand the humita on the folded end, and tap it down to remove air bubbles. Fold the other end over. Fasten with string made of torn corn leaves.

CAZUELA DE AVE
(chicken and vegetable soup)
serves 6

- 1 large chicken, cut into 6 pieces
- 2 tablespoons oil
- 1 bouquet garni
- $1/2$ teaspoon paprika
- Salt and pepper
- 1 large carrot, cut into sticks • 1 large onion, chopped • 1 medium red pepper, sliced
- 10 cups boiling water • 6 small potatoes, peeled • 2 tablespoons rice • 2 ears fresh yellow corn, each cut into 3 pieces • 6 pieces pumpkin, peeled • 1 cup sliced green beans
- Finely chopped parsley.

In a large saucepan brown the chicken in the oil and paprika. Add the onion, carrot, bouquet garni and pepper, and sauté for 5 minutes. Add the boiling water and season with salt and pepper; cover and cook over low heat, 2-3 hours until the meat is tender.

Add the potatoes, rice, corn and pumpkin and cook for another 20 minutes. Add the green beans and cook for another 5 minutes. Correct seasoning and serve topped with parsley.

SOPAIPILLAS
(pumpkin fritters)
serves 8

- 1 cup cooked pumpkin purée (butternut-squash)
- 2 cups all-purpose flour, sifted
- ¼ teaspoon salt
- 2 tablespoon margarine
- 1 tablespoon baking powder ● Corn oil.

In a bowl mix pumpkin purée with the sifted flour, baking powder, margarine and salt; form into a ball, without kneading. Spread the dough with a rolling pin to 1/2 inch thickness. Cut the fritters into 2 -inch circles. Prick with a fork.

Fry in hot oil until golden brown on both sides. Drain them on paper towels. Serve warm with green or red pebre sauce or with sweet syrup.

PASTEL DE CHOCLO
(corn and beef casserole)
serves 8

- 12 ears fresh yellow corn, grated
- 8 fresh basil leaves, chopped
- 3 medium onions, chopped
- 1 cup milk
- Salt and pepper
- 3 tablespoons oil
- 1 teaspoon cumin
- 5 tablespoons butter
- 1 pound ground beef
- 4 hard-boiled eggs, sliced
- 1 cup black olives ● 2 tablespoons sugar
- 1 whole chicken, cooked and cut into pieces
- 1 cup raisins.

In a large saucepan cook the grated corn, basil, salt, pepper and butter over low heat, stirring constantly until the mixture boils and thickens. Slowly add the milk and cook, stirring for 5 minutes; remove from the heat and set aside.

In a frying pan sauté the onion in oil until transparent. Add the ground beef and cook until lightly browned. Season with salt, pepper and cumin and cook for a few more minutes.

Spread the meat mixture in an oiled baking dish. Arrange the hard-boiled eggs, olives, raisins and the chicken over the meat mixture. Cover all of it with the corn mixture and sprinkle with sugar. Bake in a 400 °F oven, 25 minutes until golden brown.

Serve hot.

the small-batch chocolates produced in lake district tourist towns such as Pucón, Valdivia and Puerto Varas. Mass-produced chocolates are very reasonable and make a great lightweight energy source for camping.

Ice cream is available in cheap, massproduced forms on the streets, as well as in gourmet Italian-style *gelaterías*.

DRINKS

Locally produced mineral water is available nearly everywhere, and comes with or without carbonation; be sure to specify *con gas* or *sin gas*.

Soft drinks and sweetened juices are widely available, but most travelers will prefer *jugos naturales*, which are blended from real fruit – look for these in vegetarian restaurants and ice-cream bars. Another refreshing treat is *mote con huesillo*, a sweet apricot nectar served with hydrated barley, sold by the glass on the street.

Coffee is often a disappointment for foreign visitors, as most Chileans consume instant coffee such as *Nescafé*. Ground coffee is available in supermarkets, restaurants and coffee bars, where it is known as a *cafe express* or *cafe cortado*, the latter served with milk.

Black tea is commonly available, as is a wide selection of domestically produced herbal teas. Chamomile (*manzanilla*) will be familiar to most visitors; less so is *boldo*, a relaxant and digestive tea made steeped from the leaves of a tree native to central and southern Chile. *Yerba mate* is consumed in Patagonia.

All locally produced beers are lagers. Cristal is Chile's most popular beer, while Escudo, Austral, and Royal are most likely to satisfy European and American tastes.

Guinness is contract-brewed locally, but lacks authenticity. There is also one microbrewery producing bottled beer (*Kuntsmann*, from Valdivia), as well as a couple of brewpubs in Santiago. Draft beer is known as *schop*.

Chilean wine is obviously of excellent quality and very reasonably priced. Reds (especially Cabernet Sauvignon and Merlot) generally get the best reviews, though fine whites are also available. See pg. 247 for more information on Chilean wines and wineries.

Pisco is a clear spirit distilled from high-sugar grapes grown in the region surrounding La Serena. It varies in strength from 33% alcohol to 50%, with prices varying accordingly. The finest *piscos* come from limited-production *pisqueras* such as *Horcon Quemado*. Traditionally served as a *pisco sour*, it is also popular with Coca-Cola as a *piscola*. See pg. 245 for more info on pisco.

MEALS

Chileans typically start the day with a small breakfast, consisting of coffee or tea and toast with butter, cheese, avocado, cold cuts and jelly.

Lunch (*almuerzo*) is by far the most important meal, and is an indispensable social and family event. Beginning around two in the afternoon, weekend meals can last several hours. Lunchtime is also the best time to save on eating out, as most restaurants offer fixed lunches including salad, main course, desert, and a drink for US$2-8.

Once, similar to English tea, is served in late afternoon, and is very similar to breakfast. Dinner (*comida* or *cena*) is usually light or are not eaten at all, though there are many exceptions to this rule – the most notorious of which is the much-loved *asado*.

STEPPING OUT

Restaurants

Chilean restaurant fare is simple to understand and will become rapidly familiar, if not boring (see the glossary on pg. 47 for common items). Finding good food and service is largely a matter of asking locals, hotel staff, or other travelers for recommendations. Chileans typically refer to their favorite budget restaurants as *picadas*.

MACHAS A LA PARMESANA
(parmesan razor clams)
serves 6-8
- 50 whole razor clams
- ½ cup whipping cream
- Salt and pepper
- Dry Sherry • Chopped chives
- 3 ounces unsalted butter, melted
- ½ cup Parmesan cheese, grated
- 1 cup Monterey Jack cheese, grated.

Clean the clams and save the shells. Put one clam in each shell, add salt, pepper, a little Sherry, cream, chives and butter. Cover with Monterey Jack and Parmesan cheeses. Place clams in a baking sheet and broil for 6-7 minutes. Serve hot.

EMPANADAS CHILENAS
(chilean meat turnovers)

makes 20 turnovers
- 1 tablespoon baking powder
- 4 cups all-purpose flour
- 1 egg yolk
- 1 whole egg, beaten
- 1½ cups warm milk
- 1 cup melted shortening
- 2 tablespoons oil
- 1 teaspoon paprika
- ½ teaspoon chilli powder, cumin and oregano
- 4 onions, finely chopped • 1 pound ground beef
- 3 hard-boiled eggs, cut into wedges
- 20 black olives • 40 large raisins.

Sift the flour with the baking powder and salt; add the egg yolk, egg, milk and shortening. Mix to make a stiff dough; divide into 20 pieces and roll each thinly into a circle.

In a frying pan heat the oil with the paprika and sauté the onions until soft. Add the chilli powder, cumin, oregano, ground meat and salt; mix with the onions. Cook over medium heat until the meat is no longer pink. Remove from heat and let cool.

Place 1-2 tablespoons of meat filling in the center of each pastry circle; add the egg wedges, olives and raisins in each turnover. Fold the dough over the

filling making a semicircular turnover; wet the borders with a little milk and fold again to form a rectangle. Bake in a 400 °F oven, 20-30 minutes or until golden brown. Serve hot.

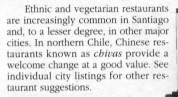

Ethnic and vegetarian restaurants are increasingly common in Santiago and, to a lesser degree, in other major cities. In northern Chile, Chinese restaurants known as *chivas* provide a welcome change at a good value. See individual city listings for other restaurant suggestions.

Bars

Santiago offers dozens of entertaining nightspots, and most other major cities should be able to satisfy most tastes. Bars in tourist centers like San Pedro de Atacama, Pucón and Puerto Varas are packed with international and Chilean travelers in the high season, much less so in the off season. Again, asking for recommendations is the best way to find what you're looking for.

Bars and pubs frequently offer two-for-one happy hours between 1800 and 2100, but those looking for social interaction won't find much then; Chile's nightlife doesn't usually get started until 2300 or midnight.

Casinos

Many major tourist destinations have casinos, often associated with a major hotel. Though not all have strictly defined dress codes, going poorly dressed to a casino is sure way to attract unwanted attention.

Discotheques

Discotheques in Chile rarely start to fill up before one in the morning, and stay open all night long; going out to a *discoteca* with a group of Chileans usually means staying out until six or seven in the morning. Most charge cover, ranging from US$4-10, usually with at least one drink included. Outside of Santiago, municipal zoning regulations often require that discotheques be located outside of town, but on Friday and Saturday nights finding public transportation is rarely a problem. Music varies from *salsa* (especially at *salsotecas*), to early 80's top forty, to postmodern techno and rave music.

MEDIA

NEWSPAPERS

On the whole, Chile's print media is overwhelmingly conservative, and only in Santiago is there any variety to choose from. *El Mercurio* is the country's oldest and most respected paper, and probably the best for international news. *La Nación* is a private daily that expounds on government policy. *La Segunda* is a weekdays-only afternoon tabloid with a brief, summarial format. *La Tercera* and *Las Ultimas Noticias* are similar to *La Segunda*, while *La Cuarta* is more of a sensationalist rag, printing a new swimsuit photo on each day's cover. Other papers include the *Metropolitano* and *El Diario*, the latter heavy on financial information. Rounding out the field are a couple of free dailies, *La Hora* and *MTG*, plus the notoriously satirical *The Clinic*.

Based in Santiago, *News Review* is the only English-language weekly newspaper, but editorial content is haphazard at best.

The best source of up-to-date Chilean news in English is undoubtedly the Internet. See the Santiago section for recommendations on where to pick up international newspapers.

Most major cities have their own local newspapers, which are a good source of information regarding movies, festivals, and other events.

MAGAZINES

Chile's tiny periodical market means a scarcity of nationally produced magazines – *Paula*, a high-gloss monthly fashion magazine with an interesting take on Chilean culture, is probably the best of the lot. Specialty-interest magazines related to outdoor sports include *Revista Outdoors* (general recreation), *Andes y Montaña* (mountaineering), and *Marejada* (surfing).

International editions of magazines like *Newsweek* and *Time* are often available at major hotels and kiosks in downtown Santiago.

TELEVISION

Seven broadcast channels currently operate in Chile. These include the private Canal 4 (*La Red*), Canal 5 (*Universidad Católica de Valparaíso*), Canal 7 (*Televisión Nacional*), Canal 11 (*Chile Visión*), Canal 13 (*Universidad Católica*) and the generally poor Canal 22 (*Gran Santiago*).

The biggest television events are undoubtedly soccer matches, either first division club rivalries (see sports) or national team (*selección*) matches.

Cable television is common in major hotels, and provides access to CNN, the Weather Channel, and ESPN, among other stations.

RADIO

Santiago has dozens of AM and FM radio stations catering to all different tastes, while outside the capital selection is much more limited. Popular FM radio stations in the capital include *Radio Concierto 88.5*, *Radio Futuro* 88.9, *Music One* 89.3, *Rock and Pop* 94.1, *Radio Tiempo* 95.9, and *Caracol* 97.1, the latter of which tends to be a bit jazzier. Radio stations in the area south of Puerto Montt often provide essential communication services for the far-flung settlers inhabiting this isolated region.

MOVIES

Chilean theaters play a more diverse range of films than theaters in the states. Unlike television, most of these are subtitled (*con subtítulos*) rather than dubbed, though this should never be assumed. *Cine Arte* theaters play art films, both new and classic. Keep your eyes open for news of periodic film festivals at cultural centers and universities.

In most Santiago theaters, Mon-Wed nights are half price.

COMMUNICATION

POSTAL SERVICE

Receiving mail in Chile is often more reliable than sending it. Post from the US and Europe usually arrives within a week to ten days, while letters posted in Chile may take two weeks or more to reach an international destination. The most reliable international sevice is undoubtedly that provided by FedEx (San Camilo 190 in Santiago, ☎ (2)3616000 , fax (2)361-6111, toll free 800-36-3030, www.FedEx.com) and UPS (Union Americana 221 in Santiago ☎ (2)689-0203, fax (2)685-0797, www.ups.com). Domestically, the best way to send packages is by bus as an *encomienda*.

Mail may be received *poste restante* at any post office, and will be held for a month, after which time it will be returned. Be sure to check general delivery lists under all possible alphabetical listings.

TELEPHONE

Chile has one of the most advanced digital telephone networks in Latin America. Local, national and international long distance calls may be made from almost any public phone or calling center (*centro de llamados*), using a variety of payment techniques. Fax service is also widely available, with international faxes normally costing about $1500 (US$3) at call centers.

National long-distance calls are handled by *carriers*, which are accessed by dialing a three-digit access code before the number you

CONVERSIONS

LENGTH, DISTANCE & AREA

	multiply by
Inches to centimeters	2.54
Centimeters to inches	0.39
Feet to meters	0.30
Meters to feet	3.28
Yards to meters	0.91
Meters to yards	1.09
Miles to kilometers	1.61
Kilometers to miles	0.62
Acres to hectares	0.40
Hectares to acres	2.47
Square miles to square kilometers	2.59
Square kilometers to square miles	0.39

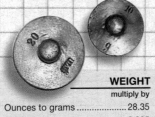

WEIGHT

	multiply by
Ounces to grams	28.35
Grams to ounces	0.035
Pounds to kilograms	0.45
kilograms to pounds	2.20
British tons to kilograms	1016
US tons to kilograms	907

VOLUME

	multiply by
Imperial gallons to liters	4.55
Liters to imperial gallons	0.22
US gallons to liters	3.79
Liters to US gallons	0.26

Five imperial gallons equal just over six US gallons.

A liter is slightly more than a US quart, slightly less than a British one.

TEMPERATURE

To convert °C to °F multiply by 1.8 and add 32

To convert °F to °C subtrat 32 and divide by 32

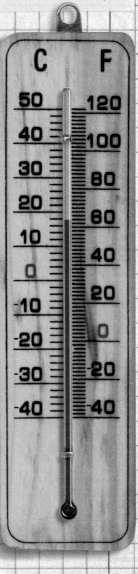

want to dial. Rates for each carrier are published daily in newspapers, but in practice rates don't vary that much. For calls within the country, dial carrier + area code + number, or carrier + 0 + country code + number for international. If you don't care which carrier you use, one will be automatically assigned; just dial 0+area code+number, or 00+country code+number for international calls.

Calling centers generally accept cash only, and are usually less expensive than coin-operated payphones. Nonetheless, international and national (pre-paid) phone cards may be used at most public phones, and provide rates similar to those charged in calling centers. If you plan on using an international calling card, be sure to verify the access number for calls from Chile before departure. Those planning to use pre-paid national calling cards should be aware that some of these use a magnetic strip, while other use a dialed code; the latter is generally more useful.

In some remote locations in northern Patagonia, the only telephone service is provided via Entel satellite telephones, for which an Entel prepaid card is required.

The yellow pages (*páginas amarillas*) can be a tremendously useful reference once you figure out the obscure headings (sporting goods, for example, are listed as 'Articles for Sports'). Travelers should also be aware that phone numbers change frequently, even among established businesses.

INTERNET/EMAIL

The Internet is undoubtedly the cheapest and most efficient method of international communication, and the network of internet cafes is steadily growing. The best way to make use of these is to open an account on one of the many free internet-based email servers, which may be accessed from any on-line computer. Rates for internet use currently vary from US$2-4/hour, though they appear to be dropping. Internet access points are listed under the corresponding city. You'll find the web's most complete index of Chilean websites at www.brujula.cl. – but you need to speak Spanish to take full advantage.

MORE DETAILS

STILL AND VIDEO CAMERAS

Though visitors are definitively encouraged to buy all photographic equipment before arrival, you can also find a good selection of used SLR cameras, accessories, and repair services in Santiago (see the Santiago listing for details). Prices for new cameras are generally higher than in the US or Europe; if you have to buy in Chile, duty-free zones in Iquique and Punta Arenas are a good place to look.

VOLTAGE

Electric current in Chile is 220V, 50 cycles. Transformers are necessary for most North American appliances, although laptop computers usually come with an internal transformer. Adapters for 3-prong US plugs are very difficult to come by, though two-prong converters may be found in any electrical supply store.

WEIGHTS AND MEASURES

The metric system is universally used for temperature, length, area, weight and volume. See the facing page for conversions.

FILM

Kodak, Fuji, and Afga color print film is readily available throughout the country, black-and-white slightly less so. Slide film is difficult to come across, even in Santiago. Film prices are basically equivalent to those in US or Europe.

Film developing can be a bit risky outside the capital. Within Santiago, however, Tecnología Uno (see the Santiago listing) offers high-quality processing at below-market prices.

LAUNDRY

At present there are no coin-op laundry services in Chile. Most laundromats (*lavanderías*) charge around US$2/kilo for clothing, which includes washing, drying, and folding within several hours.

A cheaper alternative is to have locals wash your clothing by hand (look for signs that say '*se lava ropa*') or wash clothes yourself. Not all *hospedajes* allow guests to wash clothes on the premises.

STUDENTS, SENIORS, WORKERS AND VOLUNTEERS

SENIOR CITIZENS (TERCERA EDAD)

Many of the destinations and tours described in this book are appropriate for travelers of any age. Travelers 60 years of age or older, furthermore, are entitled to discounts on many services – including hotels, buses, flights, rent-a-car, restaurants, and museums – through Sernatur's *Turismo Para el Adulto Mayor* program. These discounts are valid from April 15 to December 15 at any establishment displaying the logo below. A complete listing of over 700 participating companies is available through the main Sernatur office in Santiago.

Elderhostel (www.elderhostel.com) runs a couple of educational senior's trips each year in Chile.

OUTDOOR LEADERSHIP COURSES

Two well-known international leadership schools – the National Outdoor Leadership School (NOLS) and Outward Bound – offer outdoor leadership courses in southern Chile. NOLS has a permanent office in Coihaique, and runs 90-day semester courses combining sea kayaking and mountaineering/hiking in northern and southern Patagonia, as well as a variety of shorter courses. North Carolina Outward Bound has recently begun to run courses in PN Villarrica, near Pucón.

Spanish Language Courses

Chileans themselves are the first to admit that they speak poorly. Chilean Spanish is fast, musical, abbreviated and full of slang, and though classes are offered in many cities, Chile is not the ideal place to learn to speak Spanish. Most of the visitors who come to Chile to learn Spanish do so as part of a university exchange program. The best way for Spanish speakers to get up to speed with Chilean *modismos* is to pick up a copy of *How to Survive in the Chilean Jungle*, a dizzyingly complete dictionary of Chilean slang written by John Brennan and Alvaro Taboada.

Working

Many English-speaking travelers in Chile manage to stay on and work, most often in the tourism industry or teaching English in Santiago. Longer-term, better paying jobs are harder to come by.

It is illegal to work in Chile with a simple tourist visa, but temporary work permits may be obtained from the *Extranjería* (see Entry Requirements') with a signed contract. These permits are good for one month; citizens of some countries will have to pay a fee of up to US$100.

Obtaining a longer-term contract is more complicated, involving paperwork that can take up to a year to process.

VOLUNTEERING

A number of organizations dedicated to environmental and social change accept English and/or Spanish speaking volunteers. International organizations typically integrate volunteer experiences with travel and educational programs for a moderate cost. Local organizations are generally more informal, and qualified volunteers can often arrange to work in exchange for food and/or lodging. Stays of less than a month are usually not encouraged. See below for a list of Chilean environmental organizations.

In the UK, Raleigh International (www.raleigh.org) offers 45-day expeditions combining homestays, work projects, scientific research and adventure expeditions in the Aisén region of northern Patagonia. Earthwatch (www.earthwatch.org) offers paying volunteers the opportunity to participate in scientific research projects such as a recent study of freshwater otters in the Río Baker watershed of northern Patagonia.

RESPONSIBLE TRAVEL

Traveling in a foreign country is a pleasure that carries with it a fair measure of responsibility. Tourism can be a positive force in the thoughtful development of local communities and ecosystems, but much depends on the traveling public.

All travelers share this responsibility, and should take pains to show respect for local people. Do your best to learn some Spanish, and bring photos of your home and family to share with your hosts. Spend money locally: while buying food in a giant grocery store might be slightly less expensive, shopping in a local market will help sustain that community and its traditions.

Those traveling with an outfitter should inquire carefully into the company's attitudes and actions regarding cultural and environmental conservation. Are guides local or international? What does the company do to support the communities it visits? Do they offer literature describing the area to be visited, or recommendations regarding proper behavior of visitors? How do they manage their waste? Many companies claiming to offer *ecoturismo* have no idea what the term really means.

The decision whether to travel with a local or international outfitter is not an easy one. International outfitters are often better organized and offer higher levels of service, but how much of their income is returned to the area visited? Traveling with reliable local outfitters is a great way to get to know the country and contribute to its sustainable development.

ENVIRONMENTAL ORGANIZATIONS

The following organizations are dedicated to promoting environmental and social wellness in Chile. Interested parties are encouraged to contact them for information regarding current issues, volunteer opportunities, and other means of contribution.

Casa de la Paz
caapaz@casapaz.cl
www.casapaz.cl
Dedicated to improving the quality of life in Chile through environmental education, conflict resolution, and participatory decision-making.

CODEFF - Comité Nacional pro Defensa de la Fauna y Flora
Av. Francisco Bilbao 691, Providencia
Casilla 3675, Santiago, Chile
☎ (56-2) 2510262 - 2510287, Fax (56-2) 2518433
secretaria@codeff.cl
www.codeff.cl
The largest and most established environmental NGO in Chile, with over 4000 members.

Defensores del Bosque Chileno
Diagonal Oriente 1413, Ñuñoa
☎ (2) 2041914, Fax (2) 2092527
bosquech@entelchile.net
Specifically oriented towards preserving the native forests of southern Chile. Closely linked to Ancient Forests International.

El Canelo de Nos
Av. Portales 3020, Casilla 380, San Bernardo.
☎ (56) (2) 8571943, Fax (56) (2) 8571160
canelo@mailent.rdc.cl
Produces events and educational programs intended to foster

environmental consciousness, some of these on their 7 há property in the *campo* south of Santiago.

Fundación Lahuén
General Urrutia 592, Pucón
☎ (45) 441660, Fax (45) 441660
lahuen@interaccess.cl
Administrates the Santuario Cañi, a private nature reserve near Pucón.

GAEDA Grupo de Acción Ecológica de Atacama
Atacama 998, Copiapó
☎ (52) 216403, Fax (52) 216403
Regional organization dedicated to environmental issues in the Atacama Desert.

Greenpeace Pacífico Sur
Eleodoro Flores 2424, Ñuñoa
☎ 3437788, Fax 2040162
greenpeace@greenpeace.cl
www.greenpeace.cl
Local offices of the world's best-known environmental action organization.

IEP - Instituto de Ecología Política
Seminario 774-776 Ñuñoa, Santiago
☎ 2239059 - 2746192, Fax 2234522
iep@reuna.cl
www.iepe.org
Oriented towards finding political solutions for social and environmental issues.

Pacha-Aru Asociación Indígena Urbana
Piñones 2041, Arica
☎ (58) 222410, Fax (58) 222410
Works for the preservation and sustainable development of the Aymara culture of northern Chile.

Red Nacional de Acción Ecológica (Renace)
Seminario 774 - Ñuñoa, Santiago
Casilla 16774, Correo 9, Santiago
☎ (56) (2) 22234483, Fax (56) (2) 2258909
renace@rdc.cl
National network over 150 grassroots environmental organizations.

Terram Fundación para la Promoción del Desarrollo Sustentable
Clovis Montero 0326, depto 22, Providencia, Santiago
☎ (56) (2) 3410545 - 2742309, Fax (56) (2) 3430742
terram@mailnet.rdc.cl
Educational and investigative body oriented towards the promotion of sustainable development in Chile.

UNORCH (Unión de Ornitólogos de Chile).
Av. Providencia 1108, Santiago
☎ (56) (2) 2368178
unorch@entelchile.net

PREPARING FOR THE OUTDOORS

Most visitors will arrive in Chile wanting to get out of town and explore the country's splendid national parks and other wilderness areas. The following recommendations are intended to simplify the planning and execution of your trip. As always, you'll want to balance preparedness with the weight and volume of your luggage.

WHAT TO BRING

Clothes

Unless you are planning on limiting your visit to the beaches of northern and central Chile, you'll want a good selection of cool weather gear. For insulation, bring several layered garments instead of one bulky one, and focus on fast-drying synthetics such as Capilene or fleece rather than cotton. Down is very useful in the northern altiplano but is not worth much in the south, where rain is a constant threat. Gloves and a wool or synthetic hat are other essentials.

Raingear is another important consideration. Though waterproof-breathable garments (such as Gore-tex) are more versatile, rubberized raingear is more effective in the rainforests of the south. A brimmed hat is very useful, both for sun and rain protection.

Finally, footwear is a personal choice. A pair of lightweight hiking boots and a pair of sandals (such as Tevas) make a good, basic combination.

High quality outdoor clothing, including all the above elements, are available at reasonable prices in Santiago; see the Santiago listing for details.

Camping Equipment

A good sleeping bag is the first consideration. You'll need a good three-season sleeping bag (rated to 20°F/10°C) for most areas, and significantly warmer for sleeping at altitude. Down is a fine choice in the north, where you're relatively assured that it won't get wet, but in other parts of the country you're better off lugging the extra weight of a synthetic bag. Also, don't forget your sleeping pad.

Be sure to arrive with a good, sturdy tent, as these are hard to come by in Chile. Look for free-standing models with high wind resistance, especially if you're heading to Patagonia.

A good camp stove is another necessity. Relatively cheap butane stoves, known locally as *Camping Gaz*, are widely available in Chile, and will do in a pinch. Far preferable are white gas or multi-fuel stoves (such as the ever-popular MSR models), which can be easily cleaned and repaired in the field. White gas, known as *bencina blanca*, is sold in hardware stores and occasionally in pharmacies.

Finally, your backpack (*mochila*) is perhaps the most important item on the list. Look for a bag that can be expanded or compressed as your needs change; internal frame packs with removable top pouches are especially useful. Look out for front-loading packs that are overly dependent on zippers, as these can leave you high and dry if the zipper breaks.

Medical Kit

A good medical kit can mean the difference between a minor injury and real disaster. Many fine pre-packaged kits are currently available on the market. Even the most basic kit should contain all the following items:

- Painkillers or aspirin
- Antibiotics (no longer available over the counter in Chile)
- Antihistamine (ie. Benadryl, for congestion and swelling/itching from insect bites)
- Band-aids
- Sterile Gauze Dressing
- Medical tape
- Antibiotic cream (Betadyne)
- Iodine (for wound cleansing)
- Irrigating Syringe
- Trauma shears
- Tweezers
- Lomotin or Pepto Bismol, for nausea
- Water treatment tablets
- Moleskin (bring extra if breaking in a new pair of boots)

HEALTH CONCERNS

In addition to the basic health concerns mentioned earlier in this chapter, visitors who spend much of their time outdoors should be learned in a few common ailments. *Wilderness Medicine* by Dr. William Forgey (ICS Books) is the definitive reference on this topic.

Hypothermia is the result of a significant decrease in core body temperature. The most obvious early warning signs of hypothermia include uncontrollable shivering and lack of coordination; if someone in your party begins to display these signs, you must take immediate steps to warm them up, but *gradually*. Lack of sensation can cause near-hypothermic individuals to be badly burned by hot water or fire. Do not give alcohol.

Heat Stroke, **sunburn**, and **dehydration** are major concerns, especially in northern Chile. Always wear sunscreen (at least 30 SPF recommended) and sunglasses, especially when hiking at altitude or in the snow. As always, remember to drink plenty of water, *before* you get thirsty.

Altitude sickness is a significant concern for mountaineers and any traveler to the northern altiplano. See the general mountaineering chapter for details.

While tap water can be safely consumed in most towns in Chile, most travelers choose to treat surface water in the backcountry, either by using iodine (or chlorine) tablets or lightweight water filters. While this is a good idea when traveling through grazing country (which often extends surprisingly high up into the Andes), in many wilder areas it is not really necessary – again, use your common sense.

FIRE AND WASTE MANAGEMENT

Nothing is more frustrating than arriving at a backcountry campsite only to find it strewn with the wastes left by the previous visitors. Many Chilean campers are notoriously bad about this, so foreign visitors should do their best to set a good example and, when appropriate, let others know that they are out of line.

The first rule, of course, is if you carry it in, you carry it out. There is no excuse for leaving trash in the backcountry.

Human wastes are another important issue. Always defecate a safe distance from streams and other waterways – 100 ft is a good rule of thumb, further in high-use areas. Dig a hole six inches deep, and bury your refuse when you are done. If you must use toilet paper (river rocks or leaves are a good alternative), burn it or pack it out with you.

Finally, a word on fire. Though no one doubts the sense of comfort that fire can bring to a campsite, no other single element can be so damaging to the envi-

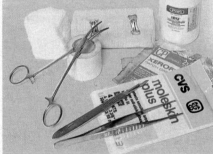

ronment. Even when campfires are kept under control, thoughtless stripping of living trees and proliferation of fire rings can do as much to ruin a campsite as a pile of left garbage. If you must make a fire, collect only downed wood and use existing fire rings; if there is none, scatter the rocks when you are done and eliminate all traces of the fire. Do not build fires on the highly flammable peat or 'duff' that collects on forest floors, and always, always make sure that your fire is completely extinguished.

NATIONAL PARKS

The *Corporación Nacional Forestal*, better known as Conaf (Av. Bulnes 259, Santiago ☎ (2) 3900125, is responsible for natural resource management on Chile's public lands and the administration of protected areas. Their main office in Santiago is a good source for National Park maps, which are occasionally out of stock at the parks themselves. Though regional offices are often more occupied with administration than serving the public, they can provide valuable information on transport to some hard-to reach parks. Addresses for these offices are found in regional chapters.

Chile's system of protected areas or Snaspe (*Sistema Nacional de Areas Protegidas del Estado*) is divided into a number of different categories: *Parques Nacionales, Reservas Nacionales, Monumentos Naturales* and *Santuarios de la Naturaleza*. Each of these has its own definitions and intended uses, and the status of protected area is occasionally upgraded or downgraded for economic or political motives.

Entrance fees range from about US$3 to the US$13 charged foreign visitors to Torres del Paine, though the latter is an anomaly. This fee is usually charged at the park entrance (*portería*), where visitors are required to sign in, though in parks with multiple sectors or those bisected by major roads there may be no *portería* or entrance fee at all. All parks have one or more ranger stations (*guarderías*) and a small staff of rangers (*guardaparques*), who can be very helpful sources of information regarding trail conditions, camping, and natural history. In some cases the rangers will give lectures or guided walks. Most parks also have a *Centro de Información Ambiental* with maps, displays on natural history, and other resources. Campgrounds and other forms of lodging may be run by Conaf or, increasingly, by a private concessionaire.

MAP AND COMPASS

No guide can completely substitute basic competency with a map and compass. In fact, this guide presupposes that independent hikers, mountaineers, and sea kayakers do, in fact, know how to find their own way. If you don't know how, get a book and learn, and practice in the field before arriving.

Maps

For road maps showing greater detail than those included at the back of this guide, check out the Turistel guidebook series, sold in three volumes: Norte, Centro, and Sur. The road maps included in these guides are the most complete and updated available.

The Instituto Geográfico Militar (IGM), at Dieciocho 369 in Santiago, produces detailed topographic maps at scales of 1:500,000, 1:250,000, 1:100,000, 1:50,000, and 1:25,000. Though many roads and trails are missing from these maps, these maps are reasonably accurate and essential for many hiking routes and other activities. Individual 1:50,000 sheets cost about US$12, while sheets from the beautiful 1:250,000 series cost about US$18. It is also possible to photocopy maps from the *Mapoteca* in Santiago's Bilblioteca Nacional. Note that many Chilean maps end abruptly at the Argentine border, so if your route takes you into Argentina, you will need to acquire maps from the Argentine IGM. Furthermore, there are few 1:25,000 scale maps of the Andes or the Atacama Desert, and no maps whatsoever for the Fitzroy area, Torres del Paine, or the Cordillera Darwin.

Excellent marine charts for sailors and sea kayakers are available from the Chilean Navy in a variety of scales. You may browse and purchase these charts at the Armada salesroom (see Useful Info in the Valparaíso entry). Nautigift (☎ (2)2357364), at Providencia 1610 in Santiago, may also be able to order charts.

Compasses

The needles on compasses from the Northern Hemisphere point down (towards the northern magnetic pole) rather than balancing flat, as they would in the north. Though the effect is lessened in liquid-filled compasses, with all others it is necessary to tilt the compass until the needle is no longer touching the base; otherwise, results are hopelessly inaccurate. The most complete solution to this problem is to purchase a compass designed for use in the Southern Hemisphere.

Magnetic deviation, indicated on IGM maps, varies from 3°E in Arica to 15°E at Cape Horn.

GPS

GPS's are now within the budget of many travelers, and for many adventures – notably sailing, sea kayaking, and ice cap expeditions – they are becoming standard equipment. Users should be aware that topography and vegetation can limit a GPS's effectiveness. Whenever possible, use compass sightings to verify GPS readings, as accuracy can vary.

SELECT BIBLIOGRAPHY

History, Exploration,& General Interest

- **A Short History of Chile.** Sergio Villalobos, Editorial Universitaria.

- **Chile, o Una Loca Geografia.** Benjamin Subercaseaux, Editorial Universitaria.

- **Historia fisica y politica de Chile.** Claudio Gay, Museo Nacional de Historia Natural.

- **Travels in a Thin Country.** Sara Wheeler, Abacus/Modern Library.

- **A Voyage towards the South Pole and Around the World.** James Cook, London.

- **Desert Trails of Atacama.** Isaiah Bowman, American Geographical Society.

- **Islas Oceanicas Chilenas.** Juan Carlos Castilla, Universidad de Católica, Santiago.

- **The Real Robinson Crusoe.** RL Mégroz, Cresset Press.

- **Aku Aku.** Thor Heyerdahl, George Allen and Unwin.

- **Ethnology of Easter Island.** Alfred Metraux, Honolulu.

- **The Underwater World of Easter Island.** Michel Garcia, S.E.E.M. Orca Ltda.

- **The Mystery of Easter Island.** Katherine Routledge, Adventures Unlimited Press.

- **Easter Island, Earth Island.** Paul Bahn and John Flenley, Thames and Hudson.

- **The Old Patagonian Express.** Paul Theroux, Penguin.

- **An Englishman in Patagonia.** John Pilkington, Century.

- **Andes Patagonicos.** Alberto D'Agostini, Buenos Aires.

- **Treinta Años en Tierra del Fuego.** Alberto D'Agostini, Ediciones Peuser, Buenos Aires.

- **Back to Cape Horn.** Rosie Swale, Collins.

- **Travel and Archaeology in South Chile.** Junius Bird, University of Iowa Press.

- **Expediciones en la Patagonia Occidental.** Hans Steffen, Imprenta Cervantes, Santiago.

- **Land of Tempest: Travels in Patagonia 1958-62.** Eric Shipton, Hodder & Stoughton.

- **In Patagonia.** Bruce Chatwin, Vintage/Penguin.

- **Patagonia: Natural History, Prehistory and Ethnography at the Uttermost End of the Earth.** Colin McEwan, Luis Borrero and Alfredo Prieto, British Museum Press/Princeton University Press.

- **The Uttermost Part of the Earth.** Lucas Bridges, Hodder and Stoughton.

- **Drama and Power in a Hunting Society: The Selk'nam of Tierra del Fuego.** Anne Chapman, Cambridge University Press.

- **Voyage of the Beagle.** Charles Darwin, Penguin/Wordworth Editions Ltd.

Guidebooks

- **TURISTEL, Guía Turística de Chile**. Turísmo y Comunicaciones S. A., TURISCOM.

- **An Uncommon Guide to Easter Island**. Georgia Lee, Booklink Distributors.

- **Guia de Campo de los Reptiles de Chile: Zona Central**. Jorge Mella.

- **Birding in Chile**. Mark Pearman, Worldwide Publications.

- **Birds of Chile**. Sharon R. Chester, Wandering Albatross.

- **Guia de Campo de la Aves de Chile**. Braulio Arraya M and Guillermo Millie H., Editorial Universitaria.

- **Introducción al estudio de los Insectos de Chile**. Luís E. Peña G. and Alfredo B. Ugarte P, Editorial Universiaria.

- **Explorando el Cielo Austral**. Jorge Ianiszewski R. Dolmen Ediciones, Santiago.

- **Wildflowers of the Chilean Desert**. Sebastián Teillier Arredondo and Herman a Zepeda F., Marisa Cuneo Ediciones.

- **Cactaceas and la Flora Silvestre de Chile**. Adriana Hoffman, Fundación Claudio Gay, Santiago.

- **Flora Silvestre de Chile: Zona Central**. Adriana Hoffman, Fundacion Claudio Gay, Santiago.

- **Flora Silvestre de Chile: Zona Araucana**. Adriana Hoffman, Fundacion Claudio Gay, Santiago.

- **Flora Silvestre de Chile: Zona Austral.** Adriana Hoffman, Fundación Claudio Gay, Santiago.

- **Plantas AltoAndinas en la Flora Silvestre de Chile**. Adriana Hoffman et al, Fundación Claudio Gay.

- **Trekking in the Patagonian Andes**. Clem Lindemayer, Lonely Planet.

- **Chile and Argentina: Backpacking and Hiking**. Tim Burford, Bradt Publications.

Fiction and Poetry

- **Curfew**. José Donoso, Picador/ Grove Atlantic.

- **The House of Spirits**. Isabel Allende Black Swan/Bantam Books.

- **Cape Horn and Other Stories from the End of the World**. Francisco Coloane, Latin American Literary Review Press.

- **Full Moon, Fleshly Apple, Hot Moon: Slected Poems of Pablo Neruda**. Translated by Stephen Mitchell, Harper Collins.

- **The Postman**. Antonio Skármeta, Hyperion.

- **The Poet is a Little God: Creationist Verse**. Vicente Huidobro, Translated byJorge Garcia-Gomez, Xenos Books.

- **A Gabriella Mistral Reader**. Translated by Maria Jacketti, White Pine Print.

- **Emergency Poems**. Nicanor Parra, W.W. Norton and Co./ New Directions.

GLOSSARY

GEOGRAPHICAL TERMINOLOGY

bay - bahía
beach - playa
bog/swamp - pantano, bofedal
(altiplano only)
border - frontera, límite
bridge - puente
campfire - fogata
campsite - sitio para acampar
cave - cueva
cliff - acantilado, farellón
coast - costa
contour lines - curvas de nivel
cornice - cornisa
crater - cráter
crevasse - grieta
earthquake - temblor, terremoto
estuary - estuario
fence - cerco
firewood - leña
fjord - fiordo
forest - bosque
glacier - glaciar, ventisquero
gorge or gully - quebrada
highway - carretera
hut or shelter - refugio
ice field - campo de hielo
iceberg - témpano
island, isle - isla
lake - lago
landslide - derrumbe
lookout, viewpoint - mirador
moraine - morrena
mountain - montaña, cerro
mountain pass - paso, portezuelo
mountain range - cordillera, sierra,
cordón
national park - parque nacional
nature sanctuary - santuario de
la naturaleza
overhang - alero
park entrance - portería
plain or steppe - pampa
ranger station - guardería
rapid - rápido
reserve - reserva
river - río
river junction - junta, confluencia
road - camino
route - ruta
salt flat - salar
scoria (volcanic landform) - escorial
signpost - cartel

spring - vertiente
stream - estero
summit - cumbre, cima
sunrise - amanecer
sunset - crepúsculo, puesta del sol
tidal wave, tsunami - maremoto
to camp - acampar
track - huella
trail - sendero
traverse - travesía
valley - valle
volcano - volcán
waterfall - salto, cascada
wave - ola

WEATHER

clear - despejado
cloudy - nublado
cloud - nube
fog, mist - neblina, camanchaca
(northern Chile only)
high/low tide - marea alta/baja
ice - hielo
rain, to rain - lluvia, llover
snow, to snow - nieve, nevar
showers - chubascos
good/bad weather - buen/mal
tiempo
wind - viento
summer - verano
fall - otoño
winter - invierno
spring - primavera
spring thaw - deshielo

CAMPING EQUIPMENT

backpack - mochila
camp stove - cocinilla
candles - velas
compass - brújula
down - pluma or plumón
flashlight - linterna
gaitors - polainas
gloves - guantes
hat - gorro de lana
pocketknife - cortaplumas
raincoat - impermeable
rope - cuerda
sleeping bag - saco de dormir
sleeping pad - colchoneta
sunglasses - lentes de sol
tent - carpa
topographic map - mapa
topográfico

trail - sendero
white gas - bencina blanca
wool - lana

ACTIVITIES

•Rafting and kayaking
eskimo roll - giro esquimal
flip - darse vuelta, volcar
helmet - casco
lifejacket - chaleco salvavidas
paddle - remo
paddling jacket - cortaviento
portage - portear
pump - bombín
raft - balsa
skirt - faldón
wetsuit - traje de goma

•Skiing
avalanche - avalancha
backcountry skiing - esquí de
randonee
binding - fijaciones
boots - zapatos de esquí
climbing skins - pieles de foca
chairlift - telesilla
off piste skiing - esquí fuera de
pista
off piste - fuera de pista
poles - bastones
powder - polvo
shovel - pala
ski - sometimes written esquí
skilift - andarivel
surface lift - silla de arrastre
to ski - esquiar
transceiver - radio trasmisor

•Biking
brakes - frenos
components - componentes
chain - cadena
helmet - casco
mountain bike - bicicleta de
montaña
panniers - alforjas
pedals - pedales
pump - bombín
rack - parrilla
seat - silla
shocks - amortiguadores
suspension - suspensión
tire - neumático
tube - cámara
wheel - rueda

- **Scuba diving**
decompression chamber - cámara de decompresión
depth - profundidad
fins - aletas
mask - máscara
regulator - regulador
snorkel - snorkel
speargun - arpón
tank - botella
to fill - llenar
underwater camera - cámara subacuática
weight - peso
wetsuit - traje de goma

- **Surf and Windsurf**
board - tabla
boom - botavara
centerboard - orza
fin - aleta or alerón
harness - arnés
mast - mástil
sail - vela
slalom - eslalom
wave - ola
wax - cera
wetsuit - traje de goma

- **Climbing and mountaineering**
belay - asegurar
bivouac - vivac
bolt - clavo or 'speed'
carabiner - mosquetón
crampons - crampones
harness - arnés
helmet - casco
ice axe - piolet
lead - puntear
mountaineering - montañismo or andinismo
rappel - rapelear
rock/ice climbing - escalada en roca/hielo
rope - cuerda
rope party - cordata
sling - cinta
sport climbing - escalada deportiva

- **Fishing**
bait - carnada
barb - rebarba, púa
fly - mosca
hook - anzuelo
licence - licencia
line - línea
lure - cuchara

net - red or malla
reel - carrete
rod - caña
to cast - lanzar
to wade - vadear

- **Overlands**
4WD - doble tracción or cuatro por cuatro
car - auto
deductible - deducible
dirt road - camino de tierra
front/rear wheel drive - tracción delantera/trasera
gas can - bidón
gas/petrol - bencina
gravel road - camino de ripio
highway - carretera
insurance - seguro
jeep - jeep
leaded/unleaded - con/sin plomo
pavement - pavimento
pick-up truck - camioneta
rent - arrendar
unlimited kilometers - kilometraje libre

- **Navigation**
anchor - ancla
boom - botavara
bridge - puente
bunk - litera
cruise ship - crucero
ferry - ferry or transbordador
keel - quilla
light motorboat - chata
mast - mástil
motorboat - lancha
motorsailer - motonave
sail - vela
sailboat - velero

- **Horseback Riding**
horse - caballo or yegua
saddle - montura
reins - riendas
stirrups - estribo
trot - trotar
canter - medio galope
gallop - galope

NUMBERS
1 - uno
2 - dos
3 - tres
4 - cuatro
5 - cinco
6 - seis
7 - siete
8 - ocho
9 - nueve
10 - diez
11 - once
12 - doce
13 - trece
14 - catorce
15 - quince
16 - dieciséis
17 - diecisiete
18 - dieciocho
19 - diecinueve
20 - veinte
21 - veintiuno
30 - treinta
40 - cuarenta
50 - cincuenta
60 - sesenta
70 - setenta
80 - ochenta
90 - noventa
100 - cien
200 - docientos
300 - trecientos
400 - cuatrocientos
500 - quinientos
600 - seiscientos
700 - setecientos
800 - ochocientos
900 - novecientos
1000 - mil

DAYS
monday - lunes
tuesday - martes
wednesday - miércoles
thursday - jueves
friday - viernes
saturday - sábado
sunday - domingo

MONTHS
january - enero
february - febrero
march - marzo
april - abril
may - mayo
june - junio
july - julio
august - agosto
september - septiembre
october - octubre
november - noviembre
december - diciembre

BASICS

yes - si
no - no
please - for favor
thank you - gracias
you're welcome - de nada, de que
where - dónde
when - cuándo
what - qué
how much - cuánto
this - este
that - eso
now - ahora
later - más tarde
open - abierto
closed - cerrado
with - con
without - sin
good - bueno/a
bad - malo/a
big - grande
small - pequeño/a, chico/a
today - hoy
tomorrow - mañana
the day after tomorrow - pasado mañana
yesterday - ayer
more - más tarde
less - menos

PHRASES

hello - hola
goodbye - adiós, chao
good morning - buenos días
good afternoon/evening - buenas tardes
see you later - hasta luego
sorry - lo siento/disculpe
excuse me - con permiso/perdón
How are you - ¿cómo esta?
I (don't) understand - (No) entiendo
Do you speak English? - ¿Habla inglés?
I (don't) speak Spanish - (No) hablo español
My name is... - Me llamo.....
What's your name? - ¿Cómo se llama?

I am...American - Soy estadounidense
...Australian - austaliano/a
...Canadian - canadiense
...English - inglés/a
...Irish - irlandés/a
...New Zealander - neozelandés/a
...Scottish - escocés/a
...South African - sudafrican/a
...Dutch - holandés/a
...Swiss - suizo/a
...German - alemán/a
...Israeli - israelita
...Belgian - Belga
...French - francés/a
...Italian - italiano/a
I want...? - Quiero...
I'd like... - Quisiera...
I need... - Necesito...
I have... - Tengo
I like... - Me gusta...
Give me... - Deme...
Do you know...? - ¿Sabe...?
Is there...? - ¿Hay...?
Do you have...? - ¿Tiene...?
Can one...? - ¿Se puede?
How do I get to...?-¿Por dónde se va a...?
Where is.... - ¿Dónde está...?
What time...? - ¿Qué hora...?
What is that? - ¿Qué es eso?
What is that called? - ¿Cómo se llama eso?

DIRECTIONS

forward - adelante
behind/backwards - atrás
up - arriba
down - abajo
right - derecha
left - izquierda
straight - derecho
north - norte/septentrional
south - sur/austral
east - este/al oriente
west - oeste/al poniente

TRANSPORTATION

bus station - terminal de buses
train station - terminal de tren, estación de ferrocarril
airport - aeropuerto
ticket - pasaje
to hitchhike - hacer dedo

LODGING

lodging - alojamiento
room - pieza or habitación
single/double - single/doble
kitchen - cocina

toilet - baño
bed - cama
towel - toalla

FOOD

●Basic Ingredients
oil - aceite
chile pepper - ají
garlic - ajo
rice - arroz
sugar - azúcar
flour - harina
egg - huevo
milk - leche
butter - mantequilla
jam - mermelada
honey - miel
bread - pan
salsa - pebre
pepper - pimienta
cheese - queso
salt - sal

●Meals
breakfast - desayuno
lunch - almuerzo
afternoon tea - once
dinner - cena or comida

●Objects
bowl - plato ondo
dining room - comedor
cooking pot - olla
spoon - cuchara
knife - cuchillo
frying pan - sartén
plate - plato
mug or cup - taza
fork - tenedor
glass - vaso

●Meat
beef - carne
pork - cerdo
lamb - cordero
ribs - costillar
goat - chivo
fillet - filete
ham - jamón
spicy sausage - longaniza
duck - pato
turkey - pavo
breast - pechuga
chicken - pollo
veal - ternero
hot dog - vienesa

●**Fruit**
apple - manzana
orange - naranja, mandarina,
　　　　clementina
pear - pera
peach - durazno
nectarine - nectarina
plum - ciruela
canteloupe - melón
honeydew - melón tuna
raspberry - frambuesa
cherry - cereza or guinda
strawberry - fresa
blackberry - mora
tomato - tomate
watermelon - sandía
grape - uva

●**Vegetables**
zucchini - zapallo italiano
onion - cebolla
green/red pepper - pimentón
　　　　verde/rojo
potatoes - papa
carrot - zanahoria
cucumber - pepino
beet - betarraga
lettuce - lechuga
spinach - espinaca
olive - aceituna
corn - maiz or choclo
avocado - palta

●**Beverages**
coffee - café
tea - té
herbal tea - agüita, té de hierbas
soft drink - bebida
beer - cerveza
red/white wine - vino tinto/
　　　　blanco
mineral water with/without carbonation - agua mineral con/sin gas
juice - jugo

●**Dining out**
The menu - la carta
The bill - la cuenta
set lunch - menú

●**Fruit and vegetables you
might not recognize**
Membrillo - quince (like a large
bitter apple), excellent sliced

and boiled, often served as
dulce de membrillo (jelly)
Chirimoya - 'custard apple,'
delicious white flesh,
sometimes served in white
wine; grows in La Serena and
Quillota, ripens in early
summer (Sep-Dec)
Tuna - fruit from a disk-shaped
cactus similar to the prickly
pear – full of seeds but very
refreshing
Pepino dulce - refreshing,
melon-like flesh
Zapallo - calabash, a huge, mild-
flavored squash, excellent in
soups and *cazuelas*.

● **Cooking styles**
A la parrilla, a las brasas - grilled
A la plancha - pan-fried
A lo pobre - with onions,
french fries, and a fried egg
Al horno – baked
Al vapor – steamed
Crudo – raw
Frito – deep fried
Pil-pil - spicy seafood sauce

●**Sandwiches**
Ave mayo - chicken and
mayonaise
Ave pimentón - chicken with
red bell pepper
Barros Jarpa - ham and cheese
Barros Luco - beefsteak and
cheese
Churrasco - thin beefsteak
Chacarero - a churrasco with
lots of toppings, including
green beans
Mechada - stewed beef
Completo - hotdog with
tomatoes, avocado, and
mayonaise

●**Fish**
Merluza - flaky white flesh, usu-
ally served fried
Lenguado - sole
Reineta - firm white flesh, similar
to flounder
Sierra - similar to reineta, but a

bit more expensive
Corvina - sea bass, excellent on
the grill or raw as ceviche
Congrio - conger eel, a staple of
Chilean seafood, served fried
or a la plancha
Albacora - swordfish, one of the
more expensive fish in Chilean markets
Salmón - a well-established Chilean export, most often served
smoked or *a la mantequilla*
(sauteed in butter)

●**Shellfish**
Cholgas, choritos, choro -
three distinct varieties of
mussels, harvested south of
Puerto Montt.
Almeja - similar to a clam,
important element in
mariscales
Macha - small razor clam. the
delicious pink foot is often
served with butter and
parmesan (*a la parmesana*)
on the half-shell
Erizo - sea urchin roe (an
acquired taste)
Jaiva - crab, often served as a
rich casserole known as
pastel de jaiva.
Centolla - king crab, harvested
on the open ocean offshore
of Punta Arenas – among
Chile's priciest and most
exquisite specialties.
Ostras - oysters, grown at
aquaculture farms in the
Chiloé archipelago
Ostiones - scallops, another
aquaculture product, usually
farmed in northern Chile.
Loco - abalone, delicious form
white flesh, periodic availability
Picoroco - enormous barnacles,
served in paila marina
Calamar - squid
Camarón - shrimp
Langosta - lobster, found in
the Juan Fernández
Archipelago only.

Trip Planning Overview

The climatic and seasonal differences implicit in Chile's 10 degrees of latitude mean that the visitor has a wide variety of options regarding when and where to visit. The desert in springtime? Forests in the fall? Patagonia in the dry season? Beaches during the low season? Each locale has a distinct appeal in every season.

When you throw in the factor of 'what' the visitor wants to do – the 'Activities,' as we call them in this book– the options multiply geometrically. Want to catch the flamingo nesting season? High water on the Futaleufú? Festival season on the altiplano? Clear skies and no wind on Aconcagua? Powder days at Portillo? If your interests are this specific and you want to get the most out of your trip, start researching now – beginning with this book. If your interests are more general, the following may provide some helpful direction.

Three weeks and two internal flights is the bare minimum for anyone hoping to 'do' Chile in one fell swoop. The 'classic' catch-all Chile itinerary would take you from **Santiago** north to **Calama or Arica** for a week, then down to **Punta Arenas** for another week, and then finally returning for a week in the south via **Puerto Montt** or **Temuco**. Depending on what you did at each stop, a trip of this sort could show you something approaching the full range of Chile's landscapes and attractions (excluding the Pacific Islands and Antarctica), though your experiences and understanding in each area will necessarily be limited. That is the tradeoff.

North

In the far north, the coastal cities of **Arica** and **Iquique** provide access to **Parque Nacional Lauca** and other parks of the **Altiplano** that are best explored over course of at least three days. Further south in the **Atacama Desert**, you could visit the oasis settlements of **Calama** and **San Pedro de Atacama** and a selection of the surrounding attractions – **RN Los Flamencos**, the **Géiseres del Tatio**, and **Río Loa Valley**, to name a few – over the course of a 5-7 day

visit. The Norte Chico merits a shorter visit, focused on the colonial city of **La Serena**, a host of nearby **beach resorts**, and the **Elqui Valley** to the east. Note that in contrast with the rest of the country, due to climatic considerations December and January are not good months to visit the altiplano; otherwise, weather isn't much of a factor in the north.

Central

A week is probably enough for most visitors to Central Chile. During that time you could explore the museums and historic *centro* of **Santiago**, the coastal cities of **Viña del Mar** and **Valparaíso** (and the chain of **beach resorts** north and south), and at least a sampler of the many ski resorts, national parks, and spectacular interior valleys of **the Andes**.

The vineyards and colonial haciendas of the **Central Valley** south of Santiago are worthy of a day or weekend trip. Springtime, from October to December, is generally the nicest season in Central Chile.

South

If you only have a week to spend in the south, you have some decisions to make. In the **LA ARAUCANÍA** region, the towns of **TEMUCO** and **PUCÓN** provide access to a wonderful variety of national parks (most notably **PN CONGUILLÍO** and **PN VILLARRICA**) and some of Chile's finest venues for hiking and adventure sports. Further south in the **LAKES AND VOLCANOES** region is the historic fluvial port of **VALDIVIA**, one of Chile's prettiest cities, as well as the remote **SIETE LAGOS** region and the rainforests of **PN PUYEHUE**. Finally, the neighboring cities of **PUERTO VARAS** and

PUERTO MONTT lie within easy distance of a number of attractions:

German-influenced villages along the shore of picture perfect **LAGO LLANQUIHUE**, the island of **CHILOÉ** (below), and national parks such as **PN VICENTE PÉREZ ROSALES** and **PN ALERCE ANDINO**. Seeing all these sites in even the most cursory manner would take about two weeks, so if you have less you'll have to choose. Most people try to visit the south during the Austral summer (Nov-Mar).

Patagonia

In Patagonia, most visitors will initially be drawn to the far tip of the continent, where the cities of **PUNTA ARENAS** and **PUERTO NATALES** provide access to **PN TORRES DEL PAINE** and a variety of lesser-known destinations, most of which require you to hop on a boat or plane. These include short cruises to **PENGUIN COLONIES** or to the **SERRANO AND BALMACEDA GLACIERS**, and longer cruises (or flights) to **USHUAIA**, **PUERTO WILLIAMS**, and the **BEAGLE CHANNEL**.

Again, you'd need at least two weeks to touch on all these sights, and this doesn't even get you near the **CARRETERA AUSTRAL**, where the city of **COIHAIQUE** is the principal settlement in a vast wilderness of temperate rainforests, glaciers, and immense rivers and lakes, including the

iceberg-strewn **LAGUNA SAN RAFAEL**. You need at least a weeks' time to explore the

northern Carretera Austral, including the **RÍO FUTALEUFÚ** and **PUMALÍN PARK**, and about the same if you want to head south towards **LAGO GENERAL CARRERA**, **COCHRANE** and the **RÍO BAKER**.

Finally, with three days on the island of **CHILOÉ** you could at least visit the principal cities of **ANCUD** and **CASTRO**, gorge on seafood, and visit a local handicrafts market. You'll need more time, however, if you want to explore the wild coast of **PN CHILOÉ** or the islands of the **CHILOÉ ARCHIPELAGO**.

The Islands

The beauty of islands – especially remote ones – is that you could as easily stay a month as a day. If you're strapped for time, however, 3-5 days in the **ARCHIPELAGO JUAN FERNÁNDEZ** (Robinson Crusoe) would probably be enough to fulfill a few island fantasies, check out the islands' endemic wildlife, and maybe go snorkeling or diving.

Because of the length of the flight, most visitors will want to stay a little longer exploring

the paradoxical archaeological treasures and Polynesian beaches of **EASTER ISLAND**.

Antarctica

Though it is possible to visit Antarctica in as little as two days (by flying from Punta Arenas), you're far better off in a boat, and most visitors will want to allow at least a week to explore the fascinating marine ecosystems, ice formations, and scientific bases along

the Antarctica Peninsula. These tours are usually arranged well in

advance, and aren't cheap, though last-minute travelers may be able to arrange cut-rate trips out of Ushuaia.

ACTIVE AND ADVENTURE TRAVEL

CIRCUITS AND OVERLAND TOURS

BIKE TOURING AND MOUNTAIN BIKING

TREKKING AND DAY HIKES

HORSEBACK RIDING

MOUNTAINEERING AND ROCK CLIMBING

SKIING AND SNOWBOARDING

FLYING

NAVIGATION

SEA KAYAKING

WHITEWATER RAFTING AND KAYAKING

SURFING AND WINDSURFING

SCUBA DIVING AND SNORKELING

SPAS AND HOTSPRINGS

FISHING

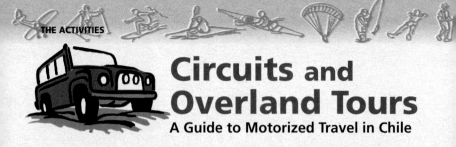

Circuits and Overland Tours

A Guide to Motorized Travel in Chile

The information on these pages is intended to help you along in the planning and execution of a Chilean road trip, whether that means signing up for a commercial 'Overland' trip or doing it on your own. Either way, having access to a private vehicle entirely changes the traveling experience, allowing for much greater flexibility and ease in reaching national parks and other remote destinations to which public transport is infrequent or nonexistent.

ON YOUR OWN

Contrary to popular images of road in South America, driving in Chile is actually quite safe. Road rules are basically the same as those in Europe or the US, and the best advice is simply to stay alert and drive defensively. This is especially true when driving in cities or on the busy Panamerican Highway.

Though visitors are technically required to have an international driver's license to drive in Chile, in practice foreign licenses are usually accepted.

Renting a Car

To rent a car in Chile, you need to be at least 25 years of age and possess a valid driver's license and major credit card. Several international rental agencies, and a host of local agencies offer rentals at most airports and destination cities.

Prices are relatively expensive, with economy-sized vehicles starting at about US$50/day. 4WD vehicles rent for about US$80-100/day in high season, though up to five people can easily travel in a four-door pickup. Longer term rentals –by the week or weekend– are often a much better deal, with economy vehicles going for about US$250/week, 4WD's about US$450/week. It pays to shop around, as prices can vary greatly between agencies. Be sure to ask carefully about insurance policies and mileage charges. A moderate fee (depending on the distance) is charged for returning vehicles at an office different from that at which the car was rented.

A special permit is required to take rented vehicles across the border into Argentina (crossing into Perú or Bolivia is not recommended). These permits generally cost US$100-150, and are valid from 1-30 days. Consult with rental agencies in advance for details.

HAVE CAR, WILL TRAVEL: ON THE LOOSE AT LAGUNA MIÑIQUES

Buying a Car

Buying a car may be less expensive than renting in the long run, but involves a far greater hassle and time commitment. Those planning on buying a vehicle should plan on at least a week to purchase the vehicle and deal with documents, and another week to sell it.

Santiago offers by far the greatest number and variety of vehicles and usually the best prices. Look in Sunday editions of *El Mercurio* or in *El Rastro*, or grab a taxi and start cruising the countless used car lots on Américo Vespucio; you can also check out the market beforehand at www.autocompra.cl. Most makes and models found in the US or Europe are available here, and choosing a vehicle is largely a question of personal taste. Don't expect odometers to provide an accurate measure of use.

Anyone purchasing a vehicle in Chile must have a RUT number, available through the *Servicio de Impuestos Internos*. Always ask if a vehicle has up-to-date papers (*papeles al día*). If so, you're in luck: just have the title signed over to you and signed by a notary public (*notario*), and you're good to go. If not, you may have to purchase insurance (*seguro*), get an inspection done (*revisión técnica*), and register the vehicle (*permiso de circulación*) for every year it has been off the road. Failing to have the *papeles al día* on your own vehicle can make it very difficult to sell.

Other alternatives to buying a vehicle in Chile include shipping a vehicle from abroad or driving from elsewhere in the Americas. Shipping generally costs about US$2-3,000 and takes about one month from either the east or west coast of the US. Used vehicles may not be legally nationalized; once in, any

vehicle from abroad must leave the country every three to six months – officials will generally give you three if you don't ask for the full six. In a pinch, used cars from almost anywhere may be sold easily in Paraguay.

Those planning on driving south from the US should solicit the South American Explorers' Club's highly informative packet *Driving in Central and South America*.

Security & Repairs

Though rural break-ins are uncommon, be cautious about what you leave in sight when leaving your car parked in cities. Locals will often offer to watch parked cars for loose change.

In case of a flat tire, what you need is a *vulcanizador*, usually indicated by a painted tire along the roadside. For more serious problems you'll have to visit a *taller mecánico*. If you don't speak much Spanish, this can be quite an experience.

Fuel

Fuel is available in leaded *rojo* (92 octane), unleaded *verde* (95 and 97 octane)

Arica — **1A**

Iquique

1C
1B

Antofagasta

1D
2

Copiapó

Easter Island

La Serena

Valparaíso — SANTIAGO — **3A**
3B

Juan Fernández Archipelago

Talca

Concepción

Temuco — **4A**
Valdivia — **4B**
Osorno — **4C**
Puerto Montt — **5**
4D

Castro
Chaitén

6A

ANTARCTIC CHILEAN TERRITORY

Coihaique

6B

Cochrane

90° 53°

SOUTH POLE

Puerto Natales
Punta Arenas — **6C**

* "Agreement between Chile and Argentina to determine precise borders between Monte Fitz-Roy and Cerro Daudet". (Buenos Aires, Dec 16, 1998).

Puerto Williams

Diego Ramírez Islands

■ See pg 6 for photo credit

and diesel. Normally, fuel is considerably cheaper than in Europe, with diesel being most economical option. Visitors should note that fuel prices are considerably inflated in some areas, especially along the Carretera Austral and in the Argentine Lake District north of Bariloche.

In some parts of the country – most notably in northern Chile and along the Carretera Austral – service stations are widely spaced, and it is a good idea to fill up whenever you get a chance. Carrying extra fuel in a plastic or metal can (*bidón* in Spanish) is a worthwhile safety measure.

OVERLAND TOURS

Commercial overland tours are often the best way to get to know a portion of the country without having to deal with making personal travel and lodging arrangements. Nothing could be easier: you just load your equipment into the operator's vehicle and away you go. Not only does this free you from the time and route constraints of public transportation, it also allows you to take advantage of an operator's experience and contacts for lodging, restaurants, and excursions.

The overland tours suggested in this guide range from single-day jeep tours to two-week traverses, and a number of international operators also include Chile as part of a longer South American circuits. Prices and services vary greatly between one trip (and operator) and the next. Questions to ask of a potential operator include:

- Is lodging in hotels, camping or both?
- How many meals are provided?
- If not all meals are provided, how much should clients expect to spend on their own? Are meals in restaurants or cooked in the field? Do clients share cooking duties?
- What options exist for side trips and excursions? Are these included in the price of the trip? If not, how much do they cost?
- How long is the average driving day?

If booking from abroad, ask for catalogues from a variety of companies in order to select the trip which best suits your budget and travel preferences. The better informed you are, the less likely you are to encounter problems once the trip begins.

WELL-EQUIPPED FORD THE ALTIPLANO

NORTHERN CHILE

Road tripping on your own or with a commercial overland tour is by far the best way to see the north. Sure, you can get around okay in a bus, but if you really want to see the sights and enjoy the vast distances, you need to get away from public transportation. Most independent travelers use public transport to get from one city to another, and then find a tour operator to take them to the sites which can't be accessed by public transport - which happens to be most of them. This at least gets you out of town.

A better way to see the sights, and to sleep beneath the stars, is to sign up for a multi-day overland tour. Overlands from 2-21 days are commonly available, including integration with the altiplano regions of Perú, Bolivia and Argentina.

If you plan to rent a car, first decide where you want it to take you. If you plan to stick to the coast and major cities, a normal passenger car is more than sufficient. A water bottle and a warm blanket or sleeping bag are

ALTIPLANO SOLITUDE

THE *MAR DE DUNAS*, NEAR COPIAPO

recommended extras in case of a breakdown, as temperatures off the coast drop considerably at night.

A 4WD vehicle is the only way to access many altiplano parks and remote beaches, and provides a lot of peace of mind. But even 4WD is by no means a guarantee of safety. In the nearly featureless Atacama Desert and in many parts of the altiplano, faint roads branch and diverge with no signposting whatsoever, and getting lost can be a grave situation indeed (some sensitive border areas are peppered with land mines). If driving in the altiplano, you need two spare tires, extra fuel, food, water and blankets or a sleeping bag. Any vehicle without fuel injection should have its carburetor ajusted for altitude.

A final consideration is that of the ALTI-PLANIC WINTER, which produces intense rainstorms in the altiplano between November and March. Erosion is rampant in this normally arid region, so these storms can make many roads impassable. Always ask local *Carabineros* about road conditions before setting out into unknown territory.

Though the circuits listed here are in the mountains, remember that there are over 2,000km of coastal roads in northern Chile, passing by hundreds of beaches and tiny *caletas*, resorts and mellow little bleached-out towns.

CENTRAL CHILE

If you're coming to Chile hoping for an adventurous road trip or an off-road safari, Central Chile is not the place: you're better off heading north or south. However, if you just want to rent a car and explore the coast and Andes on your own schedule, you couldn't pick a simpler place to do it: you'll find service stations, restaurants and other tourist infrastructure pretty much everywhere, and most of the roads are passable in any normal passenger vehicle.

Do you need to rent a vehicle to explore central Chile? Not at all – you can catch buses and scare up a ride almost anywhere along the coast or in the Central Valley, but if you want to really see the Andes and you don't want to spend your whole vacation getting there, you're far better off with a car. Most roads into the Andes are dead ends, meaning that public transport to the end of the road – where many national parks are located – is sporadic at best. If you can afford it – and especially if you don't have much time to waste – rent a car.

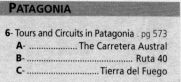
SOUTHERN CHILE

The south provides far and away the most options for road trips of any region in Chile. The beauty here is connectivity: unlike central Chile, where the roads climb into the Andes until they have to end, here the lower, broader topography allows for the presence of relatively low mountain passes connecting the various watersheds, lakes and parks of Chile and Argentina. With few exceptions, most of these roads are passable during the summer in a normal passenger vehicle, though 4WD or high clearance will always provide a measure of security. If you don't have 4WD, chains are highly recommended for back roads in winter.

Seven passes cross the Andes into the Argentine lake region, all of which are technically open year-round, though they close when it snows enough. If a big storm hits, Paso Hua Hum is usually the last to close.

A number of operators offer all or part of the routes suggested here as packaged tours. If you are traveling alone or in a small group, this is probably a more economical option than renting a car, and it saves you the hassle of navigation. And as border relations relax between Chile and Argentina, you can expect to see an increasing variety of overland tours combining the parks and lake resorts on either side of the Andes.

PATAGONIA

Simply put, there are some parts of Patagonia where you really need personal transport to take full advantage of your visit, and other areas where it is not so important.

In Chiloé, public transport connects most towns of any size, but it is the countryside itself that is most attractive; being able to stop and check out churches and tiny villages is essential. Though you don't need a four wheel drive, you should be aware that most roads are gravel and often wash-boarded. To avoid excessive vibration, large wheel diameter is highly recommended.

In northern Patagonia, if you want to really get a feel for the landscape, you need a vehicle. Public transport connects major towns, but the towns themselves are nothing – you're here for the wilderness. With a car you can camp where you wish, do side hikes, fish the innumerable rivers and lakes, stop off at hotsprings, and cross back and forth to Argentina, trading rainforest for pampa. There are 10 separate passes to Argentina in this area alone, each one different, wild, and beautiful. High clearance is key, and while four wheel drive is not essential, it does provides an added measure of security.

Most visitors to southern Patagonia do not need a car, because they are fixed upon specific destinations such as Torres del Paine or Ushuaia, and because maritime travel is such an attractive option. Nonetheless, renting a vehicle for a day or two is a great way to take in the sights around Punta Arenas – sights that you would otherwise only be able to visit by taking a tour. This is doubly true in Tierra del Fuego, where distances are immense and public transport is extremely limited.

Car rentals are available in a limited number of cities, so plan carefully. Fuel prices are inflated along the Carretera Austral, but elsewhere are comparable to the rest of Chile.

Bike Touring and Mountain Biking

Traveling by bike is unquestionably one of the finest ways to explore Chile's rural countryside and remote wilderness areas. While public transportation between major transportation centers is cheap and efficient, getting out of town without private transportation can be a challenge, and bicycles nicely release you from inconvenience of public transport, the expensive of auto rental, or the hectic pace of an organized tour.

Whether you are embarking on a long-haul independent tour, a guided and van-supported commercial tour, riding single-track or simply renting a bike for an afternoon or a weekend, the advantages of bike travel apply equally. This guide includes both suggestions for multi-day bike tours and a few single-track rides in the central region and around major tourist centers such as San Pedro de Atacama and Pucón.

SAFETY

Traffic is usually near the top of the list of bikers' safety concerns. Luckily, traffic is relatively easy to avoid in Chile, as it is concentrated in major cities, in the densely populated central region, and on the Panamerican highway that runs north-south from Arica to Puerto Montt. If you avoid these areas, you should have no problems. Dirt roads anywhere in the country are generally your best bet for avoiding traffic, but remember that no matter where you're riding, caution and visibility are your best defenses.

Dogs are often another issue for bikers, but in reality most Chilean dogs are as docile as their owners. If a dog approaches with a menacing air and you can't outrun it, the best option is to dismount, keeping the bike between you and the dog, and reach down for a rock or a stick with which to defend yourself.

HIGH ABOVE THE CORDILLERA DE LA SAL, SAN PEDRO DE ATACAMA

Though petty theft is largely confined to urban areas, all bikers should carry a stout lock and get in the habit of securing their bike whenever leaving it unattended. Most *hospedajes* have interior patios where you can leave your bike.

SEASON

The best season for biking in most of Chile is the austral spring and summer, October – March. In the north, however, consistently clear weather allows for biking year round, although those planning a trip to the altiplano should be aware of the effects of the altiplanic winter, which brings violent rain and hailstorms in December and January.

EQUIPMENT

Even if you don't plan on doing any single-track riding, you will still need a mountain bike, and front suspension is highly recommended for negotiating Chile's rocky, washboarded back roads. A gearing range of 28-front, 34-rear is recommended for anyone planning to venture beyond the gentle grades of the central valley. For long, self-supported tours, experiment with loading systems before departure, as buying further racks and panniers in Chile is rather expensive.

All visitors planning on biking extensively in Chile should plan on bringing their own equipment. High quality bikes can often be sold before departure, in Santiago and many tourist towns.

Those booking a tour with an operator should ask inquire thoroughly about the equipment provided. Though some high-quality bikes are produced domestically, the best bet is to insist on recognized brands. The same goes for short-term rentals: at the very least, take the bike for a brief spin, check the brakes aggressively, and shift through the full range of gears before agreeing to a price. Rentals typically cost about US$12-15/day.

Replacement parts are widely available in Santiago, somewhat less so in other cities; prices are slightly more expensive than in the states and Europe. Long-distance bikers arriving from neighboring countries will be overjoyed at the selection. 26", 27", 28" and 700C bike tires are all available.

Chilean bike mechanics are usually friendly, skilled, and efficient, and prices are very reasonable.

RECOMMENDED REPAIR KIT

- Tire patch kit
- Tire irons (3)
- Spoke wrench
- Spare chain links
- Chain rivet tool
- Crank arm puller
- Vise grips
- Needle-nosed pliers
- Allen wrench set (4-8mm)
- Wrench set (8-17mm)
- Phillips and flathead screwdriver
- Presta valve adaptor

*several manufacturers now offer multi-tools specifically designed for cyclists that include many of the above items.

BIKE TRANSPORT

Most domestic and international airlines do not charge excess baggage to transport bicycles, provided that the total weight of your luggage does not exceed the established limits. Nonetheless, bikes should always be packed in a bike bag or cardboard box, with both pedals removed.

Chilean bus companies most often will not charge to transport bikes, though again you should make an effort to make your bike as compact as possible, and it is a good idea to load it into the luggage compartment yourself to avoid damage. Buses in Argentina may charge to transport bikes.

Bikes must also be partially disassembled for train travel (Santiago – Temuco only). A nominal fee is charged.

Policies regarding bikes on ferries in southern Chile vary. The *Cruce de Lagos* ferry

RATINGS & SYMBOLS

Distance: Total trip distance (in kilometers) is indicated by this symbol ▶◀. Within the text itself, the distance between principal stops is indicated in parentheses.

Type of Roads: Paved **P**, gravel/dirt **D**, or single-track **ST**.

Difficulty: Routes have been categorized in one of five grades, depending on road surface, total length, vertical gain, and environmental factors such as altitude and wind.

across Lago Todos los Santos in the Lake Region charges for bikes as if they were an additional passenger, while short ferries along the Carretera Austral and between Chiloé and the mainland do not charge at all. Transmarchilay charges $5,000 to transport bikes from Puerto Montt to Puerto Chacabuco, while Navimag charges $15,000 to either Puerto Chacabuco or Puerto Natales.

GUIDED TRIPS

A growing number of outfitters offer guided biking trips in Chile, ranging from soft-adventure tours in the Lake District to more strenuous traverses in the northern altiplano and the Carretera Austral. Most of these provide a support vehicle to carry food and gear, and to transport participants when they see fit. Asking about support services, equipment, daily mileage and rest days is essential to finding the right outfitter.

NORTHERN CHILE

Though a few long-haul masochists may be tempted by the challenge of riding all the way through the driest desert on earth, challenge is about all you'll find on the Pan-American Highway. On the other hand, areas such as the northern Altiplano, the Inter-Andean Depression around San Pedro de Atacama, and the irrigated valleys and of the Norte Chico make for some safe and incredibly scenic multi-day bike trips. There are also lots of good day rides around many of the major cities and coastal resorts in the north.

Water is the biggest concern for bikers, and should be a factor in itinerary planning. See pg 263 for recommendations for dealing with water in the north.

Terrain, heat, and altitude are the other noteworthy factors. In the altiplano, you'll be dealing with elevations above 3500 meters, so you will need to spend some time acclimatizing before you begin your tour. Not all altiplano routes are the same: there is a big difference between pedaling through the relatively flat terrain of Parque Nacional Lauca and laboring through the fragmented mountain terrain around El Tatio. Luckily, temperatures are more bearable at this elevation, but by no means are bike tours in this region to be taken lightly. Consider travelling with a supported tour if unsure of your physical capabilities.

With an average elevation of 2500m, the Inter-Andean Depression is easier on your lungs, and the terrain around the San Pedro de Atacama oasis and the Salar de Atacama is almost completely flat. There are great day

THE VALLE DE LA LUNA, SAN PEDRO DE ATACAMA

■ See pg 6 for photo credit

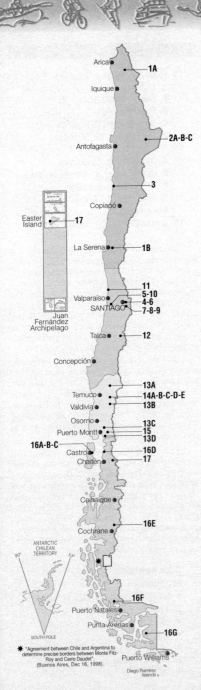

rides here for all abilities, though the heat can be brutal. The same goes for biking trips in the Norte Chico, and in general you should try to avoid riding at midday – and don't forget a hat, sunglasses, and sunscreen.

The simplest and least demanding rides are those along the coast. Though coastal day trips are not described here, Arica, Antofagasta, Caldera/Bahía Inglesa and La Serena/Tongoy are all fun to explore by bike. Rental agencies are listed below.

Winds throughout the region blow consistently out of the suthwest, increasing in intensity during the day.

> **Bike Rentals:**
> **In San Pedro de Atacama**
> - 162
> - 23
>
> **In La Serena**
> - 71

CENTRAL CHILE

With 70% of Chile's population and the great majority of its cars concentrated in the central region, this is not a great place for multi-day bike tours. There are, however, plenty of options for quality day trips and single-track rides, many of these in close proximity to the capital. Most of the listings in this section are clustered within 1-2 hour radius of Santiago, and some of them are actually within the city – so close that you can ride there from downtown.

One real trick is to choose your season carefully. As a general rule, winter and spring are the best seasons: a ride on Cerro San Cristóbal in October, when the ground is moist and the flowers in full bloom, is a far

cry from the dustbowl you'll find in March. During the summer season, ride early or late to avoid the midday heat, or head up into the cooler air of the Andes. During summer weekends, Valle Nevado runs a lift for mountain bikers; this is a great place to get up high for clean air and views and to check out the crazed downhillers in full combat gear.

Bikers who are just passing through should make a final equipment check before leaving Santiago, because you won't find selection or prices like this anywhere else. Bike shops can also be good sources of information on trails, selling gear, finding riding partners, and the like.

The rides suggested here really represent only the very tip of the iceberg; local riders can surely fill you in on other good spots. For overnight trips, many of the roads following river valleys into the Andes make for good riding with minimal traffic, although in most cases you'll have to come back the way you came.

Long-distance bike touring in the south is for experienced riders seeking a solid challenge and a hell of a workout. Although in a few places there are paved, gently-graded highways leading deep into the Andes, the roads leading north-south are almost all gravel and many are steep and in bad repair. Riding consistently with a heavy load on these roads – which are unquestionably the most scenic – requires both technique and patience.

For this reason, many bikers originally intent on long-distance touring wind up busing from one 'destination city' to another, getting their bikes out, and exploring the region in shorter tours. This allows you to freely access the parks, waterfalls, remote lakes and villages you'd otherwise have to take a tour to see, without quite the load.

The rides described here follow dirt roads, rather than trails, as most trails are too steep or rutted to be of use to all but the most advanced riders. Single-track enthusiasts will be most likely to find rideable trails on volcanic plateaus such as those in Conguillío, Villarrica, and Vicente Pérez Rosales national parks, and most likely to find information on new and developing rides in tourist centers such as Pucón and Puerto Varas.

Bike Rentals:

In Santiago, you can rent bikes by the day from
- LYS, Miraflores 537, ☎ (2) 6337600

In San Javier
- 140

In Chillán-Las Trancas
- 220   • 65

In Radal-Siete Tazas
- 89

Bike Rentals:

In Villarrica
- LA TORRE SUIZA, ☎fax (45) 411213

In Pucón
- 222
- 172
- 12

In Puerto Varas
- 26

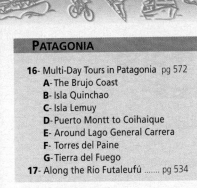

PATAGONIA

Patagonia's three regions give rise to three entirely distinct classes of bike tours.

The biking in Chiloé is that of a classic country tour, Chilean style. You ride through closely spaced little villages, camping or staying in simple, cozy inns, feasting on seafood in a waterfront restaurant or sharing a picnic on a solitary beach. Along the way, you can take a day off to browse a handicraft market or take a boat to an outlying island. Given, apart from the *Panamericana* most roads are gravel, but all in all Chiloé makes for excellent biking for all abilities.

The Carretera Austral is more of a challenge. Generally speaking, this is the most sought-after biking destination in Chile, but it's not for everyone. Though they call it a high-way, this is really a gravel road in bad repair, in many places composed of rocks as large as tennis balls, and often badly rutted. The weather can be harsh, the dust can be suffocating, and the villages are few and far between.

That said, most everyone who rides the Carretera comes out smiling. Many trans-continental cyclists heading from Alaska or Mexico to Tierra de Fuego recall this as one of their favorite sections of road, with its breathtaking landscape, abundant free camping, and friendly, generous locals. In general terms, the northern Carretera Austral is where you'll see more forests and fjords, while the southern section is more open and in places even arid, with sweeping views of glaciated peaks and the ice fields beyond. The only advice is to go well prepared, and if you're not sure exactly what that means, go with an operator.

Finally, biking in southern Patagonia is for the diehard bikers only. Unless you're heading east, you'll be battling head – or cross-winds across mile after mile of open country. If you're up to the task, you'll be rewarded with as much solitude as you're willing to handle.

PACIFIC ISLANDS

WORLD-CLASS SCENERY IN TORRES DEL PAINE

Trekking and Day Hikes

Most every visitor to Chile will eventually feel the call to get out and explore the country on foot. As experienced hikers are well aware, no other single activity is so accessible, requires so little specialized equipment, or allows such intimate contact with the natural world and local cultures.

There are hundreds, if not thousands, of worthwhile trails in Chile. We've tried to lead you to the best of them and, at the same time, point you in the right directions so you can continue exploring on your own. In order to make choosing and preparing for a trail easier, we've standardized some of the information:

GENERAL INFORMATION FOR INDEPENDENT TREKKERS

Trail Conditions

Though independent trekkers should not expect trail maintenance and signage to be up to par with that in the US or Europe, it is nonetheless safe to say that for experienced trekkers, most trails in this book pose few navigational difficulties. In general, the short hikes in the national parks – and a few longer ones in Torres del Paine – are the best marked. Elsewhere, you should bring a good topo map and a compass, and pay attention to orientation. (See pg. 42 for information on maps). For the inexperienced, the best advice is to stick to well-traveled trails in the national parks, or hire a guide. See below for more informational on local factors that can affect trail conditions.

Border Crossings

Though negotiations are under way to relax control over tourists and operators crossing over borders between Chile, Argentina, Bolivia, and Perú, this remains something of an issue. If you are hiking independently and plan on crossing the border via a non-authorized pass, you must first visit the local *aduana* (customs) post in order to get your passport stamped and inform officials of your intended route. Then, upon crossing the border, you must immediately report to the nearest customs post in Argentina.

Safety and Annoyances

Far from being a danger, Chile's mountain inhabitants can be a great source of help and information. Even women hiking alone have little to fear, though greater safety is always found in numbers.

Dogs are rarely more than a nuisance to hikers. If approached by a menacing-looking dog, grab a stout stick or bend down as if picking up a rock, and your would-be attacker will most likely turn tail and run.

Biting insects are rare and mostly restricted to the southern Lake Region and northern Patagonia. Collectively known as *tábanos*, they are attracted to dark clothing and are most common in sunny clearings. Mid-December to mid-January is normally the worst season for *tábanos*.

Mice and rats are only a problem in high-use campsites and *refugios*

ANOTHER PERFECT SUNRISE

where careless campers have left food lying about. To avoid perpetuating this problem, cook all food at least 50 feet from your tent, and hang food in a stuff sack in a different site. Do not keep food inside your tent.

On trails in national parks, bridges simplify crossings of most significant rivers. Elsewhere, however, you may have to ford rivers or streams. Springtime, obviously, is high-water season, and local rainfall at any time of year can cause rivers to rise with surprising speed. Glacially-fed rivers tend to drop in volume during the night, reaching a minimum in the early morning hours and increasing gradually throughout the day as the sun melts the glacier.

If you must cross, remember that the narrowest parts of a river are also the swiftest; the best place to cross is often at the bottom of a long pool. You should never cross a swift-moving river that is above mid-thigh, and any river above your calf should be treated with great respect. Facing upstream and leaning on a stout staff is a good crossing technique, and remember to unfasten your waist-belt before crossing, to avoid being swept downstream by your pack in the event of a fall. If planning a hike which requires fording a river, bring extra food in case you have to wait for the water level to drop.

Mountain weather in the Andes can change rapidly, both with approaching storm fronts and normal daily temperature oscillations. Always prepare for the worst, and learn to recognize the symptoms of common mountain ailments such as altitude sickness, hypothermia, frostbite, heatstroke and sunstroke.

For a suggested medical kit, health tips, weather information, notes on water availability and treatment, and low-impact camping techniques, see the Practical Information chapter.

Equipment

Day hikes in most parts of Chile require only the most rudimentary of equipment: good shoes, a water bottle, a bit of food, and an extra layer or two, depending on where you're headed. As always, plan for the worst: better to carry too much than to wish you had something you decided not to bring.

Overnight trips require a bit more planning and a bit more equipment. In fact, you'll generally require as much equipment for a two-night excursion as you will for five. Remember to pack heaviest items toward the bottom of your pack in order to maintain a

RATINGS & SYMBOLS

Duration: ⏱ Reliable information on trail length is not always available. Instead, we've given average walking times for a reasonably fit adult.

Type of trail:
Knowing that some people hate to walk out the way they came, we've indicated if the given trail is circuit ↻ (or loop), an out-and-back trail ⇄, or a traverse ↗ (ie. beginning at one point and ending at another). When a trail may be done in several ways, youll see this symbol ✛.

Difficulty: ■■□■■, varies ▣
This is a tricky one, as so many factors can influence the difficulty of a given trail. Still, we've done our best to classify each trail (into one of five grades, red being hardest), taking into account routefinding, vertical gain, probable climatic conditions, and so on.

Operators: Those that offer a given trek on horseback are followed by this icon 🐴

PARQUE NACIONAL LAUCA

low center of gravity, and when hiking in the south, use plastic garbage bags to waterproof important items such as your sleeping bag and dry clothes. Leather boots are generally better for hiking in the south than lightweight models, unless you like having wet feet. Vibram soles are best for hiking on sharp volcanic rocks, and a telescoping hiking pole can be invaluable for river crossings and for increased stability on rough terrain.

Equipment may be rented in some areas with lots of tourist traffic, such as San Pedro de Atacama, Pucón, and Puerto Natales. For further information on stoves, tents, and other camping equipment, see Preparing for the Outdoors on pg 39.

Food

Though some trekkers bring commercially available dehydrated meals with them from abroad, this is not really necessary. Chilean supermarkets – and even many small local markets – stock a wealth of nutritious, lightweight items that make great camping food. In many regions, foraging for edible plants can complement your backcountry diet.

GUIDED TRIPS

Guided hiking and trekking trips are offered in most regions of Chile, ranging from multi-day treks in which participants carry all their gear, to 'softer' overnights with horse support and lodging in comfortable *refugios*, to walking tours appropriate for travelers of any age and level of physical fitness. Asking pointed questions about

lodging, meals, required degree of physical fitness, and guide experience is key to finding the appropriate trip. As always, prices vary with the level of service.

EXPLORING

This guide does not pretend to be an exhaustive source of all possible hiking and trekking routes in Chile. We simply present a selection of what we believe to be the most noteworthy routes – either for scenery, accessibility, cultural or other values – within a framework which will allow you to continue exploring wherever your inclination leads you. One of the great things about hiking in the Andes is that trails lead almost everywhere.

The pre-Hispanic civilizations of northern Chile had no knowledge of the wheel, nor did they possess horses. Yet at the time of the

THE VAST DUNES OF THE VALLE DE LA LUNA

Spanish conquest, an active commerce united the people of the coast, the interior valleys, desert oases, sierra and altiplano. This commerce was driven by the llama – the indefatigable load-bearer of the Andes – and the equally tireless legs of messengers and traders.

The elegantly constructed roads that united the Inca empire in its late 15th century grandeur were essentially hiking trails, and walking continues to be the predominant form of travel in the sierra and altiplano. Hiking trips in this region can be extraordinarily rich cultural experiences, facilitating contact with local cultures and providing access to archaeological sites, including hundreds of petroglyphs and rock paintings.

Water and altitude are the two principal concerns for hikers and trekkers in northern Chile, and dealing with them should enter into the early stages of trip planning. See pg 263 for tips on dealing with water and altitude.

Navigation is another important issue. In the altiplano, the vastness of the landscape makes it relatively easy to find your way. Once you drop off the edge into valleys of the sierra or canyons around the Salar de Atacama, however, it can be more difficult; the highly eroded terrain makes for many choices. Remember when exploring that rivers diverge going up and converge going down, so you can always find way out to the mouth. Finding your way up the right tributary is the trick.

Daytime and nighttime temperatures in the desert and altiplano can vary up to 30°C, so if you're planning on sleeping out, be sure to pack warmly – even if it seems hot while you're throwing your stuff together in the hotel.

Coastal hikes may be less demanding because of their lower altitude, but the heat can be brutal. If you're hoping to hike along the coast, plan your trip for winter or early spring (Jul-Oct), when flowers and cactus will be in bloom, and birds will be nesting. The coastal deserts of the Norte Chico are especially beautiful this time of year.

The interior valleys of the Norte Chico present a final option for hikes in northern Chile. The uppermost reaches of the transverse agricultural valleys are steep and narrow, forming deep canyons and pools overhung with dense riparian vegetation. In springtime, these rocky creeks overflow with crystal clear runoff with the Andes, and flowers and fruit trees contrast with the arid hills. Here you can finally relax about water, and enjoy one of the most forgotten corners of the Chilean Andes.

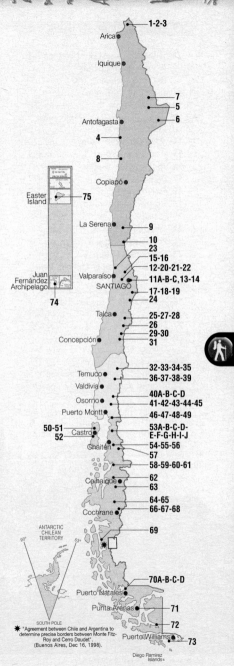

CENTRAL CHILE

GEOLOGICAL FORMATIONS IN THE UPPER COLORADO VALLEY

the classic week-long crossings of the Andes to Argentina. Right out Santiago's back door is the highest, most convoluted section of the entire Andean Cordillera, with glaciers, hotsprings, and microclimate forests hidden just beyond the first range of barren peaks. Most folks who live in central Chile have no idea of the wilderness at their doorstep.

You can hike year-round in this area, bearing in mind that routes in the high Andes will be covered in snow during the winter (attention backcountry skiers!). The best time for walking is from Oct-Jan, while the snow melts and the spring bloom hits its peak.

Water in this region should always be treated, and on some routes you'll need to carry all your water with you.

In central Chile you've got pretty much every sort of hike you could ask for, from easy afternoon strolls in the mountains or along the coast, to excellent three-day loops, to

THE SOARING PEAKS OF THE CENTRAL ANDES

CROSSING THE RIO COCHAMO

SOUTHERN CHILE

If you only have one day to spend in the south, spend it hiking. There is simply no better or simpler way to experience local forest and mountain environments and rural culture areas.

Most of the day hikes listed here, especially those in the national parks, follow clear footpaths and are reasonably well-marked, though trekkers should not expect signage to be up to US or European standards.

Many longer treks, however, are completely unmarked and receive no maintenance other than that of horses and cattle. Cattle are still allowed in many national parks, and in addition to making a quagmire of many trails, they also tend to create a labyrinth of compaths that can be very confusing to the uninitiated. Luckily, these most often lead to the same place, especially when the route leads directly up- or down-valley. A further complication is the rate of growth in Chile's southern forests, as trails not maintained for more than a year can disappear in fast-growing thickets of bamboo and other understory plants. To be on the safe side, ask park rangers or locals about trail conditions before setting off.

Once you get used to finding your own way, a whole new range of options opens up. For example, you could conceivably walk along the east side of the lakes from Riñinahue (on the SW shore of Lago Ranco) all the way to Ralún (on the Estuario de Reloncaví) crossing only one road. This network of pre-established horse trails will likely become the basis for the *Sendero de Chile*, a project-in-the-works that

THE CERRO CASTILLO TRAVERSE

would link Arica and Punta Arenas via a long-distance trail similar to the Appalachian and Pacific Crest Trails.

Bushwhacking or off-trail hiking is a simple proposition above treeline, but in the forest dense stands of bamboo (*quila* or *colihue*) can halt your progress altogether. Where bamboo grows in the trail, locals trim it with machetes, leaving long, pointy stalks that deserve a healthy measure of respect.

Though mountaineering equipment is available for rent in Pucón, it is almost impossible to rent camping equipment such as stoves, sleeping bags, or tents, and all these items should be purchased before arrival.

PATAGONIA

When most people think of trekking in Patagonia, they think of Torres del Paine, and with good reason: Torres undoubtedly has some of the wildest and most scenic trekking routes in the world. But as the listings below should demonstrate, Torres del Paine is just the tip of the iceberg. From the lush coastal forests of Chiloé to the barren tundra of Isla Navarino, this region boasts a truly awesome variety of hikes of all lengths. On most of these, you will never see another soul, but for those set on visiting Torres del Paine, the best advice is to do so in the

shoulder seasons (either Nov-Dec or Mar-April) to avoid the crowds.

Climate is a more serious factor here than in other parts of Chile, and it is essential that you come prepared with the best equipment you can afford. Tents, especially, should be stable in high winds, and good raingear is indispensable. Gaiters are an excellent idea as well, as many Patagonian shrubs produce annoying thistles and spiny seed husks that will quickly accumulate on your socks. Gaiters will also help for stream crossings.

Though you should seek to minimize your impact by using gas stoves, firewood is readily available in most areas. A look around the burned-over valleys around Coihaique, however, is reminder enough of the destructive potential of wildfires. Be sure to extinguish your fire completely.

Finally, if you spend any time at all in the Patagonian backcountry, you are sure to cross paths with rugged settlers or *colonos*, many of whom live many days' travel from the nearest town. Even if you can't speak Spanish, these *colonos* will often invite you into their home to share a mate or perhaps a meal. Declining to do so can be construed as an affront, so the best thing to do is relax, accept and enjoy the invitation. For tips on drinking *mate* like a true *colono*, see **c**.

PATAGONIA

PACIFIC ISLANDS

See pg 6 for photo credit

EXPLORING RANO RARAKU

Horseback Riding

As in the American West of the last century, horses form an inseparable part of the Chilean cultural fabric, and today can be found in nearly every rural and urban community in Chile (with the exception of those in the desert north). Chile's long-standing fascination with horses is further reflected in rodeos, rural *huaso* culture, and a popular racing circuit.

In this guide you'll find a couple of different kinds of listings. On the one hand, we've assembled a relatively complete list of stables and parks where you can rent horses on your own by the hour or the day. On the other hand is a selection of horsepacking trips – almost all of which can also be done on foot.

EQUIPMENT

Riding equipment is pretty self-explanatory, but be aware that the typical wooden Chilean stirrup is designed for narrow riding boots. If you're wearing wide-toed hiking boots, you're unlikely to fit more than your big toe into the stirrup – a precarious sensation, especially for novice riders. Whenever possible, request metal stirrups.

RIDING STABLES / RENTING HORSES

Horses are available for rent in literally hundreds of places in Chile: beaches, national parks, open lots, you name it. Prices are usually US$3-5/hour, though these prices can be negotiated, especially for longer rides. Often, horses accustomed to hourly rental have a mind of their own, dragging their heels on the way out and running full tilt on the way home. A firm hand and heels are required.

In addition to the short-term rentals listed in this book, horses may also be rented from locals for longer expeditions. Doing so requires at least a partial mastery of Spanish; prices are entirely dependent on the situation.

HORSEPACKING TRIPS

Horsepacking trips are one of the most enjoyable ways to travel in the Andes, allowing visitors of all ages and physical abilities to access remote valleys and mountain environments, and permitting a far greater daily mileage than can be accomplished on foot. A further benefit is the cultural experience provided by contact with local *arrieros*, who often subcontract guiding services and use of their horses to outfitters. Many *arrieros*, unfortunately, pay little attention to disposal of waste. You may wish to discuss this issue in advance with your outfitter.

THE CENTRAL ANDES
ON HORSEBACK

NORTHERN CHILE

1- River Valleys North of San Pedro .... pg 301

A few outfitters offer day trips on horseback, or incorporate horseback riding into longer hiking trips. These are generally limited to relatively lush oases such as San Pedro de Atacama, which for years served as an important watering hole and source of fodder for cattle trains bound from Salta, Argentina, to the nitrate stations of the Atacama Desert. You may also be able to rent horses from locals in the river valleys of the *Norte Chico*.

A CLASSICALLY ATTIRED CHILEAN *HUASO*

CENTRAL CHILE

EXPLORING CHILOE'S PACIFIC COAST

Horses are available for guided day trips and rental at numerous national parks, reserves, and beaches in the central region. If you ride in the mountains, you'll likely come into contact with some of Chile's rugged *arrieros*, while in the Central Valley, your experience may provide a glimpse of traditional *huaso* culture. The most outstanding horsepacking trips in this region are the one-week 'Cruce de los Andes' trips, leading across the high Andes to Argentina.

SOUTHERN CHILE

Horses are close to the heart of the south, having been readily adopted by the Mapuche Indians, who used them to control the cattle trade with Argentina and to spread their culture south across the *pampa*. And as Chilean and immigrant settlers arrived to claim lands usurped from the Mapuches, they too found horses to be an essential means of transport in mountain regions where roads have become a reality only in the past half-century.

Today, the mountains and forests of southern Chile and crisscrossed by thousands of kilometers of horse trails, you can rent horses and book trips seemingly everywhere. Hotels and hosterías often offer horseback riding to their guests, an in general all you have to do is ask around. From the numberless options, we've culled a few that are too good to miss or too reliable not to mention.

LOCAL HORSEMEN IN
NOTHERN PATAGONIA

> *There were several of the wild gaucho cavalry waiting to see us land; they formed by far the most savage picturesque group I ever beheld... their boots were very singular; they are made from the hide of the hock joint of the horses' hind legs, so that it is a tube with a bend in it. This they put on fresh, and thus drying on their legs it is never again removed....*
>
> **Charles Darwin**, from Charles Darwin's. The Voyage of the Beagle

PATAGONIA

Patagonia is one of those magical places where horses continue to play the same indispensable role that they did before the advent of the automobile. In the forests west of the Andes, the difficulties posed by the landscape have made slowed road-building or prohibited it altogether, and many families still live a long ride by horse or boat from

the nearest village. East of the Andes are the wide-open spaces of the pampa, home to the solitary *gaucho*: the lawless terrain that drew Butch Cassidy and the Sundance Kid when their luck had run out in the ever-tamer plains of the American West.

It is not surprising, then, that Patagonia boasts the country's best array of remote, multi-day horsepacking adventures. In addition to the trips listed here, you can find horses in just about any Patagonian town, and many hotels and hosterías can arrange trips in their local area.

PACIFIC ISLANDS

EASTERN ISLAND BY HORSEBACK

Mountaineering
and Rock Climbing

With over forty peaks above 6,000m and countless more of lesser heights that would be considered giants in most countries, Chile is a paradise for mountaineers. Vast differences in climate and geology along the 4,000km Chilean Andes create an equally vast variety of climbing conditions, including high-altitude ascents in the altiplano and the central Andes, easy walk-ups of volcanoes in the Lake District, big-wall assaults of Patagonian spires, and expeditionary climbing in the remote ranges of Tierra del Fuego and Antarctica.

Under normal conditions, most of the routes presented here require some specialized equipment, usually an ice axe and crampons. Ascents of peaks in the Coast Range and Andean foothills are found under hiking and trekking.

The information provided here is intended to be of use to climbers of varying abilities. For novice-to-intermediate climbers who wish to climb with a guide, listings and descriptions are provided for the most common or outstanding guided expeditions. For experienced climbers with their own equipment, we provide the basic information to help you select a route and bring it to execution; though we don't describe the routes in minute detail, we'll let you know what maps to use and where to look for more information.

HISTORY

The first mountaineers in Chile –and in fact the world– were subjects and priests of the Inca Empire. Discoveries of Inca artifacts and constructions throughout northern and central Chile have proven Inca ascents of at least 34 peaks, almost all of them above 5,000m. The highest of these is Llullaillaco, at 6,739m, an altitude that was not reached by modern mountaineers until 1855.

The Incas were not content with merely scaling these peaks. In many cases they built ritual stone platforms and small huts, and brought firewood up from below; in a few cases they entombed the mummified corpses of sacrificed children near the summits of sacred peaks such as Cerro El Plomo, the 5,424m giant overlooking Santiago. Accounts of early ascents in the Andes, beginning in the mid- to late-18th century, are rife with accounts of high-altitude archaeological findings and, unfortunately, the depredations of grave robbers. These last, together with unknown miners and *arriero* horsemen were probably the first in the post-Conquest era to star atop many peaks in the Andes.

The first modern mountaineers in the Andes were European aristocrats such as German Baron Alexander Humboldt, who in 1802 was turned back from the summit of Ecuador's Volcán Chimborazo at about 5,570m – a record in its era if you discount those set by

ALPENGLOW IN THE CENTRAL ANDES

the Incas centuries before. Another German, Edward Poeppig, was the first to climb in Chile, bagging the summit of Volcán Antuco in 1829; following him was Polish naturalist and explorer Ignacio Domeyko, who climbed the Nevados de Chillán in 1848 and made an attempt at Antuco that was thwarted by imminent eruption.

In the late 19th century, European aristocrats laid siege to the Andes in a series of massive expeditions. English Earl Edward Fitzgerald funded several such expeditions to Aconcagua, the highest peak in the Americas, finally summitted in 1897 by Swiss guide Matthias Zurbriggen. The necessity of resolving Argentine-Chilean border issues prompted a 14-year flurry of surveying and mapping throughout the length of the Andes, while the 1897 formation of Chile's first mountaineering club, the Club Gimnástico Alemán, opened the central Andes up to a new generation of climbers. Clubs such as this continue to play a major role in Chilean mountaineering, and are a good source of climbing information and contacts.

During the first half of the 20th century, explorers such as Alberto De Agostini, Dr. Federico Reichert, and Otto Nordenskjöld were among the first to venture among the labyrinthine glaciers and rime-encrusted peaks of Chilean Patagonia and Tierra del Fuego. Published memoirs of these early explorations are among our most fascinating works of mountain literature.

The last fifty years of mountaineering history in the Chilean Andes has focused on increasingly technical alpine rock and ice routes in the Central Andes and Patagonia. While it was émigré Germans who first dominated the climbing scene, the players in this later stage have been principally English, Italian, Polish, North American, Japanese, and – especially in the Central Andes – Chilean. Despite this recent flurry of activity, thousands of peaks in the Patagonian Andes still remain unclimbed.

GENERAL INFORMATION FOR INDEPENDENT CLIMBERS

The best available maps for most areas are those produced by the Instituto Geográfico Militar (IGM), and listings in this guide invariably refer to IGM maps. See [M] pg. 42 for details on map availability.

For multi-day trips, a sturdy mountain tent is an absolute necessity. In some regions, mountain huts or *refugios* serve as excellent base camps.

Porters, as are commonly available in the Himalayas and the Peruvian Andes, are not an option in the Chilean Andes. Horses and mules, however, are a load-bearing option for extended expeditions.

RATINGS

In Chile, mountaineering routes are usually rated using the French system, while rock climbs are rated using the Yosemite Decimal System. See [↕].

ROCK AND ICE CLIMBING

Rock climbing in Chile is growing in popularity, especially in central Chile, and there are number of quality climbing areas within an hour or two of Santiago. Here you can find both short, bolted sport routes of high difficulty and longer, more exposed sub-alpine and alpine routes, including some very daunting big walls (often on bad rock) in the Central Andes. In general, rock quality varies widely, with granitic intrusions and metamorphic rocks interspersed with crumbling volcanic formations. Upkeep is sporadic, so you should always revise and be prepared to replace fixed gear.

In recent years a number of climbing gyms have opened in Santiago, the best of which is undoubtedly Climbing Planet, located at Av. Condell 703, (☎ (2)6346391).

In the Lake District, quality rock is harder to come by, although a few small sport-climbing areas have been developed in recent years. From about 41°S, however, granitic intrusions become more prevalent, creating the famous spires of Patagonia and a nearly unknown big-wall valley known to a few as 'the Yosemite of South America.' All of these routes are difficult and committing, and the area is subject to some of the worst weather in the world.

Ice climbers will find excellent alpine ice routes in the Central and Patagonian Andes during the austral spring and summer (Nov-Mar). From Santiago south there are also a number of highly accessible glaciers where you can practice your skills during summer and fall, once the snow has melted out of the crevasses. Water ice is rarer, forming from Jun-Sep on a few select south-facing slopes in central Chile and Patagonia.

DESERT SPORT CLIMBING IN SOCAIRE

CANYONING

Long popular in Europe, canyoning trips are now offered by outfitters in Pucón, Puerto Varas, and Futaleufú. Wetsuits, helmets, and technical climbing gear are normally provided for these trips, in which participants rappel, swim, and otherwise invent their way down (or up) narrow slot canyons.

STEEP ICE IN YERBA LOCA, IN JULY

GUIDED MOUNTAIN TRIPS

Mountain guides in Chile must be certified by the *Federación de Andinismo* or by a corresponding foreign organization. Though most guides are qualified for the peaks they guide, on heavily traveled routes such as Volcán Villarrica they are worked so hard that personal attention may be lacking. If signing on for a one-day ascent, ask to meet your guide before signing on, and don't hesitate to look elsewhere if you find him (or her) less than helpful.

On multi-day expeditions guide-client relations are even more important, but these guides tend to take more pleasure in their work. In any case, always insist that safety procedures such as the all-important *self-arrest* be covered before beginning the ascent. Other concerns – as always in mountain environments – include hypothermia, frostbite, sunstroke, snow blindness, dehydration and heat exhaustion. Understanding these ailments and knowing how to avoid them is the client's responsibility as much as it is the guide's.

Many guided trips provide basic climbing equipment, including plastic boots, gaiters, crampons, and an ice axe. Single-day trips often provide mountain clothing as well, including nylon pants and jackets, mittens and sunglasses. Mutli-day trips usually provide tents and cooking equipment, but not sleeping bags, pads, or backpacks. Ask carefully about what equipment is provided, and if you have any doubt about the company you've signed on with, ask to see the equipment before you set out.

Prices vary with destination and company. The cheapest ascents are those in the Lake Region where competition between companies is fierce: the ascent of Volcán Villarica, all included, costs about US$40. Multi-day expeditions usually cost anywhere from US$100-200/day, with the most expensive peaks being big-name, logistically complicated peaks such as Ojos del Salado and Aconcagua. Don't skimp on guiding services: paying for the best guides and equipment you can afford is an investment you won't regret.

USEFUL ADDRESSES:

Federación de Andinismo, Almirante Simpson 77 (Metro Baquedano), ☎ (2)222-0888. The federation's library is supposedly open weekdays from 2000-2130 h, but call beforehand to confirm. Fairly good topos of technical routes are available here, plus a wealth of publications on climbing throughout the country. Members of the Club Andino meet

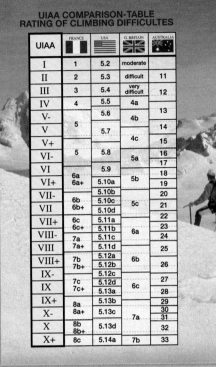

UIAA COMPARISON-TABLE RATING OF CLIMBING DIFFICULTES

UIAA	FRANCE	USA	G. BRITAIN	AUSTRALIA
I	1	5.2	moderate	
II	2	5.3	difficult	11
III	3	5.4	very difficult	12
IV	4	5.5	4a	13
V-	5	5.6	4b	13
V	5	5.7	4b	14
V+	5	5.7	4c	15
VI-	5	5.8	5a	16
VI	6a	5.9	5a	17
VI+	6a+	5.10a	5b	18 / 19
VII-	6b	5.10b	5c	20
VII	6b+	5.10c / 5.10d	5c	21
VII+	6c	5.11a	6a	22 / 23
VIII-	6c+	5.11b	6a	23
VIII	7a / 7a+	5.11c / 5.11d	6a	24 / 25
VIII+	7b / 7b+	5.12a / 5.12b	6b	26
IX-	7c	5.12c	6c	27
IX	7c+	5.12d / 5.13a	6c	28
IX+	8a	5.13b	7a	29
X-	8a+	5.13c	7a	30 / 31
X	8b / 8b+	5.13d	7a	32
X+	8c	5.14a	7b	33

Mountaintop Shrines in the Andes

The Inca religion was hylotheistic: all matter was divine. The world was alive with numinous rocks, springs, and peaks, known collectively as wak'a. These were regarded as shrines to the creator and as totemic ancestors of human groups. Some wak'a had temples and rock-hewn altars; others were left in their natural state.'

– Ronald Wright, *Stolen Continents: The 'New World' Through Indian Eyes Since 1492.*

The first modern mountaineers to ascend many peaks in northern Chile were surprised to find examples of these *wak'a* shrines at the very summits of sacred peaks such as Licancabur, Pili, Miñiques, Miscanti, Llullaillaco, Copiapó, Doña Ana, and Jotabeche. Some consisted of extensive stone constructions that served as ritual tombs for children sacrificed during the poorly understood *Capacocha* ceremony. The child, considered an intermediary between the local chief and the divine Inca ruler, would be taken to Cuzco to meet the Inca; great feasts would take place and honor bestowed on the child's family. Then the procession would climb to the summit of the holy peak, where the child would be fed *chicha* (maize alcohol) and entombed alive amongst ritual burial artifacts. Archaeologist Johan Reinhard, who has perhaps climbed more Andean peaks than any other single individual, has discovered over 40 of these high altitude ritual sites on Andean peaks in Perú, Bolivia and Chile.

INCA SHRINES ON LLULLAILLACO

upstairs on Wednesdays after 2000; this is good place to meet climbing partners.

Cuerpo Socorro Andino, ☎ 136, the Chilean mountain rescue service. Before heading to the mountains, it is a good idea to call and leave details of your route and expected return. Another option is to leave this information with local *Carabineros*.

Fronteras y Límites, ☎ (2)697-1909. Technically, foreign visitors must request permission from this government bureau for any ascent in a so-called 'border area,' which is to say anywhere in the Andes. The easiest way to avoid problems is to apply for permission in advance with a list of all the mountains you wish to climb, and estimated dates.

Conaf, ☎ (2)390-0125 (see regional chapters for local offices) for general information on national parks and other protected areas.

ALTITUDE

The major difficulty posed by many of the peaks listed in this guide – and especially those in northern and central Chile – is their extreme altitude. Not dealing properly with altitude will not only keep you from summiting, it can also be very dangerous.

RATINGS & SYMBOLS

Duration: Round-trip route duration for normal parties is given this symbol ⏱. Further information on average times is given in the text.

Difficulty: Three grades of route difficulty are given. Technical grades (when appropriate) are included within the text.

◼ Non-technical walkup at moderate altitude. No experience required.

◻ Non-technical walkup at altitude, or moderately technical routes where some experience may be required.

◼ Highly remote or technical routes where experience is required. Altitude and/or weather may be serious factors.

Here are a few suggestions to increase your chances of success at altitude:

• Climb high, sleep low. On most major peaks, you'll need to set up a number of camps before making your summit push. The idea is to ferry loads to upper camps, returning to lower camps to sleep. You'll sleep better and, after a couple of trips, be ready to move on up.

• Above 2,500m, give one day of acclimatization for every additional 300m gain in elevation. This is a general rule that can be bent if you're already acclimatized.

• Drink water, eat lightly, and avoid caffeine and alcohol. If you have a history of problems with altitude, you may try Acetazolamide (Diamox), a prescription drug that has been proven effective in minor doses of 62.5 or 125mg, twice a day, beginning with the initial ascent and concluding one day after reaching your highest point. The memory-enhancing herbal supplement *Gingko Biloba* also appears to counteract altitude sickness.

• Finally, pay attention to the warning signs. Dizziness, nausea, headache, insomnia and loss of appetite are all signs that your body is having a hard time coping. It is always better to descend or take some time off than to push your luck and risk hospitalization or even death.

NORTHERN CHILE

Most mountaineering ascents in northern Chile are non-technical walk-ups of high-altitude volcanoes, often exceeding 6,000m in altitude. Adjusting to the extreme altitude is usually the primary challenge on these altiplano peaks, so be sure to allot adequate time for acclimatization.

With base elevations normally at or above 4,000m, total vertical gain averages around 2,000m on most of these peaks, though this figure is considerably higher on super high-altitude peaks such as 6,893m Ojos del Salado.

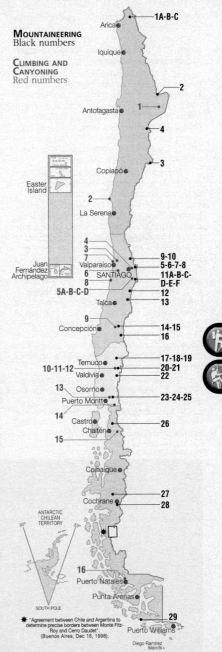

MOUNTAINEERING
Black numbers

CLIMBING AND CANYONING
Red numbers

The more commonly climbed peaks in northern Chile, such as Volcán Licancabur, near San Pedro de Atacama, may be climbed in a single day from base camp, given adequate acclimatization and fitness.

As a general rule, peaks above 6,000 meters have permanent snow or ice on their southern faces, often forming 'penitentes' – rows of snow spikes of up to a meter in height which lean toward the midday sun. Composed of crumbling rock, scree and sand, these peaks can be especially trying when not covered with snow – the classic two-steps-forward, one-step back situation.

There are two separate weather patterns at work here. Precipitation in the northern Altiplano originates in the Amazon Basin to the east and occurs almost exclusively in December and March, so plan a visit outside these dates. Further south, the effect of the Altiplanic Winter tapers off, and high peaks south of San Pedro de Atacama receive most precipitation during the Austral winter, just like the rest of Chile. During the dry seasons, you can expect perfectly clear and sunny weather, with unlimited visibility. At night, temperatures drop precipitously, and climbers are advised to get an early start to take advantage of firm snow conditions. Because of the extreme altitude, proximity to the equator, and atmospheric aridity, solar radiation is extremely intense, and sunblock, glasses and a brimmed hat are an absolute must.

Though access to these peaks might appear to be straightforward, distances on the altiplano can be very deceiving. See 'Overlands' for listing of 4WD transportation services to remote peaks such as Ojos del Salado, Llullaillaco, and Copiapó.

CENTRAL CHILE

The central Andes – training round for generations of Chilean *andinistas* – constitute Chile's greatest concentration of high altitude peaks, including the only technical high altitude climbs in the country. It is also the site of dozens of less demanding peaks in the 3-4,000m range, feasible for anyone with reasonable hiking fitness.

Choosing the right season to climb is crucial. In the winter, most folks stay out of the Central Andes, though with a good weather forecast ski mountaineering trips are great option. In spring, the storms taper off and then end

THE NORTH FACE OF PUNTA ZANZI

NEAR THE SUMMIT OF VOLCAN OSORNO

For climbers looking for a guided trip, the best advice is to look beyond Aconcagua. Sure, it's cool to say you've climbed the highest peak outside of the Himalayas, but there's a whole range of equally challenging, more aesthetic, and much more solitary peaks just waiting to be tackled.

SOUTHERN CHILE

Looming as much as 3,200m above the great lakes and glacial valleys of the Lake District, the highly active, snowcapped volcanoes of the south are the most distinctive, accessible, and popular mountaineering peaks in the country. To the present, guided trips have focused upon two peaks, Volcán Villarica and Volcán Osorno, mostly because of these peaks' proximity to major tourist centers, but independent climbers have a wealth of more remote, equally attractive peaks to choose from, at a variety of technical grades.

As elsewhere in Chile, these peaks are often covered with extensive glaciers, especially on their south and west faces. The actual extent of these glaciers varies depending on each peak's altitude and geographical position, and it is no easy task to guess which peaks you'll need ropes for and which not. Most glaciers are deeply crevassed, so you're better off exploring new routes early in the season, before the snow bridges weaken, or later on once they've disappeared altogether. Once the snow melts, these exposed crevasses and seracs are great for practicing your ice climbing skills.

Even many non-glaciated faces remain snow-covered throughout the year, and on active volcanoes, radiant heat often produces deep fractures in the snowpack, which appear as crevasses. Ski mountaineers should be especially alert regarding these fractures, as they are not always easy to spot until you're right on top of them.

Though it is possible to climb most of these peaks at any time throughout the year, the weather is the big deciding factor: there's a

altogether in mid-late October, and from then until April it's open season. The best snow conditions – important in this crumbling, talus-strewn range– last from October-January. From January on, alpine ice and 'penitentes' become more common, snow bridges across crevasses tend to disappear, and lower elevation peaks may lose all snow cover. In the southernmost part of the region (ie from Chillán south), weather patterns and climbing conditions more closely resemble those of the south.

Bad weather approaches almost exclusively from the west or SW, and as a consequence it is on these slopes that glaciers are found. North-facing slopes, of course, are the first to lose snow, and are often scoured by the strong north winds that signal an approaching front.

Though popular with Chilean climbers, the Central Andes see few ascents by foreigners. Access to these peaks can seem complicated, mostly because you can't see most of them from the Central Valley, but in many cases, buses will take you right there, and if traveling in a group, taxis are not that expensive. Santiago is also a good place to get in touch with a local climbing club for a ride to the mountains. Experienced climbers looking for a challenge should direct their attention to technical alpine walls such as the north face of Punta Zanzi, the south face of Cerro Arenas, the south face of Cerro Morado, or further south to the remote granite spires of the Cordón de Granito and the Torres del Brujo.

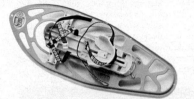

big difference between climbing on a clear day, with views of ten or more surrounding volcanoes, and slogging up into zero-visibility cloudcover. Rain and snowfall are concentrated from April – Sept, and winter storms are known to last up to a month, burying entire ski lift towers and ruling out climbing altogether. Beginning in late Sept, the fine weather starts to move in, and the peaks are prime for ski mountaineering trips. By the end of Dec on a normal year, skiing is pretty much out, and the lower slopes of the volcanoes are generally cleared of snow, which can simplify access but can make for frustrating walking upon loose volcanic ash. Without gaiters, you will spend all day emptying your boots of little rocks.

If you have experience but don't have your own gear, you can most easily rent it from operators in Pucón and Puerto Varas. If you do not have the necessary experience, you need to go with a guide, but be aware that not all guides and operators are the same. Especially in Pucón – where everyone seems to be hawking *el volcán* – you need to ask around before signing on with any company. Be sure to try on your equipment the night before, since climbs begin early in the morning. This will give you a chance to meet your guide and inspect the operator's equipment.

For the past half-century, the Patagonian Andes have fascinated the global climbing community, attracting one major expedition after another; traveling halfway around the world to wait out the weather in a grimy climbers' *refugio* has become a rite of passage for the world's climbing elite. By definition, nearly all the major ascents in this area could be considered 'extreme,' either through sheer climatic factors, remoteness, or technical difficulty.

We don't go into much detail on technical routes on the granite spites of the far south, since most of these routes – on walls of 1,200 m or greater – are beyond the grasp of most visitors. In general, most of the climbing activity of this type has been focused upon Torres del Paine and the Fitzroy/ Cerro Torre group, the former in Chile, the latter on the border but accessed via Argentina. Route information and accounts of expeditions in these areas are readily available in the American Alpine Journal and in back issues of *Climbing* magazine. If you are planning a climbing trip to Torres del Paine, you must pay a $100 per person climbing fee at the Difrol office at Bulnes 544 in Puerto Natales. There is no fee for climbing in Fitzroy or Cerro Torre.

THE WORLD FAMOUS TORRES DEL PAINE

Climbing Pioneers in Patagonia

There are pioneers and then there are pioneers. In this case, when you're talking about a region that to the present day attracts only the most seasoned (and some would add masochistic) of big-wall alpine climbers, you're talking a whole new level of suffering. These are the guys who got there first, who braved the elements in wool and leather, slept under tarps and led on hemp ropes.

The first – and in many ways most impressive – was Italian priest **ALBERTO DE AGOSTINI (1)**, who beginning in 1910 spent over thirty years working in the Salesian missions of Magallanes and Tierra del Fuego and exploring the far southern Andes. Often lugging heavy photo equipment **(4)**, Agostini visited the Torres del Paine and Fitzroy regions, nearly crossed the Southern Ice Fields, and organized the first ascents of Patagonian behemoths Monte San Lorenzo and Monte Sarmiento, in 1956.

German geologist **FEDERICO REICHERT** arrived in South America in the early 1900's under the auspices of the Universidad de Buenos Aires, to study the mineral deposits of NW Argentina and contribute to ongoing efforts to map the cordillera. Already an accomplished mountaineer, Reichert started scaling peaks in the northern altiplano, then engaged in extensive explorations of the glaciers and high peaks of the central Andes (including several unsuccessful attempts at Aconcagua), and finally looked south. Here he climbed Osorno and made attempts at Tronador and Puntiagudo, two of the most difficult volcanoes in the Lake District. In 1920, Reichert turned his attention to the Patagonian Ice Fields, visiting them on three separate occasions, in 1920, 1939, and 1940. Here, too, Reichert's dreams of climbing San Valentín, the highest peak in Patagonia, were stymied by the perpetual rain.

Following the initiative of Reichert, and getting too old for the sheer physical challenges of the Himalaya, British mountaineers **HAROLD WILLIAM TILLMAN (2)** and **ERIC SHIPTON (3)** mounted a series of hard-nosed expeditions in diverse locations on the ice fields and on Tierra del Fuego; Tillman's book 'Mischief in Patagonia' describes his adventures. Shipton visited the range repeatedly from 1958 to 1963, traversing the Darwin Range, making a first ascent of Mount Darwin, and completing the first north-south traverse of the Northern Patagonian Ice Field. For the latter endeavor, Shipton's party lugged 720 lbs of equipment and food over a course of 250 miles, spending a total of 52 days on the ice.

(1)

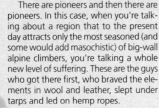

(4)

(2)

(3)

Other types of climbing in Patagonia are less technically demanding but do require stamina, perseverance, and top-rate equipment. Approaches to remote volcanoes such as Michimahuida and Melimoyu involve bushwhacking through miles and miles of dense rainforests, at altitudes low enough that it tends to rain rather than snow. Expeditions on the Patagonian Ice Fields or in the wild ranges of Tierra del Fuego can expect a couple of days of clear weather per month, if that.

While January and February are usually considered the peak summer months, they do not necessarily provide the best climbing conditions. The shoulder seasons, especially November and March -April, are often less windy and more stable climatically, though temperatures are somewhat cooler.

Very few operators run mountaineering trips in Patagonia. The few areas that are offered commercially include Torres del Paine, Monte San Lorenzo, and Monte San Valentín.

SPORT CLIMBING AT
LAS CHILCAS

Skiing and Snowboarding

Each year, more and more skiers and snowboarders are realizing that they don't have to spend the Northern Hemisphere's summer dreaming of fresh tracks – they can have them right here in the Andes. Together with Argentina, Chile is the Southern Hemisphere's top destination for skiers and snowboarders, with wonderfully diverse terrain, dependable snow conditions, resorts ranging from the plush and ultramodern to down-home rustic, and enough untracked backcountry to bring tears to your eyes. You could spend the whole winter chasing the snow from one mountain to another, and still end up feeling like you'd just scratched the tip of the iceberg. Those who think the southern Hemisphere is just for escaping the cold of winter don't know what they're missing: just ask the instructors and ski bums who come back year after year, fired up for another season in Chile.

THE TERRAIN

Though every mountain has its own characteristics, it is possible to make a few generalizations about the skiing in each geographic region. In central Chile, which is relatively close to the equator, the ski areas are way up high, and the mountains are big, rugged, and treeless. You need a lot of snow to cover up the jumbled rocks of these crumbling giants. The wide-open skiing and scale of terrain is more akin to resorts in the Alps than anywhere in the States.

In the south, the ski areas are all on volcanoes, which are the largest peaks in the region. Again, tree skiing is exceedingly rare, and the big gullies formed by lava and ash flows create natural halfpipes ideal for snowboarding.

Lift-served terrain is often not as challenging as expert skiers might desire; the true black diamond is a rarity. If you are accustomed to shredding steep chutes and slopes steeper than 40°, you should expect to hike or traverse for your turns. Your efforts will be amply rewarded.

THE SNOW

The snow, too, varies depending on latitude. The snow at the high-altitude resorts of central Chile is relatively light – not exactly Utah but good enough for guaranteed faceshots. Unfortunately, the lightest snow is the least consistent, and on dry years the ski areas above Santiago sometimes have to open late and close early in the season (if they open at all). The last ten years, as a whole, have been relatively meager – a long-time avalanche expert and backcountry guru from one of the mines in the Andes has reported storms during the 'glory years' dumping 30 feet in a week. We're all waiting anxiously for that cycle to come around again.

To the south, the snow turns gradually heavier. The season starts earlier and lasts longer, but you lose more days to bad

A WORLD OF TERRAIN, RIGHT ABOVE SANTIAGO

weather, and at the lower-elevation areas you have to look out for rain. The best bet in the south is the spring corn snow; it's hard to beat skiing in short sleeves with a multitude of lakes sprawled in the valley below.

The season throughout Chile generally begins in June and finishes up in September, though some areas in the south stay open through October. How do you know what the skiing is going to be like before you arrive? First, check out ski areas' websites for up-dated snow conditions; although the information may be a little biased, but at least you'll know if the areas are open or not. Next, you can check out global weather sites such as www.intellicast.com or www.weather.com. Pay special attention to reports on El Niño, because El Niño means fat snow in Chile.

RESORT INFRASTRUCTURE

Resort infrastructure varies widely. The big resorts of the Central Region – including Portillo, La Parva, El Colorado / Farellones, Valle Nevado and Termas de Chillán – are the best-equipped: you still won't find any high-speed quads, but lifts are more than sufficient for the number of skiers. All these areas groom their slopes, offer rentals and classes, and so on; Valle Nevado, Portillo, and Farellones/Colorado even have snowmaking. Ticket prices are a little cheaper than the

united states during high season, and go way down during the shoulder season. If you pay attention you can often save money on mid-week specials. A common complaint of skiers on a budget is the lack of mid-range accommodation at most areas, but usually you can find reasonable options near the mountain.

Villarrica-Pucón and Antillanca are mid-range areas, with fewer lifts and services than the resorts of central Chile, while Chapa Verde and El Fraile are another half-step down – though they do boast fairly respectable terrain. At the bottom of the list are tiny Lagunillas, Antuco, Lonquimay, Llaima, and Cerro Mirador. Still, the atmosphere at these community-run resorts is almost reason enough to visit, and though the lift-served terrain is appropriate only for beginners and beginning intermediates, experts can always find steep terrain above the lifts (see 📖).

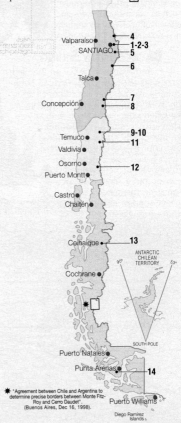

VILLARRICA-PUCON:
A SPRING SKIING

HELICOPTER SKIING

Heli-skiing is offered at Portillo, Valle Nevado, and Termas de Chillán, all of which are blessed with extraordinary terrain in the surrounding area. See the appropriate regional chapter for destination suggestions. Take note that in central Chile it is important to get out early, because as temperatures rise during the day, the air loses density and it costs more to run a helicopter. Insist on standard safety equipment such as avalanche beacons and shovels. Prices vary by destination and number of passengers.

BACKCOUNTRY SKIING

Even if you don't have all the necessary gear to stage a full-fledged backcountry ski trip, you can still open your horizons considerably just by walking a bit when skiing at a resort. With snowshoes or telemark/randonnee equipment, however, the Andes are your playground, and you don't have to be a great skier to enjoy skinning up to a glacier or into a silent araucaria forest. In this guide, we've tried to make concrete suggestions about backcountry runs near the ski resorts, as well as indicating which mountaineering and trekking routes can also be done on skis. Ski mountaineering on the volcanoes in the south is growing in popularity, and you can even rent randonnee gear and snowshoes in Pucón.

Safety, of course, is the biggest concern. During the winter months, avalanches are a serious concern, especially in the central Andes; big storms are usually accompanied by northerly winds, which create massive cornices above lee slopes. The wetter snow of the south makes for safer snow pack, but the weather is dicier. The best bet is generally to wait until after spring consolidation of the snow pack, making late September through early November the best time for backcountry ski trips.

It is often a good idea to leave details of your destination and expected return with Carabineros and the mountain rescue service, the *Cuerpo de Socorro Andino* (see Mountaineering). Always bring your beacon and shovel, and make sure you know how to use them. If you are unsure of your abilities, hire a guide.

NORDIC (CROSS-COUNTRY) SKIING

Nordic skiing is a rarity in Chile, as quality snow pack is usually only present above tree-line, in areas too steep for lightweight touring. Termas de Chillán does offer Nordic

ANDEAN POWDER SHOTS

QUICK COMPARISON CHART — RESORT INFRASTRUCTURE	Vertical drop in m.	Maximum elevation in m.	Nº of chairs	Nº of surface lifts	Nº of trails	% Easy	% Intermediate	% Difficult	% Expert	On-Mountain Rentals (snowboard, ski)	Lessons (snowboard, ski)	Snowboard park	Grooming
Portillo	836	3330	5	8	23	20	20	20	30	sb, ski	sb, ski	no	★★★
La Parva	960	3630	4	10	30	15	55	20	10	sb, ski	sb, ski	no	★★★
Farellones-Colorado	903	3333	4	12	22	40	20	30	10	sb, ski	sb, ski	no	★★★
Valle Nevado	790	3670	3	6	27	15	40	30	15	sb, ski	sb, ski	no	★★★
Lagunillas	350	2480	0	3	12	20	60	20	-	ski	ski	no	★
Chapa Verde	760	3060	1	4	22	NA	NA	NA	NA	ski	ski	no	★★
Termas de Chillán	1100	2700	4	5	28	20	30	30	20	sb, ski	sb, ski	yes	★★★
Antuco	450	1850	0	2	2	100	-	-	-	ski	ski	no	-
Lonquimay	200	1850	0	2	2	100	-	-	-	ski	none	no	-
Llaima	300	1800	0	2	5	70	30	-	-	ski	none	no	-
Villarrica-Pucón	960	2440	3	5	22	20	30	50	-	sb, ski	sb, ski	no	★
Antillanca	464	1534	1	4	11	25	50	25	-	sb, ski	sb, ski	no	★
El Fraile	800	1825	-	2	4	30	20	50	-	ski	none	no	★
Cerro Mirador	350	450	1	-	20	10	50	40	-	ski	ski	no	★

rentals and has a ski track leading through the woods around the hotel, but snow quality and trail preparation is marginal. Cerro Mirador, near Punta Arenas, also has a Nordic skiing area with relatively consistent conditions, but no equipment for rent. Hostería Ecole, in Pucón, offers Nordic skiing and snowshoeing trips in the Cañi nature reserve.

GEAR

If you're planning on doing a lot of skiing on your trip, bring your own gear. A good strong ski bag protects your equipment and holds a ton of stuff, and airlines don't charge extra for transporting skis. You may be able to sell some equipment when you leave, depending on whom you've met and how much time you have to spend.

If you're not in Chile specifically to ski, rentals are cheap and easy to come by. Every ski area rents boots, skis, and poles – though we can't vouch for quality at the smaller areas – and you can pick up a hat and gloves for a few dollars, if you don't already have them. It may be cheaper to rent equipment in town and bring it with you to the area. If you come

unprepared and plan to ski enough to make renting uneconomical, buying equipment can be a reasonable option, especially at used equipment stores in Santiago.

SKI WEEKS AND GUIDED TOURS

It's almost laughable how easy it can be to book a ski vacation in Chile. All the major resorts have websites through which you can confirm prices and book an all-inclusive ski week. They'll make your travel arrangements, get you to the resort, and send you on your way at the end of the week. The downside is that you'll have to really pay attention to even notice that you're in a foreign country, but if you're only interested in the skiing, ski weeks are the way to go.

Another option is posed by a couple of new companies (Powderquest and Casa Tours) that take you on a grand tour of Chile's ski areas, allowing you to sample the tremendous variety of Chilean ski areas and providing a more integrated cultural experience. A flexible itinerary allows you to follow the snow up and down the Andes.

Flying

From ground level, Chile is a feast for the eyes. But from the air perspective shifts completely, with spectacular results: the immense peaks to the east turn out to be only foothills of the greater Andes, immense sea-level glaciers appear as mere trickles off the Patagonian Ice Fields, and chains of volcanoes reveal long fractures in the earth's crust. This section is dedicated to the various ways in which travelers can get up into the air and broaden their perspective.

The simplest method is simply to take a **commercial flight**. All domestic flights travel north or south, to the west of the Andes; if you want mountain views, be sure to sit on the left side of the plane when flying south, on the right when flying north. It may even be worthwhile to book a ticket with more expensive fare basis, in order to reserve the right to postpone if the weather on your scheduled date is overcast.

You can only see so much from 30,000 feet, however. If you want to really get a look at the landscape, you have a couple of options:

Scenic Flights

Small planes are generally available for scenic flights at a going rate of about US$300/hour, with a capacity for five passengers.

In **central Chile**, AEROTEC offers a variety of scenic flights and aerial programs including gliders, hot air balloons, dirigibles and WW II biplane flights over the Coast Range or the Andes. Resourceful travelers with some time on their hands and a little cash in their pocket may also be able to talk their way onto one of the private planes departing from Santiago's Aerodromo Eulogio Sánchez in La Reina.

Helicopter tours and transport to the ski areas above Santiago are available through the following companies:

LÍNEA DE AEROSERVICIOS **S.A.** ....
.... ☎ (2)2735209
AERO CENTRO .... ☎ (2)2328843
ALFA HELICOPTEROS .... ☎ (2)2739999
COPTERS .... ☎ (2)2133330

Scenic flights in the **southern Lake District** may be arranged through the Servicio Aéreo Regional in Puerto Montt , ☎ (65)259131

AERIAL VIEW OF VIÑA DEL MAR AND VALPARAISO

SAF

PARAGLIDING NEAR FARELLONES

In **Patagonia**, short-haul flights in small propeller-driven planes are widely available along the Carretera Austral south of Coihaique, where on clear days you can get unbelievable views of the coast, the Andes, Lago General Carrera and the Patagonian Ice Fields. Generally speaking, these flights are not particularly expensive, and can save you hours of bus travel. For regularly scheduled flights throughout Patagonia, see the air travel section in the Practical Information chapter.

Laguna San Rafael is the most common destination for scenic and charter flights in Patagonia (see pg. 541 for details). Flights depart from Coihaique and may be arranged through the following companies:

AEROHEIN:
Coihaique .... ☎ (67) 232772
TRANSPORTES AEREOS SAN RAFAEL LTDA.
Coihaique .... ☎ (67) 232048

For charter and scenic flights elsewhere in northern Patagonia, contact the following organizations:

SERVICIO AÉREO REGIONAL
Puerto Montt .... ☎ (65) 259130.
CLUB AÉREO DE CASTRO
Castro .... ☎ (65) 632264
AEROTAXI DON CARLOS
Coihaique and Cochrane, see Practical Info for contact information.

In addtion to their regularly scheduled services throughout the **Magallanes province**, **AEROVIAS DAP** also offers scenic flights over Torres del Paine and Cape Horn and to Villa Las Estrellas, a collection of Antarctic research stations in the South Shetland Islands. Flights depart from Punta Arenas; see pg. 604 the Antarctica chapter for details.

Arica • ─1A-B

Iquique • ─2A-B-C-D

Antofagasta •

Easter
Island

Copiapó •

La Serena •

6
Valparaíso •
SANTIAGO •

3A-B-C-D-
E-F, 4
5

Juan
Fernández
Archipelago

Talca •

Concepción •

Temuco •
Valdivia •
Osorno •
Puerto Montt •

Castro •
Chaitén •

Coihaique •

ANTARCTIC
CHILEAN
TERRITORY
90°
53°

Cochrane •

✳

SOUTH POLE

Puerto Natales •
Punta Arenas •

✳ "Agreement between Chile and Argentina to
determine precise borders between Monte Fitz-
Roy and Cerro Daudet"
(Buenos Aires, Dec 16, 1998).

Puerto Williams •

Diego Ramírez
Islands

Learning to Parasail

Beginning paraglid-
ing classes typically
last 6-10 days and
include a combina-
tion of classroom and
field sessions. Paragliders come in different
sizes and models corresponding to the
pilot's weight and ability, so make sure that
the school you select has a variety of
different wings, as well as helmets, radios,
emergency parachutes, and a complete
first-aid kit – all necessities for a safe and
productive learning experience. Other
concerns include the size and regularity of
takeoff and landing zones – sand dunes are
undoubtedly the most forgiving place to
learn. Beginning courses typically cost
around US$250, not including food or
lodging – significantly cheaper than in the
united states or Europe.

PARAGLIDING SITES IN CHILE

1- Arica .... pg 277
   A- Poconchile
   B- El Morro
2- Iquique .... pg 288
   A- Duna Cerro Dragón
   B- Palo Buque
   C- Alto Hospicio
   D- Cross Country Flights
3- Around Santiago .... pg 368-369
   A- Cuesta Barriga
   B- Batuco
   C- Cerro del Medio
   D- Colina
   E- Santuario de la Naturaleza
   F- Cerro La Pirámide
4- Farellones and Valle Nevado pg 370
5- Las Vizcachas .... pg 377
6- Maitencillo and Marbella .. pg 401

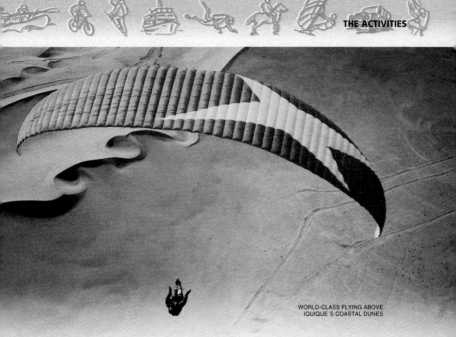

WORLD-CLASS FLYING ABOVE
IQUIQUE'S COASTAL DUNES

Paragliding

Invented by the French in the mid-1980's, paragliders are basically square parachutes formed of a series of parallel tubes, which fill with air, allowing a glide-to-descent ratio of over 9:1. With a running start off a hilltop, an expert paraglider can ride for hours on thermal and dynamic updrafts – the former caused by differential heating, the latter by local topography. As with a standard parachute, direction and speed is controlled using handheld pull-cords.

Nearly constant SW winds create ideal paragliding conditions along much of the Chilean coast and the Andes, particularly in northern and central Chile. Options for initiates include tandem flights (in which an inexperienced client is harnessed to an instructor) and paragliding lessons. Tandem flights normally cost about US$40-50 per person, and last from 15 minutes to an hour, depending upon the site and wind conditions.

Experienced paragliders should have no problem finding contacts and flying partners. Used wings can often be found in the classified pages of newspapers or through local outfitters, who may also be able to help visiting paragliders sell their gear upon departure.

Northern Chile's immense dunes and steep coastal escarpments make this one of the top destinations in the world for paragliding. Regular, unobstructed SW winds up to 40km/hr provide near-perfect conditions all day, every day, all year long.

Iquique is the capital of Chilean paragliding, with a growing number of local pilots and a couple of highly reputable outfitters offering classes and tandem flights. Above and to the south of the city, extensive dunes form a huge playground ideal for novices and classes, while experts will want to try their luck at long distance cross-country flights up the coast: the local record exceeds 185km and well over eight hours of continuous flight time.

With continued exploration, new sites are turning up all along the coast. Inland, wind conditions are much more complicated, though expert pilots will surely be tempted by the 5-6,000m volcanoes of the altiplano.

While conditions are not as consistent as those in the north, **central Chile** stands out for the sheer number of paragliding schools, shops and local contacts to get visiting pilots up to speed. You can fly along the coast or in the foothills of the Andes, and the past few years have seen a couple of truly impressive cross-country flights, including the 113km traverse from Rancagua to Colina – a total of over five hours of continuous flying.

In **southern Chile**, you may be able to sign up for a tandem flight in Pucón (either on the slopes of Volcán Villarrica or from the fields below Cerro San Francisco) through Trawen Outdoor Center.

Navigation

This section provides an overview of the numerous options for maritime and fluvial travel in Southern Chile, Patagonia, and Antarctica. Included here you'll find the following:

• **Informal motor launches**, providing access to sea lion colonies and offshore islands, or alternatively providing transport on lakes and flat-water rivers in the south. These are generally intended for use by local residents, and departure times are often irregular, so you must get used to asking questions (occasionally of several different sources) to get reliable information. These boats and services are listed individually throughout the text as follows:

INFORMAL MOTOR LAUNCHES

EXPLORING THE RIO CRUCES WETLANDS

● **Cruises and charters aboard motor yachts, sailboats, and cruise ships,** both on lakes and the extensive waterways of the southern archipelago. This includes an extremely wide range of services, with trips lasting from a single afternoon to as much as a month, on craft from ten to a hundred meters in length. As the quality of the trip depends almost as much upon the craft as it does upon the destination, it is essential that you investigate offerings and talk to operators before booking a trip. These boats and their services are listed individually or (in areas of high concentration) grouped together in the text to allow for ease of comparison. The listings are as follows.

THE MAGICAL FJORD OF NORTHERN PATAGONIA

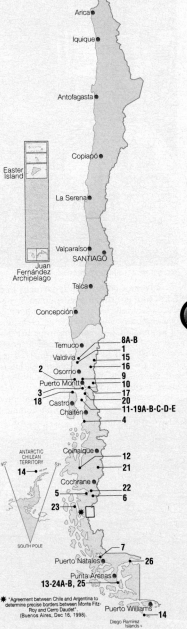

Arica
Iquique
Antofagasta
Copiapó
Easter Island
La Serena
Valparaíso
SANTIAGO
Juan Fernández Archipelago
Talca
Concepción
Temuco — 8A-B
— 1
Valdivia — 15
— 16
2 — Osorno — 9
Puerto Montt — 10
3 — 17
18 — Castro — 20
Chaitén — 11-19A-B-C-D-E
— 4
ANTARCTIC CHILEAN TERRITORY — Coihaique — 12
— 21
14 — Cochrane — 22
5 — 6
23 —
SOUTH POLE — 7
Puerto Natales — 26
Punta Arenas
13-24A-B, 25
✱ "Agreement between Chile and Argentina to determine precise borders between Monte Fitz-Roy and Cerro Daudet". (Buenos Aires, Dec 16, 1998).
Puerto Williams — 14
Diego Ramírez Islands

COMFORT AND STYLE ABOARD THE CAHUELLA

• **Ferries with fixed departures in the lakes and southern archipelago** Some of these carry vehicles and some do not, and on overnight trips you may have several choices of accommodation, ranging from armchairs (*butacas*) to bunks (*literas*) to personal cabins (*cabinas*). In high season, the ferries are increasingly booked by vacationing Chileans, and reservations are necessary for all but the shortest trips. Food and beverage are often provided, though it is a good idea to stock up on commonly marked-up items (such as beer and wine). Bikes usually go for free.

There are two major ferry companies in the south, Transmarchilay and Navimag. Their schedules vary from one year (or even one month) to the next, and it can be a challenge getting departure information ahead of time. Contact these companies in Santiago, Puerto Montt, or any other major port for updates.

Navimag .... ☎ (2)4423120
Transmarchilay .. ☎ 600600 8687

LOCAL MOTOR LAUNCH ON LAGO TODOS LOS SANTOS

THE TERRA AUSTRALIS IN THE GLACIER-STREWN FJORDS OF TIERRA DEL FUEGO

Information on short ferries is listed in the services section of the relevant town or highlight, while ferries with multiple- or long-distance services are grouped together or listed individually as appropriate.

Sea Kayaking

The watersports boom that has swept North America and Europe in the past years is arriving, slowly but surely, in Chile.

As little as a decade ago, the only way to paddle here was to stage your own expedition, bringing your boats and equipment from abroad – an operation requiring months of planning and considerable expense. Today, though the offering is still limited, a growing number of operators run guided sea kayak expeditions in the Chiloé archipelago, the northern Patagonian fjords, and the glacier-choked channels of southern Patagonia and Tierra del Fuego. Rentals of either sea kayaks or canoes are still very difficult (though not impossible) to come by.

In this guide, we focus principally upon areas that are currently served by an operator or rental agency.

GENERAL INFORMATION FOR PADDLERS

As the relative success of any paddling trip is highly dependent on the weather, the season here is restricted to the summer months, generally November-April. You are highly unlikely to find any operator functioning outside this time frame.

If planning on renting boats and paddling on your own, you should be aware that you are unlikely to be able to rent anything but the bare essentials – namely a boat, paddle, PFD and sprayskirt. All dry bags, rescue and navigational equipment, and so on should be brought from abroad. Bear in mind that water and ambient temperatures in the south can be quite cold, so you should prepare accordingly, with solid raingear and several layers of insulation. Rubber boots are very useful for paddling in Patagonia, and can be picked up inexpensively in hardware stores in Puerto Montt.

In the remote, serpentine Patagonian channels, a VHF radio (use marine channel 16) and GPS are basically indispensable. Tide charts can be obtained at the *Capitania de Puerto* (harbor master) in most ports. For information on nautical charts, see the Map and Compass section in ᴘ pg. 43.

If booking a commercial trip, in addition to obvious questions such as trip length, cost, guides, and included equipment, you should also be sure to inquire about the following details:

LAND OF CONTRASTS: VOLCAN MELIMOYU LOOMING ABOVE THE RIO PALENA

● Is the trip self-supported, or accompanied by a support vessel? This can make all the difference between comfort and misery in the event of bad weather – though it does have its cost.

● Is paddling in single or tandem kayaks? If you're not sure about your paddling abilities, a more stable tandem is the way to go.

● How many hours a day are actually spent paddling? Most inexperienced paddlers will quickly get sore if paddling more than five or six hours a day.

● What sort of cultural interaction is involved? One of the finest things about paddling in this corner of the world is the contact with local people.

SOUTHERN CHILE

For some reason, canoes and sea kayaks still haven't caught on in southern Chile, which is unfortunate when you consider the vast network of lakes, streams, and flatwater rivers that spreads throughout the Lake District, providing access to remote beaches, campsites, and hundreds of hectares of wilderness or near-wilderness. Though you may be able to scare up a canoe or sit-on-top kayak on the beach in Pucón or Lican Ray, Puerto Varas is still the only place in southern Chile where you can consistently find sea kayaks for rent.

This said, a growing number of outfitters do offer trips throughout the region, and in the coming years you can expect to see the offering continue to expand, especially in areas like the protected wetlands of the Río Cruces, near Valdivia. For the present, we focus on those areas where renting boats or booking a trip is a tangible reality.

As a general rule – valid in all Chile – bear in mind that winds tend to increase throughout the afternoon, and many big lakes tend to act as wind funnels, creating the kind of waves that most people only associate with the open ocean. Try to paddle early, and avoid exposed crossings whenever possible; the safest way to spend the afternoon is lounging on the beach, reading. This is doubly true once you leave the fresh water behind and start paddling in the Pacific.

PATAGONIA

If there is one activity that is bound to grow in popularity in Patagonia, this is it. Imagine paddling through channels and islands populated by settlers lost in time, or following an emerald river though the snowcapped Andes to the Pacific, or picking your way through an inland sea littered with icebergs. Imagine a vast, network of fjords and islands populated by sea lions, dolphins, seabirds and few solitary and resourceful fishermen. Imagine traveling silently and self-reliantly through one of the last great wilderness areas on the planet – and doing so in comfort and style.

At present, the areas in which you can feasibly paddle are rather limited. In this entire territory, there is only one agency (Dynevor Expeditions) that rents sea kayaks to independent travelers, and only one other (Patagonia Adventure Expeditions) that rents canoes. The offering by commercial outfitters is significantly broader, and continues to grow; below we've described only those areas which are currently offered as commercial trips or are likely to be offered in the near future. If you do manage to get a hold of your own equipment, the possibilities are endless – as a single glance at the map will confirm.

If you do go with an operator, it is most likely that you will be paddling with a support boat, which provides a measure of security and comfort in this region of extremely inclement weather. You could easily get five days of sun or five days of rain – there is simply no telling. Therefore, it is of the utmost importance that you come prepared, with heavy raingear and several layers of fleece.

In general terms, the Chiloé archipelago is the calmest and most sheltered place to paddle in Patagonia, and offers the most creature comforts. To the east, the continental fjords have a more challenging climate, with fierce afternoon winds channeled deep into the fjords – creating a potentially dangerous situation if you are caught offshore or in an area where the cliffs drop directly into the ocean. Finally, the glacier-strewn fjords of Tierra del Fuego constitute one of the most inhospitable – albeit rewarding – places to paddle in the world.

FACE TO FACE WITH THE ELEMENTS IN FIORDO QUINTUPEU

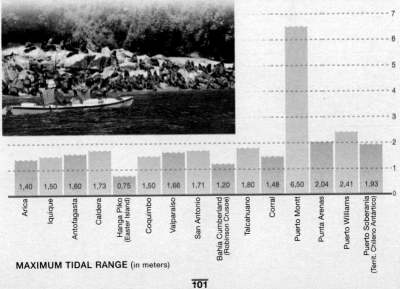

On the Virtues of the *Dalca*

Five hundred years ago, large stitched canoes known as *dalcas* were an essential means of transport for the Yamana, Alacaluf, and Chonos 'Canoe Indians,' who inhabited distinct ranges in the archipelago of southern Chile. Numbering about 8,000 individuals all told, the Canoe Indians hunted sea lions, collected shellfish, and covered their bodies in whale or sea lion blubber to protect against the constant wet and cold. The *dalcas* themselves were constructed of three boards sculpted by fire and stitched with fibers, and were designed to hold from 8-10 paddlers. Often the Indians actually lived aboard their canoes, traveling from one island to the next and actually having fires aboard – the boats reportedly leaked so much that this posed no danger. But their seaworthiness was undisputed, as Jesuit priest Diego de Rosalez reported in 1877:

'And it was impossible that any other craft should plow these seas, as it has been learned that neither ships, nor sloops, nor frigates, nor other types of vessels with which the Spanish have tried to navigate in those gulfs are as appropriate as these piraguas of three boards…. only these ride safely upon the foam. Thus not only the Indians, but also the Spanish, forget all other craft and only navigate in these, trusting themselves to three boards sewn with a string.'

SEA LIONS IN CAHUELMO

Arica	Iquique	Antofagasta	Caldera	Hanga Piko (Easter Island)	Coquimbo	Valparaíso	San Antonio	Bahía Cumberland (Robinson Crusoe)	Talcahuano	Corral	Puerto Montt	Punta Arenas	Puerto Williams	Puerto Soberanía (Territ. Chileno Antártico)
1,40	1,50	1,60	1,73	0,75	1,50	1,66	1,71	1,20	1,80	1,48	6,50	2,04	2,41	1,93

MAXIMUM TIDAL RANGE (in meters)

Whitewater Rafting and Kayaking

If you're a boater, you probably already know something about Chile's whitewater. If not, all it takes is a glance at the map and a little understanding of regional weather patterns to realize that there's something special going on here. In short, when you see storm after storm generated over the Pacific Ocean slam into the Andes and load them up with precipitation, you know that precipitation has to come back down somehow – and what you have is a recipe for what some call the best whitewater on earth. Whether you're a Zambezi veteran searching for monster waves in Patagonia, a class III kayaker hoping to improve your technique in the off-season, or a neophyte rafter just hoping to cool off on an afternoon trip, you'll find exactly what you're looking for on Chile's rivers.

In the early 1980's, the Río Biobío was catapulted to international fame as one of the world's greatest whitewater trips. It wasn't hype, either: the original Biobío trip was a seven-day romp through forgotten wilderness inhabited by a living indigenous culture, past bubbling hotsprings at the foot of a smoking volcano, with (as the first descent team described it) 'more rapids in a single day than are run in twelve days on the Colorado, and a couple as big as the biggest in the Grand Canyon.'

Despite all the press, nothing could save the Biobío from the depredations of Endesa, Chile's national power company (now privatized and in Spanish hands). In 1996, Endesa's highly controversial Pangue dam drowned the Royal Flush canyon and the Canyon of 100 Waterfalls, reducing the whitewater section of the trip to 3 days. Now construction has begun on Ralco, which will cut off flow through the remaining Class V canyon. But the greatest tragedy of the Biobío –Chile's longest and most historically significant river– is the displacement of the Pehuenche Indian families who have inhabited the valley for centuries. You can find out more information on the Biobío and the plight of the Pehuenche on International River Networks website, www.irn.org.

Still, the Biobío had turned the whitewater world's eyes on Chile, and each year more boaters arrived from around the world, running new rivers and returning with awestruck tales of waterfalls, monster holes, and wilderness canyons. The late John Foss, who died during a first descent of Peru's Huallbamba river in 1998, ran over 150 different river sections in the course of preparing his postumously completed guidebook, *Chile Whitewater, A Rafting and Kayaking Guide*. At the time of writing, the book had yet to go to press.

SPRING RUNOFF ON THE RIO ÑUBLE

The information contained in this guide is intended to be of use to both potential rafting customers with or without experience, whitewater kayakers who wish to travel with a guided tour, and independent boaters looking for an adventure on their own. Though we can't give you a blow-by-blow description of every river in Chile, we will tell you the name of the river and section, show you how to get there, and give a brief description and rating.

COMMERCIAL TRIPS

Rafting

Every year new companies join the ranks of rafting operations in Chile, and choosing among the many options can be real challenge for the uninitiated.

Among locally run companies running day trips, there exist great variations in equipment, guide training, and level of service. In Pucón, for example, intense competition between companies has driven prices so low that it is difficult to turn a profit and maintain standards. Ask your operator about such important details as a first aid kit, which is sometimes omitted from the list of trip essentials. Rafting trips on rivers rated above class III should always be accompanied by a safety kayaker.

With the Biobío no longer an option, there are very few multi-day whitewater rafting trips being offered in Chile. Aside from the San Pedro and the Futaleufú, most multi-day trips are pretty mellow, involving a bit of Class II and III and often oriented towards fishermen. This is sure to change in coming years, as Patagonia's rafting potential is further developed.

The logistics involved in running multi-days has traditionally excluded the more fly-by-night operations, but remember when booking a multi-day trip that a lot depends on your guides, and inquire carefully about all the relevant details. Price can be a good indicator of an outfitter's level of service and preparation, but it is not the only one.

Kayak Trips

Signing on for a commercial kayaking trip is a good way to save time that might otherwise be lost searching for put-ins, looking for a shuttle driver, and basically worrying over the thousand-and-one details that make a trip successful. Commercial trips are especially appropriate if you don't have anyone to paddle with, or if you're not quite sure of your abilities. The tradeoff lies in trip cost and reduced flexibility.

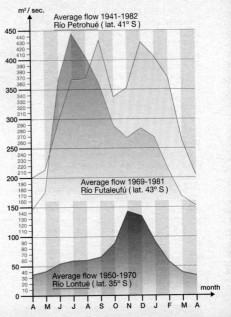

JUGBUSTER, A LOST CLASSIC ON THE BIOBIO

On most trips, you'll join a group of other boaters in a group van and travel south, beginning in Santiago or Pucón and heading south towards the Futa. In this entire area, it is rare for rivers to be separated by more than a few hours travel, and in a two-week tour you could easily paddle a different river or section every day.

Another more sedentary and relaxed option is posed by what we'll call 'paddling camps,' where you'll be put up in style along a river with a shuttle vehicle at your disposal; you won't paddle as many rivers, but you'll probably be better rested. Olympic kayaker Chris Spelius' camp on the Futaleufú was the first and remains the standard-bearer in this category.

Kayak Courses

Even if you've never even been in a kayak before, in a few short days you can learn enough of the basics to safely paddle Class II rapids. A typical three-day course consists of initial flatwater orientation, an eskimo roll session, and swiftwater instruction. If you don't speak Spanish, ask to speak with your instructor beforehand to be sure that you can communicate. Courses typically cost US$150-200.

Ducky Trips

Duckies are inflatable kayaks, far more stable and less claustrophobic than hard-shell kayaks, which means that you don't need any experience to use them. Kayakers look down their nose at duckies, but compared to rafting, it's the ride of a lifetime.

Duckies are just hitting the scene in southern Chile, and currently Anden Sport Tours (in Pucón) is the only company that has them available for rental or guided trips.

VIRGIN RAINFOREST ALONG THE RIO PALENA

Hydrospeed

Yet another toy for playing in the whitewater, hydrospeeds are plastic or foam 'sleds' that you grab onto from behind, and serve to keep you head above water and protected from rocks. You need a helmet, a padded wetsuit, swim fins and a guide, and that's it: basically you just swim down the rapids.

It may look crazy, but hydrospeed has been popular for years in Europe and is a blast. To the present, Pucón (of course) is the only place in Chile where you can get a hold of a hydrospeed.

ON YOUR OWN: PRIVATE BOATING

If you want to come to Chile and paddle, but don't have the money to pay for a guided trip, take heart: it's not that hard. Every year, dirtbag boaters from around the world converge on southern Chile to celebrate the snowmelt, swap lies, and scrounge for rides to the put-in.

First of all, it's important that you bring your own gear. Most airlines charge $60-75 excess baggage charge to transport boats, and usually buses within Chile do not charge at all. If you want to, you can usually sell gear at the end of the season, but bear in mind that most paddlers are interested in getting rid of gear at this time, so it's a buyers' market. If you don't want to bring gear, you can rent it in Pucón or Puerto Varas, but not anywhere else. Don't expect to paddle much if you don't bring your own gear.

Next, you'll need transport and someone to paddle with. Basically, if you don't want to rent a vehicle from the start, your best option is to head straight for Pucón. Pucón is the start of the paddler's circuit, and it's entirely feasible to show up there with your boat and put together a bigger group to make renting more affordable. Once you have a vehicle, you're golden.

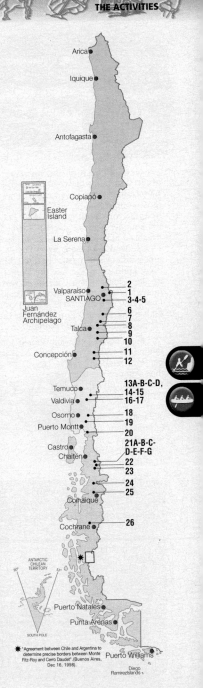

CENTRAL CHILE

(*) Indicates that a given river section is offered as a commercial rafting trip.

Sure, the heart of Chilean whitewater is in the south, but between Santiago and the Biobío alone there are enough rivers to make most countries envious. Fed by snowmelt from the Andes – it literally does not rain in the summer – these glacially-formed rivers run hard and early, peaking in December. As a general rule, these rivers have a consistent gradient and relatively few eddies, but there are exceptions, like the Siete Tazas of the Río Claro, which consists of seven perfect waterfalls carved through a basalt lava flow. Few of these rivers are run commercially, the one exception being the Río Maipo, Santiago's local favorite.

Kayakers headed south should consider beginning with a week or ten days in the central region; in that time you can easily tick off seven or eight separate runs, as it's usually just a couple of hours from the takeout of one river to the put-in of the next.

Though hydropower schemes have brought the mighty Biobío to its knees, the Lake District still contains the greatest diversity and concentration of accessible whitewater in the country. Unfortunately for rafters – and fortunately for kayakers – only a few of these rivers are runnable in a raft.

Whitewater in the south centers on the same two poles as most other activities: Pucón and Puerto Varas. Pucón is definitely more of an all-round boater's destination, with hordes of rafting companies and at least 7 different runs in the immediate area. Many kayakers headed south make this their first stop, and usually get hung up for at least a week running waterfalls and hanging out at the beach and in the bars. This is also a great place to buy or sell gear. Puerto Varas also has a couple of rafting companies, but there are fewer local runs and less of a scene.

The boating itself defies description. You find a little of everything here, from steep, densely forested gorges with big waterfalls and tranquil pools, to big-water runs though massive glacial riverbeds, to mellow crystal-clear streams and steep granite creeks. The most characteristic rapids are those formed over basalt ledges, which means big, abrupt drops with big recovery pools at the bottom, perfect for neophyte rafters. River levels depend on a combination of snowpack and rainfall; peak flows generally occur from October to December, but the season usully lasts well into February.

RIVER RATINGS

Class I Flat, moving water.

Class II Moving water with slight obstacles. 'Easy.'

Class III Significant obstacles such as waves, holes and rocks. 'Fun.'

Class IV More and larger obstacles, requiring significant manoeuvering; rafting customers should be prepared to swim and self rescue. All commercial trips should use a safety boater. 'Advanced.'

Class V Major obstacles requiring aggressive evasive action, with the possibility of long and/or dangerous swims. Previous experience required for raft trips. 'Expert.'

Class VI Unrunnable without serious risk of injury or death.

LOW WATER ON THE BIOBIO LAVA SOUTH

PATAGONIA

(*) Indicates that a given river section is offered as a commercial rafting trip.

It is no exaggeration to say that Patagonia boasts some of the most remote, powerful, and beautiful wilderness river trips in the world. Though most paddlers have heard only of the Futaleufú, that is really only the tip of the iceberg. Further south, the rivers keep spilling west out of the Andes, hell-bent for the Pacific.

It is almost impossible to generalize about the rivers here, because of the variety of geologic and hydrologic forces at work. The Futaleufú, for example, flows out of dam-release reservoirs in Argentina and drops through a number of different sections, some drop-pool, some intensely continuous. Just south, the Río Palena, which would appear to have a similar profile, has almost no rapids at all. And near the end of the Carretera Austral, the glacially-fed Río Baker and Río Pascua tend to run high when other rivers are bone dry, due to exaggerated melting of the surrounding glaciers. In general, peak flow occurs during the winter and early spring (Oct-Nov), but you're not looking for peak flow. December - February is the best time to paddle here.

Logistically, paddling on the Futaleufú is not difficult. Numerous outfitters now offer guided trips for rafters and kayakers, several of these with luxurious basecamp accommodations; day trips are also increasingly available. Private boaters are best off to rent a truck and arrive self-sufficient, but in a pinch you can transport your boat by ferry and bus and hook up with fellow boaters once you arrive. Renting kayaking equipment is not an option.

South of the Futa, logistics are trickier. Aside from the Río Baker, there are no 'local' raft companies on any of these rivers; if you want to paddle, you'll have to arrange a trip ahead of time or, if you're a private boater, come prepared to run your own shuttles and be entirely self-sufficient. At least for the present, it is very unlikely that you'll see another party on these rivers.

Though high pressure systems often strike the region for weeks on end, you should come fully prepared for paddling in rain and cold weather. If booking a commercial trip, ask your outfitter about what is included and what you should bring.

...ANOTHER PERFECTLY
CLEAN 25-FOOTER

Surfing and Windsurfing

SURFING

Surfing in Chile began in the central region in the early seventies. Since then, hundreds of great breaks have been discovered all along the Chilean coast, from the tubes and reef breaks of the desert north to the wild, stormy, largely undiscovered coastline of the south. The number of Chilean surfers – and especially bodyboarders – continues to grow every year, but foreign surfers are still relatively rare. Localism is highest in northern Chile, where most surf spots are close to urban populations.

Waves and Wave Reports

In addition to cold water, the Humboldt Current brings very consistent, powerful swells to the Chilean coast. Winter low-pressure systems and resulting winds over the Pacific make for even bigger waves (4-5m) but also tend to create messy conditions. Summer (Nov-Apr) generally produces the cleanest waves in most of Chile.

Prevailing winds in most of Chile are south or SW, averaging 15-20 knots. In the winter, north or NW winds of similar velocities are more common, but prevailing winds continue from the SW. Differential heating of air over the continent and over the ocean produces offshore winds at night (stronger at river mouths), with calm mornings and building onshore winds in the afternoon.

The internet is far and away the best source of wave forecast information, and experienced surfers will more than likely already have their sources wired. If you don't know where to start, visit www.stormsurf.com for an excellent collection of weather maps, buoy reports, and wave forecasts specifically focused on the Pacific Ocean.

Equipment

Bring all your gear with you – if you wish, you can probably sell it before departure. Ding kits and extra fins should also be brought, as well as a strong leash and a board bag for traveling. Wetsuits are required throughout the country, though thickness varies with region and season. If you can bring two boards, bring one 7-8' and another 6-6.5'.

More Info:

Maps and break-by-break descriptions of the entire Chilean coast are available from The Surf Report, PO Box 1028, Dana Point, CA 92629. You can pick up a copy of the excellent Chilean surf magazine *Marejada* at board shops throughout the country.

The Surf

The surf in **northern Chile** is big, powerful, and consistent, with the waves during the Chilean winter (April-November) over 15'. In the southern portion of the region (La Serena), expect a variety of beach breaks, points and rock reefs. Reefs and tubes are the general rule in Arica and Iquique, making the area more suitable for expert surfers.

In winter, a full wetsuit is necessary throughout the north, though in summer a springsuit works for the area from La Serena to Antofagasta, and you can probably get by with boardshorts in Iquique and Arica. Cold-water wax is best for La Serena and Antofagasta, tropical wax for Iquique and Arica.

WINDSURFING

Windsurfing is not nearly as widely practiced as surfing in Chile, but conditions are similarly reliable. Although many sites are good year-round, the most consistent winds and benevolent climatic conditions are concentrated in the spring and summer months (Sep – Mar). Prevailing westerly breezes usually begin in early afternoon and last until dark, reaching a peak of 40 knots in some areas. Inland lakes and especially artificial reservoirs often have excellent conditions, and many sites better known for surfing also provide excellent wave sailing for advanced sailors.

Good windsurfing spots can often be identified by paying attention to coastal topography. The diagram below shows how peninsulas like that at Quintero cause SW winds to accelerate as they bend around a rocky headland to fill the vacuum behind. Greatest wind speeds are at points A and B.

RIPPING WINDS ON LAGO TODOS LOS SANTOS

As always, if you want to avoid crowds, get out early; Iquique and Arica tend to get rather crowded in the afternoons. Tide has a minimal effect on most breaks in the north.

Central Chile is a great place for visiting surfers to travel, because transport along the coast is such a breeze; you can easily hitch and catch buses to most breaks. You'll find the cleanest waves during the spring and summer (Sept-May), when the wind blows consistently out of the south. The big highlight here is Pichilemu where you'll find 4 separate points in 5 kilometers, including the one of the longest, most consistent lefts in Chile. This place is hands down world class.

Easter Island gets swell all year and from all directions. Though almost all the breaks here are over lava reefs, conditions on the northwest and south shore are entirely different.

The surf on the northwest shore – particularly around Hanga Roa – is safe and consistent, good for beginners and intermediates. The south shore, on the other hand, requires huge swell to set up, but when it does, look out: clean waves up to 18' have been reported here. If you're visiting with hopes of surfing the south shore (the austral winter is the most consistent season) you'll need at least an 8' board.

Due the abrupt coastal topography, getting into and out of the water can be a challenge, so be sure to scout your entrance and exit carefully. Water temps vary from 67° in winter to 72° during the summer months, so the most you'll ever need is a springsuit. Tides are minimal and have little effect on the surf.

Unlike many Pacific Islands, Easter Island still sees relatively few visiting surfers, and as a consequence there is very little local attitude.

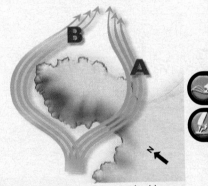

Boarding equipment is considerably more expensive in Chile than abroad, and those who plan to sail a lot are encouraged to bring their own equipment – rentals are frightfully hard to come by. As long as they have cargo space available, most airlines will not charge to carry boarding gear, though it is always a good idea to confirm ahead of time. If you wish to lighten your load, high-quality equipment may often be sold before departure

Visiting sailors without their own equipment are best off in **central Chile**, simply because they'll have better chances of renting a board or hooking up with other sailors. A good contact in the Santiago area is Windsurfing Chile (☎ (2)2156089), at Las Carmelitas 30 in Las Condes. They sell a full range of equipment, can give information on contests and esvents, and have a windsurfing school and rentals on Laguna Aculeo in summer.

SURFING

...HEAD-HIGH AND GLASSY...

WINDSURFING

NORTHERN CHILE

1- The Mejillones Península ... pg 291
   A- La Rinconada
   B- Isla Santa María
   C- Juan López
   D- Playa Las Palmeras
   E- Playa Amarilla
2- Bahía Inglesa .... pg 315
3- Punta Choros .... pg 318
4- In and Around La Serena ... pg 323
   A- La Herradura
   B- Puerto Aldea
5- Embalse La Paloma .... pg 328
6- Los Vilos and Pichidangui .. pg 329

CENTRAL CHILE

7- Laguna Aculeo .... pg 368
8- Caleta Higuerillas .... pg 401
9- Quintero .... pg 401
10- Algarrobo .... pg 405
11- Santo Domingo .... pg 405
12- Around Navidad .... pg 411
   A- Las Boca
   B- Matanzas
   C- Pupuya
   D- Punta Topocalma
   E- Pichilemu
   F- Llico
13- Punta Parrón and Curanipe . pg 416
14- Dichato .... pg 425
15- Laguna Grande San Pedro pg 425
16- Quidico .... pg 426
17- Tirúa .... pg 426

SURFING Black numbers

WINDSURFING Red numbers

✱ "Agreement between Chile and Argentina to determine precise borders between Monte Fitz-Roy and Cerro Daudet". (Buenos Aires, Dec 16, 1998).

Scuba Diving
and Snorkeling

Chile's marine environments are among the most important and accessible of the country's biomes. No matter where you are, the Pacific is never far off, and to the attuned traveler – one who learns the ocean's rhythms and inhabitants – the ocean is an ever-present companion and source of wonder.

There's no better way to get to know the ocean than to immerse yourself in it, whether it comes down to nothing more than packing a basic snorkel outfit for a trip through the north or signing up for a full-blown dive vacation on one of Chile's unique Pacific Islands. Either way, it's a world apart.

CONTINENTAL CHILE

The marine ecosystem of greater continental Chile is strongly influenced by the Humboldt Current, which carries cold, low-salinity water north from Antarctica. Some 300m deep and 80-150km wide, this immense current contains high concentrations of dissolved oxygen and carbon dioxide, which favors the growth of phytoplankton and zooplankton, the basis of all marine ecosystems. For this reason, these coasts have historically been among the world's most productive fisheries, and divers will be amazed above all at the number of fish they find here.

The cold water – we might as well face it, most of Chile's coast has cold water – favors the development of benthic algaes, which reach extremely high levels of diversity here, with over 500 species; algae collection is an important economic activity for many coast dwellers. Where the cold water of the Humboldt Current meet with the warmer waters of the Perú countercurrent, a unique transitional ecosystem exists, in which benthic algae with a 32% endemism rate and clear affinities with Sub-Antarctic regions coexists with marine fauna from the tropics.

As a general rule, Chile's Pacific coast is big and exposed, with powerful waves and currents. On the downside, this means that you must pay special attention to safety and navigation, and wait a few days after a big swell for the sand to settle. On the positive side, however, this means a huge number of diveable shipwrecks from 4 centuries of highly adventurous shipping. There is a long if factually incomplete list of ship-

DIVER AMID A SCHOOL OF PAMPANOS, JUAN FERNANDEZ ARCHIPELAGO

wrecks along the Chilean coast at http://www.geocities.com/ Yosemite/Gorge/8743/ naufraga.html. Note that in order to visit submarine archaeological sites (including any shipwreck over fifty years old) you need authorization from the *Consejo de Monumentos Nacionales*, located in the Sala Andres Bello, on the second floor of Santiago's Bilblioteca Nacional (National Library).

Diving conditions vary along the length of the coast. Visibility and temperatures are lowest in the south, where the best diving options usually lay in protected fjords or freshwater lakes. In the north, visibility is much better and water temperatures are higher, but a relative lack of infrastructure make a guided trip a necessity for scuba diving in many regions. The central coast provides a good compromise, with intermediate temperatures and visibility, dozens of shipwrecks, and plenty of qualified schools and guide services. Offshore, Easter Island and the Juan Fernández Archipelago stand apart by virtue of their abundant and highly endemic marine fauna, crystal clear water, and unique submarine topography.

LESSONS

If you're not already qualified to dive, many schools in Chile offer both basic and advanced courses. The international organizations offered and recognized here include PADI, NAUI, CMAS and SSI. PADI courses are the most common, and usually cost from $300-400, with full equipment, classroom, pool, and open water sessions. If you already have basic qualification, a number of schools offer advanced and specialty courses, up to Dive Master.

For those on the fence as whether to certify or not, one-time introductory dives are a good alternative. So-called «*bautismos submarinos*» usually run about $50-80.

GUIDED TRIPS

For the casual snorkeler or spear-fisherman, a guide is probably not necessary. There are thousands of places along this coast where you can carry your gear to the shore, suit up and lose yourself in the submarine world. Use caution in unknown waters, however. A good precaution is to observe the sea for a good half an hour before entering, keeping an eye out for current and wave patterns.

If you want to really dive, however, hiring a guide is more than just helpful – it can be downright essential. Imagine trying to find a shipwreck in 20 meters of water, with 5 meters of visibility and a 6-knot current; imagine trying to barter with fishermen for a boat every time you wanted to get offshore. Guides transform the impossible into reality.

If you wish, you can book a trip with all diving equipment included, which makes diving excursions a real possibility for qualified divers who didn't think or chose not to bring any gear. Underwater video and photography are often available options. Single-day trips usually cost around $60 pp, or $80 pp with equipment.

If you decide to do things on your own – bring the gear, rent the car, find the spots and rent boats when necessary – filling tanks is likely to be the single largest limiting factor. In addition to the dive outfitters and local contacts listed in regional chapters, you can sometimes fill up at fishing villages (*caletas de pescadores*) or wherever commercial divers are working (such as aquaculture farms). These guys may also take you out in their boats, and are a great source of information. It usually costs about $5 to fill tanks to 3000 psi.

Three final things. If diving with a private party, always leave personal information and dive plans with the Capitanía de Puerto in the nearest town. If going with an outfitter, make sure that they are currently registered with the Chilean army (this is required), and note down all relevant company information. If you have an emergency, you can dial marine rescue (*rescate marítimo*) at 137, free from any telephone.

DECOMPRESSION CHAMBERS IN CHILE

Iquique Hospital de la Armada

Antofagasta Hospital de la Armada
'Servisub'

Coquimbo Hospital Regional

Valparaíso Hospital Naval
Partida de Salvataje

Santiago Hospital de la FACH

Talcahuano Hospital Naval
Partida de Salvataje

Puerto Montt Hospital Naval

Ancud Sindicado de Pescadores

Punta Arenas ENAP (Empresa Nacional
del Petroleo)
Partida de Salvataje

HYDROSTATIC PRESSURE TESTS

Indura ☎ 600 600 3030
AGA ☎ 600 600 0242

NORTHERN CHILE

The unusual marine ecosystems of northern Chile are the result of a complex oceanographic situation. On the one hand you have the mighty Humboldt current surging north from Antarctica, sending biomass – sheer number of fish – through the roof, and providing habitat for cold-water dwellers like penguins and sea lions. On the other, you have the Perú-Chile Current bringing warmer waters south from the tropics, mixing up the diversity of species near Arica and Iquique. When El Niño hits, this coastal current is amplified, and its effects broaden and stretch further south.

The continental shelf in northern Chile is narrower than elsewhere on the continental coast, for the same reason that visibility is better: it almost never rains. You'll find most marine life around rock reefs and points, in the intertidal zone. The effect of the tides is minimal.

Aside from a few big cities, the population along the northern coast is pretty sparse. Most of the places listed here are in urban or semi-urban areas - the only places, most often, where you'll find any rentals or other dive infrastructure. Some of the most attractive areas, however, are remote beaches and islands, far from any services. Guided dive expeditions are often the only option for diving in these areas.

If you just want to snorkel, you're in luck. You can dive up and down this coast on your own, using public transportation; if you have a spear gun, you can eat for free every night. Just be careful and remember, you will need a wetsuit.

- Temperature: 18-27°
- Visibility: 15-20
- Wetsuit: Minimum 5mm

DIVE OPERATORS & CONTACTS

In this guide, operators visiting a given dive destination are listed by number, just like those in other activities. For a few destinations in the north, we also suggest local contacts who may be able to help out with equipment, boats, filling tanks, and so on.

ANEMONES, ROBINSON CRUSOE ISLAND

CENTRAL CHILE

Central Chile is the easiest part of the country to take a dive course or arrange an expedition, for simple demographic reasons: this area concentrates the vast majority of Chilean divers and dive outfitters. Most of these outfitters have offices in major population centers – principally Viña del Mar and Santiago – though their trips and courses visit distinct locales all along the central coast. Some also organize excursions to the Pacific Islands and select sites in the Norte Chico.

Submarine topography in this region reflects the climatic pattern of seasonal precipitation. During the rainy winter season, fluvial deposition upon the continental shelf increases, reducing visibility and producing, over time, a more extensive submarine platform. Spring and fall bring the clearest conditions, as the increase in plankton during the summer months can also cloud the water. Allow 3-4 days after a rainstorm or big swell for the sediment to settle.

Shipwrecks constitute a major attraction for divers in this area: almost every port seems to boast at least one wreck.

- Temperature: 17-19°C summer, 12-14°C winter
- Visibility: 5-15m
- Wetsuit: Mininum 7mm (or use a drysuit)

ACTINIAS, ROBINSON CRUSOE ISLAND

SOUTHERN CHILE

Diving is an essential part of life for many coastal inhabitants in southern Chile, especially in the region south of Puerto Montt, where many make their living diving for the salmon farms or collecting shellfish. Mussels, oysters, abalone and urchins abound in these protected channels, together with a diverse range of seaweed including impressive 'forests' of up to 15m in height. With heavy precipitation and correspondingly low visibility in coastal waters, this region is unlikely to attract travelers specifically for the diving, but certified divers can certainly spend an enjoyable day or weekend exploring this productive maine ecosystem and/or a couple of well-preserved shipwrecks. A single dive outfitter in Puerto Montt, Ecosub, offers excursions in the surrounding area.

Another unique and attractive option is poised by great lakes at the foot of the Andes. A few of the lakes stand out: along the south shore of Lago Colico, for example, is a near-vertical wall that plunges over 400m into the depths, while Indian dugout canoes have been discovered submerged in Lago Rupanco. Note that diving in the lakes creates a couple of special situations. First of all, because fresh water is not as dense as salt water, you need less weight to create the same bouyancy. Secondly, many of these lakes are situated at altitude, which changes dive time charts: because air pressure is reduced at altitude, decompression at the surface is exaggerated, so you're allowed less time at a given depth than when diving in at sea level.

At present, there are no companies specifically offering fresh water diving in the south, but you can certainly consult with Ecosub or other operators in the central region for guided trips. Note that special certification is required to lead dive excursions at altitude.

ANEMONES, ROBINSON CRUSOE ISLAND

PACIFIC ISLANDS

ARCHIPELAGO JUAN FERNANDEZ

Though the Juan Fernández Archipelago has a warm temperate climate similar to that of central Chile, the surrounding ocean is considerably warmer and clearer, and the marine flora and fauna differ greatly from those on the continent. The extreme isolation of the island, however, has led to high rates of endemism: about 15% among coastal and neritic fishes, 32% among benthic algaes. Excellent visibility, an abundance of schooling fish, and endemic species such as the Juan Fernández Fur Seal (*Arctocephalus philippi*) make Juan Fernández a top priority for divers in Chile. Endémica Expediciones is the island's local dive center, though you can also arrange to visit with an operator from Santiago or the central coast.

EASTER ISLAND

Isolated in the center of the vast Pacific, Easter Island is renowned among divers around the world for its crystal-clear water (over 50m average visibility), dramatic submarine rock formations, abundant coral and colorful tropical fish species. Endemism rates are even greater than those of Juan Fernández, reaching 27% in coastal fishes and 14% in

PARAPERCIS DOCKINSI, ENDEMIC TO THE JUAN FERNANDEZ

algaes, but this ecosystem is characterized by much greater affinities with tropical and subtropical regions of the West Pacific, such as Hawaii, the Marshall Islands, New Zealand and Australia. Outstanding fish species include the endemic Blue Toby (*Canthigaster sp*) and the brightly colored Wrasse (*Pseudolabrus semifasciatus*).

Though coral (especially varieties of *Scleractinia*) flourishes on the sandy submarine platform off the island's north coast, the powerful storms that hit the island in winter impede the formation of barrier reefs. The exposed southeast and southwest coasts feature some of the island's most impressive submarine topography with an abundance of steep sea cliffs, caves, pillars and arches. There are two dive centers on the island, Orca and Mike Rapu.

LOCAL DIVERS ON EASTER ISLAND

Spas and Hotsprings

At a rate of some ten to fifteen centimeters a year, the oceanic Nazca plate slowly slides to the east, 'subducting' beneath the South American plate in the Atacama Trench, 7,635m below sea level. This subduction zone extends along the coast of South America from about 8°N all the way 48°S, giving rise to the highest peaks of the Andes and one of the most tectonically and geothermically active regions in the world.

Over 240 thermal springs lie scattered throughout the Andes from Arica to Cochrane. Some owe their existence to purely volcanic phenomena, which is to say that groundwater or precipitation is heated near the surface of the earth. Others are attributed to major or minor geological faults, which allow the filtration of precipitation to great depths, where it is superheated and subsequently rises to the surface.

The combination of these factors means that rarely in Chile will you find yourself more than an hour or two from the nearest hotsprings. In many areas, in fact, you often have to choose between several different options.

Temperature is obviously an important factor, as options range from tepid (20-25°C) coastal springs to dangerously hot (>80°C)

altiplano geysers. Whenever possible, we give spring temperatures for featured hotsprings, but it must be understood that these do vary over time. Of equal importance is the extent to which a spring has been 'improved': visiting a luxury spa is a vastly different experience from hiking into remote natural baths. To make things easier, we have included an 'infrastructure rating' (see 🚿) for each spring. Whenever possible we've also included the spring's entrance price and telephone number.

Nudity is not accepted at commercial hotsprings in Chile. At remote backcountry springs there are no set 'rules,' and the best advice is simply to use your best judgement.

RATINGS & SYMBOLS

N🚿 Non-commercial hotspring. These may be entirely natural or moderately 'improved' with wooden tubs, rustic buildings, and so on, no fee is charged.

C🚿 Rustic commercial. A fee is charged for use of springs, but infrastructure is low-key.

🚿 Spas and Hotels.

DESERT BLISS: THE BAÑOS DE PURITAMA, NEAR SAN PEDO DE ATACAMA

NORTHERN CHILE

The northern sierra and altiplano constitutes one of three geothermal 'hotspots' in the Chilean Andes, with a high concentration of active volcanoes along the Bolivian border and over 70 thermal springs documented from 17-25°S. Most springs here are situated at altitude, close to the axis of volcanic activity. The nearby presence of geysers or smoking *fumaroles* usually indicates an extremely hot source spring where extreme caution is advised.

In comparison with the more southerly regions of Chile, relatively few of the hotsprings in northern Chile have been harnessed for commercial use. In the altiplano, where distances are immense and roads are unreliable, most springs consist of simple pools along riverbeds or salt flats, often with strange mineral formations and surrounded by spectacular wide-open scenery. They make splendid campsites, but as most thermal springs are highly mineralized, you will usually have to bring your own water, and a lot of it: the combination of high altitude and hot water is a serious recipe for dehydration. Also, remember that nighttime temperatures in the altiplano are very cold, and there is no firewood. You need a bike or your own transport to visit most hotsprings in the altiplano, while the scattered hotsprings and cool, refreshing *cochas* of the sierra are significantly more accessible – though sometimes crowded on weekends.

The *Norte Chico* (from 25-33°S) exhibits lower levels of volcanic activity than any other region in Chile, and hotsprings are relatively scarce. Aside from the Termas de Socos near Ovalle, the hotsprings of the Norte Chico are situated at altitude near the Argentine border, near the head of steep, V-shaped river valleys. If nothing else, these springs are a great excuse for exploring the seldom-visited upper reaches of these transverse valleys.

A MORNING BATH AT POLLOQUERE

CENTRAL CHILE

SOUTHERN CHILE

This region is another of Chile's geothermal 'hotspots,' with the Pocuro fault giving rise to over 35 documented hotsprings.

Most of these springs have been known for centuries, and have grown up into hotel and resort complexes catering to families from Santiago and other urban areas. Usually located in the foothills of the Andes, these hotels make a relaxing base for further explorations, and a few offer bike rentals, horseback riding, and other activities. Lodging at these places is not cheap, but at most of them you can just pay to use the pools.

Only the remotest springs, tucked away deep in the Andes, have remained in a purely natural state. Anyone who has ever camped beside natural springs in a high mountain valley does not need to be told how magical the experience is. Many of the biking, hiking and mountaineering trips recommended in this chapter are associated with these remote springs.

Over 30% of all the hotsprings in Chile are concentrated in the Araucanía and the Lake District, thanks to a combination of two geological factors. The first and more obvious factor is the high level of local volcanic activity, dramatically apparent in nearly every aspect of the landscape. The second factor is the Liquiñe-Ofqui fault, which extends nearly 1,000km along the main axis of the Andes, facilitating the filtration of rain and snowmelt and its subsequent, seemingly miraculous reemergence in thermal springs.

That's the science behind it. In practice, all you need to know is that no matter where

THE TERMAS DE PUYUHUAPI, OUTSIDE...

you wander in the southern Andes, there are always hotsprings nearby. These come in all varieties, from luxury hotels and family resorts, to rustic wooden tubs, to natural stone *pozones* alongside a mountain river. Nearly all the springs mentioned here have been commercialized in one form or another, however.

Though there may be fewer hotsprings in Patagonia than in many other parts of Chile, what the region lacks in number it more than makes up for in quality. By and large, these springs are hard to reach and overwhelmingly beautiful, set along the shores of the great fjords or remote rivers, in the midst of the temperate rainforest. Here you find both Chile's top spa hotel and its least-visited wilderness springs.

PATAGONIA

...AND IN

Fishing

The secret is out: southern Chile is the jewel of trout fishing in the southern hemisphere.

Trout and salmon are not native here. Brown, rainbow, and brook trout were introduced for sport in the late 1800's by Isidora Goyenechea, wife of a wealthy mining boss, while cohos, steelheads, king and Atlantic salmon didn't happen upon the scene until the last decade or two, when they were brought for the aquaculture industry. All of these species quickly established themselves and over time have marginalized the native percatrucha and other endemic species. Today there are both resident and coastal trout and salmon in most major river systems in the south, though true sea-run fish are relatively rare.

Though it is possible to fish in lakes and high mountain streams in the central Andes, population pressure and irregular stream flows make this area less than ideal as trout habitat. The real action is in the

Lake District and Patagonia, so that is where we concentrate our energies. Note that deep sea fishing and surf casting are popular all along the Chilean coast, but conditions are consistent enough that detailed description is not necessary. Sole, sea bass, and *robalo* are among the most common and desirable saltwater catches.

Though Chilean sport fishing began in the area around Pucón, in the past decades this area has become increasingly developed and more intensely fished. This is not to say that fishing in this area is not worth the trouble – far from it – but if you want trophy fish and lots of action, you are better off in the area roughly from Lago Llanquihue south. Here, abundant precipitation and extensive lake and river systems assure cool, oxygen-rich conditions, while the proximity of the ocean increases your chances of hooking a big sea-run or coastal fish. Additionally, fisherman visiting the big, productive waters of Chilean Patagonia can combine their trip with a visit to one of the fine dry fly fisheries across the border in Argentina.

SALMO SALAR

ONCORHYNCHUS MYKISS

SALVELINUS FRONTINALIS

ONCORHYNCHUS KYSUTCH

SUBMERGED LOGS ABOUND IN THE RIVERS OF NORTHERN PATAGONIA

RECOMMENDED EQUIPMENT

Rods
For trout, 8'6"-9', 5-7 weight.
For sea-run fish, 9-9.5', 6-9 weight.

Reels
Good drag systems are essential, with 50-150 yds of backing.

Lines
Floating lines, Sinking Tips, and Shooting Lines.

Leader-Tippet
0x – 6x. Extra fine tippets are rarely necessary.

Flies
● Woolly buggers in olive, black, gray, brown, and especially white, sizes 2-8
● Variety of streamers (Gray Ghost, Muddlers, and Mickey Finns) sizes 2-8

● Crayfish (*Pancora*) in olive, sizes 4-10
● Dragonflies, caddisflies, stoneflies, mayflies in dry and nymph patterns (Wulffs, Adams, Hoppers, Damsels, Coachman, bead-head recommended), sizes 6-18

Other
Strike indicators

Clothing
Neoprene waders are usually required in Patagonia, though on warm days (and in the Lake District) you may be able to get away with Gore-tex. Rain gear, wading boots, cap and polarized sunglasses are essential.

SALMO TRUTTA

ONCORHYNCHUS TSHAWYTSCHA

In general, conditions are similar to those in the western US. Expect principally freestone rivers with many submerged logs, and an abundance of cold, clear lakes. Good streamer and nymph fishing normally occur throughout the season, while hatches of caddis and mayflies generally occur during the high summer (Jan-Feb). In the major rivers west of the Andes you can expect to fish a lot of streamers and nymphs, while the spring creeks and streams to the east generally offer the best surface action. Hatches are generally less abundant than those in North American rivers.

GUIDES AND LODGES

There are dozens of places in the south to rent boats and hire fishing guides.

At the lower end of the scale, you should expect to pay US$70-80 per person (or per boat, normal capacity 2 passengers) for a day trip with local boatmen, though prices vary greatly.

At the upper end of the scale are the top-level fishing lodges and outfitters catering principally to North American guests. These typically offer all-inclusive week-long packages, ranging in cost from US$250-550/day; in Patagonia it is also increasingly possible to arrange a fishing trip based aboard a motor yacht, at similar prices. When booking a trip, ask carefully about the following issues:

● **Guides** What is the client-to-guide ratio? What languages do the guides speak? How much experience do they have in the local area?

● **Infrastructure** What kind of boats does the lodge or outfitter use? Does it offer equipment or fly-tying services to its guests? Where do the guests sleep? How many guests are present at the lodge at once?

● **Type of fishing** How many different bodies of water can be fished from the lodge? Is fishing mostly in rivers or lakes? What are the principal modalities (wading, floating, belly boats, dry flies or nymphs/streamers, etc)? What kind of travel time is involved?

Arica

Iquique

Antofagasta

Copiapó

Easter
Island

La Serena

Valparaíso
SANTIAGO
Juan
Fernández
Archipelago
Talca

Concepción

Temuco — 1
Valdivia — 2
— 3
Osorno — 4
Puerto Montt — 5-6
— 7
11 —
Castro — 9-10
Chaitén
— 11
— 12
— 13
Coihaique — 14
— 15
Cochrane

ANTARCTIC
CHILEAN
TERRITORY

SOUTH POLE

Puerto Natales

Punta Arenas

— 16
— 17
Puerto Williams

Diego Ramírez
Islands

"Agreement between Chile and Argentina to
determine precise borders between Monte
Fitz-Roy and Cerro Daudet".
(Buenos Aires, Dec 16, 1998).

THE RÍO PUELO

Finally, it should be mentioned that it is not necessary to spend hundreds of dollars a day to have a good time fishing in Chile. Certainly, if fishing is your prime objective and you have limited time to spend, you are best off booking a guided fishing trip. On the other hand, if you just want to wet a line from time to time, there's no reason why you can't just bring your rod and fish on your own – though a guide will always improve your chances.

Whether you are fishing alone or with a guide, you should bear a couple of things in mind. First, always ask permission before crossing private property. Second, remember that fisheries are fragile; the fishing is as good as it is in the south simply because these waters are not often fished. Catch-and-release fishing is a great way to experience the thrill of the sport without damaging the resource for future generations.

TECHNICALITIES

To fish in fresh and salt waters in Chile, you need a license from Sernapesca, the national regulating authority. A one-year license currently costs about US$13 and is often included in commercial trips. An additional fee (US$20) is required of those fishing the protected waters of the Río Cumilahue, Río Sur, and Río Pescado, all located in the Lake District. If fishing on your own, you can

Chile

GUÍA DE PESCA
FISHING GUIDE
GUIDE DE PÊCHE

124

get a license in the local *Municipalidad* (municipality) or through local outfitters and fishing supply shops; you can find a complete listing of participating locales at www.sernapesca.cl, or just ask around. Saltwater fishing is permitted throughout the year, as is freshwater fishing in trans-Andean lakes such as Lago Cochrane. Otherwise, the freshwater season lasts from Nov 15 to May 15 in the area north of Lago Las Torres (near the Río Cisnes in Aisén), and from Oct 15 - April 15 from here south. The season on Lago Llanquihue lasts from Sep 15 - May 15.

SOUTHERN CHILE

Sport fishing got its start in Chile about seventy years ago, when fishing guides in Pucón first started floating rivers in the flat-bottomed skiffs now common throughout the south. Passengers arrived in Villarica by train and then traveled by boat across the lake, to the hotel pier. From there, they explored the lakes and rivers by rowboat and horseback, fishing first for the native *percatrucha*, then increasingly for the trout and salmon that were introduced in the late 19th century.

Today, you can find boats for rent, guides, equipment, and a wide variety of fishing lodges throughout the Lake District. Access is significantly easier than in Patagonia, which means that on the one hand, the fish are smaller, but on the other hand, you can do a lot more on your own. Remember, the banks of rivers and lakes are public up to 5m above the high-water line.

The fishing here is quite varied, as you can fish a single watershed all the way from its source to the sea. High in the mountains to the east you find small, clear Andean lakes and cold, fast creeks and rivers that are easily fished from the bank. These steep rivers collect in the chain of glacial lakes, where the trout bulk up to six kilos or more; the eastern shores of many lakes have no road access, and the mouths of the creeks (*bocas*) attract big trout and seasonal salmon runs, especially in the Lago Llanquihue region. Most of the lakes are drained to the ocean by bigger, lazier rivers that are best fished from a boat.

To the south, near Puerto Varas, the scale and abruptness of the landscape changes, and the ocean incurs upon the lake region, so that mountain rivers such as the Puelo flow directly into the ocean. Here you find an increasing proportion of stocky coastal and sea-run fish, including Coho, Atlantic, and King salmon, hybrid strains of rainbow and brown trout, and the occasional steelhead. The fish are often bigger here, but access is more complicated than in areas further north. Still, anglers searching for a remote experience without the travel time involved in a trip to Patagonia should focus upon this area.

Fishing Supplies:

In Pucón
- El Pescador Don Ele, on Urrutia between Ansorena and Fresia
- Mario's Fishing Zone, O'Higgins 590.

  In Puerto Varas
- Gray Fly, San Francisco 447 or San José 192.

  In Puerto Montt
- Fly Box, corner of San Martín and Benavente

AN AVERAGE COASTAL RAINBOW ON THE RIO PUELO

PATAGONIA

In a world in which new, 'unexplored,' and increasingly exotic fly fishing destinations are proliferating like mayflies at the height of an evening hatch, Patagonia claims a spot near the top of the list. Few regions in the world can compete with the quality, variety, and sheer abundance of fishable rivers and streams here, and nowhere will you find such a variety of reliable and comfortable lodges in an area with such minimal fishing pressure and breathtaking scenery. As lodge owners and outfitters are fond of mentioning, most fish here have never seen a fly, and many never will.

Fishing here ranges from pristine spring creeks and clear dry-fly streams, to abundant remote lakes and immense freestone rivers, to highly productive saltwater estuaries where you can fish year-round. As the area discussed here ranges from 42-55° S – a distance of over a thousand kilometers – you can expect to find a great variety in both resident fish populations and the timing and scale of seasonal runs of migratory fish. Nonetheless, there are a few constants: throughout Patagonia you can expect moderate to high winds, cold water, abundant (though highly localized) hatches, and big, strong fish. Resident species generally average 2-3 kilos, but are also taken in the 5-6 kilo (25-30") range, with trophy browns up to 10 kilos coming out of the lakes to spawn in the fall (April). Sea-run and coastal fish may be even larger.

If you're planning a fishing trip to Patagonia, you should be aware that booking a trip at the tried-and-true fishing lodges is not your only option. Several independent outfitters now offer fishing tours in the coastal fjords fjords and other remote watersheds with little to no fishing pressure at all; access to these areas may be on foot, by horseback, or by motor yacht and zodiac. More independent travelers may also consider renting a car and travel overland along the Carretera Austral, hiring local guides and boats by the day. In a two-week trip of this sort, you could sample a good portion of the rivers in northern and central Patagonia, which concentrates the majority of Chile's world-class trout streams.

At the far southern tip of the continent, the island of Tierra del Fuego has long been renowned for its enormous sea-run browns, which regularly grow to 7-8 kilos. You need a fast action 8-9' rod and heavy sinking lines to fish this wildly remote area, which is served by a couple of international-level fishing lodges.

> **Fishing supplies:**
> **In Coihaique**
> - Ferretería Brautigan, Calle Horn one block from the plaza.

PATAGONIAN SOLITUDE

BACKGROUND INFORMATION

GEOLOGIC TIME SCALE

Era	Period	Epoch	YBP	Event
PALEOZOIC			590-248 mya	• Pangea complete.
MESOZOIC	TRIASSIC		248-213 mya	• Pangea splits apart, Chile part of new supercontinent Gondwanaland. • South America Linked to North America via land bridge.
	JURASSIC		213-144 mya	• Land bridge between North America and South America sinks. • Appearance of Araucaria trees.
	CRETACEOUS		144-65 mya	• Africa separates from Gondwanaland. • Angiosperms arise in Gondwanaland, spread rapidly. • Volcanic activity in southern Chile forms 'primitive Andes'.
CENOZOIC	TERTIARY	Paleocene	65-55 mya	• Beginning of modern Andean Orogeny. • Most of South America tropical. Oceans cover Patagonia to 45° S latitude.
		Eocene	55-38 mya	
		Oligocene	38-25 mya	• Oceans rise to 35° S latitude.
		Miocene	25-5 mya	• South America separated from Antarctica and Australia; formation of Humboldt current begins to bring cold water north from Antarctic Forests, large mammals in present-day Atacama Desert.
		Pliocene	5-2 mya	• Uplift of Central American Land Bridge. • Influx of more highly competitive animals from North America. • Formation of Juan Fernández Archipelago. • Reduction of tropical forests to present limits. • Ice covers Antarctica and surrounding islands. • Volcanic activity in central-southern Andes.
	QUATERNARY	Pleistocene	2 mya-10,000	• High volcanic activity in northern Altiplano. • Andes attain present heights. • Glaciers cover southern Chile. • Humans arrive in Chile.
		Holocene	10,000-present	• Decrease in volcanic activity in northern Altiplano. • Climate warming, extinction of megafauna. • Disappearance of 'vegetal bridges' linking coast and Altiplano.

Cooling of global climate.

PALEOCLIMATE AND GEOMORPHOLOGY

Some 200 million years ago, in the Mesozoic era, it is believed that all the world's landmass was concentrated in a single supercontinent, known as Pangea (from the Greek, *pan*=all, *gea*=earth), inhabited by flora and fauna vastly different from those of the present day.

Throughout the Mesozoic, Pangea gradually split apart, forming two sub-continents, known as Laurasia and Gondwanaland, separated by the Tethys Sea. Formerly linked to modern-day North America, South America now formed part of Gondwanaland, together with Africa, India, Australia and Antarctica. In the region now known as Patagonia, dinosaurs over 120 feet in length roamed freely from the 'Atlantic' coast to the 'Pacific,' unimpeded by the as-yet-uncreated Andean *cordillera*.

Tremendous changes were to occur in the Cretaceous period. Somewhere in Gondwanaland, the first flower-bearing *angiosperms* arose and quickly spread throughout the world, mutating and adapting at a rate far exceeding that of the gymnosperms (such as conifers) that had previously dominated the world's flora. Extensive forests of *Nothofagus* and *Podocarpus* established themselves in modern-day Chile, Argentina, South Africa, Australia, New Zealand, and Antarctica.

By the mid-Cretaceous, Africa and India had split completely from Gondwanaland, leaving South America largely isolated, connected to the Antarctic/Australian landmass only at its southernmost point. In this isolated environment, and with the age of the dinosaurs having come to its catastrophic end, a great and singular diversification occurred among South American fauna. Marsupials became the dominant carnivores, while placental mammals ruled herbaceous life. Glyptodons, Megatheria, Milodons and Maucrauchenia, as well as dozens of other now-extinct species and a few modern survivors (such as the condor and avestruz) flourished in South America – and only in South America – throughout the early and mid-Tertiary.

By the end of the Cretaceous, the Andean orogeny was well under way, as the eastward-moving Nazca oceanic plate subducted beneath the South American continental plate, giving rise to massive faulting, uplift and volcanism.

DISTRIBUTION OF GONDWANA FORESTS

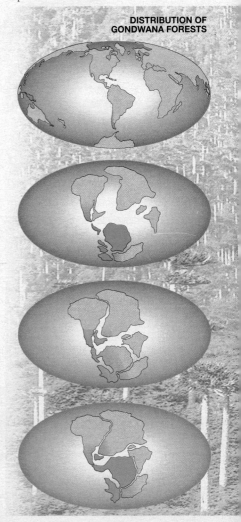

MEGATHERIUM

MYLODON

HIPPIDION

GLYPTODON

PALAEOLAMA

MACRAUCHENIA

The mountain-building processes that characterized the Tertiary period, combined with ongoing climatic changes, wrought great changes upon South American flora and fauna. In the Paleocene, most of South America was covered in tropical forests, with some subtropical elements present in southern Chile and temperate forests in Antarctica. After a period of climatic warming in the Eocene and Oligocene, during the Miocene global temperatures began to drop and continued uplift created the first Andean forest ecosystems.

By the Pliocene, the Drake Passage had finally separated South America from Antarctica, changing patterns of southern ocean circulation and giving rise to the Humboldt Current, which brings Antarctic water north along the Chilean coast.

Not until the late Tertiary and early Quaternary, however, did Chile's topography and biogeography begin to approximate that which exists today. The Andes became more active than ever, spewing out tremendous quantities of ash and lava and rupturing the landscape into the 3 vertical bands – Coast Range, Central Valley, and Andes – which now characterize most of Chile. In northern and central Chile, desert and *matorral* scrub began to replace sub-tropical forests, while in eastern Patagonia, temperate forests were replaced by the high desert or 'pampa.' Far to the west, the volcanoes of Easter Island and the Juan Fernández Archipelago began to nose above waters of the Pacific. The great temperate forests of Antarctica finally gave way to the encroaching ice.

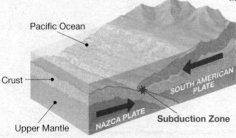

Pacific Ocean

Crust

Upper Mantle

SOUTH AMERICAN PLATE

NAZCA PLATE

Subduction Zone

CLIMATE AND FLORAL CHANGES

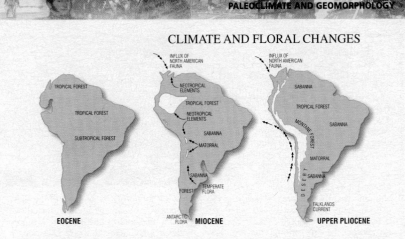

EOCENE — TROPICAL FOREST, TROPICAL FOREST, SUBTROPICAL FOREST

MIOCENE — INFLUX OF NORTH AMERICAN FAUNA, NEOTROPICAL ELEMENTS, TROPICAL FOREST, NEOTROPICAL ELEMENTS, SAVANNA, MATORRAL, SAVANNA, FOREST, TEMPERATE FLORA, ANTARCTIC FLORA

UPPER PLIOCENE — INFLUX OF NORTH AMERICAN FAUNA, SAVANNA, TROPICAL FOREST, SAVANNA, MONTANE FOREST, MATORRAL, DESERT, SAVANNA, FALKLANDS CURRENT

The most significant change for South American fauna was the uplift of the Central American land bridge, which transformed a scattered chain of islands into a veritable highway for faunal migration from North America. Horses and *paleollamas*, mastodons, rodents, felines, foxes, and deer flooded in and continued south, using the heights of the Andes as 'stepping stones' through the dense tropical forests that covered most of South America. Most of these new species had the edge on native species in competition for resources, and over time the 'original' fauna of South America began to disappear from the fossil record. Today many Chilean endemics are survivors from this early Quaternary invasion.

Still, the formation of modern Chile was not complete. As global temperatures dropped in the Pleistocene, immense glaciers carved great fjords and cirques throughout the Andes and scoured the forests off of Tierra del Fuego. Meanwhile far away to the north, sea levels dropped, linking the Americas to Asia, providing a new corridor for the migration of Asian fauna and the *homo sapiens* that followed close behind.

FITZ ROY, CERRO TORRE AND THE
SOUTHERN PATAGONIAN ICE FIELDS

Chile's Glaciers

The glaciers present throughout the length of Chile may best be understood as part of an ongoing process of expansion and contraction that has continued unabated since about 1 million years before present. Since that time, world climate seems to have passed through a series of temperature intervals in which cold snaps lasting about 100,000 years were interspersed with warmer periods lasting 10-15,000 years. Considering that the last glacial interval began about 115,000 years ago, and that the last great advance of the glaciers dates from about 14,500 years ago, it would seem as if global climate is poised for another ice age – though the proliferation of greenhouse gases could well have interrupted this cycle.

In northern Chile, where glacial coverage was never particularly extensive, gla-

LAGUNA SAN RAFAEL

ciers are found on the summits of the highest peaks, exclusively at elevations above 6,000m. In Central Chile, they are far more widespread, clinging to shady SW slopes in the Andes, in some cases extending down onto the U-shaped valley floor.

In the south, although the landscape has been intensely modified by past glaciations, present-day glaciers are only found above tree-line, near the summits of the highest volcanoes. In Patagonia, on the other hand, the situation is very different: numerous glaciers extend down past tree-line and in many places even reach sea level. The San Rafael glacier, in fact, is recognized as the most equatorial glacier in the world to reach the ocean.

South of San Rafael, dozens of other glaciers plunge directly into lakes or the sea. Over fifty of them spill off the sides of the Patagonian Ice Fields, or *Campos de Hielo*, an enormous cap of ice covering over 18,000 square kilometers – an area nearly the size of New Jersey. Divided into two entities, the Northern and Southern Ice Fields extend from 46-52°S and constitute the world's third-largest continental mass of ice, after Antarctica and Greenland. These fields are so large that they create huge blank spots on the map, creating ongoing border tensions between Chile and Argentina.

GEOGRAPHY AND TOPOGRAPHY

ANTARCTIC CHILEAN TERRITORY	1.250.000 km²
NORWAY	385.935 km²
SWEDEN	449.964 km²
UNITED KINGDOM	244.045 km²
GERMANY	356.868 km²
FRANCE	547.026 km²
ITALY	301.225 km²
SOUTHERN KOREA	98.955 km²
UNITED STATES	9.363.498 km²
SPAIN	504.750 km²
JAPAN	377.643 km²
CHILE (Continental)	756.252 km²
EGYPT	1.001.449 km²
SENEGAL	196.192 km²

CHILE COMPARED WITH US & EUROPE

Descriptions of Chile's geography invariably begin with the contrast between the country's length and width. Extending from 18°-56°S, a distance of 4,300 km, Chile's length is equal to a tenth of the world's circumference. Superimposed upon Europe, Chile would stretch from Norway to Morocco, while in the states it would easily span the distance from New York to Los Angeles.

Meanwhile, in no place does the country exceed 400km wide, and it averages less than half that. With an area of some 750,000 km² (not including Chilean Antarctica), Chile is the fourth smallest country in South America, though its area is still greater than that of France and roughly equal to that of Texas. Over 80% of this territory is considered mountainous, a huge contributing factor to Chile's diversity of climates, ecosystems, demographics and economy.

CERRO ACONCAGUA, THE HIGHEST PEAK IN THE AMERICAS

Arica
Iquique
Antofagasta
Eastern Island
La Serena
Juan Fernández Archipelago
Valparaíso
SANTIAGO
Concepción
Temuco
Valdivia
Osorno
Puerto Montt
Coihaique
Cochrane
Chilean Antarctic Territory
90°   53°
POLO SUR
Puerto Natales
Punta Arenas
Puerto Williams
Islas Diego Ramírez

*"AGREEMENT BETWEEN CHILE AND ARGENTINA TO ESTABLISH THE PRECISE ROUTE OF THE BOUNDARY FROM MOUNT FITZ-ROY TO MOUNT DAUDET".
(Buenos Aires, 16 December 1998).

VOLCAN VILLARRICA'S ACTIVE CRATER

Chile's Volcanoes

The Andean Cordillera leads all other mountain regions in the world in sheer number of volcanoes, with a total of 204. Of these, 112 are considered 'Holocene' volcanoes, having formed or erupted within the last 10,000 years.

Most of the historically active volcanoes in South America are in Chile – some 36 of them, all told, including the world's highest, Ojos del Salado. Most of these are what are known as composite volcanoes or stratovolcanoes: steep-sided, relatively symmetrical cones caused by the buildup of layers of lava flows, volcanic ash, and other volcanic material. These usually have a central crater or vent, as well as lateral vents on the flanks of the volcano, often indicated by steam emissions known as fumaroles.

In central and southern Chile, the peaks of these volcanoes are often covered by extensive glaciers. Major eruptions have been known to cause sudden melting of these glaciers, resulting in potentially dangerous mudflows (known as *labars*) that surge down-valley at great speeds, taking forests, boulders, even villages with them. Lava flows themselves often contribute to local geomorphology, redirecting rivers and forming new lakes, while major eruptions can have wider-ranging effects: the August 1991 eruption of Volcan Hudson, for example, buried the

GEYSERS DEL TATIO

region under a thick layer of andesitic pumice (ash), with deposits reaching as far as the Falkland Islands/Islas Malvinas.

When stratovolcanoes become extinct, erosive processes strip away soft sides of the cone, leaving only the hardened magma in the throat of the volcano and in the dikes leading to the fissures and vents on the volcanoe´s flanks. Volcán Puntiagudo is an example of an extinct volcano in the midst of this erosive process.

Other volcanic and geothermal features of the Chilean landscape include geysers, hotsprings, and lava tube caves, the last formed by the cooling and hardening of the outer layer of a lava flow. For definitive information of volcanic activity in Chile and around the globe, visit the website of the Smithsonian Institution's Global Volcanism Program at www.volcano.si.edu/dvp.

VOLCAN PETEROA

CHILE'S PRINCIPAL VOLCANOES

ARICA
- Tacora 5988 m
- Tarapacá 5815 m
- Parinacota 6330 m
- Tutapalca 4876 m
- Guallatiri 6063 m
- Isluga 5530 m

IQUIQUE
- Puchuldiza 4447 m
- Irruputuncu 5163 m
- Olca 5407 m
- Aucanquilcha 6176 m
- Ollagüe 5863 m
- San Pedro 5974 m
- Tatio 5208 m
- Putana 5890 m
- Sairécabur 5971 m
- Licancábur 5916 m

ANTOFAGASTA
- Láscar 5154 m
- Llullaillaco 6739 m
- Lastarria 5697 m

COPIAPO
- Ojos del Salado 6893 m

ISLANDS
San Félix
San Ambrosio
Salas y Gómez
Eastern
Alejandro Selkirk
Robinson Crusoe

LA SERENA

VALPARAISO
SANTIAGO
- Tupungatito 5682 m
- San José 5856 m
- Maipo 5323 m

TALCA
- Tinguiririca 4300 m
- Peteroa y Planchón 3991 m
- Descabezado Chico 3750 m
- Descabezado Grande 3830 m
- Azul 3810 m - Quizapú 3050 m

CONCEPCION
- Chillán 3122 m
- Antuco 2985 m
- Copahue 2969 m
- Callaqui 3164 m
- Tolhuaca 2806 m
- Lonquimay (Navidad) 2865 m

TEMUCO
- Llaima 3125 m
- Villarrica 2840 m
- Quetrupillán 2009 m
- Mocho Choshuenco 2415 m

VALDIVIA
El Mirador 700 m
- Carrán 900 m
- Riñinahue 900 m

OSORNO
Cordillera Nevada o Cordón de Caulle 576 m
- Puyehue 2240 m
- Azufreras de Puyehue 1400 m

PUERTO MONTT
- Osorno 2652 m
- Calbuco 2015 m
- Huequi 1050 m

CASTRO
- Michinmahuida 2404 m
CASTRO
- Corcovado 2300 m

COIHAIQUE
- Macá 2960 m
- Hudson 2500 m

COCHRANE
- Lautaro 3380 m

"Agreement between Chile and Argentina to determine precise borders between Monte Fitz-Roy and Cerro Daudot". (Buenos Aires, Dec 16, 1998).

- Viedma
- Aguilera
- Reclus

PUERTO NATALES
- Burney 1750 m

ANTARCTIC CHILEAN TERRITORY

PUNTA ARENAS

PUERTO WILLIAMS

- Penguin 180 m
- Paluet 350 m
- Decepción 576 m

THE ANDES

The Andean cordillera is the world's longest mountain range, extending some 8,000km from 11°-56°S, forming part of a greater mountain chain which continues, with a few interruptions, all the way from Alaska to Antarctica. Like most of the ranges along the Pacific 'Rim of Fire,' the Andean Cordillera is a volcanically and seismically active range. Its formation dates to about 65 million years ago.

Over half the length of this immense mountain chain lies within or partially within Chilean territory. In northern Chile, near the borders of Bolivia and Perú, the range consists of a broad, high altitude plateau, the *altiplano*. Averaging over 3,500 meters in elevation, the altiplano is formed of volcanic depositions from dozens of high altitude volcanoes, many of which are still active. This unbroken barrier prevents moisture-laden storms originating in the Amazon basin from reaching the desert along the Pacific coast.

Towards the south, the peaks of the Andes continue to surpass 5000m, but the range narrows and the broad plains of the altiplano give way to a sea of abrupt, jagged peaks. From 28-32°S, all volcanic activity has ceased, though this activity begins again in the central region, where the Andes reach their greatest heights: at 6,962 meters, Cerro Aconcagua is the highest peak in both the Western and Southern Hemispheres.

From here, the range begins to lose height. By 37°S, the range is almost purely volcanic, and the highest peaks of the region are set in a rough line west of the continental divide. A number of low-altitude Andean passes – and trans-Andean lakes – facilitate passage through the *cordillera* to Argentina.

South of about 41°S, the range changes character yet again. Though volcanic activity still remains high, harder intrusive rock types (such as granite) become more prevalent. Glaciers – relegated to the south side of the highest volcanoes in the Lake District – begin to appear with greater frequency, and with the submergence of the Central Valley, the Andes suddenly become a coastal range, directly exposed to Pacific weather systems. Many Chilean roads and settlements in this region lie in the benevolent

A Small Earthquake in Chile'

COLECTA
Pro DAMNIFICADOS
Terremoto 1960

Chile has a long and occasionally catastrophic history of earthquakes, another product of ongoing plate tectonics. Known as *temblores* or *terremotos*, most earthquakes are frightening but not particularly dangerous; if you happen to be inside when one hits, the common advice is to seek shelter beneath a doorway or other structural element of the building.

Historical data indicates that major earthquakes tend to hit Chile every 25 to 100 years. The one that struck on May 22, 1960, holds the title of the largest earthquake in registered history, with an intensity of 8.6 on the Richter scale. Emanating from an epicenter 160km off the coast of Valdivia, this temblor devastated Puerto Montt, Valdivia, and dozens of smaller villages, demolishing some 60,000 homes and killing hundreds, if not thousands, in southern Chile. Corollary effects of the quake included the triggered eruption of Volcán Puyehue and a landslide that blocked the Río San Pedro for two months, until a round-

PLATE TECTONICS

COCOS PLATE

AFRICAN PLATE

NAZCA PLATE

PACIFIC PLATE

SOUTH AMERICAN PLATE

ANTARCTIC PLATE

→ Relative plate movement
⠿ Earthquakes
▬ Rift zone (seafloor spreading)
▬ Subduction zone

AFTERMATH OF THE 1960 EARTHQUAKE

the-clock siege of heavy machinery succeeded in breaking the dam in a controlled fashion, preventing the complete destruction of Valdivia Meanwhile, the tremor created a tidal wave or tsunami that affected the entire Pacific basin, destroying archaeological sites on Easter Island, killing 61 in Hawaii, overturning boats in Los Angeles harbor, and even causing minor disturbances in coastal towns in Alaska.

rain shadow east of the highest peaks, in a transitional zone between the Patagonian forests and the pampa.

From about 47°30' to 51°S, two Patagonia ice caps inundate the Andes, fed by annual precipitation exceeding 8,000 mm/year. Protruding above the ice are peaks such as Monte Valentín, at 4,058m the highest peak in the southern Andes, and granite towers such as Cerro Fitzroy and Cerro Torre, both of legendary renown among climbers the world over.

South of the Patagonian Ice Caps, the Andes become progressively more fragmented, penetrated by deep, glaciated fjords, eventually breaking into a universe of islands. Here we find the Cordillera Sarmiento and, further south, where the Andes begin to curve east to Cape Horn, the peaks of the Cordillera Darwin. These heavily glaciated ranges are among the world's most inhospitable mountain regions.

GLACIAL EROSION

THE COAST RANGE

Chile's Coast Range extends over 3000 km, from Arica south to the Taitao Peninsula. Formed during the late-Tertiary uplift that raised the Andes to their current stature, the Cordillera de la Costa is a lower, gentler range, composed largely of granite and sedimentary depositions. It reaches its greatest height in northern Chile, topping out at 3,114m on Cerro Vicuña Mackenna, near Antofagasta.

In places the Coast Range drops directly into the Pacific, while in others a coastal plain, formed of uplifted marine sediments or fluvial depositions, lies between the mountains and the ocean. As most weather patterns arrive from the west, the local topography of the Coast Range often plays a key role in determining climatic conditions on the coast and in the interior. Western slopes are typically wetter and richer in vegetation, while the rain shadow to the east may extend well into the Central Valley. Where the Coast Range is higher, steeper, or more continuous, this effect is magnified.

NORTHERN CHILE'S DRAMATIC DESERT COAST

THE CENTRAL VALLEY

In the Lake Region, the Coast Range steadily loses height, to the point where it becomes little more than a series of rolling hills. Interrupted by the Canal de Chacao, it rises again to form the backbone of the *Isla Grande* of Chiloé, again exerting a noticeable influence over the local climate. South of Chiloé, the Chonos Archipelago and the Taitao Peninsula are the only portions of the Coast Range to break the surface of the Pacific.

Range. From Santiago south to the río Biobío, it achieves its most classic form: perfectly flat, punctuated by the peaks of *cerros* as yet uncovered by sediments, with steep peaks visible to the east and west. South of the Biobío, the Central Valley is not nearly as tangible, as the foothills of the Andes extend further to the west, while glacial and fluvial processes have transformed the landscape into a series of rolling hills and valleys.

South of Puerto Montt, the Central Valley sinks below the surface of the Pacific, forming the Gulf of Ancud, which lies between Chiloé and the Patagonian mainland.

Viña del Mar
Valparaíso

Santiago

Central Valley

Sedimentary Deposits

PACIFIC OCEAN   COAST RANGE   INTERMEDIATE DEPRESSION   ANDES RANGE

THE CENTRAL VALLEY

Sunk between the Andes and the Coast Range, the Central Valley has over millions of years been filled with material eroded from both ranges – though principally from the younger, softer rocks of the Andes. The gentle east-west slope of the Central Valley (also known as the Intermediate Depression) is a modern-day reflection of these depositional processes, as is the fact that the peaks of the Coast Range almost invariably appear higher from the coast than they do from the interior.

Between Copiapó and the río Aconcagua, the Central Valley is interrupted by a series of transverse valleys and mountain ranges that link the Andes and the Coast

OCEAN CIRCULATION ALONG THE CHILEAN COAST

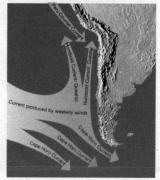

CLIMATE

As a general rule, temperatures drop and rainfall increases as one moves through Chile from north to south. Though north-south temperature variation is basically a function of latitude, understanding the vast range of climates present here requires a basic understanding of Pacific weather patterns, Amazonian weather patterns, and the modifying influence of local topography.

THE PACIFIC OCEAN

The Pacific Ocean is the world's largest body of water, and creates massive circulation patterns with myriad global effects, as has been illustrated in recent years by the el Niño / la Niña phenomenon (see 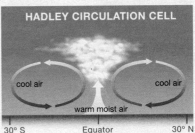).

HADLEY CIRCULATION CELL

cool air   cool air

warm moist air

30° S   Equator   30° N

Circulation in the Pacific, and in fact throughout the global atmosphere, is largely a result of the transfer of heat from the tropics towards the poles. The basic mechanisms for this transfer are so-called 'Hadley Cells' in which warm air rises at the equator and flows toward the poles at altitude. Between 20-30° north and south this air, now cooled, drops towards the surface of the ocean. As it falls, it is compressed and warmed again, causing clouds to evaporate and creating a weather-stabilizing high pressure system or anticyclone.

Just off the Pacific coast of South America is a powerful high pressure system known as the semi-permanent Pacific anticyclone. As descending air is compressed over the eastern Pacific, it flows out from center; as it does so it is spun by the rotation of the earth (the Coriolis effect) a counterclockwise direction. Migrating north (in winter) and south (in summer), the Pacific Anticyclone drives away storm systems, and is largely responsible for the clear skies which characterize northern Chile throughout the year and central Chile in the summer months.

In summertime, moisture-laden southwesterly winds originating in the 'planetary frontal zone' between subtropical and polar air masses are simultaneously repelled by the Pacific Anticyclone and attracted by low pressure systems that form over the Patagonian *pampa*. The result is that while rainfall decreases in the south during the summer months, winds in Patagonia tend to increase.

A complicating factor in Chilean weather is the Humboldt Current, in which cold upwellings of Antarctic water are carried north along the Chilean coast. In addition to moderating temperature along the entire coast, the Humboldt Current cools westerly breezes and reduces oceanic

SEASONAL WEATHER VARIATIONS

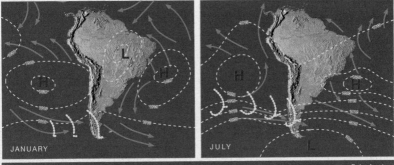

JANUARY   JULY

Wind direction   - - - Atmospheric pressure (in millibars)   •••••••• Polar fronts

OCEAN TEMPERATURES ALONG THE CHILEAN COAST

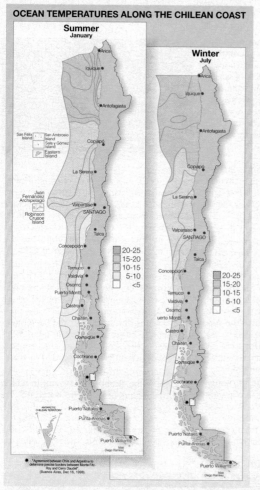

Summer
January

Winter
July

20-25
15-20
10-15
5-10
<5

20-25
15-20
10-15
5-10
<5

*Agreement between Chile and Argentina to determine precise border borders between Monte Fitz-Roy and Cerro Daudet (Buenos Aires, Dec 16, 1998).

evaporation, contributing to the formation of deserts in the north.

AMAZONIAN WEATHER

During the austral summer, the angle of incidence of sunlight upon the Amazon basin nears vertical, resulting in increased evaporation from the tropical rainforest. Easterly winds drive storm clouds formed over the Bolivian *Yungas* and Argentine *Chaco* towards Chile; as these clouds are forced over the Andes, their temperature drops and water vapor condenses, falling

upon the Chilean altiplano as rain and snow. This phenomenon, common in northern Chile in December and January, is known as the altiplanic or Bolivian winter (*invierno boliviano* or *invierno altiplanico*).

EFFECT OF LOCAL TOPOGRAPHY

Chile's mountain topography has a serious modifying effect upon regional and local climate. Though the Pacific may modify temperatures throughout Chile, this effect is much more evident to the west of the Coast Range than it is to the east. Likewise, though it is true that rainfall is greater in southern Chile than in the north, equally great differences may exist between the coast, the central valley, and the Andes at any given latitude.

On a large scale, for example, mountain topography plays a large role in the aridity of the Atacama Desert: the Andes block passage of storms from the Amazon Basin, while the Coast Range traps Pacific mists known as *camanchaca*. In Patagonia, meanwhile, westerly storms slam into the Andes and drop their load of moisture, creating a vast desert – the pampa – in the rain shadow to the east.

Where topography creates a local climatic anomaly, the result is what is called a *microclimate*. Typical Chilean microclimates include coastal mist-fed ecosystems in the desert north, Andean valleys in the Central Valley which trap passing rain clouds, and sunny Patagonian settlements hidden in the lee of the rain-soaked Andes.

SEASONS

Seasons here are offset by six months from those of the Northern Hemisphere. The summer solstice, longest day of the year, occurs on December 21, and the shortest day occurs on June 21. December-February are the hottest months throughout the country.

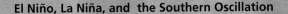

El Niño, La Niña, and the Southern Oscillation

These days the internet and the popular press are replete with the latest on the climatic phenomenon known as El Niño. But just in case you haven't caught the drift yet, here's a brief primer:

The name El Niño (the little boy or, more obliquely, the Christ child) originated in coastal Perú, where the inhabitants used it to refer to a south-flowing current of warm water that occurred once every 2-7 years, usually beginning around Christmas. This current of warm water brought unseasonably heavy rains to the arid coast and produced wide-ranging changes in marine and terrestrial ecosystems, most notably a significant decline in the productiveness of these normally abundant fisheries.

In broader terms, El Niño is an aberration or 'warm phase' of a complex oceanographic/atmospheric system known as the Southern Oscillation, the main features of which are focused on the tropical Southern Pacific but whose effects span the entire globe. During 'normal' Southern Oscillation conditions, the intense high pressure over the southeastern Pacific is paired with an area of low pressure over the southwest Pacific. The Coriolis effect and the flow of air from high to low pressure areas creates constant easterly winds along the equator (the trade winds), which serve to draw warm water away from the Southern American coast and create warm ocean conditions in the

west. During normal conditions, sea level in Indonesia is typically half a meter higher than it is off the coast of Ecuador.

During an El Niño event, the gradient between these paired high and low pressure systems eases, the trade winds relax, and warm water piles up on the South American coast. Precipitation increases in the Andes and the thermocline (the barrier between cold deep-ocean water and warm surface water) drops. What's more, El Niño (and its counterpart La Niña, the 'cold phase' of the Southern Oscillation) create far-reaching changes in global atmospheric circulation: the 1982-83 El Niño is thought to have resulted in losses of as much as US$8 billion to the global economy.

EL NIÑO 1982-83

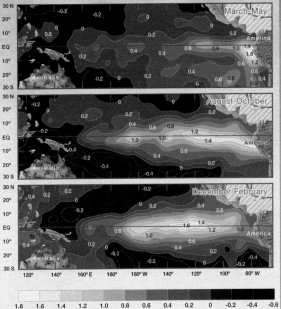

The actual seasons vary by region. Northern Chile basically receives no rain, aside from that of the altiplanic winter (see [↑]), which only affects the altiplano. Central Chile has a Mediterranean climate, which is to say that rainfall is concentrated in the four months from May-August; the rest of the year is basically dry and sunny.

Further south, rainfall is more equitably divided throughout the year, though is still heaviest in the winter months. Spring and fall are longer and more pronounced than in areas further north. In southern Patagonia, the westerly winds which plague hikers and climbers during the summer months decline considerably during the winter.

PREHISTORY

HIPPIDION

The 'first Americans' were not explorers in the normal sense of the word. Instead, they were nomadic hunter-gatherers, migrating on the heels of the mastadons and other now-extinct megafauna that clothed and fed them; the idea that they had discovered an entirely new hemisphere was obviously well beyond them. Studies of the Bering seafloor have revealed that a drop in sea level of only 45m would make crossing the Strait entirely feasible; with an additional 25m drop a second bridge would be formed, and with a 100m drop from present sea level, the entire continental shelf would be revealed. However, when sea levels were lowest, continental glaciers would have covered most routes linking Alaska with the rest of North America. Reconstructing the routes by which the Americas were populated requires synthesizing paleoclimate studies with the data available from early Paleolithic sites – a sketchy, theoretical process at best.

MYLODON

In any case, by 12,000 years before the present (BP) such nomadic groups had clearly spread over a great portion of North and South America. While most of the Paleolithic sites discovered in Chile – and in fact throughout the Americas – seem to correspond to bands of highly mobile hunters and gatherers inhabiting open terrain, new sites in southern Chile (at Monte Verde) and in the Amazon basin have begun to challenge assumptions about how, when and where Paleolithic peoples lived.

Modern understanding of the changes that transpired between the initial arrival in Chile of *homo sapiens* and that of the first Europeans some 13,000 years later is highly dependent on local environmental conditions. In northern Chile, the arid conditions perfectly preserve residential and burial complexes, foodstuffs, textiles and other artifacts, providing for a relatively complete reconstruction of cultural change and interaction. Further south, the wetter climate and dense vegetation tends to obfuscate the archaeological record. You'll find information on regional prehistoric development in the introductions to regional chapters, and a general overview of the indigenous groups inhabiting Chile at the time of the Spanish conquest in **c**.

MUMMY FROM THE CHINCHORRO CULTURE

OCCIDENTAL CONTACT AND CONQUEST

Beginning in the late 1400's, Chile's indigenous inhabitants got their first taste of invasion. Under the rule of Tupac Yupanqui, the Inca empire rapidly expanded south into Chile from highland Perú, imposing their solar-based religion, installing Quechua work parties known as *mitimaes*, and demanding periodic tribute in the form of labor. Inca influence in Chile was most strongly felt in the north, and petered out completely a few hundred kilometers south of Santiago, where the Mapuche Indians fiercely held their ground.

ALMAGRO LEAVING CUSCO, OIL ON CANVAS BY SUBERCASEAUX

The rise of the Incas was paralleled by the rise of other large administrative and religious dynasties throughout Latin America. After Columbus' 'mistake' opened the door to the Spanish conquest, this existing hierarchy and conglomerate tendency worked to the Spaniards' advantage, and in many cases they maintained control over native peoples by installing a puppet ruler in the post of the traditional Indian leader. Unlike North America, where native cultures under increasing pressure from the whites could always escape into the vast western frontier, in most cases the Indians of Latin America inhabited a narrow ecological niche and had nowhere else to go.

PEDRO DE VALDIVIA

The speed at which the South American continent was 'discovered' and 'conquered' defies the imagination, for never before or since has so vast a region been so completely transformed in such a short period of time. In 1494, the pope granted Spain all the lands west of Brazil (with the stipulation that they convert the inhabitants), and the free-for-all began: equipped with swords, crossbows, horses, vicious war dogs and an accompanying horde of pestilent diseases never before seen in the Americas, the often-degenerate soldiers of fortune known as *conquistadors* used whatever means necessary to bring native populations to their knees.

Following Hernán Cortez' 1521 defeat of the Aztec empire, two conquistadors, Francisco Pizarro and Diego de Almagro, organized an expedition to seek out the fabulously rich Indian cities rumored to exist further south. When they arrived in Perú, they found the Inca empire torn by factional fighting, and through a combination of luck, deception, and sheer meanness, the Spanish managed to conquer the once-great Andean nation with a force of only 180 men.

Soon afterwards, in 1535, Diego de Almagro followed the Inca trail south to undertake the *conquista* of the land known as Chile. Almagro wasn't the first to lay eyes on Chilean territory – Ferdinand Magellan, who sailed through the Strait of Magellan in 1520, claims that distinction – but he may have been the most disappointed. After nearly perishing during a crossing of the frigid altiplano, Almagro's party continued south to the Aconcagua valley, found none of the riches they'd been hoping for, and returned promptly to Perú. Three years later Pedro de Valdivia mounted a second expedition – this time opting for the marginally more benign route through the Atacama Desert – and in 1541 founded the city of Santiago, the first Spanish settlement in Chile.

THE COLONIAL ERA

Though Valdivia's precarious 'city' was very nearly eradicated on several occasions by the local Picunche Indians, over time the Spanish were able to consolidate their holdings in central and northern Chile. As elsewhere in America, their energies were initially focused almost exclusively upon mining for gold and silver, and in order to work the labor-intensive mines, individual Spaniards were awarded the rights to use local Indian labor, known as an *encomienda*. Though the owners of *encomiendas* were ostensibly required to offer their subjects religious instruction in return, in reality most *encomiendas* turned out to be virtually indistinguishable from slavery.

When Chile's gold and silver mines continued to yield less than the anticipated bounty, the nascent colony became more and more focused on the agricultural and pastoral industries. Beginning in 1550, Valdivia began to explore the southern part of the country, and through the latter half of the century, the south became the principle arena of Spanish activity – that is, until the Mapuche Indians revolted and definitively ousted the Spanish from their territory in 1598. Thus arose a singularly defining element of Colonial and early Republican Chile: *La Frontera*.

Throughout the Colonial era, the Spanish were forced to maintain a standing army along *La Frontera*, the division between Spanish and Mapuche that hovered around the latitude of the Rio Biobío. The needs of this army, combined

CHILI MAGELLAN-LAND, 1709

with those of the Spanish mines in Perú and Bolivia, created a substantial demand for horses, leather, and foodstuffs, particularly wheat. And as agriculture continued to increase in importance throughout the 17th and 18th centuries, the *hacienda* arose as the dominant organizational feature of the rural Chilean landscape.

With nearly every last bit of land held by a few great landowners, Chile's increasing population of mixed-race *mestizos* gravitated naturally towards the haciendas, where they became *inquilinos*. In return for the use of a small plot of land, *inquilino* families were required to work for the hacienda, and later, they were required to provide a son or daughter to serve in the main house or *casa patronal*. This arrangement continued with few modifications until the agrarian reforms of the mid-20th century.

Extending from the Río Loa south to the Biobío, colonial Chile was only a fraction the size of the modern nation. Both the desert north and the island of Chiloé (settled by Spaniards in the 16th century) pertained to the more powerful Viceroyalty of Perú.

'Exports from Chile: Gold (Principally from Valdivia); Hemp: To Perú; Mules: to Potosí (via Atacama), Almonds: to Perú; vegetables. Imports from Spain to Chile: Cows, Pigs, Horses, Dogs.
-Alonso González de Najera, 1614.

HOMBRE DE CAMPO, BY J. RAVENET, 1793

MAPUCHES FROM CLAUDIO GAY'S *ATLAS*

INDEPENDENCE AND THE NEW REPUBLIC

HOMBRE A CABALLO,
BY ALPHONSE GIAST

As happened throughout the Americas, over time a new generation of Chilean-born Spaniards or *criollos* began to chafe under Spain's strict and inefficient governance. Not only were they subjected to the indignity of being ruled by imported officials (known as *peninsulares*), but furthermore, the crown's harsh trade regulations were costing *criollo* merchants money. As the 18th century drew to a close, with revolutionary sentiment permeating intellectual circles on three continents, Chile's *criollos* were becoming increasingly preoccupied with self-governance.

The opportunity presented itself in a curious fashion. After Spanish King Ferdinand VII was toppled by Napoleón in 1908, local governing bodies known as *juntas* were formed throughout Spain and the Spanish colonies in Ferdinand's name. The same occurred in Santiago in 1810, where a six-man junta adopted a number of measures intended to increase Chile's decision-making autonomy – while still remaining loyal to the deposed king. This junta, however, was soon usurped by another, more radical one, headed by José Miguel Carrera. When colonial authorities in Perú caught wind of these events, they sent a bat-

BERNARDO O'HIGGINS

talion of Royalist troops south to bring to heel the so-called 'Patriots.' The Patriots – originally commanded by Carrera and later by the more capable Bernardo O'Higgins – managed to hold the Royalists off for some time, but were finally forced to flee east across the Andes after being routed in the 1814 'Disaster of Rancagua.'

Meanwhile, King Ferdinand had returned to the throne in Spain. His heavy-handed attempt to re-establish control of the country's American colonies, known as the Reconquest, only cemented the *criollo* convictions about the need for independence. But bold strokes were needed to oust Spanish power from its stronghold in Perú.

Chile's struggle for independence coincided with those being fought throughout the Spanish colonies. While Simón de Bolivar's liberation army was fighting its way south from Venezuela, José de San Martín was sequestered in the mountains of Mendoza, just across the Andes from Santiago. With his troops bolstered by those of Bernardo O'Higgins, San Martín orchestrated

BATALLA DE MAIPU,
OIL PAINTING BY
P. SUBERCASEAUX

one of history's great tactical invasions, won a couple of decisive battles, and in April of 1818 finally terminated Spanish rule in Chile at the Battle of Maipú. From there, Scotsman Lord Thomas Cochrane, the founder of Chile's navy, was dispatched north to undertake the siege of Callao (Perú), which finally fell in 1820.

In the wake of independence, Bernardo O'Higgins was made Chile's first 'Supreme Director.' Setting a standard of authoritarian rule, he nonetheless enacted a number of important reforms, including the legal abolishment of the *mayorazgo* system that allowed so much land to remain concentrated in the hands of so few. However, the high taxes that O'Higgins was forced to levy (to recuperate war costs) eventually riled the landed classes to the extent that he was forced to seek exile in Perú.

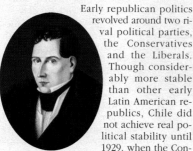
DIEGO PORTALES

Early republican politics revolved around two rival political parties, the Conservatives and the Liberals. Though considerably more stable than other early Latin American republics, Chile did not achieve real political stability until 1929, when the Conservatives definitively seized power under the quiet leadership of Diego Portales. Portales' 1833 constitution, which bestowed sweeping powers upon the president, was to determine the course of Chilean politics for nearly a hundred years.

With power firmly but constitutionally concentrated in the hands of a few, Chile enjoyed a period of sustained growth throughout the mid-1800's. Not only did the economy grow – fed principally by mining in the Norte Chico – but the country's national territory expanded as well. Little by little, the Mapuche homeland in the south was chipped away by the work of the army and the Church, while usurped lands were immediately distributed to an influx of European immigrants. In 1843, Chile established sovereignty over the Strait of Magellan, the only known shipping route between the Atlantic and Pacific Oceans. And in the

THE WAR OF THE PACIFIC

north, the Chilean victory over Perú and Bolivia in the War of the Pacific (1879-1880) secured the country's rights over the immense – and immensely valuable – nitrate reserves of the Atacama Desert. Finally, in 1888 Chile annexed Easter Island, 4,000km west in the middle of the Pacific Ocean.

In this atmosphere of growth and affluence, the presidency of José Manuel Balmaceda nonetheless demonstrated the intrinsic flaws in Portales' authoritarian constitution. Balmaceda's insistence on wielding his executive powers created a rift with Congress that finally precipitated in a bloody civil war pitting the country's army and navy against one another. In the aftermath of the conflict, which is thought to have claimed some 10,000 lives – including that of Balmaceda, who committed suicide in the Argentine embassy – Portales' constitution was scrapped in favor of a Parliamentary Republic in which Congress, rather than the president, held the balance of power.

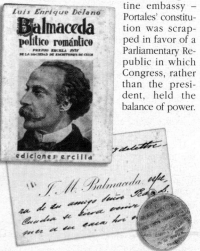

Luis Enrique Délano
Balmaceda
político romántico
PREMIO ERCILLA 1957
DE LA SOCIEDAD DE ESCRITORES DE CHILE

ediciones ercilla

THE TWENTIETH CENTURY

TALCA IN THE EARLY 20TH CENTURY

The vast profits generated by the nitrate fields of the Atacama Desert fueled a number of important changes during the early years of the twentieth century. On the one hand, tax dollars were used to build important industrial and transportation infrastructure throughout the country, diversifying the economy and creating conditions favorable to the growth of the middle class. On the other hand, as thousands of Chileans moved from the haciendas of central and southern Chile to the mines of the north, the working classes began to develop a sort of political consciousness. With no other means of protest available to them, the rudely exploited Chilean nitrate workers increasingly resorted to strikes as a means of lobbying for change – and in return were brutally repressed by government forces.

When the bottom fell out of the nitrate market in 1914, these same workers returned to their homes in the south, carrying with them a newly formed sense of class solidarity and struggle. During the early 1920's, the charismatic Arturo Alessandri Palma attempted to address the growing discontent of Chilean workers with a number of reformist measures, but was blocked by Congress until a power play by the military forced the legislature to accept the

ARTURO ALESSANDRI

changes. This intervention by the military was a sign of things to come, as the exiled Alessandri was soon succeeded by General Carlos Ibáñez del Campo, the first true dictator in the country's history. After attempting to revive the Chilean economy through a series of state sponsored enterprises – including the formation of LanChile, the national airline – Ibáñez was also ousted when the Great Depression sent copper prices tumbling, and the Chilean economy with it.

Though civil rule was restored in 1932, Chile's long slate of unresolved social and economic issues made for an increasingly complicated political playing field. The vast majority of agricultural land remained in the hands of a few landed oligarchs, the copper mines remained in the hands of US corporations, and Marxist rhetoric become increasingly prevalent among the lower classes. Though Carlos Ibáñez del Campo, the old dictator, was re-elected in 1952, this represented the last democratic gasp of Chile's right. By the late 1950's it had become clear that the political climate in Chile had definitively shifted to the left.

Allende and the Unidad Popular

In the 1958 elections, a middle-class Socialist doctor named Salvador Allende, running on the ballot of the leftist FRAP (*Frente de Acción Popular*, Popular Action Front), finished a close second to the conservative Jorge Alessandri, son of Arturo. This shocked both Chilean conservatives and the communist-wary US government into action, and both threw their weight solidly behind Eduardo Frei, the candidate for the Christian

CHRONIC SHORTAGES DURING THE ALLENDE YEARS

Democrats, who defeated Allende by a solid margin in the 1964 elections. In accordance with his party's platform, Frei soon began a program of progressive agrarian reform, but the measures were at once too lenient for the militant left or too harsh for the landed elite. As the 1970 elections approached, Chilean society in general, and the Christian Democrats in particular, had become irreconcilably polarized.

Salvador Allende, now running on the ballot of the newly-formed coalition known as the UP (*Unidad Popular*, Popular Unity), won the 1970 election by the slimmest of margins, making him the world's first and only democratically elected Socialist president. He immediately set into motion a wide-ranging program of social and economic reform, including appropriation of all haciendas over 80 hectares and nationalization of major industries, including the Chilean copper mines – without compensating the US owners.

However, Allende's measures did not satisfy many of the more extreme factions of his party, who urged ever swifter and more sweeping reforms, and his image was increasingly injured by the actions of the MIR (Movimiento Izquierda Revolucionaria, Leftist Revolutionary Movement), which began seizing haciendas on its own initiative. In response, panicked landowners began selling off stock and machinery as fast as they could in order to risk losing it altogether, with the result that Chilean food productions dropped dramatically, obliging Allende's administrations to import staple foodstuffs, sending inflation through the roof. A worldwide drop in copper prices and a nationwide trucker's strike.

By mid-1973, the situation had reached critical stages. Despite Allende's efforts to regain stability by appointing military leaders to key cabinet posts, the end was at hand. On September 11th, the Chilean military took to the streets of Santiago under the command of General Augusto Pinochet. As the air force bombed the presidential palace, Salvador Allende, holed up inside, made one final poignant radio address to his supporters before taking his own life.

Pinochet and the Military Dictatorship

Pinochet's *golpe de estado* was swift and brutal. Leftist sympathizers were herded into the National Stadium, where many were tortured or killed as examples. Within weeks, thousands had died or 'disappeared' and tens of thousands had fled the country to seek asylum.

THE BOMBING OF LA MONEDA

AUGUSTO
PINOCHET

In the aftermath of the coup, Pinochet installed himself at the head of a military junta that was to rule the country for the next 17 years. Opposition parties – in fact all political parties – were summarily banned, the press placed under strict control, and a fearsome secret police force, the DINA (Directorio de Inteligencia Nacional, National Intelligence Directorate) routinely violated human rights in its campaign to control 'subversion.'

Meanwhile, Pinochet embarked on the restoration of Chile's economy, enlisting the aid of a troupe of free market economists, known as the Chicago Boys, who had studied under the guidance of University of Chicago economist Milton Friedman. With government spending and import tariffs reduced, the already shattered economy took an even sharper turn for the worse.

By the late 1970's Chile's economy had begun to recover, and in 1980 the Pinochet government took advantage of improved public opinion to have a new constitution approved in a national plebiscite. Under the new constitution, Pinochet would rule through 1988, at which point another plebiscite would determine whether or not the regime would continue in power – this time until 1997.

Early in the 1980's, however, a regional debt crisis again induced a downward turn in the Chilean economy, and opposition to the regime increased, both within Chile and abroad. As the 1988 plebiscite approached, the various opposition parties finally united in the famous 'No' campaign, and in October of that year, Christian Democrat Patricio Aylwin – running for the *Concertación para la Democracia* (Concertation for Democracy) party – was elected with a majority of 55%. Contrary to many expectations, Pinochet stepped down peacefully.

The Transition to Democracy

In the years following Chile's return to democracy, its government has largely followed the economic policies established by Pinochet and the social policies advocated by Aylwin. In 1993, Christian Democrat Eduardo Frei was elected to the presidency, and in 1999 Ricardo Lagos, a Socialist, was elected to the post. Both were backed by Aylwin's *Concertación para la Democracia* party.

EDUARDO
FREI R.

EL MERCURIO

Aylwin juró como Presidente

Confianza en el pueblo de Chile expresó Aylwin

Chile reanudó relaciones con cinco naciones

RICARDO
LAGOS

In 1998, Augusto Pinochet's arrest in a London hospital and his subsequent extradition to Spain briefly refocused the world's press on the atrocities committed during the regime's 17-year tenure, and recently declassified US documents have revealed the depth and intensity of the CIA's role in the coup. In Chile, however, little has changed, and the populace remains divided and deeply injured by years of dictatorship and fear. Resolving human rights issues and finally leaving *la dictadura* in the past is a process that will not occur overnight – and not, some would add, without restructuring of Chile's military, which continues to operate as if it were a distinct social caste.

CHILE TODAY

Today, the Chilean economy is among the most competitive in Latin America, though it remains heavily dependent on the exportation of non-value-added natural resources. Copper is far and away the country's biggest cash cow: 1997 exports topped US$7 billion, though more of that goes to the foreign-owned private sector than to state-owned Codelco. That bounty, at least, appears unlikely to run out soon, as over a quarter of the world copper reserve lies in Chilean earth.

WINE CELLARS AT VIÑA LA POSADA

Forestry brings in another US$1.3 billion a year, most of that derived from plantations of Monterrey pine that are expected to cover a total area of 2 million há by the year 2010, in many cases replacing slower-growing native hardwood forests, which now cover about 13.4 mil há. Tragically, most native hardwoods are converted into low-value pulp for export to Japan.

The fresh fruit industry is another big winner, with Chilean fields producing 44% of South America's winter fruit crop, or some 14% of world fruit exports. Salmon farming is perhaps the biggest success story of the last decade, and Chile now ranks second only to Norway in salmon exports. Finally, tourism brings in about US$900 million/year, or 4% of GDP.

This focus on growth has not come without its social and environmental costs. The distribution of wealth is still extremely uneven, and minimum wages have not significantly increased since Pinochet's 1980 Constitution. Eager to attract foreign investment, Chilean legislators have been loathe to tighten up the country's environmental regulations, and today Chile ranks among the world's top ten producers of sulphur dioxide; 90% of that comes from the country's copper smelters. Deforestation, desertification, and the pollution of water-ways are other themes that will need to be addressed in the coming year, as proponents of sustainable development seek to raise environmental awareness and shift to and economy based on value-added goods.

Chuquicamata Copper mine

COPPER READY FOR EXPORT

FIELD GUIDES

Natural Attractions

Most of South America, as well as Central America, the Carribean, Mexico, and Baja California, is covered by what is known as Neotropical flora, which consists of a mixture of tropical rainforests, scrub forests, deserts and high steppe, plus an nearly infinite spectrum of intermediate 'ecotones.' The flora of the southernmost part of the continent is of distinct origins, and corresponds to the so-called Antarctic floral kingdom. In a certain sense, Chile represents the meeting of these two floral kingdoms, across a sharp north-south gradient of temperature and precipitation. The peculiarity of this situation manifests itself in unusually high levels of biodiversity and endemism.

Diversity in Chile is not species-rich like the tropical rainforest regions of the Amazon basin. Instead, Chilean ecosystems exhibit extraordinary richness of the higher orders, from forests to cactus, penguins to flamingos. The proximity of incredibly distinct environments makes Chilean diversity simple to appreciate.

Endemism – which means simply that a species lives here, and nowhere else – is a more complex matter, arising from a variety of geographical phenomena. The roots of Chilean endemism lie in the long period of isolation experienced by the South American continent from the Cretaceous to the late-Tertiary – some 200 million years, during which entire families of unique organisms

evolved in an environment of relatively mild competition for resources. Many Chilean endemics, such as marsupials, edentates (armadillos), numerous invertebrates and several bird species, are relics of this continental diversification.

But why did these species survive in Chile, and nowhere else? For this we must thank Chile's unusual geography, which – isolated by the mountains, the Pacific, and the Atacama Desert – has transformed the territory into a *biological island*. This has served to preserve relict species that otherwise would not be able to compete for resources with better-adapted species. Discontinuity of ecosystems within the country is further responsible for high endemism rates, as isolated populations in neighboring valleys will develop along their own evolutionary paths. Some botanists estimate that as many as 50% of all Chilean plant species grow nowhere else on the planet, and in some areas endemism rates are even higher.

Solid efforts have been made in recent years to protect Chile's native flora and fauna, its unique and invaluable genetic patrimony. Conaf's national system of protected wildlands (Snaspe) includes some 13.8 million hectares, including five national parks that have been incorporated into Unesco's World Biosphere Reserves program: Lauca and Fray Jorge in the north, Torres del Paine and Laguna San Rafael in Patagonia, and the Juan Fernández Archipelago.

Chile currently ranks seventh in the world and third in the Americas in terms of percentage of landmass protected, a figure which does not take into account private conservation initiatives (such as Douglas Tompkins' 317,000 hectare Pumalin Park). Still, environmental degradation is rampant, especially in terms of native forest conservation, desertification, urban air quality, and native forest conservation, and many endangered species and even entire ecosystems are not represented within the Snaspe system. On the plus side, new parks and reserves are approved every year. You can get a list of priority conservation areas proposed for protected status from Conaf.

Mammals

Chile is home to over 80 species of native mammals, representing the orders *Marsupiales* (marsupials, three species), *Quiropteros* (bats, 11 species), *Edentados* (edentates, 3 species), *Roedores* (rodents, 45 species), *Carnivoros* (carnivores, 15 species), *Arciodactilos* (camelids and deer, 6 species) and pinnipeds (seals and sea lions, 9 species). Of all terrestrial mammals, only marsupials and edentates are 'original' South American orders, the rest having arrived with the Pleistocene uplift of the Central American land bridge.

Birds

Over 430 species of birds have been registered in Chile. Of these, nine are endemic to continental Chile, three are endemic to the Juan Fernández Archipelago, five are endemic to northern Peru and southern Chile, and another 75 species are only found in the southern cone (Chile/Argentina). With lesser diversity than that of the tropics, Chile offers a good introduction to bird families of the Neotropical region. Birders with experience in Neotropical birding will likely focus upon Chilean and regional endemics.

For more information on birding in Chile, contact the Union de Ornitólogos de Chile at (see pg 37 for contact info) for more information on birding in Chile.

CHILE'S ENDEMIC BIRDS
- Slender-billed parakeet
- Crag chilia
- Chilean Seaside-Cinclodes
- Dusky-tailed Canastero
- Chestnut-throated huet-huet
- Moustached Turca
- White-throated Tapaculo
- Dusky Tapaculo
- Chilean mockingbird
- Juan Fernández Firecrown
- Juan Fernández Tit-tyrant
- Masafuera Rayadito

Reptiles

Scientists have thus far identified a total of 100 species of reptiles in Chile, including 88 species of lizards and salamanders, five species of snakes, and seven species of migratory tortoises. At least 55 of these species are endemic to Chile, and all are considered threatened. The capture of reptiles has been prohibited since 1993, in order to curb a black market pet trade that exported nearly two million reptiles between 1985 and 1993.

CONTENTS

THE NORTHERN COAST

Marine ecosystems along northern Chile's coast are relatively homogeneous, largely due to the effects of the Humboldt current, which maintains consistent water temperatures across a broad range of latitudes. Terrestrial ecosystems along the northern coast are characterized by plants and animals that are able to maximize scarce water resources, occasionally lapsing into dormancy to survive long periods of drought.

ALGAE

Some 550 species of benthic algae grow along the Chilean coast, with increased diversity towards the higher latitudes. The livelihood of an estimated 9-10,000 Chilean fishermen depend fully or partially upon the harvest of algae.

1. *Porphyra columbina*, commonly known as 'luche,' grows just below the high tide line. The wide, tapered leaf measures 6-10cm long and up to 4cm wide. Common from Coquimbo to Chiloé, it is one of Chile's important commercial varieties.

2. *Ulva rigida* is found from Arica to Magallanes, but is most common in exposed rock outcroppings north of Puerto Montt. It may be recognized by its stiff, multi-lobed, dark green oblong leaves.

3. *Iridaea laminarioides* is found south of Coquimbo, preferentially on exposed, rocky coasts. Composed of up to 50 tapered leaves up to 30cm long and 5cm wide, they are anchored to the rocks by a root structure known as a holdfast.

4. *Gelidium lingulatum* is endemic to South America's temperate Pacific coast. They are common between Puerto Montt and Valparaiso, in lower to middle intertidal zones with consistent waves. The plant consists of a long cylindrical stem with numerous small holdfasts; between these sprout vertical stems with upper ramifications.

5. *Macrocystis integrifolia* is commonly known as 'huiro,' and grows from Arica to Concepción. The plant attaches to the rocks with a flat, bulky rhizome, from which numerous stems extend up to 30m in length; the leaves have air bladders at their base, causing them to float to the surface.

6. *Durvillaea antarctica*, also called cochayuyo, is a staple in many coastal kitchens. Common from Valparaíso to Tierra del Fuego, this kelp grows from the intertidal zone to depths of 15m, forming a 'kelp forest' in protected bays. In the water, you'll recognize the conical holdfast and dark brown leaves, but cochayuyo is easier to spot in tightly wound bundles at local markets.

7. *Lessonia nigrescens* is the most common algae on exposed and semi-exposed coasts from Arica to Tierra del Fuego. They measure up to 4m long, with olive green to black fronds; the holdfast measures up to 50cm in diameter.

CACTI

Believed to have originated in México, the family Cactacea is an almost exclusively American phenomenon, with only one genus growing anywhere outside the Western Hemisphere.

Unique climatic conditions have made Chile into something of an evolutionary laboratory for these highly adapted xerophytic plants: though estimates of the total number of Chilean species vary from as many as 154 to as few as 84, botanists generally agree that over 80% of these are endemic. The vast majority of cactus species inhabit coastal environments in the north, where they benefit from nightly *camanchaca* mist; the rest grow in the *sierra* and altiplano (at elevations up to 4500m), as well as in the Norte Chico and central Chile.

The cactus family currently has more species in danger of extinction than any other major plant group. Please do not contribute to its extinction by removing plants as souvenirs or purchasing handicrafts made from cactus.

Candelabra Cactus (*Browningia candelaris*): Grows at elevations from 1,700-300m, reaching 3-5 meters high and up to 50cm thick at the base. Heavily exploited for firewood and handicraft use, this majestic cactus is most easily sighted along Ruta 11 to Putre and PN Lauca.

Genus *Opuntia*: 200 species found throughout the Americas. Common Chilean varieties include Chuchampe (*O. atacamensis*), found in the Inter-Andean Depression, and tuna (*O. ficus-andina*), a Mexican native grown commercially throughout northern and central Chile for its delicious fruit.

Genus *Echinopsis*: 50 species. Quisco (*E. chilensis*) is extremely abundant from the Elqui Valley south through much of central Chile, where it generally grows on sunny north-facing slopes. Known variously as 'Cactus cardón' or 'Cactus Gigante,' *E. atacamensis* grows at elevations from 2,600-3,800m, and may reach 7m tall and 70cm in diameter. Once common in the Inter-Andean depression (near San Pedro de Atacama), *E. atacamensis* has been severely overexploited for use in 'traditional' handicrafts, and today may be best observed in the altiplano northwest of Cariquima and in the hills above Toconce.

Genus *Copiapoa*: The 18 species of the endemic genus *Copiapoa* consist of groups of small globes forming dense cushions up to 1m high and 2m in diameter. Common in PN Llanos del Challe and PN Pan de Azúcar, as well as other coastal environments, *Copiapoa* cacti suffer from illegal exportation and sale to collectors; please leave them in their place.

Sandillón de los Ratones (*Eriosyse rodentiophila*): Found between Taltal and Flamenco (south of Chañaral), this endemic species grows to anywhere from 15-70cm in diameter. Its small wooly flowers and fruit grow as a crown on the plant's apex.

**Red-backed Hawk
Aguilucho**
(*Buteo polyosoma*)
In northern Chile this
species nests in cactus and
feeds upon lizards, rodents,
small birds and insects. Its
plumage varies with age:
juveniles (shown in photo)
are brownish, while adults
are white beneath with a
contrasting back (black in
males, red in females).

Chinchilla
(*Chinchilla lanigera*)
Famous for its
remakably soft fur, this
rodent is endemic to Chile.
At the turn of the century,
nearly half a million
chinchilla pelts were
exported annually from
Chile; though protected
since 1929, only one wild
population is known to
survive, in RN Las Chinchi-
llas near Illapel.

THE FLOWERING DESERT

The *Desierto Florido* is a periodic phenomenon that generally
occurs during springtime of an El
Niño year, when the Norte Chico receives greater than normal amounts
of precipitation. Local vegetation in the
region, which normally varies from a
scrubby matorral in the south to the near-
absolute desert near Copiapó, transforms
between the months of Au-
gust and November into a
fantastically diverse community of rare and beautiful flowers. Many cacti
also flower during
El Niño events.

Though different
plants flower at differ-
ent times, the peak of
the event usually occurs
between the first week in September and the second week in
October. The area surrounding
the Huasco valley – and particularly PN Llanos de Challe, north
of Huasco – is generally regarded
as one of the best sites for observation of this spectacular, ephem-
eral natural phenomenon. Please
leave all flowers in their place –
many are rare or endangered.

Garra de León (*Leontorchir
ovallei*): This rare endemic is
found almost exclusively in PN
Llanos de Challe.

Añañuca
(*Genus
rodophiala*):
Grows in yellow,
orange, and red
varieties. Flowers
in mid-September

RELICT FORESTS

In a few sites along the coast of the Norte Chico, the
high peaks of the Coast Range trap *camanchaca* mist in
quantities sufficient to support forest communities more
similar to the temperate rainforest of southern Chile than the
matorral scrub which typifies vegetation throughout the rest
of the region. Known as relict forests, these unlikely ecosystems are remnants of the forests that appear to have covered much of the region as recently as the Pleistocene,
when increased precipitation and decreased temperatures

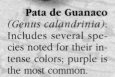

Terciopelo *(Genus argylia radiata)* This endemic genus appears in yellow, orange, and dark brown varieties, flowering in mid-September.

Huille *(Genus leucocoryne)*: Grows in white and lavender, flowers in mid-September.

Pata de Guanaco *(Genus calandrinia)*: Includes several species noted for their intense colors; purple is the most common.

Family Alstroemeria: Several species, flowers in mid-September to late-October.

Vaquitas del desierto *(Genus gyriosomus)*
These unusual black, grey and white beetles appear in great numbers during flowering desert events. Like the flowers, they dedicate their short lives almost exclusively to reproducing. You might spot them running across the dunes, the males hot on the trail of their prospective mates.

permitted the northward migration of 'Antarctic' flora. Olivillo, canelo, arrayan are among the most common species found in the relict forests of central and northern Chile. See below for description and species guides for temperate forest ecosystems.

- PN Fray Jorge
- PN Altos de Talinay
- Quebrada el Tigre

Bottle-nosed Dolphins
(Tursiops truncatus)

Though they inhabit temperate and tropical waters throughout the world, bottle-nosed dolphins are something of an anomaly in Chile; a single population, found in Reserva Nacional Los Pingüinos, is thought to have arrived during the 1978 El Niño event. Large males may grow to 3.7m in length and weigh up to 450kg.

Grey Gull
Gaviota garuma
(Larus modestus)

An exclusive inhabitant of northern Chile and southern Perú, this species may be often spotted on the beach in large groups, feeding upon sand fleas. Known for its melodious call, the Grey Gull nests in colonies up to 50km inland, in the very midst of the desert.

Peruvian Booby
Piquero *(Sula variegata)*

This species may be most easily identified while fishing: tucking its wings close against its body, the Peruvian booby dives from heights up to 10m in pursuit of the ubiquitous anchovy its most common prey. Length up to 75cm, with a white head, neck and underside brown or black edged wings, greyish-blue beak. Common from Arica to Chiloé.

Humboldt Penguin
(Spheniscus humboldti)

Endemic to the Humboldt current, this species forms large breeding colonies on islands just off the coast. Like other penguins, they feed primarily on fish, especially anchovies. Length up to 70cm, back slate black or brownish grey, head black with a white band which begins at the top of the beak and curves around the eyes to join with white underbelly. Found from Arica to Chiloé, Humboldt penguins may be observed in northern Chile in PN Pan de Azúcar and RN Pingüino de Humboldt.

Guanay Cormorant
Guanay
(Phalacrocorax bougainvilli)

This species was formerly of great economic importance in northern Chile and Perú, where its copious droppings were mined (for use as fertilizer) from the breeding colonies of the offshore islands. Length 68cm, black with white throat and underside, found from Arica to the Strait of Magellan.

Chilean Pelican
Pelícano
(Pelecanus thagus)

Often found lurking around local fishing ports, the Chilean Pelican is the most eye-catching of all birds on the Chilean coast. They generally breed on the rocky islands of the Peruvian coast, migrating south in April or May. Pelicans are commonly observed from Arica south to Valdivia, and occasionally as far south as Puerto Montt and Chiloé.

Guanaco
(*Lama guanicoe*)
Intermediate in size between the llama and the alpaca, the versatile guanaco once abounded throughout Chile, but centuries of hunting have reduced its range to a national parks and other protected areas. In the north, PN Pan de Azúcar is a good place to spot guanacos. See The Altiplano (⬇) for more on camelids, which are also known as 'American camels.'

Chungungo (*Lutra felina*)
Once common on exposed coastlines throughout the length of Chile (prefentially in habitats characterized by forests of cochayuyo seaweed), this native sea otter feeds upon sea urchins, abalone, fish and molluscs. Today, hunting and habitat destruction have caused the chungungo to all but disappear along the populated coast. The same is true of the slightly larger **huillín** (*Lontra provocax*), which inhabits both freshwater and protected marine habitats in southern Chile and Patagonia. The destruction of wetlands habitat currently threatens the huillín's survival as a species.

FOXES
Two highly adaptive foxes live in the coastal desert, feeding on lizards, insects, rodents, and even the fruit and seeds of the scant vegetation. The reddish, mountain-dwelling **Andean Fox** or **Zorro culpeo** (*P. culpaeous*) is the larger of the two; the finer-featured **Grey Fox** or **Zorro chilla** (*Pseudalopex griseus*) lives throughout the country and is frequently seen in PN Pan de Azucar, where it has learned that where there are humans, there's food.

CHILEAN IGUANA

LAGARTO CORREDOR

LIZARDS
Lizards are well adapted to the arid environments of northern and central Chile. Along the coast, look out for the **Lagarto Corredor** (*Tropidurus peruvianis*), which feeds upon green algae and a variety of insects near the high tide line. Also found in coastal environments in the north, the endemic **Chilean Iguana** (*Callopistes palluma*) grows to a total length of over half a meter, making this the largest of the Chilean lizards. The **Lagartija lemniscata** (*Liolaemus lemniscata*) inhabits inland environments in the Norte Chico and central Chile.

ZORRO CULPEO

LAGARTIJA LEMNISCATA

THE ATACAMA DESERT

The Atacama Desert is the driest desert in the world. Some interior regions have never been rained on, and in a good portion of the desert there is no vegetation – and apparently no life – at all. Wherever the slightest trickle of water appears, it gives rise to diverse communities of supremely adapted plants and animals. This is one of the most unique and unusual ecosystems in Chile.

Tamarugo (*Prosopis tamarugo*)
Highly resistant to aridity and saline soils, the tamarugo was once common in northern Chile, but was overexploited as fuel during the nitrate era. Today plantations and some native forests may be observed at RN Pampa del Tamarugal, and in the Tambillo sector of RN Los Flamencos. Mature trees can reach up to 15m tall and 1m in diameter. The tiny **Tamarugo Conebill** (*Conirostrum tamarugense*) lives exclusively in tamarugo forests.

CHAÑAR

Chañar
(*Geoffroea decorticans*)
Algarrobo
(*Prosopis chilensis*)
Found in *quebrada* valleys and desert oases throughout northern Chile, these two drought-resistant trees produce sweet, abundant fruit that served as a staple foodstuff for the region's early indigenous inhabitants.

Tropical Birds
Several species of tropical birds live and nest in the desert, including swifts, tanagers, cuckoos, and the colorful Vermillion Flycatcher or **Saca-tu-real** (*Pyrocephalus rubinus*), which exhibits pronounced sexual dimorphism. Tropical hummingbirds in this area include the Chilean Woodstar or **Picaflor de Arica** (*Eulidia yarrellii*), the Peruvian Sheartail or **Picaflor de Cora** (*Thaumastura cora*), and other recently registered species.

SACA-TU-REAL

PICAFLOR DE ARICA

Peruvian Thick-knee
Chorlo cabezón
(*Burhinus superciliaris*)

This unusual nocturnal plover inhabits valleys and quebradas of the extreme north. During the day, it seeks refuge among the rocks, waiting out the heat in groups of up to 20 individuals.

Burrowing owl
Pequén
(*Athene cunicularia*)

This small, primarily nocturnal owl feeds on insects, lizards, small rodents and birds. Often spotted in the Pampa del Tamarugal, the Burrowing owl lives (as its name would suggest) in underground burrows. Shown in the drawing is the larger, more readily adaptive, **Great Horned Owl** or Tucuquere (*Bubo virginianus*) which lives throughout the Americas.

Black-hooded Sierra Finch
Cometocino del Norte
(*Phrygilus atriceps*)

This small (15cm long), colorful finch inhabits streambanks and quebradas throughout the desert and altiplano. The male's coloration is noticeably more intense than the female's.

Chilean Mouse Possum - Llaca
(*Thylamys pallidior*). This tiny marsupial feeds on insects and makes spherical nests for its young, at times occupying abandoned birds' nests.

THE CORDILLERA DE LA SAL, NEAR SAN PEDRO DE ATACAMA

THE ALTIPLANO

The altiplano is a broad volcanic plateau with an average elevation of over 4,000 meters. Though it receives more rain than the Atacama Desert to the west, the harsh climatic conditions at this altitude make this an extremely selective environment in which only the most specialized of plants and animals can survive. The vast majority of the landscape is covered by a relatively heterogeneous floral community of coarse, bright yellow bunch grasses known as *pajonales* (principally Genus *festuca*) and clusters of the resilient Tolar shrub (Genus *parastrephia*), though in a few specific niches you'll find other ecosystems of surprising diversity.

ALTIPLANO WETLANDS

Scattered throughout the vast basins of the altiplano are a number of unique wetland environments, including desolate-looking salt flats, brightly-colored mineralized lakes, and marshy *bofedales*. Attracting over a hundred species resident and migratory birds (including three species of flamingos), these wetlands are undoubtedly the most productive and unusual ecosystems in the north, and constitute a major highlight for visiting birders and naturalists. Vicuñas, vizcachas, and domesticated llamas and alpacas are also drawn to the relatively rich grasses that thrive in altiplano bofedales.

At right is a list of important wetlands in northern Chile; those marked with an asterisk have been incorporated into the Ramsar list of wetland environments of international importance. Signed in Ramsar, Iran, in 1971, and currently recognized by 123 member nations, the Ramsar treaty is intended to promote 'the conservation and wise use of wetlands by national action and international cooperation as a means to acheiving sustainable development throughout the world.' Other Chilean Ramsar sites include Humedal El Yali in central Chile, and the Santuario Rio Cruces, near Valdivia. Visit www.ramsar.org for more information.

Queñoa (*Polylepis besseris* or *Polylepis tarapacana*) This twisted, scrubby tree is considered the highest-growing tree in the world.

QUEÑOA

Llareta (*Azorella spp*) Found throughout the high Andes, Llareta or 'cushion plant' is a colonial organism composed of thousands of tiny individual

LLARETA

plants growing together in dense, low-lying clusters – part of an adaptive strategy intended to conserve heat and moisture. Its overexploitation as fuel by the mining industry has led to grave conservation issues.

PAJA BRAVA IN THE ALTIPLANO
NEAR LAGUNA MISCANTI

Lago Chungará
Bofedal de Parinacota
Río Lauca Wetlands
Salar de Surire*
Laguna Arabilla, Laguna Parinacota
Salar de Huasco*
Salar de Uyuni
Salar de Ascotán
Salar de Atacama
Laguna Colorada
Laguna Verde
Laguna Miscanti, Laguna Miñiques
Bofedal de Soncor*
Salar de Tara*
Salar de Pujsa
Salar de Pedernales
Salar de Maricunga
Laguna Negro Francisco*
Laguna Verde
Laguna Santa Rosa*

THE SALAR DE ATACAMA

FLAMINGOS

(Family *Phoenicopteridae*)

Flamingos are an extremely old group of birds from an evolutionary point of view, having been present in the fossil record since the Cretaceous. Of the world's six surviving species, three are inhabitants of Chile. The flamingos' pinkish color is attributed to pigments contained in tiny crustaceans such as brine shrimp (*Genus artemia*) – better known to aquarium hobbyists as sea monkeys – that thrive in the salty mud of the flats and form the basis of the flamingos' diet.

Chilean Flamingo

(*Phoenicopterus chilensis*)

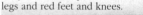

ANDEAN FLAMINGO

Intermediate in height between the James and Andean Flamingo, the Chilean Flamingo inhabits coastal and lake habitats throughout the length of Chile, with concentrations in the far north and southern Patagonia. The largest population has historically been in the Salar de Surire, northeast of Iquique. They are whitish-pink in color, with greyish legs and red feet and knees.

IMMATURE JAMES FLAMINGO

James Flamingo (*P. jamesi*)

The smallest of the three species, the James Flamingo prefers extremely high-altitude habitats in the north of Chile, with the greater part of its population living above 4,000m. The Salar de Surire, the Salar de Tara, and Laguna Negro Francisco are favorite gathering places for the James Flamingo, which may be identified by its characteristic red legs.

Andean Flamingo

(*P. andinus*)

The rare, yellow-legged Andean Flamingo preferentially inhabits elevations lower than that of the James Flamingo. The Salar de Atacama is the most important site for Andean flamingos in northern Chile, and lesser concentrations may be found in the Salar de Maricunga, the Salar de Surire, and Laguna Negro Francisco.

CAMELIDS

Early precursors of the family *Camelidae* are thought to have originated in North America, though none of their modern offspring survive there. Instead, some appear to have migrated west into Asia, where they encountered an arid habitat to which they were specially adapted; over time they would become modern camels. With the Pliocene uplift of the Central American land bridge, camelids known as *paleollamas* migrated into South America.

Modern camelids are divided into four species, two domesticated, two wild; though guanacos may be found throughout the country, the other three species are inhabitants exclusively of the northern altiplano and high sierra.

Llama (*Lama glama*) The largest and hardiest of the South American camelids, llamas are capable for going for extended periods without water, which made them the ideal transport mechanism for trade throughout the Andes and the Atacama Desert. Furthermore, their meat may be eaten fresh or dried into *charqui*, and their wool – courser and itchier than alpaca wool – is often used for textiles. Now as ever, llamas are the economic basis of altiplano cultures.

Alpaca (*Lama pacos*) Somewhat smaller than a llama, alpacas have a similar history of domestication but are not pack animals. They are more selective eaters, feeding exclusively in *bofedal* wetlands, but their soft, fine wool, makes them worth the extra trouble. The average alpaca produces over five kilos of wool every two years, and as with the llama, its meat is a staple of the altiplano diet.

Vicuña (*Vicugna vicugna*) The exquisite, long-fibered wool of this relatively small camelid was once worn by Inca royalty – in fact, it was reserved for their use – but the arrival of the Spanish was almost the species' undoing. By 1970, hunters had driven the population of vicuñas on the Chilean altiplano to a low of 600 individuals, but aggressive conservation efforts have resulted in one of the country's most dramatic environmental success stories. In 1990, Chile's vicuña population was measured at over 17,000 individuals.

Vicuñas live at elevations from 3,800m to over 5,000m. They feed bofedales and the altiplano steppe, and are commonly sighted in PN Lauca and RN Las Vicuñas. Conaf has plans to begin limited hunting of vicuñas, selling the exorbitantly expensive wool as a means of providing supplemental income to struggling altiplano communities.

BIRDS

Andean Hillstar
Picaflor de la Puna
(*Oreotrochilus stella*)
This high-altitude hummingbird (one of two in Chile of the genus Oreotrochilus) lives exclusively at elevations surpassing 3000m, where it feeds on the flowers of cactus and other plants. Its feet are unusually large for a hummingbird.

BOFEDAL WETLAND NEAR
THE SALAR DE PUJSA

Andean Goose - Piuquén
(*Chloephaga melanoptera*)
This lovely black and white goose inhabits altiplano lakes and *bofedales*.

DUCKS

Several species of ducks inhabit the altiplano wetlands. The most common are the **Puna Teal** or Pato puna (*Anas puna*), easily recognized by its bright blue beak, the brownish **Chilean teal** or Pato jergón chico (*Anas flavirostris*) and the large **Crested duck** or Pato juarjual (*Lophonetta specularioides*), with its characteristic crest of dark feathers.

PUNA TEAL

COOTS

(*Fulica spp*)
Known in Spanish as Taguas, these heavy, short-winged aquatic birds inhabit lakes and wetlands throughout the country. The **Giant Coot** (*F. giganta*) may be found nesting in the springtime in Lago Chungara, while the rare **Horned Coot** (*F. cornuta*) nests further south in Laguna Miñiques.

GIANT COOT

**Andean gull
Gaviota Andina**
(*Larus serranus*)
Commonly spotted in bofedales and altiplano lakes, the Andean Gull may be easily identified during the mating season by its characteristic black hood. In Laguna Miñiques, these gulls nest alongside horned coots and occasionally prey upon their eggs.

Ñandú, **Avestruz**, or **Rhea**
(*Pterocnemia pennata*)
One of two species of South American ostrich, the ñandú inhabits is an inhabitant of the northern altiplano, and is often spotted in PN Lauca and the chain of parks to the south. Males of this species mate with up to seven females and single-handedly hatch and raise up to twenty young.

Andean avocet - Caití
(*Recurvirostra andina*)
Commonly spotted in lakes and salt flats throughout the altiplano, the Andean avocet feeds on acquatic invertebrates by drawing its beak back and forth across the surface of the water.

MAMMALS

Vizcacha (*Lagidium viscacia*)
Looking more than anything like a rabbit with a long tail, the vizcacha is an inhabitant of the high Andes throughout Chile. They are most commonly spotted in rocky bluffs above altiplano streams and wetlands, becoming active in the morning and spending the afternoon largely immobile on sun-soaked rocks. The vizcacha warns its companions of approaching danger by emitting a sharp whistle similar to that of the North American pica. The best place to spot and photograph vizcachas is near the Las Cuevas ranger station in PN Lauca.

Chilean Butterflies

Battus archidamas

Eurema deva

Hypsochila huemul

Cynthia carye

Colia vauthieri

Colia weberbaueri

Yrgmea cytheris

Cosmosatyrus chilensis

THE NIGHT SKY
Astronomy in Chile

Stellar Cluster NGC 1850 in the LMC
(VLT UT1 + FORS1)

With over 300 cloudless nights a year and one of the most transparent skies on the planet, northern Chile is a paradise for stargazers. Whether you're set visiting the Southern Hemisphere's greatest concentration of high powered telescopes, or simply want to make the most out of a night out under the stars, the tips on this page will help orient you in your exploration of the southern firmament.

Recommendations for stargazers

Remember that light and dust contamination are the greatest detriments to proper viewing – find a spot where there are no visible lights, preferably away from trafficked roads. This star chart depicts the sky at 30° S (approximately that of the Elqui Valley) at 0100 on the 21 of Nov, at 2300 on the 21 of Dec, and at 2100 on the 21 of Jan; to use it, cover your flashlight with a piece of red cellophane and hold the chart overhead, using landmarks or known constellations to orient you. Remember, nights with no moon provide the best viewing.

What to look out for

CONSTELLATIONS: The Southern Cross is visible year-round in the southern sky. If you measure the long axis of the cross with your fingers and project 4.5 times that distance past the bottommost star, you will have found the Southern Celestial Pole: the southern equivalent of the North Star, a

OBSERVATORIO CERRO PARANAL

fixed point around which the heavens rotate. Alongside the Southern Cross is the Coal Sack, a dark cloud (nebula) of dust and gas, while surrounding the Cross is the constellation Centaurus. Also, note that Orion appears upside down or sideways during spring and summer, and the Great Bear (also known as the Big Dipper) is not visible at all.

GALAXIES: During the winter months, earth's orbit puts us in position to look towards the brilliant center of the Milky Way. Located just on the far side of the Southern Celestial Pole from the Southern Cross, The Clouds of Magellan are the closest 'satellite galaxies' of our Milky Way, and are only visible from the Southern Hemisphere. From Oct to Jan, the Andromeda Galaxy – twice as large as the Milky Way, but some 2.2 million light-years away – is visible near the northern horizon.

OBSERVATORIO INTERAMERICANO CERRO TOLOLO

TELESCOPIO DE 8,2m
CERRO PARANAL

* 1st Magnitude

* 2nd Magnitude

* 3rd Magnitude

Open clusters

Globular clusters,
galaxies and nebulae

NORTHERN CHILE'S OBSERVATORIES

Located just east of the Panamerican Highway between La Serena and Vallenar, **La Silla Observatory** features a 15 meter parabolic antennae for radio observations, as well as 15 smaller telescopes. Visits every Sat at 1330 with reservations (Casilla 567 La Serena, ☎ (2)2285006), closed Jul and Aug.

Nearby La Silla is **Las Campanas Observatory**, where the Carnegie Institution is currently finishing two new 6.5 meter telescopes, known collectively as the Magellan Project. Visits Sat from 1430-1730 with reservations (Casilla 601 La Serena, ☎ (51)224680, fax (51)227817).

At the **Cerro Tololo Inter-American Observatory**, southwest of Vicuña, current installations are being complemented by the new 8.1-meter Gemini telescope (an identical telescope is under construction on Hawaii's Mauna Kea island, for viewing of the northern hemisphere's skies), and a 4-m telescope pertaining to Southern Observatory for Astrophysical Research (Soar). Visits Sat 0900-1300h,with reservations (Casilla 603 La Serena, ☎ (51)225415, fax (51)205212).

Of greatest relevance to travelers is the recent opening of the **Cerro Mamalluca Observatory**, the only local observatory available for use by the public. With a 12" Smith-Cassegrain 1x200 telescope, donated by the Cerro Tololo observatory, Cerro Mamalluca may be visited throughout the year; tours are offered in summertime at 2000, 2200, and 2400, and in winter at 1800, 2000, and 2200. To visit, make reservations in advance (especially during summer months) at the observatory office at Gabriela Mistral 260 in Vicuña (☎(51)411352, fax (51)411255). The observatory also features digital photography and computer equipment for the use of experienced astronomers.

OBSERVATORIO
ASTRONOMICO LA SILLA

THE CENTRAL VALLEY AND CORDILLERA

Biotically speaking, central Chile may be considered an area of transition between the arid north and the water-rich forests of the south. During the intense climatic changes of the Pleistocene, this area served as a sort of refuge for marginalized species from both the north and the south, and for this reason central Chile concentrates the country's greatest diversity in forest composition.

Climatically and floristically similar to southern California, this region – from about 30-37°S – is characterized by a sunny dry season lasting from eight months in the northernmost portion, to five to six months in the central region, to four to five months near the region's southern limit. Floristic formations shift through a variety of 'ecotones' in response to these changing climatic conditions, which often depend as much on altitude and distance from the coast as upon latitude. Throughout the region, however, resistance to seasonal drought and tremendous year-to-year variations in rainfall are the limiting factors governing vegetative development.

Solar radiation in this region is blindingly intense, and as a consequence the northern and southern sides of a given valley often support completely different flora. Generally speaking, sunny north-facing slopes are inhabited by cactus and spiny matorral shrubs like espino and guayacán, while south-facing slopes and valley floors are inhabited by sclerophyllous species such as boldo, peumo, and litre. In many nonprotected areas, foreign species such as eucalyptus, monterrey pine, and the pestilent blackberry threaten to crowd out native flora.

Visiting birders will be drawn to Central Chile's rapidly disappearing network of wetlands or *humedales*. Protected wetland environments in this region include (from north to south) Santuario de la Naturaleza Laguna del Peral, Reserva Nacional El Yali, and Santuario de la Naturaleza Reloca. Many rivermouths (such as that of the Río Aconcagua near Concón) also provide important wetlands habitat.

SHADY SLOPE

VEGETATIONAL PROFILE OF QUEBRADAS IN CENTRAL CHILE

Belloto

Patagua

SUNNY SLOPE

Quintral

Parrilla Blanca

Espino

Quillay

Chilca

Peumo

Quisco

Salvia Blanca

Maravilla de Cerro

Litre

Molle

Barbones

Tevo

Litre

Boldo

COCOS

Boldo (*Peumus boldus*)
This endemic tree (or shrub) is recognizable by the look and smell of its shiny, dark green, deeply veined leaves. The leaves (lighter on their undersides) may be steeped to make a tasty digestive tea.

Espino
(*Acacia caven*)
Extremely common in the Central Valley and foothills of both ranges, this xerophytic tree (or shrub) can be recognized by its feathery leaves, thorns and bright yellow globular flowers. A similar-looking species is **Guayacán** (*Porlieria chilensis*), which is smaller, with fewer ramifications and no thorns.

Chilean Palm (*Jubaea chilensis*)
This unmistakable Chilean endemic grows further south than any other palm in the world. Once abundant on the western slope of the Coast Range from 32-35°S, this species was ruthlessly harvested for the sap that fills its bulbous trunk, which is made into *miel de palma*, still available in grocery stores. The small round nuts (*cocos*) are also collected and sold both in their green and mature form, and are delicious either raw or candied. Today the only remaining stands of Chilean palm are found in the Ocoa sector of PN La Campana and in Cocalán, near Lago Rapel.

Chagual or **Cardón**
(*Puya spp*)

The endemic, drought-resistant chagual is common on sunny slopes throughout central Chile. The base consists of a radiant bunch of fleshy, spiny leaves, and from the center of the plant sprouts a flowering stem over a meter long, with fragrant yellow or bluish flowers, depending on the species. In the spring you can sip the pollen from the enormous flowers, which also serve to incubate the larva of *Castnia psittachus*, a moth known as the Mariposa del Chagual.

Peumo
(*Cryptocarya alba*)
The endemic peumo is similar to boldo, though with less prominent veins; the leaves also have a distinctive astringent fragrance. The reddish oblong fruit is edible.

Litre
(*Lithrea caustica*)
As its Latin name implies, the bark of this common tree/shrub can cause allergenic reactions in some individuals. The leaves of the litre are oblong, with non-serrated borders and distinctive white veins.

Colliguay
(*Colliguaja odorifera*)
One of the most common native species in the central region. Look for its opposed, oblong, serrated leaves and red-yellow flowers growing in rocky soils up to 1,200m in elevation.

Quillay
(*Quillaja saponaria*)

Currently endangered, the quillay is an extraordinarily resilient tree, growing on both sunny and shaded slopes in the central Chile, at altitudes up to 2,000m. The bark has long been used as a detergent and shampoo, due to its high concentrations of soapwort. The simple evergreen leaves are notched with a few irregular teeth.

Doca
(*Carpobrutus aequilaterus*)

Widespread on the central coast, doca is often used to stabilize dunes and prevent erosion. The edible berries are called *frutillas del mar* (sea raspberries).

Quintral
(*Tristerix spp* and *Phrygilanthus spp*)

Commonly found growing on the *quisco* cactus in central Chile, this parasitic plant may be recognized by its spiny red flowers.

Andean cóndor
(*Vultur gryphus*)

A member of the vulture family, the Andean cóndor is the largest of the world's raptors, with mature adults measuring up to 110cm in length and boasting wingspans of over three meters. Nesting in cliffs high in the Andes, condors are often spotted riding thermals above mountains throughout Chile, searching for carrion. Apart from their size, condors may be identified by their black chest and body, silver wingbacks, white tufted collar and bare head and neck.

Burrowing Parrot - Tricahue
(*Cyanoliseus patagonus*)

The largest (45cm) and most colorful parrrot in Chile, the tricahue is now threatened in most of its formerly extensive range, and can be most easily be observed RN Río Los Cipreses, RN Radal Siete Tazas, and other microclimate valleys in central Chile.

Chimango Caracara Tiuque
(*Milvago chimango*)

This relatively small but aggressive raptor is known to attack hawks and other larger predatory birds. Frequently encountered from Atacama to Tierra del Fuego, this versatile caracara has also been introduced on Easter Island.

Giant Hummingbird Picaflor gigante
(*Patagona gigas*)

Found from Atacama to Arauco, this hummingbird is almost twice as large as Chile's next-largest species, with a total length of 21-24cm.

Austral Thrush Zorzal
(*Turdus falcklandii*)

This highly adaptive and abundant bird may be spotted in forests, gardens and urban habitats from Chañaral to Cape Horn, including the Juan Fernández Archipelago. The head of the male is black, while that of the female is grey.

Chilean Tinamou - Perdiz Chilena
(*Nothoprocta perdicaria*)

This endemic species is found in grasslands from Huasco to Llanquihue, as well as on Easter Island, where it is an introduced species. The males mate with several females and hatch the eggs on their own, and the young are able to walk and feed themselves immediately upon hatching.

Chilean Mockingbird
Tenca (*Mimus thenca*)
Identifiable by its melodious call, long tail and black legs, this endemic mockingbird inhabits dense shrubs or *matorral* from Copiapó to Valdivia.

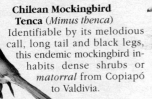

PATO NEGRO

PATO CUCHARA

Ducks
Ducks commonly encountered in central Chile's wetlands include the **Chiloe Wigeon** (*Anas sibilatrix*), the **Brown Pintail** (*A. georgica*), the **Chilean Teal** (*A. flavirostris*), and the **Black-headed Duck** (*Heteronetta atricapilla*), which often raids the nests of neighboring coots. Other, less common species include the **Cinnamon Teal** (*A. cyanoptera*) and the **Red Shoveler** (*A. platalea*), identifiable by its distinctive spoon-shaped beak. The **Ruddy Duck** and the **Lake duck** (*Oxyura spp*) are noted for their exceptional underwater swimming ability. The supremely adapted **Torrent Duck** or **Pato cortacorrientes** (*Merganetta armata*) inhabits whitewater rivers throughout central and southern Chile, feeding on insects that inhabit aerated water.

PATO REAL

The females are reddish brown, while the males have a sharply contrasting black and white pattern across their back and wings.

White-backed Stilt
Perrito (*Himantopus mexicanus*)
Named for its piercing 'bark,' the perrito may be identified by its long, red legs, which allow it to wade at will along the shores of lakes and marshes, where it feeds on insects and other invertebrates. Found from Huasco to Llanquihue.

Southern Lapwing
Queltehue
(*Vanellus chilensis*)
Easily identified by its sharply contrasting brown, black, and white plumage, the queltehue is a noisy, gregarious fixture in the Chilean *campo*. As they nest on the ground, the queltehue's young are rather exposed, and adults utilize a variety of ploys to drive intruders away, from aggressive mock attacks to feigning injuries.

Geese
Several species of geese and swans inhabit lakes and marshes in central Chile. The most common is the easily identified Black-necked Swan or **Cisne de cuello negro** (*Cygnus melanocorypha*). The **Coscoroba Swan** or **Cisne coscoroba** (*Coscoroba coscoroba*) is much rarer, inhabiting a few scattered coastal wetlands; this lovely goose is almost completely white, with a red beak and legs and black-tipped wings. **The Andean Goose** or **Piuquén** (*Chloephaga melanoptera*) inhabits principally highland lakes, and may be identified by its white head and body, red beak and feet, and black tail and wings.

Moustached Turca
Turca (*Pteroptochos megapodius*)
Endemic to Chile, this diminutive inhabitant of Central Chile's matorral lives underground and uses its large, powerful feet to dig for insects, worms and other prey. Identified by its low, vigorous flight and unique territorial call, the curious turca will often follow hikers.

CISNE CUELLO NEGRO

COOTS
(Fulica spp.)

At least three species of coots may be spotted in the central Valley, including the **tagua común** (*Fulica armillata*), the **tagua de frente roja** (*F. rufifrons*), and the **tagua chica** (*F. leucoptera*).

Madre de la culebra
(Acantinodera cummingi)

This immense beetle takes the prize as Chile's largest insect – adult females measure up to 10cm long and are so heavy that they are unable to fly. The adults of this species appear for only a few days in December, when the males (who are able to fly) are invariably drawn to windows and other light sources.

female

male

Cururo
(Spalacopus cyanus)

This endemic rodent is responsible for the caves and burrows commonly seen in open terrain in the central Valley and Andean foothills. Its name derives from its curious alarm whistle (*cu-ru-ru-ru-ru...*)

Coipo
(Myocastor coypus)

Chile's largest rodent inhabits lakes throughout central and southern Chile. A powerful excavator, it builds elaborate burrows on the lakeshore, accessed via underwater tunnels.

LAGARTIJA ESBELTA
(male and female)

REPTILES AND AMPHIBIANS

Over 60 species Lizards of the genus *Liolaemus* inhabit lowland environments in central and southern Chile – 34 of which are endemic. Most, including the **Lagartija Esbelta** (*L. tenuis*), are chameleons, brightening in color with increasing temperature. Also common in the Central Valley and precordillera is the **Culebra de cola larga** (*Philodryas chamissonis*), the largest of the Chilean snakes. Reaching a total length of almost two meters, it feeds primarily on rodents and other reptiles.

RANITA
ARBOREA

SAPO DE RULO

Notable amphibians include the endemic **Sapo de rulo** (*Bufo chilensis*), which in its mature form lives almost entirely independent of water, inhabiting arid hills and valleys throughout the central region. Further south, the unusual **Darwin's Frog** (*Rhinoderma darwinii*) is a rainforest ground-dweller with a very interesting behavioral trait: after the female lays her eggs, she leaves them in the care of the male, who swallows the young one by one as they hatch, guarding them in his vocal sac. When the tadpoles have matured, he spits them out. Also of note is **Ranita arbórea** (*Hylorina silvatica*), a tiny green tree-dwelling frog with enormous eyes.

CULEBRA DE
COLA LARGA

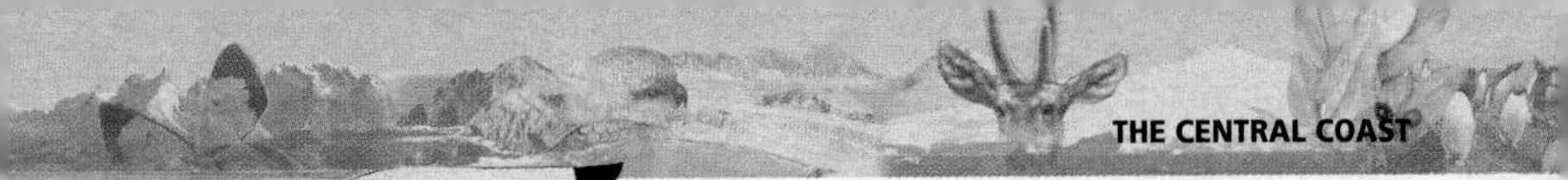

THE CENTRAL COAST

Kelp gull
Gaviota dominicana
(*Larus dominicanus*)
The most common gull along the central coast, readily identifiable by its black wings, the Kelp gull feeds on everthing from fish to crustaceans to carrion and trash.

Brown-hooded gull
Gaviota cáhuil
(*Larus maculipennis*)
Smaller than the Kelp gull, this common gull sports a dark hood during the mating season, much like the Andean gull.

Olivaceous cormorant
Yeco
(*Phalacrocorax olivaceus*)
The most abundant of Chile's six species of *Phalacrocorax*, the Olivaceous cormorant is the only one with completely black plumage. It nests in clamorous offshore colonies and occasionally spotted in interior lakes and rivers.

Red-legged
Cormorant Lile
(*Phalacrocorax gaimardii*).
This is a smallish grey cormorant with a red beak and legs, and two white oval marks on the back of the neck. It reproduces in cliffs on the offshore islands, using seaweed and other detritus to construct its nest.

Playero blanco (*Calidris alba*)
Sanderlings arrive on the coast of Chile each year in springtime and depart in fall, bound for their nesting grounds in northern Canada and Alaska. Often spotted sprinting along the beach in groups of twenty or more, sanderlings have ash-grey backs with with fine brown streaks, a black band on the wings, and a white head and underside.

Whimbrel
Zarapito
(*Numenius phaeopus*)
Another visitor from the arctic, the Whimbrel is spotted on beaches from Arica to Tierra del Fuego. Its plumage is mostly grey and greyish-yellow, with a white throat and underside and a long, black, downcurved beak.

American
Oystercatcher
Pilpilén
(*Haematopus palliatus*)
A non-migratory inhabitant of the Pacific coast from Ecuador to Chiloé, the American Oystercatcher feeds largely on shellfish, opening the shells with its crimson red, yellow-tipped beak. The head, neck and part of chest are slate black, with a white underside and brown back. They nest in dunes from Oct.-Dec. Equally conspicuous and abundant is the Blackish Oystercatcher (*H. ater*).

Sea lion colonies may be observed in central Chile in the following locations:
- Isla Cachagua
- Islote de los Lobos, Punta Curaumilla
- La Lobería, Quintay
- Cartagena
- Piedra de la Lobería, Cobquecura

SOUTHERN CHILE'S FOREST ECOSYSTEMS

PIÑON

All told, there remain nearly 12 million hectares of native temperate forests in Chile and Argentina, which makes this the world's second-largest reserve of this dwindling resource. (The Pacific Northwest is first). Considered the most diverse temperate forests in the world, Chile's forest ecosystems are traditionally broken up into 12 forest types, including the mesomorphic formations of the central region (above). Within and between these 'types' are dozens of distinct forest communities, which shift gradually or suddenly in response to soil type, topography, temperature and precipitation. There are more than 50 tree species in Chile's temperate forests, most of which are endemic to Chile and Argentina.

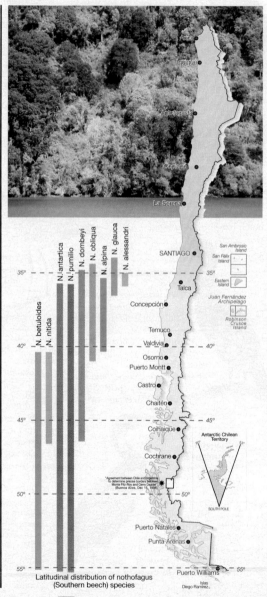

Latitudinal distribution of nothofagus (Southern beech) species

Both evergreen and deciduous forests grow here. Evergreen or 'Valdivian' rainforests grow in more benign climatic conditions – generally at lower elevations and on the coast. Deciduous forests tend to grow at higher elevations, though this threshold elevation declines with increasing latitude. Poorer in species than their evergreen counterparts, these deciduous forests erupt into brilliant shades of yellow and red in the austral fall, reaching peak in most regions in mid-May.

The most common trees in these forests pertain to the genus *Nothofagus* (southern beech, 10 species, all endemic to the southern Andes) and *Podocarpus* (3 species), both of which are closely related to other Godwanaland species in Australia and New Zealand. Laurels (genus *Laurelia*) and cypresses (family *Cuppressaceae*) are other common trees.

HIGHLAND FORESTS OF LA ARAUCANÍA

The most characteristic element of southern Chile's highland forest is undoubtedly the ARAUCARIA or 'monkey-puzzle' tree, *Araucaria araucana*. Ancestors of the araucaria first appeared in the fossil record some 200 million years ago, during the Jurassic age, and today several species of the genus *Araucaria* are found in Oceania, south Brazil, and the Misiones province of Argentina.

Known to the Mapuches as **pehuén**, *Araucaria araucana* is endemic to Chile and Argentina. In the Andes, these singular trees inhabit an extremely limited range from 37°27' to 37°50'S, at elevations from 900-1,700m. In the Coast Range, two widely separated populations exists, both in the Cordillera Nahuelbuta at elevations between 600-1,400m. Mature trees may reach 50m in height and 3m in diameter.

Araucaria is found either in pure stands or mixed with high-altitude *Nothofagus* species; on sunny northern slopes, it often mixes with ñirre near the vegetional limit, while on shady southern slopes it is found at a somewhat lower niche, where it mixes with lenga. Over seventy species of insects are thought to inhabit the trunk and canopy of a mature araucaria tree, which also produces edible nuts known as **piñones**, the traditional dietary base of the Pehuenche Indians.

- Alto Biobío: Cuesta Las Raíces
- RN Malalcahuello Nalcas, RN Tolhuaca
- PN Conguillío
- PN Villarrica
- PN Huerquehue
- El Cañi Reserve

ARAUCARIAS IN PARQUE NACIONAL CONGUILLÍO

Coigüe (*N. dombeyi*)
The evergreen coigüe is one of the most impressive and representative trees of southern Chile, easily identified at a distance by its tremendous stature and stout, truncated branches. The coigüe grows from Colchagua to Aisén at a variety of elevations, though preferentially at altitude.

Raulí (*N. alpina*)
Common from the Rio Teno to Valdivia, raulí generally grows at elevations above 500m. Mapuche artisans utilize its fine-grained, reddish wood to make bowls, utensils, and other handicrafts. Faster growing than most other species of southern beech, this is an important species for reforestation projects.

Ñirre
(*N. antactica*)
Found from Talca to Tierra del Fuego, the scrubby ñirre is highly resistant to cold and snow, and generally grows right at timberline. In the northern part of its range it is often found in mixed stands with araucaria, while in Aisén and Magallanes it grows all the way down to sea level. In the fall, its leaves turn a bright, almost searing red.

Mañío
Several different species known as mañío grow in the south. These include the fast-growing colonizer *Podocarpus nubigena*, the long-leaved *Podocarpus salgna*, and the densely branched *Saxe-gothaea conspicua*, identifiable by its short, narrow leaves, which give it the appearance of a conifer.

Roble or **Hualle** (*N. obliqua*)
Common from the Río Aconcagua to Chiloé, the roble (known as a *pellín* in its mature form) normally grows at low elevations, topping out at about 1,800m at the northern limit of its range. Under ideal conditions, this tree can grow to over 40m in height. Central Chile's great stands of robles are especially attractive in autumn (April-May), when their leaves turn yellow or orange. In August and September, a round edible mushroom known as a **dihueñe** grows on the branches of the roble.

DIHUEÑE

Lenga
(*N. pumilio*)
Occupying a vertical niche just below the nirre, lenga also grows in two distinct forms: scrubby in the north, tall and straight in the south. Like the ñirre, lenga is deciduous.

PARAKEETS

Endemic to Chile and Argentina, the **Austral Parakeet** or **Cachaña** (*E. ferrugineus*) may often be spotted in auracaria forests, feeding on *piñones*. The smaller **Mountain Parakeet** or **Periquito Cordillerano** (*Bolborhynchus aurifrons*) inhabits two distinct ranges, one in the far north and one in central Chile – though in the latter range it has become quite scarce. The most abundant parakeet in Chile is the endemic **Slender-billed Parakeet** or **Choroy** (*Enicognathus leptorhynchus*), which feeds principally on tree-dwelling insects, hopping nimbly from branch to branch,

CHOROY

using its tail as a counterbalance. All these species are threatened by poachers who steal young out of the nests to sell as pets.

CACHAÑAS

Magellanic Woodpecker
Carpintero negro
(*Campephilus magellanicus*)

The male of this species, which lives exclusively in old-growth forests, sports an unmistakably bright red head. Like all woodpeckers, this *carpintero* feeds on insects and carves its nest in the trunks of dead trees.

Ringed Kingfisher
Martín Pescador
(*Ceryle torquata*)

This surprisingly large and abundant kingfisher feeds on fish in aquatic environments (inland and coastal) from the Biobío to Tierra del Fuego. A smaller species, the **Green Kingfisher** or **Martín pescador chico** (*Chloroceryle americana*), is an inhabitant of northern Chile.

Buff-necket Ibis
Bandurria
(*Theristicus melanopis*)

Commonly sighted in open fields and meadows in the south, the bandurria makes a distinctive clacking call while flying. The males and females are almost identical.

Puma
(*Puma concolor*).

Known in North America as a cougar, the shy, mostly nocturnal puma lives throughout the Andes, surviving anywhere that it can find sufficient habitat and prey. They are powerful hunters, measuring over two meters from head to tail when fully grown, and their preferred prey are guanaco and huemul. The young are born with spots that gradually disappear with age. Other Chilean cats include the **colocolo** (*Lynchailurus colocolo*), the spotted **güiña** (*Oncefelis giugna*), and the **gato montes andino** (*Orealurus jacobita*).

PUMA

THE VALDIVIAN RAINFOREST

The evergreen Valdivian Rainforest or *selva valdiviana* is found in areas with optimal growing conditions: abundant rainfall, low elevation, and minimal temperature fluctuations. At higher elevations, Valdivian Rainforest communities generally give way to deciduous species, and occasionally form mixed stands with alerce. In addition to the arboreal species listed below, this forest type is notable for its unique tree ferns and abundant creeping vines and epiphytes – every square centimeter of available surface area, it seems, is covered by a resplendent carpet of green.

Valdivian Rainforest formations are found along the coast from about 38-47°S, in the Andes below 1,000m from 40°30' to 47°S, and in the lowlands of the Central Valley south of 40°S. Thanks to its broad distribution, you can check out the *selva valdiviana* in almost any protected area between Valdivia and Coihaique.

VALDIVIAN RAINFOREST SPECIES

ALERCE

Known as **lahuén** to the Mapuche indians, *Fitzroya cupressoides* is the second longest-lived tree in the world, after the California Bristlecone Pine; carbon-14 readings of an alerce stump of over four meters in diameter gave an age of 3621 years at the time the tree was felled. Unfortunately, the size of the tree and the quality of its wood led to intense overexploitation during the late 19th and early 20th centuries, and today this magnificent species is restricted to a few remote reserves. Whereas once there were some 250,000há of alerce forest just between Puerto Montt, Puerto Varas, Calbuco and the Río Maullín, today there remain only an estimated 300,000há of *alerzales* in the entire country – a minor proportion of which are on protected lands.

Today, the alerce inhabits a discontinuous range from 39°50' to 34°30'S, with the greatest concentration of *alerzales* found between the Estuario de Reloncaví and Volcán Hornopirén. In general, the slow-growing alerce thrives in two areas that are marginal for most species: poorly-draining lowlands in the central Valley (glacial·moraines), and at 700-1,000m in the Andes, near the limit of vegetation. Most of the lowland stands have been cut, leaving a few remote stands in the Coast Range and the Andean highlands.

You can visit alerce forests in the following spots:

- PN Alerce Andino
- Parque Lahuén Nadi
- El Alerzal
- El Arco
- Parque Pumalín

Pelu
(Sophora microphylla)

Closely related to the toromiro of Easter Island, the pelu grows along rivers and streams from the Río Maule to Palena, at elevations below 500m. From Aug-Sept, its bright, drooping yellow flowers attract hordes of insects and hummingbirds.

Lingüe
(Persea lingue)

Endemic to Chile, the evergreen lingüe grows from the Rio Aconcagua to Chiloé, at elevations below 700m. You can identify it by its elongate, alternate leaves, from 6-7cm in length. The usefulness of the bark for drying and curing leather has led to its overexploitation, and today there remains almost no first-growth lingüe.

Avellano (*Gevuina avellana*)
Found from Valparaíso to Aisén, the evergreen avellano produces reddish-brown nuts that are tasty and nutritious either raw or roasted (avellano translates as 'hazelnut'). The highly elastic wood is used to make boats, paddles, and musical instruments.

Notro
(*Embothrium coccineum*)
Endemic to Chile and Argentina, the shrubby notro grows on hilltops from the Río Maule to Magallanes. It is most easily identified by its spiky, bright red flowers, which bloom from Sept-Jan.

Olivillo
(*Aextoxican punctatum*)
Adapted to stable temperatures and salt air, the olivillo often forms pure stands near sea level, from the relict forest in PN Fray Jorge all the way south to Chiloé. Its name is derived from its spherical seed, which is similar in appearance to a small olive.

Ulmo
(*Eucryphia cordifolia*)
Common from Concepción to Chiloé, mainly in the Cordillera de la Costa, the ulmo blooms into lovely white flowers in January and February. These flowers, so abundant as to make the tree appear covered in snow, are pollinated by bees that use the nectar to produce *miel de ulmo* a specialty of the south.

Tepa
(*Laurelia philippiana*)
Relatively common from Cautín to Chiloé, the tepa may be identified by its simple, opposite, serrated leaves, which when crushed produce a strong, acrid odor. The trunk is often thickly wrapped with vines.

Canelo (*Drimys winteri*)
The sacred tree of the Mapuches, used as a symbol of peace during the Arauco War, the canelo grows from the Río Limarí to Cape Horn, and is considered one of the most ancient angiosperms on the planet. Poultices and teas made from canelo have long been used to treat infected wounds and stomach ailments. This tree is known in English as 'Winter's Bark,' a reference to one 'Captain Winter' who used the Vitamin C-rich bark to treat scurvy among his crew in 1578.

Arrayán
(*Luma apiculata*)
Inhabiting the humid shores of rivers and lakes from Colchagua to Chiloé, the arrayán may be identified by its smooth, red trunk, with scattered patches of white where bits of bark have fallen away. The blackish berries are tart but edible.

VEGETATIONAL PROFILE OF THE COAST RANGE NEAR VALDIVIA

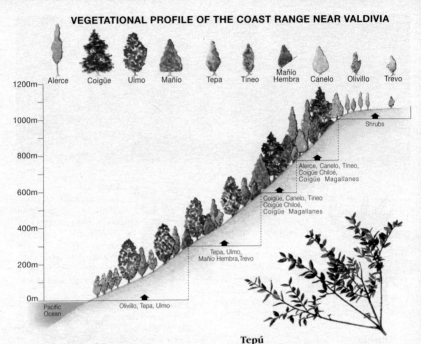

Alerce Coigüe Ulmo Mañío Tepa Tineo Mañío Hembra Canelo Olivillo Trevo

1200m
1000m
800m
600m
400m
200m
0m

Shrubs

Alerce, Canelo, Tineo, Coigüe Chiloé, Coigüe Magallanes

Coigüe, Canelo, Tineo Coigüe Chiloé, Coigüe Magallanes

Tepa, Ulmo, Mañío Hembra,Trevo

Pacific Ocean

Olivillo, Tepa, Ulmo

Tepú
(*Tepualia stipularis*)

Similar in appearance to the arrayán, the shrubby tepú grows in moist, often swampy habitats from the Río Maule to Magallanes. In some areas, most notably in PN Chiloé, it forms dense monotype stands known as *tepuales*. The wood burns even when wet.

Copihue (*Lapageria rosea*)

Mapuche legend has it that the copihue, Chile's national flower, took its color from tears of blood shed by native women who climbed trees to watch their men at battle. First described by Spaniards Hipólito Ruíz and Juan Antonio Pavon in the late 18th century, it is the only species in its genera, and has been afforded protected status. Like its bright orange cousin, the coicopihue (*Philesia magellanica*), the vine of the copihue climbs up the trunks of other trees towards the faint light filtering through the rainforest canopy.

Chilco
(*Fuschia magellanica*)

Extremely abundant in the south, the lovely wild fuschia flowers from Aug.-April, when it becomes a veritable magnet for hummingbirds. The fig-like fruit of the chilco may be consumed in late autumn.

184

Nalca (*Gunnera tinctoria*)

The unmistakable nalca, with its enormous 'elephant ear' leaves, grows throughout the south in areas of extreme humidity. The young stalk of the plant may be peeled and eaten as a sort of acidic celery (better with salt).

Chucao Tapaculo
Chucao (*Scelorchilus rubecula*)

The loud, clucking call of the chucao is a defining characteristic of Chile's southern forests. If you enter the nearby undergrowth and sit quietly, this curious bird will approach within a meter or less, hopping nimbly from branch to branch. Length 18cm.

Ciervo volante
(*Chiasognathus grantti*)

This large, metallic-colored beetle, whose name translates as 'flying deer,' is named for the prominent mandibles on the head of the male.

Chilean opossum
Monito del monte
(*Dromiciops gliroides*)

This marsupial nests in stands of quila (bamboo) and stores fat for its winter hibernation in its thick, furry tail. Strangely, its marsupial pouch opens at the bottom rather than the top. Even stranger is the **Comadrejita trompuda** (*Rhyncholestes raphanurus*), which has no pouch at all. First discovered in 1922, the Comadrejita trompuda inhabits old-growth rainforest from Osorno to Chiloé.

Pudú
(*Pudu pudu*)

A mere 40cm tall at the shoulder, this shy pygmy deer inhabits dense forests from the Río Biobío south to Aisén and the northern forests of Magallanes. They are most often spotted in the forests of western Chiloé.

Huemul (*Hippocamelus bisulcus*)

The huemul is an extremely shy, extremely rare Andean deer that was nearly hunted to extinction during the Colonial era and early years of the Republic. It was originally thought to be a strange species of native horse, and even appeared on Chile's first coat of arms as an ungulate horse with a long tail. Living in the highlands during the summer, and descending into the forest in winter, the huemul has been reduced to such small, scattered populations that its continued viability as a species is in doubt. In central Chile there remains only one population (of about 50 individuals) in the Nevados de Chillán. The rest principally inhabit the remote wildlands of the southern Aisén province. RN Tamango is noted as a good place to spot huemules. Even rarer is the **taruca** or **huemul del norte** (*Hippocamelus antisensis*), which inhabits an extremely limited range in the precordillera east of Arica.

THE SOUTHERN FJORDS AND ARCHIPELAGO

QUINTUPEU FJORD

Chile's southern fjords and canals are characterized by high levels of precipitation (over four meters annually in some areas) and relatively stable temperatures, which has favored the growth of dense forests along the steep shores of the fjords and islands. These forests – which in most areas grow almost all the way down to the high tide line – range from species-rich Valdivian Rainforest in the northern fjords to Magallanic lenga forests in the extreme south.

The cold, protected, nutrient-rich waters of the immense archipelago support a thriving marine ecosystem characterized by kelp forests, abundant fish and shellfish, marine mammals and a limited but interesting variety of seabirds. The great extent and inaccessibilty of this ecosystem has helped it remain in pristine conditions, though the growth of the salmon farming industry has resulted in the degradation of some areas, particularly in Chiloé and the fjords of northern Patagonia.

Kelp Goose - Caranca
(*Chloephaga hybrida*)
Endemic to Chile and Argentina, the caranca inhabits rocky shorelines and islands from Chiloé to Tierra del Fuego, feeding principally upon marine algae. The species exhibits striking sexual dimorphism: the male is completely white with yellow legs, while the female is black with white stripes on the chest, a pink beak, and yellow feet.

female

male

Southern Giant Petrel
Petrel gigante
(*Macronectes giganteus*)
This largest of the petrels may be recognized in flight by the long, narrow silouette of its wings, which stretch over two meters from tip to tip.

Blue eyed cormorant - Cormorán imperial
(*Phalacrocorax atriceps*)
One of six species of cormorants in Chile, the Imperial cormorant is an inhabitant of the coast from Valdivia south. It may be identified by its sharply constrasting back and underside. Also found in this region is the **Rock cormorant** or **Cormoran de las rocas** (*Phalacrocorax magellanicus*), which may be differenciated from the former by its black neck.

Penguin Colonies in Patagonia

- Pingüinera Puñihuíl
- Ahuenco
- Isla Metalqui
- Pingüinera Seno Otway
- Pingüinera Isla Magdalena

Access to penguin breeding sites at Pingüinera Puñihuíl (in Chiloé) and on Isla Magdalena and Seno Otway (near Punta Arenas) is regulated by the Fundacion Seno Otway. Visits may be arranged through operators or directly through the foundation at the following addresses:

- Antonio Varas 629, of. 5&7 Pto. Montt
  ☎ (65)315494, fax (65)315494

- Casilla 444 Correo Punta Arenas
  ☎ fax (61)219532

- Otwafund@ctcinternet.cl

- Otway@telsur.cl

Numerous agencies in Punta Arenas can arrange visits to Isla Magdalena or Seno Otway.

Steamer duck
Quetro no volador
(*Tachyeres pteneres*)
This enormous duck is an able diver, and often feeds on shellfish collected from the seafloor. Though unable to fly, when threatened it flees across the surface, paddling furiously and beating its wings. This is one of the most characteristic species of the southern canals. The **Flying Steamer Duck** or **Quetro volador** (*T. patachonichus*) is similar though smaller and with larger wings; capable of flying, it is also spotted in freshwater environments in the extreme south.

Magallanic Penguin
Pingüino de Magallanes
(*Spheniscus magellanicus*)
Of nine species of penguins, only two inhabit areas outside the Antarctic and Sub-Antarctic regions. The Humboldt penguin is found from Chiloé north to Perú (see the Northern Coast, above, for drawing and description), while the Magallanic penguin is found from Chiloé south to Tierra del Fuego. The two species are of very similar appearance; the Magallanic penguin may be differentiated by an additional band of black which separates the white eye-ring and underbelly.

DOLPHINS AND WHALES

Endemic to Chile's southern coast, the dark-colored **Chilean dolphin** or **Delfin chileno** (*Cephalorinchus eutropia*) may be distinguished by its rounded dorsal fin. The **Delfin oscuro** (*Lagenorinchus obscurus*), identified by its sickle-shaped dorsal fin, inhabits a more ample range, and may be seen near the coast in groups of anywhere from three to several hundred individuals. The Delfin austral (*L. australis*), often spotted in the Strait of Magellan, is similar in appearance with somewhat whiter sides. The smaller, black and white **Tonina overa** (*C. commersoni*) also inhabits the strait, where it feeds on fish and squid.

TONINA

DELFIN OSCURO

ORCA

The **killer whale** or **orca** (*Orcinus orca*) is occasionally spotted throughout the Patagonian fjords and archipelago, though its presence is more common at the higher latitudes and in Antarctica. Most easily identified by its meter-high dorsal fin, the orca feeds on sea lions, seals, and a variety of fish.

Southern Elephant Seals

The largest of all pinnipeds, southern elephant seals grow to nearly 7m in length and weigh up to three tons. Their name derives from the males' large, curved proboscis, which is often inflated as a display of dominance during the spectacular annual mating ritual. Most of the species' adult life is spent in the frigid waters between southern Patagonia and Antarctica, though they come ashore in spring to mate and again in autumn to molt, sloughing off large pieces of skin and hair. Hunted to near extinction in the 19th century, the elephant seal is now protected and has recovered its long-term viability as a species.

Southern Sea Lions (*Otaria flavescens*)

The southern sea lion is considerably larger than its counterpart in the Northern Hemisphere, with males reaching a total length of up to 3.5m, and a weight of over 500kg. Beginning in September, dominant or 'Sultan' males begin to occupy mating positions on remote rock outcrops or *loberías*, attracting a harem of 10-15 females; pups are usually born from late December to mid-February, and mating occurs almost immediately afterwards, on account of the species' 12-month gestation period. Non-harem bulls often congregate in nearby 'bachelors' clubs,' in hopes of taking advantage of a stray female. The orca or killer whale is the sea lion's main predator, though protective local fishermen (and workers at the salmon farms) are also known to hunt them.

Sea Lion Colonies in Southern Chile and Patagonia:
- La Arena
- Fiordo Cahuelmó
- Fiordo Reñihue
- Chaitén

PATAGONIAN STEPPE ECOSYSTEM

CINEREOUS HARRIER

Extending from the east slope of the Patagonian Andes to the Atlantic Ocean, the Patagonian steppe or pampa is considered one of the five largest deserts in the world, with an extension of over 670,000 square kilometers. Characterized by relatively cold temperatures and incessant arid winds from the west, the pampa's vegetal community consists primarily of tussock grasses known as *coironales* and scattered shrubs and low trees.

Wildlife on the pampa is abundant and surprisingly easy to spot. The majority of the bird species found in far southern Chile and Argentina live here rather than in the dense forests to the west of the Andes, as do guanacos, foxes, ñandus and flamingos.

PN PALI AIKE

Ñandú
(*Pterocnemia pennata*)
See the altiplano, above, for description

CANQUEN

GEESE

Three species of geese inhabit fresh and salt-water habitats in southern Patagonia. The endangered **Ruddy-headed Goose** or **Canquén colorado** (*Chloephaga rubidiceps*) inhabits a very limited range from southern Magallanes to northern Tierra del Fuego; its recent population decline may be due to the introduction of the predatory Grey Fox in Tierra del Fuego. The **Upland Goose or Caiquén** (*Chloephaga picta*) feeds in grasslands from central Chile to Tierra del Fuego, and exhibits pronounced sexual dimorphism, in contrast to the **Ashy-headed Goose** or **Canquén** (*Chloephaga poliocephala*), the most common of the three species.

CAIQUENES

Black-chested Buzzard Eagle
Aguila (*Geranoaetus melanoleucus*)

The largest of Chile's predatory raptors, this eagle builds large nests in cliffs and trees, often remaining for several years in the same nest. Unlike Chile's several species of hawks, it is not commonly seen at altitude. It can be most easily recognized by its pointed wings and short, wedge-shaped tail. Length 70cm, wingspan up to two meters.

Cinereous Harrier
Vari
(*Circus cinereus*)

Found throughout the length of Chile, this acrobatic raptor nests in burrows near lakes and marshes. Males are ash-colored and slightly larger than the reddish-plumed females.

Peregrine falcon
Halcón peregrino
(*Falco peregrinus*)

Considered the fastest creature in the world, the peregrine falcon dives at speeds up to 160km/hour in pursuit of the small birds on which it feeds. It dwells on cliffs, occupying nests abandoned by eagles, hawks and ibises. Peregrines mate for life.

Guanaco (*Lama guanicoe*)

Relatively common in Torres del Paine and on Tierra del Fuego, guanacos are usually spotted either in large groups of males or smaller family groups consisting of one male together with a harem of females and their young. The guanaco is a preferred prey of the puma.

Grey Fox
Zorro chilla (*Pseudalopex griseus*)

Highly adaptable and often fearless of humans, this fine-featured fox is often spotted in Torres del Paine. The park entrance at Laguna Amarga is an especially good place to spot them. The smallish **Chilote Fox** or **Zorro chilote** (*Pseudalopex fulvipes*), on the other hand, is extremely hard to spot, inhabiting two very limited ranges, one on the island of Chiloé and another in the densely forested Cordillera de Nahuelbuta, south of Concepción.

ZORRO CHILLA

Calafate (*Berberis sp*)

Tasting something like a slightly tart, seedy blueberry, the calafate is the source of an interesting tidbit of local mythology: the saying goes that he who eats it will return, sooner or later, to Patagonia. You'll find this waist- to head-high thorny shrub growing in open terrain and edge environments throughout Patagonia.

THE JUAN FERNANDEZ ARCHIPELAGO

EVERGREEN RAINFOREST

The flora of the Juan Fernández Archipelago consists of some 77 families of vascular plants, divided into 213 genera with a total of over 360 species. Although fully 40% of these species are introduced, another 127 species, 12 genera, and one entire family (*Lactoridaceae*) are endemic to the archipelago. Overall, this fascinating and unusual ecosystem boasts a greater number of endemic species per unit of landmass than any other island group in the world, and any visiting botanist will soon realize that most of the plants seen here do not exist anywhere else in the world.

The origins of the archipelago's flora are relatively diverse. While the majority (80%) of native plant species appear to be linked to plants in the southern cone, another 10% appear to have originated in Oceania and another 7% are related to the Neotropical flora of Central America and the northern portion of South America. Especially noteworthy are the islands' 51 species of ferns, including a variety of tree ferns surpassing that of Chile's Valdivian Rainforest.

Four basic formations may be identified here. At lower elevations (and especially in the damp *quebradas*) is an **evergreen rainforest** consisting of trees such as the endemic luma, the canelo, and the chonta palm. Forests of tree ferns are common here as well at higher elevations, where the rainforest gives way to a sparser **heath** formation. The third island ecosystem is the **grassy steppe** found in the arid western portion of Isla Robinson Crusoe. Finally, an interesting, poorly studied **alpine ecosystem** has been identified on the highest slopes of the younger, steeper Isla Alejandro Selkirk, which itself has a number of endemic species not found elsewhere in the archipelago.

Luma (*Myrceugenia fernandeziana*)
Together with the canelo, the endemic luma is most common arboreal species in the island's rainforests. It is similar in appearance to the arrayan (*Luma apiculata*) found in central and southern Chile.

Canelo (*Drimys confertifolia*)
Occasionally considered a subspecies of *Drimys winteii*, the sacred tree of the Mapuche Indians, this lovely endemic tree may be identified by its leathery green leaves and white-petaled flowers.

FOREST OF LUMA AND CANELO

Chonta
(*Juania australis*)

One of only two palms native to Chile. Overharvesting nearly led the once abundant chonta down the same path as the extinct sandalwood, until the 1935 creation of PN Juan Fernández brought a fortunate end to its exploitation.

Dendroseris litoralis

One of eleven endemic species of the Genus Dendroseris found in the archipelago, this unusual arboreal Composite belongs to the same family as the common daisy. Its yellow flowers are a favorite food of the Juan Fernández firecrown (below). Several examples of this species grow in the plaza in San Juan Bautista. Another species of Dendroseris, known as the **cabbage palm** (*D. pinnata*), was a favorite food of visiting mariners, including Alexander Selkirk himself.

THE ARID WESTERN END OF THE ISLA ROBINSON CRUSOE

FEMALE

Tree ferns

In and around the islands' arboreal rainforests are exceedingly strange stands of endemic tree ferns, most notably *Thyrsopteris elegans* and *Dicksonia berteroana*; also keep an eye out for species of the Genus *Hymenophyllum*, which grow as epiphytes on the trunks of these tree ferns. The endemic *Blechnum cyadifolium* is common on the high peaks of Isla Robinson Crusoe. All told, there are 25 species of endemic ferns on the island, most of them of southern South American origin.

Juan Fernández Fur Seal
(*Arctocephalus philippi*)

Between 1797-1804, North American sealers killed over three million Juan Fernandez Fur Seals for their pelts, and by the late 1800's the species was actually considered extinct. Today the *lobo fino* has recovered, and is commonly sighted in the islands. The only active breeding colony is in Bahía Tierras Blancas, in the western sector of Isla Robinson Crusoe.

Juan Fernández Firecrown
Picaflor de Juan Fernández
(*Sephanoides fernandensis*)

This endemic hummingbird may be spotted feeding on the purple flowers of *Rhaphithamnus venestus* (a highland shrub) and the cabbage palm (above). In recent years its population has declined inexplicably, and the species is now considered endangered. Note the pronounced difference between the male and female. The male shown in the drawing is immature.

MALE

ANTARCTIC FLORA AND FAUNA

Antarctica's terrestrial and marine environments present one of the most striking contrasts on the planet. Consistently cold temperatures, a lack of ice-free landmass, and months on end of pure or partial darkness create exceedingly difficult conditions for the growth of terrestrial plants, while the cold, nutrient-rich waters of the Southern Ocean provide for the world's most productive marine ecosystem.

TERRESTRIAL FLORA AND FAUNA

The flora of the Antarctic continent is highly limited, consisting principally of a variety of microscopic fungi, 300 species of lichens, 80 species of mosses, and about 400 species of algae; the latter includes unusual 'snow algae' that grows in colorful patches on the surface of coastal snowfields. The only two species of vascular plants found on the Antarctic mainland are the hearty **Antarctic hairgrass** (*Deschampsia antarctica*) and **Antarctic pearlwort** (*Colobanthus quitensis*). Antarctic terrestrial fauna is even more limited, consisting of about 100 species of insects and a few landbird that live and nest on the ice-free shores of the Sub-Antarctic islands.

ANTARCTICA'S MARINE ECOSYSTEM

Though seabirds, seals, and whales may be the most visible and dramatic members of the Antarctic marine ecosystem, they are far from the most important. This honor falls upon a single species of zooplankton known as **krill** (*Euphasia superba*), which feeds upon Antarctic phytoplankton and is the base of the marine food chain. Nearly every species of higher Antarctic fauna depends, either directly or indirectly, upon the health of krill populations, making this one of the shortest – and therefore most vulnerable – food chains in the world. Annual production of krill in the Southern Ocean is estimated at between 200 and 600 million tons of total biomass.

PENGUINS

Seven species of penguins (out of a world total of 18) inhabit the mainland coast and offshore islands of Antarctica. These highly adapted birds, who 'surrendered' their ability to fly millions of years ago in

COLONY OF GENTOO PENGUINS

exchange for their extraordinary swimming ability – form nesting colonies (or rookeries) of over a million individuals, and feed primarily upon krill, fish, and squid.

MACARONI

Antarctic penguins of the genus *Eudyptes* include **Macaroni** and **Rockhopper** penguins, both identified by their yellow crests. Members of the genus *Pygoscelis* include **Gentoo**, **Chinstrap**, **Adelie** penguins, the latter of which is the most common of all Antarctic penguins. Finally, **King** and **Emperor** penguins are classified as genus *Aptenodytes*. Emperor penguins stand out not only as the largest of the world's penguins (reaching an average height of one meter tall and a weight of over 30 kilos), but also as that with the most unusual breeding techniques: both males and females incubate their eggs on top of their feet, spending up to three months standing immobile on the Antarctic ice while they wait for their young to hatch.

KING

ADELIE

WHALES

Fifteen species of whales visit Antarctica during the summer months, including the famously endangered **Southern Right Whale** (*Eubalaena australis*); named the 'right' whale by whalers because of its relative ease of capture and commercial value, this species was hunted to near extinction by the mid-1800's. The immense **Blue Whale** (*Baleanoptera musculus*), considered the largest mammal on earth, also frequents these waters, as do **Minke Whales** (*B. acutorostrata*) and a variety of toothed whales and dolphins. In 1994, the International Whaling Commission established the Southern Ocean Whale Sanctuary in the waters south of 40° S, thus prohibiting all commercial whaling in this area.

WEDDELL SEAL

SEALS

Six species of seals inhabit Antarctic waters. Four of these – including the **Weddell seal** (*Leptonychotes weddelli*, a superb diver thought to reach depths of up to 600m), the krill-eating **Crabeater seal** (*Lobodon carcinophagus*), the predatory **Leopard seal** (*Hydrurga leptonyx*), the rare, poorly understood **Ross seal** (*Ommatophoca rossii*), and the immense, highly territorial **Elephant seal** (*Mirounga leonina*) – belong to the family *Phocidae*, known as the 'true seals.' Prized by sealers for its fine, double-layer pelt, the **Antarctic fur seal** (*Arctocephalus gazella*) belongs to the family *Otariidae*.

SEA LIONS

Cultural Attractions

Chile's history and modern cultural panorama reflects the convergence of many worlds: native and European, industrial and scientific, religious and secular. Beneath even the strangest custom and most obscure artifact is a unique historical trajectory, a context that brings sense and life to the unknown.

In this section, we've highlighted some of the most significant, beautiful or extraordinary manifestations of Chile's modern and historical culture. You'll find them here organized by interest, and fleshed out with contextual information and concrete suggestions for where and when to visit.

CONTENTS

NATIVE PEOPLES OF CHILE,
Circa AD 1600

The Prehistoric era in Chile ended in the early 1500's with the arrival of the first Spanish explorers and *conquistadors*. Though the Spanish had no manifest interest in archaeology or native culture, they could not help but notice the diversity and number of native cultures, and the first written records of Chile's natives are those written by the *cronistas* who accompanied each expedition. From these and later writings, combined with archaeological data and the oral histories of surviving cultures, it has been established that the groups listed below inhabited Chile at the time of the Spanish conquest. It should be remembered that while the cultures of northern and central Chile were profoundly influenced by the great empires of the Central Andes (particularly Tiwanaku and the Incas), the people of the southern portion of the continent had little contact – and less in common – with Central Andean cultures.

You'll find a more complete cultural chronology of each of Chile's regions in the appropriate regional chapter, and more indepth accounts of selected indigenous cultural phenomena throughout this field guide.

The **AYMARA INDIANS** of Chile's northern altiplano live on the fringe of the great Aymara homeland stretching north through Bolivia and southeastern Perú. Living principally from the husbandry of llamas and alpacas and the cultivation of high-altitude crops (especially tubers, several hundred varieties of which grow in the Andes), the Aymaras are in a period of marked cultural decline within Chilean territory, as villages are abandoned and children leave home to seek work in the great cities along the coast. The Aymaras are especially well known for their fine weavings and colorful festivals, which blend Christian and native beliefs.

Throughout the northern coast, communities of now-extinct **CHANGO MARINE NOMADS** lived principally from fishing, the collection of algae and shellfish, and the hunting of marine mammals. The Changos, who traded the products of the sea with native groups from the interior oases and highlands, are

SELK'NAM

thought responsible for many of the petroglyphs and rock paintings found along the coast of northern Chile.

In the oases of the río Loa, the río Salado, and around the Salar de Atacama, groups of **ATACAMEÑO INDIANS** lived from small-scale agriculture, the domestication of American camels, and the fruits of trees like algarrobo and chañar. The Atacameños' cultural development was very much a reflection of their intense exchange with the highland cultures of NW Argentina, Bolivia, and Perú.

In the transverse valleys of the Norte Chico, the **DIAGUITA INDIANS** practiced a similar economy as the Atacameños. Occupying a sizeable territory on both sides of the Andes, the Diaguitas made life in the north difficult for the Spanish through the early years of the colonial period. They are best remembered now for the singular beauty of their ceramic designs.

At the time of the Conquest, the **ACONCAGUA INDIANS** of Central Chile apparently spoke *mapudungun*, the language of the **MAPUCHE INDIANS**. In fact, between the Río Aconcagua and Chiloé nearly all indigenous groups appear to have adopted many of the cultural traits of the Mapuches, whose name in mapudungun means 'the people of the land.'

Thus, while each individual culture may have had their own economy and lifestyle – ranging from the **TEHUELCHE** hunter-gatherers of the Argentine pampa to the relatively sedentary **PICUNCHES** of the Central Valley around Santiago – all were somewhat united by language. The heartland of this great Mapuche nation, however, lay in the region now known as La Araucanía, where a combination of hunting, gathering, and slash-and-burn agriculture appears to have been the norm. Over the course of 300 years of resistance to the Spanish and later the Chilean state, the Mapuches proved again and again the resilience and adaptability of their culture.

In the Chiloé archipelago and along the coast of Palena and Aisén, the **Chono**, **Cunco**, and **Caucahue Indians** spoke distinct languages, as did the **Aónikenk** (or Southern Tehuelche) of the southern Patagonian pampa. The Indians of the archipelago practiced slash-and-burn agriculture and fished and hunted the channels aboard loosely stitched canoes known as *dalcas*, while the Aónikenk depended mainly upon the abundant guanaco and other fauna of the grassy steppe.

The Indians of Tierra del Fuego were also divided into so-called 'Foot Indians' and 'Canoe Indians.'

The **Huash and Selk'nam Foot Indians** were terrestrial hunters of guanaco, rheas and other prey. The Huash lived in the remote southeastern corner of the island, while the more aggressive Selk'nams occupied a broad range including the northern and central pampas and forested *hirsk* woodlands.

The **Yamana and Kawéskar Canoe Indians** inhabited the fragmented southern and western coast of Patagonia. Subsisting on fish, shellfish, and marine mammals, they lived and even built fires aboard their canoes, travelling constantly among the islands of this stormy archipelago.

With a few dramatic exceptions, the Fuegian Indians avoided sustained contact with the whites until the late 19th century, when gold prospectors and sheep ranchers began to invade the Great Island of Tierra del Fuego. Within the space of a few decades, these magnificent cultures had been almost entirely extinguished.

On tiny Easter Island, 4,000km west in the very midst of the Pacific, the **Rapa Nui** culture was apparently on the brink of ecological disaster and cultural decline at the time of the first contact with Europeans in the early 1700's. By the end of that century, intertribal warfare had broken out on the island, leading the destruction of the island's magnificent stone monuments. Polynesian in origin and substance, the Rapa Nui culture witnessed by European observers was but a pale shadow of the great monument-building civilization of the past.

AYMARA

ISLANDS
San Félix
San Ambrosio
Salas y Gómez
Eastern
Robinson Crusoe
Alejandro Selkirk

SYMBOLOGY
○ Inca Settlements
Unoccupied territories
Permanent Inca occupation
Periodic Inca occupation
⟺ Continuation of group territory
⟸ Penetration from the pampa

Changos
Atacameños
Aymaras
Picunches
Diaguitas
Chiquiyanes
Mapuches
Pehuenches
Cuncos
Puelches
Huilliches
Yaganes
Rapa Nui
Poyas
Alacalufes
Onas
Tehuelches
Chonos

RAPA NUI

MAPUCHE

AÓNIKENK

Agreement between Chile and Argentina to determine precise borders between Monte Fitz-Roy and Cerro Daudet. (Buenos Aires, Dec 16, 1998).

ANTARCTIC CHILEAN TERRITORY

YAMANA

ARCHAEOLOGY

Max Uhle, 'Father of the South American Chronology'

German Max Uhle (1856-1944) was the first archaeologist to make extensive excavations in South America. A linguist by training, he was turned on to the Central Andes in 1898 by a friend recently back from Perú. By 1892, when he first arrived in Buenos Aires, Uhle had already written a book and several articles on language and archaeology in the Central Andes.

Once ashore, Uhle dedicated himself to fieldwork. He began in Argentina and later moved on to Bolivia, where he found the army using Tiwanaku sculptures as targets. The rate of his new finds was astounding: in two years of excavating in Perú, he collected over 9000 artifacts spanning over 3000 years of prehistory. When he lost his funding from Germany, Uhle moved to the States, where he had the fortune to meet the wealthy amateur archaeologist Phoebe Hearst (mother of William Randolph Hearst), his future wife and sponsor for the next ten years of excavating.

In his later years, Uhle moved on from pure excavation and focused on establishing a basic archaeological chronology of South America. Though it has been continually refined over the years, his chronology still underlies modern understanding of cultural development in the Andes.

Pukaras and other Pre-Hispanic ruins of Northern and Central Chile

PUCARA DE QUITOR (MN)

Early cultural development in northern Chile was typified by localized economies and small, relatively impermanent dwellings. The Tiwanaku empire, however, introduced a structured and hierarchical society that required more elaborate constructions. The most common are stone forts known as *pukaras*, built in strategic positions overlooking valleys and oases. More pukaras were built following the demise of Tiwanaku near 1000 AD, when regional kingdoms vied for control of the routes linking the coast and the altiplano.

The Incas brought a new wave of construction, reflecting the remarkable organization of the greatest empire in the Americas.

Over 1,500km of Inca roads have been identified in northern and central Chile, varying from 60cm to 3m in width, and often paved with stones at the entrance to villages or *tambo* storehouses. Other Inca sites include a regional administrative center, a metalworking plant, and a number of high altitude mountaintop shrines.

VIEW OF THE VALLE DE AZAPA FROM
THE PUCARA DE SAN LORENZO

VALLE DE AZAPA

The Azapa Valley's dependable water supply and proximity to the ocean made it a top priority for resource-poor cultures from the altiplano. Two 12th century pukaras and dozens of geoglyphs on the south side of the valley reflect the intense trade which characterized this valley during the pukara epoch.

(1) **Aldea Cerro Sombrero** A group of over 400 habitations, covering 6.5há.

(2) **Pukara Tumulo** Overlooking the valley east of Alto Ramírez.

(3) **Pukara de San Lorenzo** Dates from the 12th century.

THE SIERRA OR PRECORDILLERA

Here you find the north's highest concentration of defensive constructions, most of these strategically located at the head of the great *quebradas* and often associated with cultivated terraces known as *andanarías*.

This niche was probably utilized for the cultivation of tubers, for produc-

tion of long-lasting *chuño*; above here the land is suitable only for pasture.

(4) **Pukara de Copaquilla**: 12th century.

(5) **Tambo de Zapahuira**: These ruins are actually thought to be a group of Inca *colqas*, used for storing food, textiles and other tribute to the Inca. On nearby Cerro Huaycuta is a group of circular pre-Inca habitations, and 150m south is a group of *chullpa* funeral structures, rare outside the altiplano.

(6) **Pukaras in Belén**: In the Belén area are a number of Inca and pre-Inca pukaras. Across from the Belén cemetery is Ancopachane, composed of over a hundred circular and rectangular dwellings; nearby is

THE PUCARA DE LASANA AND THE RIO LOA VALLEY

demonstrate the importance that these arable valleys held for pre-Hispanic cultures with imperialist aspirations.

⑦ Pukara de Lasana 12th century construction, built on a mound on the west side of the Loa, upriver of Chiu Chiu.

⑧ Pukara de Turi The largest of the Atacameño pukaras, but in poor repair. 12th century construction, later occupied by Inca administrators.

SAN PEDRO DE ATACAMA

⑨ Pukara de Quitor Covering 2.5há, this 12th century construction, most likely fortified during the brief period of Inca rule, commands a tremendous view over the San Pedro oasis. Francisco de Aguirre stormed the pukara with 30 mounted soldiers and a backup of 1,000 *yanaconas* (Spanish-friendly Indians) in 1540, during his brutal pacification of northern Chile.

⑩ Catarpe Inca Administrative Center Formed of a series of rectangular rooms, built on a terrace overlooking the Río Grande or San Pedro. The site is protected to the east by the labyrinthine formations of the Salt Range; you can get here (with luck or a guide) through the Garganta del Diablo.

⑪ Tulor The earliest site of permanent habitation in the valley, Tulor consists of a series of interconnected circular dwellings dating from 800 BC-500 AD, representing the Toconao phase of regional Atacameño

the Inca Pukara de Chajpa. 5km south, on a well-preserved section of the Inca trail which leads towards the Quebrada de Laguame, is the Pukara de Huaihuarani, with some 500 dwellings and cave paintings under an overhang to the SE. 500m east of Belén, the Pukara de Incaullo is the most elaborate construction in the area.

THE RÍO LOA WATERSHED

The Río Loa, the only river to reach the Pacific from 20-27°S, has seen heavy traffic ever since the first episodes of vertical exchange between the coast and the altiplano. The immense pukaras at Turi and Lasana

PICTOGRAPHS IN TAIRA

culture. This site was inhabited by a people practicing a mixture of agriculture, recollection of chañar and algarrobo, and hunting of camelids, birds, and rodents.

THE COPIAPÓ VALLEY

This complex valley system is set in a transitional area between the Atacama Desert and the Norte Chico. The valley's agricultural and mineral wealth, numerous ecological niches, and relative proximity made it exceptionally attractive to the Inca Empire, but the high levels of local organization and technology made its conquest and control a challenge. As a consequence, this area boasts Chile's highest concentration of Inca *tambos*, *pukaras*, and other ruins.

The best known and most accessible of these is **Viña del Cerro**, an Inca copper foundry designed to channel wind into its 26 separate kilns. The majority of the sites, however, occupy commanding sites near the headwaters of the Río Copiapó tributaries, between the Río Jorquera and the Río Manflas. All told, local archaeologists have discovered over 70 Inca sites, including mountaintop shrines on the Copiapó and Jotabeche volcanoes. Visits to these sites can be arranged through Copiapó's Museo Regional de Atacama.

• **Pukara de Chena** SW of Santiago, near the Hacienda de Calera de Tango, this Inca fortress was probably built around 1480, 70-odd years before the foundation of Santiago. The fortress, of nine rectangular rooms overlooking the Maipo valley, has been partially restored. At one time there were two Inca cemeteries on the SW flank of the hill; there is now a picnic area on the site.

Rock Art: Geoglyphs, Petroglyphs, and Pictographs

Scattered throughout northern Chile are literally thousands of examples of rock art, representing 10,000 years of human history and the full range of human economies.

GEOGLYPHS

Often found adorning hillsides along desert trade routes in the region between Nazca, Perú, and the Río Loa, geoglyphs are the largest and most impressive of northern Chile's manifestations of primitive art. Geoglyphs may be formed in one of two ways: 'positive' representations are created by placing dark colored rocks upon the lighter substrate, while 'negative' designs were created by clearing oxidized superficial rocks away, leaving a lighter line. Some 90% of all images in northern Chile's geoglyphs are of camelids, suggesting the important role that these animals played in the highly interdependent Neolithic societies of the coast, desert, sierra and altiplano. Other images include pumas, serpents, stylized human images and geometric designs. The earliest geoglyphs in Chile are thought to date from around 700 BC.

⑫ **Geoglifos de Lluta** On the south side of the Lluta Valley, on the route to Putre and PN Lauca.

⑬ **Geoglifos de Azapa** 5 separate panels on the south side of the valley, from Cerro Sombrero to Alto Ramírez.

⑭ **Geoglifos de Chiza** Visible from the bridge on the south side of the Quebrada de Chiza.

⑮ **Geoglifos de Tiliviche** Represents a group of llamas, 2km off the Panamerican on the north side of the Quebrada de Tiliviche (signposted).

GEOGLIFOS DE PINTADOS

16 Geoglifos de Pintados

Located in RN Tamarugal east of Iquique, Pintados consists of nearly 1000 separate figures arranges in thematic panels and extending over nearly 4km of arid hills. This is the highest concentration of geoglyphs in the north.

17 Cerro Unita - El Gigante de Atacama

On the route from Iquique to PN Isluga, the Giant of Atacama is a stylized human figure in a cat mask measuring 86m in height – making it the world's largest humanoid image. The image is on the west side of the hill, and is not visible from the highway.

PETROGLYPH IN MN
VALLE DEL ENCANTO

18 Chug-Chug

Just north of route 24 from the Panamerican to Calama, along the ancient trade route from the upper río Loa to the coast. Designs include representations of coastal hunters aboard rafts made from inflated sea lion pelts.

PETROGLYPHS AND PICTOGRAPHS (ROCK-PAINTINGS)

Though they incorporate many of the same design motifs as geoglyphs, petroglyphs are smaller and simpler – usually the work of a single individual. Pictographs are usually found beneath overhangs (*aleros* or *abrigos*), and are sometimes found in combination with petroglyphs. This list does not include the many coastal and interior sites in Central Chile.

- **Putre**

There are three collections of pictographs in this area. The Alero de Vilacaurani lies about 10km down-valley on the trail to Socoroma, but has unfortunately been damaged by vandals. Better preserved are the sites above Putre, Incanny (13km) and Viluvio (18km). Consult in Putre's *municipalidad* for guided day tours to these sites.

- **Quebrada el Medano** Hundreds of pictographs, including representations of men hunting whales from sea-lion rafts, adorn the upper portion of this *quebrada* (between 1300-1700m elevation). Walking access is from the coastal highway near Paposo, south of Antofagasta

- **Finca de Chañaral** An oasis along the Inca Trail 19km NW of Inca de Oro, with paintings and petroglyphs on the valley walls. Nearby is the Quebrada de las Pinturas, also with abundant rock art.

PETROGLYPHS ALONG THE RIO SALADO

Diaguita Ceramics

Created for both ritual and domestic purposes, the intricate ceramic designs of the Diaguita Indians are grouped into four evolutionary phases, based on shape and decorative styles. The Museo Antropológico in La Serena and the Museo de Limarí in Ovalle contain Chile's finest collections of Diaguita artifacts.

Las Animas (800-1000 AD). Dates from an era of transition from the Las Animas culture. Characterized by geometric designs such as crosses and steps.

Diaguitas I (1000-1200 AD). Characterized by black and white geometric designs over a red base. Pieces are larger than Las Animas, with heavily painted exteriors and narrow bands painted on the interior. First appearance of human forms.

Diaguitas II (1200-1470 AD). Considered the classic phase of Diaguita pottery. Plates and bowls have rounded base and straight walls. First appearance of *jarros patos* or 'duck jars' — asymmetrical vessels with handles, made to resemble animals. Increased variety of decoration, including first relief work. Anthropomorphic figures are also common.

Diaguitas III (1470-1536 AD). Influenced by Tawantinsuyo, the Inca empire. Changes include new designs (jars with small upper handles, different animal shapes) and decorative motifs (mainly triangles and strips in checkerboard design).

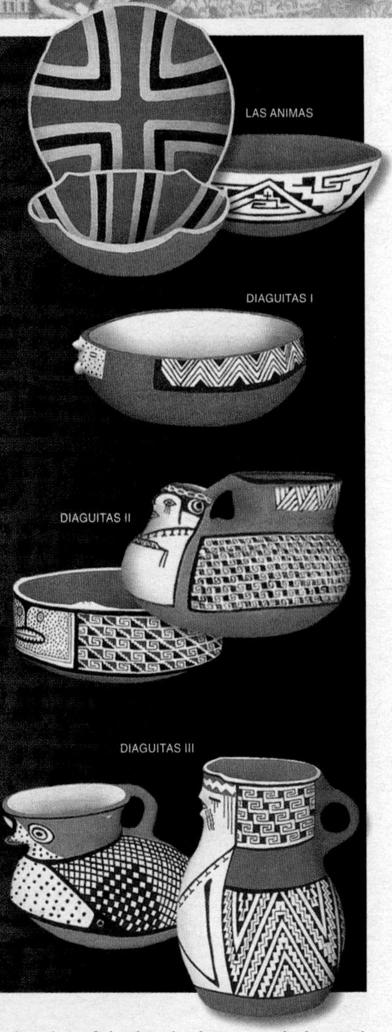

LAS ANIMAS

DIAGUITAS I

DIAGUITAS II

DIAGUITAS III

• **Río Loa Watershed** Sites include a collection of pictographs under the *Abrigo de Aiquina* overhang (on the south side of the río Salado Valley, 3km west of Aiquina), and some 76 petroglyphs (look for painted numbers) on rocks along the east side of the Río Loa, above the road between Chiu Chiu and the Pukara de Lasana. There is also an impressive collection of paintings and petroglyphs on the west side of the Rio Loa valley in Taira, 56km above Lasana.

• **Río Salado** There are over a dozen well-preserved panels of petroglyphs on both sides of the lovely desert wash, located an easy day's bike ride and walk north of San Pedro de Atacama.

• In the **Quebrada de Tulan** between Lagunas Miniques and Miscanti and the village of Tilamonte, there are two spectacular pictographs, one depicting a puma attacking a llama, another a group of shamans. You need a guide to find these panels.

NORTE CHICO

• **Piedra del Guanaco** This large rock, located in a grassy pasture near the entrance to the Quebrada de Pangue in Cochiguaz, is carved with numerous images of guanacos and other designs.

• **Valle del Encanto** The principal attraction at this national monument SE of Ovalle is a collection of 30 petroglyphs and 20 stone mortars attributed to the El Molle culture (300 BC-700 AD). Best viewed in early afternoon.

• **RN Río Los Cipreses** The petroglyphs are located far up the Los Cipreses watershed, about a day and a half walk from the trailhead. Ask park rangers for details.

PATAGONIA

• **MN Manos de Cerro Castillo** Just west of Villa O'Higgins, this well-preserved site features over 100 of the hand paintings common throughout northern Patagonia, dating from up to 10,000 BP. These images were created by filling the mouth with dye and expelling it forcefully around a hand placed on the wall.

• **Cueva de las Manos** Located in RN Jeinimeni, this is one of Patagonia's greatest concentrations of the hand paintings described above.

EASTER ISLAND

Among Easter Island's 15,000 archaeological sites is a fascinating array of petroglyphs, pictographs and stone sculptures. Most of the design motifs are associated with the Birdman Cult (a relatively late phenomena) rather than with the moai-building phase on the island. Nonetheless, some of the moai have images etched upon them, including one at Orongo with a birdman on its back and one at Rano Raraku with a three-masted ship on its chest. Some of the designs utilized in Easter Island petroglyphs also appear in the island's *rongo rongo* script.

PETROGLYPHS IN THE BAHIA DE LAPEROUSE, EASTER ISLAND

• In **Mata Ngarau**, the 'ceremonial village' at Orongo, there are 1700 separate petroglyphs, including Tangata Manu birdmen, *komari* vulvas images, and representations of Makemake, the creator-god.

• **Moto Nui**, the island off the coast of Orongo, has a large cave with red paintings and numerous petroglyphs. The trip to the island is exposed and only possible with very calm conditions.

• **North along the coast from Ahu Tepeu**, the site at Omohe features a unique spindly figure thought to represent an *aku aku*, one of the island's protectorate spirits.

• **Rock outcrops near Ahu Tongariki** are carved with numerous petroglyphs, including a tortoise and a bonito, both of which were traditionally reserved for consumption by the island's religious nobility.

• **Near the eastern end of the Poike Península**, the site known as Papa ui hetu'u is thought to have been a center for astronomical observation. Its name translates as 'The-Rock-for-seeing-stars.'

MATA NGRAU, EASTER ISLAND

• Half an hour south along the coast from Hanga Roa, the **Ana Kai Tangata** lava tube cave has red and white stylized birds painted on its ceiling.

Ahu, Moai and other elements of Easter Island archaeology

The richness, variety, and mystery of Easter Island's archaeological treasures place the island in a category all its own. As North American archaeologist William Mulloy put it, the island truly is 'a great open-air museum.'

The island's most conspicuous artifacts are the stone ceremonial platforms (*ahu*) and gigantic stone statues (*moai*). The ahus, the earliest of which have been carbon-dated to the 8th century AD, represent the earliest constructive phase on the island. They are almost invariably located along the coast, and generally feature a high, finely finished seaward wall and a sloping inner wall; quality varies from one to the next, perhaps by the intended purpose or era in which each ahu was built. Ahu Vinapu, for example, is constructed of large stones so closely fitted that the platform really does resemble Inca masonry, though it should be noted that even the finest ahus consist of a finished facade backfilled with rubble – a far cry from the impeccably thorough building techniques of the Incas.

Each ahu appears to have been associated with single kinship group, whose lands extended from the coast inland. The higher ranking members of each clan lived near the base of the *ahu*, often in eliptical (or 'boat-shaped') stone and reed houses known as *hare paenga*, while common folks lived further inland. When a member of clan died, his or her bones might be concealed within the ahu, increasing the magic or *manu* of the site.

Not until the second constructive phase (following the sequence established by Thor Heyerdahl) did the first moai begin to appear. Ranging in height from about two meters to a gigantic 21 meters (but averaging about 4m), the moai were hewn from the volcanic tuff of the Rano Raraku crater using basalt tools known as *tokis*. They were carved *in situ*, face up, and left connected to the bedrock by a narrow spine or 'keel' until ready for transport. Though no two are identical, nearly all demonstrate a marked stylistic similarity, with their long, angular faces, sharp brows, and elongate ears.

Once the statues were nearly complete, the islanders faced the arduous task of transporting them to their respective ahus. Visitors have long puzzled over how the gigantic statues, which weigh up to eighty tons, could possibly have been moved – especially given the island's total lack of trees, which could be used for leverage or as rollers. However, excavations have indicated that forests once covered at least a portion of the island, and theories such as William Mulloy's 'fulcrum method' appear quite plausible – though proving anything, as always, is impossible. Regardless of the method used, the carving and transportation of the statues clearly required massive amounts of manpower, though it appears that this work was that of a privileged artisan class and not that of slaves or forced laborers.

Once the moai were in place, they had to be raised atop their respective ahus. Here the method used ap-

RESTORED AHU ON EASTER ISLAND

EASTER ISLAND'S UNUSUAL BOAT-SHAPED HOUSE

pears to be a relatively simple one, in which the statue was levered up by long poles and supported by a pile of stones wedged underneath until the moai could finally be rocked upright with the aid of ropes. In 1955, a team of locals under the encouragement of Thor Heyerdahl used precisely this method to raise the moai at Ahu Ature Huki, near Playa Anakena. The *pukao* topknots that adorned many moai were apparently set in place afterwards, though no one yet claims to understand how. Finally, the moai were completed with inset eyes of white coral and, in some cases, earplugs of the type presumably used by the island's so-called Long-ears.

Other *in situ* archaeological attractions on the island include the ceremonial constructions at Orongo and a scattering of stone towers of unknown origin known as *tupas*.

One thing you won't see on Easter Island, however, is a genuine **rongo rongo** tablet. Legend has it that there once existed some 67 of these elegantly carved tablets, but many were destroyed or lost and the 24 remaining examples are held by foreign and Chilean mainland museums (including Santiago's Museo de la Merced and Museo de Historia Nacional). First discovered in the mid-19th century, they constitute another of the island's great unsolvable mysteries.

The rongo rongo script consists of about 150 basic elements, including many of the same images that appear in island petroglyphs. The tablets, which are carved from the beautiful dark wood of the toromiro, are read from left to right beginning with the bottom line; at the end of the line the tablet is turned upside down and the reading continues on the next line. Reading them was the task of select priests known as *Tangata moari rongo rongo*, the last of whom died in Peruvian guano mines in the 1860's.

Though the rongo rongo script and its associated rituals were lost by the time the first serious ethnological and archaeological studies were carried out on the island, ancestor worship appears to have endured well into the twentieth century. For decades, missionaries on the island had heard (and ignored) rumors of secret family heirloom caves, but none were discovered until Thor Heyerdahl's 1955 expedition; convinced that Heyerdahl was a 'Norwegian Long-ear,' several islanders invited he and his companions into hidden caves crammed with sacred carvings in wood and stone. Usually, the visitors were required to appease the *aku aku* guarding the cave by first partaking of a chicken baked in an *umu* (ritual earth oven). Like the rongo rongo, however, most of the unusual, highly stylized statues were whisked away to foreign museums.

RONGO RONGO TABLET

Monte Verde: A Clue in the Search for the First Americans

Few archaeological sites have had as profound an impact upon recent understanding of human occupation of the Americas as that discovered at Monte Verde, just NW of Puerto Montt. Excavated from 1977-1985 by a team of 80 researchers headed by the University of Kentucky's Dr. Tom Dillehay, Monte Verde consists of a creekside habitational complex that was covered by a peat bog beginning about 13,000 years ago, protecting the site from bacterial attack and decay. Excavations have turned up hundreds of artifacts, including stone and wooden tools, bola stones, wooden house foundations, 42 species of edible plants, twine made from local grasses, and bones from mastadons and other prey.

What is fascinating about Monte Verde is not just the extraordinarily well-preserved condition of the site, nor even the findings of edible plants and semi-permanent houses that contrast so strikingly with previous assumptions about the economies and lifestyles of early hunter-gatherer cultures. What is perhaps most exciting is that the widely accepted validity

POSSIBLE PRE-CLOVIS SITES

Cordilleran Glacier

Laurantide Ice Sheet

Hebior Schaefer ▲

▲ Meadowcroft

Channel Islands ▲

Clovis ▲

▲ Cactus Hill

▲ Topper

HUMAN FOOTPRINT

Tainta ▲ Taima

Pedra Pintada ▲

Pedra Furada ▲

Quebrada Tacahuay ▲ Quebrada Jaguay

Monte Verde ▲

of Monte Verde has broken a 60-year stalemate in the search for answers regarding the possible dates at which humans could have first entered the New World. For years, sites attributed to the Clovis people – the earliest of which has been dated at 11,500 years before present – represented the earliest dateable evidence of human occupation in the Americas. Though many believed that pre-Clovis sites might exist, nothing could be proved – until now. The dating of the Monte Verde site at 12,500 ybp clearly establishes that humans had entered the Americas no later than 13,000 ybp – at which time the inland route south from Alaska would have been summarily closed by glaciers. Monte Verde strongly suggests that either the first Americans migrated south via a coastal route, or that they in fact arrived much, much earlier – sometime before 20,000 ybp, which marked the onset of the last glacial maximum.

While Monte Verde doesn't provide any definitive answers, it does provide some new clues as to what questions we should be asking. As Alex Barker of the Dallas Museum of Natural History has been quoted as saying: 'Monte Verde is real. It's old. And it's a whole new ballgame.'

ARCHITECTURE

SOCOROMA PUTRE

PARINACOTA (MN) CAQUENA

GUAÑACAGUA CASPANA (MN)

AIQUINA (MN)

ISLUGA (MN)

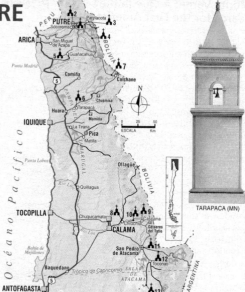

TARAPACA (MN)

Colonial Churches of the Desert and Altiplano

The colonial churches of northern Chile mostly date from the 17th century. Erected in the *pueblos de indios* established by the Spanish in order to control the native population, these churches are almost invariably the oldest post-contact construction in any given settlement.

The churches themselves – built as a single nave with a single door in the facade, and surrounded by an adobe or stone wall that defines a sacred space – generally predate the bell towers. The design of the towers is derived from a combination of Spanish and indigenous influences, and often reflects the proportions of native and Spanish inhabitants in a given village at the time of construction.

Most churches are built of stone and abobe, whitewashed annually with chalk; roofs and doors

IGLESIA DE PARINACOTA (MN)

CHIU CHIU, IGLESIA DE SAN FRANCISCO (MN)

are often built of panels of *cardón* cactus. The interiors of these churches often contain impressive 18th century gold leaf altarpieces and religious images, while the nearby cemeteries range from the barren steel crosses at Poconchile to elaborate pastel and paper-flower crypts in San Pedro de Atacama and Toconao.

(1) **Socoroma** (1560) and (2) **Putre** (1670)
Bell towers reflect a pronounced indigenous influence.

(3) **Parinacota**, (4) **Guallatire**, and (5) **Guañacagua**
In the Andean Baroque style, brought from Arequipa.

(6) **Tarapacá** 17th century, pronounced Spanish influence.

(7) **Isluga** 17th century, considered one of the finest of the altiplano churches.

(8) **Chiu Chiu** (1675) Reflects Atacameño design influence.

(9) **Caspana** (1641) Andean Baroque.

(10) **Aiquina** Andean Baroque.

(11) **San Pedro de Atacama** The church dates from 1641; the bell tower is a 1964 addition.

(12) **Toconao** (1744) Predominantly Spanish design.

(13) **Peine** (1750) Built of white *liparita* volcanic stone.

SOCAIRE

PEINE (MN)

SOTOCA (MN)

MATILLA (MN)

GUALLATIRI

TOCONAO (MN)

SAN PEDRO DE ATACAMA (MN)

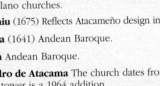

CACTUS-WOOD ROOF

IGLESIA DE SAN PEDRO DE ATACAMA (MN)

Santiago in 1900

Turn-of-the-century Santiago was a dynamic and rapidly changing city. With tax incomes flowing steadily south from the nitrate fields, the Chilean government contracted foreign architects and embarked on colossal beautification projects. Looking about at Santiago's most noteworthy urban highlights, it is hard to find one that doesn't date from this era. The gardens and terraces of Cerro Santa Lucía, the Mercado Central, Parque Forestal and the Museo de Bellas Artes, the Quinta Normal and Museo de Historia Natural, and the Virgen de San Cristóbal all date from Santiago's golden age.

SANTIAGO'S ALAMEDA IN THE EARLY 20TH CENTURY

• **Ex-Congreso Nacional** Built on lands previously occupied by the Compañía de Jesús. The present building was begun by French architect C.F. Brunet de Baines in 1858, and completed in 1876.

• **Municipalidad de Santiago** This Neoclassic / Renaissance edifice was inaugurated in 1885, on the site of the Colonial town hall and jail. The architect was Eugenio Joannon.

• **Iglesia de las Agustinas** This NeoRenaissance church, designed by Italian Eusebio Chelli, was consecrated in 1888.

• **Correo Central** Built over the site of the Colonial Government Palace, the central post office building was begun in 1881 by R. Brown and finished in 1908 by R. Fehrman.

• **Edifico Comercial Edwards** Prefabricated in France, this steel building was finished in 1893, following the plans of E. Joannon.

• **Palacio de los Tribunales de Justicia**
Built on the site of the Colonial Tribunal del Consulado, where independence was first declared in a town meeting in 1810. The actual building was erected from 1901-1929 by Emilio Doyere and Emilio Jéquier. Note the French influence and vaulted glass ceiling.

• **Teatro Municipal** Begun in 1853 under the direction of C.F. Brunet de Baines and finished – after major fire damage – by his compatriot L Henault together with E. Chelli, R. Brown, and P. Lathoud.

• **Palacio Errázuriz**
Built in 1872 by Eugenio Chelli, in the Italian Neoclassic style.

• **Palacio Cousiño** Lavish private residence built from 1870-1878 by French architect Paul Lathoud.

• **Palacio Edwards**
Neoclassic, built in 1888 as a private residence by J.E. Fehrman.

Parks and Gardens

Architects weren't the only ones to cash in on the bourgeois aspirations, fat checkbooks and European tastes of Chile's turn-of-the-century elite. With the completion of irrigation works and the formation of the exotic tree nursery at the Quinta Normal in Santiago, elaborate, well-manicured parks and gardens became marks of prestige in the capital and at *haciendas* throughout the Central Valley. French landscape artist Gustave Renner pulled the most weight, designing the terraces and gardens for **CERRO SANTA LUCÍA**, **PARQUE MACUL** and **VIÑA SANTA RITA**, while Irishman William O'Reilly got the nod at **PARQUE DE LOTA**, near Concepción.

Today most of the trees in Chile's parks and plazas are over a hundred years old, and they are almost invariably the most elegant and relaxing component of urban design. Other noteworthy parks include the **QUINTA VERGARA** in Viña del Mar, **PARQUE PEÑALOLÉN** in Santiago, and **PARQUE CONCHA Y TORO** in Pirque.

HACIENDA CONCHA Y TORO, PIRQUE IN THE 19TH CENTURY

Haciendas

Until the early 18th century, Santiago was the only city in all of central Chile. In the absence of urban nuclei – and with nearly all the land concentrated in the hands of a few large landowners – the *hacienda* emerged as the center of rural life. Producing food, clothing, leather goods, candles, and wine (to name just a few items), the hacienda was a self-sufficient unit run by a *patrón* and worked by landless servants and sharecroppers known as *inquilinos*.

16th, 17th, and early 18th-century hacienda architecture reflects the uncertainties of life in the colonial era, with thick walls fully enclosing an interior patio space. Towards the mid-18th century, the perceived threat of Indians and bandits had subsided, and hacienda design began to open up more, permitting better efficiency in attending to a wide variety of agricultural tasks. Constructions from this era tend more towards U-shaped buildings or lineally arranged compounds, with a large *casa patronal* facing the more modest homes of the inquilinos. Towards the end of the 19th century, many homes were bought by nou-

CASAS DE CALERA DE TANGO (MN)
original design

CHAPEL
ADMINISTRATION   CORRAL
OVENS
ORPHANS & DEPENDENTS   SLAVE QUARTERS
BLACKSMITH & SILVERSMITH
GENERAL WORKSHOP   RESIDENTIAL QUARTERS

N
Building Layout in 1767

veau riche who built European-inspired mansions or complemented existing structures with elaborate parks and gardens.

The haciendas and colonial villages between San Fernando and Pichilemu are described below in wine tours, and in general you can often combine hacienda visits with wine tasting.

The Aconcagua Valley

Lo Vicuña 10km north of Putaendo, this hacienda dates from 1790. The actual church was built from 1839-1880, the *casa patronal* in 1915. You can ask for permission to see the grounds.

Panquehue Bought in 1870 by Maximiliano Errázuriz and subsequently transformed into what at the time was one of the largest vineyards in the world, the Hacienda Panquehue unfortunately preserves little of its rural heritage. Still, you can tour the park and visit the Viña Errázuriz Panquehue with previous notice (☎ (2)2036688).

Santiago

Calera de Tango In 1685 the Jesuit order purchased the hacienda and began the long process of building irrigation canals; these were some of the first intensely irrigated lands in the Central Valley. More than half of the present buildings date from 1741-1761, and are among the best-preserved representations of the walled complexes common until the end of the 18th century.

When the Jesuits were expelled from the Spanish colonies, the hacienda passed into the hands of colonial administrators, and was later sold to the Ruiz-Tagle family. In 1912, the hacienda was returned to the Jesuits, and since 1970 many buildings have been restored. Visits are allowed on a sporadic basis. Just south are the San Miguel de Tango and Santa Helena de Lonquén haciendas.

Colchagua

Los Lingues This extremely well preserved hacienda (now a hotel) has remained in the hands of the same family since 1599, when it was given by the Spanish crown to don Melchor Jufre de Aguila, then mayor of Santiago, in return for his services as a writer and historian. The central buildings date from the 17th and early 18th century, while the exterior wings were added a century later. Bavarian monks from the Hacienda Calera de Tango (⌖) carved several of the wooden doors.

Visits to Los Lingues include a gourmet lunch and a tour of the house –with antique furniture and an excellent art collection– and the 3,500há grounds. Nearly as impressive as the house is the horse farm or *caballeriza*, with its lovely mosaic floor. The 'Aculeo' horses bred here have been registered since 1860, and are considered descendents of Berber horses brought by the Moors to Spain. Top-notch lodging is also available at Los Lingues.

HACIENDA LOS LINGUES, INTERIOR AND EXTERIOR VIEWS

La Sanchina 3km east of Rancagua, this is a classic early-19th century construction, rectangular with outdoor corridors. Today it is a university; visits are allowed during the day.

San José del Carmen de El Huique 50km west of San Fernando, on the road to Pichilemu. The *casa patronal* and other buildings were begun in 1829, finishing in 1857 with the chapel. Visits by guided tour only.

Quinta de Tilcoco 59km SE of Rancagua, near the Cachapoal valley. Around the plaza are 18th and 19th-century constructions, including the 1880 Casa de Ejercicios Espirituales, which at one time had 14 separate interior patios. Nearby are the colonial villages of Guacarhue and Zúñiga, with roofed corridors running along the streets. The church in Guacarhue is a Toesca design. Just north of here is the town of Doñihue, famous for its weaving.

TALCA

Villa Cultural Huilquilemu The hacienda dates from a 1603 *merced* from the Church to Spanish captain Flores de León. The main house, with its interior patio and long exterior corridors, dates from mid-19th century, as does the well-maintained garden. The house is currently a museum and exhibition space.

The *Ascensores* of Valparaíso

One of Valparaíso's most distinguishing features is undoubtedly its 15 funicular railways or *ascensores*, which efficiently and elegantly connect the flat financial and commercial district (*El Plan*) with the steep residential *cerros* that surround the harbor. Dating from the late 19th century, these ascensores typically feature two counterweighted cars, one of which rises while the other descends.

Today, funicular railways are still in use in a number of cities around the globe, most notably San Francisco, Lisbon, and Shimla, India. Valparaíso's *ascensores* have all been declared national monuments, though upkeep is an increasingly problematic burden. Efforts are under way to secure funding and protection through Unesco's World Heritage program.

QUINTA DE TILCOCO

Spanish Forts

Scattered throughout southern Chile are the remains of dozens of stone and wooden forts, built by Spanish and Chilean troops during 330 years of regional instability in 'La Frontera.'

Spanish colonial presence in the south never amounted to more than fortified military installations, which paradoxically allowed the Mapuche Indians to obtain metal, arms, and horses from circumspect traders; after a time of peace, the Mapuches inevitably rallied and destroyed the fort, sending the Spanish scurrying north. Spanish accounts reveal the desperate nature of this historical moment, with tale after tale of earthquakes, fires and treason, long sieges, and near escapes down the river to the ocean.

The ocean, however, was far from safe. In addition to the Mapuches, the Spanish had to contend with fleets of marauding Dutch and English pirates, who periodically occupied and burned Spanish settlements and threatened to set up their own.

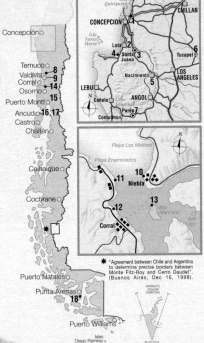

CORRAL, CASTILLO SAN
SEBASTIAN DE LA CRUZ (MN)

Most colonial and Chilean forts defended strategic points along the Río Biobío, at the entrance to Andean passes, along coastal rivers and at ocean ports. The interior mostly remained under Mapuche control until 1881. The forts have a variety of styles, depending on their location and purpose. Most were hastily erected wooden fortresses, built to secure a military advance; those known as *plaza fuertes* were associated with neighboring civilian populations, who would seek refuge inside in the event of an attack. Along the coast were more substantial stone fortresses, most of which were built in the 16th and 17th century and improved during the 18th.

Many forts retain their original artillery, and a few have been restored with exhibits, tours and even historical re-enactments.

(1) La Planchada Built in 1687, this impressive stone fort dominates the waterfront in Penco, 14km north of Concepción. The actual construction replaced the adobe fortresses built during the 16th century, when this was the principal Spanish settlement in the south; the city of Concepción

THE PERIMETER WALL AT NACIMIENTO

was originally founded here. The fort was attacked by the Dutch in 1694 and 1720.

② Lota This 1661 *plaza fuerte* is located on the steep peninsula 3km south of Lota.

③ Santa Juana de Guadalcázar This fort on the Río Biobío was originally built in 1626, and was repeatedly destroyed by the Mapuches. The actual edifice is a faithful reconstruction of the 1739 fort, surrounded on all sides by deep trenches. There is a traditional restaurant inside.

④ Ballenar This 1788 fort, located 15km east of Antuco, was intended to defend against Pehuenche incursions from the upper Laja valley. Only the stone platform remains.

HISTORIC RE-ENACTMENT AT FUERTE SAN SEBASTIAN (MN)

⑤ Nacimiento The original fort was founded by the Spanish in 1603 and destroyed three times by the Mapuches; on more than one occasion the Spanish escaped down the Biobío on rafts. The actual construction, dating from 1749, features a *plaza fuerte* and a fortified brick wall overlooking the Río Vergara. Originally the fort was separated from the civilian population by a dry moat, which today forms the Calle Lastra.

⑥ Tucapel The site of the 1552 original fort, where Pedro de Valdivia was defeated and killed by Mapuche *cacique* Lautaro, has never been located. The Tucapel fort in Cañete, which overlooks the Río Cañete valley, was founded in 1868 during the 'Pacification of *La Araucanía.*'

⑦ Purén The actual fort is a reconstruction of an 1869 wooden fortress. You may consult at the fort for nearby attractions including Mapuche burial mounds, petroglyphs, and the remnants of two earlier Spanish forts. This general area was the site of the 1598 'Disaster of Curalaba,' which set off the general Mapuche insurrection that expelled the Spanish from La Araucanía.

⑧ Built in 1647 on a bluff above the Río Cruces, **Fuerte San Luis de Alba de Cruces** was intended to defend the route between Valdivia and the missions and agricultural lands upriver. Though remodeled by the Spanish in 1774, it was abandoned soon after independence; excavations begun in 1967 have restored the original walls, towers, moats and a bridge. The interior of the fort holds a reconstructed church and the *Casa del Castellano*, with exhibits of artifacts discovered during the excavation.

FUERTE DE SANTA JUANA DE GUADALCAZAR (MN)

RIO BUENO, FORTIN SAN JOSE DE ALCUDIA (MN)

⑨ VALDIVIA

Following Hendrick Brouwer's 1643 attempt to establish a Dutch colony in Valdivia, the Spanish sent 10 ships and 1200 men to Valdivia with the task of transforming the port into a vast, impenetrable fortress. The mouth of the Río Valdivia was protected by forts at Niebla, Corral, and Isla Mancera, while the city itself was enclosed by a high barrier and defended by four towers and 10 cannons. A further fort upriver on the Río Cruces completed the arsenal, which together allowed Valdivia to become the third largest settlement in Chile during the 17th century, and an essential link in the precarious coastal road to Chiloé.

⑩ In Niebla, the **Fuerte La Pura y Limpia Concepción de Monfort de Lemus** was originally built in 1671, and renovated in 1767 with major stone walls and a cannonball foundry. At one time the fort contained 18 cannons, which overlapped the range of those from Mancera and Corral. The fort has been restored on several occasions; there is an on-site museum with exhibits on colonial Valdivia.

⑪ Located in Corral, the **Fuerte San Luis de Alba de Amargos** was built between 1655 and 1661. In 1679, its size was doubled to include a total of 12 cannons.

⑫ The largest and most powerful of the forts at the mouth of the Río Valdivia, the **Fuerte San Sebastián de la Cruz** consists of three separate batteries, built between 1645 and 1767. At one time the fort contained some 21 cannons. During the summer season, local actors produce daily re-creations of civic and military life in the Spanish forts.

⑬ Located on Isla Mancera, the **Fuerte San Pedro de Alcántara** was the first of the forts built at the mouth of the Río Valdivia, and from here the entire defense system was coordinated. In the interior of the fort is a small church and convent.

⑭ **San José de Alcudía** With a commanding view over the Río Bueno, this fort dates from 1778. Several of the original cannons are still in place.

⑮ **Reina María Luisa** This fort on the east side of the Río Rahue was built in 1793, during the reoccupation of Osorno. Only the defensive wall remains.

⑯ **San Antonio** North of Ancud's port, this 1770 stone fort was the second-to-last in the Americas to fly the Spanish flag. The base structure is all that remains.

⑰ **Agüi** This stone fort was held by the Spanish from 1779 to 1826, when it was finally taken by nationalist forces, along with the fort at San Antonio. The remains include stone walls and a few cannons; visits may be arranged in Ancud.

⑱ **Bulnes** Dating from 1843, Fuerte Bulnes was the first Chilean (not Spanish) settlement on the Strait of Magellan. The founding party consisted of eight soldiers and two wives, who remained on the site for five years before relocating to Punta Arenas. The wooden fort has been faithfully reconstructed, and may be visited by tour from Punta Arenas.

FUERTE BULNES

German Settlement in the Lake Region

During the second half of the 19th century, the Chilean government – anxious to consolidate the unknown lands in the south – granted large swaths of land to European homesteaders, particularly Germans. The first group of settlers arrived on Valdivia's Isla Teja in 1850; two years later, a boatload of 212 Germans arrived on the shores of modern-day Puerto Montt and forged inland to claim their territory on the shores of Lago Llanquihue.

Each colonist in the Lago Llanquihue region was granted an ox team, a pregnant cow, 500 boards, a hundred pounds of nails, a monthly stipend, all medical services for a year, and Chilean nationality, provided that they build a house and clear and fence the surrounding land. As first lumber and then agricultural produce began to flow out of the recently settled lands, professionals and businessmen established themselves in the fast-growing cities of the south. Thus the relics of German settlement span the rural-urban spectrum, including everything from handmade rural implements to elegant wooden mansions. Valdivia, Osorno, Puerto Octay and Frutillar all have museums with displays and photographs from the era of German settlement; see city listings for details.

PUERTO VARAS

Historic constructions in Puerto Varas mostly date from 1912, when the city was connected to Santiago via rail. Eight of these homes have been declared national monuments.

CASA JÚPNER (1910)

CASA GOTSCHLICH (1910 APROX.)

CASA OPITZ (1915 APROX.)

CASA ALEMANA (1914)

CASA YUNGE (1932)

CASA KUSCHEL (1915)

VALDIVIA

The principal historic constructions are clustered along the waterfront on Calle General Lagos, south of the Mercado Fluvial.

CONJUNTO INDUSTRIAL HAVERBECK

CASA WERKMAISTER

CASA DE CALLE GENERAL LAGOS 1036

CASA CONRADO STÜCKRATH (MN)

OSORNO

Six homes along Calle Mackenna east of the plaza have been declared national monuments.

CASA FEDERICO STÜCKRATH (MN)

CASA SCHÜLLER (MN)

CASA SÜRBER (MN)

CASA H. STÜCKRATH (MN)

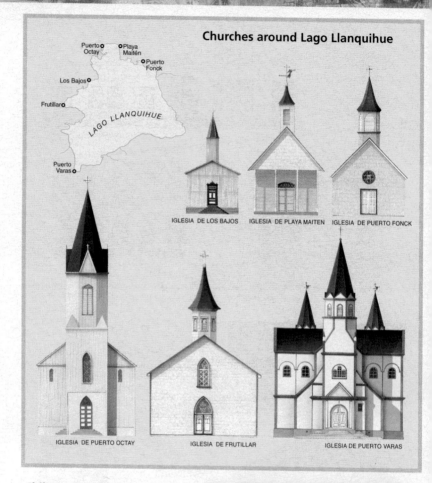

Churches around Lago Llanquihue

Puerto Octay
Playa Maitén
Puerto Fonck
Los Bajos
Frutillar

LAGO LLANQUIHUE

Puerto Varas

IGLESIA DE LOS BAJOS IGLESIA DE PLAYA MAITEN IGLESIA DE PUERTO FONCK

IGLESIA DE PUERTO OCTAY IGLESIA DE FRUTILLAR IGLESIA DE PUERTO VARAS

Chilote Churches

Over 150 elegant wooden chapels adorn the rolling countryside and scattered islands of the Chiloé archipelago. These are the legacies of the Jesuit order, which aimed to transform the archipelago into a so-called 'Garden of the Church.' Such was the fervor of the Jesuits that it is rare in the whole of the archipelago for one chapel to be separated from the next by a distance greater than 10km.

The oldest chapel in Chiloé is in Achao. Originally constructed entirely of wood, using pegs as fasteners in

CASTRO, IGLESIA DE SAN FRANCISCO (MN)

place of costly nails, Achao's church displays the classic architectural elements favored by the early Bavarian priests. Note the semi-circular arches over the external patio, and the upper facade that merges seamlessly with the facade of the bell tower.

The Neoclassical influence of the 19th century brought a number of design changes. In Chonchi, for example, the upper facade is set forward from the bell tower, while in Tenaún a horizontal frieze appears on the facade above the arches. The arches themselves appear increasingly flattened, and in some cases (such as in Chelín) are omitted altogether.

Many of these churches also have nearby cemeteries and outbuildings known as *casemitas*, which were occupied by missionaries during their yearly tours of the islands.

Nine of these chapels have been declared national monuments, and efforts to preserve them are currently supported by a number of national and international organizations. In July 2000 Unesco voted unanimously to designate 16 Chilote churches as World Heritage sites.

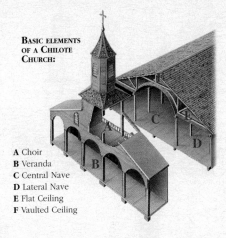

BASIC ELEMENTS OF A CHILOTE CHURCH:

A Choir
B Veranda
C Central Nave
D Lateral Nave
E Flat Ceiling
F Vaulted Ceiling

QUETALCO

APIAO

LLAU LLAO

HUYAR

VILUPULLI (MN)

QUILQUICO (MN)

DETIF (MN)

QUICAVI

CHELIN

QUEHUI

ACHAO (MN)

ALDACHILDO (MN)

DALCAHUE (MN)

QUINCHAO (MN)

NERCON (MN)

RILAN (MN)

CHONCHI (MN)

TENAUN (MN)

IGLESIA DE TENAUN (MN)

Magallanes in 1900

EDIFICIO DE LA GOBERNACION

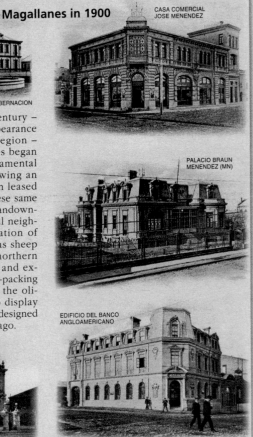

CASA COMERCIAL JOSE MENENDEZ

PALACIO BRAUN MENENDEZ (MN)

EDIFICIO DEL BANCO ANGLOAMERICANO

Beginning in the late 19th century – less than fifty years after the appearance of the first settlements in the region – southern Patagonia or Magallanes began to experience a rapid and fundamental economic transformation. Following an early boom in sheep ranching on leased lands, the government offered these same lands for sale, allowing already landowners to overbid their less powerful neighbors, resulting in the accumulation of ever-greater properties. Finally, as sheep ranching operations spread to northern Patagonia and Tierra del Fuego and expanded to include shipping, meat-packing and other commercial interests, the oligarchs of Punta Arenas strove to display their wealth in opulent mansions designed to compete with the best of Santiago.

PALACIO SARA BROWN (MN)

RELIGION AND MYTHS

Religious Festivals and Ceremonies

By and large, Chile's religious ceremonies and festivals are the country's most visible manifestations of the ongoing fusion of Catholic and indigenous traditions that characterizes life throughout the Andes.

Every church has at least one **patron saint**, and celebrates its **saints' day(s)** with a religious procession. The integration of singing and dancing is most common in the altiplano, where many villages remain empty throughout the better part of the year, coming alive on saints' days with a strange and colorful blend of Andean and Catholic iconography.

Carnaval is celebrated throughout South America, most famously in Brazil and in Oruro, on the Bolivian altiplano. Catholic in origin, it takes place during the last weeks in February, ending on a Tuesday (known as Mardi Gras in New Orleans), 40 days before Easter Sunday. The forty days, known as lent, are a period of abstinence in accordance with Jesus' desert fast, and Carnaval – in its present incarnation – is the last chance for the

LA TIRANA

devout to release any demons, to get their fill before buckling down. Altiplano Carnaval masks are a unique twist on the European custom of Carnaval masquerades. At the end of lent is *Semana Santa* (Holy Week), which is celebrated widely throughout the country, culminating on Easter Sunday.

Other widely celebrated religious festivals and holidays include Christmas (*Navidad* or *Pascua*), *San Pedro* (Patron Saint of fishermen, June 29), and the *Fiesta de Cuasimodo*, held in late March or early April. Notable celebrations of these and other religious festivals are listed under special events in the corresponding regional chapter.

A few religious festivals have attained true pop-culture status, attracting traditional dance groups and thousands of tourists and vendors:

The *Fiesta de la Virgen del Carmen* (July 12-18) in **La Tirana** attracts close to 80,000 people, including dozens of dance troupes in Carnaval masks, pilgrims with their offerings to the Virgin, vendors and tourists. The celebration centers around the Santuario de la Tirana,

FIESTA DE ANDACOLLO - ATLAS DE CLAUDIO GAY, 1854

ANDACOLLO TODAY

FIESTA DE CUASIMOSO, IN THE EARLY 20TH CENTURY

CERAMIC REPRESENTATION
OF RIDER IN THE
FIESTA DE CUASIMODO

where there is a museum displaying dance costumes. Other celebrations at the sanctuary include *Pascua de los Negros* (Jan 5-6) and Semana Santa.

• Copiapó's *Fiesta de La Candelaria* (Feb. 1) draws over 3000 traditional *bailarines chinos* (literally, 'chinese dancers') to the Santuario de la Candelaria. The religious dances combine religious and popular imagery from all over the world.

• In **Andacollo**, set in a narrow canyon in the the heart of Norte Chico mining country, two major festivals have attracted pilgrims and dancers since 1580. The carved wooden Virgin honored by these festivals was apparently the Patron Saint of early La Serena until the Diaguita Indians destroyed the city; an anonymous Spaniard saved the figure and hid it in these hills. For the *Fiesta Grande* (23-27 Dec), some 150,000 of the devout converge on the 1789 Templo Antiguo (home of the Virgen del Rosario, the new patron of the sanctuary) and the unmistakable Templo Grande or Basilico, built in 1893 to accommodate the hordes of pilgrims. The *Fiesta Chica* is a smaller event, held the first Sunday in October.

Mapuche Religion

The modern history of the Mapuche nation is one of adaptation and transformation, and, at the same time, one of remarkable resilience. At the core of this resilience is the Mapuche system of religious beliefs, known collectively as *feyentún*. As ethnographer Ramón Curivíl points out, Mapuche culture is 'eminently religious... Their culture, values, art, music, folklore, cosmovision – in one word their life is religious.'

Feyentún is not exclusive. Indeed, most modern Mapuches actually consider themselves Christians, a seeming paradox that is wonderfully illustrative of the nature of Mapuche religiosity: *feyentún* embraces all that permits contact with the sacred, the mysterious, and the magical. From this viewpoint, all religions are inherently valid.

CANELO

Traditional Mapuche ceremonies are conducted by religious figures known as *machis*, who may be male or female and continue to be among the most important individuals in any community. The largest

RHEWE

and most important ceremony is the *ngillatún*, the central artifact of which is the *rhewe*, a ritual staircase carved from the sacred canelo (*Drymis winteri*), which represents access to the sacred realms overhead. Music is played on the *trutruka*, a wind instrument consisting of a bull's horn attached to long bamboo shaft, and the *kultrún*, a drum painted with ritual designs representative of the Mapuche cosmovision. An important act in fostering community solidarity in the face of increasing acculturation, the *ngillatún* is typically off-limits to outsiders – who are known in mapudungún as *winka*.

Chilote Myths

Isolated for hundreds of years from colonial Chile, caught in a spiritual hinterland between Jesuit orthodoxy and the animistic beliefs of the Huilliche and Chonos Indians, the increasingly *mestizo* population of the Chiloé archipelago developed a singular and occasionally very graphic mythology.

PINCOYA

In the beginning, Chiloé's creation myth recounts, the island was united to the mainland and the world was ruled by two great serpents: *Tenten-vilu*, who ruled the seas, and *Caicai-vilu*, who ruled the ocean. One day *Caicai-vilu* induced the sea to rise, flooding the Central Valley and threatening to submerge the entire island. Finally *Tenten-vilu* intervened, a fantastic battle transpired, and the rise of the waters was halted. But the damage was done; Chiloé was an island.

INVUNCHE

Defeated, *Caicai-vilu* ceded power to an equally unusual creature, the *Millalobo*. Described as having the torso of a man, the lower body of a sea lion, and a face somewhere in between, the golden-fleeced *Millalobo* wooed himself a wife, known as *La Huenchula*, from among the island's

MAPUCHE RHEWE (RITUAL STAIRCASE) WITH VOLCAN LLAIMA AND VOLCAN VILLARRICA IN THE BACGROUND

inhabitants. Together, the unlikely pair had three children: *la Pincoya*, who sows the seeds with fish and shellfish, *la Sirena*, a lovely mermaid, and *El Pincoy*, an extraordinarily handsome cross between a human and a seal.

TRAUCO

Together, the three siblings make sure all runs well in the ocean; when Chilote sailors are lost at sea, they lead them to *El Caleuche*, a ghost ship under the command of Chiloé's many *brujos*, or witches. Often spotted in the fog, *El Caleuche* and its crew bring prosperity to their loved ones and ruin upon those who abuse the sea's resources.

Land-based Chilote myths are equally instructive. *El Trauco* is a repulsive little troll who lives in the forest, and whose gaze, inexplicably, is irresistible to young maidens. *El Trauco* gets the

CAICAI-VILU

blame for most unwanted pregnancies on the island. Even more horrible is *El Basilisco*, a weird rooster-shaped creature with a long serpent's neck. If allowed to hatch from its leathery little chicken's egg, the *Basilisco* will steal into the house nightly, sucking the phlegm from its victim's lungs and throats, leaving them to wither and die, one by one. The only remedy is to burn the house.

Perhaps most hideous, however, is the man-eating *Invunche*, guardian of the witches' cave near Quicaví. Stolen from his human parents at the age of nine days, the *Invunche* was fed on human flesh stolen from the graveyard. Viewed from the front, he would appear to have a single antennae wobbling above his head, which in reality is one of his legs, twisted there by the *brujos* during his brutal metamorphosis.

BASILISCO

The Hain

Often dismissed by early explorers as ignorant, uncivilized savages – James Cook called the Huash Indians 'as miserable a set of people as are this day upon earth' – the hunter-gatherer cultures of Tierra del Fuego were, in fact, an able and highly adapted society with a remarkably complex cosmology. Thanks to the efforts of individuals such as Salesian priest Martín Gusinde and Tomas and Lucas Bridges, extensive ethnographic records and photos allow us to reconstruct the social and ritual life of these fascinating cultures.

One element common to both the Selk'nam and Huash cultures was the male initiation ceremony, known as the *Hain*. In the times of plenty before the

MATAN

whites came to the island, these ceremonies lasted up to a year, and would bring together all the normally combative clans (*haruwens*) in one encampment. During the first days of the ceremony, the male initiates (*kloketens*) were assembled together with the rest of the men in a conical wooden hut (also known as a *Hain*). Here, they were confronted by masked 'spirits' they had been taught to fear since childhood, and forced to unmask them. Having determined that the 'spirits' were in fact no less human than themselves, the kloketens were told a story which takes place in the mythical time (*hoowín*) of their ancestors. The story goes basically like this:

ULEN

Long ago, Sun and Moon lived on earth as husband and wife. Like the other women, Moon was a tyrannous wife, forcing Sun to hunt, cook and even care for the children. In order to maintain power over the men, the women had invented a ruse ceremony in which they would dress up and act out the roles of vicious, vengeant spirits. The spirits – whom the men thought to be real – made it clear that if they challenged the women's hierarchy, both they and the women would be mercilessly punished, even killed. The most terrifying of the spirits was *Xalpen*, who lived in the earth and would appear in a burst of flame visible from outside the hut, demanding meat and threatening to slaughter the women if her needs were not met. Of course, all this was an act put on by Moon and the other women, but the men were convinced and continued in abject servitude.

One day, Sun happened to overhear two of the women talking, and realized that the ceremony was all a hoax, and one day at his cue the men rose up in the midst of the ceremony and attacked the women. All the adult women were killed save Moon, who escaped into the heavens, pursued by Sun. Now that they had the upper hand, the men staged a ceremony of their own, painting their bodies and carving elaborate masks to represent a whole cast of spirits. And to the present day the women had remained subservient. The only thing was that they could never know that the Haín was anything but real.

The *Hain* was part ritual, part theatre, in which the women themselves actually participated, preparing the paint for the actors but nonetheless sustaining the belief that the spirits were real. For months on end, the men lounged in the hut or set out on long hunting excursions, staging periodic presentations in the 'stage' space that separated the hut from the women's camp. Each spirit had its own characteristic personality and gestures, and great actors from past Hains were recalled and emulated. One spirit, *Shoort*, constantly haunted the women's camp, poking and hitting the women, disrupting their camp, and basically making a nuisance of himself. Others in the cast were silly, shy, beautiful or insane.

The climax of the *Hain* occurred when *Xalpen* arose from her underground abode (with a show of fire and smoke emerging from the ritual hut), 'killed' the *kloketens* initiates, and returned to her lair. Later the *kloketens* were 'restored' to life and thenceforth considered *maars*, adult men.

The last *Hain* on Tierra del Fuego was held in 1923, during the decline of the Selk'nam. Father Martín

KATAIX

Gusinde was present during the ceremony, and managed to create a series of remarkable photographs of the highly ritualized body paintings and masks created by this unique culture. Today, the Museo Martín Gusinde in Puerto Williams features a replica of the traditional hut used in the Hain.

TANU

INDUSTRY AND DEVELOPMENT

MINNING ACTIVITY IN THE COLONIAL CHILE, BY SCHMIDTMEYER

Mining history

The spice trade may prompted the discovery of the Americas, but it was the search for precious metals – especially gold and silver – that served as the principal motivation for their initial exploration. Pizarro's windfall bounty of Inca gold and the colossal deposits of Cerro Rico in Potosí seemed too good to be true, while the abundance of labor – thanks to the convenient *encomiendas* system – made mining in the Colonial era extremely lucrative. Mining activity in colonial Chile consisted largely of low-capital, labor intensive exploitation of gold placer mines in the central region, in La Serena, Combarbala, and the Huasco Valley.

Silver production in colonial Chile was of minor importance, amounting to a mere 270 metric tons – small change compared to the 7,800 metric tons produced in the 19th century alone. Far more significant to the colonial economy were the various industries – leather, grain, and shipping among them – associated with the Spanish mine at Potosí. Of 165 mines registered at the end of the 18th century, 67 were gold, 35 were silver, 61 were copper and the rest quicksilver or mercury.

Following independence, the nascent republic undertook the exploration of its territory, triggering a series of important discoveries that would transform the nation in a matter of decades. In 1811 silver was discovered at Agua Amarga, near Vallenar, and in 1832 prospector Juan Godoy revealed his discovery of silver at Chañarcillo, near Copiapó – which turned out to be the third most productive silver deposit in the Americas. In three years, the population of Copiapó tripled to 12,000, as prospectors were lured by tales such as that of a single 2,700-kilo chunk of nearly pure silver. By

1855 Chañarcillo was already in decline, but copper, coal, and nitrate (see 🔖) were coming into their own.

Copper, the preferred metal of native populations, wasn't mined significantly until after independence. Early 19th century copper mining focused upon the high-grade oxide ores of the *Norte Chico*, which were smelted in rustic ovens fired by bellows; in 1830 Charles Lambert's 'reverberating oven'

RUINS OF THE FOUNDRY AT HUANCHACA, ANTOFAGASTA

PIRQUINEROS

Small-scale mining continues in mountain towns of the Norte Chico such as Andacollo and Combarbala. Employing techniques virtually unchanged since the 19th century, independent miners known as *pirquineros* grind their ore in rented *trapiche* mills. The largest gold particles remain at the bottom of the trapiche, while medium-sized particles are attracted to mercury-covered copper plates. The smallest particles are extracted using chemical flotation techniques similar to those used in large-scale mining. The remains are sold to processing plants for further extraction.

revolutionized the industry, allowing the utilization of significantly lower-percentage ores. From 1840-1850, copper from the Norte Chico accounted for 30% of world totals, a figure which grew to 44% in the 1860's. Meanwhile, railroads and smelters created a growing demand for coal, which was extracted from Matias Cousiño's mines at Lota, south of Concepción, transforming this area into the country's primary industrial center during the late 19th century.

At the beginning of the 20th century,

worldwide copper demand began to grow exponentially. The industrial revolution had begun in Europe, and copper was needed for telegraph and telephone lines, electric railways, and other electric installations. Supply met demand in 1911, when the Guggenheim brothers of New York City – already big players in the nitrate industry – bought the Chuquicamata mine. Incorporating high-capital, large-scale mining techniques developed in the States, the Guggenheims began to exploit Chuqui's unfathomable reserves of subterranean low-grade porphyry ore. Under the management of the US-based Anaconda Corporation, who bought the mine from the Guggenheims, copper production at Chuquicamata increased by a factor of 22 between 1915 and 1922.

By the 1960's, Anaconda and Kennecott (owner of El Teniente) accounted for 60% of Chile's total exports and 80% of tax revenues. In 1971 the copper industry was nationalized, and the two mines fell under the ownership of the Corporación del Cobre de Chile (Codelco), which in 1973 paid the two companies for their loss of assets. Still the largest mines in a country which contains an estimated 25% of world copper reserves and relies upon copper for some 40% of all exports, El Teniente and Chuquicamata are both open to visitors. You can also tour the coal mines in Lota, which extend for several kilometers beneath the seafloor.

COPPER
FOUNDRY

AERIAL VIEW OF THE OLD MINER'S CAMP AT EL TENIENTE, TAKEN IN THE 1950'S

• Mining Tours of Chuquicamata pg 297

• Mining Tours of El Teniente pg.407

• Mining Tours in Parque El Lota pg. 425

The Nitrate Boom:
Oficinas Salitreras

No industry has had as great and visible effect upon the landscape, history and architecture of northern Chile as that of nitrate, which near the turn of the century accounted for over 50% of the country's tax base.

Used by Indians to fertilize the river valleys of the Norte Grande, nitrate or *salitre* was largely neglected by the Spanish, who concentrated their energies on gold and silver extraction; the once-abundant guano reserves of the Peruvian offshore islands fulfilled the colonies' agricultural needs. Not until the early 1800's, when German scientist Tadeo Haenke made possible the conversion of sodium nitrate into potassium nitrate (an important basic ingredient in the manufacture of gunpowder) was a commercial market found for *salitre*. Haenke's discovery coincided perfectly with the era of Latin American revolutions, and mining grew rapidly in the nitrate fields of the Tarapacá province, at that time part of Perú. Meanwhile, the industrialization of agriculture in Europe created a new demand for fertilizer, and in 1830 the first shipment of nitrate left Iquique bound for Europe and the US. Between 1840 and 1870, production of nitrate grew from 73,000 tons to 500,000 tons, and by 1917, three million tons were being exported annually from the *Norte Grande*.

Oficina salitrera „Agua Santa" Canchas de Salitre

At first, the raw material, known as *caliche*, was mined only where it occurred in very high concentrations, 50-60% sodium nitrate by weight. Independent miners used dynamite to blast apart deposits of *caliche*, the raw mineral, and then carted it to the buyer's office (*oficina*), where the *caliche* was dissolved in boiling water which was later evaporated, leaving concentrates of nitrate and iodine.

The *oficina* fires were fueled by salt and drought-resistant trees such as tamarugo, algarrobo, and chañar, eliminating the north's few forests. Water was brought by boat from Arica to Iquique, and then by mule-cart to the desolate *oficinas* - and when the highest concentrations of *caliche* were exhausted, the *oficina* pulled up stakes and moved on. But with technological developments continually lowering the minimum nitrate content, *oficinas salitreras* multiplied throughout the Tarapacá province, and railroads linked the desert and the coast.

Until 1866, nitrate was an exclusively Peruvian industry. In this year, however, Chilean José Santos Ossa received exclusive rights from the Bolivian government to mine and export nitrate in the Antofagasta region. Together with Gibbs House, an English company with nitrate interests in Perú, Ossa began developed Antofagasta as a nitrate port, and in the following eight years the city grew from 300 to 8500 inhabitants, of whom

NITRATE WORKERS

85% were Chilean. But in 1879 the Bolivian government raised taxes on Ossa's Antofagasta Nitrate and Railway Co, and when the company refused to pay, seized its assets. The Chilean government responded by occupying Antofagasta – the first act in the War of the Pacific.

Meanwhile, in 1875 Perú had nationalized its own nitrate industry, issuing bonds that it was later unable to honor because of a failed loan. The bonds plummeted in value, and when Perú sided with Bolivia in the War of the Pacific, British speculators anticipating a Chilean victory bought them up at as little as 10% of their value. The gamble paid off: after the war Chile honored the Peruvian bonds, and the British share of the nitrate market grew from 16% to 70%. The biggest winner was 'Nitrate King' John Thomas North, who by 1889 owned 15 nitrate companies, four railroads and a water company, among other interests.

Following the war, the industry continued to rise, now faster than ever, and by 1910 northern Chile was exporting some 65% of the world's supply of nitrate fertilizer. The Georgian architecture of Iquique's historic district and the Neoclassic construc-

THE MARKET AT OFICINA SANTIAGO HUMBERSTONE (MN).

tions of downtown Santiago both date from the so-called 'Nitrate Era.'

By 1917 the nitrate industry had reached its peak, but a fall was imminent. Naval blockades during the early years of WWI took a big bite out of exports, and though a resurgent gunpowder market gave new impetus to the industry, the invention of synthetic nitrate signaled the beginning of the end. As Chile's share of the world nitrate market plummeted (to a mere 10% in 1930), 90 of 134 nitrate *oficinas* stopped producing, and tens of thousands of workers were left jobless. Only the largest nitrate plants – such as that at Maria Elena, inaugurated in 1930 and still in operation – could survive in this new climate. For the most part, all that is left are the abandoned *salitreras* and the fading glory of the nitrate ports.

AROUND IQUIQUE
Oficina Santiago Humberstone

This is the best preserved of the dozens of abandoned *oficinas salitreras* along the Panamerican near Iquique. Much of the original machinery and buildings are still in place, preserved by the total aridity of the Atacama Desert. Historical information in English and Spanish and guided tours (Sat and Sun only) may be available; if not,

OFICINA SANTA LAURA

SWIMMING POOL AT OFICINA SANTIAGO HUMBERSTONE (MN)

ask at the gate for directions to the theater (the seats are still in it), the swimming pool (made from an old ship's hull), and the tennis club.

AROUND ANTOFAGASTA

Oficina de Chacabuco

Built between 1922 and 1924, this was the last and greatest of the 'Shanks system' *oficinas*; in 1938, 7000 people inhabited this self-contained company town. A highlight is the Teatro Filarmónica, restored in 1992.

Hours: Tue-Sun 10-17.
Entrance: $1000, $500 children.

María Elena, Pedro de Valdivia

These are the only two functioning nitrate plants in northern Chile, built in 1926 and 1931 respectively, using the patented Guggenheim system and large economies of scale to exploit low-yield *caliche*. Pedro de Valdivia's town was abandoned in 1996, though the area surrounding the plaza has been declared a national monument. Maria Elena is the site of the Museo Arqueológico e Histórico, with historical information and exhibits on the native cultures of the upper Río Loa.

Open Mon-Sat 9-13, 16-19, Sun 10-13, 17-20.

Nitrate Tokens

The use of tokens in Chile originally dates from the Colonial era, when most manufactured coins were of excessive value for daily use. In the remote nitrate *oficinas*, each company essentially minted its own currency, creating a closed economic system that obliged workers to return almost all their earnings to their employer. A total over 3000 designs have been catalogued: the first single-sided bronze and copper disks began to appear in 1850, and the first real mintings began in 1865, producing tokens in copper, bronze, nickel, aluminum, lead and *alpaca* (an alloy of copper, nickel, and zinc). Especially noteworthy are tokens made of *ebonita*, made of fired rubber and dyed a variety of colors; originally ordered from abroad, from about 1880 all ebonita tokens were minted in Valparaíso. Production ended in 1924 when a new law required that salaries be paid in legal currency.

OFICINA DE CHACABUCO (MN),
IN THE CENTER OF THE PHOTO IS THE THEATER

SULPHUR PLANT, REFINERY, AND FOUNDRY

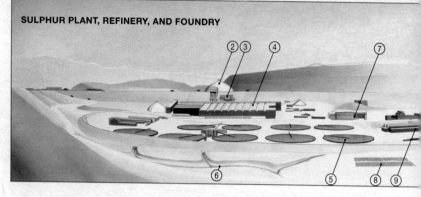

FLOW DIAGRAM

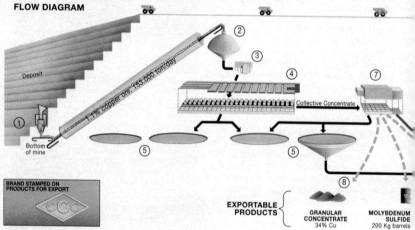

BRAND STAMPED ON PRODUCTS FOR EXPORT

EXPORTABLE PRODUCTS

GRANULAR CONCENTRATE
34% Cu

MOLYBDENUM SULFIDE
200 Kg barrels

Chuquicamata

Chuquicamata is the world's largest open-pit mine: 4,300m long, 3,000m wide, and 720m deep. Over 500,000 tons of raw materials are extracted from the pit every day, leading to an annual production of 600,000 tons of refined copper. Though guided tours no longer visit the smelting plant, the following diagram explains the smelting process.

1- Primary crusher: Raw material of 1.1% copper content is crushed and sent via subterranean conveyor belt to the

2- Collection dome, which is sealed to minimize dust. From here the crushed material passes to the

3- Secondary crusher, and from here to the

4- Concentration plant. Two processes are carried out here:

A- WET MILLING: Crushed material is mixed with water and hundreds of ball bearings and milled between huge metal cylinders, forming a wet paste.

B- FLOTATION CELLS: The paste is transferred into hundreds of rectangular tanks, where it is mixed with more water and chemicals and injected brusquely with air. Copper particles adhere to air and form

a dense layer of foam containing 32% copper and 1% molybdenum, silver, and gold, known as collective concentrate. The tailings from the bottom of the cell are sent to the

5- Thickening tanks, where the water is treated for reuse in flotation cells. Waste material flows down the

6- Relief channel to holding tanks in the desert.

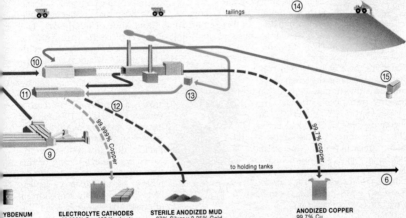

**YBDENUM
RIOXIDE**
Kg barrels

ELECTROLYTE CATHODES
99.999% Cu - 155 Kg sheets
2,2 Ton bales

STERILE ANODIZED MUD
27% Silver y 0.25% Gold

ANODIZED COPPER
99.7% Cu

7- Molybdenum plant. Collective concentrate is subjected to another chemical flotation process in order to extract the 1% molybdenum. Final products from this plant include Molybdenum sulfide and Molybdenum oxide. A certain portion of the concentrate is transferred to the

8- Solar drying fields, which produce granular concentrate for transport to national and international smelting plants.

9- Drying plant. The greater portion of the concentrate is transformed into

dry concentrate, containing 35% copper. The next step is the

10- Copper smelter, where the dry concentrate is processed first in a Teniente conversion oven and then in a refinery oven, producing plates (known as Anodized copper or Blister) measuring 1m x 1m x 2 cm thick and containing 99.98% copper. These plates are then transferred to the

11- Electrolyte refinery, where they are subjected to electrolysis in tanks of sulfuric acid and thereby transformed into electrolyte cathodes, which are exported for conversion into

copper wire. The remains (known as anodized mud) are sent to the

12- Noble metals plant, which produces a concentrate containing 27% silver and 25% gold.

13- Sulfuric Acid Plant: extracts sulphur from the smoke produced in the smelting process and produces sulfuric acid for use in electrolysis.

14- Tailings: Composed of waste material deposited at a rate of over 355,000 tons a day.

15- Oxygen Plant: Separated from the rest of the plant to reduce risk of explosion.

PUENTE PETRUFIQUEN,
RAILROAD BRIDGE, CIRCA 1900

Chile's Railroads

HENRY MEIGGS

Like most technological innovations in Chile, the growth of the railroad began with a foreign initiative. In this case it was Massachusetts native William Wheelwright, who passed through the town of Copiapó in 1840 to sing the praises of the great steam-powered railways that were revolutionizing transport in the US and Europe. By 1851, Wheelwright had rallied investors and Chile had its first railroad, the third in South America: 81km of track between Copiapó and Caldera, powered by a Norris Brothers 4-4-0. Today the oldest surviving locomotive on the continent, the *Copiapoa* is currently on display on the campus of the University of Atacama.

MATEO CLARK, BUILDER OF THE FERROCARRIL TRASANDINO

Soon new railroad projects sprung up throughout the country. Mining was the driving force in the north, where lateral lines leading inland from the coast were linked by the costly (and never very effective) *Red Norte*; in its finest hour, the Santiago-Iquique run took a grueling 95 hours. In central Chile, North American Henry Meiggs brought the costly Santiago-Valparaíso line, with its multiple bridges and tunnels, to hard-fought completion in 1863. Later, tourist trains from the capital spawned seaside resorts in Cartagena and Pichilemu, while the southern *Red Sur* facilitated the export of forest products and contributed to the rapid growth of Temuco and Puerto Montt, to which rail service arrived in 1913.

The most impressive engineering feats, however, were those that connected Chile with their trans-Andean neighbors. The building of the *Ferrocarril TransAndino*, which connected Los Andes with Mendoza, was a twenty-year effort finally concluded in 1908; its long cog sections were surmounted by an English-made Kitson-Meyer now on display at Santiago's Museo Ferroviario. Designed to provide a direct overland link betweeen Buenos Aires and the Pacific, the railway lost significance with the opening of the Panama Canal. It never made money, left off passenger service in 1971, and finally retired from international service in 1984.

In the north, the Calama – Uyuni line, united under ownership of the Antofagasta and Bolivia Railway Company in 1909, is the only trans-Andean railway still in operation. Today as always, the ride across the altiplano is long, slow and bitterly cold, with an interminable wait at the border while a Chilean engine is swapped for a Bolivian one. Culturally, however, the experience can't be beat, as the train is usually packed with Bolivian Indians.

LOCOMOTORA 3349

Arica historically had two international lines, but the one to La Paz – completed in 1913 out of an obligation to provide the Bolivian capital with port access – no longer carries passengers. Still, you can check out the old engine, a 1924 German Esslingen, at the train station in Arica. Daily trains still connect Arica with Tacna, Perú. The trip lasts 1.5 hours (significantly longer than by road) but the ambiance is worth it.

Other functioning passenger lines in Chile include narrow-gauge service from Tacna to Concepción and daily service south from Santiago as far as Temuco, using classy Linke-Hoffman/ Breslau sleeper cars imported from Germany between 1929 and 1935.

LAGO RAPEL HYDROPOWER PLANT

HYDROPOWER

In this era when free-flowing rivers are becoming ever scarcer, few environmental issues incite as much controversy as large-scale dam projects, and Chile – with its chronic power shortages and vast hydropower potential – is at center stage in the issue. Endesa, the formerly state-owned power company now owned by Spanish interests, reportedly has a folder of some 220 potential hydropower projects planned for Chilean rivers.

The most famous and controversial dams are those on the Río Biobío, which for the past decade has been a rallying point for Chilean environmental and indigenous rights groups. Six separate dams are planned for the upper Biobío watershed, capable of producing 2700 megawatts of energy – more than doubling the country's current output. The energy is intended to benefit industry and urban communities in south-central Chile, while in the upper Biobío, the dams would flood the ancestral lands of the Pehuenche Indians, one of the most traditional indigenous communities left in the country. Defense of the Biobío has focused on the rights of the Pehuenche via Chile's Indigenous Rights Act.

The first of the dams, Pangue, entered into operation in 1996. This was the only dam approved by the World Bank, which originally provided funding for the project; yet without the further dams upriver, Pangue can't work at capacity. Construction has already begun on the second dam, Ralco, which would displace many more Pehuenches to unsuitable highland areas and cut off flow to the river's only remaining rapids of any size.

Meanwhile, environmentalists and river runners have spotted a darker threat on the horizon. For years, rumors have been circulating of Endesa's plans to harness the still vaster potential of the Río Futaleufú, the famous whitewater river in the Palena province of Chilean Patagonia. As it turns out, Endesa owns a very significant portion of water rights on the Futaleufú: with 622 m³/sec at one point and 560m³/sec at another, Endesa owns enough water to build a 910 megawatt dam right now. Local and international interest groups are currently attempting to consolidate public opinon, mobilize resistance, and above all promote sustainable economic development in the Futaleufú valley, so that locals will have some ammunition when and if Endesa comes knocking. The failure of the Indigenous Rights Act to save the Biobío has made it more than clear that mere rhetoric won't do for the Futa. For more information or to contribute to the campaign to save the Futaleufú, contact the Futafriends at www.futafriends.org.

TRANQUE SLOMAN (MN) NEAR QUILLAGUA

THE ARTS

For more suggestions of Chilean prose literature, see the suggested reading section on pg. 44.

GABRIELA MISTRAL (1889-1957)

South America's first Nobel prize-winning poet, Gabriela Mistral was born in the Elqui Valley and raised in the tiny village of Monte Grande. Raised by her sister, the village postmistress and schoolteacher, Mistral (whose given name was Lucila Godoy Alcayaga) developed an early fondness for poetry, and for anonymity: her first works, published in a local periodical, were signed *Alguien* ('Someone'), *Soledad* ('Solitude'), and *Alma* ('Soul').

By the age of 15, the young poet had begun her career in education, and at 17 she met Romelio Ureta, a 23-year-old railroad employee, her first love. Three years later Romelio committed suicide in Coquimbo, an event grimly recalled in *To See Him Again*:

> *And shall it be never be again, never?*
> *Not on nights filled*
> *with tremblings of stars, or by the pure light*
> *of virginal dawns, or on afternoons of immolation?*
>
> *Never, at the edge of any pale pathway*
> *that borders the field, or beside any*
> *tremulous fountain white under the moon?*
>
> *Never, beneath the tangled tresses of the forest*
> *where, calling out to him, nigh descended on me?*
> *Nor in the cavern that returns my echoing outcry?*
>
> *Oh, no! Just to see him again, no matter where –*
> *in little patches of sky or in the seething vortex,*
> *beneath placid moons or in a livid*
> *horror!*
>
> *And, together with him, to be all springtimes*
> *and all winters, entwined in one anguished knot*
> *around his bloodstained neck!*

The latent morbidity of Mistral's work (in 1914 she published a collection entitled 'Sonnets on Death,' and in 1922 another called 'Desolation') contrasted sharply with the bright enthusiasm she showed for her work as a teacher. In Chile, the poet worked in public schools from Antofagasta to Punta Arenas, and in 1922, she was invited to México in order to participate in the country's educational reform and the organization of public libraries.

In 1926, Mistral was assigned a post in the League of Nations, and beginning in 1932 she filled a series of consular posts in Italy, Spain, Portugal, and Brazil. Travelling, writing, and continuing to work for children everywhere, she lived the life of that noblest of Latin American personalities: the poet/diplomat.

With the Nobel Prize in 1945, Mistral's fame passed to an entirely new level, and further awards and honorary degrees – combined with her ongoing consular work – kept the poet continually on the move. In 1957 Gabriela Mistral died in Hempstead, New York, but not before willing the rights all her works published in South America to the children of Monte Grande, her childhood home. Mistral's mausoleum and the Casa Escuela y Correo, where she grew up, are both open to visitors.

MISTRAL RECEIVING THE NOBEL PRIZE IN 1945

PABLO NERUDA (1904-1973)

Known to his friends as *el vate* (the seer), to himself as an 'anti-intellectual,' and to Gabriel García Márquez as 'the greatest poet of the twentieth century, in any language', Pablo Neruda wrote with the voice of his country and his continent. In addition to being Chile's second winner of the Nobel Prize for Literature, he is also thought to be one of the most-read writers in human history, thanks in part to enormous editions in Chinese and Russian.

Born in Parral, Neruda (whose real name was Neftalí Ricardo Reyes) attended school in Temuco, where he fell briefly under the tutelage of Gabriela Mistral. Mistral helped him get a scholarship to study French in Santiago, where he fell in with writers and intellectuals in a scenario vividly captured in Isabel Allende's House of the Spirits (in which Neruda is referenced simply as 'the Poet'). His *Veinte Poemas de Amor y una Canción Desesperada* – which remains his favorite work among Latin American audiences –came out in 1924.

Named to the Chilean Consular Service in 1927, Neruda began a long series of travels throughout the Far East, in Burma, Celon, Djakarta, and Singapore. *Residencia en la Tierra*, published in 1933, reflects Neruda's lonely, somewhat disillusioned state of mind during this period:

I wander from one point to another, absorb illusions,
converse with the tailors in their nests:
and these, time and again, in a cold, fatal voice
Sing out and drive off the curses.
(from *Walking Around*)

Serving as consul in Spain, Neruda made friends with García Lorca and his circle of highly political poets. When civil war broke out (and Lorca killed), Neruda was forced to resign his consulship but continued working to help political refugees and speak out against Franco and for the republic.

Upon returning from Spain, Neruda joined the communist party, and his work assumed a more political slant. The deaths of Lorca and other friends in Spain haunted his work, as is evident in these excepts from *I'm Explaining a Few Things*:

My house was called
The house of the flowers, because everywhere
Geraniums exploded: it was
A lovely house
With dogs and little boys.

Raul, do you remember?
Do you remember, Rafael?
Federico, do you remember
Below the earth,
Do you remember my house with balconies where
The light of July drowned with a mouthful of flowers?

Brother, brother!

Right before us I have seen the blood
Of Spain rise up
To drown us in a single wave
Of pride and knives!

You will ask why his poetry
Doesn't speak of dreams, of the leaves,
Of the great volcanoes of his native land.

Come and see the blood in the streets.
Come and see
The blood in the streets.
Come and see the blood
In the streets!

NERUDA'S HOUSE (MN)
AT ISLA NEGRA

Despite his increasing allegiance to the Communists, Neruda's lyric elegance and generous vision allowed him to avoid the pitfalls of the political poet. *Odas Elementales* – with its odes to everyday items such as socks or onion – was supposedly written out of a perceived obligation to write to the masses, but the lines reverberate with a fullness that is reminiscent of haiku.

The pinnacle of Neruda's art is generally though to be the *Heights of Machu Picchu*, in which Neruda retells the history of the South American continent. Richly grounded in geography and myth, this series of poems represents the embodiment of Neruda's uniquely American vision: 'I thought about ancient American man,' he writes. 'I saw his ancient struggles linked with present struggles.'

In 1948, while serving in the Senate, Neruda published an open letter denouncing President González Videla (who had outlawed the Communist Party) and was forced to go into hiding, escaping across the Andes into Argentina. Once Videla's term had expired, the poet returned to Chile and continued his political activities while setting up his home in Isla Negra, the most famous and whimsical of his three houses. In 1969 he was actually on the presidential ballot, but stepped down in deference to his friend

NERUDA'S 1971 NOBEL

Salvador Allende, who upon election sent Neruda to France as his ambassador. When issued the Nobel Prize in 1971, Neruda was living in France, but returned to Chile upon hearing of the military coup. He died Sept. 23, 1973, 12 days after Allende.

Today, Pablo Neruda is the only thing many people know about Chile. His houses – La Chascona in Santiago, La Sebastiana in Valparaíso, and Isla Negra, on the coast south of Valparaíso – have been transformed into museums, and are open to the public. All are well worth a visit, reflecting the poet's eclectic style and packrat tendencies.

NICANOR PARRA (1914)

Two Nobels and counting...... who will be the next Chilean poet to receive the call from Sweden? Some in Chile's literary community think it should be Nicanor Parra, a physicist/poet best known for his so-called 'antipoetry,' a style defined by the poet as 'maximum content, minimum words.... economy of language, no metaphors, no literary figures.'

Roller Coaster

For half a century
Poetry was the paradise
Of the solemn fool.
Until I came along
And built my roller coaster.

Go up, if you feel like it.
It's not my fault if you come down
Bleeding from your nose and mouth.

THE CUECA

Chile's national dance, the *cueca*, is an essential element of the September 18 *Fiestas Patrias* (Independence Day), and can be observed at many lesser local events – basically anytime that traditional music is being played. Reputedly introduced to the country by a Spanish battalion of African slaves, the *cueca* in its most classic Chilean form is performed by decked-out *huasos* in ponchos (*chamantos*), spurs, and the traditional straw hat or *chupaya*. In a pinch, however, the only absolutely necessary implements are the bandanas wielded by each partner, alternately twirled extravagantly above the head and clasped coquettishly behind the back. In Santiago, you can catch nightly performances of the *cueca* at Los Adobes de Argomedo (Metro Irarrazabal, ☎ (2)2222104).

THE *ZAMACUECA*
OIL PAINTING
BY M.A. CARO

NUEVA CANCIÓN:
THE NEW SONG MOVEMENT

Dating from the early 1960's, *nueva canción* is part protest music, part folk music: a poignant and heartfelt expression of solidarity discontent with Latin American power politics and inequality. In Chile, the movement got its start with singer and songwriter Violeta Parra, who collected peasants' songs and blended them with traditional Andean instruments such as the *charango* and the *quena* (pan flute). Despite her suicide in 1967, Violeta's legacy inspired her children, Angel and Isabel, to open the *Peña de los Parra*, a legendary nightclub where the gifted singer and songwriter Victor Jara often performed.

Brutally assassinated by the 1973 military junta, Jara is among *nueva canción's* best-known and best-loved artists. His fate was intended as a warning to other musicians of his creed: songs of protest would not be tolerated under the new regime. Groups such as Inti Illimani and Illapu, however, continued to perform in exile, raising consciousness of the military coup, while fans at home in Chile, Argentina, Uruguay and other Latin American countries continued to learn the forbidden songs by heart. Today, the common Chilean's repertoire of memorized songs – many of these songs of protest – is a subtle but impressive reminder of the repression of a the past.

REGIONAL SPECIALTIES

Northern Chile

ALTIPLANO FOOD is not the most flavorful, but those looking for an experience should try alpaca or llama steaks (ask in Parinacota), *charqui* (dried alpaca or llama meat) and *chuño* (freeze dried potatoes). Those suffering from altitude sickness should look for *chachacoma*, which is made into tea or simply crushed and its odor inhaled.

MANGOS

TROPICAL AND CITRUS FRUITS (including lemons and limes, oranges, grapefruit, guayavas, and mangos) are grown in sierra oases such as Camiña, Mamiña, and Pica, all located east of Iquique.

Excellent **OLIVES** and small-batch **OLIVE OIL** are produced in the Huasco Valley, especially in Freirina. Also look for locally-produced Horcón Quemado *gran pisco*; you can visit the distillery in San Félix Mon-Sat during business hours.

The Elqui valley is famous in Chile for its **SWEETS** and **FRUIT**; look for fresh chirimoya, dried figs, and fresh, canned or candied papayas. Another regional specialty is white *manjar* or *dulce de leche*. These products are available in La Serena's La Recova market, as well as in most towns in the Elqui Valley.

The Elqui and Limarí Valleys are the center of Chile's *pisco*-producing region. Though you may purchase most varieties of *pisco* almost anywhere in the country, here you may visit the distilleries and sample their distinct varieties.

- **PISCOTECA PISCO CONTROL**, in La Serena on Rengifo just north of Brazil. Hours: Tue-Sat 1030-1330, 1530-1930. Sun 11-1430.
- **PISCO CAPEL**, in Vicuña. Hours: Jan-Feb: Mon-Sun, 0930-1800. Mar-Dec: Mon-Fri 0930-1200, 1430-1900, Sat-Sun, holidays 0930-1230.
- **EL SOLAR DE PISCO TRES ERRES**, in Pisco Elqui. The oldest distillery in the Elqui valley, producer of Pisco Tres Erres. Free tours Mon-Sat 1030-1230, 1430-1830.
- **PISCO CONTROL** has two plants in the Limarí valley, one at the eastern end of Sotaquí, the other just east of Monte Patria. For visits, contact Pisco Control's main distillery in La Serena (☎ (51)207800).

PISCO SOUR CHILENO
(chilean pisco sour)
serves 4

- 2 cups Chilean Pisco (35°)
- 1/4 cup corn syrup
- 1/2 cup lemon or lime juice
- 1/2 teaspoon finely grated lemon zest
- 1 egg white
- Crushed ice to taste

Shake all the ingredients in a cocktail mixer until foamy. Pour into cocktail glasses. Serve immediately.

Huge **SCALLOPS** are cultivated and sold (both live on the half shell and shelled in one-kilo bags for takeaway) at the seafood market on the south side of the peninsula at Tongoy.

CHIRIMOYAS

PEPINOS

PAPAYAS

SCALLOP

Local farmers in many parts of the Norte Chico produce exquisite *queso de cabra* (**GOAT CHEESE**) during spring and early summer (Sept-Dec). If buying locally, be circumspect with sanitation standards, and bear in mind that in reality goats are an ecological disaster, removing the very roots of the grasses they feed on and contributing to desertification.

Pisco: History and Production

Though the name *pisco* is relatively unknown in the US and Europe, the drink itself is fairly common: known as *grappa* in Italy and *raki* in Greece, distilled grapes are a staple liquor in most Mediterranean climates.

Chileans and Peruvians argue endlessly over who really invented pisco. Chilean lore maintains that the drink was developed in response to the continued failure of sweet wines or 'musts' from La Serena and Copiapó to survive shipment to Potosí in the 16th century. Distillation solved the problem, creating a strong, flavorful alcohol, and when El Callao (Perú) became a dry port, the neighboring port of Pisco began to receive the contraband spirits, giving the drink its name. Another theory asserts that the name is derived from the Quechua word for the conical vessels in which the liquor was transported.

In 1931, during the presidency of General Carlos Ibáñez del Campo, pisco was declared a 'denomination of origin' for the alcohol distilled from Moscatel grapes in Regions III and IV. In 1939, the town of Unión in the Elqui Valley changed its name to Pisco Elqui, effectively blocking a Peruvian attempt to acquire international exclusivity to the name Pisco.

Today, *pisco* is a mainstay of Chilean popular culture. Most commonly served to tourists as a *pisco sour*, it is more often consumed in bars and at parties with Coca-Cola – a concoction known as a *piscola*. Of 60 million bottles produced annually, 90% of those are consumed internally, which works out to something like 4.5 bottles per capita.

Climate and Soils: Drier and hotter than the wine-producing valleys of central Chile, with more alkaline and less water-retentive soils, the valleys of Chile's III and IV region produce slow-growing grapes with high sugar content.

Grape Varieties: Of a total of 13 varieties of grapes utilized in pisco production, the most important are Moscatel de Alejandría or Blanca Italia, Moscatel Rosada or Moscatel de Pastilla, Moscatel de Austria, Pedro Jiménez, and Torontel. Some 10,000 hectares are planted with these vines.

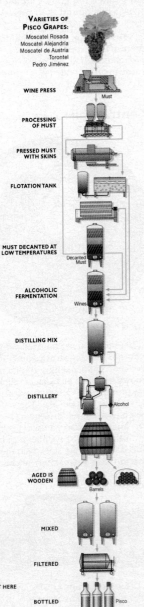

VARIETIES OF PISCO GRAPES:
Moscatel Rosada
Moscatel Alejandría
Moscatel de Austria
Torontel
Pedro Jiménez

WINE PRESS — Must

PROCESSING OF MUST

PRESSED MUST WITH SKINS

FLOTATION TANK

MUST DECANTED AT LOW TEMPERATURES — Decanted Must

ALCOHOLIC FERMENTATION — Wines

DISTILLING MIX

DISTILLERY — Alcohol

AGED IS WOODEN — Barrels

MIXED

FILTERED

BOTTLED — Pisco

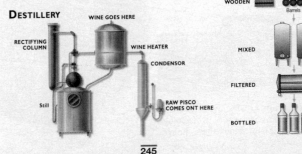

DESTILLERY

WINE GOES HERE

RECTIFYING COLUMN

WINE HEATER

CONDENSOR

Still

RAW PISCO COMES ONT HERE

FERMENTATION: Grape harvest (*vendimia*) lasts from mid-February to the end of May, after which the grapes are measured for sugar content and then pressed and fermented as an ordinary wine.

DISTILLATION: The fermented wine is then transferred to copper stills and brought to a boil; the vapors produced are subsequently condensed, forming a liquid of 55-65% alcohol.

AGING: The distilled *pisco* is aged in barrels, usually of American oak, for 3-6 months.

FINAL PREPARATION: After aging, distinct varieties of pisco are mixed for flavor and aroma. The mixed product is then diluted with distilled water to reach the various grades at which *pisco* is sold commercially: *Tradicional* 30° and 32°, *Reservado* 35°, *Especial* 40°, and *Gran Pisco* of 43°, 46°, and 50°. Finally, the finished *pisco* is filtered and bottled.

Central Chile

DULCES CHILENOS

Scattered along the Panamerican Highway near La Ligua are some 400 white-frocked vendors selling traditional sweets known as DULCES DE LA LIGUA. Similar sweets are produced in Curacaví, on the road from Santiago to Viña del Mar. The vendors often board buses to sell their goods.

MIEL DE PALMA, a sweet syrup made from the sap of the Chilean palm, is produced from private stock near the palm forests in Ocoa. You can buy miel de palma in most major supermarkets.

MIEL DE PALMA

EMPANADAS and fresh clay oven-baked breads called **TORTILLAS** are sold by seemingly numberless vendors in stands along the road

to the Cajón del Maipo. Be aware that not all empanadas are the same (many are almost pure onion) and that tortillas often come with *chicharrones*, similar to salt pork.

In the Feria de Chillán, look out for **DRIED FRUITS** including apricots, pears, and cherries: they're not intended to be eaten as is, but rather boiled with sugar to make a tasty juice, great for travelling. The classic example is **MOTE CON HUESILLO** – sweet apricot juice with hydrated barley for substance – some 4,000 glasses of which are sold daily in stands on the north side of the market.

MOTE CON HUESILLOS

EMPANADAS

CHILEAN WINE

Winemaking in Chile dates back over 400 years. Legend has it that father Francisco de Carabantes first planted the noble vine in Concepción in 1548, and during the colonial era the religious orders were responsible for cultivating grapes and making wine for the sacrament. Growing conditions proved to be ideal, with a long, dry growing season, daily temperature fluctuations of up to 60°F, relative humidity of 55-60%, and porous, well-drained volcanic and fluvial soils. During *La Colonia*, Chile supplied much of the wine that helped keep Spanish America pious.

These hearty wines, made from the black país grape (known as the Mission grape in California) and aged in barrels of native *roble*, didn't change much for about three hundred years, until the second half of the 19th century. Around this time, as Jan Read observes in her book *Chilean Wine,* 'it now became the fashion of wealthy owners of coal and silver mines to vie with one another in bringing back noble stocks from their travels in Europe and in establishing vineyards and wineries.' Cabernet Sauvignon, Merlot, Pinot, Riesling, Sauvignon Blanc, Semillon, and most other noteworthy Chilean stocks date from this era, as do Chile's most distinguished traditional wineries.

VIÑA SELENTIA

Meanwhile, disaster struck in Europe. A devious beetle known as phylloxera spread like a plague across the continent, devouring the roots of over one million hectares of vineyards. French oenologists, left jobless at home, arrived in Chile and set the new vineyards straight: by 1887 Viña Santa Teresa was exporting wine to Europe, and by 1903 production had reached a high of 275 million liters/year, leaving the country with something of a drinking problem.

It wasn't until the 1970's, however, that Chilean wineries really took it to the next level. In 1978, Spanish oenologist Miguel Torres bought Viña Manquehue and incorporated new equipment and techniques, including stainless steel fermentation tanks and cold fermentation of white wines. Torres' gamble paid off when his new Chilean wines won one gold and two silver medals at the 1985 Olympia wine fair in London.

In the aftermath of Torres' success, the Chilean wine industry has caught on in a big way, thanks to competitive advantages in labor and land costs and a non-grafted rootstock with a useful life of over a hundred years (as compared to thirty in Europe and California). In 1998, some 84

Also available through Ediciones Turiscom, the *Guía de Vinos de Chile* is an annual bilingual publication providing background information and reviews of each year's finest Chilean wines. Ask for your copy at fine bookstores everywhere in Chile or www.turistel.cl

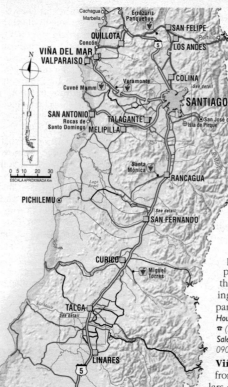

Viña Errázuriz Panquehue See Haciendas, , for details. No direct sales. ☎ (2)2036688.

Viña Sánchez de Loria The free tours at this small vineyard are run by the owner himself.
Salesroom is open 0800-1800.
☎ (34) 591054.

THE MAIPO VALLEY

The Maipo is Chile's most traditional winemaking region, and producer of its most distinguished Cabernet Sauvignons and Merlots. Happily, it's also the closest to Santiago.

Viña Cousiño Macul Another feather in the cap of the mighty Cousiño family, this is the oldest vineyard in the country; in 1550 wine produced here was already being exported to Perú. Visits include a tour of the cellars and bottling plant, and a tasting. Of special note is the surrounding park, of Gustave Renner design.
Hours: Mon-Sun 1100, with previous reservations
☎ (2) 284101 1, x45
Salesroom open Mon-Fri 0900-1300, 1400-1800, Sun 0900-1300. In Feb, closed Sat.

Viña Santa Carolina The winery dates from 1875; visits include a tour of the cellars and the colonial *casa patronal*, and a tasting. Minimum ten people.
Reservations ☎ (2) 4503000, US$10 per person.

Viña Concha y Toro Chile's biggest and best-known winery. Visits to the winery in Pirque include a tour of the turn-of-the-century mansion (pictured on Santa Emiliana labels), the Gustave Renner-designed park, and the wine cellars, concluding with a tasting.
Hours: Tours in Spanish Mon-Fri 1100, 1430, 1630, Sat at 1100. In English Mon-Fri 1000, 1200, 1430, Sat at 1000, 1200. Reservations ☎ (2) 8217000. Tour is free, tasting costs US$0.80 glass.

Viña Undurraga The vineyard was started in 1885 by Francisco Undurraga Vicuña, who introduced Riesling, Sauvignon Blanc, Cabernet Franc, Merlot and Pinot Noir rootstock to Chile. Visits include the bottling plant, the cellars, and the French-designed park. No direct wine sales.
Hours: Visits Mon-Fri 1000-1600, free guided tour.
Reservations ☎ (2) 3722900, 3722932.

Chilean wineries exported US$502 million in wines; as a country, Chile ranks third in exports to the US. A solid reputation for flavor and value has been bolstered by a recent report that ranks Chilean cabernets first in levels of flavanol, a natural antioxidant. That means Chilean wines are not only tasty and cheap – they're also *healthy*.

You can buy great Chilean wines in any major supermarket, and even the wines that come in one-liter boxes (ideal for camping and picnicking) are surprisingly palatable. If you'd like to get a closer look at the process, wine tours are offered at wineries throughout central Chile. The best of these are listed below, organized by region.

THE ACONCAGUA VALLEY

With just 405há of vineyards, the Aconcagua Valley is not a major wine region. Still, you can visit the following vineyards with advance notice:

WINE CELLARS AT VIÑA TARAPACA

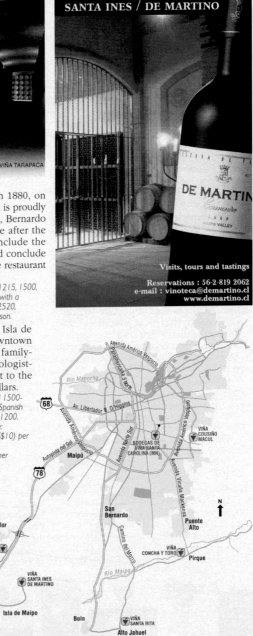

SANTA INES / DE MARTINO

DE MARTINO

Visits, tours and tastings

Reservations : 56-2-819 2062
e-mail : vinoteca@demartino.cl
www.demartino.cl

Viña Santa Rita Founded in 1880, on the site of a colonial hacienda. As is proudly proclaimed on Santa Rita's labels, Bernardo O'Higgins hid in the cellars here after the 'Disaster of Rancagua.' Tours include the bottling plant and the cellars and conclude with a tasting. There is also a fine restaurant on the premises.

Hours: Guided tours Tue-Fri 1030, 1130, 1215, 1500, 1600; Sat-Sun 1230, 1530. Reservations with a minimum 2 days anticipation, ☎ (2) 3622520, 3622000. Tour costs aprox. US$5 per person.

Viña Santa Inés Located in Isla de Maipo, just an hour south of downtown Santiago, this traditional Italian family-owned winery offers daily oenologist-guided tours, ending with a visit to the Tuscan-style tasting room and cellars.

Open to visitors Mon-Fri 1030-1330 and 1500-1830, and Sat 1030-1330, with tours in Spanish starting at 1100 and 1600, in English at 1200. The following choice of tours are available:
a) For the «knowledgeable» - $6,000 (US$10) per person (tasting of 2 reserve wines).
b) For the «fanatic» - $12,000 (US$20) per person (tasting of 4 Premium wines).
Tour and lunch have a cost of $21,000 (US$35) with unlimited reserve wine.
Call ☎ (2) 8192062 for reservations and details.

Viña Tarapacá Ex-Zavala Founded in 1874. Tours include visits to the cellars and to an on-site wine museum, and a tasting.

Minimum 10 people, reservations ☎ (2) 8192764. US$10 per person, including tasting.

de Colchagua in Santa Cruz or call ☎ (72) 823199 for reservations.

The route (from east to west) leaves San Fernando and passes through Nancagua, with colonial architecture and a lovely park; here you can visit **VIÑA PUEBLO ANTIGUO**. Next you pass Cunaco, once the largest hacienda in the valley (closed to the public). Following this are **VIÑA VIU MANENT**, **VIÑA SANTA LAURA** and **VIÑA LA POSADA**, the latter two in the town of Santa Cruz.

THE CASABLANCA VALLEY

The wineries of the Casablanca Valley are located west of the Coast Range, where lower temperatures create an extended ripening season. Casablanca is known principally for its white wines, especially Chardonnay. These are the closest wineries to the Valparaíso / Viña del Mar area.

Viña Veramonte *Open Mon-Thu 0930-1800, Fri-Sat 1000-2000. Reservations ☎ (32) 742421.*

Cuveé Mumm Producer of sparkling wines.
Open Mon-Fri 0900-1300, 1430-1730; Sat 0930-1300. Reservations ☎ (32) 742421.

THE CACHAPOAL VALLEY

The Cachapoal valley is a major producer of Chilean reds, especially Merlots. Though relatively few of wineries in this area merit a trip on their own, they are located in an interesting area near the colonial villages of Guacarhue, Quinta de Tilcoco, and Doñihue.

Viña Santa Amalia Visits of this winery in Requinoa include a free tour of the vineyard and cellars; tastings are apart.
Visits Mon-Sat 0800-1200 and 1330-1800. Reserve one day in advance, ☎ (72) 551230.

Viña La Ronciere Oenologist-guided tours include a free tasting.
Visits Mon-Sat 0800-1200, reserve one day in advance, ☎ (72) 471571.

THE COLCHAGUA VALLEY

The Colchagua valley is a focal point of Central Valley culture and colonial architecture. Seven wineries in the region have joined forces to create an excellent tour of the region, mixing wine tours and tastings with cultural activities. Consult at the Museo

West of Santa Cruz, on the road to Pichilemu, are **VIÑA SANTA LAURA**, **VIÑA SIEGEL**, **VIÑA MONT GRAS** and **VIÑA BISQUERTT**. Another option from Santa Cruz is to continue to the coast at Bucalemu, site of an important hacienda presently occupied by the Chilean military. Along the route is San Pedro de Alcántara, an interesting colonial village.

THE CURICÓ VALLEY

There are two top-notch vineyards just outside of Curicó, but only **Viña Miguel Torres** is open to visits. Bilingual tours include a free tasting.
Open Mon-Fri 0900-1200 and 1400-1800, ☎ (75) 310455.

THE MAULE VALLEY

The Maule Valley is Chile's largest wine-producing region, containing 27% of the country's vineyards. Local vineyards have joined forces to create 'wine route' similar to that in Colchagua, including guided visits to **VIÑA CARTA VIEJA**, **VIÑA BALDUZZI**, **VIÑA CREMASCHI**, **VIÑA DOMAINE ORIENTAL**, **VIÑA SEGU**, **VIÑA TABONTINAJA**, **VIÑA EL AROMO**, **VIÑA HUGO SASANOVA**, **VIÑA J. BOUCHON**, **VINOS DEL SUR**, **VIÑA TERRANOBLE**, and **VIÑA LA CALINA**. Contact the Ruta del Vino at ☎ (73) 323657 or wineroute@entelchile.net for information and reservations.

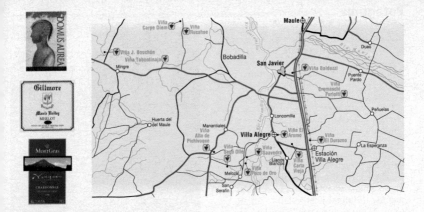

Southern Chile

PIÑONES

Piñones are the fruit of the Araucaria tree, and the traditional dietary base of the Pehuenche Indians. They are harvested and appear in supermarkets throughout the south beginning in March. When boiled they taste something like a potato.

Kuntsmann beer is brewed in Valdivia to the specifications of the brewery's German founders. Bock, lager, and pale ale are the standard varieties. Visits to the pub/brewery are highly recommended, but you can also find bottled Kuntsmann in *botillerías*, and find it on tap at a growing number of bars and restaurants.

Sweets including **gourmet chocolate** and **homemade pastries** such as *kuchen* are the culinary legacies of European settlers in the Lake District. Bariloche is the undisputed chocolate capital of the south, famous for its *chocolate de ramas*; you can get a taste of the good life at the Bariloche-based El Turista café in Pucón. Kuchen – in English

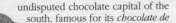

MARZIPAN

KUNTSMANN BEER

you'd call it a torte – is widely available in the Lago Llanquihue Region, especially Frutillar. The Entrelagos café in Valdivia gets our vote as the best catch-all sweet tooth fix in the south.

KÜCHEN

Beyond the rows of handicraft stalls, Puerto Montt's sprawling waterfront market at Angelmó displays the produce of the Chiloé archipelago. In the fish market, look out for vacuum-packed **smoked salmon**; other worthwhile items include **miel de ulmo**, a flavorful honey derived from the fragrant ulmo tree, and a wide selection of **homemade cheese** (don't be afraid to ask for a taste). Also keep an eye out for colorful **fruit liquors** made from aguardiente mixed with blackberries, raspberries, sour cherries, or lesser-known local berries such as grosella and murta. **Licor de Oro** is a similar golden-colored spirit commonly served as an after-dinner drink in Chiloé.

Patagonia

Beyond doubt, the most characteristic dish of the Chiloé archipelago is **CURANTO**, a hearty steamed dish similar to the New England clambake. In its traditional form, the dish is cooked in a hole in the ground using red-hot rocks, covered by the thick leaves of the nalca plant. Today, unless it is specifically called *curanto en hoyo*, it is more often cooked in a pot. Traditional ingredients include mussels, clams, pork ribs, sausages, chicken, cabbage, and a couple of unique Chilote creations, *milcaos* (made from potatoes) and *chapaleles* (made from flour dough).

Though you might be invited to an *asado* almost anywhere in Chile, in Patagonia the ritual is elevated to an art form. **ASADO AL PALO** usually consists of a whole or half lamb (*cordero*) cooked on a spit over an open fire. Another special treat to look out for in rural areas is *jabalí*, or wild boar.

With many towns in Chilean Patagonia located on the eastern side of the Andes, cultural exchange with Argentine is at its strongest here. This is especially conspicuous in the widespread consumption of *mate*, a highly nutritious, highly caffeinated herb known as *yerba mate* (*Ilex paragua-riensis*) that is traditionally served with a gourd (*mate*) and metal straw (*bombilla*). Drinking mate is a social event

ASADO AL PALO

MATE AND BOMBILLA

with very specific rules: the host pours the water and passes it to the guests, who drink it dry and pass it back to be refilled. Nobody but the server moves the straw, and you don't say *gracias* until you don't want any more.

Keep an eye out in restaurants in Punta Arenas for **CENTOLLA** or king crab; since it is only encountered in the frigid seas off the southernmost part of the continent, it's always freshest and cheapest here.

Pacific Islands

Most of the cultivated crops on Easter Island are Polynesian in origin; the most common is the *camote* or **SWEET POTATO**, which comes as a side with many meals. **TROPICAL FRUITS** such as pineapple, guayabas, and bananas flourish in cave gardens known as *manavai*.

Easter Island's most coveted seafood includes the delicious white-fleshed **TOREMO** and freshly-caught **BONITO** or *atun*, often served within a piping-hot *empanada*.

The *langosta* or **SPINY LOBSTER** is the most outstanding culinary highlight of the Juan Fernández archipelago. Those who enjoy foraging for their meals (*a la* Robinson Crusoe) will find **WILD CELERY** growing along the shores of the Bahía Cumberland.

SPINY LOBSTER

SEAFOOD MARKET ON EASTER ISLAND

HANDICRAFTS (ARTESANÍA)
AND OTHER THINGS TO BUY

Northern Chile

Traditional **AYMARA TEXTILES** in llama and alpaca wool (remember that llama wool is irritating to some) are widely available at markets in the altiplano, the sierra, and most cities.

Noteworthy traditional markets include the following:

ALPACA WOOL

- Aymara market every Wed. and Sat. in **CHARAÑA**, across the border from Visviri.
- Aymara market every Sunday, north of Visviri at the **TRI-PARTIDE BORDER** of Chile, Perú and Bolivia.
- Kespikala Centro de Arte y Cultura Indigena, in **MAMIÑA**.
- In the seldom-visited altiplano sector east of Mamiña, the Aymara artisans in **LIRIMA** produce fine alpaca sweaters and other textiles primarily for export. You must visit the town to purchase their work domestically.

Hand-spun, vegetable-dyed rugs and other textiles are produced in the altiplano village of **CHAPILCA**, east of La Serena on the route to Argentina via Paso Agua Negra.

COMBARBALITA is a semiprecious multicolored stone composed of silicone, quartz, clay, and copper and silver oxides. Declared the Chilean National Stone in 1993, it is mined in the outskirts of Combarbalá – the only place in the world where it is known to occur – and sculpted into a variety of figures by local artisans. Other minerals commonly available in the Norte Chico include **QUARTZ CRYSTALS** and **LAPISLAZULI**, mined from the upper Río Grande valley, east of Ovalle. Found only in Chile and Afghanistan, lapizlazuli is available in countless jeweler's shops in Santiago's Bellavista district.

LAPIZLAZULI

Central Chile

Earthy, attractive, incredibly inexpensive pottery is produced in the 'Indian town' of **POMAIRE**, SW of Santiago. You can find Pomaire ceramics in handicraft fairs throughout the region. For finer rustic pottery designs, visit the museum store at the Museo de Santiago.

Chile's finest traditional *chamantos* are produced in the village of **DOÑIHUE**, SW of Rancagua. These huaso ponchos typically take three months to weave, and cost up to US$1200.

Inexpensive, attractive furniture and artwork in wicker is produced and sold in **CHIMBARONGO**, on the Panamerican south of San Fernando.

POMAIRE

Artisans in **QUINCHAMALI**, SW of Chillán, produce unique ceramic figures in their homes; you can visit and see how they are shaped and fired in wood-fired kilns.

DOÑIHUE

CHIMBARONGO

QUINCHAMALI

For **TRADITIONAL** *HUASO* **CLOTHING** and accessories (including a wonderful selection of hand-made *sombreros*), visit *Donde Golpea El Monito*, at 21 de Mayo 707 in Santiago.

HAT
(CHUPALLA)

STIRRUPS
(ESTRIBOS)

SPURS
(ESPUELA)

Southern Chile

The Mapuche Indians learned to work silver from the Spanish, and during the 18th century they adapted these new techniques to their own singular aesthetic, creating an entirely unique style of women's jewelry. You can find reproductions of **MAPUCHE JEWELRY** at the Universidad Católica's *Taller Artesanal* in Temuco.

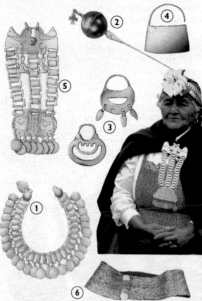

(1)*Trarilonco*: Worn around the head, this piece began as a simple headband adorned with polished coins.

(2)*Punzón*: Used to pin clothing or blankets.

Earrings known as (3)*Chawai* are the most widely reproduced form of Mapuche jewelry. The simple trapezoidal form is known as (4)*Chawai Chapell*.

(5)*Akucha* breastplates were developed only in the late 19th century, on the eve of the decline of Mapuche silverwork. These were traditional hung by a *Punzón*.

(6)*Nitrowe* or *Pollqui* are long woolen strips up to 4m long, covered with hundreds of tiny silver beads and traditionally used as an elaborate hair tie.

MAPUCHE INSTRUMENTS include the *kultrun*, a round, wood-and-leather drum painted with representations of Mapuche cosmology, and the simple *trutruka*, a wind instrument measuring up to 3-4m in length, made from a cow's horn and a shaft of bamboo. You can find these items at Temuco's Mercado Municipal, and at handicraft markets throughout the country.

Local Mapuches carve attractive **WOODEN BOWLS**, platters, utensils and other decorative/functional items from native *rauli*. The best selection of these carvings is found in handicraft markets in Villarrica, but you can find them throughout the south.

WOOLEN GOODS produced in the Chiloé archipelago (see 🔅) are displayed in great quantities in the handicraft stalls in Angelmó, in Puerto Montt. *Taller Raíces* at Av Angelmo 571 has a marvelous selection of naturally-died sweaters and hats, as well as some very fine reed baskets.

MAPUCHE WOODEN UTENSILS

TRUTRUKA

KULTRUN

Patagonia

Chile's finest and most charismatic **HANDICRAFTS MARKET** is held on Sundays on the waterfront in Dalcahue, on the east coast of Chiloé. Handmade sweaters and baskets stand out among the many inexpensive items sold here by local vendors just in from the outlying islands. This is also a great place to gorge on a traditional *curanto en hoyo* or *asado al palo*, or pick up a whole smoked salmon for the road.

The Pumalin Park visitor's center in **CALETA GONZALO** also offers a variety of handmade crafts made by local inhabitants.

Pacific Islands

The most representative Easter Island carving is the **MOAI KAVAKAVA**, a gaunt, bearded statue with hideously projecting ribs. Said to represent an *aku aku* spirit glimpsed by King Tuu-ko-iho, these striking figures are commonly available in the island's many handicraft markets and shops. Other commonly available items involve wooden representations of the *moai* and an abundance of Tahitian jewelry.

EASTER ISLAND CARVINGS

SPORTS

How it works:

The event starts when the bull enters the *apiñadero*, where the *collera* awaits him. The bull and riders make two passes around the apiñadero before the door is thrown open and they enter the main *cancha*. The rider behind simply herds the bull around the ring, while the forward rider, in the last 10m before the *atajada* (marked by the *Linea de Postura*), must turn his horse sideways and maintain its chest against bull's shoulder. Once the bull reaches the *atajada*, he must pin the bull against the wall; this is the crux of the event, as points are awarded for the positioning and technique employed in the *atajada*.

The event consists of four passes, two in each direction, with the riders alternating each direction. On the fourth pass the bull is herded out the gate through which he entered.

The Federación del Rodeo Chileno organizes and regulates the event, and has over 10,000 members between Copiapó and Punta Arenas. For more information, contact the Federación at ☎ (2)6990115.

Rodeo

Even most Chileans don't understand the finer points of the Chilean rodeo. Like its counterpart in the US, the Chilean rodeo is an elegant synthesis of rural culture and sport, having arisen from the necessity of separating livestock and delivering them to their respective owners. During Central Valley roundups, cattle were herded into circular corrals, where pairs of riders would select an animal and run it along the fence to the gate, with one of the riders maintaining guiding pressure with the chest of his horse. This technique, in which the forward horse is forced to run sideways, is the basis of the Chilean rodeo.

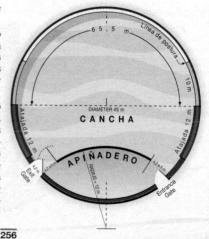

ENVOLTURA
COGOTE LIBRE
PALETA LIBRE
COSTILLA LIBRE
0 POINTS 2 POINTS 3 POINTS 4 POINTS

Today, there are over 300 official rodeo competitions in Chile each season, which lasts from Sep 1st to May 1st. Each event lasts two days (usually Sat-Sun), and involves some 300-350 young bulls. The bulls are only run once in their lifetime.

The National Rodeo Championships in Rancagua runs annually for three days at the end of the March. Regional championships held 45 days before the event determine who will fill the field of 90 competing teams (known as *colleras*). After 10 eliminatory rounds, the championship round closes the festivities on Sunday afternoon.

CANCHA
DIAMETER 45 m
APIÑADERO
Linea de postura
10 m
6 5,5 m
Atajada 12 m
Atajada 12 m
Entrance Gate

Soccer

Soccer is Chile's greatest passion, and news of the sport dominates the airwaves and the printed press. Being able to talk about Chilean *futbol* will win you immediate friends wherever you go.

Chile's professional season runs from Mar to Dec, with games played on Sat, Sun, and Wed. Most cities have first league teams, but the best of them are all from Santiago: Universidad de Chile, Universidad Católica, and Colo Colo are almost always the top contenders. The *Copa Libertadores* is an important Latin American club championship, taking place each year in during the austral winter. The Chilean national team, or *selección*, is also known as *La Roja*, for the color of their jerseys.

If you want to kick the ball around, you can almost always get in on a neighborhood soccer match, or *pichanga*.

Spanish speakers can get an interesting take on Chile's futbol-obsessed culture by checking out Chilean director Andrés Woods' film *Historias de Futbol*.

Palín

Reminiscent of field hockey, the Mapuche sport of *palín* was originally played on a field up to 2km long, with matches and associated festivities lasting three days or more. Today the game has shrunk to more manageable proportions, but many of the traditional elements are still incorporated: each match begins with brief ceremony conducted by a local shaman or *machi*, and the players compete barefoot, using colored headbands to differentiate between teams. Points are scored when the wool-and-leather ball crosses the endline.

From North to South

NORTH

PACIFIC ISLANDS

CENTRAL

SOUTH

PATAGONIA

ANTARCTICA

90°   53°

SOUTH POLE

PERU

Vn Tacora
5983
Co
Cosapilla
5200

PUTRE
Socoroma
Parinacota
Vn Parinacota 6330
Portezuelo de
Tambo Quemado 4660
Vn Guallatiri 6063

ARICA

San Miguel
de Azapa

Camiña
5

Vn Isluga
5530
Paso
Cerrito Prieto
Colchane

Huara
IQUIQUE

La Tirana
Pica
Matilla
Geóglifos
de Pintados
Vn
Irruputuncu
5163
Vn Olca
5407
BOLIVIA

Vn Ollagüe 5863
Ollagüe

Quillagua

Tranque
Sloman
Vn San Pablo
5334
Vn Linzor
5610

TOCOPILLA
Chuquicamata
Lasana
Río Loa
Chiuchiu
Chapana

CALAMA
Puntana
Vn Licancábur
5916

San Pedro
de Atacama
Toconao
Nvs de Poquis
5756

Isla Santa
María
Baquedano
Trópico de Capricornio

ANTOFAGASTA
SALAR
DE
ATACAMA
Vn Láscar
5154
Paso Jama

Paso de
Guatiquina
4296

Vn Socompa
6050
Paso
Sico
4079

Co.
Llullaillaco
6739

Laguna de
la Azufrera
Vn Azufre
o Lastarria 5697

Taltal

El Salvador
Salar de
Pedernales
Laguna
Resca

CHAÑARAL
Salar de
Maricunga
Paso
San Francisco
4726

Caldera
Bahía Inglesa
Cerro Ojos
del Salado 6893
Co
Tres Cruces
6749

COPIAPO
5

ARGENTINA

VALLENAR

Co del Toro
6380

LA SERENA
COQUIMBO
Vicuña
Paihuano
Paso del
Agua Negra
4765

Tongoy
Andacollo

Ovalle

Combarbalá
Paso del Verde

Paso de la Laguna
de la Overa

ILLAPEL

Los Vilos
5

Océano Pacífico

Mar Chileno

N

ESCALA   Km
0   25   50

OFICINA ALIANZA
2
PULPERIA

CORREOS DE
40 C

The North

While some parts of Chile might remind you of other parts of the world, that is not the case in the north. There truly is no place like this on earth.

The greater portion of the north is desert - a vast, colorful desert, with limitless views, bizarre geological formations, spellbinding sunsets and brilliant traces of green following trails of water from the Andes to the ocean. Archaeologists and those interested in native cultures are in seventh heaven here, as the natural aridity preserves artifacts and ruins from early local cultures and the great expansions of the Tiwanaku and Inca empire. Naturalists will find the ecosystems of the high Andes to be exceedingly rich and visually resplendent. Surfers and sun-worshippers have a universe of beaches to choose from.

Apart from the coast, the principal features of northern Chile are the Atacama Desert, the Altiplano, and the valleys of the Norte Chico. Each has its own topography, climate and ecosystems, its own history and culture.

NORTHERN CHILE

GEOGRAPHY AND TOPOGRAPHY

The Norte Grande

From Arica south to Copiapó, the Norte Grande is characterized by a number of relatively well-defined topographic features which create natural divisions in the landscape.

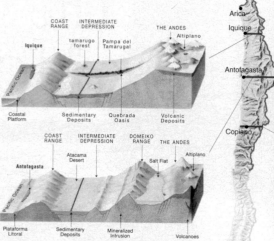

The **Coast Range** begins at El Morro, the historic mound overlooking Arica, and from here to Iquique it clings resolutely to the coast. Travelling north or south on the Panamerican highway, you'll cross a series of incredibly abrupt river valleys, known as *quebradas*, which crosscut through the desert, busting through the Coast Range and providing the only passage to the Pacific. South of Iquique, a narrow uplifted marine platform at the foot of the range allows for the presence of a chain of beaches and a recently completed coastal highway. The *Cordillera de la Costa* reaches its greatest height in all of Chile at Cerro Vicuña Mackenna (3,114m), southeast of Antofagasta.

To the east, the Atacama Desert is composed of sedimentary depositions from the rapidly eroding Andes. These depositions have formed a broad *pampa* that slopes gently from east to west, reaching nearly to the top of the Coast Range, broken by the protuding peaks of rows of striking multicolored hills. The sedimentary deposits are exceedingly rich in mineral content: over

millions of years, water heated by the barely subterranean magma underlying the Andes has continually leached soluble minerals out of the soil, drawing them to the surface and leaving them here in vast salt flats and nitrate fields. As the Atacama Desert is now known as the driest region on earth, it is difficult to imagine water flowing off the Andes in sufficient quantities to produce these deposits. Still more impressive is the formation of the huge quebradas mentioned above; research suggests that these may have been formed during the cataclysmic release of water from the huge 'paleolakes' that once filled vast basins in the altiplano.

In the northernmost portion of the region, from 18-21°S, the area of transition between the desert and the Andes is known as

THE VALLE DE LA LUNA

the *sierra* or *precordillera*. This is a band of arid, rocky foothills rising from 1,200m to 3,500m, heavily eroded into complex series of ridges and quebradas. Precipitation filtered through the porous soils of the altiplano rises to the surface in scattered springs throughout the sierra.

South of 21°S, the transition from the intermediate depression to the altiplano is interrupted by the mineral-rich **Domeyko Range**, which splits off the main Andean chain at 27°S, the approximate latitude of Copiapó, and runs north for some 400km. The two parallel ranges form an orographic V open to the north, trapping runoff from the altiplano in the **Inter-Andean Depression** and creating vast salt-flats and oases.

Caldera

Copiapó

Pacific Ocean

Coastal Platform   Transvere Valley   Agricultural Valley
    COAST RANGE   Conected to   THE ANDES

To the east of the desert, the **Altiplano** is a broad, undulant volcanic plateau with a minimum elevation of 3,500m, extending from the border with Perú south to about 28°S. Composed primarily of volcanic depositions from the late Cenozoic, this is still among Chile's most active volcanic regions, and site of the world's highest volcano, Ojos del Salado (6,893m). Salt flats, lakes and marshes lie in the basins which once held the huge lakes of the Pleistocene.

The Norte Chico

South of Copiapó, the landscape changes completely. No longer is it possible to differentiate between the Coast Range and the Andes; instead, the entire region is mountainous, fragmented by endlessly branching river valleys, most of which, paradoxically, are dry throughout most of the year. Five principal rivers have a constant water supply and hold the vast majority of the region's population. Like the Atacama Desert, the mountains of the Norte Chico are extraordinarily rich in mineral deposits.

Increased precipitation and fluvial erosion in this region has produced an extensive coastal shelf and numerous

---

Dealing with water and altitude

Independent travelers in northern Chile need to be prepared to deal with two very important factors: water and altitude.

The issue with water is simply that there isn't very much of it. In oasis towns, selling bottled water is big business, but what to do when you're off the beaten track? The best idea is to bring as much with you as possible: if driving, buy a big water tank and keep it filled, and if walking or biking, count on consuming 4-5 liters a day, per person. What you can't carry, you'll have to find along the way; almost all villages have reliable water sources, but it may not be potable, so bring a filter or water treatment tablets. Even where it is potable, high mineral content can cause off flavors. Don't count on finding water between villages, as much surface water is brackish or too high in minerals to be consumed.

As far as altitude is concerned, the best advice is simply to budget time for acclimatization, eat lightly, stay hydrated, and avoid alcohol. Coca leaves, a common remedy in Perú and Bolivia, are rarely available in Chile, but you can ask in altiplano villages for *chacacoma*, a fragant native herb that relieves *soroche* (altitude sickness) when made into tea or crushed and inhaled. See the general mountaineering chapter for more tips for success at altitude.

COCA

PACIFIC ANTICYCLONE A

EASTERLY WINDS A

HUMBOLDT CURRENT

POLAR FRONT

created. Moist maritime air never forms rain-bearing clouds; instead, it is driven against the high, unbroken peaks of the Coast Range, forming a dense morning fog known as *camanchaca*. This camanchaca is responsible for the existence of diverse ecosystems composed of cacti and succulents, and sustains isolated **relict forests**, composed of similar species as the evergreen forests of south-central Chile.

These forests date from the Pleistocene, an era in which cooler global temperatures and greater precipitation produced extensive forests of drought-resistant tree species throughout the Atacama Desert. But climate change, followed by the depredations of the mining industry, reduced these forests to a limited range along the coast, a few river valleys, and a single protected tamarugo forest east of Iquique.

GIANT LLARETA PLANT IN THE ATACAMA DESERT

beaches, especially near river mouths. Towards the east, the peaks grow gradually in height and river valleys become increasingly steep and narrow. There is no volcanic activity of any sort in the Andes from 28-32°S, though the highest peaks along the Argentine border frequently exceed 5,000m.

CLIMATE AND BIOGEOGRAPHY

The arid climate of Northern Chile is the product of a unique synthesis of oceanographic, atmospheric, and topographic conditions.

Just west of the Chilean Coast between 20-30°S, the Semi-Permanent Pacific Anti-Cyclone is a region of nearly constant high pressure, which pushes storm systems away to the north and west. During the day, however, air heated over the desert rises, drawing an onshore breeze. This breeze is relatively dry, because the waters which bathe this coast are cooled – and therefore less subject to evaporation – by the north-flowing **Humboldt Current**.

Passing over the Humboldt Current, these onshore breezes drop in temperature, and as upper strata of air are being constantly heated by the sun, a temperature inversion is

THE FLOWERING DESERT

East of the Coast Range, the fertile quebrada valleys and the oases of the sierra and intermediate depression receive almost none of their precious water from the Pacific Ocean.

Instead, this water originates in the Amazon basin; during the summer months, increased solar radiation over the Amazon creates a low-pressure system of moist, rising air, which is displaced towards the west. These easterly storms must pass over the heights of the altiplano, and in doing so, they are drastically cooled and consequently drop their load of moisture, creating intense storms during the so-called **altiplanic winter**. While precipitation has never been recorded in some parts of the Atacama

CARDON

ALSTROEMERIA

COPIAPOA

Desert, rainfall reaches up to 500mm/year in the altiplano, 300mm/year in the sierra.

Regional ecosystems reflect this sharp gradient in precipitation: while the altiplano supports a variety of hardy grasses, shrubs, and a few woody plants, floral diversity drops in the increasingly arid precordillera. Cacti occupy a narrow niche between the highlands and the desert, and below 3,000m, areas with no groundwater support no vegetation whatsoever.

Towards the south, the effect of the Semi-Permanent Pacific Anti-Cyclone eases a bit, bringing a gradual increase in precipitation and a consequent vegetal gradient from the absolute desert of the Norte Grande to the Mediterranean climate of Central Chile. Drought-resistant grasses and shrubs become more common on the hills separating each river valley, while in the valleys themselves, coastal camanchaca extends inland as much as 40km, and increased precipitation in the Andes provides runoff which is trapped in reservoirs and utilized in extensive irrigation systems. During **El Niño** events, seasonal rains increase significantly, prompting dormant flowers to germinate and cacti to flower, transforming the entire landscape in a phenomenon known as the **flowering desert**.

Temperatures on the coast of northern Chile are moderated by the ocean, but the crystal-clear skies of the desert and altiplano create enormous differences in daytime and nightime temperatures.

PREHISTORY

The earliest dated archaeological site in northern Chile corresponds to a highly mobile group of hunter-gatherers who inhabited the Quebrada de Quereo near Los Vilos, in the Norte Chico. Like **Paleolithic cultures** all across the Ameri-

The Altiplanic Winter

While most of northern Chile is apt for travel any time of year, the altiplanic winter, also known as the 'Bolivian Winter,' can complicate travel in the altiplano from December to February. Sudden rainstorms can produce serious erosion, with some roads washing out entirely, year after year.

Unlike the rest of Chile, therefore, the best time to plan a trip to the altiplano is from April to October, when the risk of precipitation is practically nil. Bear in mind, that the effect diminishes towards the south, petering out at the approximate latitude of San Pedro de Atacama.

cas, they subsisted on now-extinct megafauna such as mastadons, American horses and camels, deer and South American endemics like the milodón. Artifacts from Quereo are thought to date from around 13,000 years before the present (BP).

Sites found in caves and beneath overhangs in the northern altiplano are only slightly more recent (10,000-8,000 BP), yet findings here reflect the great changes which occured in the interval. Gone are the megafauna that characterized the Paleolithic, and in their place vicuñas, guanacos, tarucas, rodents and birds have emerged as the principal prey of these **Neolithic** hunter-gatherers. The reasons for this early holocene extinction are thought to reside in some combination of human and environmental factors.

This smaller, faster prey required a refinement of hunting techniques, and the fragmentation of ecosystems caused by climate change resulted in a further specialization of local economies. Whereas a single group would once have followed prey between the coast and the Andes, the disappearance of so-called 'vegetal bridges' across the Atacama Desert appears to have prompted some groups to move

MASTADON

CHANGO INDIANS, IN A DRAWING BY FREZIER

permanently to the coast, beginning around 8,000 BP. The findings at coastal sites such as Playa Chinchorro (6,000 BP), Caleta Huelén (7,000 BP), Tiliviche (10,000 BP), and Quebrada de las Conchas (9,000 BP) may be understood as the Neolithic precursors of the coastal Indians known to the Spaniards as **Changos**.

At the time of the Spanish conquest, these Changos inhabited the better part of northern Chile's coast. They gathered shellfish and algae along the shore, and fished and hunted marine mammals from atop ingenious rafts made from two sewn and inflated sea lion skins. Numerous **cave paintings** and **petroglyphs** depict human figures using them to hunt prey as large as whales.

In the interior, geography and climate conspired to create a number of vertical niches, where only certain products could be obtained. The chal-

lenge to Neolithic societies lay in maximizing a niche and obtaining what they lacked through trade with communities occupying other ecological tiers. This concept of **verticality** is key to understanding culture in the Andes, where a single 200km cross-section includes twenty of the world's 34 life zones.

During the **pre-Ceramic period** (7,000-6,000 BP) the hunter-gatherers who had established themselves around altiplano lakes took the first steps towards the **domestication of camelids**, and the first cultigens from the highlands and tropics were introduced along the coast. Hunting and gathering continued to be of great importance: guanacos, vicuñas and ñandus were readily available in the altiplano, and in the oases and valleys, drought-resistant trees like chañar and algarrobo provided fruits that were ground into flour or fermented into *chicha*. During the 4,000-2,800 BP **Initial Period**, the cultivation of beans, maize, gourds, quinoa and other crops was well under way in the **Azapa Valley** east of Arica, and vertical trade between the coast and the Andes had begun to increase. From this era on, connections with technology-rich highland cultures would play an increasingly important role in regional development in northern Chile.

Changos
Atacameños
Aymaras
Picunches
Diaguitas
Chiquiyanes

○ Inca Settlements
Unoccupied territories
Permanent Inca occupation
Periodic Inca occupation
Continuation of group territory
Penetration from the pampa

MUMMY FROM THE ATACAMEÑA CULTURE

CHINCHORRO BURIAL SITE AND MUMMY

The Alto Ramírez culture (~2,500 BP), usually associated with sites in the Azapa Valley, is exemplary of this stage of rapid cultural development. Copperwork, basketry, weaving, ceramics and the **ritual inhalation of hallucinogens** were among the advances which Alto Ramírez borrowed from the cultures of the altiplano, in exchange for agricultural products and dried fish from Arica's rich coast. A similar exchange was under way in the oases of the Inter-Andean Depression, where the Toconao (2400-2100 BC) and Sequitor (100 BC- 400 AD) cultures were becoming increasingly sedentary, benefiting from their location near a crossroads of desert commerce. Increasingly conspicuous is the consumption of hallucinogenic drugs such as *cebíl*, brought over the Andes from NW Argentina.

At this stage of cultural development, exchange was still fairly localized: Azapa traded with cultures from Perú and Bolivia, **San Pedro de Atacama** traded with the tribes of NW Argentina, and the cultures of the transverse valleys of the Norte Chico were relatively isolated. The typical Andean pattern of *ayllu* kinship groups, by which single families could control niches on the coast, sierra, and altiplano, may have already been manifest. With the rise to prominence of the first of the Central Andes' highland empires, Tiwanaku, the native cultures of northern Chile were further incorporated into the greater Central Andean culture area.

Tiwanaku

Tiwanaku began its rise to dominance in the Callao Basin of NW Bolivia and SE Perú around 400 BC. Using raised-bed

TIWANAKU 4-POINTED HAT

and shoreline irrigation techniques on the southern bank of 12,600 ft **Lago Titicaca**, Tiwanaku grew to house from 25,000-40,000 individuals in one of the greatest Andean platform complexes ever built. The rise and fall of Tiwanaku are poorly understood: Thor Heyerdahl's comparison of monoliths in Ti-

Expansion of the Tiwanaku empire

wanaku and Easter Island led him to propose that the same culture was responsible for both.

Tiwanaku valued the Azapa Valley for its agricultural and marine resources. Its influence in this region involved the introduction of new agricultural techniques and the installation of *cabuza* administrators and colonies of workers from the highlands, whose remains are found concurrently with those of Alto Ramírez. In San Pedro de Atacama, on the other hand, Tiwanaku was mainly interested in mineral resources such as copper, turquoise and malachite, and dealt only with the *Atacameño* elites. Trade between the coast and the Andes rose to unprecedented levels, and massive, stylized works of rock art known as **geoglyphs** appeared along desert trails throughout the north.

Tiwanaku design motifs appear repeatedly in geoglyphs and petroglyphs, ceramic and textile designs throughout northern Chile. Other physical manifestations of the Tiwanaku empire include the use of ritualized wooden, stone or copper tablets for the inhalation of hallucinogens, and characteristic four-pointed hats.

TABLET FOR INHALING HALLUCINOGENS

Around 1000 AD, Tiwanaku entered into decline, possibly due to drought in the Lago Titicaca basin. Contact was broken with satellite communities throughout Bolivia, Argentina, Perú and Chile, and in the **Pukara period** which followed, the diverse tribes of the Bolivian and Argentine altiplano rose in bellicose competition for the suddenly available resources of the Chilean desert and coast. In the sierra east of Arica, numerous defensive forts called *pukaras* were erected at commanding sites at the head of the steep quebradas that link the coast to the altiplano. Further pukaras were erected in the **Río Loa basin** north of San Pedro de Atacama.

In the **Norte Chico**, the isolated tribes of the Copiapó, Huasco, Elqui, Limarí and Choapa valleys followed a similar pattern of development, though their integration with altiplano cultures was later and less intense. Irrigated agriculture and the domestication of camelids formed the economic basis of the varied cultures of the **El Molle period** (2,300 YBP - 700 AD), while the subsequent Las Animas period (700-1000 AD) is characterized by the appearance of metallurgy and increased similarities with the cultures of NW Argentina. Beginning in 1000 AD, the **Diaguitas culture,** differentiated by its stunning ceramic designs, supplanted Las Animas throughout the region, though each valley appears to have maintained its own language.

CERAMICS FOUND NEAR ARICA

Tawantinsuyo: The Incas

Meanwhile, in the highlands of southern Perú – also the scene of feuding regional kingdoms – a great empire was taking form. Known as *Tawantinsuyo*, the Land of the Four Corners, the civilization we now know as Inca began in Cuzco, Perú. In Quechua, the term Inca literally means 'archetype,' or 'the original model of all things'. In more practical terms, the term referred to the reigning political leader – considered a divine descendant of *Inti*, the sun – and his ayllu kinship group. When one

Inca was succeeded by the next, the land he had conquered remained under the power of his kinship group, and only the army passed on to the successor. In this way, territorial expansion was institutionalized.

When Pachacuti Inca Yupanqui, the ninth Inca, assumed power around 1438, his predecessors had already consolidated lands around Cuzco, which translates as 'navel.' By the time his son Topa Inca Yupanqui took the throne in 1471, the empire already comprised great portions of Ecuador and Perú. Topa Yupanqui continued the expansion, spreading south through the Bolivian altiplano and NW Argentina. In Chile, Inca dominion extended as far south as the Río Maule, near modern-day Talca.

The Incas used a variety of techniques to implement and maintain their rule over this vast empire. Imposition of the state religion, based upon the worship of *Inti*, was almost universally imposed, as was the Quechua language, today the most widely-spoken native language in the Americas. A standing army was frequently employed to overcome resistance, but the Incas also incorporated many cultures under more hospitable terms. The major form of exchange was in labor (*miti*), with local communities required to contribute to road and irrigation projects. In some situations, Inca colonists were placed among local populations to aid in implementation of new technologies and maintain administrative presence. In northern Chile, the Incas

THE INCA TRAIL

See pg 6 for photo credit

occupied many existing pukaras and built new ones, as well as administrative centers, metalworking plants, ritual platforms and **mountaintop shrines.** The Inca road system, extending for some 30,000 - 40,000km, united the most distant parts of the empire. Inca design motifs exerted a profound influence over local artistic production.

By the early 16th century, European diseases were already decimating native populations in the Americas. When Huayna Capac, successor to Topa Yupanqui, died of sickness in 1527, his sons Atahualpa and Huáscar each claimed the kingdom, the former from Quito, the latter from Cuzco, and war broke out between the two factions. Atahualpa had just defeated Huáscar and was camped in Cajamarca, on his way to Cuzco to claim his throne, when he was betrayed to the recently arrived Spaniands by his half-brother, Manco Inca. Captured by **Francisco Pizarro,** Atahualpa was held ransom for gold and then executed. The year was 1532.

ROYAUME DE CHILI, 1683

D. FRAN PIZARRO

THE CONQUEST AND COLONIA ERA

Among Pizarro's partners in the conquest of Perú was one **Diego de Almagro,** who for his efforts was awarded possession of the newly defined territory of Nueva Toledo. Nuevo Toledo extended roughly from the latitude of Cuzco south to Taltal, and east to the limit of Spanish jurisdiction as defined by the Pope in 1494. Almagro, taking advantage of the roughness of the borders, promptly seized control of Cuzco, assuming the Inca capital fell under his jurisdiction. This was not what Pizarro had in mind, however, and the two partners were at the point of bloodshed when Almagro decided to head south to undertake the **conquest of Chile**.

Generating interest in the expedition was not difficult. The Spanish soldiers who had arrived too late to claim a share of Atahualpa's fortune were anxious to get their hands on the realms of gold described by the natives, who were more than happy to send the Spanish off to the south. In mid-june of 1535, Almagro left Cuzco at the head of a column of 500 soldiers, 100 African blacks and 10-15,000 natives. Atahualpa's brother Pablo Tupac and Inca priest Villac-Umu also accompanied Almagro.

Marching south through southern Bolivia and NW Argentina, the expedition encountered ever more difficult conditions. The barren soils and salt flats of the altiplano increased the soldiers' dependence on dwindling food supplies, Indian servants disappeared in the night, nighttime temperatures plummeted and the altiplano Indians posed a constant threat. Crossing the 4,726m Paso San Francisco into Chile in the mounting winter, Almagro was forced to leave the bulk of his stuggling men behind and forge on with twenty riders in search of supplies. In May of 1536, the Spanish entered the Copiapó valley for the first time.

From here, the now much-reduced expedition continued south, meeting up with a re-supply ship in Los Vilos, the only one of three to have survived the voyage from Perú. In the Aconcagua Valley, dismayed by the diminishing wealth and increasing hostility of the natives the further he got from Cuzco, Almagro called a halt to restock on provisions and promptly returned to Perú. Northern and Central Chile had been officially 'discovered,' and succinctly discarded.

The next Spaniard to try his luck in northern Chile was **Pedro de Valdivia,** who arrived in Perú in 1537 and soon found himself helping Francisco Pizarro fight against - strangely enough – Diego de Almagro. Though richly rewarded with land, mines, and plenty of Indians to work them, Valdivia had grander designs, and

PEDRO DE VALDIVIA

DIEGO DE ALMAGRO

from Cuzco
from Cuzco
to Cuzco

Tarapacá

Chiu Chiu
San Pedro
de Atacama

Paso de
San Francisco

La Serena

EXPEDITIONS

Diego de Almagro
(1535-36)

Pedro de Valdivia
(1540-53)

Santiago

to Concepción

Ahead of them, the Indians of the Norte Chico burned their crops, slaughtered their animals, hid their gold and mounted what opposition they could muster against the strange mounted soldiers. In 1541 the city of Santiago was founded, and Valdivia focused upon the placer mines of central Chile and the green pastures of the south. Northern Chile, with its implacable desert and troublesome natives, remained a thorn in Valdivia's side, complicating communication between his precarious colony and the Viceroyalty of Perú.

asked permission to occupy the territory abandoned by Almagro.

This time it wasn't so easy to rally troops, and when Valdivia departed from Cuzco in 1540, his expedition numbered only around 150 Spaniards and a few Indians who had no choice in the matter. In the Lago Titicaca basin, Valdivia met up with other pillaging conquistadors including **Francisco de Aguirre**, and together this ragged group began the conquest of Chile.

Following the Inca trail along the coast and through the sierra, the Spanish made their way to San Pedro de Atacama, where they rested before continuing south.

DUTCH AND
BRITISH'S CORSAIRS

POTOSI

The saying goes that the Spanish could have built a bridge back to Spain with the silver they mined from Cerro Rico, the mother lode of Potosí, which produced some 40% of the silver discovered in the New World. By the beginning of the 17th century, Potosí had grown to be one of the largest cities in the world, with almost 200,000 inhabitants – this at a time when there lived a mere 75,000 within the walled city of London. As Potosí is too high for agriculture of any sort, the task of keeping the masses fed and the silver flowing towards Spain fell upon the sierra and oasis communities of northern Chile. Today, mining cooperatives continue to exploit the dwindling reserves of Cerro Rico, and occasionally the miners come across a corpse that was simply walled in during the Colonial era.

La Serena, founded in 1544, was the first 'city' in the north, but was shortly attacked and destroyed by the Diaguitas. Five years later, Valdivia's strongman Francisco de Aguirre was dispatched to the north to rebuild the settlement and secure the route to Perú. The Indians who survived Aguirre's attacks and the constant threat of European diseases were subjected to the *encomiendas* labor system in the few Spanish settlements established in the region.

With its difficult topography, relatively sparse Indian population and predominantly low-grade metal ores, northern Chile was largely neglected by the Spanish. Mining during La Colonia was mostly limited to the Norte Chico; in the northernmost province, Tarapacá, the irrigated valleys of the coast and sierra were utilized for agriculture, mostly to supply the mule trains that transported silver from **Potosí** (see sidebar) to the port of Arica. Guano was mined from a few rookeries along the coast, but the Atacama Desert was almost entirely uninhabited; San Pedro de Atacama and Chiu Chiu, on the río Loa, were the largest settlements in the region. Catholic missionaries from Arequipa were charged with the task of converting the natives, supposedly legitimizing the tragedy of the *encomiendas* system. Marauding Dutch and English pirates repeatly sacked Spanish ports.

At the time of independence, northern Chile was divided between the Viceroyalty of La Plata, which included the Inter-Andean Depression and the Puna de Atacama and was governed from Buenos Aires, and the Viceroyalty of Perú, with its capital in Lima. The latter was further subdivided, with the area south of the Río Loa pertaining to the Audiencia – soon to be the Republic – of Chile.

Post-Independence

With independence, the Spanish monopoly on trade was lifted, and northern Chile's mineral wealth began to attract entrepreneurs and explorers from far and wide. During the 19th century, these charismatic individuals wrought great changes upon the social and economic landscape of the region and the country.

At first, activity was focused upon the city of **Copiapó**, located on the very cusp of the Atacama Desert. New mines were discovered weekly, and get-rich-quick hopefuls arrived from the south in droves. Copiapó became the country's new intellectual and financial center, and artists, writers, politicians and naturalists held company with the town's ever-wealthier

The Explorers of the Atacama

During the colonial era, the vast, nearly unpopulated Atacama Desert was known as the Despoblado de Atacama, and most of the trails and oases were known only by the Indians. But with the burden of the Spanish crown lifted and new mineral deposits being discovered left and right, curiosity started to get the best of folks.

Copiapó-born **Diego de Almeyda (1)**, who fought for independence and was imprisoned by the Spanish on Isla Robinson Crusoe, came home in 1824 and began the first of an endless series of brutal expeditions, slogging along desert trails all the way past the Salar de Atacama, discovering dozens of mines.

Almeyda's finds, and the growing wealth of areas adjacent to the Despoblado, attracted other explorers. José Antonio Moreno, a disciple of Almeyda, walked from Copiapó north along the coast to modern-day Antofagasta, discovering important copper and nitrate deposits. **José Santos Ossa (2)** left Huasco at 19 to move to the port of Cobija, discovering important nitrate reserves and brushing frequently with death in the absolute desert.

During the later half of the century, scientific and geopolitical interests joined the fray. In 1853, German naturalist **Rudolfo Amando Philippi (3)** was contracted by the Chilean government to prepare a description of the geography, mineralogy, and natural history of the region, and Almeyda guided the seven-month expedition. From 1883-1888, Francisco San Roman spent summers in the Atacama, mapping and giving names to places. Two years later **Federico Philippi**, son of the famous naturalist, traveled 90 days by mule up the length of the Inter-Andean Depression, writing a botanical and zoological description of the region and collecting plant and animal specimens for Santiago's Natural History Museum.

CHILEAN SOLDIERS

entrepreneurs. But for the vast majority, life in the desert didn't get any easier, and as class struggle became an increasingly salient characteristic of daily life, the identity of the Chilean miner was forged.

Further north, the growth of the nitrate industry in the Atacama Desert raised the stakes for the three countries with claims to the region. When the Republic of Bolivia was created in 1825, Simón Bolivar petitioned Perú for the port of Arica, was denied, and settled for Cobija, just north of Antofagasta. The Chilean government, whose original constitution had defined the republic's northern limit vaguely as 'the Atacama Desert,' agreed tacitly in 1842 to grant the Bolivians a swath of land between the río Loa and parallel 23°S. After years of difficulties, new treaties and rising hostilities, in 1874 the border was definitively moved south to 24°S, with the stipulation that Bolivia not raise taxes on Chilean companies operating between 23° and 24°S for the next 25 years.

IRENE MORALES

Meanwhile, Bolivia entered into a secret defense agreement with Perú, with each country committed to defending the territory of the other. When the Chileans learned of this alliance, they stepped up their orders

for ironside ships from England, which turned out to be a good idea. In 1876, Bolivian General Hilarión Díaz seized power and raised taxes on the Chilean nitrate companies, and when these refused to pay, seized their assets. This obliged the Chilean government to act: in 1879, Chile occupied the Bolivian port of Antofagasta, Bolivia declared war on Chile and invoked its agreement with Perú, and Chile declared war on both countries.

The War of the Pacific

Chile's first move was to blockade Iquique, Perú's principal nitrate port, while the majority of the fleet headed north towards Callao to engage the Peruvians. Meanwhile, the Peruvian ironclads *Huáscar* and *Independencia* were headed south, and on May 21, 1879 the *Huáscar* sunk the *Esmeralda* – captained by Chilean hero Arturo Prat – in the **Battle of Iquique**. A bit further south, however, at Punta Gruesa, the Chilean *Covadonga* ran the *Independencia* aground and shelled it to pieces, evening the score and leaving the Peruvians with only one remaining ironclad. In October of the same year, the *Huáscar* was captured and the Peruvian naval threat negated.

ELEUTERIO RAMIREZ

On the terrestrial front, during the month of November successive battles incurred heavy losses upon the Chilean army but left them, at the end of the month, in control of Perú's vast and lucrative nitrate reserves. The following winter, the Chileans came ashore near Tacna, and beat the combined Peruvian and Bolivian forces so

PAINTING OF THE BATTLE OF IQUIQUE, BY TOMAS SOMERSCALE

soundly that the alliance between the two was broken and Bolivia withdrew from the fracas. Following the Peruvian defeat in the **Battle of the Morro**, representatives of the three countries met aboard a US frigate in Arica's harbor to negotiate peace. The attempt failed, and in early 1881 the Chilean army attacked and occupied Lima, obliging the Peruvian government to accept the conditions imposed upon them. When the negotiations were concluded, Bolivia wound up landlocked – an economic curse which Bolivians will never forgive – while Chile was left with the immense wealth of the Atacama Desert completely under its jurisdiction.

NITRATE OFFICE

THE NORTH IN THE 20TH CENTURY

As the bottom dropped out of the nitrate market, large-scale mining operations such as that at **Chuquicamata** were growing rapidly on a steady diet of foreign capital. Today, Chuqui continues to dominate the mining sector of a national economy in which mining provides some 40% of GNP – a situation slightly better than that which caused Chile to be hit harder than any country in the world by the Great Depression.

In the far north, Arica and Iquique developed big fishmeal industries over the last twenty years, but overfishing has led to a drastic decline in the industry; small scale fishing, seaweed harvest and aquaculture are among the more sustainable industries in the region. From Copiapó south, agriculture plays an increasingly large role in the local economy, thanks in large part to big investments in irrigation beginning in the early 1980s. Today, agricultural land in the Copiapó valley, which produces table grapes for holiday export to the States and Europe, are among the most expensive in Chile. The designation of the Tarapacá province as a duty-free zone (*Zona Franca*) has stimulated trade in the region, and tourism is increasingly important to the north's economy, a trend that should be applauded and supported, considering this is among the north's only non-extractive industries. Increased integration with Perú, Bolivia and Argentina can only add to the still-underexploited touristic potential of the north.

LA ESCONDIDA MINE

Arica
Pop. 161,333 (☎ city code 58)

Located at the mouth of the Río Azapa, Arica is Chile's northernmost city, and one of its liveliest. The Peruvian border is only 18km away, and it's an easy day's bus ride to La Paz, which explains Arica's international atmosphere and the popularity of its beaches. There are also excellent archaeological sites and a top-notch museum nearby.

Long inhabited by native populations, Arica served as the principal port for the Spanish silver mines at Potosí until 1776, when the Viceroyalty of La Plata was created, and silver traffic was rerouted through Buenos Aires. Shortly thereafter, the Spanish abandoned Arica because of chronic malaria (now extinguished), though after independence Perú reoccupied. With the 1880 **BATTLE OF THE MORRO**, which signaled the end of the War of the Pacific in this region, Arica became part of the Chilean republic.

In recent years, Arica's once-strong fishing and manufacturing industries have entered into somewhat of a decline, and trade is probably the most significant sector of the local economy. Everyone in Arica, it seems, is either headed to or coming back from Tacna, shuttling cigarettes, automobile parts, and a plethora of other products this way or that.

In-town attractions

The Morro Dominating the city and port of Arica, the Morro is the northernmost peak of Coast Range and site of a decisive battle in the War of the Pacific. Among the several monu-

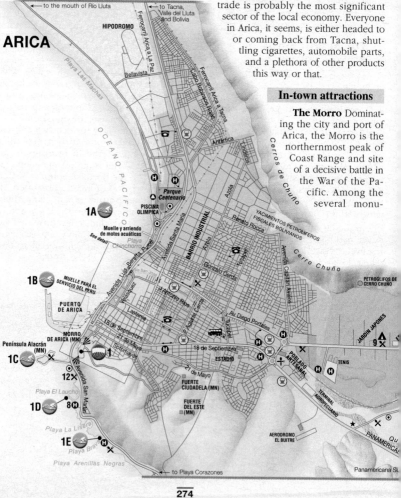

ments and defensive fortifications above the cliffs you'll find the **MUSEO HISTÓRICO Y DE ARMAS** (History and Arms Museum), but the view is far and away the biggest selling point. Walking access is via a trail from the southern end of Calle Colón.

National Monuments The most impressive buildings are clustered around the three plazas north of the Morro, and were prefabricated in Paris by Gustave Eiffel and erected in 1876. These include the **CATEDRAL SAN MARCOS**, east of Plaza Colón, the **EX-GOBERNACIÓN** (Minister of the Interior) and the **EX-ADUANA** (Customs house), which now houses the **CASA DE CULTURA**. North across Calle 21 de Mayo is the 1913 train station.

The Agro For thousands of years, Arica has been a hub of vertical trade between the coast, the irrigated internal valleys, the altiplano and the Amazon rainforests. Today, the immense Agro agricultural market is a vibrant living manifestation of this ongoing tradition. Access via taxi colectivo or micro marked 'Agro.'

Beaches

Arica has some of Chile's nicest beaches and warmest water. To the north of town, you can camp for free on the immense **PLAYA LAS MACHAS**; closer to town is the popular **PLAYA CHINCHORRO**. The most protected (and most crowded) beaches are south of town, at the foot of the Morro: **PLAYA EL LAUCHO** and **PLAYA LA LISERA** are the best beaches for swimming, while **LAS ARENILLAS** and **PLAYA BRAVA** are considerably rougher. 8km south is

ARICA'S «COSTANERA» WITH EL MORRO IN THE BACKGROUND

PLAYA LOS CORAZONES, a spectacular beach flanked by steep cliffs. You can camp for free, but you must bring all your water from Arica. Transport by micro in summer only.

 Warm water, tropical fish, and a protected shore south of town make this a fine dive site for snorkelers and scuba divers alike. There are also a couple of shipwrecks off the Extremo Molo lighthouse. For info and equipment contact:
• Ludwig Duarte, Alonso Ovalle 1347, ☎ (58)241396, (09)5179027.

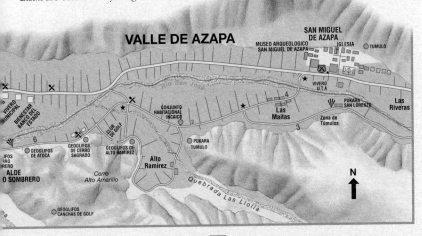

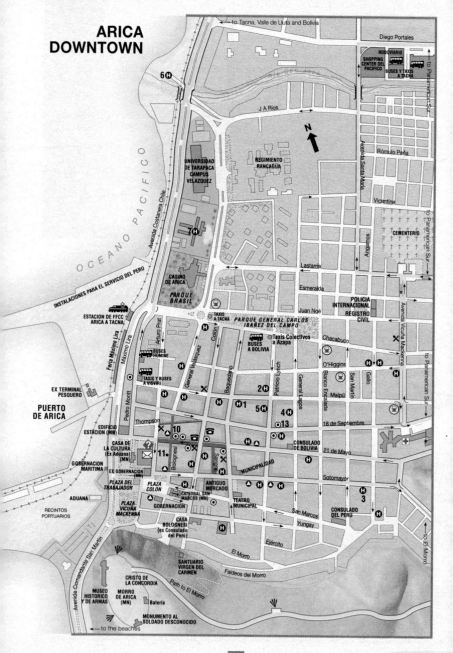

ARICA
DOWNTOWN

Sernatur Prat 305, 2nd floor, open
Mon-Fri 0830-1300, 1500-1900.
Conaf Vicuña Mackenna 820, open
Mon-Fri 0900-1300, 1400-1700.

BANKS AND MONEY CHANGERS
Many money changers and ATMs
downtown, especially on 21 de Mayo.

HOSPITAL
18 de Septiembre 1000, ☎ 232242.

POST OFFICE
Prat 305.

INTERNET CONNECTION
LABS, General Lagos 596.

ACCOMMODATION
1 *Residencial La Blanquita* $, Maipú
472, ☎ 232064.
2 *Residencial Chungara* $, Patricio
Lynch 675, ☎ 231677.
3 *Hostal Jardín del Sol* $, Sotomayor
848, ☎ **232795**.
4 *Hotel Americano* $$, General
Lagos 571, ☎ 257752.
5 *Hotel Lynch* $$, Patricio Lynch 589,
☎ 231581.
6 *Hotel Bahía Chinchorro* $$, Luis
Bretta Porcel 2031, ☎ 241068.
7 *Hotel El Paso* $$$, General
Velásquez 1109, ☎ 231965.
8 *Hotel Arica* $$$, Comandante San
Martín 599, ☎ 254540.

CAMPING
9 *El Refugio de Azapa*, km 3.5 in the
Valle de Azapa.

Free Camping on Playa Las
Machas, no water.

RESTAURANTS
10 *La Scala*, corner of Bolognesi and
21 de Mayo. Sandwiches, juices.
11 *La Fontana*, Pasaje Bolognesi.
Arica's best ice cream.
12 *Restaurant Maracuya*, San
Martín 321. Seafood, expensive,
ocean views.

AIRPORT
Chacalluta Airport, 18km north
on Panamerican.

AIRPORT TRANSPORT
Lanchile & Ladeco have courtesy vans.

AIRLINE OFFICES
LanChile, 21 de Mayo 345 ☎ 251641.
Ladeco, 21 de Mayo 439 ☎ 252021.
Aerocontinente, ☎ 6002092358.

TAXI COLECTIVOS
To the *Valle Azapa*, corner of
Maipú and Patricio Lynch.
To *Tacna*, Av. Chacabuco, between
Baquedano and Colón.

TRAINS TO TACNA
Máximo Lira 889, ☎ 231115.
Departures 1200 and 1800 Mon-
Sat, duration 1.5 h.

RENT A CAR
American, Gral. Lagos 559 ☎ 252234.
Avis, Chacabuco 180 ☎ 232210.

BUS STATION AND/OR OFFICES
Bus station at Diego Portales 948,

reached by taxi colectivo from 18
de Septiembre.
*Buses to the Valle Lluta, Poconchile,
Putre and Belén:* Buses la Paloma,
corner of G. Riesgo and Tucapel.
Buses to Visviri and Parinacota:
Transp. Martínez, Pedro Montt 620,
or Transp. Humire, Pedro Montt 622.

ENTERTAINMENT
13 *Bar Barrabás*, 18 de Septiembre 520.
Pub atmosphere, disco next door,
popular. Discotheques on the road
to Azapa, access by taxi colectivo.
Casino in Parque Brazil, just north
of downtown. Open seven days a
week from 1200-0400.

SHOPPING
Pasaje Bolognesi Artisans market
off Plaza Colón between
Sotomayor and 21 de Mayo.
Poblado Artesanal Ceramics,
alpaca and llama woolen goods,
musical instruments and other
altiplano handicrafts may be
purchased at this replica of an
altiplano village, east of downtown
near the route to the Panamerican.
Take taxi collectivo #3.

SPORTS
Golf 18-hole course in Valle de
Azapa, open Tue-Sun.
Tennis Club de Tennis Centenario,
Av. España 2640.
Swimming Pool at Parque
Centenario, open Tue-Sat
0830-1830.

EX ADUANA, CASA
DE LA CULTURA

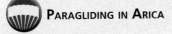

PARAGLIDING IN ARICA

● Poconchile
The takeoff site for flights over the dramatic
Lluta valley is accessed from the paved
switchbacks on the route to Putre. Its northward
orientation can make takeoff somewhat complicated.
Operator: 9

● El Morro
A takeoff from the SW edge of Arica's most
prominent landmark allows you to fly above the
city and land on Playa Chinchorro or Playa Las
Machas, north of town.
Operator: 9

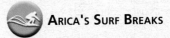

ARICA'S SURF BREAKS

● Playa Las Machas & Playa Chinchorro
Beach breaks, best at high tide.

● La Puntilla
Lefts at low tide with medium to large swell.

● Isla Alacrán
Lefts and rights off the north of the island
with medium to large swell, waves at all tides.

● El Buey
Lefts off Playa el Laucho, also rights on big
days, best with low tide and no wind.

● Playa Brava
Beach breaks at mid – to high tide.

● La Capilla
Lefts and rights over a rock reef, works on big
days only. 3km paddle from shore.

Around Arica

Museo Arqueológico San Miguel de Azapa

Located in the **AZAPA VALLEY** 14km east of Arica, *(Jan-Feb Mon-Fri 0900-2000, rest of the year 1000-1800. Entrance: $700, children $200)* this museum features excellent, well-labeled exhibits on regional development in the Norte Grande, beginning with the sand-preserved mummies of the Chinchorro culture, from approximately 8000 BC. The museum also boasts the best collection of textiles in the north and provides a good introduction to the concept of vertical trade in the Andes. Along the south side of the Azapa Valley are a number of geoglyphs and archaeological sites . There is also an excellent upmarket cabaña complex in the Azapa Valley, the *Hotel Saint Georgette.* Access by taxi colectivo.

Up the Valle de Lluta

Accessed via the Panamericana 9km north of Arica, the Lluta Valley is a worthwhile day trip and is the standard route for those heading to Putre.

The valley itself is a miracle of contrast, with its patchwork of irrigated maize fields flanked by pale, sandy, utterly lifeless desert hills. Keep an eye out to the south as you enter the valley for several panels of geoglyphs (), which testify to the importance of this valley as a regional trade route. 35km from Arica is the pre-Hispanic town of **POCONCHILE**, with a stark cemetery and restored colonial church; shortly beyond, the paved highway leaves the valley and climbs steeply into the *sierra*. Soon you'll begin to see scattered examples of candelabro cactus, and at about 100km from Arica you'll pass the funky, hippie-owned *Posada Taki,* which offers meals, lodging, and local tours. Just beyond is the **PUCARA DE COPAQUILLA**, the first of the pre-Inca ruins in the area, (see for details) and at 111km from Arica is the **CRUCE DE ZAPAHUIRA**, where you can veer south to visit the Belén Precordillera or continue on the main road to Putre. Public transport from Arica is provided by Buses La Paloma.

Playa Corazones

At the mouth of the dramatic Quebrada de Corazones lies an isolated beach and tiny fishing village which makes a great camping spot (but bring all your water). Transport by bus to the Quebrada de Camarones bridge, then walk 11km downvalley to the beach.

Visviri

Chile's northeasternmost village lies 127km NE of Putre; on Sundays there is a tri-national Aymara market across the border in Charaña. Transport with Buses Martínez from Arica.

Putre & PN Lauca

PUTRE is 145km east of Arica, access by daily bus with Buses La Paloma. One-day trips to the altipano are offered from Arica but are not recommended due to the extreme change in altitude.

PUTRE, WITH THE NEVADOS DE PUTRE IN THE BACKGROUND

See Pg 6 for photo credit

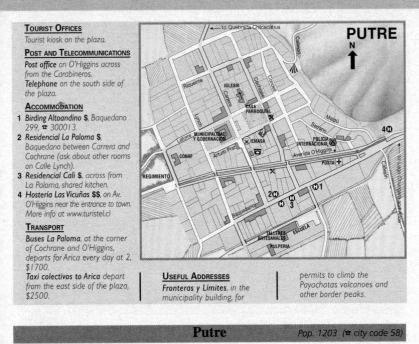

PUTRE

N ↑

TOURIST OFFICES
Tourist kiosk on the plaza.

POST AND TELECOMMUNICATIONS
Post office on O'Higgins across from the Carabineros.
Telephone on the south side of the plaza.

ACCOMMODATION
1 *Birding Altoandino* $, *Baquedano 299,* ☎ *300013.*
2 *Residencial La Paloma* $, *Baquedano between Carrera and Cochrane (ask about other rooms on Calle Lynch).*
3 *Residencial Cali* $, *across from La Paloma, shared kitchen.*
4 *Hosteria Las Vicuñas* $$, *on Av. O'Higgins near the entrance to town. More info at www.turistel.cl*

TRANSPORT
Buses La Paloma, at the corner of Cochrane and O'Higgins, departs for Arica every day at 2, $1700.
Taxi colectivos to Arica depart from the east side of the plaza, $2500.

USEFUL ADDRESSES
Fronteras y Límites, in the municipality building, for permits to climb the Payachatas volcanoes and other border peaks.

Putre

Pop. 1203 (☎ city code 58)

Putre occupies an interesting ecological niche between the rich agricultural lands of the coastal valleys and the high pasturelands of the altiplano. Though alfalfa, orégano, and a variety of tubers grow in Putre, the town's regional importance due to its role as a crossroads of trade and travel.

The town sits on a long, narrow, sloping terrace, surrounded on all sides by a maze of steep quebrada valleys. Below the town, an age-old network of trails link Putre with the other villages of the sierra, while to the east more roads and trails branch out into the altiplano. Llamas raised in the alti-plano for export are typically kept here for several weeks in order to ease the transition to sea level.

Accommodation in the town is basic but adequate for most tastes and overnight tours from the coast almost always stay here. If you walk around Putre´s cobblestoned streets and surrounding *chacras* you can find orégano farms and llama corrals; in town on the north side of the plaza is the IGLESIA DE PUTRE, constructed in 1670 and restored in 1871 after being destroyed by an earthquake. Ask at the *Municipalidad* for the keys to visit the interior.

Around Putre

Day Hikes Around Putre

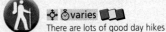 ☼ ⏱varies 📖

There are lots of good day hikes along pre-Hispanic trails in the Putre area. From the prominent radio tower next to the highway SW of town, an obvious trail leads 7km downvalley to the prehispanic village of Socoroma, where you'll find a modest *residencial* and a 1560 church, the Iglesia de San Francisco. The 150-odd villagers live mostly from the cultivation of alfalfa and orégano. Buses La Paloma runs from Socoroma to Putre Tue and Sat at 1130, but you could also arrange a pickup beforehand or simply walk the 4km uphill to the highway and hitch back.

Alternately, you can hike to the Incani, Viluvio, Anocarini, and Vilacaurani rock paintings; for directions or guided hikes, ask for Justo Blas in Putre's *Municipalidad*. Other possibilities include the long day hike to the base of the Nevados de Putre above town, and the moderate walk through open country above the town to the Baños de Jurasi.

Baños de Jurasi

 free

Set in an idyllic quebrada with expansive views over the precordillera, this 66°C spring has been piped into concrete pools in a tiny, community-built wooden shack. The springs lie 3km south of the highway from Putre to PN Lauca (signposted turnoff 7km from Putre).

The Belén Precordillera

The precordillera is a region of steep, arid hills separated by narrow fluvial valleys. The towns here are of pre-Hispanic origin, and doubtlessly were valued because of the strategic position they command over the agriculturally rich quebrada valleys below. With the Spanish conquest, natives from the surrounding area were forced to resettle in these towns, and were charged with the task of providing alfalfa for the mule trains from Potosí to the coast. Catholic priests from Arequipa built many of Chile's oldest chapels in this area.

There are modest *residenciales* in **Socoroma** and **Belén**, and a hosteria in **Codpa**; the latter is also the site of an annual *Fiesta de la Vendimia*, held near the end of each May in celebration of the harvest of grapes for the sweet, locally produced *vino pintatani*. There are lovely colonial churches in all of these towns, as well as in Guañacagua and Livilcar (the latter of which is accessible on foot only). Other attractions include the high concentration of *pucara* defensive forts (), and the singular possibility of spotting a rare *taruca*, an Andean deer that appears to survive nowhere else in Chile. The precordillera is accessed from Arica with Buses La Paloma, which runs to Belén on Tue and Fri at 0645, and to Codpa/Tignamar on Mon and Fri at 1600.

Parque Nacional Lauca

See map

INFORMATION

*The Conaf ranger station at Las Cuevas, at the western entrance to the park, is a good source of information on flora and fauna, hiking routes and road conditions in the altiplano. **Carnaval** is celebrated in altiplano villages during the week before Ash Wednesday (late Feb).*

ACCOMMODATION

Putre is the only nearby town with any variety of accommodation. In the park itself, Conaf has rustic refugios and campsites at Las Cuevas, Parinacota and Chungará; call the office in Arica for reservations. You may also be able to rent a bed or a room from local villagers in Parinacota or any of the sierra villages.

TRANSPORT

To Parinacota by twice-weekly bus from Arica.

Comprising 137,883há of high-altitude altiplano habitat (ranging from 3,200-6,300m in elevation), Lauca is a true gem in Chile's network of protected areas. The park has been declared a Unesco World Biosphere Reserve, largely for its unique, plentiful and surprisingly docile wildlife: vicuñas, vizcachas and foxes are easy to spot and photograph, and rheas, condors, giant coots, flamingos and dozens of other bird species visit or nest in high altitude lakes, marshes and rivers.

Paved Ruta 11 from Arica to La Paz runs right through Lauca. From Putre, the road climbs steeply through arid hills, then levels out once it hits the altiplano; the ranger station at **Las Cuevas** marks the park entrance. Nearby, among the jumbled rocks above the Río Lauca, is an excellent place to photograph vizcachas.

Further up on the left, at 4,450m, is the Aymara pueblo of **Parinacota**, with a 17th century church and a Conaf refugio. The town sits on eastern edge of the **Bofedal de Parinacota**, where the locals graze their llamas and alpacas; behind the *bofedal* are the snowcapped peaks of the Nevados de Putre. East of town, dirt roads lead through the strange volcanic landscape and scattered lakes of the **Lagunas de Cotacotani**, which receive their water via filtration from Lago Chungará, just east. The Río Lauca carries the water south through the park, creating wetlands habitat along its winding course into Bolivia.

Considered among the world's highest lakes, 4,570m **Lago Chungará** is a very powerful place: between the extreme clarity of the air, the physiological effects of altitude, and the tremendous scale of the lake and the Payachata volcanoes just to the northeast, you can hardly help but be overwhelmed. In October, the spectacle increases as thousands of giant coots build their nests and

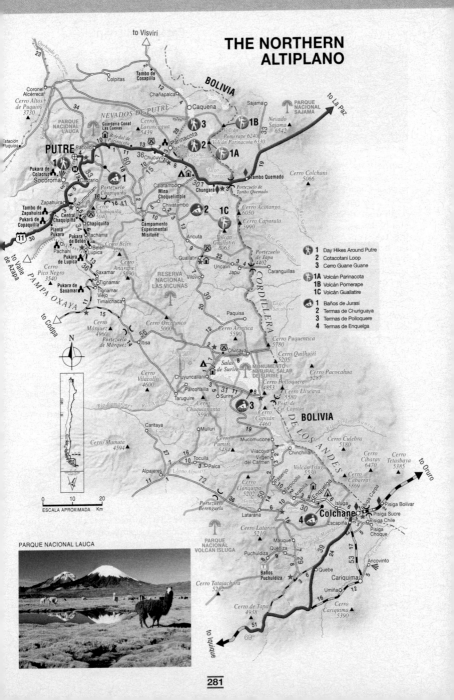

THE NORTHERN ALTIPLANO

PARQUE NACIONAL LAUCA

VOLCÁN PARINACOTA

compete for mates in the shallow water along the south shore of the lake, in plain view of Conaf's **REFUGIO CHUNGARÁ**.

If you have a car, you can take a road south from the customs checkpoint near the end of the lake and continue over a pass to the **TERMAS DE CHURIGUAYA**. From here you can head west, rejoining the Río Lauca valley and the route to RN Las Vicuñas; for a good day trip you can circle back to Parinacota or Las Cuevas, or loop south and then west on one of the roads through the precordillera . Despite the popularity of Lauca's central attractions, once you're off the highway you are unlikely to come across other tourists.

Termas de Churiguaya

N free
This tiny roadside pool is good for washing up but not quite big enough for soaking. Still, as the only hotspring to speak of in Lauca, it can provide much-needed relief from the dust and chill of the altiplano.

Catacotani Loop

⟳ ⏱4h
From the Conaf administration center in Parinacota, this easy hike leaves leads through small bofedales and along the western shore of the Lagunas Cotacotani.

Cerro Guane Guane (5,096m)

⇄ ⏱4-6h
Though Cerro Guane Guane's altitude would make it a serious mountaineering expedition in most countries, once you're accustomed to the air at Parinacota (4,450m), this peak just north of the village makes a relatively easy day hike. Climb the east flank for incredible views of the park.

Volcán Parinacota (6,330m)
Volcán Pomerape (6,240m)
Volcán Guallatire (6,060m)

⏱5d return from Putre
IGM 1:250,000 Arica
These three peaks constitute the country's second-greatest concentration of peaks over 6,000m. Both Parinacota and Pomerape (together known as the Payachatas) may be climbed in one-day pushes from a single base camp to the NW, accessed via Caquena. Just east, Nevado Sajama (6,542m) is of similar elevation, though the presence of extensive glaciers makes this a more serious undertaking. Note that to climb the Payachatas you need authorization from Fronteras and Limites, available in Putre.

Operators: 31 - 49 - 199

RN Las Vicuñas, Monumento Nat. Salar de Surire See map

INFORMATION
Conaf ranger stations at Guallatire and on the east side of the Salar de Surire.

ACCOMMODATION
4-person refugios at both Conaf ranger stations.

TRANSPORT
No public transport (for nearest public access see Putre, above); otherwise by tour or 4WD vehicle only.

PROVISIONS
Nearest provisions in Putre and Colchane. Bring all fresh fruit and vegetables from Arica or Iquique.

Together, this reserve and adjacent natural monument protect a total of 226,631há of altiplano habitat, forming a vital wildlife corridor between Lauca and Volcán Isluga national parks. This is the site of some of the best overland and bike traverses in the country, with abundant wildlife, stunning landscapes and fairly good roads throughout most of the year.

Most visitors will arrive from the north, via Lauca. From here, the road south passes through wetlands along the Río Lauca en route to the delapidated Aymara village of Guallatire, where there is a Conaf ranger station (but little else). South of Guallatire, the route continues through arid grasslands used by locals as pasture for alpacas and llamas; vicuñas and ñandús also abound in this area.

Further south, the **Salar de Surire** produces mixed emotions. It is difficult to understand why mining is being permitted in a natural monument, but unfortunately that is the case, and visitors have to put up with the eyesore of huge trucks rumbling out and back across the vast expanse of the salar. The Conaf ranger station on the east side of the salar has a bird's eye view of the operations.

The south end of the salar, however, is entirely pristine. Four snowcapped peaks above 5,000m hem in the salar to the north and west, forming a spectacular backdrop for the hotsprings and extensive thermal fields at **Termas de Polloquere,** the best campsite along this stretch.

Termas de Polloquere

 N free

One of the more spectacular termas in the altiplano, consisting of a large thermal lake and mineralized stream flowing through the Salar de Surire. Spring temp 85°C, exposed camping on-site.

CHILEAN AND ANDEAN FLAMINGO CHICKS IN THE SALAR DE SURIRE

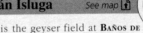

Parque Nacional Volcán Isluga   See map

INFORMATION / ACCOMMODATION
Conaf ranger station, 4-person refugio in Enquelga.

TRANSPORT
No public transport; nearest public access by bus Iquique-Colchane.

This 174,744há national park protects altiplano habitats and landscapes similar to those just of PN Lauca, but with far fewer visitors. As with Lauca, you can arrange single-day tours from the coast (departing from Iquique), but this is not recommended. The best option by far is to link all the altiplano parks in a single tour.

Colchane is the nearest 'town' to the park, but don't expect a wealth of services – fuel may be available in a pinch, but that's about all. Park administration is in the village of **Enquelga**, near the southern entrance; Conaf has a refugio here, and there are hotsprings just down the road. There are also hotsprings near the northern entrance to the park, on the road to Chinchillani. Perhaps the impressive spectacle, however,

is the geyser field at **Baños de Puchuldiza**, on the border of the park SW of Colchane. Unlike the more famous geysers at El Tatio, these erupt constantly throughout the day and are rarely visited by tourists. During the winter, the water vapor from the geysers freezes into a huge block of ice that looks like a misplaced iceberg.

Other highlights include the Aymara village of **Isluga** and a wealth of bird habitat centered around the *bofedales* and two lakes (Parinacota and Arabilla). Isluga's church is among the most picturesque of all the altiplano churches and should not be missed. Sadly, the town is slowly being abandoned, and today many of the houses do not even have roofs.

Termas de Enquelga

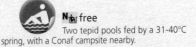 **N** free

Two tepid pools fed by a 31-40°C spring, with a Conaf campsite nearby.

Iquique   Pop. 145,139 (☎ city code 57)

Iquique probably boasts the most impressive location of any major city in Chile, consuming every square foot of a triangular coastal shelf that juts into the Pacific from the base of the Coast Range. If arriving from the east, you'll pass through a notch in the mountains and suddenly see the city laid out far below, surrounded by immense dunes. The view is unforgettable, by day or night.

Once you're down on the flats, Iquique sports a couple of different faces. Towards the southern end, the scene is all about the beach: there's a palm-lined boardwalk, throngs of surfers, hotels and condominiums, and discotheques that don't close their doors until well into the morning. Further north is the central historic district, with charming turn-of-the-century constructions and the grimier port district. The effect of Iquique's massive duty-free zone, the ZOFRI, is unmistakable, and flashy vehicles are serious status symbols among Iquique's youth.

During the colonial era, Iquique was a tiny, forlorn settlement whose utility was limited to the guano reserves of its offshore islands; even the silver mine at Huantajaya, located in the Coast Range above the town, was incapable of increasing the port's prestige. With the growth of the nitrate industry, however, Iquique (at the time part of Perú) began to grow by leaps and bounds, reaching a population of 2,500 by 1855 and 10,000 by 1878. In 1879, just as Iquique was reaching its peak, the War of the Pacific broke out, and by the end of the year the city was in Chilean hands.

The years 1880-1920 were the nitrate industry's peak years, and Iquique was the greatest nitrate port of all. When nitrate declined, fishing stepped up, though Iquique's glory days had passed. Now, with fishing on the decline, trade and tourism have become top priorities in Iquique.

In-town Attractions

Walking tour of the Historic District Start at the corner of O'Higgins and Baquedano, at the PALACIO ASTORECA, a 1904 mansion providing a vivid glimpse of the splendor of the nitrate era.

Hours: Mon-Fri 1000-1400, 1600-2000, Sat 1000-1300.
Entrance: $300, children and seniors $150

Walk north along Calle Baquedano, taking note of the handsome Georgian-style buildings that line the street, most built of imported Douglas fir. Just past calle Zegers, on the left, is the MUSEO REGIONAL with exhibits on local prehistory – including Chinchorro mummies and remains of two Inca youths

IQUIQUE

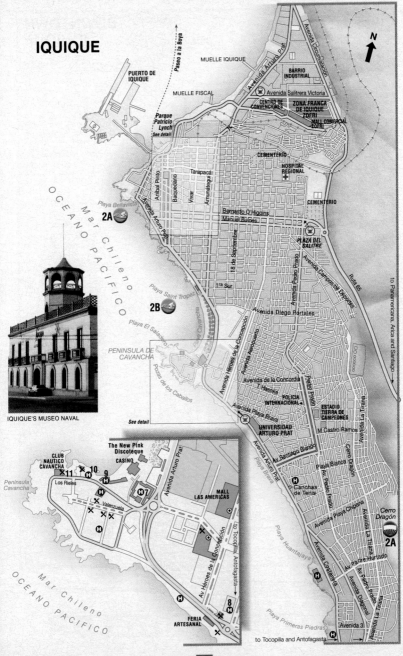

IQUIQUE'S MUSEO NAVAL

PUERTO DE IQUIQUE

MUELLE IQUIQUE

Paseo a la Boya

MUELLE FISCAL

Parque
Patricio
Lynch
See detail

Avenida Arturo Prat

Avenida Circunvalación

BARRIO
INDUSTRIAL

Avenida Salitrera Victoria

CENTRO DE
CONVENCIONES

ZONA FRANCA
DE IQUIQUE
ZOFRI

MALL COMERCIAL
ZOFRI

CEMENTERIO

HOSPITAL
REGIONAL

CEMENTERIO

Playa Bellavista

Mar Chileno

OCEANO PACIFICO

Aníbal Pinto

Baquedano

Vivar

Amunátegui

Tarapacá

Avenida Arturo Prat

2A

Bernardo O'Higgins

Manuel Bulnes

PLAZA DEL
SALITRE

18 de Septiembre

Avenida Pedro Prado

Avenida Campos de Deportes

Ruta 65

to Panamericana, Arica and Santiago

1ra Sur

Playa Saint Tropez

2B

Playa El Saladero

PENINSULA DE
CAVANCHA

Pozas de los Caballos

Avenida Cavancha

Avenida Héroes de la Concepción

Avenida Aeropuerto

Avenida de la Concordia

T. Henna

POLICIA
INTERNACIONAL

Avenida Diego Portales

Pedro Prado

ESTADIO
TIERRA DE
CAMPEONES

M. Castro Ramos

Avenida Tirana La Tirana

Avenida Playa Brava

UNIVERSIDAD
ARTURO PRAT

Av. Santiago Blanco

Playa Blanca

Av. Pedro Prado

Cerro Dragón

See detail

The New Pink
Discoteque

CASINO

CLUB
NAUTICO
CAVANCHA

11

10

9

Los Rieles

Peninsula
Cavancha

Valenzuela

Avenida Arturo Prat

7

MALL
LAS AMERICAS

Canchas
de Tenis

Avenida Playa Chipana

Avenida La Tirana

Avenida Diagonal

Cerro
Dragón

2A

Mar Chileno

OCEANO PACIFICO

to Tocopilla and
Antofagasta

Av. Héroes de la Concepción

8

FERIA
ARTESANAL

Playa Brava

Playa Huantajaya

Avenida Costanera

Avenida Padre Hurtado

Av. Padre Hurtado

Playa Primeras Piedras

to Tocopilla and Antofagasta

Avenida 3

Avenida La Tirana

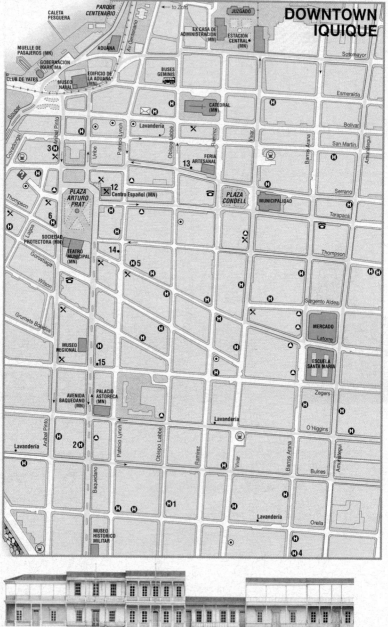

DOWNTOWN IQUIQUE

HOUSES ON CALLE BAQUEDANO

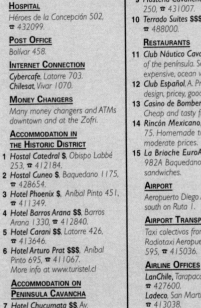

TOURIST INFORMATION
Sernatur, Serrano 145, open Mon-Fri 0800-1330, 1500-1800.

HOSPITAL
Héroes de la Concepción 502, ☎ 432099.

POST OFFICE
Bolívar 458.

INTERNET CONNECTION
Cybercafe, Latorre 703.
Chilesat, Vivar 1070.

MONEY CHANGERS
Many money changers and ATMs downtown and at the Zofri.

ACCOMMODATION IN THE HISTORIC DISTRICT
1 **Hostal Catedral $**, Obispo Labbé 253, ☎ 412184.
2 **Hostal Cuneo $**, Baquedano 1175, ☎ 428654.
3 **Hotel Phoenix $**, Aníbal Pinto 451, ☎ 411349.
4 **Hotel Barros Arana $$**, Barros Arana 1330, ☎ 412840.
5 **Hotel Carani $$**, Latorre 426, ☎ 413646.
6 **Hotel Arturo Prat $$$**, Aníbal Pinto 695, ☎ 411067.
More info at www.turistel.cl

ACCOMMODATION ON PENÍNSULA CAVANCHA
7 **Hotel Chucumata $$**, Av. Balmaceda 850, ☎ 435050.

8 **Hotel Terrado Club $$$**, Avenida Aeropuerto 2873, Playa Brava, ☎ 447371.
9 **Hostería Cavancha $$$**, Los Rieles 250, ☎ 431007.
10 **Terrado Suites $$$**, Los Rieles 126, ☎ 488000.

RESTAURANTS
11 **Club Náutico Cavancha**, at the tip of the península. Seafood, expensive, ocean views.
12 **Club Español**, A. Prat 584. Moorish design, pricey, good mango sours.
13 **Casino de Bomberos**, Serrano 520. Cheap and tasty fixed lunches.
14 **Rincón Mexicano**, Patricio Lynch 75. Homemade tortillas, moderate prices.
15 **La Brioche EuroAmericana**, 982A Baquedano. Real coffee, sandwiches.

AIRPORT
Aeropuerto Diego Aracena, 41km south on Ruta 1.

AIRPORT TRANSPORT
Taxi colectivos from Plaza Prat; Radiotaxi Aeropuerto, Aníbal Pinto 595, ☎ 415036.

AIRLINE OFFICES
LanChile, Tarapacá 465, ☎ 427600.
Ladeco, San Martín 428, local 2 ☎ 413038.
Aerocontinente, ☎ 6002092358.

BUS STATION AND/OR OFFICES
Bus station at north end of Patricio Lynch, but most companies have separate offices around the mercado on Barros Arana, Latorre and Sargento Aldea. Tur-Bus is at the corner of Ramírez and Esmeralda.
Buses to Pica, Mamiña, Matilla corner of Sargento Aldea and Barros Arana.
Colectivos to Humberstone, Pozo Almonte, La Tirana corner of Sargento Aldea and Barros Arana.

RENT A CAR
Budget, Bolívar 615 ☎ 416095.
Hotel Charlie Inn, T. Bonilla 989 ☎ 413835.
Jofamar, Libertad 1156 ☎ 423489.

ENTERTAINMENT
Barracuda, Gorostiaga 601. Mellow pub with snacks, a variety of beers, tasteful music.
Discotheques on Península Cavancha.
Casino on the north side of Península Cavancha, open seven days a week from 2000 to 0345. Entrance to slot rooms costs US$50, card tables US$2.

SHOPPING
Main shopping drag on calle Tarapacá, between Plaza Prat and Plaza Condell. North of town, the immense Zofri duty-free zone is a good place to pick up cameras, film, and electronic goods. Access via northbound colectivos or micros.

---

sacrificed on nearby Cerro Esmeralda – plus photos and artifacts from the nitrate era.
Hours: Mon-Fri 0900-1300, 1600-2000, Sat 1000-1300, 1600-2000, Sun 1000-1300.
Entrance: $300, children and seniors $150, foreigners $ 600).

Continue north to Plaza Prat. As you walk into the square, you'll see the 1889 TEATRO MUNICIPAL (Municipal Theater) to your left. The centerpiece of the plaza is the 1877 TORRE RELOJ, and at the northeast corner is the moorish-styled 1904 CENTRO ESPAÑOL, now transformed into a restaurant and worth a visit.

If you walk four blocks north on Calle Uribe, you'll run smack into the 1871 EDIFICIO DE LA ADUANA (Customs Building) and the MUSEO NAVAL, featuring exhibits on the 1879 Battle of Iquique.
Hours: Tue-Sat 1000-1300, 1500-1800. Sun and holidays 1000-1300.

Here you can turn left towards the 1901 MUELLE DE PASAJEROS (passenger pier), where you can catch a boat tour to check out the sunken wreck of the Esmeralda,

Arturo Prat's ship. Otherwise, bear right from the Museo Naval, follow Calle Centenario to a triangular intersection, and bear right again on Calle Sotomayor. Three blocks east, on the left, is a small plaza where you'll find the buildings of the old train station, which date from 1883. A block south is Iquique's Cathedral.

Beaches
PLAYA CAVANCHA is the best and most popular beach in Iquique. South of Península Cavancha is PLAYA BRAVA, a long, rough beach that extends south to PLAYA HUANTAJAYA and the massive dunes of Cerro el Dragón.

The Iquique coast is better suited for surfing than diving, but there are a couple of outfitters in town that organize classes and excursions. If you have your own equipment, you can probably fill your tanks at the aquaculture farms at Pozo Toyo and Punta Chipana, off Ruta 1 south of the city. For info and equipment contact:
• Carlos Guerrero Medel ☎ (09)7747240

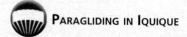

IQUIQUE'S SURF BREAKS

• Intendencia
Powerful, hollow left over a rock reef, experts only.

• Playa Saint Tropez
Six separate breaks, rights and lefts, tubes, best at low tide.

• Huayquique
Sandbar break with small- to medium swell.

PARAGLIDING IN IQUIQUE

• Duna Cerro Dragón
This 350-meter sand dune receives constant westerly sea breezes throughout the day, making it an ideal site for beginners and classes. This is the closest place to fly in Iquique.

• Palo Buque
There are two sites here, 15km south of Iquique. The *cerro* itself is 50m high, with good SW exposure, and is good for beginner courses. Nearby is an extensive 1,100m sand dune receiving clean, laminar winds directly off the ocean.

• Alto Hospicio
At 500m above sea level, this takeoff site lies just south of the road from Iquique to the Panamerican, near where the road flattens out through a break in the coast range. From here you can fly out over the city, landing on Playa Brava or Playa Cavancha.

• Cross Country Flights
There are three common takeoffs for cross country flights along the coast south of Iquique: Patillos lies at 60km south, Pabellon de Pica is at 83km, and Cabo Paquica is at 185km. All three sites have good SW exposure for takeoff, but are recommended for experienced pilots only; the entire traverse from Cabo Paquica has only been accomplished a couple of times, and these with perfect wind conditions. Note that you must first solicit permission if you intend to pass through the airspace of Iquique's airport, located along the coast south of the city.

IQUIQUE SEEN FROM A PARAGLIDER

Around Iquique

Oficina Humberstone

47km east of Iquique, this is the best preserved of the abandoned nitrate offices 🎧. Transport by colectivo to Pozo Almonte or any northbound bus (ask to be dropped off and flag one down for a ride back).

La Tirana

66km SE of Iquique, La Tirana annually hosts Chile's largest religious festival 🎧. Note that there is no lodging at all in town, though there is a rather interesting MUSEO DE SALITRE (Nitrate Museum) across from the church. Transport by taxi colectivo.

Reserva Nacional Pampa de Tamarugal

69km SE of Iquique, this 102,264há reserve contains the Atacama Desert's last remaining native *tamarugo* forest, as well as extensive plantations of *tamarugo* and *algarrobo*. The highlight of the reserve, however, is the collection of geoglyphs on CERRO PINTADOS (see 🎧 for info on this and CERRO UNITA, another notable geoglyph site near Iquique). Conaf maintains a campground near the reserve headquarters, 25km south of Pozo Almonte. Transport by southbound bus or tour.

IGLESIA DE MAMIÑA

Mamiña

125km east of Iquique, Mamiña began as a defensive *pucara* and Inca administrative center; its name is said to mean 'Girl of my Eyes,' in reference to an Inca princess who regained her sight in one of the oasis' hotsprings. The terraces and archaeological sites in the valley and the cliffs overlooking the city are Inca and pre-Inca in origin, while the Iglesia de Nuestra Señora del Rosario dates from 1632. The many hotsprings attracted a great deal of tourist traffic during the nitrate boom, and though small, Mamiña still sports plenty of accommodations, the best of which is *El Cardenal*. Transport by regular bus.

🏊 c🛁🏠 Chinos $500
Tambo, Ipla free

Mamiña has a number of springs, each with differing temperatures and mineral properties. The major spring is Termas el Tambo (45-57°C), source for the pools at historic Hotel Refugio del Salitre. The rustic Baños de Ipla has four pools with a source temperature of 30-35°C, providing water for a number of nearby hotels and residenciales. Further upvalley are the mud baths at Barros Chinos Manantial (go in the morning to avoid afternoon winds).

Pica

108km SE of Iquique, Pica marks the site of a copious underground spring, where water filtered down through the porous soils of the altiplano reemerge cool and crystal clear – a true rarity in this region. The oasis' reliable water supply made it an important *tambo* on the Inca trail, and after the conquest Pica became famous for its wine, sold from Arequipa to Potosí. The valley is now dedicated to the cultivation of citrus fruit including mangos, guayabas, grapefruit and Chile's favorite limes (*limones de Pica*); be sure to try the fresh juices sold at kiosks on the streets. Most constructions in town date from the turn of the century nitrate era, when the town attracted the north's *nouveau riche*. Today Pica's water supply is threatened by diversion to Iquique, but you can still swim in refreshing pools such as the COCHA RESBALADERO, Pica's top attraction. Two km up the road to the altiplano is an excellent view of the oasis, and another 1km beyond is a trail to cave paintings in the quebrada de Quisma. Just downvalley is MATILLA, locally famous for its *alfajor* sweets. There are abundant accommodations in town in all price ranges, including the recommended *Hotel El Emilios*, *Residencial El Tambo*, and *Camping Miraflores*. Transport by regular bus from Iquique.

Colchane and Parque Nacional Isluga

Colchane is 245km from Iquique. The road to the park passes by the colonial village of TARAPACÁ (with Saints' Days celebrations on Aug 10 and Nov 30), and the TERMAS DE CHUSMISA. See 🏕 for park details. Transport to Colchane by daily bus.

Termas de Chusmisa

N free

The hotel is presently closed, and the mineral water bottling plant shut down, at this thermal resort 5 km south of the Iquique-Colchane highway. Nonetheless, persistent visitors may be able to talk their way into the pools, which are fed by a 40-46°C spring (ask in the village below town).

Pisagua

Located 167km north of Iquique, Pisagua sits at the mouth of the Quebrada de Tiliviche, and is accessed via a spectacular paved road through the Coast Range from the Panamerican Highway. It was once the third-largest of the nitrate ports, and was the site of a major battle in the War of the Pacific: on November 2, 1879, the Chilean infantry stormed the beach, beginning the bloody campaign which ousted Perú from the Tarapacá province. Today the town is home to a mere 160 inhabitants, but many of its tattered buildings have been declared national monuments. Check out the 1892 TEATRO MUNICIPAL (Municipal Theatre) and the 1887 clock tower. The public jail, now a hotel, was a detention center during the military dictatorship. There's also a nice beach and a municipal campground with hot showers, but no direct public transport.

10km north of the turnoff to Pisagua, the Panamerican highway crosses the QUEBRADA DE TILIVICHE; if you veer left before the bridge you can visit the Hacienda de Tiliviche, and its haunting British Cemetery. On the far side of the bridge is a turnoff from which you can get a good view of the Tiliviche geoglyphs. Transport along the Panamerican is provided by frequent buses.

The Coast from Iquique to Antofagasta   See map

ACCOMMODATION
Free camping on beaches, but bring water and all supplies. Hospedajes, hotels in Tocopilla, Mejillones, and Juan López; best variety in Tocopilla.

TRANSPORT
Frequent northbound and southbound buses ply this route, providing access everywhere but Mejillones and Juan López, which are reached by micro from Antofagasta. Otherwise you can just ask to get dropped off at any beach and flag down another bus when you are ready to leave.

Recently paved, this stretch of Ruta 1 has now replaced the Panamericana as the normal bus route, and provides access to dozens of beaches with free camping and good fishing. Unfortunately, the ease of access has caused many once-pristine beaches to become littered with trash; in general, the beaches are cleaner the further you get from Iquique. About 10km south of town, PLAYA BLANCA is recommended for swimming, while at POZO TOYO (and at PUNTA CHIPANA, further south), cultivated scallops and oysters are available for purchase. PLAYA CHANABAYITA is also good for camping and swimming, with local seafood restaurants and a *caleta pescadores* where you can buy your fish direct from the fishermen. PLAYA EL AGUILA, declared a *Santuario de la Naturaleza* because of nesting tortoises, is another good campsite, but bring all water and supplies. Further south is the sea lion colony at PUNTA DE LOS LOBOS and the idyllic PLAYA IKE-IKE, also known as Playa Peruana.

Beaches in TOCOPILLA include BALNEARIO EL SALITRE, nearest to downtown, and the smaller BALNEARIO COVADONGA, in the rocky coast to the south. Further down is HORNITOS, a lovely beach flanked by seacliffs and good for swimming and sunbathing.

Just north of Antofagasta, MEJILLONES and JUAN LÓPEZ occupy the northern and southern ends of the Península Mejillones, a wide uplifted marine platform. Once the site of South America's greatest railroad yard, Mejillones is now a small industrial and fishing town, popular with weekending *antofagastinos* for its beaches. Plans are brewing to build the continent's largest port on this bay. Juan López is smaller and more pleasant, though condominiums are cramping its ramshackle fishing village ambience. You can find reasonable accommodation at *Hostería Sandokan*, or else camp for free on the beach.

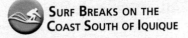

SURF BREAKS ON THE COAST SOUTH OF IQUIQUE

● **Punta Gruesa**
Lefts on big days, rides to 300m.

● **Palo Buque**
Killer left point with big swell, tubes.

● **Caramucho**
Right point, best at low tide with medium to large swell.

● **Caleta Loa**
Beach breaks, best at low- to mid-tide.

● **Tocopilla**
Right point, tubes with big swell, low tide best.

● **Hornitos**
Beach breaks, good without wind.

● **La Portada**
Good rights on windless days.

● **La Chimba**
Fast, hollow lefts over rock reef.

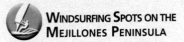

WINDSURFING SPOTS ON THE MEJILLONES PENINSULA

All these areas are good for beginning and intermediate windsurfers, with flat water and afternoon winds to 20 knots.

● **La Rinconada**

● **Isla Santa María**

● **Juan López**

● **Playa las Palmeras**

● **Playa Amarilla**

ANTOFAGASTA, LA PORTADA

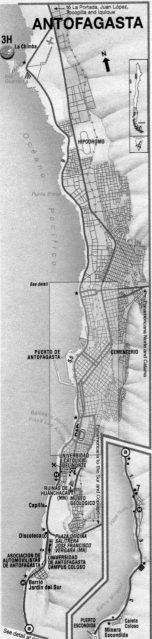

Antofagasta
Pop. 225,316 (☎ city code 55)

ANTOFAGASTA DETAIL

TOURIST INFORMATION
Sernatur, Maipú 240, open Mon-Fri 0930-1300,
1530-1930, Dec-Mar also Sat-San 1000-1400.
Information kiosk at Balmaceda and Prat.

BANKS AND MONEY CHANGERS
Casas de cambio, ATMs downtown on Baquedano.

HOSPITAL
Avenida Argentina 1962.

POST OFFICE
Washington 2613.

INTERNET CONNECTION
Intitour, Baquedano 460, ☎ 266185.

ACCOMMODATION
1 **Hotel Brasil** $, J.S. Ossa 1978, ☎ 267268.
2 **Hotel Tatio** $, Av. Grecia 1000, ☎ 247561.
3 **Apart-Hotel Don Luis** $$, Prat 819, ☎ 262599.
4 **Apart-Hotel El Arriero** $$, Condell 2644 ☎ 264371.
5 **Hotel Antofagasta** $$$, Balmaceda 2575,
  ☎/fax 228811.
6 **Holiday Inn Express** $$$, Grecia 1490,
  ☎ 800 366666.
  More info at www.turistel.cl

CAMPING
7 **Las Garumas**, in Caleta Coloso.
  Free camping on Playa Huáscar.

RESTAURANTS
8 **Café Caribe**, Prat 482. Coffee, juices, breakfast.
9 **Club de Yates**, Balmaceda 2705. Expensive,
  seafood, ocean views.
  Nuevas Raíces, O'Higgins 1892. Pub with live
  Andean music.

AIRPORT
Aeropuerto Cerro Moreno, 25km north.

AIRPORT TRANSPORT
Micro #1 from the Terminal Pesquero. Shared
taxis (US$3) from airline offices. Radiotaxi
Aerobus (US$6), ☎ 262727.

AIRLINE OFFICES
LanChile, Arturo Prat 445, ☎ 265151.
Ladeco, Washington 2589, ☎ 269170.
Aerocontinente, ☎ 6002092358.

BUS STATION AND/OR OFFICES
Long-distance companies operate out of their
offices, mostly on Latorre between Sucre and
Bolívar, also east of Plaza Colón. Local buses (to
Tocopilla, María Elena, Taltal, Chañaral) operate out
of the Terminal de Buses Rurales, Riquelme 513.
Minibuses to Mejillones, Juan López (summer
only), and Hornitos (summer only): Latorre
between Sucre and Bolívar.

RENT A CAR
Avis, Balmaceda 2499 ☎ 221073.
Budget, Baquedano 300 ☎ 452137.
Retablo Rent a Car, E. Pérez 7972 ☎ 278314.

TRAIN
Train to Uyuni, Bolivia, leaves from Calama;
tickets are available at Tramaca offices at Uribe
936 and Sucre 375, ☎ 251770.

ENTERTAINMENT
Pubs, discoteques on Av. Grecia and in Caleta
Coloso, south of town.

Antofagasta is the largest city and most important port in northern Chile, handling the export of copper from Chuquicamata and the bulk of Bolivia's shipping trade. Of the north's coastal cities, it is probably the least attractive to tourists due to its largely industrial character and lack of in-town beaches. Still, the city has an interesting history and is worth a look if you're passing through.

Antofagasta's curious origins date from 1856, when Juan López, a prospector from Copiapó known as 'El Chango,' settled with his family in La Chimba, now a natural reserve north of the city. When Chilean business magnate José Santos Ossa was granted permission by the Bolivians to begin nitrate extraction in their territory, he called upon 'El Chango' and began explorations in the desert east of the city's present site. Ossa soon discovered nitrate in the nearby Salar de Carmen, and the boom was on. Disputes over taxation of Chilean companies operating in the Bolivian-controlled Antofagasta region instigated the War of the Pacific, and in 1879 Antofagasta became the first Bolivian city to be occupied by Chile.

As throughout the Norte Grande, most of Antofagasta's historic architecture dates from the 40 years between the end of the War of the Pacific and the beginning of WWI, when the bottom fell out of the nitrate market. Unlike other ports in the north, however, Antofagasta was able to switch smoothly from nitrate to copper, and today the city remains as dependent upon mining as ever.

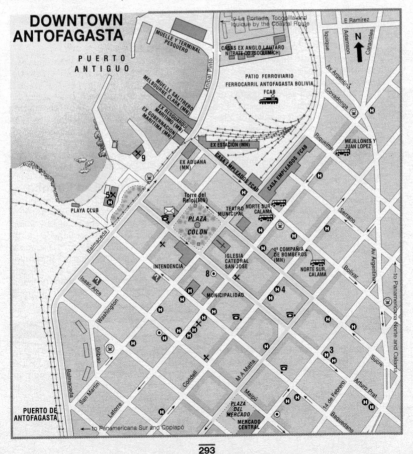

DOWNTOWN ANTOFAGASTA

In-town attractions

Walking tour of the Historic District

Start at the 1872 MUELLE SALITRERO (Nitrate Pier) northwest of downtown. South of the pier are the 1910 EX RESGUARDO MARÍTIMO (Naval Defense Building) and the similarly dated EX GOBERNACIÓN MARÍTIMA (Port Authority). Across the street to the east is the EX ADUANA (Customs House), built in 1868 in Mejillones and transferred to the current site in 1888. Upstairs is the MUSEO REGIONAL *(Tue-Sat 1000-1300, 1530-1830, Sun 1100-1400)*, with exhibitions on regional geology, paleontology, ecology, archaeology, the War of the Pacific and the nitrate era.

North across Calle Bolívar from the Aduana are the various buildings of the FERROCARRIL ANTOFAGASTA-BOLIVIA (FCAB, railway station), which date from 1885-1887.

Walk southeast on Bolívar until you come to San Martín, and turn right; one block down is the Plaza Colón, the centerpiece of which is the TORRE RELOJ, a small-scale replica of Big Ben.

Terminal Pesquero Just north of the historic port, the fishing pier and market is a good place to visit at mid-morning, when local fishermen come off the water with their night's catch.

Avenida Grecia This is the longest boardwalk in Chile and the most pleasant part of Antofagasta, with numerous restaurants and bars. There is a small beach at the Balneario Municipal.

Around Antofagasta

Beaches

Antofagasta´s best beaches are 9km south at Balneario Huáscar and Caleta Coloso. There are a couple of commercial campgrounds nearby, as well as Antofagasta's top discotheques; to get there, take micro #3 on Calle Washington. For out of town beaches to the north, see Beaches from Iquique to Antofagasta, above.

 The best diving in the Antofagasta area is to be found in the calm waters off Juan López and the rocky, remote coast to the south. For info and equipment contact:
  • Víctor González R., Armando Carrera 0235, ☎ (55)211226 or
  • María Verónica Toro Santana, Salvador Reyes 1145, ☎ (55)268370, 257952, (09)2182214.

La Portada

Antofagasta's most famous natural spectacle is located 15km north of the city. Declared a national monument, this natural offshore arch is composed of a base of Jurassic andesites, covered by alternating sandstones and marine sediments, then uplifted and eroded to its current dimensions over the course of the past 3 million years. There is a restaurant at the overlook. Access by micro #15 from the Terminal Pesquero.

Reserva Nacional La Chimba

 This small (2,583há) coastal reserve is located 15km north of town, just to the SE of La Portada. Like other coastal parks in northern Chile, it features a *camanchaca*-fed microclimate, supporting xerophytic plants, foxes, guanacos, and many bird species. You can camp for free in the reserve. Transport via micros #14 and 29 as far as park turnoff, 3km walk required.

The Coast from Antofagasta to Pan de Azúcar

This section of coast – one of few in the *Norte Grande* not yet accessed by paved roads – features some of the north's most diverse and endemic coastal vegetation. Those with their own transport can explore the area surrounding PAPOSO (about 180km south of Antofagasta), which is near the top of Conaf's priority list of new protected areas, or camp on the pristine beach at Playa Cifuncho (no infrastructure, bring water). If using public transport, you are pretty much limited to the urban beaches in Taltal, which may be accessed by regular bus from Antofagasta. See pgs. 307-308 for information on Chañaral and PN Pan de Azúcar.

Quebrada El Médano

⇄ ⏱ 1d ▭
The Quebrada El Médano intersects unpaved coastal Ruta 1 about 150km south of Antofagasta. From the highway, head east up the *quebrada* to an elevation of about 1,300m, where you'll find the first of hundreds of Chango rock paintings spread over nearly five kilometers of cliffs. There is no water at all on the route, which makes for a full days' walk.

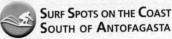

SURF SPOTS ON THE COAST SOUTH OF ANTOFAGASTA

● **Las Pozas**
Beach breaks, best at low tide.

● **Puerto Fino**
Left point with medium to large swell, long rides, best at low tide.

● **Villa Alegre**
Beach breaks, best at low tide.

● **Balneario Flamenco**
Left point with medium to large swell, best at low tide.

PARQUE NACIONAL PAN DE AZUCAR

See pg 6 for photo credit

Calama
Pop. 121,300 (☎ city code 55)

Situated on the banks of the Río Loa, clean, orderly Calama is the largest of northern Chile's oases. It's a good place to rest up from explorations in the desert and altiplano, and if heading to San Pedro de Atacama, Calama is an obligated stop.

Like most desert oases, Calama began as a supply point – called *tambos* by the Incas – along on of many trade routes through the desert. The Spanish overlooked the site in favor of nearby Chiu Chiu, which was preferable for agriculture. After independence, however, Bolivia transferred its regional administration to Calama, which lay on the supply route between Salta, Argentina and the Bolivian port of Cobija.

In 1879, soon after the outbreak of the War of the Pacific, Chilean forces occupied the city. Significant growth began with the beginning of operations at CHUQUICAMATA, the world's largest open-pit copper mine, which is responsible for the prosperity which Calama currently enjoys. In 1956, with the diversion of water from the acrid Río Salado for use in the mine, water quality in the Río Loa improved and agriculture spread in the surrounding area.

In-town Attractions

Museo Arqueológico y Etnológico Located in Parque El Loa, south of town on Av. O'Higgins, Calama's only museum features exhibits on regional archaeology and ethnology.
Hours: Open Tue-Fri 1000-1300, 1500-1930. Transport via taxi colectivos #5 or #18 from Latorre and Vicuña Mackenna.

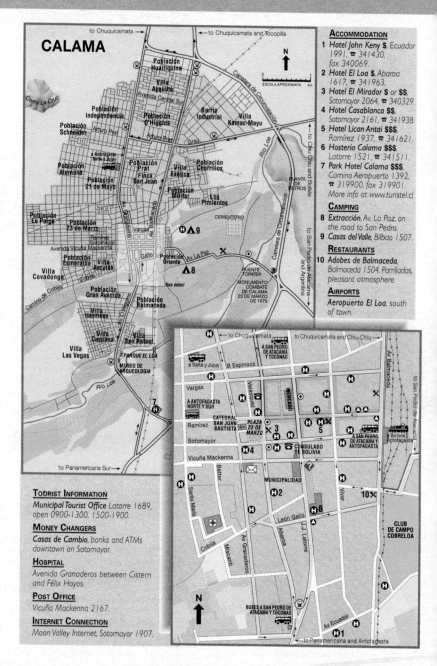

CALAMA

AIRLINE OFFICES
LanChile, Latorre 1499, ☎ 313927.
Ladeco, Eleuterio Ramírez 1858,
☎ 312626.
Aerocontinente, ☎ 6002092358.

BUS STATION
No central terminal. Company
offices on Sotomayor between Vivar
and Balmaceda, on Vivar between

*Ramírez and Vargas, and Antofagasta
between Abaroa and Latorre.*
Colectivos to Chuquicamata: On
the plaza.
Colectivos to Tocopilla: Corner of
Balmaceda and Vargas.

RENT A CAR
Avis, P. Gallo 1985-A ☎ 319797.
Budget, Granaderos 2875 ☎ 361072.

TRAIN STATION
Balmaceda 1777. Tickets for
Wed night trains to Ollagüe
and Uyuni are available at
terminal and at Tramaca
offices in Calama (Sotomayor
1961, ☎ 340000),
Antofagasta, and Santiago.
Trains depart at 0400.

Around Calama

Chuquicamata

16km north of Calama, the town of Chuquicamata exists for one reason and one reason only: to provide housing and amenities for the employees of the homonymous open-pit copper mine just north. Free bus tours of the mine depart daily at 1000 from the north end of J.M. Carrera; be sure to arrive at least an hour early. Regular taxi colectivos run to Chuqui from Calama's plaza. See 🄲 for details on the mine at Chuqui.

Geoglyphs at Cerro Chug Chug

The north's second-largest collection of geoglyphs lies 82km west of Calama on the road to Tocopilla. From the turnoff, it's 13km to the base of the *cerro*, so if you don't have your own transport it may not be worth the walk. See 🄲 for more details.

The Río Loa Watershed

CHIU CHIU is 31km east of Calama. There is no public transport; but a taxi there will cost you about $7000. 🄳

El Tatio Geysers

114km from Calama. No public transport, access by tour only. 🄳

San Pedro de Atacama   *pop. 1,446 (☎ city code 55)*

Set in a pleasant oasis at the north end of the Salar de Atacama, San Pedro de Atacama is the center of Atacameño culture and a pivotal landmark in regional history and prehistory. Today, this hip little adobe town is the number one destination for Chilean and foreign visitors to northern Chile, and during peak season San Pedro's numerous hotels, campgrounds, restaurants and bars fill to overflowing. No other destination in the north can compete with San Pedro for the number and variety of nearby attractions, relaxed atmosphere, spellbinding light and unforgettable sunsets.

San Pedro's dependable water supply and proximity to the altiplano made it a hub of Neolithic development in the north, and the area's mineral wealth and importance as a desert crossroads attracted the attentions of the Tiwanaku empire during the first millenium AD. The same characteristics later attracted the Incas, who established their regional administration at Catarpe, upriver on the Río Grande, during the 15th century.

San Pedro entered into the history of the conquest in 1536, when Diego de Almagro passed through the oasis on his way back to Perú to fight with the Pizarro brothers. Four years later, Francisco de Aguirre stormed in at the head of a large contingent of Spanish-friendly Indians (known as *yanaconas*), paving the way for the arrival of Pedro de Valdivia, who alledgedly slept in the CASA INCAICA, the ancient but unremarkable structure on the east side of the plaza. In 1547, the Spanish established their first mission in San Pedro (which they called *Atacama la Grande*), and subjected the local Atacameños to the virtual enslavement of the *encomiendas* system.

SAN PEDRO DE ATACAMA

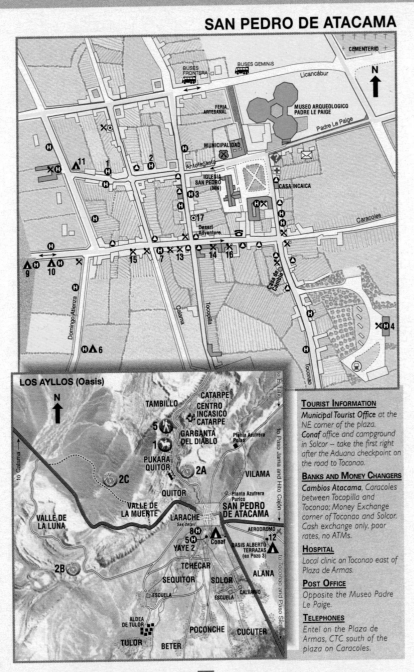

TOURIST INFORMATION

Municipal Tourist Office at the NE corner of the plaza.
Conaf office and campground in Solcor – take the first right after the Aduana checkpoint on the road to Toconao.

BANKS AND MONEY CHANGERS

Cambios Atacama, Caracoles between Tocopilla and Toconao; *Money Exchange* corner of Toconao and Solcor. Cash exchange only, poor rates, no ATMs.

HOSPITAL

Local clinic on Toconao east of Plaza de Armas.

POST OFFICE

Opposite the Museo Padre Le Paige.

TELEPHONES

Entel on the Plaza de Armas, CTC south of the plaza on Caracoles.

With independence, San Pedro became a vital link on the supply route from the port of Cobija to Salta, Argentina; later, as the nitrate industry exploded in Chile, it served as an essential watering hole for cattle driven west from Argentina to the desert *oficinas*. These cattle drives ended with the inauguration of the Antofagasta-Bolivia railroad, and today San Pedro lives by tourism, small scale agriculture, and mining in the Salar de Atacama.

Divided into 15 sectors known as *ayllus*, San Pedro de Atacama is tiny but can be somewhat confusing, as almost all the streets and buildings look the same; use Volcán Licancabur, the conical peak directly east of town, to orient yourself. There is electricity in town only from sunset to midnight, though some restaurants and hotels have generators. Still, firelight and candlelight are still the rule, rather than the exception, in San Pedro.

In-town attractions

Museo Arqueológico Padre Le Paige
A must-see for any visitor to San Pedro de Atacama, with over 380,000 archaeological artifacts depicting the many phases of development in the Inter-Andean depression. The collection represents the life's work of the late Belgian Jesuit Gustavo Le Paige, and contains extensive collections of ceramics, copper and gold work, and artful utilitarian objects. Note the tablets and straws for the inhalation of hallucinogenic *cebil* and San Pedro cactus, the mummies exhibiting practices of skull deformation, and the exhibits on local petroglyphs and cave paintings.
Hours: Open Jan-Feb Mon-Sun 1000-1300, 1500-1900; Mar-Dec Mon-Sun 0900-1200, 1400-1800.

Iglesia de San Pedro On the west side of the plaza, San Pedro's church was originally built in 1641, though the present structure dates from 1774 and the tower was built only in 1964. Note the lovely algarrobo rafters and the ceiling and doors made from cardón cactus.

Around San Pedro

Pucara de Quitor and Catarpe Administrative Center
These pre-Hispanic ruins along the Río Grande make for an easy half-day trip from San Pedro: Quitor is a mere 3km north, while Catarpe lies another 3km upvalley. You can walk, bike, ride a horse, or take your pick of tours to these sites. **G**

Ayllo de Tulor
The oldest habitational site in the valley lies 9km SW of San Pedro. Access is by bike or tour; the latter are often combined with visits to the Valle de la Luna. **G**

Valle de la Luna

San Pedro's most popular attraction is set 14km west of town in the heart of the *Cordillera de la Sal* (Salt Range). Nearby is the similar but lesser-known Valle de la Muerte; access to each is by bike or tour. See 🔲 for details on this and other attractions in Reserva Nacional Los Flamencos.

El Tatio Geysers

The geysers and steaming fumaroles of the El Tatio Geyser field are set at an elevation of 4,321m, making this the highest such geothermal field in the world. Once targeted by the state development agency Corfo for geothermal development, el Tatio is best visited at sunrise, when changing atmospheric pressure causes the geysers to erupt, spewing steam up to 10m high. Winds at this hour are minimal and low angle sunlight heightens the contrast of rising steam, bizarre mineral deposits, and the surrounding peaks. Use special caution to avoid breaking through the thin crust surrounding the vents.

Access to El Tatio is by private vehicle or tour from San Pedro or Calama only. You must leave San Pedro by 0400 to arrive at sunrise; most tours also stop off at the Baños de Puritama.

Baños de Puritama

 C 🛏 free
This large 30-35°C pool (and waterfall) are located at an elevation of 3,475m, about 30km from San Pedro on the route to El Tatio. You can camp nearby but must bring all food and water.

River Valleys North of San Pedro

 🔦 ⏱5d ▯
This excellent hike may be begun right in the town of San Pedro. Start by heading north up the Río Grande, continuing past the Pucara de Quitor and the Catarpe Inca administrative center to the villages of San Bartolo and Río Grande. From here, continue up the Penaliri river gorge to the village of Machuca, at 3,500m. The descent leads past the Baños de Puritama, down a lovely gorge of white tupirite to the Guatín river valley and the village of Guatín. The final day follows the Guatín river valley south into the San Pedro oasis. Some operators offer the first stage of this trek on horseback, and shorter versions are often available.
Operators: 10 - 22 - 31 - 49 - 102 - 132 - 212

VALLE DE LA LUNA

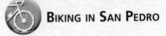 BIKING IN SAN PEDRO

Operators: 31 - 102 - 137 - 162 - 164
Bikes are tremendously useful for seeing the sights in and around San Pedro de Atacama. The trips listed here all make good, relatively easy day trips, and if you have camping gear and are in good riding shape, there is no reason why you couldn't ride from north San Pedro towards the El Tatio Geysers and the upper Río Loa, east into the Puna de Atacama, or south along the Salar de Atacama. With van support, you can ride the whole area in eight days or so.

● Archaeological sites along the Río Grande
▶16km◀rt to Catarpe ⏱½d ▯ ▯
From San Pedro (0km), head north out of town on Calle Tocopilla, along the Río Grande. The Pucara de Quitor (3km) is on a bluff on the west side of the river. Further up is a T intersection (3km): the left road leads to the Catarpe Inca administration center (2km), while the right road leads into the labyrinthine Garganta del Diablo (Devils Gorge). Another 4 km past Catarpe is the entrance to the Río Salado valley, on the left; if you stash your bike here and continue another 2 km up the Salado, you'll find a remarkable collection of petroglyphs.

● Ayllo de Tulor, Valle de la Luna
▶40km◀rt w/ trip to Tulor ⏱½d ▯ ▯
From San Pedro (0km), head west out of town on Calle Caracoles. Past the bridge head left at the fork and continue through open country. Take the left (3km) towards Coyo and continue south through the village, passing the soccer field (4km) and continuing south until you see signs for Tulor (2km). The route is a little confusing and you may have to ask for directions. From Tulor, return to the crossroads (6km) and turn left, climbing (gradually at first, and then steeply) into the Valle de la Luna (11km). Return via the same route.

● Valle de la Muerte
▶10km◀rt ⏱½d ▯ ▯ ▯
May be combined with either of the above routes; all three would make a big day, but still feasible. From San Pedro (0km) head west out of town on Licancabur, towards Calama. At a signaled crossroads (3km), turn right onto a dirt road and continue up a steepening grade into the Cordillera de la Sal. From the top of the pass you can continue on to rejoin the highway to Calama, or return the way you came.

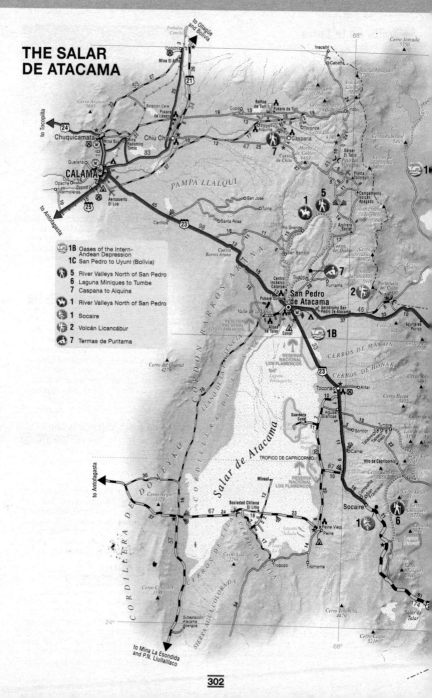

THE SALAR
DE ATACAMA

1B Oases of the Intern-
    Andean Depression
1C San Pedro to Uyuni (Bolivia)

5 River Valleys North of San Pedro
6 Laguna Miniques to Tumbe
7 Caspana to Aiquina

1 River Valleys North of San Pedro

1 Socaire
2 Volcán Licancábur
7 Termas de Puritama

Reserva Nacional Los Flamencos

Created in 1990, Reserva Nacional Los Flamencos consists of seven separate sectors, mostly to the southeast of San Pedro de Atacama, with a total area of 73,986há. The park was ostensibly created to provide protected nesting habitat for three species of South American flaminges, though it also includes sectors such as the Valle de la Luna, which have little to do with flamingo conservation.

A visit to Conaf's *Centro de Informaciones Ambientales* on the way out of San Pedro is highly recommended to orient you within the reserve – all of its sectors merit a visit.

The geological formations of the **VALLE DE LA LUNA** constitute the park's most popular and accessible attraction. On the approach from San Pedro, you'll see the Salt Range on the horizon to the west; climbing past the first range of crumbling hills, you'll enter a broad, wind-sculpted basin, in the center of the which are a couple of huge sand dunes that you can can climb for views (and an exhilarating descent). Further north is the dramatic rock formation known as the **TRES MARÍAS**, and from here you can either backtrack or continue north to join up with the paved highway to Calama.

Tours to the Valley de la Luna are often combined with visits to the archaeological site at **TULOR**. If at all possible, plan your visit to coincide with sunset or the full moon, but note that camping is not allowed.

The **TAMBILLO** sector, between San Pedro and Toconao, is probably the least worthwhile section of the park for most visitors, consisting of a plantation of salt-resistant tamarugo trees.

Further south (38km from San Pedro) is the pre-Hispanic village of **TOCONAO**. Built entirely of white *liparita* volcanic stone, Toconao has a lovely 18th century church and bell tower in the plaza, while just southeast is a remarkable cemetery strewn with thousands of paper flowers brought by the families of the deceased and perfectly preserved in the arid, rarified air. Above the town to the east is the **QUEBRADA DE JEREZ**, a deeply inset irrigated valley with swimming holes, rocks to climb on, and trails through pomegranate and quince orchards.

Southwest of Toconao in the Salar de Atacama are some of the best places in the reserve to spot and photograph Chilean and James flamingos. Most tours visit **LAGUNA CHAXA**; just south of here are **LAGO BARROS ARANA** and **LAGUNA AGUILAR**, where most courtship and nesting takes place. Binoculars are a good idea, though the flamingos are accustomed to humans and occasionally come quite close.

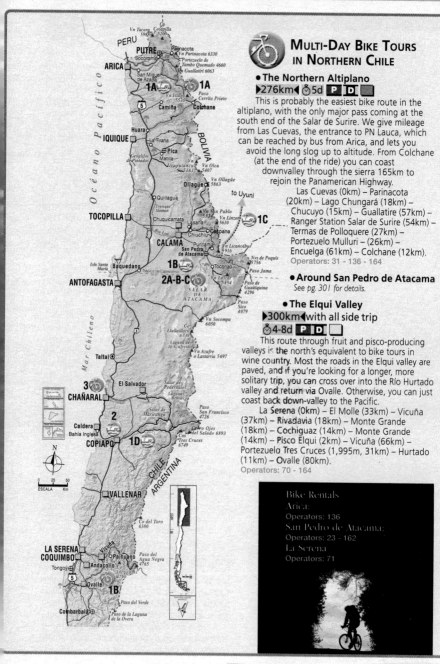

MULTI-DAY BIKE TOURS IN NORTHERN CHILE

• The Northern Altiplano
▶276km◀ ⏱5d P D ▭

This is probably the easiest bike route in the altiplano, with the only major pass coming at the south end of the Salar de Surire. We give mileage from Las Cuevas, the entrance to PN Lauca, which can be reached by bus from Arica, and lets you avoid the long slog up to altitude. From Colchane (at the end of the ride) you can coast downvalley through the sierra 165km to rejoin the Panamerican Highway.

Las Cuevas (0km) – Parinacota (20km) – Lago Chungará (18km) – Chucuyo (15km) – Guallatire (57km) – Ranger Station Salar de Surire (54km) – Termas de Polloquere (27km) – Portezuelo Mulluri – (26km) – Encuelga (61km) – Colchane (12km).
Operators: 31 - 136 - 164

• Around San Pedro de Atacama
See pg. 301 for details.

• The Elqui Valley
▶300km◀ with all side trip
⏱4-8d P D ▭

This route through fruit and pisco-producing valleys is the north's equivalent to bike tours in wine country. Most of the roads in the Elqui valley are paved, and if you're looking for a longer, more solitary trip, you can cross over into the Río Hurtado valley and return via Ovalle. Otherwise, you can just coast back down-valley to the Pacific.

La Serena (0km) – El Molle (33km) – Vicuña (37km) – Rivadavia (18km) – Monte Grande (18km) – Cochiguaz (14km) – Monte Grande (14km) – Pisco Elqui (2km) – Vicuña (66km) – Portezuelo Tres Cruces (1,995m, 31km) – Hurtado (11km) – Ovalle (80km).
Operators: 70 - 164

Bike Rentals
Arica:
Operators: 136
San Pedro de Atacama:
Operators: 23 - 162
La Serena
Operators: 71

OVERLANDS AND CIRCUITS IN NORTHERN CHILE

• Northern Altiplano and Sierra Circuit
At least ⏱5d

This extraordinary route takes you through some of Chile's richest wildlife parks and Aymara culture areas. From Arica, principal stops include the Lluta Valley, Putre, PN Lauca (Parinacota, Lago Chungará), RN Las Vicuñas, MN Salar de Surire, PN Volcán Isluga (Enquelga, Isluga, Termas de Puchuldiza), and Colchane, descending to Iquique. This route may also be varied to include villages and oases of the arid sierra. 4WD required for altiplano section.
Operators: 10 - 31 - 37 - 49 - 73 - 136 - 153 -170

• Around San Pedro: Oases of the Inter-Andean Depression
At least ⏱4d

San Pedro makes a great base for explorations or a relaxing stopoff on an overland route linking the Altiplano with the Atacama Desert. With a rented vehicle, you could see all the 'major' attractions in four or five days, but you need 4WD (or at least high clearance) to visit El Tatio and other altiplano attractions.
Operators: 10 - 22 - 23 - 31 - 49 - 77 - 102 - 120 - 153 - 170 - 209 - 212 - 223

• San Pedro to Uyuni (Bolivia)*
⏱3-4d

Probably the most spectacular way to cross from Chile into Bolivia, this trip takes you into the Bolivian altiplano just south of Volcán Licancabur, and stopping at Lagunas Verde and Colorada, a major nesting site for James flamingos. From here, the route leads across the Salar de Uyuni, the world's largest salt flat, stopping at the eerie Isla del Pescado. 4WD is required.
Operators: 10 - 22 - 31 - 49 - 133 - 170

• The Copiapó Altiplano*
⏱2d minimun

The valleys and altiplano east and northeast of Copiapó are remote, extremely varied, and rich in fauna and archaeological significance. An excellent circuit takes in the Inca ruins of the upper Copiapó and Jorquera Valleys en route to Laguna Negro San Francisco, Laguna Santa Rosa and the Salar de Maricunga, PN Tres Cruces, Laguna Verde and Volcán Ojos del Salado, returning via the Salar de Pedernales and El Salvador. PN Llullaillaco, further north, is accessed from the north via the Escondida mine. 4WD is required for all these routes.
Operators: 143 - 153 - 200

*these routes are not recommended for independent travelers due to navigational difficulties.

At the southern end of the Salar de Atacama is the oasis village of PEINE. The Inca Trail passed through here, and there are refreshing pools for swimming, called *cochas*.

The three altiplano sectors of the RN LOS FLAMENCOS are a little more difficult to access, and tours are somewhat more expensive – but well worth it. From San Pedro, you can see the paved road to the altiplano (Ruta 27 to Salta), climbing steeply up the incline south of VOLCÁN LICANCABUR. Following this route past the initial incline, the terrain levels out into vast basins and salt flats such as the SALAR DE PUJSA which serves as nesting habitat for the Andean flamingo. Further on toward Argentina, via an unmarked turnoff before the Salar de Aguas Calientes, is the SALAR DE TARA, flanked by startling geological formations; vizcachas and Andean geese may often be spotted here. You need 4WD to access these sectors.

Further south, via Ruta 23 to Argentina via Paso Sico, are LAGUNA MIÑIQUES AND LAGUNA MISCANTI. Set at the base of two immense volcanoes (also named Miñiques and Miscanti), these altiplano lakes are fringed with salt deposits and surrounded by brilliantly colored clumps of *paja brava*, creating a singular visual experience. You can loop past both lakes and rejoin the highway to the southeast. On your way to the lakes, check out the terraced agriculture and colonial church in SOCAIRE.

Between the two highways lies a vast altiplano region with more lakes and salt flats. The old highway to Argentina leads through the tiny Aymara village of TUMBRE and past VOLCÁN LASCAR to LAGUNA LEJÍA. These regions are not protected by the park, but are so remote that it hardly matters. You need a 4WD and probably a guide to access this area.

Climbing in Socaire

Local climbers have thus far established over 100 routes on the clean, reddish volcanic walls in the quebrada above the village of Socaire. The routes are generally short and dynamic, featuring a mix of finger cracks and bolted face climbing. Routes vary from 5.8-5.12c, with a majority of routes in the 5.11 range. All routes are equipped with bolt anchors.
Operators: 191

Laguna Miñiques to Tumbre

🥾 ⏱3d ☐
This hike leads through high, remote country in the altiplano sector of Reserva Nacional Los Flamencos. From Ruta 23, follow the western shore of Laguna Miñiques past Cerro Miñiques and on to the Quebrada de Nacimiento. Continue north, around the western flank of Cerro Lejía and cross the old road to Argentina en route to Laguna Lejía (4,350m). A long last day passes over Lascar Pass (4,500m) and descends to the tiny Aymara village of Tumbre. If doing this hike on your own (recomended for strong, experienced parties only), you'll want to arrange a pickup beforehand to avoid a long, thirsty walk out to the highway.

Operators: 31

Volcán Licancabur (5,916m)

⏱3d return from San Pedro ☐
Dominating the skyline east of San Pedro, Licancabur was routinely scaled by Inca priests, who built a stone *pirca* and left piles of firewood on the rim of the lake-filled summit crater. Today, the ascent is usually made either from the south (off Ruta 27) or from a base camp on Laguna Verde in Bolivia. The route is nontechnical, usually involving a long, tiring slog up loose scree. Other noteworthy ascents in the area include Volcán Apagado (5,700m), Volcán Sairecanbur (6,100m), Cerro Toro (5,600m), Volcán Chiliques (5,778m), the intensely active Volcán Lascar (5,400m), and Cerro de Pili (6,044m), which also has an Inca ritual site on the summit. Climbing conditions on all these peaks are similar to those on Licancabur.

Operators: 31 - 83 - 102 - 191 - 212

The Río Loa Watershed

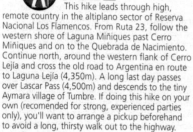

ACCOMMODATION / FOOD AND DRINK
Hospedajes and limited provisions in Chiu Chiu only.

TRANSPORT
No public transport. Access by taxi from Calama ($7000), or by tour from Calama or San Pedro (often combined with visits to the El Tatio Geysers).

Accessible from Calama or San Pedro de Atacama, the Río Loa and its several tributaries – the Río Toconce, Río Salado, and Río Caspana – are among Northern Chile's most significant and accessible sites of pre-Hispanic and early colonial civilization.

Located near the confluence of the Loa and the Salado, **CHIU CHIU** is the largest and most 'prosperous' pueblo in the area. Having long served as an important crossroads for trans-Andean llama caravans, in the early 17th century the town was baptized *Atacama la Chica* by the Spanish, for whom it served as an important missionary center and supply point in the Potosí – Cobija silver route. Chiu Chiu's thick-set **Iglesia de San Francisco** dates from 1675 and is one of the north's finest representations of the fusion of Spanish and Native design.

To the north, the Río Loa enters a box canyon, and if you walk upriver you can check out the numerous petroglyphs engraved in soft *liparita* volcanic stone along the east side of the valley. 8km up this same road from Chiu Chiu is the Pucara de Lasana, an immense defensive fort dating from the post-Tiwanaku epoch of Atacameño culture (12th-century). From here Ruta 21 continues north past the Salar de Ascotán to **OLLAGÜE** and Bolivia.

East of Chiu Chiu along the Río Salado valley, **AIQUINA** is perhaps the most beautiful of the stone oasis villages; check out the overlook from the hilltop behind the church. Further east, well-preserved **CASPANA** boasts a surprisingly good museum depicting local culture and a small handicraft market with textiles in llama and alpaca wool. Finally, the terraced village of **TOCONCE** gets marks for its spectacular location near the mouth of the Río Toconce gorge, in the midst of a vast, rocky plateau begging for exploration on foot.

North of the irrigated valleys are the fields of the **VEGAS DE TURI**, a traditional pasture area now in decline due to water-diversion schemes. Here you'll find the sadly deteriorated **PUCARA DE TURI**, the largest of the pre-Hispanic fortresses, also dating from the post-Tiwanaku epoch and later occupied by Inca administrators. Tours from San Pedro are often combined with a visit to the El Tatio Geysers.

Caspana to Aiquina

🥾 ⏱1d ☐
Beginning in Caspana, head down the Caspana Valley, continuing past the confluence with the Río Salado until you reach Aiquina. The route follows beautiful box canyons, and some wading is required.

Operators: 31

Chañaral
pop. 12,008 (☎ *city code 52*)

Set at the mouth of the Río Salado, Chañaral was an important colonial port for the nearby oasis of Finca de Chañaral, and later handled independent Chile's first exports of copper. Unfortunately, history is about all Chañaral has going for it.

The broad beach in front of the town was once much smaller: beginning in 1920, tailings from the Potrerillos and El Salvador mines, upriver on the Río Salado, backfilled the bay with 320 million tons of toxic sand. In 1988, a successful citizen's suit against Codelco – the first of its kind in Chile – required the company to contain its wastes in the desert.

Today, the only reason to stop off in Chañaral is to visit the coast to the north, which is noted for its beaches and highly endemic vegetation. Most visitors hurry through this industrial town and head straight to PN Pan de Azúcar.

Around Chañaral

Beaches to the South

There are dozens of beaches along this stretch of coast, all with easy access from the Panamericana. **BALNEARIO FLAMENCO** is the most developed beach destination in the area, with locally grown oysters and scallops. Further south, there are a number of small beaches in and around the **SANTUARIO DE LA NATURALEZA GRANITO ORBICULAR**, protected for its unique geological formations. Transport by regular bus. See pg.294 for beaches to the north of PN Pan de Azúcar.

RECOMMENDED LODGING

1 *Hotel Mini* **$**, San Martín 528, ☎ 480068.
2 *Hostería Chañaral* **$$**, Miller 268, ☎ 480055.

TRANSPORT

Bus station on Merino Jarpa between Los Baños and Conchuela. Many buses pass by town but will stop to pick up passengers on the Panamerican. Turismo Chango (☎ 480484, 480668) runs minibus service to PN Pan de Azúcar, departing from in front of the Municipalidad, consult for times.

CHAÑARAL

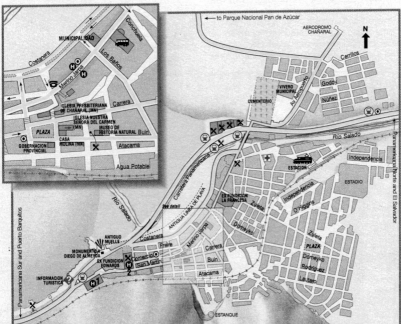

Parque Nacional Pan de Azúcar

INFORMATION
Conaf ranger station at Caleta Pan de Azúcar.

ACCOMMODATION
Campsites at Caleta Pan de Azúcar, Playa Piqueros, and Playa Blanca. Isolated cabañas north of the caleta. Water available at park administration.

TRANSPORT
By minibus from Chañaral. Hitching is possible but depends on the season. If you have your own vehicle, you can also access the park from the east, via the turnoff at Las Bombas, 45km north of Chañaral.

PROVISIONS
A small store in Caleta Pan de Azúcar sells dry and canned goods, but much better to buy provisions in Chañaral or - even better - Copiapó or Antofagasta.

Pan de Azúcar is a coastal park, ranging in elevation from sea level to 900m, with an extension of 43,769há. Within the park are several white-sand beaches ideal for camping, and the camanchaca-fed microclimate supports a surprisingly varied floral community of over 20 species of cactus and other xerophytic flora. This is also one of the few coastal environments that still supports healthy populations of guanacos.

Most infrastructure is located in the southern sector of the park near the administration at **CALETA PAN DE AZÚCAR**, where Conaf maintains a labeled cacterium and a local concessionaire runs a simple campsite and a couple of cabañas. Local fishermen in

the caleta offer boat trips *($3500/ pp, minimum six passengers)* around **ISLA PAN DE AZÚCAR**, which is home to sea lions and otters (*chungungos*), and is a nesting site for Humboldt Penguins. **PLAYA PAN DE AZÚCAR** is the large beach to the north of the *caleta*, while the more solitary **PLAYA PIQUEROS** and **PLAYA BLANCA** are located just south.

In the northern sector of the park, perched over the ocean at an elevation of 700m, **LAS LOMITAS** may be accessed by road from Caleta Pan de Azúcar. The road is usually closed by a locked barrier, and you must pay an entry fee to Conaf in the *caleta* to have it opened. There may be water here, collected from the *camanchaca*, and foxes are commonly spotted. The road between Las Lomitas and Caleta Pan de Azúcar shows you the full range of ecosystems present in the park.

 ▶varies◀ ⏱varies P D

From a base camp at Caleta Pan de Azúcar, you can ride on dirt roads and single-track trails throughout the park, including the 60km round-trip up Quebrada Pan de Azúcar to Las Lomitas. Aside from the standard entrance via the coast from Chañaral, another good option is to have a bus drop you with your bike at the top of the quebrada (45km north of Chañaral on the Pan-American), and ride west through the coast range into the park.

Operators: 164

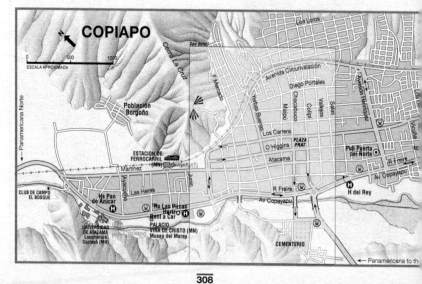

♿ ⏱varies ⬛
Hiking trips in Pan de Azúcar are especially worthwhile in spring, when the surprising vegetation of the Coast Range comes into bloom. From the park administration in Caleta Pan de Azúcar, you can hike east into any of several relatively lush *quebradas*; Conaf has done some trail work in Quebrada Castillo, accessed via a transverse track which splits east from the coastal road to Chañaral, just south of the *caleta*. Guanacos are frequently spotted near the entrance to the quebrada. To the north of the caleta, you may hike to the overlook at Mirador Pan de Azúcar; ask rangers for details.

COPIAPÓ'S MUSEO MINERALÓGICO

Copiapó

Pop. 98,188 (☎ city code 52)

Poised at the southern edge of the inhospitable Atacama Desert, Copiapó has a long and illustrious history that has been largely obscured by a century of economic decline and foreign ownership of industry. Today, you have to look hard to notice the beautiful mansions and public buildings erected during Copiapó's heydey in the mid-to-late 19th century, and most travelers pass the city by. But Copiapó is worth a visit, and provides access to excellent beaches, labyrinthine Andean valleys loaded with archaeological sites, and a remote and seldom-visited section of the altiplano.

The Inca empire erected dozens of forts and tambos in the Copiapó valley, and from here shipped metals and agricultural products over the altiplano to Cuzco. Diego de Almagro followed the Inca Trail here in 1536, and the estimated 5,000 Indians of the Copiapó valley were the first in Chile to catch a glimpse of his ragged band of conquistadors limping down off Paso San Francisco. The valley was also the first of the territories claimed by Pedro de Valdivia upon his arrival in Chile in 1540, but the lack of significant mineral finds limited Copiapó's importance during the Colonial era.

In 1832, however, the discovery of silver at nearby **CHAÑARCILLO** gave the nascent settlement the only impetus it needed. For the next twenty years, Copiapó was the single most important settlement in the north, attracting a new class of Chilean elites, many of whom would go on to become important players in other sectors of the national economy. Most of the city's historic architecture dates from this era.

Since the decline of Chañarcillo, a succession of other mines have buoyed Copiapó's economy, though most of these have been foreign-owned and thus impart limited local benefits. The same is true for agriculture, which focuses on the production of export-quality table grapes. Many locals see tourism as the answer to the city's economic straits, but lack of paved roads to Argentina has created a sense of isolation that has proved difficult to overcome.

The long, narrow city is located on the north bank of the Río Copiapó and surrounded by high, arid hills. The streets are somewhat confusingly offset with respect to the cardinal directions, but Copiapó is not big and you can easily visit all of the city's historic attractions on foot.

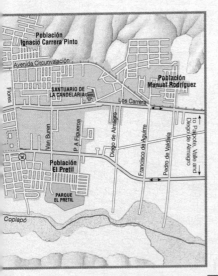

COPIAPO DOWNTOWN

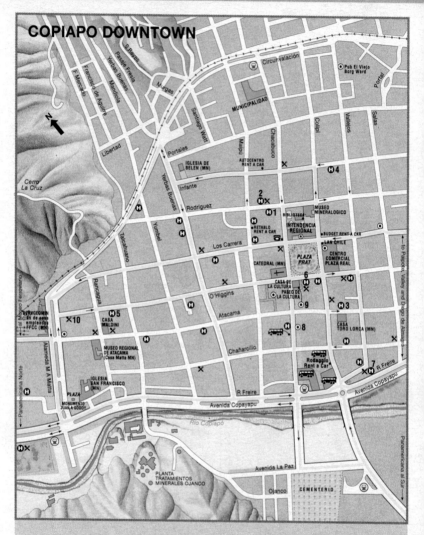

TOURIST INFORMATION

Sernatur is on the north side of Plaza Prat, open Mon-Fri 0830-1730.
Conaf is at Atacama and Salas, ☎ 212571.

HOSPITAL

Corner of Los Carrera and Vicuña.

MONEY CHANGERS

Banks, ATMs downtown.

POST OFFICE

In the Intendencia Regional, Los Carrera 691.

INTERNET CONNECTION

Zona Virtual, Colipí 610

ACCOMMODATION

1 *Hotel El Sol* **S**, Rodríguez 550, ☎ 215672.

2 *Residencial Ben-Bow* **S**, Rodríguez 541, ☎ 217634.

3 *Hotel Palace* **SS**, Atacama 741, ☎ 212852.

4 *Hotel Montecatini I* **SS**, Infante 766, ☎ 211363, fax 214773.

5 *Hotel La Casona* **SS**, O'Higgins 150, ☎fax 217278.

6 *Hotel Diego de Almeyda* **SSS**, O'Higgins 656, ☎fax 212075.

7 *Hotel Miramonti* **SSS**, Ramón Freire 731, ☎ 210440.
More info at www.turistel.cl

In-town Attractions

Walking tour of historical sites Begin in the **PLAZA ARTURO PRAT**, the center of city life and one of the nicest plazas in the north, with giant *algarrobos* and *pimiento* trees dating from 1880. The *pimientos* have brilliant magenta flowers in springtime. The 1851 **CATEDRAL** is at the eastern corner of the plaza, and kitty corner to it is the **EX-MUNICIPALIDAD**. Now known as the **CASA DE CULTURA** (Cultural Center), the building hosts art exhibitions and features a pleasant interior courtyard with handicrafts and a café.

A block northeast of the plaza, on Colipí, is the **MUSEO MINERALÓGICO**. With over 2000 samples, this is the second most complete mineral museum in South America, and provides a good introduction to local and general mineralogy.

Hours: Mon-Fri 1000-1300, 1530-1900, Sat 1000-1300.
Entrance: $300, children $100).

From the Plaza, walk northeast on O'Higgins to calle Rancagua, where you'll find the unassuming **CASA MATTA**, site of the **MUSEO REGIONAL DE ATACAMA**, with exhibitions on local prehistory and history. Ask here for tours of archaeological sites in and around the Copiapó Valley.

Hours: Tue-Thu 0930-1245, 1500-1915, Fri 0930-1245, 1500-1815, Sat 1000-1245, 1500-1715, Sun 1000-1245.
Entrance: $500, children $250.

Continue past the museum to Alameda Matta, shaded by large algarrobos; to the right, towards the mountains, is the recently restored **CASA DE EMPLEADOS DEL FFCC** (Railroad Employees Building), from 1860. Just northeast on calle Martínez is the **ESTACIÓN DE FERROCARRILES** (Train Station) and the **MUSEO FERROVIARIO** *(Railroad Museum, Jan-Feb: Mon-Sun 0900-1300, 1500-2100. Mar-Dec: 1000-*

INCA METALLURGICAL CENTER AT VIÑA DEL CERRO

1300, 1500-1900). Built in 1854, this was the eastern terminus of the Copiapó-Caldera line, which carried silver from the mine at Chañarcillo to port.

Backtrack southeast, towards the river. Near where Matta runs into Kennedy is the 1872 **IGLESIA SAN FRANCISCO**, in front of which is a small plaza and a monument to Juan Godoy, the discoverer of Chañarcillo.

Take a right on Kennedy. About a kilometer down on the left is the **PALACETE DE LA VIÑA DEL CRISTO**, an opulent Gregorian mansion dating from 1860. A few blocks further west is the pleasant campus of the **UNIVERSIDAD DE ATACAMA**, where you can check out the 'La Copiapó' locomotive, an 1850s Norris Brothers from Philadelphia, among the first trains to function in South America.

Santuario de la Candelaria On Los Carrera east of downtown, this is the site of an important popular-religious festival, attracting over 3000 'chinese dancers' on the first Sunday in February. The sanctuary originated as the home of a tiny (14cm) cult icon of the virgin, found in 1780 in the Salar de Maricunga. Transport by regular taxi colectivo.

RESTAURANTS

8 *Café Real*, sandwiches, beer. Chacabuco between Atacama and Chañarcillo.

9 *Bramada Café*, ice cream, sandwiches, juices. In the patio behind the Casa de Cultura.

10 *Y se Llama Perú*, O'Higgins 12. Peruvian cuisine.

AIRPORT

Aeropuerto Chamonate, 15km west.

AIRPORT TRANSPORT

LanChile minibuses ($1500) depart from office and pass by the south side of the plaza. Taxi $2000-3000.

Copiapó's bus station is at Chacabuco 112. Pullman Bus has separate terminal at Colipí 109, TurBus at Chañarcillo 680.

Colectivos to Santuario de la Candelaria depart from O'Higgins on the plaza, take #1 or #7.

AIRLINE OFFICES

LanChile, Colipí 484 local 102-A ☎ 213512.
Ladeco, Colipí 354 ☎ 217285.
Aerocontinente, ☎ 6002092358.

RENT A CAR

Avis, Peña 102 ☎ 213966.
Budget, Freire 466 ☎ 216030.
Retablo, Carrera 955 ☎ 219384.

SPECIAL EVENTS

Feb 1 Festival de la Candelaria.

Around Copiapó

Caldera and Bahía Inglesa

Caldera is 74km from Copiapó; transport by frequent bus and taxi colectivo.

Interior Valleys

Over 70 INCA ARCHAEOLOGICAL SITES have been discovered in the valleys east of Copiapó, including mountaintop shrines and the metallurgic center VIÑA DEL CERRO (88km east). 126km east of Copiapó are the ruins of the IGLESIA COLORADA, thought to be the first church ever built in Chile; you need a guide to find the site. Transport by bus as far as Embalse Lautaro, departing 1250, returning 1700.

Desert Archaeology Sites

There are extensive rock paintings at the QUEBRADA DE LAS PINTURAS and FINCA DE CHAÑARAL (80 and 115km from Copiapó, repectively). Transport by tour only; consult at the Museo de Atacama in Copiapó for details.

Desert Jeep Tours

 Contact local 4x4 enthusiasts for adventures in the altiplano, along the coast, or through the *Mar de Dunas* – a veritable sea of dunes sprawled across the Coast Range just north of the Copiapó Valley.

Operators: 200

Parque Nacional Tres Cruces / Ojos del Salado

INFORMATION / ACCOMMODATION
Conaf ranger station on the south shore of Laguna del Negro Francisco, 6-person refugio at ranger station from Sep-May. Mountaineering refugios on Ojos del Salado.

TRANSPORT
No public transport. Access by 4WD vehicle or tour from Copiapó.

East of Copiapó, near the Argentine border, lies one of the most remote and spectacular altiplano regions in the country. Designated a national park in 1994, 59,082há Parque Nacional Tres Cruces consists of two sectors, one centered around Laguna Santa Rosa, the other around Laguna del Negro Francisco. Further to the east, along the Argentine border, is the surreal Laguna Verde, surrounded by some of the highest peaks in the Americas. Unlike PN Lauca and the San Pedro de Atacama region, this area sees very few visitors.

The standard access to this region is via international Ruta 31, which climbs the Quebrada San Andrés; you can also get there via the Quebrada Paipote, but the more southerly routes shown on some maps are not recommended without a guide.

From Copiapó, Ruta 31 winds through a bleak desert landscape before entering the narrow, labyrinthine valleys eroded from the west side of the Cordillera Domeyko, a parallel spur of the Andes. 161km from Copiapó, the road crests the 4,500m Portezuelo Codecedo, where you'll get your first views of the Salar de Maricunga and the inter-Andean depression. From the pass, it's another 20km down to the San Francisco border station, situated on the east side of the salt flat, and from there another 25km south to Laguna Santa Rosa, set at an elevation of nearly 3,700m. There is a Conaf ranger station and a rustic *refugio* on the west side of the lake, accessed via a dirt track branching to the north of the main road. The road up the Quebrada Paipote accesses Laguna Santa Rosa more directly from Copiapó.

Dominating the horizon to the south of Laguna Santa Rosa is 6,052m Volcán Copiapó, and in order to reach Laguna Negro Francisco, you have to make a long (85km) detour around the east side of the volcano. Significantly larger than Santa Rosa, Laguna del Negro Francisco is home to a wide variety of birdlife, including all three species of flamingos. The Conaf ranger station and 10-person *refugio* are located on the south shore of the lake.

To get to Laguna Verde, you simply continue east about 85km on Ruta 31 from the San Francisco border station. The lake's bright turquoise water contrasts brilliantly with the surrounding peaks, creating a scene that is nothing short of surreal. Thirteen of these peaks exceed 6,000m in elevation, including 6,892m Volcán Ojos del Salado, the highest volcano in the world and the highest peak in Chile. There is a Carabineros post just southwest of the lake, and right across the road are the Termas de Laguna Verde hotsprings, which makes a good place to camp. From here it's another 20km east to the Argentine border.

Termas Laguna Verde

 N free

These 45-48°C natural pools are housed in a rustic shack at the west end of the lake. For the full treatment you can jump in the mineral-charged lake between baths.

Termas Juncalito

 N free

These remote springs are located in the Cordillera Claudio Gay, 30 km up the Río Juncalito from La Ola, on the route from Diego de Almagro to PN Tres Cruces. Spring temp. 30-40°C.

Cerro Ojos del Salado (6,893m)
Cerro Incahuasi (6,621m)
Cerro Tres Cruces (6,753m)
Cerro Copiapó (6,060m)

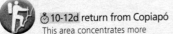 10-12d return from Copiapó

This area concentrates more 6,000m peaks than any other region in the Andes. Ojos del Salado, the highest active volcano in the world.

The non-technical route up Ojos climbs the NW face, beginning at a base camp at Laguna Verde, at 4,200m in PN Tres Cruces. Acclimatize here for a day or so and then begin the ascent, staying at huts at 5,100m and 5,750 (you can reach the first hut by 4WD). The push to the summit usually takes about 8hrs from high camp, with a scramble to the summit (not so easy at this altitude) protected by fixed ropes. The crater, now covered with ice, last erupted in 1956.

After Ojos, Nevado Incahuasi, Nevado Tres Cruces, and Volcán Nacimiento (in Argentina, 6,492m), are probably the most-coveted ascents in the region. Cerro Copiapó is often climbed as an acclimation peak, usually requiring two days round trip from Laguna del Negro Francisco. There is an inca pirca on Copiapo's summit.

Operators: 10 - 13 - 30 - 31 - 49 - 137 - 199

Volcán Llullaillaco (6,739m)
Volcán Lastarria (5,697m)

 10d return from Copiapó

Llullaillaco is the sixth highest peak in South America, and the stone pirca discovered on its summit is considered the world's highest archaeological site. Though the ascent is not technically demanding, this is a remote, challenging peak; the best time to climb is generally during winter (May-Oct) since snow is the only source of water on the route. 50km south is Volcán Lastarria, an extremely active sulphurous volcano that makes an excellent acclimation peak. Access to this mountain region is via the Mina Escondida mine to the north.

Operators: 30

Laguna Verde

Salar de Maricunga

Co. Maricunga 4,985m

Co. Mulas Muertas 5,897m

Co. Tres Cruces 6,753m

Co. Ojos del Salado 6,893m

Co. Copiapó 6,060m

See pg 6 for photo credit.

CALDERA AND BAHIA INGLESA

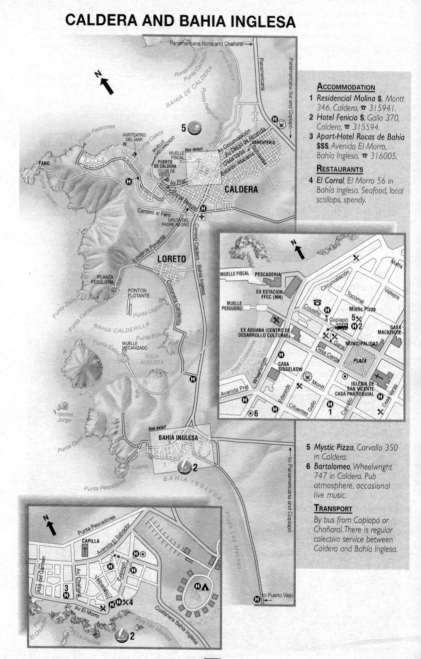

ACCOMMODATION

1 *Residencial Molina* **$**, *Montt 346, Caldera,* ☎ *315941.*

2 *Hotel Fenicia* **$**, *Gallo 370, Caldera,* ☎ *315594.*

3 *Apart-Hotel Rocas de Bahía* **$$$**, *Avenida El Morro, Bahía Inglesa,* ☎ *316005.*

RESTAURANTS

4 *El Corral, El Morro 56 in Bahía Inglesa. Seafood, local scallops, spendy.*

5 *Mystic Pizza, Carvallo 350 in Caldera.*

6 *Bartolomeo, Wheelwright 747 in Caldera. Pub atmosphere, occasional live music.*

TRANSPORT

By bus from Copiapó or Chañaral. There is regular colectivo service between Caldera and Bahía Inglesa.

Caldera and Bahía Inglesa

These are the principal beach resorts for folks from the Copiapó area, and in the summer months they are very popular with vacationing *santiaguinos*. The rest of the year, the beaches are empty and the mood is wonderfully laid-back; this is a great place to just lose yourself for a few days.

Though you wouldn't guess it today, Caldera was once Chile's second-largest port, having been launched to prominence in 1849 with the inauguration of the railroad between here and Copiapó. You can visit the 1850 **Ex-Estación**, currently under restoration, on the waterfront near the fish market. The beaches are north of town.

Bahía Inglesa is smaller and much prettier. It's brilliant white beaches are separated by rock outcroppings that form pleasant pools for swimming, and there are cabins, hosterías, and an expensive campground behind **Playa Las Machas**, which stretches out to the south. You can also camp for free on the beach.

South of Bahía Inglesa is a chain of beautiful, remote, white-sand beaches (Playa La Virgen is considered the best of the bunch). You need a vehicle and all your own provisions, including water, to visit this area; with 4WD you can continue south all the way to PN Llanos del Challe, described below.

With its mellow atmosphere and abundance of protected beaches, this is a great place to spend a few days taking a course or diving on your own. Bahía Inglesa has the calmest water, though experienced divers will likely be drawn to the *Cali*, a shipwreck off Punta Caleta in Caldera. You may also be able to arrange expeditions to Pan de Azúcar with operators here.

Operators: 156

On days with waist- to shoulder-high swell, a rock reef off Caldera's Playa Brava produces clean rights and occasional tubes.

Bahía Inglesa is a favorite place with beginning windsurfers, with maximum winds of about 15 knots, though you need all your own equipment.

Vallenar

Pop. 42,725 (☎ city code 51)

Shady and relaxed, Vallenar lies equidistant from the coast and the narrow valleys of the Andes, and well off the beaten tourist track. On El Niño years, the town is the logical base for explorations of the flowering desert .

Located on the north bank of the Río Huasco, Vallenar was founded in 1789 by order of Governor Ambrosio O'Higgins. Originally called Villa de Vallenar, the town's name is a corruption of O'Higgins's birthplace: Ballenagh, Ireland. In 1811, a silver strike at nearby Agua Amarga spurred early local development; later progress included the installation of the Huasco-Vallenar rail-

way in 1892, and the beginning of iron ore extraction by the Compañía Minera del Pacífico, in 1959. Like many towns in the Norte Chico, Vallenar continues to live on a mixed mining-agriculture economy.

In-town attractions

Museo del Huasco At the corner of Alonso de Ercilla and Sargento Aldea, this museum features exhibits on local archaeology and mineralogy, as well as a collection of historic photographs.

Hours: Open Mon-Fri 1000-1300, 1530-1830, Sat 1000-1300. Entrance $350, children $200.

THE FLOWERING DESERT

VALLENAR

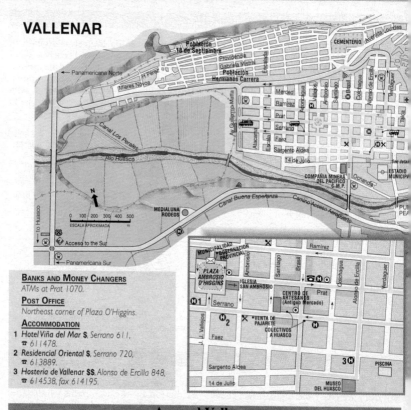

BANKS AND MONEY CHANGERS
ATMs at Prat 1070.

POST OFFICE
Northeast corner of Plaza O'Higgins.

ACCOMMODATION
1 Hotel Viña del Mar **$**, Serrano 611,
☎ 611478.
2 Residencial Oriental **$**, Serrano 720,
☎ 613889.
3 Hostería de Vallenar **$$**, Alonso de Ercilla 848,
☎ 614538, fax 614195.

Around Vallenar

Beaches

The beaches around **HUASCO** (57km from Vallenar) make an easy day trip. Though there are beaches right in town, your best option is to head north from Huasco Bajo to **TRES PLAYITAS** (12km north), which makes a great campsite. This coast is especially beautiful in spring, when coastal vegetation is in flower. The beaches at **CARRIZAL BAJO** are a good place to camp when visiting PN Llanos de Challe . Public transport to Huasco only, by taxi colectivo from Vallenar.

Parque Nacional Llanos de Challe

Set on the western slope of the Coast Range north of Huasco, this 45,000há park is probably the best place to observe the phenomenon of the **FLOWERING DESERT**. There are two Conaf ranger stations, one on the coastal road from Huasco (Sector Los Pozos) and another on the interior road to Vallenar (Sector Administración). Short trails depart from each *guardería*, but camping is not permitted in the park. Transport to **CARRIZAL BAJO** by irregular bus (3/week) from Vallenar.

Valle El Carmen, Valle El Tránsito and Conay

Above Vallenar, a paved road follows the Río Huasco upriver into the Andes, through vineyards and past the Santa Juana Dam to the junction of the Río del Carmen and the Río del Tránsito. If you turn up the Río del Carmen, you'll soon come to the village of **ALTO DEL CARMEN**, where there is a pisco bottling plant; there is another 26km further on in **SAN FÉLIX**, where there are also

---

316

a couple of basic places to stay. The northern branch leads 30km upvalley to the pleasant village of **EL TRÁNSITO**. This makes for an idyllic day trip or overnight camping excursion, with geological formations and marine fossils in the **QUEBRADA DE PINTE** (7km past El Tránsito) and swimming holes in a deep canyon further on near **CONAY** (30km from El Tránsito). Transport up both valleys by regular buses and colectivos; consult in Vallenar.

HOSPITAL
Corner of Merced and Talca.

TRANSPORT
Vallenar's bus station is at the corner of Matta and Ramírez. Tur-Bus is at Merced and Aconcagua. Most other company offices downtown on Serrano.

Taxis colectivos to Huasco and Freirina depart from the corner of Brazil and Serrano.

ENTERTAINMENT
Cinema at Prat 1094, ☎ 611501.

Reserva Nacional Pingüino de Humboldt

INFORMATION
Conaf administration at Punta de Choros. Hours Dec-Mar 0900-1800, Apr-Nov 0900-1700. Entrance $1200, children $500.

ACCOMMODATION / FOOD AND DRINK
Camping at Punta de Choros and Isla Damas (with previous authorization from Conaf). Basic provisions, seafood in Punta de Choros.

TRANSPORT
Transport by taxi from Vallenar ($35,000, max. 4 pax) or tour from La Serena ($25,000 pp) with one of the following operators:
Operators: 85 - 123 - 185

This 859há reserve protects three tiny islands and one of the most fascinating and unusual marine ecosystems in the country. For those without their own transport, however, it's not cheap or easy to visit.

The reserve's two access points lie more or less midway between Vallenar and La Serena. The more northerly of the two, **CALETA CHAÑARAL**, is a tiny fishing village where you can rent motor launches to take you on the 2.5hrs tour to **ISLA CHAÑARAL**. The boat is usually accompanied by a pod of playful bottlenosed dolphins, which are found nowhere else along the Chilean coast; when you make it out to Isla Chañaral you're in for an even greater surprise, as you may see

Humboldt penguins nesting in the rocky, cactus-strewn interior of the island. Note that camping is not allowed on the island, and there's nowhere to stay in the *caleta*.

Further south, **PUNTA DE CHOROS** is the point of departure for motor launches heading out to **ISLA DAMAS**, the only one of the three islands on which camping is permitted. There is a Conaf visitor center in Punta de Choros, as well as a campground run by Darwin Expeditions; boats out to Isla Damas cost about $30-35,000 for six people, and if you wish to camp you should make reservations in advance with Conaf in La Serena. The marine ecosystem here includes many of the same species as Isla Chañaral.

This is probably the single most important dive site in the north, with an entirely unique and well-protected marine ecosystem, including Humboldt Penguins, bottlenosed dolphins, sea otters, sea lions, and tortoises in season (Sept-Mar); another attraction is the shipwrecked *Lynch* off the north point of Isla Damas. In addition to the operators listed below, Camping Tío Pepe (☎ 09-4332751, (2)2391874) on Punta de Choros offers equipment and guided dive excursions in the reserve.
Operators: 53 - 112 - 113

Punta de Choros is one of the most popular windsurfing spots in the north, with winds to 14 knots and relatively flat conditions ideal for course-race and slalom.

Climbing on Isla Damas

In the center of the island are some small granite spires with excellent crack and face climbing. There are no bolts, but a top-rope can be set up with long slings. There is also an extensive bouldering area, also on granite, on the west coast of the island.

La Serena / Coquimbo Pop. 220, 172 (☎ city code 51)

La Serena combines well-preserved colonial charm with one of Chile's most popular and best-equipped beach resorts. The small coastal and mountain valley towns which lie just a stone's throw from the city make its appeal that much greater, making this one of the prime destinations in the north. It is also a convenient stopoff for those heading north or south, and makes for an easy weekend trip from Santiago.

Juan Bohón, Pedro de Valdivia's lieutenant, founded La Serena in 1544, in order to facilitate communication between Valdivia's Reino de Chile and the Viceroyalty of Perú. Soon after, the Diaguita Indians completely destroyed the city; according to colonial chroniclers, only two Spanish survived the uprising. In 1549, the city was refounded by Francisco de Aguirre, who subsequently undertook the heavy-handed pacification of the local natives. From 1649 until 1744 La Serena was the only city in the region – the rest of the territory was divided into great haciendas – and an important missionary center. Today there are some **29 churches** in the city.

Though downtown La Serena maintains a distinctly colonial appearance, the truth is that few colonial buildings managed to survive the city's long history of earthquakes and rampaging British pirates. Beginning in 1948, however, Chilean President Gabriel González Videla's 'Plan Serena' began an ongoing process of urban renovation with a noted preference for constructions in the colonial California style. In recent years, rapid growth in La Serena has spawned real estate projects such as Serena Norte, a planned development north of town with a projected capacity of 35,000 residents and tourists.

The port of **Coquimbo** is the grittier side of greater La Serena. Though the port itself has been utilized since the colonial era, it wasn't until 1826 – near the date when silver was discovered at Arqueros, and copper mining in the region began in earnest – that the first installations began to appear on the península. By 1858, three copper refineries had been established around the port, including Guayacán, at the time the world's largest.

La Serena's In-town attractions

Churches At the corner of Eduardo de la Barra and Balmaceda, the **Iglesia de San Francisco** was built between 1585 and 1627 in the Italian Renaissance style. Its age and quality of construction – the walls are over a meter thick – make it one of the most important architectural works of the Colonial era in Chile. At the time of writing, the **Museo de Arte Religioso** housed within the church was temporarily closed for renovations.

Other noteworthy churches in town include the **Iglesia San Agustín**, at the corner of Cantournet and Cienfuegos near the Recova market, built by Jesuits in 1755 and restored following a 1975 earthquake. On the corner of Zorrilla and Justo Donoso (northeast of downtown) is the **Casa de la Providencia**, a Neoclassical church and orphanage dating from 1872. On the east side of the Plaza de Armas, the **Iglesia Catedral** was built in 1844-1856 by French architect Juan Herbage. On the corner of Pedro Pablo Muñoz and Cordovez is the stone **Iglesia Padres Carmelitas**, with a convent and interior plaza, dating from 1755; the belltower dates from 1912.

Museo Arqueológico At the corner of Cordovez and Cienfuegos, this museum specializes in the prehistory of the Norte Chico, with a superlative collection of Diaguita ceramics.
Hours: Open in summer Tue-Fri 0900-1330, 1500-1930, Sat 1000-1300, 1600-1900, Sun 1000-1300; in winter Tue-Sat 0900-1300, 1600-1900, Sun 0900-1300.

LA SERENA AND COQUIMBO

TOURIST INFORMATION

Sernatur is on west side of La Serena's plaza, open Mon-Fri 0830-1830.

BANKS AND MONEY CHANGERS

Banks, casas de cambio, ATMs downtown in La Serena.

HOSPITAL

La Serena: Balmaceda 916, emergency entrance at corner of Larraín Alcalde and Anfión Muñoz.
Coquimbo: Corner of Videla and Darío Salas.

POST OFFICE

La Serena: Corner of Matta and Prat.
Coquimbo: Varela between Bilbao and Las Heras.

INTERNET CONNECTION (LA SERENA)

Netcafé, Cordovez 285.

ACCOMMODATION NEAR THE CENTRO

1 *Casa Gilberto* $, on Cienfuegos, ☎ 211287
2 *Residencial Limmat* (hostal) $, Lautaro 914, ☎fax 211373.

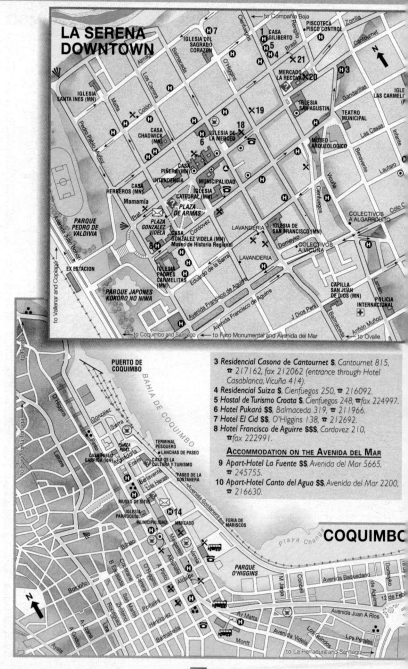

LA SERENA DOWNTOWN

COQUIMBO

3 *Residencial Casona de Cantournet* **$**, *Cantournet 815,*
☎ *217162, fax 212062 (entrance through Hotel Casablanca, Vicuña 414).*
4 *Residencial Suiza* **$**, *Cienfuegos 250,* ☎ *216092.*
5 *Hostal de Turismo Croata* **$**, *Cienfuegos 248,* ☎/fax *224997.*
6 *Hotel Pukará* **$$**, *Balmaceda 319,* ☎ *211966.*
7 *Hotel El Cid* **$$**, *O'Higgins 138,* ☎ *212692.*
8 *Hotel Francisco de Aguirre* **$$$**, *Cordovez 210,*
☎/fax *222991.*

ACCOMMODATION ON THE AVENIDA DEL MAR

9 *Apart-Hotel La Fuente* **$$**, *Avenida del Mar 5665,*
☎ *245755.*
10 *Apart-Hotel Canto del Agua* **$$**, *Avenida del Mar 2200,*
☎ *216630.*

11 *Cabañas Alborada* **$$**, *Avenida del Mar 5695*, ☎ *246124.*
12 *CT Jardín del Mar* **$$$** *Av. Costanera 5425*, ☎ *242835.*
13 *Hotel Club Resort La Serena* **$$$** *Avenida del Mar 1000*, ☎ *221262.*
More info at www.turistel.cl

ACCOMMODATION IN COQUIMBO
14 *Hotel Iberia* **$**, *Lastra 400*, ☎ *312141, fax 326307.*

ACCOMMODATION IN LA HERRADURA
Villa Náutica **$$**, *Av. Costanera 1223*, ☎*fax 260895.*

CAMPING (LA SERENA)
15 *Hippocampo*, *Avenida del Mar 4600.*
16 *Antares, Los Pescadores 4655, Peñuelas.*
17 *Sole di Mare, Parcela 66*, ☎ *312531*

RESTAURANTS (LA SERENA)
18 *El Cedro, Prat 572. Arabic food, moderate prices.*
19 *La Mia Pizza, O'Higgins 360. Artsy café serving pizza and good breakfasts.*
20 *La Recova Market, Cantournet and Cienfuegos. Cheap fixed lunches.*
21 *Donde El Guatón, Brasil 750. Parrilladas, live music on weekends.*
22 *Le Creperie, near Playa La Barca. Crepes, lively atmosphere.*
Andalucía, Costanera 5425. Spanish cuisine, ocean views, moderate prices.

AIRPORT
East of La Serena on Ruta 41.

AIRPORT TRANSPORT
Cabs from downtown La Serena about $1500.

AIRLINE OFFICES
LanChile, Alberto Solari 1400, ☎ *221531.*
Ladeco, Cordovez 484, ☎ *225753.*

RENT A CAR
Avis, Av. F. de Aguirre 068 ☎ *227171.*
Budget, Av. Balmaceda 3820 ☎ *290241.*
Daire, A. Prat 645 ☎ *226933.*
La Florida, Camino Aeropuerto ☎ *217029.*

BUS STATION AND OFFICES IN LA SERENA
Bus Station: Corner of Amunátegui and Av. El Santo.
Buses to Andacollo and the upper Elqui Valley (Vicuña, Monte Grande, Pisco Elqui): Frontier Elqui, corner of Juan de Dios Peñí and Coquimbo.
Buses to San Juan and Mendoza, Argentina, via Paso Agua Negra (summer only): Buses Covalle, Infante 538.

BUS STATION AND OFFICES IN COQUIMBO
Company offices near corner of Videla and Av. Juan Ríos.

TAXIS COLECTIVOS IN LA SERENA
To Tongoy, Andacollo, and the Elqui Valley: Domeyko 524 (between O'Higgins and Balmaceda).

ENTERTAINMENT
Pubs on Avenida del Mar, discos on Avenida 4 Esquinas. Downtown at Prat 470 is the Café del Patio, with live jazz on weekends.
23 *Casino de Peñuelas next to the Club Hípico de Peñuelas, where the Avenida del Mar changes into the Costanera de Coquimbo.*

Slots open Sun-Thu 2100-0300, Fri, Sat, nights before holidays 2100-0400, entrance free. Vip salon Sun-Thu 2100-0500, Fri, Sat, nights before holidays 2100-0600, entrance $2500.

SPECIAL EVENTS
January is the month for exhibitions and other events in La Serena. Ask at local tourist offices for exact dates and locations for events such as the Feria Regional de Artesanía (handicrafts), the Encuentro Musical de La Serena, and the Encuentro Regional de Pintores (paintings).

SHOPPING
Visit the La Recova market (on Cantournet between Cienfuegos and Rengifo) for regional handicrafts, manjar sweets, candied papaya, semiprecious stones such as lapizlazuli and combarbalita, and other regional specialties.

Casa Histórica González Videla On the corner of Cordovez and Matta, this 1890 adobe house is the only 19th century building on the Plaza. Exhibits recount the life of Gabriel González Videla, creator of the 'Plan Serena' and president of Chile from 1946-1952. The museum also contains regional historical information and Chilean paintings.
Hours: Tue-Sat 0900-1300, 1600-1900, Sun 0900-1300.

Beaches The AVENIDA DEL MAR provides access to the extremely popular beaches which extend from Avenida Francisco de Aguirre south to Peñuelas, a full 6km. The beaches themselves are quite nice but some visitors may be turned off by the Cancúnesque condos and high rises.

Coquimbo's In-town attractions

Plaza de Armas, Calle Aldunate Check out the 1862 IGLESIA LA MERCED, across from the Plaza de Armas, and the MUSEO DEL SITIO (Jan-Feb, Mon-Sat 0930-2030, Sun and holidays 0930-1400). The latter is an *in situ* display of a burial site corresponding to the Las Animas culture, (900-1000 AD), containing 39 corpses of humans and llamas. Further north on Aldunate are interesting 19th and early 20th-century wooden buildings.

Caleta Pescadores Just off the Avenida Costanera near the corner of Benavente, this is a good place to buy seafood, or hop a boat to La Serena. 10 boats operate in summer from 1000-2100, departing when full; in winter 2 boats provide service on weekends and holidays. $2000 p/p.

Iglesia de Guayacán At the west end of Los Rieles in the town of Guayacán (on the south side of the Coquimbo península), this metallic structure was built in Gustave Eiffel's workshops in Belgium. Maximiliano Errázuriz purchased it in 1888 and had it assembled here.

AERIAL VIEW OF LA SERENA'S BEACH

Around La Serena & Coquimbo

The Elqui Valley

Vicuña is 66km east of La Serena. Transport by regular bus or colectivo from La Serena 🏍.

Andacollo

Two hugely popular religious festivals are held in this tiny mining town 53km SE of La Serena. Transport by bus or colectivo from La Serena 🚌.

Beaches

The popular beaches south of La Serena are described below. If headed north, a dirt turnoff 40km north of the city (at the beginning of the switchbacks up Cuesta Buenos Aires) leads to CALETA TOTORALILLO (59km), PLAYA EL TEMBLADOR (68km), and CALETA CHUNGUNGO (73km). Of these, El Temblador has the nicest beach, with white sand and calm waters, but no water or infrastructure of any kind. Chungungo has the only potable water along this stretch. Further north is the RN Pingüino de Humboldt 🏍. No public transport.

Astronomical Observatories

This area features the Southern Hemisphere's greatest concentration of high-powered observatories 🔭.

Beaches South of Coquimbo

TRANSPORT
Regular taxi colectivos connect most towns with La Serena and Coquimbo. Tur-Bus also offers direct buses from Santiago to Tongoy (Dec-Feb).

The nicest beaches in the La Serena area are undoubtedly those to the south of Coquimbo. In fact, if you've come looking for rest and relaxation, you're probably better off avoiding La Serena altogether and heading straight here. Be advised, however, that the crowds can get a little heavy in February, and you should definitely reserve lodging in advance. Any one of these places makes for a great weekend escape from Santiago.

2km south of Coquimbo, **LA HERRADURA** has a protected half-moon beach, dozens of seafood restaurants and hotels, and a couple of commercial campgrounds. Due to its proximity to the city, however, it generally lacks the peace of the beaches further south.

Totoralillo (15km from Coquimbo) has pretty beaches and rock formations where you can camp for free; if you want a roof over your head, there is also a Polynesian-style cabaña complex on the jetty jutting into the ocean. There are no provisions, however, so purchase everything ahead of time if traveling without a vehicle. Just south is **LAS TACAS**, a plush Mediterranean-style resort. Beyond that, the 10km **PLAYA GRANDE** has a number of commercial campgrounds.

Guanaqueros (35km from Coquimbo) is a picturesque if slightly tattered fishing village on a bluff at the end of the beach, with locally harvested seafood and some reasonable lodging. On the south side of the Guanaqueros península is the tiny, privately owned **PLAYA BLANCA** (campground, restaurants and cabañas, entrance charged). Beyond this is **PUERTO VELERO**, a luxury time-share resort with a fine restaurant. **PLAYA SOCOS** continues south to Tongoy.

Tongoy (48km from Coquimbo) is the coolest little town on this coast, built on a rocky headland between the Playa Socos and the Playa Grande. Lodging can be tight here in summertime, so call ahead for reservations at the recommended *Hotel Panorámico* or *Cabañas Linda Vista*; there are also both free and paid campsites on the beach south of town. One of the best things about Tongoy is the excellent open-air seafood

market on the south side of the peninsula, serving locally-cultivated scallops and oysters, which you can also sample at the fine restaurants along the beach. At the far end of the 14km Playa Grande is **PUERTO ALDEA**, a tiny fishing village.

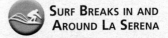 The best diving in this area is normally off the rocky points separating the beaches. La Herradura, Totoralillo, and Tongoy are all recommended; in Tongoy you may be able to fill tanks at the scallop farm. There is also a fully equipped dive shop at the Hotel in Las Tacas. For info and equipment visit Comercial Ocaranza at Av. Aldunate 932 in Coquimbo.
Operators: 78

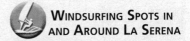

SURF BREAKS IN AND AROUND LA SERENA

● **La Barca (La Serena)**
Beach breaks on windless days.

● **Totoralillo**
Point breaks off either side of island, best at low tide.

● **Playa Socos (Tongoy)**
Left point off the peninsula with big swell.

WINDSURFING SPOTS IN AND AROUND LA SERENA

● **La Herradura**
Very safe, winds to 15 knots, good for beginners.

● **Puerto Aldea**
Winds off the point up to 40 knots in the afternoon.

The Elqui Valley (Valle del Elqui)

Extending east from La Serena into the Andes, the Valle de Elqui has become a landmark in Chilean cultural geography: home to great poets, heart of pisco country, beacon for esoteric groups and astronomers.

Vicuña is the largest settlement in the valley and has a reasonable range of accommodation. While in town you might stop in at the **MUSEO ENTOMOLÓGICO E HISTORIA NATURAL** *(Jan-Mar: Mon-Sun 1000-2100. Apr-Dec: Mon-Fri 1030-1330, 1530-1900, Sat-Sun 1030-1900. Entrance $350, children $200)*, which contains a surprising collection of some 26,000 items, including displays on entomology, paleon-

tology, shellfish and local avifauna. Just outside of Vicuña are the **OBSERVATORIO CERRO MAMALLUCA** (for info on stargazing see), and the **PISCO CAPEL BOTTLING PLANT**.

Upriver from Vicuña in the town of Rivadavia, the road splits. The northern branch leads up the Río Turbio to **BAÑOS EL TORO** and over Paso Agua Negra to Argentina. The road soon turns to dirt and climbs high up into the Andes. There is no public transport.

The main branch heads south, following the Río Elqui to **MONTE GRANDE**, childhood home and resting place of Gabriela Mistral, who won the Nobel Prize for Literature in 1945.

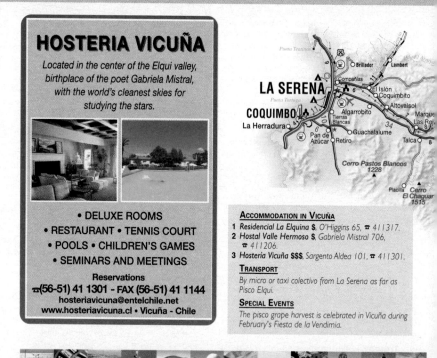
ACCOMMODATION IN VICUÑA

1 *Residencial La Elquina* $, O'Higgins 65, ☎ 411317.
2 *Hostal Valle Hermoso* $, Gabriela Mistral 706,
   ☎ 411206.
3 *Hostería Vicuña* $$$, Sargento Aldea 101, ☎ 411301.

TRANSPORT

By micro or taxi colectivo from La Serena as far as
Pisco Elqui.

SPECIAL EVENTS

The pisco grape harvest is celebrated in Vicuña during
February's Fiesta de la Vendimia.

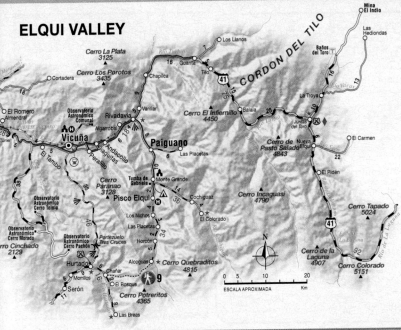

ELQUI VALLEY

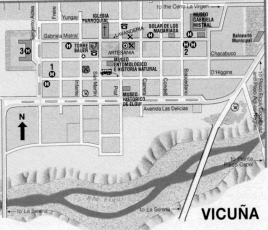

VICUÑA

On a rock outcrop over-looking the town and the valley is the poet's mausoleum, and a museum in her honor may be visited inside the **CASA ESCUELA Y CORREO**. As a child, the poet lived here and studied with her sister, the postmistress.

Here the road splits again, the route due south (right) leading up the río Claro to **PISCO ELQUI**. Originally known as Unión, the town's name was changed in 1939 in order to keep Perú from registering exclusivity to the name 'pisco.' Today it is shady and relaxed, and is slowly becoming something of a resort town, with fine outdoor restaurants, cabañas and hosterías; recommended places to stay include the *Hotel Elqui*, *El Tesoro del Elqui*, and a pleasant campsite, *Los Olivos*. In town you can visit the **SOLAR DE PISCO ELQUI**, the oldest distillery in the region. Upvalley from Pisco Elqui the road turns to gravel, and the valley becomes less populated. There are *pisquerías* in **PISCO PERALTO** and **LOS NICHOS**, and swimming holes near the bridge 14km upriver of Pisco Elqui.

From Monte Grande, the northern (left) branch of the road leads up the **COCHIGUAZ**

VALLEY, locally famous for the growing presence of groups dedicated to various disciplines of holistic and new age therapies; claims of UFO visitations are frequently reported here. There are cabañas all along the road, the closest of which is *Spa Naturista* at 2km from Monte Grande, followed by *El Albaricoque* at 5km. About 12km up is the 'town' of Cochiguaz, where a dirt road leads off to the north past the Piedra del Guanaco, an enormous boulder decorated with petroglyphs. This is the center of esoteric energy in the valley, and the surrounding hills are reportedly chock full of quartz crystals, creating a natural conduit for the 'energy' that draws visitors here. Just beyond you'll find upmarket lodging at *Cabañas Casa del Agua*, and at the end of the road 15km from Monte Grande, the riverside *Camping Cochiguaz*.

Most travelers visit the Elqui Valley from La Serena, but if you have a car you can also enter from the south, via a remote pass from the Río Hurtado.

Alcohuaz to Río Hurtado

 🥾 ⏱2-3d ▢
This recommended traverse connects an upper tributary of the Valle de Elqui with the Río Hurtado valley, just south. From Alcohuaz, 14 km up the Río Claro valley from Pisco Elqui, head south over a mountain pass and down the Quebrada el Chañar to the town of Chañar. There is a simple hospedaje 6km down the road in Chañar, and nice hiking further up the Río Hurtado valley, which is planted with apricot and walnut trees. Return to Ovalle by bus. Note that there is very little water on this route, which is best done in winter or early spring.

Ovalle   *Pop. 53,515 alt. 200m (☎ city code 53)*

Ovalle is a small agricultural town on the north bank of the Río Limarí. Though it can claim few attractions of its own, it does provide access to some interesting sites along the coast and in the interior. Few

travelers stop off here at all – which for some may be an attraction in its own right. A big earthquake in 1997 destroyed many of Ovalle's historic adobe buildings.

OVALLE

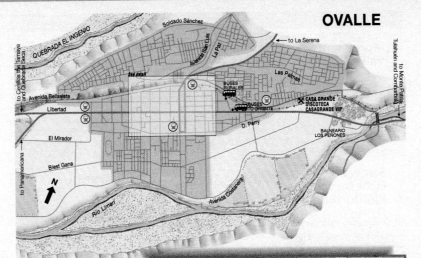

TOURIST INFORMATION
Kiosk at SE corner of Plaza de Armas.

BANKS AND MONEY CHANGERS
Cash exchange at Aguirre 373; ATMs at Vicuña Mackenna and Victoria.

HOSPITAL
Ariztía Poniente, between Socos and Los Pescadores.

POST OFFICE
Vicuña Mackenna between Victoria and Miguel Aguirre.

ACCOMMODATION IN OVALLE
1 Hotel Roxy $, Libertad 155, ☎ 620080.
2 Hotel Turismo $$, Victoria 295, ☎ 623536.

TRANSPORT
Bus company offices on Ariztía. Taxi colectivos to Monte Patria and Embalse La Paloma at Benavente 114.

SHOPPING
Local agricultural products, ceramics, semiprecious stones at the Feria Modelo, located on the north side of Benavente (east end of town).

In-town Attractions

Museo del Limarí Located in the old train station at the corner of Antofagasta and Socos, Ovalle's only museum contains the country's finest collection of Diaguita ceramics, with a total of over 1,800 artifacts.
Hours: Open Mon 0900-1300, 1500-1900, Tue-Fri 0800-1300, 1500-1900, Sat-Sun, holidays 1000-1300. Sat summer only 1700-2000.

Feria Modelo de Ovalle East of downtown near the bus offices, this is the largest agricultural market in the north.

Keep an eye out for dried fruit (especially figs) and locally-produced goat cheese.

PANORAMIC VIEW OF OVALLE

Around Ovalle

Monumento Natural Valle del Encanto

This national monument features abundant petroglyphs and stone mortars attributed to the El Molle culture. Camping is permitted and there is water available on the site, the turnoff to which lies 19km west of Ovalle. Southbound buses can drop you off here, from which point you'll have to walk in about 5km.

Santuario de la Naturaleza Pichasca and the Río Hurtado Valley

The main attractions at Pichasca (45km NE of Ovalle) include a petrified araucaria forest and fossilized dinosaur remains. Continuing on takes you up the fruit-producing Río Hurtado Valley, and over a pass into the Valle de Elqui. Transport to Hurtado by regular bus.

Andacollo

One of the north's most important popular-religious festivals (🎻) takes place in this tiny mining town, 83km north of Ovalle via the paved highway. Transport by regular bus.

Beaches

South of Ovalle are a number of excellent, uncrowded beaches ideal for camping, none of which has any water or infrastructure; the best is probably **HUENTELAUQUÉN**. The nearest services are in **LOS VILOS** and **PICHIDANGUI**, described below. Transport by any southbound bus. See 📖 for beaches to the north of Ovalle.

Embalse La Paloma

38km east of Ovalle, this manmade reservoir is popular for camping and windsurfing, with reliable afternoon winds from 18-24 knots. Transport by regular bus from Ovalle.

Termas de Socos

☎ (53)681021 🏠free NA
This hotsprings resort lies just off the Panamerican, 33km west of Ovalle. The large pool and private tubs are fed from a 26-30°C source spring; if you don't care to pay for the hotel there are also campsites available. Transport by any southbound bus from Ovalle.

Baños del Gordito

 ⟳ ⏱2-3d
☐ N🛏free
This relatively unknown hike begins in the tiny stone-and-adobe village of Tulahuén, 45km up the Río Grande from Monte Patria. From here the road continues up another 28km to Las Ramadas, set in a narrow river canyon rife with swimming holes and campsites. The fumaroles and thermal pools at Baños del Gordito lie another 7hr walk upvalley, at an elevation of 2,975m. You can rent mules for the trip in Tulahuén.

PARQUE NACIONAL FRAY JORGE   See 📖

INFORMATION
Conaf visitor center at park entrance. During summer, the park is open Thu-Sun and holidays, 0900-1800; the rest of the year it's open Sat, Sun, and holidays only (same hours). Conaf may permit camping during the week as well.

TRANSPORT
Public transport via northbound buses bypassing Ovalle along the Panamerican; ask to be dropped off at the turnoff and walk the 22km to park entrance. Otherwise by tour from La Serena or Ovalle.

Parque Nacional Fray Jorge

Fray Jorge is a 9,959há national park and Unesco World Biosphere Reserve set in the Altos de Talinay, an unusually abrupt section of the Coast Range southwest of Ovalle. Rising directly from the ocean to an elevation of 667m, this range serves as a natural collector for the thick *camanchaca* mist that blows in off the Pacific. Annually, this mist contributes the equivalent of 1,000mm of rainfall to the local ecosystem, allowing for the continued survival of a unique 'relict forest' more akin to the Valdivian Rainforest of southern Chile than the scrub desert of the Norte Chico. Species found here include canelo, olivillo, arrayán, and numerous vines and epiphytes. Springtime (Oct-Nov) is the best time to visit.

The park is named for Franciscan monk fray (friar) Jorge, who used wood from this forest to construct the Iglesia de San Francisco in La Serena. It would appear as if he wasn't the only one to take advantage of this locally scarce resource, as Fray Jorge's once-extensive relict forest has today been reduced to a single stand of only about 400há.

Access to the park is relatively difficult, as the entrance and information center lay well west of the Panamericana, and there is no public transport. Activities in the park are largely limited to walking the short trail (Sendero El Bosque, 1km) through the misty cloud forest at the top of the ridge. From the visitor center, it's 3km to the campground at El Arrayancito, and from there another 7km on to Sendero El Bosque.

Los Vilos, Pichidangui, and the Coast South

TRANSPORT
Access by any northbound or southbound bus. The Panamerican runs all along this section of coast.

SPECIAL EVENTS
The Fiesta Virgen del Carmen del Palo Colorado is an important religious festival held every July 16 in Quilimari, just east of Pichidangui.

This section of coast is close enough to Santiago to receive a fair number of weekend and summer visitors from the central region, making the mood here quite different than other parts of the north. Los Vilos is extremely popular in the high season, but there are some excellent restaurants and a fish market in Caleta San Pedro. You can also hire a boat in the *caleta* to ISLA LOS HUEVOS and ISLA DE LOS LOBOS, two offshore islands with nesting birds and sea lions. PLAYA LA PRINCIPAL extends north from the caleta, while PLAYA LAS CONCHAS is just south.

Pichidangui is the center of Chilean sailing and windsurfing, with a good variety of restaurants and lodging, including an excellent beachfront campground, *Bahía Marina*. There are horses for rent on the beach near the rivermouth north of town, and a large cave further north, the CUEVA LA QUINTRALA.

Another 10km south of Pichidangui is the village of LOS MOLLES, set on a lovely beach with good campsites and couple of cabañas for rent along the waterfront. North of the village are interesting geological formations, including a noisy blowhole known as 'El Puquén.'

SURFING AND WINDSURFING AROUND LOS VILOS AND PICHIDANGUI

- **Chigualoco**
  Right and left points with medium to large swell, best at low tide.

- **Pichidangui**
  The cradle of Chilean windsurfing. Open ocean conditions, good for slalom and course-race, very consistent winds up to 30 knots. There are also a variety of beach breaks on small days.

- **Los Vilos**
  An excellent place to learn wave jumping, with consistent SW winds to 30 knots.

• Diving in Los Molles

Los Molles ranks alongside RN Pingüino de Humboldt as one of the top dive spots on the continental coast. There is a small fishing village on the peninsula, which closes off the large bay and sand beach to the south; dive attractions include unusual geological formations and one of the best preserved marine environments in the region, with sea lions, kelp forests and nesting seabirds.
Operators: 112

Central Chile

Central Chile is not only such in a geographical sense. It is also the center of national government, industry, agriculture, finance and education. Some 75% of Chile's inhabitants live between the Río Aconcagua and the Río Biobío, and each year more people leave their homes in the *campo* to look for work in the big cities of the central region. This sort of centralization is ubiquitous in Latin America, and Chile is among the most centralized countries of all.

This is also the heartland of mainstream Chilean culture. The hacienda-based legacy of the Colonial era manifests itself most strongly in the Central Valley south of Santiago, now occupied by vineyards and fruit orchards, while the working port of Valparaíso recalls the economic growth and international influences of the early independence years. In its best moments, Santiago recalls the paradise it must have been at the turn of the century, when well-traveled elites collaborated with European architects and designers to transform the capital with new parks, gardens, and other public works. The influences of this leisure class are further reflected in the Mediterranean-inspired design of the 25 beach resorts lining the central coast.

Central Chile shows us other faces too: flashy cars and cellphones sported by newly-rich *cuicos*, high rises and condominium complexes from a twenty-year construction boom, bohemian neighborhoods where the left lives on, and an ever-expanding sea of residential neighborhoods and *callampa* slums. Excellent tourist infrastructure makes it easy to escape to the mountains or the coast, and you can practice pretty much any sport imaginable within an hour and a half of Santiago. The diversity of landscapes and proximity of wild places to the major population centers are two of the greatest things about central Chile.

CENTRAL CHILE

GEOGRAPHY AND TOPOGRAPHY

Though the area comprised in this region extends north to the Río La Ligua, the area from 32-33°S actually has more in common geographically with the Norte Chico, where the Andes and the Coast Range are virtually indistinguishable. South of the Chacabuco Ridge, the geography of central Chile assumes its most classic form, as the Coast Range, the Central Valley, and the Andes are all clearly defined.

The **Coast Range** is older, harder, and more rounded than the Andes, composed of granitic batholiths mostly dating from late Mesozoic. It is an impressive range in its own right, and snowfall is not uncommon on the summits of such peaks as Cerro La Campana (1,910m) and Cerro el Roble (2,222m), northwest of Santiago. Towards the south the range loses elevation, and is increasingly eroded by the numerous rivers flowing west out of the Andes.

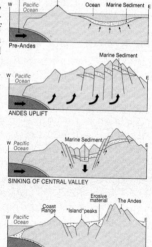

To the west of the Coast Range, uplifted marine sediments form a broad, undulant **coastal shelf**. In places this shelf drops off steeply into the Pacific, forming dramatic sea cliffs with deeply incised coves and half-moon beaches. In others – mostly at the mouths of river valleys – the coast is low and expansive, with broad dunes and miles and miles of beaches.

East of the Coast Range lies the **Central Valley**. Ever since the beginnings of the Andean orogeny, this basin has been continually filling with sediments of fluvial, glacial, and volcanic origin, covering irregularities in the landscape and forming a relatively flat, west-sloping plain. The few Central Valley peaks protruding above this plain appear as islands, and if you climb Cerro San Cristóbal in Santiago you'll see how the valley to the south of the park has been filled with sediments to a level much higher than the valley to the north.

The sunken geography of the Central Valley is most tangible in and just south of Santiago, where the basin is no more than 80km wide, hemmed in by the peaks of the Andes and the Coast Range. To the south, however, the valley widens and is less visibly sunken, and the valley floor is increasingly modified by the rivers crossing it on their east-west run to the Pacific. The Panamerican highway runs straight down the center of the valley, so you can observe the changes as you head south.

The Andes cut an imposing figure in central Chile, rising steeply from a base elevation of 600m to peaks frequently exceeding 6,000m; just across the border in Argentina is 6,962m Cerro Aconcagua, the highest peak in the world outside the Himalaya. The scale of these abrupt peaks is humbling.

The formation of the range is attributed to Tertiary and Quaternary volcanism and tectonic uplift; in addition to volcanic ash and metamorphic rocks, uplifted marine deposits comprise a good portion of the Central Andes, and marine fossils are commonly found in the mountains above Santiago. The intense glaciations of the past million years, however, have completely modified the topography of the relatively soft central Andes. Most river valleys are broad and U-shaped, littered with huge gravel bars left by retreating glaciers, and everywhere you look the Andes have been sculpted into an intricate series of cirques and subranges. The remnants of the great glaciers of the Pleistocene now occupy SW slopes on high peaks throughout the range.

South of about 35°S, the Andes begin to lose height, and numerous sub-ranges extend west from the main cordillera, reaching like fingers into to the Central Valley. Volcán Chillán is the northernmost of southern Chile's chain of volcanoes.

CLIMATE AND BIOGEOGRAPHY

Central Chile enjoys what is known as a **Mediterranean climate**, with a moderating maritime influence and a seasonal regimen consisting basically of dry, sunny summers and mildly rainy winters.

During the summer months, the semi-permanent Pacific anticyclone exerts its influence over the central region of the country, obstructing passage of moisture-bearing lows from the southern Pacific. Constant southerly or southwesterly breezes indicate continuing high pressure and clear weather. Central Chile's dry season typically lasts from late September to April.

During the winter, the Pacific anticyclone migrates north and west, away from the continent, and the rains which sustain the forests of the south extend their reach into Central Chile. Precipitation almost invariably originates in the west, but interestingly, the approach of bad weather is usually signaled by northerly winds. Central

Average temperature in hottest and coldest month			Location	Precipitation in driest and wetlest months	
mean maximum (c)	mean minimum (c)	month		month	rain fall (mm)
31,6	12,4	Ene	Los Andes	Ene	2,8
16,3	2,8	Jun		Jun	77,2
26,7	11,6	Ene	Quillota	Mar	2,2
16,7	5,3	Jul		Jun	125,4
22,5	13,3	Ene	Valparaíso	Feb	2,6
16	8,3	Ago		Jun	134,1
29,4	12,4	Ene	Santiago	Ene	3,3
14,5	3,2	Jul		Jun	93,5
20,2	10,5	Ene	El Teniente	Dic	9,2
8,6	0,4	Jun		Jun	250,1
27,7	12,5	Ene	San Fernando	Dic	6,5
12,2	3,7	Jul		Jun	209
30,8	12,7	Ene	Talca	Ene	7
13,6	3,7	Jul		Jun	189,6
18,7	11,9	Feb	Chanco	Ene	8,7
13,2	7,3	Jul		Jun	192,3
18,8	11,5	Ene	Concepción	Ene	10,6
13	6,7	Ago		Jun	182,7
26,2	10,1	Ene	Contulmo	Ene	42,7
13,6	4,8	Jul		Jun	340,2

Smog

Most folks agree, if it weren't for the smog, Santiago would be another city altogether. But what actually creates smog, and why is it so bad here?

One of the problems is obviously emissions: Santiago is jam-packed with vehicles, many of which don't even have catalytic converters. Circulation of non-catalytic vehicles is currently restricted, based on a rotating cycle of license-plate numbers. If the digits for the day appear on your plate, you can't drive.

A good part of the problem, however, is just plain dust. Widespread deforestation and an abundance of unpaved roads in the Santiago region means lots of airborne particulates, which contribute significantly to decreased visibility and air quality. If you travel at all in the central region, you'll notice a widespread haze, common even in rural areas, which is due primarily to dust particulates.

The final and most damning factor is Santiago's geographical location. Like many other smog-plagued cities, Santiago sits in an intermontane depression, surrounded on all sides by mountains. During the day, sunlight heats the air above the city, but the contaminated air in the Santiago basin remains cool and stagnant, forming a temperature inversion that worsens in winter, when the 'ceiling' drops to a mere 300-400m above the city. If anything, southwesterly daytime winds tend to exacerbate the problem, as most of Santiago's industry is located – guess where? – southwest of the city.

DROUGHT-RESISTANT FLORA IN CENTRAL CHILE

Chile's winter normally begins in May and ends in September, but on **El Niño** years, the winter is longer and more intense – a skier's dream.

Though these general patterns are valid throughout the region, local weather depends to a great extent upon the effects of topography. Temperatures along the coast are warmer in winter and cooler in summer than at equivalent latitudes inland, and remain more constant throughout the day; precipitation is greater along the coast than anywhere except the high Andes. When it rains in Santiago, it snows in the Andes, and mornings following a big storm – with the air cleaned of smog and the cordillera shimmering white – are the finest of the year.

The **flora** of central Chile combines elements of the arid north and forested south. The dramatic climatic changes which effected the north and south during the Pleistocene made this region a sort of refuge for marginalized species from both regions, as is reflected in the diversity of ecosystems found here. The classic ecosystem of central Chile is called *matorral*, consisting of drought-resistant shrubs and trees similar to California's *chaparral*. However, such topographic factors as latitude, slope aspect, and elevation exert tremendous influence over the distribution of central Chile's flora. There are sclerophyllous forests on the coast and in quebrada valleys in both ranges, cactus on north-facing slopes throughout the region, and highly endemic shrubs and grasses in the steep, isolated valleys of the Andes.

PREHISTORY

Very little is known about **Paleolithic cultures** in Chile's Central Region. The site at Tagua Tagua, located in the Central Valley south of Santiago, is the only confirmed site from this remote era. Tagua Tagua dates from 11,500-10,000 years before the present (BP) and includes remains of mastodons, American horses, milodons and other now-extinct Pleistocene megafauna.

Notable findings from post-extinction **Neolithic hunter-gatherers** include that along the Río El Manzano (10,200-9,850 BP), in the Cajón del Maipo southeast of Santiago, and at Punta Curaumilla (10,500 BP), a dramatic cape southwest of Valparaíso. Central Chile's earliest known ceramics also come from Punta Curaumilla; dated at 2,860 (BP), they probably represent a period of increased contact with the cultures of the *Norte Chico* and NW Argentina.

Agriculture followed close on the heels of ceramics, beginning about 2,300 (BP). Sites in Concón and Santiago, dated from the beginning of the modern era, mark the integration of New World crops such as maize, squash, beans and tubers into a traditional economy based on fishing, gathering of shellfish, and hunting of the guanaco and other mammals. Links with cultures to the north and west are reflected in sites corresponding to the Bato culture (250-600 AD), which show widespread use of *tembeta* labial adornments, and in the ritual skull deformations of the Llolleo culture (150-900 AD).

This pattern of cultural exchange appears to have been broken around 900 AD, with the appearance of the **Aconcagua culture**. Sites excavated from the Río Aconcagua to the Río Cachapoal reveal a culture with a mixed economy similar to that of their local predecessors, but with completely distinct decorative styles and utilitarian artifacts. The origin of the Aconcagua Indians, who left numerous petroglyphs in the Andean valleys east of Santiago, remains the subject of speculation.

The 15th-century **Inca expansion**, which incorporated northern and part of central Chile into the realm of *Collasuyo*, is generally thought to have reached as far south as the Río Maule. However, the area effectively occupied by the Incas probably reached only as far south as Cerro La Compañía, south of Rancagua, where there remains an Inca *pukara*. This and other Inca fortifications are an indication of the opposition the Incas likely faced as they expanded south towards the Mapuche homeland.

At the time of the Inca expansion, the Aconcaguas and other culture groups of central Chile spoke the Mapuche language, *mapudungun*, indicating the widening influence of this vital Amerindian culture. Known to the Mapuche of the southern heartland as the **Picunche** (people of the north), the Indians of central Chile entered abruptly into the history of the conquest beginning in 1536.

CONTACT AND CONQUEST

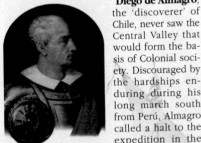

DIEGO DE ALMAGRO

Diego de Almagro, the 'discoverer' of Chile, never saw the Central Valley that would form the basis of Colonial society. Discouraged by the hardships enduring during his long march south from Perú, Almagro called a halt to the expedition in the Río Aconcagua valley. A small retinue of soldiers, sent to the coast to look for the three ships that were supposed to be supporting the expedition, found the tiny *Santiaguillo* (the lone survivor) at anchor in the future port of Valparaíso. As soon as they judged themselves ready, the embittered Spaniards made tracks back to Cuzco.

Five years later, an expedition under the command of **Pedro de Valdivia** made its way south over the Chacabuco Ridge and into the Mapocho valley, present-day site of Santiago. Impressed by the climate and the number of natives available for *encomiendas*, the Spanish set up camp at the base of Cerro Santa Lucía, the prominent hill known by the natives as *Huelén*. Here, in February 1541, they founded Chile's first city, **Santiago de Nueva Extremadura**. Land was distributed among the soldiers, and European crops and domestic animals appeared for the first time in the valley. Pedro de Valdivia established a local government, emphasizing his independence from Perú and Pizarro.

Next Valdivia turned his attentions to gold. The Incas had mined gold from Estero Marga Marga, the narrow stream which runs through modern-day Viña del Mar, and it was to this spot that the local chief **Michimalongo** led the Spaniards. Soon Valdivia had a huge placer mine up and running, with an *encomienda* work force of nearly 2,000 natives.

Not all the conquerers were so lucky, however. The non-irrigated land of the Central Valley wasn't quite what the Spanish had hoped, the threat of attack by the Indians was a constant strain, and mutiny was easy to sow among the discontent. Some six months after the founding of Santiago, a conspiracy to murder Valdivia and escape to Perú was uncovered and the conspirators executed, but a ball had been set in motion. Taking advantage of the general confusion, the Indians revolted. Setting off with 90 soldiers to put down the rebellion, Valdivia left the 'city' with his second in command, Alonso de Monroy. In his absence, Michimalongo attacked and burned Santiago, leaving the Spanish in more precarious straits than ever, and Monroy was sent back to Perú to seek assistance. The trip there and back took him a year and a half, but the colony was saved.

As soon as he could, Valdivia sent a party north to secure the road to Perú. Another expedition ranged into the south, and returned with tales of rich agricultural lands and thousands upon thousands of Indians. Once again, Valdivia sent off to Perú for more soldiers, horses and weapons.

In typical Colonial fashion, however, Valdivia's emissaries to Perú were not heard from for several months, having become embroiled in a new round of factional fighting.

El Ejército Libertador de los Andes

Few acts in the Latin American independence movement stand out like the brilliantly planned and executed campaign of José de San Martín's Army of the Andes, which definitively broke the Spanish stronghold on central Chile.

San Martín was a professional soldier. Born in Yapeyú (Argentina) but educated and trained in the art of war in Spain, he returned to Buenos Aires in 1812, ready to fight for independence. Argentina was already free, and in fact the only remaining bastions of Spanish power in the entire continent were right across the Andes, in Bajo Perú (Lima) and Chile.

In late 1814, San Martín was sent to Mendoza and began to transform the city into a massive staging ground. Speaking to no one of his greater plan, he set to producing arms, weapons, uniforms and provisions. For the better part of two years, the preparations continued and the army swelled to over 5100 men, including those who had fled across the Andes with Bernardo O'Higgins after the Disaster of Rancagua. Meanwhile, San Martín began negotiations with the Pehuenche Indians, who still controlled the Andean passes south of Santiago. As 1817 approached, he asked the Pehuenches for permission to send his army across the Andes at the approximate latitude of Talca.

As San Martín had predicted, the Pehuenches told the Spanish what to expect. Meanwhile, the real plan was revealed to a select few: six separate battalions, crossing the Andes simultaneously in six different locations.

Security was such that the officers of the decoy battalion, led across Paso del Planchón by Ramón Freire, actually believed that the rest of the army was coming up behind them. Joined at the border by Chilean *guerrillas*, they met the bulk of the Spanish army on February 4, 1817. Meanwhile, the five other battalions were stealing across the Andes and catching the Spanish unawares. Copiapó fell on Feb 11, and La Serena on Feb 12, while a group of barely 50 soldiers set another decoy in the Cajón del Maipo.

Meanwhile, the two major battalions crossed the Andes almost directly west of Mendoza. Crossing via Paso del Camino de los Patos and Paso Uspallata (site of the actual Los Andes – Mendoza highway), the two forces reunited in San Felipe/Los Andes and continued south to defeat the outnumbered and unprepared Spanish forces at the Battle of Chacabuco, on February 12th. Led by O'Higgins and San Martín himself, the victorious *libertadores* marched into Santiago two days later. The Spanish escaped to the south, but their days were numbered.

BATALLA DE MAIPU, OIL PAINTING BY M. RUGENDAS

THE SANTIAGO VALLEY, IN THE 19TH CENTURY, BY CLAUDIO GAY

When Valdivia heard of these new developments in Perú, he too rode north to fight for the king, and distinguished himself in the final defeat of the *pizarristas*. In 1549, Valdivia returned to Chile, finally well equipped and secure in his position as Governor and Captain of *Nueva Extremadura*.

In the space of a couple of years, the Spanish rebuilt the town of La Serena and founded a score of towns and forts south of the Biobío. The arable lands of the south, far better for wheat production than those of central Chile, were rapidly claimed by the governor's cronies, and for the next 50 years the south was the focus of agricultural activity. When the Mapuche rose up and expelled the Spanish from their homeland, however, agricultural production shifted back to the Central Valley. For two centuries, Santiago was remain the only city in the entire region, as the self-sufficient agricultural unit known as the **hacienda** came to dominate rural life.

COLONIAL CHILE

Most of the agricultural land in the region was originally distributed in plots of 300 to 1,500há. Additionally, the Spanish Crown awarded distinguished families with larger properties known as *mayorazgos*, which were passed on to the eldest son, indivisible and free of taxation, contributing to the rooted establishment of a land-owning oligarchy. The **religious orders**, especially the Jesuits, were perhaps the greatest landowners of all.

With the land thus divided into major *hacienda* agricultural holdings, a new class of peons arose, known as **inquilinos**. These *inquilinos* received a borrowed piece of land on which to farm, in return for which they were required to work for the landowner, with worker-land-owner relationships enduring for generations. By 1760 it had become customary for tenants to provide a son or daughter for household duties, a trend which is reflected today in middle- and upper-middle-class Chileans' dependence on live-in housekeepers.

Early economic demand in Chile focused upon livestock, as horses, leather, grease and tallow were needed to supply the mines in Bolivia and the ongoing war with the Mapuches. But when a 1687 earthquake destroyed the Peruvian wheat crop, it allowed superior quality Chilean wheat to gain an edge in supplying the work forces of the Peruvian mines. Throughout the 18th century, wheat prices determined land prices in Central Chile.

By the end of the 18th century, after two and a half centuries of colonial rule, Santiago had been destroyed once by Indians and twice by earthquakes, but had grown nonetheless to hold some 40-50,000 inhabitants. New constructions, such as La Moneda Government Palace and the Cal y Canto Bridge, had added unaccustomed elegance to the city, and new cities had been founded to the north and south of Santiago. Merchants in the port of **Valparaíso** were anxious to market the surplus produced by the *haciendas*. In short, the region and the country were primed for independence.

INDEPENDENCE

Chile's independence movement began in 1810 with the formation of a local *junta* in Santiago, and the great majority of the battles between the 'Royalists' and 'Patriots' took place in Central Chile. By 1818, following a devastating defeat in Rancagua and the heavy-handed Spanish 'Reconquest,' the Patriots finally succeed in ousting the Spanish once and for all from the Chilean heartland, opening the door to a century of changes that were to completely transform the country and its landscape.

In 1822, Valparaíso was declared a free port, and quickly became the country's primary financial center, intimately linked with mining interests in the north and Arauco, and later with urban development and ranching in Patagonia. As the first port of call for ships rounding Cape Horn, the city grew organically from the narrow flats up into the surrounding hills, as mariners and traders arrived,

Claudio Gay and Ignacio Domeyko

In the mid-19th century, dozens of European naturalists and scholars arrived in Chile to participate in the exploration and documentation of the country's fascinating and poorly-understood natural history. Some (such as Charles Darwin) stayed only a few months, while others became hooked and stayed on for the better part of a lifetime.

Claudio Gay (1), a native of Draguignan, France, was initially contracted to teach in a Santiago day school. After a couple of years his lot improved when the Chilean government charged him with the enviable task of traveling the length of the country, studying the nation's flora, fauna, geography and geology, forming a catalogue of mineral and thermal springs, and producing maps and drawings. A gifted artist, Gay spent the better part of ten years exploring from the Atacama Desert to Chiloé. Beginning in 1842, he began the herculean task of compiling his notes and drawings into the Physical and Political History of Chile, an immense tome of 30 volumes published in 1855.

(2)

Polish exile **Ignacio Domeyko (2)** arrived in Chile in 1837, at the behest of English railroad magnate Charles Lambert, to teach chemistry and mineralogy at the nascent Universidad de Chile. He assumed the post with enthusiasm, participating in the construction of laboratories and building a curriculum from scratch; the summers he spent exploring the mountains and making the first recorded ascents in the Central Andes. For forty years, the tireless Pole continued to broaden his interests and work for the bettering of the University, helping to build programs in architecture, civil and industrial engineering, painting and sculpture. He last visited his homeland in 1888, returning to Chile with a sack of Polish soil.

Did the two know each other? Of course: the native violet, *Viola domeykoana*, was named by Gay for his well-rounded and well-grounded colleague.

(1)

PLATES FROM GAY'S ATLAS

MODERN-DAY SANTIAGO

liked what they saw, and decided to stay.

Meanwhile, *hacienda* owners began to build their own merchant marine and install warehouses all along the coast. As well-traveled elites returned from vacations in the Mediterranean with a taste for the beach life, these coastal *bodegas* were transformed into **summer resorts**.

In the interior, the construction of over 30 major canals brought the entirety of the Aconcagua, Santiago, Rancagua and Cachapoal basins under irrigation. By 1851, the first **vineyards** were appearing in the region, and by 1900 **fruit production** was well under way. Santiago was booming, as tax revenues from the mines and nitrate fields of the north funded such works as the channeling of the Mapocho, the creation of the park on Cerro Santa Lucía, the Quinta Normal and Natural History Museum, and a score of Neoclassical buildings in the city center. Private parks and gardens became popular signs of worldliness and taste. Photos from turn-of-the-century Santiago reveal what must have been a true paradise for the fortunate.

The vast majority of the population, however, continued in their role of servitude to the landed oligarchy. Though Bernardo O'Higgins outlawed the *mayorazgos* upon independence, the vast majority of agricultural land continued to be held in immense *fundos* until the mid-1900's, when many of the largest properties were finally broken into smaller holdings known as **minifundios**. Meanwhile, the growth of mining increasingly drew workers off the haciendas, and when the mines were exhausted, the miners limped back to Santiago, where industry had been retarded and jobs were few. The Great Depression of the 1920's, coming close on the heels of the collapse of the nitrate industry, capped a period of increased social divisions and calls for land reform.

THE TWENTIETH CENTURY

In central Chile, the 20th century has brought a continual increase in urbanization and industrialization. From 1900-1920, Santiago's population grew from 300,000 to over 600,000, and by 1952 it had more than doubled again, to 1,438,000. Today, 86% of Central Chile's population lives in cities and 40% in Santiago.

Throughout the first half of the century, electricity and telephone lines were strung throughout the region, the Panamerican highway grew north and south from the capital, and the first hydroelectric plants began to make use of runoff from the Andes. WWII provided a much-needed boost to Chilean industry, but the jobs produced were not sufficient to quell continued concerns about **land reform**, which was a central issue in the 1970 elections.

Primed by the free-market economics of Pinochet's 'Chicago Boys' – and encouraged by slack-to-nonexistent zoning laws – the **construction boom** of the 1980's has continued unabated until the present day, and has completely transformed the cities and coastal resorts of central Chile. The economy of the region is the most diverse in all of Chile, with mining, agriculture, forestry, fishing, finance, and manufacturing all playing significant roles.

Outside the big cities and the commercial corridor along the Panamerican highway, the *campo* of the Central Valley seems to belong to another era. With its tiny colonial villages, old haciendas, fruit orchards and subsistence farms, the rural landscape of the Central Valley maintains a timeless rhythm and aesthetic that stands in stark counterpoint to the hectic pace and com-

Santiago
Pop. over five million (☎ *city code 02*)

'Santiago is waiting for an interpretation that goes beyond habit and customary vision. We have not yet realized that Santiago is a strange and profoundly original city....'
- Benjamin Subercaseaux, Chile, o Una Loca Geografía

Almost everyone who visits Chile spends some time in Santiago, and everyone who lives in Chile has an opinion about the capital. How could you not? With over five million inhabitants – a number that grows every year – Santiago contains over 40% of Chile's population and is far and away the financial, educational, and cultural center of the country. Santiago often gets a bad rap because of its air quality issues, but the truth is that enjoying Santiago, like many big cities, just requires a bit of familiarity and a bit of good weather. In the springtime, with new leaves on the trees, fresh breezes airing out the city, and snow-covered mountains looming to the east, Santiago is a pleasant and entertaining city.

HISTORY

Santiago was officially founded by Pedro de Valdivia on February 12, 1541, in a ceremony at the base of Cerro Santa Lucía. Originally named *Santiago del Nuevo Extremo*, Valdivia's encampment was completely destroyed six months later by the Mapuches, but the Spanish rebuilt immediately, laying out the city's first streets around today's Plaza de Armas. The initial street plan incorporated the area limited on the north by the Río Mapocho, to the south by the Alameda, to the east by Cerro Santa Lucía, and to the west by Calle Brazil.

SANTIAGO'S ORIGINAL LAYOUT

Growth in the capital lagged with the Spanish focus upon settlement and agriculture in the south, but with the Mapuche uprising of 1599 and the consequent Spanish retreat to the north, Santiago's political and financial hegemony was restored. Still, it remained little more than an outpost in the wilderness, populated by a few Spanish soldiers, colonists, and tradesman, a much larger population of not-quite-peaceful Indian servants and wives, and a growing population of mestizos. The interaction of Spaniards and Indians was mediated by the various orders of the Catholic Church, which together controlled nearly a third of urban Santiago.

Successive earthquakes in 1647 and 1730 basically leveled the city, leaving the 1618 Iglesia de San Francisco as the only remaining construction from the early Colonial years.

CERRO SANTA LUCIA IN THE MID-19TH CENTURY

CAL Y CANTO BRIDGE

In the later half of the 18th century, however, growing prosperity and the arrival of new ideas and architects from Europe began to impart elegance and substance to Santiago. The Río Mapocho, which had flooded the city every spring for over two centuries, was finally contained by dikes, and the Cal y Canto bridge, built over the course of 13 years, linked Bellavista and «el Centro». Italian architect Joaquín Toesca and his disciples added Neoclassic style to the capital with such works as the Palacio de la Moneda (1805), the Iglesia Catedral (1785), the Iglesia de la Merced (1795), Iglesia de Santo Domingo (1808), and the Real Audiencia (1808), today the site of Santiago's Museo Histórico Nacional.

Ideas of independence germinated in Europe and North America took root in this atmosphere of newfound growth and potential. The move towards independence began in 1810, when Chile's first *Junta Nacional* was formed in the Plaza de Armas, and the stop-and-start struggles of the following decade largely impended any significant improvement of the city; the first major change of the post-independence era was Bernardo O'Higgins' creation of the *Alameda de las Delicias*, a broad, tree-lined avenue built upon the old channel of the Mapocho. Today this avenue, known as Avenida Libertador Bernardo O'Higgins or simply the Alameda, is the city's principal east-west axis.

The late 19th century brought political stability, increasing revenues from the northern mines, and a pervasive atmosphere of national growth and consolidation that was manifested in the urban transformation of the capital. Benjamin Vicuña Mackenna, named *Intendente* of Santiago in 1872, gave the initial impulse to this movement, building new streets, initiating horse-drawn carriage service, and ordering the creation of gardens and terraces on Cerro Santa Lucía. Wealthy,

VICUÑA MACKENNA

well-traveled miners and entrepreneurs not only built sumptuous private residences, but also funded parks and public buildings such as Parque O'Higgins, donated to the city by Luis Cousiño in 1877. By 1910, the Parque Forestal and Museo de Bellas Artes had appeared along the banks of the Mapocho, electric cable cars clattered along the cobblestoned streets of the *centro*, and Santiago's landed elites – in the midst of a growing population of 300,000 mostly poor and landless immigrants from the countryside – spent their afternoons enjoying the city's new elegance, its shady avenues, fountains and parks stocked with exotic trees.

In the twentieth century the city expanded at an ever-increasing rate, initially towards the east and then in all directions. By the 1960's the capital held nearly two million inhabitants, and the construction of new high rises began what would become a complete tranformation of Santiago's look and feel. This tendency for uncontrolled growth (and attendant vehicular congestion and contamination) has continued unabated to the present, and today these rank among the most important of the many issues that city planners must confront in the coming years.

CERRO SANTA LUCIA AND PLAZA V. MACKENNA IN THE LATE 19TH CENTURY

■ See pg 6 for photo credit

Orientation

Santiago is huge, distributed in thirty-two comunas covering a total of nearly 1,400km². However, the area of real interest is relatively small, and if you key on a few obvious landmarks you should have no problem navigating within the city.

The main axis extends roughly east-west, along the Alameda (Av. Bernardo O'Higgins) and Avenida Providencia, which run more or less parallel to the Mapocho. The main line on the Metro, Línea 1 (see 🚇) runs along this same axis, which is what Santiago residents are referring to when they say *arriba* (up) or *abajo* (down): up is east, towards the mountains, and down is west, towards the coast. Most areas of interest to travelers lie within walking distance of this main axis.

The historic Centro has the rough shape of a triangle, bordered by the Mapocho to the north and the Alameda to the south, with Plaza Baquedano forming the eastern apex of the triangle. Plaza Baquedano is an important spot to key on: here the Alameda becomes Avenida Providencia, and here the Pío Nono bridge crosses the river to the north, providing access to Bellavista. Providencia continues east, paralleling the Mapocho as far as Los Leones, where the river veers north; from here the *barrios altos*, Las Condes and Vitacura, expand to the east in a vast array of high-rises and residential neighborhoods. The main axis continues east up Av. Apoquindo, which turns into Av. Las Condes and eventually follows the Mapocho into the mountains, towards the ski areas.

When navigating in Santiago, use the Metro as your anchor, and key on such landmarks as the Panamerican or Ruta Norte-Sur, which limits the Centro to the west; Cerro San Cristóbal, which looms to the north of Barrio Bellavista and basically cuts the city in two; and Avenida Américo Vespucio, which makes a tremendous loop around the city.

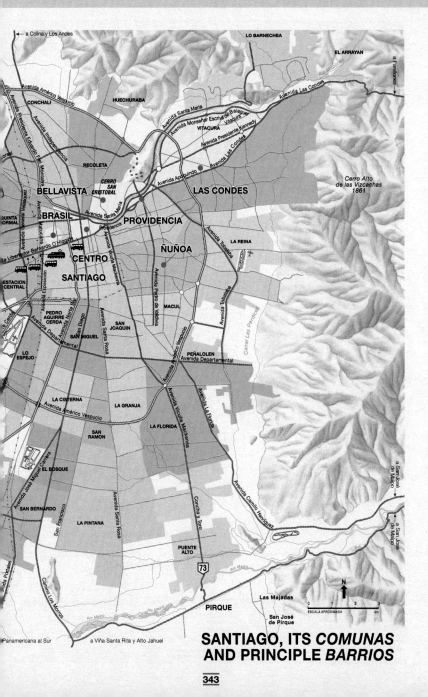

SANTIAGO, ITS *COMUNAS*
AND PRINCIPLE *BARRIOS*

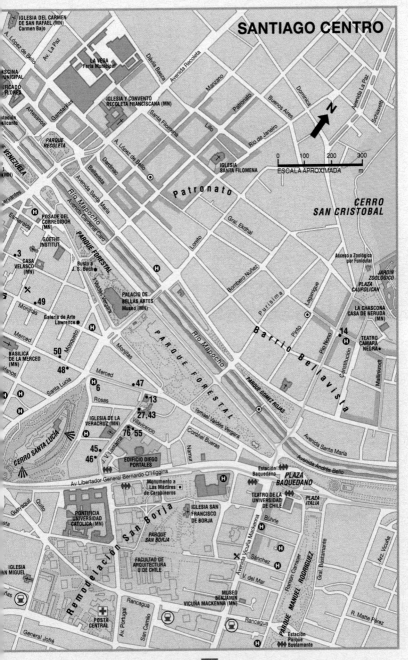

SANTIAGO CENTRO

ESCALA APROXIMADA

0   100   200   300
m

IGLESIA DEL CARMEN DE SAN RAFAEL (MN)
Carmen Bajo

LA VEGA
Feria Municipal

IGLESIA Y CONVENTO RECOLETA FRANCISCANA (MN)

PARQUE RECOLETA

IGLESIA SANTA FILOMENA

Patronato

CERRO SAN CRISTOBAL

POSADA DEL CORREGIDOR (MN)

GOETHE INSTITUT

PARQUE FORESTAL

3 **CASA VELASCO (MN)**

Busto a J. S. Bach

PALACIO DE BELLAS ARTES Museo (MN)

49

Galería de Arte Lawrence

Acceso a Zoológico por Funicular

JARDIN ZOOLOGICO

PLAZA CAUPOLICAN

LA CHASCONA CASA DE NERUDA (MN)

14

TEATRO CAMARA NEGRA

BASILICA DE LA MERCED (MN)

50

48

6

47

Barrio Bellavista

PARQUE GOMEZ ROJAS

13

27,43

IGLESIA DE LA VERACRUZ (MN)

76   55

45

46

EDIFICIO DIEGO PORTALES

Av. Libertador General Bernardo O'Higgins

CERRO SANTA LUCIA

Monumento a Los Mártires de Carabineros

Estación Baquedano

PLAZA BAQUEDANO

TEATRO DE LA UNIVERSIDAD DE CHILE

PLAZA ITALIA

PONTIFICIA UNIVERSIDAD CATOLICA (MN)

IGLESIA SAN FRANCISCO DE BORJA

PARQUE SAN BORJA

FACULTAD DE ARQUITECTURA U DE CHILE

Remodelación San Borja

IGLESIA SAN MIGUEL

MUSEO BENJAMIN VICUÑA MACKENNA (MN)

POSTA CENTRAL

Estación Parque Bustamante

<u>TOURIST INFORMATION</u>

Sernatur is at Providencia 1550, on the corner of Santa Beatriz (Metro: Pedro de Valdivia or Manuel Montt). Open weekdays 0900-1700, Sat 0900-1300. There is also a kiosk on Paseo Ahumada between Agustinas and Huérfanos, offering free guided walking tours during the summer.

Oficina Municipal de Turismo in the Casa Colorada, Merced 860, open weekdays 1000-1800.

<u>BANKS AND MONEY CHANGERS</u>

The highest concentration of banks and money changers is in the Centro on Huérfanos and Agustinas, but you can find banks in many places, especially in Providencia and Las Condes. Another concentration of 'casas de cambio' is on Pedro de Valdivia and Orrego Luco, north of Providencia. ATM's are literally everywhere. Remember that banks are only open 900-1400; money changers also close at 1400 but most re-open 1500-1800. Banks are closed Saturday and almost everything is closed Sunday.

American Express is near the US embassy at Av. Andrés Bello 2711, 9th floor, ☎ *3506700.*

Citybank has many branch offices in the capital. In the Centro there are offices at Ahumada 40, Huérfanos 1201, Huérfanos 770, and Teatinos 180. In Providencia there are offices at Av. Providencia 655, Av. 11 de Septiembre 1363, Orrego Luco 58, Av. 11 de Septiembre 2302, and Providencia 2653.

Thomas Cook representative is Turismo Tajamar, Orrego Luco 032, Providencia, ☎ *2329595.*

<u>HOSPITALS AND MEDICAL SERVICES</u>

Posta Central, Av. Portugal 125, ☎ *6341650, (Metro: Univ. Católica). For medical emergencies. Note that taking a cab is usually faster than waiting for an ambulance.*

Clínica Universidad de Católica, Marcoleta 367 (Metro Univ. de Católica), ☎ *6332051.*

Clínica Alemana, Av. Vitacura 5951 and Av. Manquehue Norte 1410, ☎ *2101111, emergency,* ☎ *2101334.*

Clínica Las Condes, Lo Fontecilla 411, ☎ *2114000, emergency,* ☎ *800211800.*

Clínica Indisa, Av. Santa María 1810, ☎ *3625555, emergency,* ☎ *3625333.*

<u>LANGUAGE SCHOOLS</u>

Centro de Idiomas Bellavista, Crucero Exeter 0325, ☎ *7375102,*

---

fax 7357651, www.cib.in.cl, fdo@cib.in.cl
Highly recommended, excursions.

Escuela Violeta Parra, Lagarrigue 362-A, ☎ *7358240, fax 2298246.*

Instituto Goethe, Esmeralda 650, ☎ *6397371.*

<u>POST OFFICE</u>

Main office on the Plaza de Armas, open weekdays 0800-1900, weekends 0800-1800. Post restante list kept in main hall. Other offices at Moneda 1155 and Av. Providencia 1466.

<u>EXPRESS / INTERNATIONAL COURIER</u>

FedEx is at Av. Providencia 1951, ☎ *2315250.*

DHL Express is at Santa Rosa 135, ☎ *6392171, or Suecia 072,* ☎ *2327539.*

<u>INTERNET CONNECTION</u>

Café Virtual, Alameda 145, 2nd floor.
Navegación@internet, Providencia 1413.
Cybercenter, General Holley 170.
Sicosis Pub, José Miguel de la Barra 544.
Corner of Alameda & Subercaseaux, 2nd floor.
Corner of Alameda and Almirante Pastene, 2nd floor.
Entel, Morandé 315.
Cibercafe, Alameda 2292 (corner of República).

<u>TRAVEL AGENCIES</u>

Outbound international plane tickets are offered at dozens of travel agencies, concentrated in the Centro and Providencia. The AmEx representative is Turismo Cocha, Av. El Bosque Norte 0430 (Metro Tobalaba), ☎ *2301000, fax 2035110. Student tickets and friendly assistance are available from the **Student Flight Center**, Hernando de Aguirre 201, of. 401, (Metro: Tobalaba),* ☎ *3351175.*

<u>ACCOMMODATION</u>

IN THE CENTRO

1 **Hotel Nuevo Valparaíso $**, Morandé and San Pablo, ☎ 6715698.
2 **Hotel Caribe $**, San Martín 851, ☎ 6966681.
3 **Residencial Santo Domingo $**, Santo Domingo 735, ☎ 6396733.
4 **Residencial Londres $**, Londres 54, ☎ 6382215.
5 **Hotel Paris $**, París 813, ☎ 6640921.
6 **Foresta Hotel $$**, Victoria Subercaseaux 353, ☎ 6396291
7 **Hotel Libertador $$**, Av. Bernardo O'Higgins 853, ☎ 6398366.
8 **Hotel Majestic $$**, Santo Domingo 1526, ☎ 6958366.
9 **City Hotel $$**, Compañía 1063, ☎ 6954526.

---

10 **Hotel Vegas $$**, Londres 49, ☎ 6322496.
11 **Hotel Carrera $$$$**, Teatinos 180, ☎ 6982011.
12 **Hotel Plaza San Francisco $$$$**, Alameda 816, ☎ 639332.
13 **Hostal del Parque $$$**, Merced 294, ☎ 6392694.

IN BELLAVISTA

14 **Monteverde $$**, Pío Nono 193, ☎ 7773607.

IN PROVIDENCIA AND THE BARRIOS ALTOS

15 **Hotel Santa María $$$**, Santa María 2050, ☎ 2323376.
16 **Marver Deptorent $$$**, Nueva de Lyon 114, ☎ 2312542.
17 **Hotel Victoria $$$**, Lota 2325, ☎ 2330458.
18 **Park Plaza $$$$**, Ricardo Lyon 207, ☎ 2336363.
19 **Hotel Sheraton San Cristóbal $$$$**, Av. Santa María 1742, ☎ 2335000.
20 **Montebianco $$$**, Isidora Goyenechea 2911, ☎ 2325034.
21 **Diego de Almagro Apart-Hotel $$**, Apoquindo 3397, ☎ 3350787.
22 **Hotel Rugendas $$$**, Callao 3121, ☎ 2466000.
23 **Radisson $$$$**, Vitacura 2610, ☎ 2036001.
24 **Hotel Intercontinental $$$$**, Luz 2920, ☎ 2342200.
25 **Plaza El Bosque $$$**, San Sebastián 2800, ☎ 3621600.
81 **Golden Tulip Hotel Presidente $$$**, Eliodoro Yáñez 867, ☎ 2358015.
82 **Apart-Hotel Club Presidente Santiago $$$**, L.T. Ojeda 558, ☎ 2335652. (see ad inside front cover)

IN BARRIO BRASIL AND AROUND THE BUS STATION:

Hostal Río Amazonas $, Rosas 2234, ☎ 6719013.
Hostelling International $, Cienfuegos 151, ☎ 6718532.
SCS Habitat $, San Vicente 1798, ☎ 6833732.
Hotel Turismo Japón $$, Almirante Barroso 160, ☎ 6984500.
More info at www.turistel.cl

<u>FOOD AND DRINK / ENTERTAINMENT</u>

CAFÉS AND BAKERIES

Many cafés serve expresso and café cortado in the downtown area; these are typically stand-up bars with waitresses in risqué clothing, but are patronized by men and women. The most common are Café Haití and Café Caribe, both with locales on Paseo Ahumada.

26 **Tavelli**, Providencia 2211 in the Galería Drugstore. Outdoor tables, wildly popular for 'once.'
27 **Pérgola de la Plaza**, Plaza Mulato Gil de Castro. Quiet, cozy art café.

28 *New York Bagel Bakery*, Roger de Flor 2894, El Bosque. Bagels and gourmet coffee.

29 *Café Melba*, Don Carlos 2898. American-syle breakfast.

RESTAURANTS
IN BELLAVISTA

30 *Azul Profundo*, Constitución 111. Seafood, poetic ambiance.

31 *Etniko*, Constitución 172. Very stylish, sushi, good bar.

32 *Le Tasca Mediterránea*, Purísima 161. Good lunches, tapas, live music.

33 *Todo Fresco, Cocoa*, and *El Otro Sitio* Three quality Peruvian restaurants, all on Antonia López de Bello between Lagarrigue and Purísima.

34 *El Caramaño*, Purísima 257. Chilean food, no sign, very popular.

35 *Alí Babá*, Santa Filomena 102. Tasty arabian cuisine, cozy atmosphere, good value.

36 *La Bodeguita del Julio*, Antonio López de Bello 0108. Cuban food, live music on weekends.

37 *Kilométre 11680*, Dardignac 0145. Hearty fare, excellent wine list.

38 *La Esquina al Jerez*, Mallinckrodt 102. Spanish food, tapas.

39 *Off the Record*, Antonia López de Bello 0155. Art café, films, readings.

40 *Don Simón*, Pío Nono 261. Chilean cuisine, 2nd floor balcony.

IN THE CENTRO

41 *Bar de la Unión*, Nueva York 11. Classy old-school bar, entrance only in company of club members.

42 *Confitería Torres*, Alameda and Dieciocho. The oldest restaurant in Santiago. Classic Chilean food, somewhat overpriced.

43 *Cocoa*, Lastarria 297. Tiny, classy Peruvian restaurant. There is another locale in Bellavista, above.

44 *Mercado Central*. Lots of cheap stalls, the best-known is Donde Augusto.

45 *Gatopardo*, Lastarria 192. Artsy, imaginative cuisine, a Santiago standard. Live jazz on weekends.

46 *Don Victorino*, Lastarria 138. Chilean food, cozy ambiance.

47 *Les Assassins*, Merced 297. Reasonably priced French cuisine.

48 *Luzakaya Yoko*, Merced 456. Affordable Japanese cuisine, sushi.

49 *Da Carla*, Mac Iver 577. Splendid Italian food, charming decor.

50 *Big Market*, Merced 501. Take-out sandwiches and meals, inexpensive, great portions.

51 *Roof Garden Restaurant*, Hotel Carrera, Teatinos 180. Spendy, executive lunches, excellent views.

52 *Majestic*, Santo Domingo 1526. Indian cuisine, good vegetarian menu.

53 *El Naturista*, Moneda 846. Vegetarian food, busy at lunchtime.

54 *El Vegetariano*, Huérfanos 827. Vegetarian food, desserts, pleasant atmosphere.

55 *Café del Dizgaf*, Villavivencio 398. Coffee, sandwiches, lunch.
Puro Chile, Maipú 363. Seafood, good wine list, hip bar.

IN PROVIDENCIA, EL BOSQUE AND THE BARRIOS ALTOS

56 *El Huerto*, Orrego Luco 054. Vegetarian, eco-hangout, next door to Gaia bookstore.

57 *Phone Box Pub*, Av. Providencia 1670 Loc. 1. Dark wood booths, lunches.

58 *Café del Patio*, Providencia 1670. Vegetarian food, interesting menu.

59 *Aquí Está Coco*, La Concepción 236. Unique seafood menu, maritime decor.

60 *Casa de Cultura de México*, Bucarest 162. Chile's best Mexican food.

61 *Camino Real*, on Cerro Cristóbal. Excellent views, good wine list, tastings.

62 *El Mesón de Calvo*, El Bosque Norte 083. Chilean food, asados, big portions.

63 *Taj Majal*, Isidora Goyenechea 3215. Indian cuisine.

64 *Shoogun*, Enrique Foster Norte 172. Japanese cuisine, traditional decor, private rooms available.
Hostería Doña Tita, Camino Los Refugios 15125, El Arrayán.
Chilean cuisine, pleasant patio.
Gran Vista, La Reina Alta, Talinay 11040 (Club de Equitación).
Unbeatable views, Patagonian fare.

65 *Le Fournil*, Av. Vitacura 3841 or Don Carlos 2879. Moderate French cuisine, excellent breads and lunches.

66 *Munchen*, El Bosque Norte 204. German cuisine.

67 *Isla Negra*, El Bosque Norte 0325, Chilean food, fine seafood.

68 *Giogia*, Isidora Goyenechea 3456. Italian cuisine, excellent wine list.

69 *Le Due Torri*, Isidora Goyenechea 2908. Outstanding Italian cuisine

70 *Angus*, El Bosque Norte 0111. Upscale steak house.

71 *El Club*, El Bosque 0380. International cuisine and drinks, professional clientel.

BARS
IN BELLAVISTA

La Boheme, Bombero Núñez 336. French-owned, friendly, hip.

72 *Etniko*, Constitución 172. Chic, modern, cool patio.

73 *Libro-Café Mediterráneo*, Purísima 161. Artsy bookstore-café.

IN THE CENTRO

74 *La Chimenea*, Príncipe de Gales 90. Films, live music, central location.

75 *777*, Alameda 777. Scruffy, popular with students, cheap beer.

76 *El Biógrafo*, Lastarria and Villavicencio. Traditional 'intellectual' hangout, friendly.

IN PROVIDENCIA, EL BOSQUE AND THE BARRIOS ALTOS

78 *Liguria*, Av. Providencia 1373. Wildly popular, good food.

79 *Geopub*, Encomenderos 83. Irish theme, gringo hangout, Guiness on tap, live music weekends.

80 *Clavo Oxidado*, Nueva de Lyon 113. Hip, artsy, decorated with recycled materials.

IN ÑUÑOA

Bar Sin Nombre, on Irarrázaval one block west of the plaza. Hip, modern, somewhat cramped.
Club de Jazz, Av. José Pedro Alessandri 85, Ñuñoa. Live jazz Thu-Sat.
La Batuta, Jorge Washington 052, just north of the plaza. Live rock music Wed-Sat.

DISCOTHEQUES / NIGHT CLUBS

Discotheques in Santiago don't usually start happening until after 1 AM. Concentrations of discotheques are found on Calle Suecia in Providencia (big, American-style dance places, with little character), and in Bellavista, which has a more eclectic offering.
La Feria, Chucre Manzur L. 6.
Boomerang, on General Holley.
Tantra, Lagarrigue 154.

FILM

There are many big US-style movie houses, showing principally Hollywood films but also European and Latin American releases; look in the newspaper for listings. There are also several art-film venues, with independent releases:
El Biógrafo, Lastarria 181
☎ 6334435.
Cine Normandie, Tarapacá 1181, ☎ 6972979.
Centro de Extensión de la Universidad Católica, Alameda 390, ☎ 6866500.

THEATER, MUSIC AND DANCE

Teatro Municipal, Agustinas 749, ☎ 6332804. International chamber and orchestra music, ballet.
Teatro Universidad de Chile, right next to Metro Baquedano at 043 Baquedano. Fall season of music and dance.
Teatro de la Universidad Católica, on Plaza Ñuñoa, ☎ 2055652.

SMALL THEATERS IN BELLAVISTA:
Teatro Bellavista, Dardignac 0110, ☎ 7356264.
Teatro Taller, Lagarrigue 191, ☎ 2351678.
Teatro El Conventillo, Bellavista 173, ☎ 7774164.

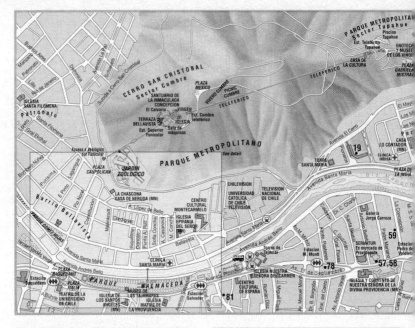

AIRPORTS

Aeropuerto Comodoro Arturo Merino Benítez, or Pudahuel, lies 26km west of downtown. There are separate terminals for international and national flights, but they are right next to each other.
Aeródromo de Los Cerrillos lies southwest of downtown, off Av. Pedro Aguirre Cerda. Some flights to Isla Robinson Crusoe depart from here.
Aeródromo Tobalaba (also known as Eulogio Sánchez) is in La Reina, SE of downtown. Scenic and glider flights, as well as some flights to Isla Robinson Crusoe, usually take off here.

AIRLINE OFFICES

LanChile, Huérfanos 926, ☎ 5262000.
Ladeco, Huérfanos 1157, ☎ 6613990.

AIRPORT TRANSPORT

Bus Service: Buses Centropuerto ($640 ow, $1100 rt) and Tour Express ($1000 ow, $1600 rt) depart every 15 min or so from Metro Los Héroes, stopping at marked pick-up spots along O'Higgins. Tour Express also departs from the bus station. The buses run 0530-2200 every day.
Minibus Transfers: AeroExpress, ☎ 6773000, fax 6994958. Tour Express, ☎ 6019573. Blue Line, ☎ 7764150.
Radio Taxis: Most companies $7000 one way, 4 person maximum; see the local transport section below.

BUS STATION AND/OR OFFICES

There are four separate terminals in Santiago, but the best bet is to head for Terminal Alameda and/or Terminal Santiago, which are right next to each other near the west end of town (Metro; Univ. de Santiago).

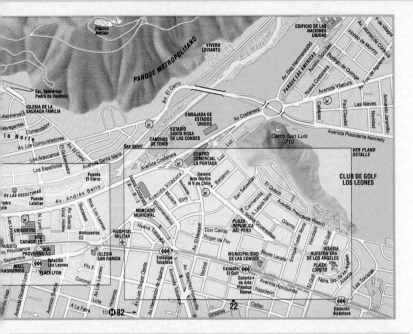

Terminal Alameda is a private terminal belonging to Tur Bus and Pullman Bus, while Terminal Santiago is used by all other companies; between them, they cover every major destination in the country. If heading for the Viña del Mar / Valparaíso area, the fastest option is to take the metro to Pajaritos and flag down a westbound bus, but don't try this on a Friday before a holiday weekend. See Practical Info for company info and destinations.
Terminal Los Héroes, Tucapel Jiménez 21, ☎ 6969080, fax 6969082 (Metro: Los Héroes)
Terminal San Borjas, Alameda 3250 (Metro: Estación Central). Located just west of the main railway station at the rear of a crowded shopping gallery.
Torres del Tajamar, on the north side of Providencia between Metro Salvador and Metro Manuel Montt.

LOCAL TRANSPORT

Though the area of interest to visitors is relatively small compared with the overall size of the city, you will need to use public transport to move between the distinct sectors. The Metro is unquestionably the most user-friendly of Santiago's

transport options, and is a good tool for orientation. Taxis and radio taxis are also good, simple, inexpensive options. Micros and taxis colectivos are a little more difficult, requiring at least basic knowledge of the city. Santiago's Metro is clean, efficient, and inexpensive – its greatest drawback is its limited extension. Still, even when the Metro won't get you exactly where you need to go, you can use it to get close to your destination and then take a taxi or combination Metrobus. Peak hours are uncomfortably crowded, but if you need to get somewhere at this time it's a toss-up between a short period of suffering on the Metro or a long wait in a bus or taxi on the surface.

Signs at the entry to the platforms indicate direction of travel. The main line, Línea 1, runs between the Escuela Militar station (Dirección Las Condes) at the intersection of Apoquindo and Américo Vespucio, and the San Pablo station at the west end of town (Dirección Pudahuel). The Metro does not reach the airport. The other two lines run north-south: Línea 2 intersects with the main axis at the Los Héroes Terminal, while Línea 5 crosses at Baquedano.

Metro stations also make good meeting places, and free event boards along the platforms can be good sources of information. Most stations have phones, and all have good maps of the surrounding area to help you get oriented.

If you forsee using the Metro a lot, you'll get more rides for your money if you buy a multi-use ticket for about US$6. The magnetized tickets are inserted into the turnstile slot, and pop back out if you have any money left on your ticket. Several people may use the same ticket. Single rides cost from $180-260, depending upon the time of day. Hours are Mon-Sat 0630-2230, Sun and holidays 0800-2230.

MICROS

Over 10,000 city buses known as micros crowd Santiago's narrow streets, contributing hugely to air and noise pollution but providing essential transport for millions of Santiaguinos. To most visitors the micro system is rather confusing: the buses follow a fixed route, the principal streets and destinations of which are listed on the windshield and side of the bus. This means that if you're heading for an address on Av. Apoquindo, you look for the word Apoquindo on the sign. However, the micro may not follow the entire street, and next thing you know, you're off the main drag and heading for the barrio. At the time of writing, the rapidly rising single-ride fare on Santiago micros is $290.

RADIO TAXI
RadioTaxi Las Condes, ☎ 2114470. El Golf, ☎ 2200873. 33 Ltda., ☎ 6381508. Cheaper than street taxis for the airport.

TAXIS
Foreign visitors will find Santiago taxis to be very reasonable, but not all drivers know the city as you might expect. All taxis are required to use their meter, but some will attempt to take advantage of foreigners by neglecting to do so and then overcharging. Your best recourse is simply to insist upon meter use, and get another taxi if the driver refuses. Santiago taxis charge $150 at pickup and another 60 or 70 pesos per 200 meters.

RENT A CAR
Automóvil Club ☎ 6019828. Avis, Hotel Sheraton ☎ 2747621. Budget, F. Bilbao 1439 ☎ 3623200. Full Fama's, F. Bilbao 1049 ☎ 3430604.

TRAIN STATION
The Estación Central is at Alameda 3322 (Metro: Estación Central), open 0700-2300. You can also purchase tickets at Galería Libertador, Alameda 853, Local 21, ☎ 6398247, open weekdays 0830-1300, Sat 0900-1300. Another option is Galería Comercial Sur, Local 25, at the Escuela Militar station, ☎ 2282983, same hours.

CULTURAL CENTERS
Centro de Extensión de la Universidad Católica, Alameda 390, ☎ 2220275 (Metro: Univ. Católica). Art exhibits.
Centro de Arte Violeta Parra, Carmen 340, ☎ 6352387. Films, folklore music.
Corporación Cultural de la Estación Mapocho, south side of Río Mapocho at the end of Bandera, ☎ 6972990 (Metro: Puente Cal y Canto). Concerts, theater, café, art exhibits, special events.
Instituto Chileno Británico de Cultura, Santa Lucía 124, ☎ 6382156. Newspapers in English.
Instituto Chileno Francés de Cultura, Merced 298, ☎ 6398433.
Instituto Chileno Alemán de Cultura / Goethe-Institut, Esmeralda 650, ☎ 6383185. Films, exhibitions.

Instituto Chileno de Cultura Hispánica, Providencia 927.
Instituto Italiano de Cultura, Triana 843.
Instituto Chileno Israelí de Cultura, Moneda 812, of. 613.
Instituto Chileno Japonés de Cultura, Providencia 2653, of. 1902.
Instituto Chileno Norteamericano de Cultura, Moneda 1467, ☎ 6963215. Films, library, job board, language courses.
Instituto Cultural del Banco del Estado, Alameda 123. Art exhibitions, theater, etc.
Instituto Cultural de Providencia, Av. 11 de Septiembre 1995 (Metro Pedro de Valdivia). Art exhibitions, theater, etc.
Instituto Cultural Las Condes, Av. Apoquindo 6570. Art exhibitions, theater, lectures.

SHOPPING
BOOKSHOPS
English-language newspapers and magazines are sold at upmarket hotels and at kiosks on the corner of Huérfanos and Bandera.
Feria Chilena del Libro, Huérfanos 623. Largest selection of books, in Spanish and English.
Librería Chile Ilustrado, Av. Providencia 1652 Local 6 (behind Phone Box Pub), ☎ 2358145. Social and natural sciences, history, exploration, folklore, all about Chile. Rare and old books. Next door, Books sells and trades books in English.
Librería Albers, Vitacura 5648, Las Condes, ☎ 2185371, fax 2181458. Books in Spanish, English, and German.
Librería Inglesa, Huérfanos 669, Local 11, also at Pedro de Valdivia 47. Books in English.
Gaia Centro de Difusión Ecológica, Orrego Luco 054. Excellent selection of books on flora and fauna, coffee table books, postcards.

CAMPING EQUIPMENT
Lippi, Av. Italia 1586. Domestically manufactured fleece and outerware, packs, etc. High quality and reasonable prices.
Lucy Montaña, Portal de Lyon Gallery, Subterranean Local 14 (corner of Providencia and Ricardo Lyon). The grande dame of the Chilean Andes. Buys and sells new and used gear.
Mountain Service, Paseo Las Palmas 2209, Local 016, Providencia (entrance to Los Leones Metro). Outerwear, climbing and camping hardware, etc.
Outdoors and Travel, Encomenderos 206 Las Condes. Brand-name outerwear and soft goods.

Patagonia, corner of Helvecia and Ebro. Patagonia retail store.
Patagonia Sport inside the Federación de Andinismo at Almirante 77. Mountaineering and camping equipment, maps.

CAMERA REPAIRS
Many camera shops sell new and used equipment and will repair cameras. Suggestions include Interfoto, Merced 832 Local 9, FotoMundo, Merced 832 subte. and Casa Pavez, San Antonio 568.

FILM AND PROCESSING
Tecnología Uno, Av. Santa María 0120. Fast, inexpensive, high quality slide processing.
Reifschneider, main office at Av. José M. Infante 1639, many branch offices. Best selection of Fuji film, discounts for bulk purchases.

HANDICRAFT MARKETS & SHOPS
Feria Artesanal La Merced, corner of Merced and Mac Iver.
Centro Artesanal Cerro Santa Lucía (Metro Santa Lucía). Traditional handicrafts, leather goods, hippy stuff, jewelry.
Poblado Artesanal de Manquehue, at the corner of Manquehue and Los Milagros, just south of Apoquindo. New, highly recommended handicraft market.
Los Graneros del Alba, Av. Apoquindo 9085, ☎ 2464360, open 1100-1930 (Metro: Escuela Militar, then take a micro marked 'Los Dominicos'). Santiago's largest variety of imported and domestic crafts, including antique furniture and other upscale items. Many stalls are closed during the week.
Artesanías de Chile, Antonio Varas 475, Providencia, also in the Estación Mapocho, ☎ 2363315.

MALLS
Parque Arauco, on Av. Kennedy east of Américo Vespucio (Metro Escuela Militar, then take the Metrobus).
Alto Las Condes, Av. Kennedy 9001.
Mall Panorámico, corner of 11 de Septiembre and Ricardo Lyon (Metro Pedro de Valdivia or Los Leones).

MARKETS
The Mercado Central, with its excellent fish and shellfish market and inexpensive restaurants, is on the south side of the Río Mapocho between Puente and 21 de Mayo (Metro Cal y Canto). Across the river is a huge vegetable market, La Vega Central.

MUSIC
Best selection at the Feria del Disco, with locations at Ahumada 286 and at the corner of Providencia and Suecia.

WINE

The Wine House, Vitacura 2904.
El Mundo del Vino, Isidora
Goyenechea 2931.
Vinopolis, El Bosque 038, Pedro de
Valdivia 036, and in the
international airport.

SPORTS

FOOTBALL / SOCCER

The professional season runs Mar-
Dec, with most games played on
Sat, Sun, and Wed. The three local
teams are Colo Colo, who plays at
home at the Estadio Monumental
in Macul (Metro Pedrero, Línea 2);
the Universidad Católica, who plays
at home at San Carlos de
Apoquindo in Las Condes; and the
Universidad de Chile, who plays at
the Estadio Nacional, at the corner
of Grecia and Marathon in Nuñoa.
Contact the clubs directly for tickets:
Colo Colo, Cienfuegos 4 I, ☎ 6952251;
Univ. de Chile, Campos de Deportes
565, Nuñoa, ☎ 2392783; Univ.
Católica, Andrés Bello 2782,
Providencia, ☎ 2312777.
If you're really lucky, you might
catch the Chilean national squad
(La Roja) playing a friendly or
qualifier. If they happen to be
playing, you can get tickets at the
Estadio Nacional.

HORSE RACING

Two large hippodromes, very
popular, nice at sunset.
Club Hípico, Blanco Encalada
2540, ☎ 6836535 (Metro: Unión
Latinoamericano). Races every Mon
and every other Thu, beginning at
1430 in summer and 1400 in winter.
Hipódromo Chile, on Av. Fermín
Vivaceta, ☎ 7369276, in Recoleta.
Races every Sat, every other Thu,
beginning at 1430.

SWIMMING POOLS

There are two public pools in
Parque Metropolitano, open
summer only Tue-Fri 1000-1800,
weekends and holidays 1000-
1900. Entrance to each costs
about US$10.

USEFUL ADDRESSES

Conaf: Av. Bulnes 285,
☎ 3900000 (Metro: Moneda).
Instituto Geográfico Militar (IGM):
Dieciocho 369, ☎ 6968221
(Metro Toesca), open Mon 0900-
1730, Tue-Fri 0900-1750.

METRO

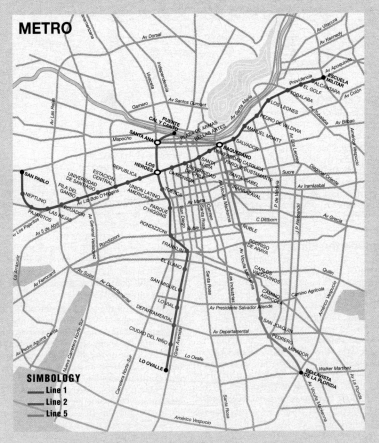

SIMBOLOGY
— Line 1
— Line 2
— Line 5

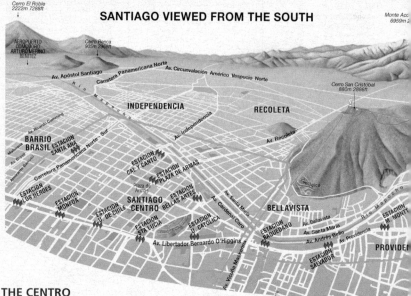

SANTIAGO VIEWED FROM THE SOUTH

THE CENTRO

The Centro is Santiago's downtown, the heart of the city. Most of Santiago's historic architecture and museums, are concentrated here, somewhat hidden among the clustered high rises reflecting the modern focus of the Centro: business. On weekdays, and especially at rush hour, the Centro is overwhelmingly modern and fast paced – and some might add crowded and noisy. Weekend mornings, and evenings after the rush, are the best times to sightsee.

Around the Plaza de Armas

The Plaza de Armas lies four blocks north of the Alameda, and has its own Metro stop; if coming from the Alameda the nicest way to walk there is up the Paseo Ahumada pedestrian mall. Commercial arcades line the eastern and southern sides of the Plaza, while to the north are the 1882 **CORREO CENTRAL** (Post Office, museum upstairs,), the 1807 **PALACIO DE LA REAL AUDIENCIA** (now site of the **MUSEO HISTÓRICO NACIONAL**,), and the 1895 **Municipalidad**. The entire west side is consumed by the 1775 **IGLESIA CATEDRAL**, a neoclassical work by Joaquín Toesca. There is a small religious museum inside.

Two blocks south of the plaza, on the east side of Estado, is the green and yellow

TEMPLO SAN AGUSTÍN, the third church built on the site, last touched up in 1863; the earlier churches were destroyed by earthquakes. Legend has it that during the *terremoto* of May 1647, the crown of thorns worn by the Cristo de Mayo, now on the north altar, fell down around his neck, and when an attempt was made to raise the crown to the wooden figure's head, it began to bleed. One block further east, on the corner of Agustinas and San Antonio, is the 1857 **TEATRO MUNICIPAL** (Municipal theatre, see P for box office info).

Just east of the plaza on Merced, to the right, are the 1892 **EDIFICIO COMERCIAL EDWARDS** and the 1769 **CASA COLORADA**, the latter built by Mateo de Toro y Zambrano, first president of the 1810 Junta Nacional. Inside is the **MUSEO DE SANTIAGO** (see). If you continue another two blocks east, to Calle Mac Iver, you'll see the **BASÍLICA DE LA MERCED**, the third church erected on the site, finished in the late 18th century by Joaquín Toesca. There is a nice courtyard inside the convent next door to the church; upstairs is the **MUSEO DE LA MERCED** .

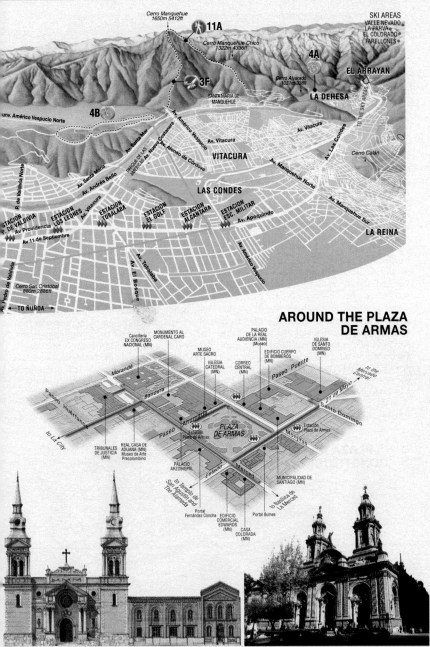

SKI AREAS
VALLE NEVADO
LA PARVA
EL COLORADO
FARELLONES

Cerro Manquehue
1650m 5412ft

11A

Cerro Manquehue Chico
1322m 4336ft

4A

3F

Cerro Alvarado
1031m 338ft

EL ARRAYAN

Santa María de
Manquehue

LA DEHESA

unv. Américo Vespucio Norte

4B

Av. Vitacura

Av. Santa Mar

Av. Américo Vespucio

Av. Las Condes

Av. Vitacura

PARQUE DE LAS
AMERICAS Av. Nueva Costanera Av. Alonso de Córdova

VITACURA

Av. Manquehue Norte

Cerro Calán

Av. Andrés Bello

Av. Santa María

LAS CONDES

Av. Vitacura

**ESTACIÓN
LOS LEONES**

**ESTACIÓN
TOBALABA**

**ESTACIÓN
EL GOLF**

**ESTACIÓN
ALCÁNTARA**

**ESTACIÓN
ESC. MILITAR**

Av. Manquehue Sur

**ESTACIÓN
P. DE VALDIVIA**

Av Providencia

Av. Apoquindo

Av. Américo Vespucio

LA REINA

Av 11 de Septiembre

Av. Pedro de Valdivia

P. de Valdivia Norte

Av. Tobalaba

Av. El Bosque

Cerro San Cristóbal
880m 2886ft

TO ÑUÑOA

AROUND THE PLAZA DE ARMAS

Cancillería
EX CONGRESO
NACIONAL (MN)

MONUMENTO AL
CARDENAL CARO

MUSEO
ARTE SACRO

IGLESIA
CATEDRAL
(MN)

CORREO
CENTRAL
(MN)

PALACIO
DE LA REAL
AUDIENCIA (MN)
(Museo)

EDIFICIO CUERPO
DE BOMBEROS
(MN)

IGLESIA
DE SANTO
DOMINGO
(MN)

Morandé

Bandera

Paseo Puente

to the
Mercado
Central

Paseo Huérfanos

21 de Mayo

Santo Domingo

Paseo Ahumada

to La City

Paseo

**PLAZA
DE ARMAS**

Estación
Plaza de Armas

Monjitas

Estación
Plaza de Armas

TRIBUNALES
DE JUSTICIA
(MN)

REAL CASA DE
ADUANA (MN)
Museo de Arte
Precolombino

PALACIO
ARZOBISPAL

Estado

Merced

MUNICIPALIDAD DE
SANTIAGO (MN)

to Templo de
San Agustín and
The Alameda

Portal
Fernández Concha

EDIFICIO
COMERCIAL
EDWARDS
(MN)

CASA
COLORADA
(MN)

Portal Bulnes

to Basílica de
La Merced

IGLESIA AND MUSEO DE LA MERCED

PLAZA DE ARMAS AND CATEDRAL (MN)

PALACIO DE LA MONEDA (MN)

One block north of the plaza, on Santo Domingo between Puente and 21 de Mayo, is the **TEMPLO DE SANTO DOMINGO**, the fourth church built on the site, the rest having fallen victim to earthquakes and fires. The current structure was last restored in 1963. Two blocks further north is the 1868 **MERCADO CENTRAL**, an elegant metal structure prefabricated in England, now site of the city's best seafood market. West along the Mapocho is the 1812 **ESTACIÓN MAPOCHO**, once the terminal for trains to Valparaíso, now a cultural center and concert hall, with a café and bookstore inside. To the east, along the south bank of the Mapocho, are the **PARQUE FORESTAL** and the **PALACIO DE BELLAS ARTES**, described below in Parks and Gardens.

One block west of the plaza, on the south side of Compañía, lies the 1805 **REAL CASA DE ADUANA** (Customs House); on the second floor is the **MUSEO CHILENO DE ARTE PRECOLOMBINO**, one of Chile's very finest museums, (see 🔼). On the next block west, on the north side of Compañía, is the 1858 **EX-CONGRESO NACIONAL** (Chile's Congress now convenes in Valparaíso), and the quiet, fenced gardens designed by Gustave

Renner. Across the street is the 1907 **PALACIO DE LOS TRIBUNALES**; you can check out the glass-roofed interior hall if you leave ID with the guards.

If you walk two blocks south on Morandé, you'll come to the austere **PLAZA DE LA CONSTITUCIÓN**, on the southern side of which stands the 1784-1799 **PALACIO DE LA MONEDA**, designed by Joaquín Toesca and considered one of the finest works of Neoclassical architecture in Latin America. Designed as the colonial mint, it later served as the presidential residence, and though Chilean presidents no longer live here, La Moneda still serve's presidential headquarters. The building was bombed by the Fuerza Aérea in 1973, while Salvador Allende took his own life inside. You can check out the changing of the guard at the entrance on Plaza de la Constitución every other day at 1000, and from 0900-1800 daily you can walk through the building's two interior patios from the Plaza de la Constitución to the Plaza de la Libertad, on the Alameda.

PLAZA DE LA CONSTITUCION

Free tours of the interior of La Moneda can also be arranged at Morandé 130, in Plaza de la Constitución, but approval can take up to 20 days.

MERCADO CENTRAL (MN)

Along the Alameda

One block east of Plaza Bulnes, on the north side of the Alameda on the corner of Bandera, stands the **Club de la Union**, an elegant business and social club open only to members. North of the club, between Bandera and Nueva York, is the **Bolsa de Comercio**

BOLSA DE COMERCIO (MN)

known as the **Barrio París Londres**, that has been declared a national monument.

Another block east, the entire block between Mac Iver and Miraflores is consumed by the 1925 **Biblioteca Nacional** (National Library). Among the largest libraries in Latin America, this is a great resource and a nice place to escape from the city noise and heat – be sure to walk upstairs and poke your head inside the elegant *Sala Medina*.

IGLESIA DE SANTO DOMINGO (MN)

(stock market). If you leave ID at the door, you can go in and observe the trading on weekday mornings.

A couple of blocks further east, on the south side of the Alameda, is the **Iglesia San Francisco**. Built under the direction of Franciscan monk Fray Antonio between 1586 and 1628, this is reputed to be the oldest building in Santiago, having survived the numerous earthquakes that toppled lesser constructions. The small figure on the main altar is the Virgen del Socorro, brought by Pedro de Valdivia from Perú.

Next door to the church is now occupied by the **Convento y Museo de San Francisco** ⬇; south of the convent is a neighborhood of narrow, winding cobblestone streets,

CENTRO CULTURAL ESTACION MAPOCHO (MN)

East of Cerro Santa Lucía

Between Cerro Santa Lucía and Plaza Italia is a pleasant little neighborhood of crooked streets that somehow escapes the noise of the *centro*. Here on Calle Lastarria is the Plaza Mulato Gil de Castro, with a couple of cafés, an art gallery, and the excellent **Museo Arqueológico de Santiago**; nearby is the El Biógrafo art-film theater, as well as numerous cafés and bars, restaurants, bookstores, and galleries.

Palacio Cousiño

Hours: Tue-Sun 0930-1330, 1430-1700.

This opulent mansion was built from 1870-1878 by French architect Paul Lathoud for Isidora Goyenechea, widow of Luis Cousiño and a member of one of Chile's most prestigious families. Fashioned with imported construction materials and furniture, it was the first building in Chile to have an elevator and central heating. Tours in English and Spanish visit the well-preserved interior.

East of the Palacio Cousiño are a series of pleasant malls and parks, with fountains and large open spaces, at the far end of which

lies the **Basílica de los Sacramentinos**, a striking church with multiple domes and towers. In front of the Basílica there are a group of stalls selling old and rare books.

You can access Palacio Cousiño directly from Metro Estación Toesca (Línea 2), or else walk there from the Alameda via either Paseo Bulnes or Calle Dieciocho, the latter of which concentrates a number of other impressive turn-of-the-century buildings.

INSIDE THE PALACIO COUSIÑO (MN) AND CARVING ON THE FROM DOOR

THE BASILICA LOS SACRAMENTINOS (MN)

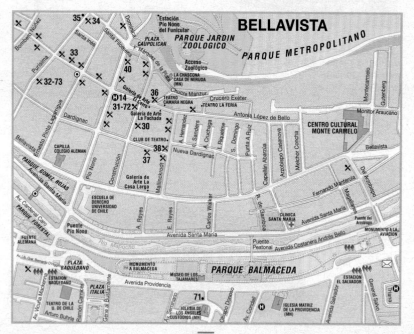

NERUDA'S LIBRARY AT LA CHASCONA (MN

CEMENTERIO GENERAL

BELLAVISTA

North of the Río Mapocho, right at the foot of Cerro San Cristóbal, Bellavista is at once Santiago's mellowest and most happening barrio, and should not be missed by any visitor. Its shady, tree-lined streets, rows of old houses, scattered art galleries and abundant restaurants make the so-called 'bohemian district' a great place to spend a relaxed afternoon or step out at night. The energy here on weekends is really surprising.

Pío Nono Bridge (Metro Baquedano) is the standard way to access Bellavista. The street itself, lined with street vendors and beer halls that fill up with students at night, is probably the least pleasant part of Bellavista. The side streets to the east and west are where you'll find the best restaurants and bars, but some are well hidden and it's best to have an idea where you're heading before setting out. There are also numerous boutiques selling handicrafts in *lapizlázuli*, a blue semiprecious stone (see P for recommendations).

At its northern end, Pío Nono runs into Plaza Caupolicán, where you can catch the funicular railway to the zoo and the top of Cerro San Cristóbal 🔽. This is one of Santiago's coolest little corners – you can see why Pablo Neruda chose to have his home here.

La Chascona (Museo Neruda) Nestled up against the side of Cerro San Cristóbal at Fernando Márquez de la Plata 0192, just east of Plaza Caupolicán, La Chascona is the home that Pablo Neruda built for and named after his third wife, Matilde Urrutia. Like Neruda's other homes in Valparaíso and Isla Negra, La Chascona houses a delightful collection of artifacts collected during the poets travels, though it is the intricate, intensely private design of La Chascona that is perhaps most intriguing. Be sure to check out the floor of the dining room, which is made of *combarbalita*, a semiprecious stone from northern Chile, and the immense table made from a single slab of Araucaria. La Chascona also houses a select portion of Neruda's 6000-volume library.

Hours: Aug-May/Tue-Sun 1000-1300, 1500-1800, Jun-Aug/1000-1300, 1430-1730.
Entrance: $1500, children, students and seniors $750.

Cementerio General About 10 blocks north of the Mapocho, on the west side of Av. Recoleta, Santiago's municipal cemetery is a unique window on Chilean family life and society. On Sundays, the cemetery fills up with families visiting the graves of their deceased, which range from house-sized mausoleums to block upon block of modest tenement graves known as *nichos*; all, however, are lovingly adorned with flowers and personal icons. At the main entrance to the cemetery is an enormous white marble plaque adorned with the names of thousands of *desaparecidos* from the 1973 military coup and dictatorship.

PROVIDENCIA

Providencia is an orderly business and residential district east of downtown. It occupies a sort of middle ground between the hubbub of the center and the expansive, snooty barrios of Las Condes and Vitacura. There are malls, ice-cream shops, music and bookstores, excellent restaurants, happy-hour cafes, and hyped-up discoteques. Providencia may lack the soul of Bellavista, but it's cleaner and probably safer at night.

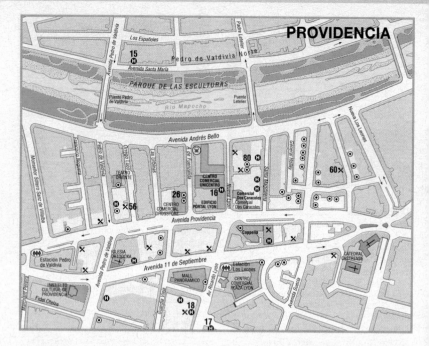

The main drag, Avenida Providencia, begins at Plaza Baquedano, but the heart of Providencia begins ..bout 10 blocks up, around Metro Manuel Montt, and extends up to Los Leones. In a couple of places, the eastbound and westbound lanes separate into two streets; the westbound keeps the name Providencia, while the eastbound is called Av. 11 de Septiembre.

ÑUÑOA

Ñuñoa has something of Bellavista's mood, though it's not so scruffy and is a little further off the beaten path. Most of the action centers around Plaza Ñuñoa, where there are a couple of good bars popular

with students (some of them with live music), and a theater run by the Universidad Católica. Just southwest, Santiago's Estadio Nacional hosts occasional concerts and soccer matches. To get to Plaza Ñuñoa, look out for micros on the Alameda marked 'Irarrázaval – Plaza Ñuñoa.' You can also take a micro in Providencia from the corner of 11 de Septiembre and Suecia, and get off at the corner of Grecia.

WEST OF THE CENTRO

Between the Los Héroes and República Metro stops, on the north side of the Alameda, are a couple of older neighborhoods in the process of urban renewal, as artists and students have taken an interest in these unassuming homes with high ceilings and lovely doors. Just off the Alameda is the

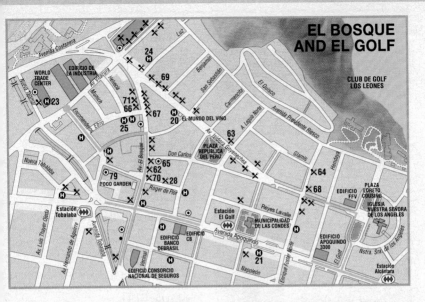

EL BOSQUE AND EL GOLF

BARRIO CONCHA Y TORO, with a tiny plaza accessed by winding, cobblestoned streets. Further north is BARRIO BRASIL, with some good restaurants and bars surrounding the plaza. There is a great antique fair here on Sundays.

Further west along the Alameda is ESTACIÓN CENTRAL, accessed by the Metro stop of the same name. This ornate 1896 train station – more impressive from the Alameda than from the cluttered interior– continues to provide train service to the south.

THE BARRIOS ALTOS: EL BOSQUE, VITACURA AND LAS CONDES

The *Barrios Altos* are the pride of Santiago modern, spotless, and expansive neighborhoods of office buildings, top-notch hotels and restaurants, shopping complexes, and endless suburbia. As part of a general tour of the city, this area is worthwhile to give you an idea of the range of architectural styles and living standards in the capital, but otherwise this area holds little in the way of tourist attractions.

The restaurants and hotels in the western part of these neighborhoods, such as those around Av. El Bosque, lie within walking distance of Providencia and have a similar in-town feel. Further east, however, the Metro comes to an end, and getting around becomes a little more complicated: unlike older parts of the city, these neighborhoods were designed with the automobile in mind. Av. Vitacura, Av. Kennedy, and Av. Apoquindo/Las Condes are the main east-west thoroughfares, while Av. Tobalaba, Av. Manquehue, and Av. Américo Vespucio are the main north-south drags.

Two attractions in the Barrios Altos stand out. At the east end of Av. Apoquindo is the Iglesia Los Dominicos and the LOS DOMINICOS HANDICRAFT MARKET. The craft market itself is somewhat more expensive than others in Santiago, but has a better quality and variety of items, though many stands only open on weekends. Across from the Alto Las Condes mall is the MUSEO DE ARTES DECORATIVAS, described in Museums 🔽.

MUSEUMS IN SANTIAGO

Museo de Santiago In the Casa Colorada, Merced 860. Presents the history of Santiago in a series of unique dioramas. Worth a visit.
Hours: Tue-Fri 1000-1800, Sat 1000-1700, Sun 1100-1400.
Entrance: $500, children $200.

Museo de La Merced Mac Iver 341, 2nd floor. Religious iconography, handicrafts, and an interesting Easter Island exhibit, including one of few *rongo rongo* tablets still in Chile 🅒.
Hours: Tue-Fri 1000-1300, 1500-1800.
Entrance: $500, children $250.

Convento y Museo de San Francisco Londres 4. Diverse exhibits, including religious icons and paintings from the Cuzco school, and a magnificiently carved cedar door.
Hours: Tue-Sat 1000-1330, 1500-1800, Sun 1000-1400.

Museo de Arte Contemporáneo Located in the back half of the Bellas Artes building, this contemporary art museum under the direction of the Universidad Católica hosts a wide variety of temporary exhibitions.
Hours: Tue-Sat 1100-1900, Sun 1100-1400.
Entrance: $300, students $150.

Palacio de Bellas Artes Parque Forestal s/n, just south of the Loreto bridge. A lovely Neoclassical building with an open central hall beneath an arched, iron-and-glass ceiling. The museum was inaugurated on Chile's centennial celebration, in 1910, and features excellent rotating exhibits from around the world.
Hours: Tue-Sun 1000-1900.

Parque Museo Ferroviario In the Quinta Normal. An open-air railroad museum with 15 steam engines, including the original engine from the Mendoza-Los Andes trans-Andean line.
Hours: Tue-Fri 1000-1730, Sat-Sun 1100-1830.
Entrance: $600, children $400.

Museo Nacional de Historia Natural In the Quinta Normal. Though lacking solid information in English, this museum presents a good introduction to Chile's flora and fauna. Interesting exhibits include the body of the 12-year- old boy found in an Inca shrine near the summit of Cerro El Plomo, and remains of a Milodón from southern Patagonia.
Hours: Tue-Sat 1000-1730; Sun from Sept-Mar 1100-1830, Sun from April-Aug 1200-1730.

Museo Arqueológico de Santiago Tucked in a corner of Plaza Mulato Gil de Castro, this unassuming museum is smaller than the Museo de Arte Precolombino, but focuses more on Chilean culture groups. Merits a visit.
Hours: Mon-Fri 1000-1400, 1530-1830, Sat 1000-1400.
Entrance: free.

Museo Postal y Telegráfico Upstairs in the post office. Stamps from Chile and around the world, antique telegraph machines, and the like.
Hours: Mon-Fri 0900-1700.

Museo Ralli Alonso de Sotomayor 4110, on the corner of Candelaria Goyenechea. Contains a private collection of contemporary art from around the world, with a focus on Latin American artists.
Hours: Summertime Tue, Wed, Fri, Sat, Sun 1100-1700, winter 1030-1600.
Entrance: free.

Museo Histórico Nacional Plaza de Armas 951. Displays on colonial and early republican history. Not one of Santiago's better museums.
Hours: Summer Tue-Sat 1000-1730, Sun 1000-1330; winter Tue-Sun 1000-1730.
Entrance: $600, children 8 to 18 $300.

Museo de Artes Decorativas Opposite the Alto Las Condes Mall at Kennedy 9350. An eigthteenth-century *casa patronal*, with well-preserved antiques and a collection of lovely Spanish coffers.
Hours: Tue-Fri 1000-1730, Sat 1100-1730, Sun 1400-1730.
Entrance: $500.

Museo Chileno de Arte Precolombino Upstairs in the Real Casa de Aduana, Bandera 361. Santiago's best museum, a must-see for anyone interested in Amerindian culture and archaeology. The permanent exhibitions cover 80 separate culture areas from México to Tierra del Fuego, divided into four areas: Mesoamérica, Intermedia, Andina and Surandina. Attractive, well-ordered and labeled displays.
Hours: Tue-Sat 1000-1800, Sun 1000-1400.
Entrance: $1500, children and students free.

Museo Artequín In the Pabellón París building, Av. Portales 3530, south of the Quinta Normal. Interactive art museum for children, with reproductions of classical works.
Hours: Dec-Feb/Tue-Fri 1030-1830, Sat-Sun 1100-1930. Mar-Nov/Tue-Fri 0900-1700, Sat-Sun 1100-1800.
Entrance: donations requested.

Museo Interactivo Mirador (MIM) At Av. El Mañío 6410, 800m from Metro Mirador Azul (Línea 5). Fascinating new interactive museum for children and adults.
Hours: Tue-Sun 0930-1830.
Entrance: $3000, students $1.500, children and seniors $2000.

PARKS AND GARDENS

Cerro Santa Lucía

Known to the native inhabitants as *Huelén*, Cerro Santa Lucía lends shape to the otherwise homogenous landscape of the centro. Pedro de Valdivia and his soldiers were apparently drawn to the hill, camping at its base for the first time on Dec. 13, 1540, and renaming it in honor of that day's patron saint, Santa Lucía. Until the late 19th century, however, Santa Lucía remained nothing more than a 'pile of offensive and useless rocks, a refuge for criminals,' as it was described by Benjamín Vicuña Mackenna, who in 1872 put the prisoners from Santiago's jail to work converting the hill into a public park. That same year the first walkways were opened to the public, and over the next thirty years Santa Lucía continued to evolve, with French landscape artist Gustave Renner collaborating on garden design. The elaborate gateway and staircases were completed in 1902.

There are two entrances to the park, and a stroll through Santa Lucía can easily be incorporated into a walking tour of the centro. The principal entrance is on the Alameda just east of the Santa Lucía Metro station; from here, winding staircases lead up past fountains to a series of shady terraces frequented by families and lovers, with excellent views of downtown Santiago. The other entrance is at the north end of the park, near the Palacio de Bellas Artes. Note that Santa Lucía is open only during daylight hours, and that visitors are required to sign a guest book.

CERRO SANTA LUCIA

Riverside Parks

Upriver of the Cal y Canto bridge, a series of parks lines both sides of the Mapocho. With well-maintained lawns and lots of trees and benches, these make for a great momentary escape from the city, and are popular with runners and walkers. Two areas stand out:

Parque Forestal

Dating from Chile's 1910 centennial, Parque Forestal extends along

PARQUE FORESTAL

the south bank of the Mapocho between the Museo de Bellas Artes and Plaza Baquedano. Unfortunately, the park is cut off from the river by a four-lane expressway, which makes it a bit difficult to escape from the sound of the traffic, but it certainly beats walking up the Alameda. At the east end of the park, there's an interesting fountain donated to the city by Chile's German community.

Parque de las Esculturas

Located on the north bank of the Mapocho between Pedro de Valdivia and Padre Letelier, Parque de las Esculturas is an easy walk from downtown Providencia. In addition to a number of outdoor sculptures, there's a sunken gallery in the center of the park, with temporary exhibitions. The park entrance is on Padre de Letelier; there are green areas east and west of the park along the river, and the neighborhood to the north, called Pedro de Valdivia Norte, is a great place to take a stroll or a leisurely bike ride.
Hours: Daily 1000-1400, 1500-1800.

Parque Metropolitano / Cerro San Cristóbal

Cerro San Cristóbal is the steep, elongate hill that extends from Cerro La Pirámide far into the Santiago basin, dividing the city in two. Most of it has been converted into a park, the Parque Metropolitano – the largest open space within city limits. The park is extremely popular with Chileans, who flock there on the weekends to ride bikes, do aerobics, take a stroll, have a picnic, and take in the birds-eye view of the city. The best time to visit is in the early morning, before the smog kicks in and obscures your view, and the best season is unquestionably springtime, when the *matorral* scrub which covers most of the hill erupts into flower.

The park has two principal access points. **From Plaza Caupolicán in Bellavista**, a funicular railway climbs up the steepest part of the hill to the **Zoológico** (Santiago Zoo, details 🔲), with examples of native fauna, including pudú, puma and cóndor. The funicular continues up to Terraza Bellavista and the Virgen de la Inmaculada Concepción, which has been gazing out over Santiago since 1908. Behind the virgin is the uppermost station for the *teleférico* cable car, 🔲. If you have a car or a bike, you can also ascend San Cristóbal via a road from Plaza Caupolicán that wraps around the north side of the park.

FUNICULAR RAILWAY

Hours: Mon 1300-2000, Tue-Sun 1000-2000; closes one hour earlier in winter.
Cost: Round trip $1000 (children $700), one way $700. Tickets may also be purchased in combination with the teleférico, see below.

ZOOLÓGICO

Hours: Tue-Sun 1000-1800.
Entrance: $1600, children $500.

THE PARK ENTRANCE AT THE NORTHERN END OF PEDRO DE VALDIVIA provides the most convenient access to the Tupahue sector of the park. This is the standard route for cyclists and joggers, though the views are better if you ride the *teleférico* cable car to the top 🔲. In Tupahue, there's a public swimming pool, a botanical garden with labeled native plant species, and the Camino Real restaurant, with a nice patio and inexpensive wine tastings.

East of Tupahue, the road climbs to the Antilén swimming pool and a cul de sac with a little playground. From here, roads and trails continue east along both sides of the ridge to the gap where Av. Américo Vespucio crosses the ridge into the northern part of the city. From here, a bridge over Vespucio connects the park to the foothills of Cerro La Pirámide, where there are more trails apt for walking, running, and biking, though muggings are occasionally reported here – use your judgement.

FUNICULAR RAILWAY ON CERRO SAN CRISTOBAL

LOCOMOTORA 18

LOCOMOTORA 306

TELEFÉRICO

Hours: Mon-Fri 1430-2000, Sat, Sun, holidays 1030-2030; closes 1 hr earlier in winter.
Entrance: Round trip $1400, children $700; one section only $700, two sections $900.

QUINTA NORMAL

This 40há park dates from 1830, when it was begun as a nursury for the propagation of exotic plant species for public and private parks throughout Santiago. In 1875, the **MUSEO NACIONAL DE HISTORIA NATURAL** was inaugurated for Santiago's international expo, and throughout the turn of the century this cool, forested park was a traditional *paseo* for the city's rich. Today the Quinta Normal is far less exclusive, filling up on summer weekends with picnicking *Santiaguinos*, and is a nice place to escape the noise of the city and maybe get in on a pickup soccer match. In addition to the Natural History Museum, the **PARQUE MUSEO FERROVIARIO** and **MUSEO ARTEQUÍN** are also worth visiting 🔲.

The Quinta Normal lies west of downtown; to get there, take the Metro to Estación Central, and then catch a northbound micro or colectivo on Matucana. The main entrance is at Matucana 502, near the corner of Catedral, four blocks north of the Alameda.
Hours: 0800-2000. *Entrance:* free

PARQUE O'HIGGINS

Donated to the city in 1873 by Luis Cousiño, this 80há park began, like the Quinta Normal, as a retreat for the city's rich. Today it is anything but that, and the gardens and ponds have supplanted by family-oriented installations such as an amusement park (**FANTASILANDIA**, *open on weekends and holidays in winter, in summer Tue-Fri 1400-2000, weekends 1100-2000*), tennis courts, a public swimming pool, a roller-skating rink, an aquarium, and a minor zoo. There are also a couple of museums: the **MUSEO DEL HUASO**, with exhibits on traditional rural clothing and implements (great hat collection), and the **MUSEO DE INSECTOS Y CARACOLES**, featuring the city's best collection of insects and snails.

The **CLUB HÍPICO** (horsetrack) is just west of Parque O'Higgins; 🅿 for details.

Day Trips out of Santiago

See The Río Mapocho Valley, the Cajón del Maipo, and Parque Nacional La Campana (all below) for more recommended day trips.

Pomaire

80km SW of Santiago on the road to San Antonio, Pomaire is famous throughout Chile for the inexpensive, tasteful and functional pottery which, it seems, every single inhabitant of the town either makes or sells: the streets are literally lined by one overflowing pottery stand after another. This is a popular weekend trip for Santiaguinos, culminating in a traditional Chilean lunch at one of Pomaire's many rustic eateries. Transport by regular bus from Santiago.

Wineries and Haciendas

Several wineries make easy, inexpensive day trips from Santiago, but be advised that most require you to book visits in advance. Closest to town is VIÑA SANTA CAROLINA, located at Rodrigo de Araya 1341 in Macul; other options include VIÑA COUSIÑO MACUL (at Av. Quilín 7100 in Macul, take micro #390 or 391 from the Alameda to the corner of Tobalaba and Quilín), VIÑA UNDURRAGA (at km 34 on the road to Melipilla, access by bus from Terminal San Borja), VIÑA SANTA RITA in Alto Jahuel, and VIÑA CONCHA Y TORO in Pirque. See for more complete information on vineyards and wine tours.

Pirque

Located about 20km south of downtown Santiago at the mouth of the Cajón del Maipo, Pirque is a popular and relaxing weekend destination for families from Santiago. Near the northern entrance to town is the Concha y Toro vineyard , and in the village itself are a number of colonial-style buildings, as well as a handicrafts fair (on weekends) and a host of traditional restaurants. To get to Pirque, catch a taxi colectivo from the south side of Plaza Italia or follow the directions to RN Río Clarillo, .

Reserva Nacional Río Clarillo

This 13,185há reserve SW of Pirque makes for one of Santiago's most peaceful, relaxing day trips – provided that you have your own transport. On weekends, Santiago families flock to Río Clarillo to picnic on the banks of the clear-flowing Río Clarillo, and to swim and lounge on the smooth, white granite

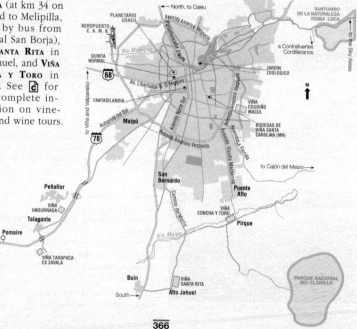

boulders in the streambed; if you're looking for solitude, you can usually find some by continuing up past the footbridge at the end of the road. The native vegetation in the park ranges from sclyrophyllous forest to cactus and *matorral*, and short interpretive trails allow visitors to identify characteristic species of the central region. Note that if using public transportation, you need an early start to avoid traffic, and you'll have to walk to 5km from the park entrance to the picnic areas. Camping is not allowed in the park.

Hours: daily 0830-1900
Entrance: Mon-Fri $2500, children $700, Sat-Sun $3500, children $1500

TRANSPORT
By Metrobus 80 from Bellavista de la Florida (Línea 2) to the end of the line, then walk the 2km to the park entrance. The picnic areas are another 5km up. The last buses leave around 2100 on weekends.

Santuario de la Naturaleza El Arrayán

Located in a narrow canyon above the upper-class community of El Arrayán, the Santuario is a popular destination for weekend picnickers from Santiago, with tables and barbecue pits scattered along the shady streambank. There is also a nice 1-2 day hike along the Estero El Arrayán, but if you only have one day to spend, there is equally good hiking (for free) on nearby Cerro Pachoco and on the trails of the Contrafuertes Cordilleranos system 🛈. One of the big advantages of the Santuario is the fact that horses are regularly available for rent on the premises, making this the easiest place near Santiago to mount a spur-of-the-moment riding trip.

Hours: Daily 0900-2000

TRANSPORT
By micro from the Alameda to Plaza San Enrique in El Arrayán, then by taxi or colectivo to the park entrance. From here it's another 2-3 kilometers to the picnic area. Consider making pickup arrangements beforehand if you don't want to get stuck walking out.
Entrance: Adults $1500, children $1300.

SANTIAGO'S CLOSEST DAY HIKES

Cerro Manquehue

 ✥ ⏱ 5-6h 📷
Cerro Manquehue is the steep, flat-topped peak looming to the north of Vitacura; its ascent makes a good, challenging day hike, with amazing views over the city and foothills. The trail begins at an unmarked trailhead at the end of

Calle Villa Roja (in Lo Curro), and climbs steeply up an obvious ridge to the summit. From here, you can return the way you came, or to make a circuit, walk west down the ridge towards Cerro La Pirámide (steep descent, use caution), passing south of the peak of La Pirámide and ending above Américo Vespucio, where you can catch a cab or micro back into town. Note that solo hikers should avoid the La Pirámide area, as muggings are occasionally reported here.

Cerro Pochoco

 ⇄ ⏱ 3h rt 📷
One of Santiago's most popular and accessible day hikes. To reach the trailhead, take the Calle Pastor Fernández from Plaza San Enrique as if going to the Santuario de la Naturaleza, but instead of turning left on the Camino El Cajón, continue on and take the next right on the Camino El Alto. At the end of the road is an old observatory; the trail from the end of the road leads steeply uphill about 1.5hrs to the 1,805m summit. There is no water on the route.

Operators: 49 - 137

Up the Santuario

🐎 🚶 ⇄ ⏱ 7-8h rt 📷
From the picnic area at the bridge (3km from the park entrance), head west up the hill on a dirt road for about 5 min, at which point a trail heads off to the right (east). Follow this trail about 45 min to a bridge over the stream; from here the route continues up the east side of the valley about 3-3.5hrs through native matorral and sclyrophyllous forest to a major stream confluence. Most hikers turn back here, returning the way they came, although it is possible to make a 2-3 day loop by crossing a pass to the east and descending the Quebrada de los Perros to the Río Mapocho canyon.

Operators: 39 🐎 - 137 🐎

SINGLE-TRACK IN SANTIAGO

La Dehesa

🚲 ▶varies◀ ⏱ varies **D** **S** 📷
This is the best single-track within riding distance of Santiago. Getting there takes a bit of map work: take Avenida La Dehesa north across the Mapocho from Las Condes, turning right on Av. El Rodeo, then a left on Camino El Huinganal. At the end of the street is a metal gate with a wooden gate beside it; enter here and have at it. This area is very popular with Santiago cyclists, so you might be able to tag along behind someone or ask for suggestions.

LAGUNA DE ACULEO

N

Laguna Aculeo

Calm in the morning hours and windy in the afternoon, Laguna Aculeo is Santiago's backyard nautical sports playground; on weekends the lake fills up with waterskiers, powerboaters, sailboats and windsurfers. Lining the NE shore of the lake is a series of upscale campgrounds, cabaña complexes, and private clubs (where you can rent motor boats and other toys), while just SE of the lake is the picturesque village of Pintué, originally the seat of the immense Hacienda de Aculeo. At the SW corner of the lake is the town of Rangue and a recommended campground, *Los Alamos*. Four kilometers west of Rangue on the road to Melipilla is a mountain pass, Cuesta El Cepillo, with excellent views over the lake and an unmarked trailhead leading south to through roble forests to the rocky summit of 2,706m Cerro Horcón de Piedra. Frequent buses from Santiago to Rangue access all the areas described above.

Biking on Cerro San Cristóbal

▶varies◀ ⏱varies ST ▢

While most Santiago cyclists stick to the paved roads, Cerro San Cristóbal also has a ton of fast and highly technical single track trails, mostly along the ridgetop east of the Antilén swimming pool and along the southern flank of the cerro. Winter and spring are by far the best times to ride; in summer and fall the trails get a little dusty.

Caleu

Set on the southern flanks of Cerro Roble, Caleu is a charming adobe village that provides access to one of the finest native roble forests in Central Chile. Hiking, biking, and horseback riding are all possibilities in this nearly forgotten enclave in the Coast Range. Caleu may be reached by micro from Santiago via the town of Tiltil.

Cerro El Roble

▶20km◀ D ▢
⏱4-5h rt

This route leads from Caleu up a dirt road in good repair to the very summit of Cerro el Roble (2,200m), a climb of 1,000m in 10km. There are excellent views of the coast and the Andes from km 4, as well as stands of native roble. This is also a great place to check out the fall foliage in April-May.
Operators: 70

One of the few places in Chile where you can rent high-quality boards and equipment, Aculeo boasts consistent winds from 1630 and areas for beginners and experts alike.
Operators: 43 - 233

PARAGLIDING AREAS NEAR SANTIAGO

Operators: 15 - 38 - 187

• Cuesta Barriga

There are two takeoffs just off the paved road over the Coast Range SW of the capital. Winds from the south are channeled up a canyon directly to the principal takeoff, creating principally dynamic wind conditions. With wind from the north, you can fly off the other side of the pass, making this a good choice when conditions are poor elsewhere.

● Cerro del Medio

This isolated 1,000m peak above La Dehesa receives the direct force of the venturi formed between Cerro Alvarado and Cerro Lo Curro. Access is on foot or by vehicle through the private Lomas de la Dehesa housing development. With consistent conditions throughout the year, this area is commonly used by classes. Expert pilots can potentially fly here from La Pirámide, thereby significantly extending their flight.

● Colina

About 40 min north of Santiago, this is a popular area for classes, with reliable and relatively gentle conditions throughout the year and a couple of different takeoffs.

● Santuario de la Naturaleza

Intermediate flight zone in the Santiago precordillera, generally accessible only to members of the Asociación Chilena de Vuelo Libre. Access to the takeoff is via a 15km mountain road from the entrance to the reserve. Expect primarily thermal uplift during peak season, from Oct-Apr.

● Cerro La Pirámide

The ample takeoff zone for Cerro La Pirámide is reached via a 15 min. walk uphill from the micro stop just east of Américo Vespucio. This site features consistent southerly winds with dynamic and thermic uplift from Oct-Apr. Because of the central location, pilots must have a D.G.A.C. and carry VHF radios and emergency parachutes, in addition to all regular equipment. Flying is prohibited on weekends and holidays.

● Batuco

Located approximately 35km NW of Santiago, the 300m cerro above the town of Batuco is commonly visited by paragliding schools and beginning-to-intermediate pilots. Note that you must either pay a daily fee, be a member of a paragliding association, or be enrolled in classes to fly here. Access to the takeoff is via 4WD vehicle only.

Sport Climbing in Las Chilcas

Located about 60km north of Santiago, Las Chilcas is the largest sport climbing area in central Chile, and often (depending on traffic) the fastest to reach from the capital. You'll recognize it by a huge white spot painted on a cliff just south of the Panamerican Highway at the bottom of a steep gorge surrounded by congomerate crags. There are currently about 90 established routes rated from 5.5-5.14, with the majority 5.11 or above. If you're stuck in Santiago, there is a pretty nice bouldering wall below the Piscina Tupahue on Cerro San Cristóbal, as well as a couple of climbing gyms ▣.

The Río Mapocho Valley

See map ▣

If you want to get a feel for the scale of the Andes and you don't have much time, this is your best bet. To get there by car, you simply follow Av. Las Condes east along the Mapocho; if using public transport, you'll want to catch a micro to Plaza San Enrique in El Arrayán and then hire a taxi.

100m before the bridge at Puente Ñilhue, 6km from the turnoff to El Arrayán, a signposted turnoff off to the right provides access to the *Area de Protección Contrafuentes Cordilleranos*, trailhead for hikes to Vallecito, Alto del Naranjo, Cerro Provincia

and Cerro de Ramón ▣. From here the road climbs up above the gorge along the north wall of the valley, passing the police post at La Ermita (chain rental in winter) at km 13. At km 16 is a turnoff on the left to the La Disputada mine, and shortly thereafter begins the series of 40 switchbacks leading to the ski areas.

At Curve #15 (km 23) is the entrance to **Santuario de la Naturaleza Yerba Loca** *(Entrance $1000, children $500. Administration hours May-Nov 0900-1700, Dec-Apr 0800-2000)*. From here, it's 4.2km up a dirt road to Villa Paulina, where Conaf has an administration center, a picnic area, and a number of campsites.

Farellones, the first of the ski areas, lies 32km from the turnoff to El Arrayán.

Vallecito, Alto de Naranjo & Cerro Provincia

⏱ 6-8h to summit

This is the largest interconnected trail network in the Santiago area. Beginning at the trailhead above Puente Ñilhue, a trail leads steeply up to the powerline road and continues up and over a ridge to Vallecito (1-2hrs), where there is a waterfall and pleasant (if sometimes dirty) camping in a native sclrophyllous forest. This alone makes for an easy morning hike; if you feel like continuing on, continue climbing the ridge west of Vallecito to the campsite at Alto del Naranjo (1,868m, no water) in about 2hrs total from Puente Ñilque. From here you can either descend west to San Carlos de Apoquindo, or continue up the ridge another 4.5hrs to the summit of Cerro Provincia (2,750m). The ascent of Cerro Provincia makes for a very long day trip, which can be extended into a three-day traverse, over the summit of Cerro de Ramón and down into the El Manzano valley, ending in the Cajón del Maipo.

Operators: 49 - 137

The Yerba Loca Valley

⏱ 1-2d

From the campground at Villa Paulina, head up the the well-marked trail on the east side of the Yerba Loca valley. The route climbs at a moderate grade through scrubby andean vegetation, arriving at the rustic stone refugio at Piedra Carvajal in about 4-5hrs (this is the normal campsite). From here it's another two hours round-trip to the foot of the La Paloma glacier. Yerba Loca can also be linked on foot (or even bicycle) with the La Parva ski area, while mountaineers can continue on Cerro La Paloma and Cerro El Altar (see Mountaineering). Note that while you should not drink the water in the Estero Yerba Loca due to its high mineral content, tributary streams provide plenty of fresh water along the route.

Operators: 10 🐎 - 137

Flying in Farellones & Valle Nevado

The ski areas above Santiago provide for spectacular flying on thermal updrafts, with limitless views of the Andes and the Central Valley. The classic takeoffs are from the summit of Cerro Colorado and the road to Hotel Tupungato, and there are good landing areas at Curva #30 and just above the entrance to Villa Paulina at Curva #15. Tandem flights are often available at Valle Nevado during the ski season, but note that private pilots must obtain previous permission to fly at the ski areas in winter. This area is not recommended for novice pilots.

Cerro La Paloma (4,910m)

⏱ 3d

This heavily glaciated peak dominates the north end of the Yerba Loca valley. From Villa Paulina, follow the trail upvalley about 4hrs to the Casa de Piedra Carvajal; from here you can see the standard route up the south face, which follows the right side of the left-hand glacier, the Glaciar del Rincón, ending on the west face. Set your base camp at Casa de Piedra or another 2km up, on the terminal moraine below the glacier. From here it's 5-8hrs to the summit. A rope is indispensable on this route, which can be combined with an ascent of 5,222m Cerro Altar, just south. Backcountry skiers should check out the stunning chutes on the south side of the Cordón de los Españoles, visible to the north of the Yerba Loca valley on the approach to La Paloma.

Cerro El Plomo (5,424m)

⏱ 3-4d

This classic peak is the most accessible of the 5,000m summits near Santiago, and as it presents few technical challenges, is often used as an acclimation climb for ascents of Aconcagua. It is also famous for the presence of an Inca shrine at 5,140m, where the corpse of a young boy was discovered in 1954 (on display at the Museum of Natural History). The approach leads from the La Parva ski resort over Portezuelo Franciscano, dropping into the Río Cepo valley, east of Cerros Pintor and La Parva, with a first camp at the fields of Piedra Numerada. Most parties reach La Olla (final camp), at the base of the El Plomo glacier, on the second day. From La Olla, the standard route follows the SW ridge up talus, to the right of the main glacier. Towards the top the route trends left, past the Inca shrine and across ice to the summit ridge. A more challenging alternative route climbs the main glacier.

Operators: 10 - 31 - 49 - 137 - 199

Cerro La Falsa Parva (3,888m)
Cerro La Parva (4,047m)
Cerro Pintor (4,180m)
Cerro La Leonera (4,954m)

⏱ 1-2d

This chain of peaks extends immediately NW of the La Parva ski area, and the closer peaks (La Parva and La Falsa Parva) may be easily hiked and skied from the resort. As with El Plomo, access is via Portezuelo Franciscano, but instead of dropping into the valley, the route veers left up the ridge to the summit of La Falsa Parva. From here, continue NE, passing (or summiting) La Parva and Cerro Pintor, arriving at the vast Cancha de Carreras in 4-6 hours total from La Parva (this makes a good campsite). The summit of La Leonera is another 4-5 hours walk, with no technical difficulties.

Operators: 49 - 137

Cerro de Ramón (3,249m)

⏱2d ■

Cerro de Ramón dominates the immediate Santiago skyline, and makes for a great mid-altitude climb with no special equipment required. The fastest access is from the Quebrada de Peñalolén, from which point you can walk to a campsite at Casa de Piedra in about 4 hours; from here it's another 5 hours or so on a clear trail to the summit. The other route begins at Puente Ñilhue on the Río Mapocho and includes a camp at Alto de Naranjo (no water in summer) and an ascent of Cerro Provincia. Either route can be continued west to the Quebrada del Manzano, in the Cajón del Maipo. Take note that conditions on Cerro de Ramón vary drastically throughout the year. The best season is undoubtedly spring (Oct-Nov), while there's still snow left on the peak.

La Parva to Yerba Loca

▶23km◀ ⏱1d P D ST ■

If you're feeling fit, start this ride at the entrance to SN Yerba Loca: the 14 kilometers of paved switchbacks to the ski area should get your heartrate up and keep it there. Otherwise, you can make this ride much easier by catching a ride to La Parva. From the base of the ski area, follow a dirt road north about 1km to a cluster of shacks, then continue down the ridge towards Santiago until you come to an abandoned refugio. From here a trail drops precipitously north into the Yerba Loca Valley, where you can catch a trail back out the to the main road.

Río Mapocho (IV+)

⏱2h

This great little class IV+ creek is a spring classic. The put in (below the chapel in La Ermita) lies just 45 minutes from downtown Santiago, and the takeout is at the Puente Ñilhue bridge. Look out for strainers.

Ice Climbing in Yerba Loca

About four hours up from Villa Paulina, on the north side of the valley, is a variety of waterfalls and ice couloirs up to 400m in height. Routes established here to the present are in the WI3-WI5 range, but there remain many unclimbed lines. The ice is usually in condition from June to September.

Ski Areas above Santiago

Just 32km from Santiago lies Chile's greatest concentration of lifts and most accessible skiing – and the views over the capital and the Andes make the trip worthwhile even for non-skiers. A combined ticket lets you ride lifts in all three areas, each with a distinct character and terrain.

ACCOMMODATION

If you're on a budget, finding lodging up at the ski areas can be a real challenge. The best mid-range options are the hosterías and refugios in Farellones, of which the Hostería Posada de Farellones is especially recommended (though a bit pricey). Otherwise, you can stay in the hotel at Valle Nevado or Colorado, or look in the classified section of Santiago newspapers for private condominiums available for rent.

RESTAURANTS

Valle Nevado has the best variety of restaurants in the area, with everything from elegant fondues at Le Montagnard to on-mountain burgers at the Jazz grill. In Farellones, there are cheap stands along the access road and restaurants in most of the refugios. The selection is more limited in La Parva; a recommended choice for mountain cuisine is La Marmita de Pericles.

TRANSPORT

Transport to the ski areas (as well as transport and other services) is available from Ski Total, Apoquindo 4900 Loc. 39 - 42, ☎ 2460156 or 2466881. Departure 0845 AM, return 1730 PM.
Destinations and Prices: La Parva, US$11. El Colorado - Farellones, US$11. Valle Nevado, US$12. Portillo, US$180 (8 - 11 passenger van).
Hotel Pick up Service (Hotel - Ski Area- Hotel) US$20.

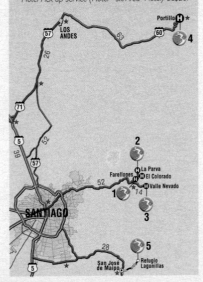

Santiago's Backcountry

• Colorado provides access to short but very steep lines dropping through the cliff bands above Farellones. Though most look unskiable from the road, the cliffs become less continuous further north, where there are great lines, accessed from the Cono Este lift, dropping down to the road to Valle Nevado. Bear in mind that you'll have to hitch back or arrange a shuttle. Some of this terrain can also be accessed from Valle Nevado, by traversing south from the top of the #4 lift. This terrain is of relatively low elevation.

• La Parva provides the best backcountry access of the three areas. From the top of the Piuquenes lift (#12), you can hike up the headwall to the skiers right (west) of the lift, accessing a broad ramp that terminates at the top of La Chimenea, a narrow, 50° chute that gets shade all day. You can easily spot La Chimenea from the access road to the area. Other backcountry areas from La Parva involve longer hikes, often with more difficult snow conditions. La Falsa Parva, directly above the lifts, has a couple of nice lines, while Cerro La Parva, just beyond, has some of the steepest, narrowest shots you could ever ask for. You need an early start to ski Cerro La Parva, and the runout takes you down to Valle Nevado.

• Some of the best backcountry at Valle Nevado is in the Río Molina valley to the east of the hotel. There are steep, untracked lines dropping into this valley from both sides (eg. from the hotel or the ridge below Cerro Tres Puntas), but once you get to the bottom, you must hike out or get a helicopter to come get you. Continuing out the bottom of the valley is not a real possibility. The Cerro Tres Puntas lift also provides access to the endless terrain extending north towards Cerro el Plomo, but access is easier from La Parva.

Heli-Skiing

Valle Nevado is the only area to offer heli-skiing to its guests. Standard destinations include Cerro La Parva, Cerro Pintor, and La Meseta; you can also ski into the Molina Valley, described above, and have the chopper pick you up at the bottom. Prices start at about US$50/pp for the Molina valley run, and vary by destination and number of passengers. Remember that for best fuel efficiency (and prices) it is important to fly in the morning, before the air heats up.

Symbol	Legend	Symbol	Legend
—	Expert	Ⓗ	Hotel
—	Dificult	🅐	Ski School
—	Intermediate	🅡	Restaurant
—	Easy		Ski Patrol
—	Free Skiing	☎	Emergency Telephone
	Skating Rink		Heliskiing
	Chairlift		Restrooms
	Double Chair		Ski Rental
	Triple Chair	Ⓣ	Tickets
	Quad Chair	Ⓔ	Car Park
	Poma		Cafeteria
	T-Bar		Paragliding

Farellones - Colorado

Farellones was an early focal point of mountain sports and living in Chile. As early as 1931, mule trains organized by the Ski Club Chile were bringing eager *Santiaguinos* into the mountains for their first ski experience. In 1935, the first stone refugios were built, and today Farellones retains the most authentic ski village atmosphere of any resort in the Chilean Andes. It also contains the greatest variety of accommodation, and its central location allows you to ski La Parva, El Colorado, and Valle Nevado from a single base.

FARELLONES / COLORADO

The bottom of the area, Villa Farellones, is a favorite spot for sledders and families from Santiago, but the real base area and trails are above the large cliffs (*farellones* in spanish) in Villa El Colorado. You can catch the lift up from Villa Farellones or, for closer access, drive up and park at El Colorado.

The trails are mostly on the south and SW faces of cone-shaped Cerro Colorado. The western slopes are scoured by prevailing winds, and to get to La Parva you must drop down into Valle Nevado and then traverse over from the Tres Puntas lift (#9 on area map). The scoured snow is generally deposited on the east face (Cono Este), where a pitch drops to the El Prado lift (#4) at Valle Nevado. Remember to stop at the bottom of the Cono Este lift (#16) if you don't have a combined ticket.

Farellones / Colorado is the lowest of the three areas, so on hot days the snow can get awfully soupy. Take advantage of morning conditions.

LA PARVA

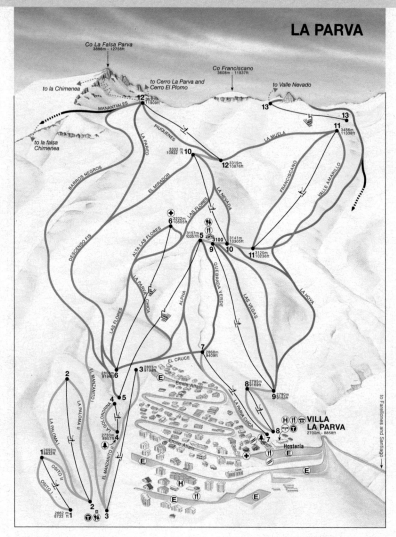

La Parva

Six km west of Farellones, La Parva is the highest of the three areas, and though it lacks steep groomed runs, it does provide access to some great off-piste and backcountry skiing. As a resort, La Parva has a reputation for exclusivity, and finding lodging here can be a real challenge.

Most steep pitches are relatively short, followed by a long intermediate runout. Las Vegas, beneath the mid-mountain restaurant at 3,100m, is probably the best long, steep cruiser. If you don't need to ski the steeps, you have a whole mountain of well-groomed, undulant cruisers to choose from.

From the top of the Piuquenes lift, you can traverse west to access the Falsa Chimenea, a steep chute that drops back east to Barros Negros. On the far side of this ridge is an expansive off-piste area, with the best advanced terrain on the mountain. Be aware that ridgetops are often heavily scoured by winds, and the rocky substrate means that a lot of snow is needed for complete coverage, especially off-piste.

To reach Valle Nevado from La Parva, follow the cat track to the skiers left (SE) from the top of the Las Tórtolas lift (#13).

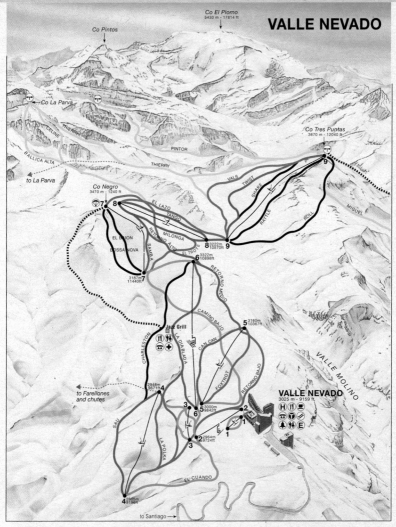

VALLE NEVADO

Co El Plomo
5430 m - 17814 ft

Co Pintos

Co La Parva

CELINE

THIERRY

B ALLICA ALTA

to La Parva

PINTOR

THIERRY

Co Tres Puntas
3670 m - 12040 ft

VALS

TWIST

SHAKE

RATTLE

ROLL

MIGUEL

Co Negro
3470 m - 1240 ft

EL LAZO

TANGO

MILONGA

RETORNO ALTO

EL BAJON

BOSSA NOVA

SAMBA

EL TROTE

3222m
10570h

3322m
10898ft

RETORNO MEDIO

3187m
11440ft

CAMINO BAJO

Jazz Grill

CHARLESTON

LA DIABLADA

CAN CAN

FOXTROT

RETORNO BAJO

3160m
10367ft

VALLE MOLINO

2948m
9671ft

to Farellones
and chutes

SAU

LA POLKA

3000m
9842ft

2964m
9724ft

VALLE NEVADO
3025 m - 9159 ft

EL CUANDO

2965m
9196ft

to Santiago

Valle Nevado

Of the three areas, Valle Nevado is the most specifically geared to the international guest. The hotel is big, modern and aesthetic, the ski school is top-notch, and grooming and other services are on a par with many areas in the US.

Valle Nevado ('Snowy Valley') is named as it is for a reason: much of the snow blown off of La Parva and Colorado is deposited here, and huge avalanches occasionally bury the access road under meters of debris. If you're not staying at the hotel when this happens, and you can't afford the helicopter transfer, you miss out on the bonanza.

This area has better variety of terrain than La Parva or Colorado, and if you pay attention to the movement of the sun throughout the day, you can ski in great conditions all day long. There are big cornices and other dramatic features to ski or ride off Cerro Negro, and good chutes and pitches off the ridge south of Cerro Tres Puntas. Most of the steepest pitches are fairly short, but if you're willing to hike you can access a ton of steep, untracked headwalls.

To reach Colorado from Valle Nevado, take the Cono Este lift (#16 on the El Colorado map). To reach La Parva, traverse NW along the cat track from the top of Cerro Tres Puntas.

THE CENTRAL ANDES

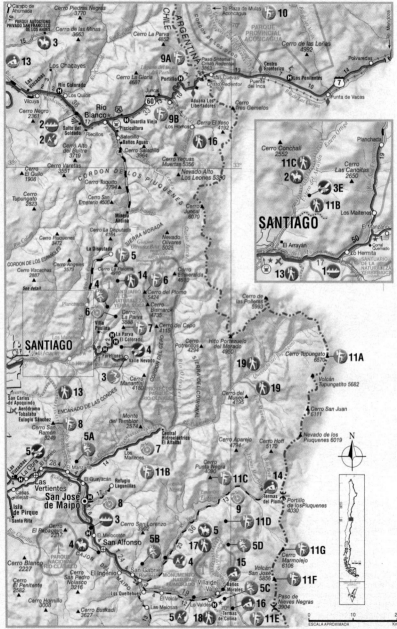

The Cajón del Maipo
See map

PRACTICAL INFORMATION
There are no banks or ATMs in the Cajón, so bring money with you.

ACCOMMODATION
There are campgrounds, cabañas, and hosterías everywhere in the Cajón, and where you stay will depend on what you want to do. The nicest area for most tastes is probably the stretch between San José and San Alfonso.

TRANSPORT
Buses depart from Metro Parque O'Higgins and Metro Lo Ovalle for San José de Maipo daily, continuing on the Baños Morales weekend mornings from Sept-May. Turismontaña (☎ 8500555 ir 8518381) also runs minibuses to Baños Morales from Plaza Italia, weekends at 0730 year-round; call ahead for reservations. If driving, a normal passenger car will do, but the road may be washed out above San Gabriel in winter.

The Cajón del Maipo is Santiago's favorite weekend retreat, and it's easy to see why. If you get out early and beat the traffic, you can be out of Santiago and into the Cajón in under an hour, cruising past almond and cherry plantations, sleepy mountain villages, and roadside stands selling fresh-baked bread and empanadas; further up, the valley splits into a labyrinth of tributaries branching out into the high, glaciated Andes, creating a mountain playground that would literally take a lifetime to explore. The potential for sporting activities in the Cajón del Maipo is really staggering: there is a ski area, two commercial rafting sections on the Río Maipo and numerous runnable tributaries, several hotsprings, rock and ice climbing, hordes of peaks to bag, and hiking and mountain bike trails galore.

On weekends after midday, the traffic gets pretty bad, but you can avoid it by taking the first paved turnoff on the right past the Las Vizcachas intersection (km 0). After crossing the river below the diversion dam, this secondary road leads up the south side of the valley, rejoining the main drag in El Toyo, past San José de Maipo.

Paragliding in Las Vizcachas

Just before the intersection at Las Vizcachas, on the left (north) side of the road, you'll see the bright-yellow climbing wall at GEOEXPEDICIONES. The hills east of here are frequented by paragliders, and you can arrange lessons and tandem flights on the spot. Private pilots are charged a minor fee to use the well-maintained takeoff zone.

If you continue on the main drag, at 18km past Las Vizcachas you'll cross a bridge over the Estero El Manzano, a popular bathing spot. Just past the bridge on the right is a recommended restaurant, the *Tratoria Italiana*, and further up on the left is the entrance to an immense *fundo* that includes the entirety of the El Manzano valley. The entrance is marked *Zona de Picnic Estero El Manzano*, and entrance is charged. Above the stream to the east is one of central Chile's best rock climbing areas.

At 22km is another bridge and a turnoff on the left which leads up the Río Colorado valley, a massive watershed extending NE towards Volcán Tupungato, with endless hiking and mountaineering possibilities, including the soon-to-be-developed Parque Nacional Río Olivares. You must solicit permission from the army (Ejército de Chile, Comando de Ingenieros, Departamento Propiedades, ☎ 6813700, fax 6813350) and the power company (Chilgener, ☎ 6868377) to continue upvalley past the hydroelectric plant at El Alfalfal. This area is noted as an important nesting site for condors.

Alfalfal / Los Maitenes Loop

This loop starts at the Los Maitenes hydropower plant, 14km up the Río Colorado from the turnoff past the bridge, and follows the paved road another 7.5km to El Alfalfal.

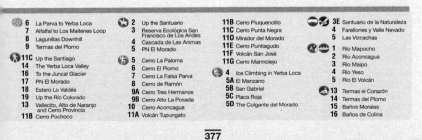

Here, find the little road west of the village that leading up and left to the Estero Quempo, then head downvalley through high country north of the river. 5km from the stream, the route crosses a 1,680m pass and then descends to Estero El Durazno. Several hundred meters after the stream is another small pass, from which point the route continues down the southern ridge of Cerro Durazno, passing a section of steep switchbacks en route to the bridge over the Río Colorado. From here it's 1km back to the starting point in Los Maitenes.

Back on the main road up the Cajón, 25km from Santiago, is **SAN JOSÉ DE MAIPO,** the valley's principal town; there are restaurants around the plaza and markets where you can stock up for the day. Just east of town is the turnoff to Centro de Ski Lagunillas, which lies 16km up a winding dirt road.

Centro de Esquí Lagunillas

16km above the town of San José, tiny Lagunillas offers skiing for the common Chilean, in a down-home, family atmosphere. The area is owned and administered by the non-profit Club Andino de Chile.

LODGING AND RESTAURANTS

Bunks at the somewhat run-down Refugio Club Andino costs $6000/pp. There are a couple of reasonably priced restaurants at the base area, open in winter and spring.

TRANSPORT

Though there is no regularly scheduled transport to Lagunillas, the Club Andino, ☎ (2)6338054 may be able arrange a ride or offer suggestions. Otherwise, you can hitch or take a taxi ($15,000) from San José de Maipo.

While in-bounds skiers are probably better off sticking to the larger areas, backcountry skiers will find Lagunillas to provide a lower-key alternative, with a wealth of steep, easily accessed terrain that never gets skied out. The steepest terrain is off of Punta Satler, directly above and to the east of the refugio, but note that this area gets lots of sun and must be skied immediately after a storm. Other options include Morro Bayo, which drops north into the Río Colorado Valley off the ridge leading to Cerro Piuquencillo, and La Vela, a long, low-angle run leading from the top of the La Lola lift all the way down into the Cajón del Maipo. For the former of these lines, you must hike back out the way you came; for the latter, you can walk out to the road below San José.

Single-ride lift tickets are not presently available at Lagunillas, which is too bad because it's what the place most needs. Hopefully, in time the backcountry ski world will catch on and start to apply some pressure.

Lagunillas Downhill

▶32km◀ ⏱4-5h rt **D S↑** ■

From San José de Maipo, the gravel road to Centro de Ski Lagunillas rises 1,230m in 16km; riding up will take you at least 3h. To descend, you can either stick to the road or explore the horse trails that cross it periodically – either way it's world class, with little traffic and expansive views of the valley below. You can also ask operators (or taxis in San José) for a lift to the top.

Operators: 164

At 36km is hip, shady **SAN ALFONSO,** with its tiny side streets overhung with vegetation. Recommended lodging includes *Hostería Los Ciervos* and *Cascada de las Ánimas,* a private park with campsites, cabins, excursions and a kayak school, plus the Cajon's coolest pub, *La Tribu.* You can ask permission here to walk to the cascada, a 20m waterfall on a southern tributary of the Mapocho.

At km 47 from Las Vizcachas, the police checkpoint in San Gabriel marks the end of the paved road. Just beyond the bridge over the Río Yeso, a turnoff on the left leads 23km up the Yeso valley to the **EMBALSE EL YESO,** a spectacular reservoir surrounded by high peaks. A 4WD road continues on from the reservoir to the Termas del Plomo hotsprings.

Termas El Plomo

▶25km◀ ⏱1d rt **D N** free ■

Though their location can't be beat, these simple mineral-charged pools are not, unfortunately, particularly hot. Nonetheless, this a great place to camp and makes for a great bike trip, as the road is bad enough to keep vehicular traffic down (you'll need 4WD if driving). The route begins at the far end of the Embalse el Yeso and follows a jeep track that climbs gradually up the north bank of the Río Yeso. If you don't have your own transport, you'll have to start at San Gabriel, adding another 23km in either direction.

Continuing up the main road, at km 50 the road forks; the right fork dead-ends at a hydroelectric plant, while to the left the road follows the Río Volcán further into the mountains, with ever-grander views. At km 59 is the crumbling mining village of El Volcán (where local residents sell marine fossils), and at km 69 a turnoff on the left leads to Baños Morales.

Baños Morales itself isn't much – just a collection of semi-abandoned private *refugios* set in a stand of poplars on the north side of the valley. The attraction, however, is that from here you can access **MONUMENTO NACIONAL EL MORADO** *(Entrance adults $1200, children $800)*, a 3,009há glacial valley extending north from Baños Morales to the base of 5,060m Cerro El Morado. Snow covers the valley entirely in winter, making skis or snowshoes a necessity until the spring consolidation; after the snow has melted, the park makes an excellent day or overnight trip of moderate difficulty, leading past a mineral spring and small alpine lake to the San Francisco glacier. Local *arrieros* have horses for rent near the park entrance.

On the south side of the valley across from Baños Morales is the mountain hamlet of Lo Valdés. Here you'll find the *Lo Valdez Mountain Center*, offering cozy lodging, meals and a variety of excursions, open all year. About 10km past the refugio, the hotsprings at Baños de Colina make a good base camp for further explorations, though they can get crowded on summer weekends. During the winter, the road is to the springs is usually closed.

Baños Morales

 C🛏 **$1,000, children $400**
The cement pools at Baños Morales are warm (22-28°), rather than hot; if you've really come to soak, you're better off continuing on to Baños de Colina. Still, they do feel nice after a hike in El Morado, and inexpensive lodging is available in the village.

Baños de Colina

 C🛏 **$9,000, children $4,000**
Scorching hot natural pools (up to 60°C), high in the Andes. During the summer (and especially on weekends), this place fills up with busloads of *Santiaguinos*, so try to visit on weekdays or at night; you can camp for free near the springs. There's a restaurant and horse rentals on site in summer, while in winter you can have the springs all to yourself – provided you can get there. This is a good place to base a short backcountry ski trip.
Operators: 49

TREKKING IN THE CAJÓN

Parque Nacional El Morado

 ⇄ ⏱5-7h rt ☐
From Baños Morales, this route climbs north up the broad, glacial El Morado valley to the Laguna el Morado (5km) and Glaciar San Francisco (8km), providing excellent views of the surrounding peaks and the layered geological formations of the Cajón del Maipo valley. There are campsites around the lake and bivouac spots on the moraine below the glacier. Local *arrieros* rent horses near the entrance to the park in Baños Morales; in winter this makes a superb ski tour.
Operators: 199

Estero Lo Valdés

 ⇄ ⏱3-4h rt ☐
This short but challenging hike leads south from the Refugio Alemán up the valley of the Estero Lo Valdés. In order to enter the upper valley, you must cross to the east side of the stream and switchback steeply up the ridge for about an hour; after that, the trail levels off somewhat as it returns to the streambank. This is the best place near Santiago to look for fossils.
Operators: 199

Cascada de Las Animas

 ☎ (2)2327214
Home to Cascada Expediciones, this private nature reserve near San Alfonso serves as a trailhead for numerous routes through the high country south of the Río Maipo. There is a stable on site, and here you can arrange a wide variety of guided hikes and rides, ranging from simple half-day tours to the 12-day crossing of the Andes to Laguna del Diamante in Argentina. Cascada also offers lodging (camping and cabañas) here on the banks of the Río Maipo, and runs rafting trips and whitewater kayaking and climbing courses throughout the year.

Up the Río Colorado

⇄ ⏱3-5d ☐
From the hydroelectric plant at El Alfalfal (ask ahead of time for permission to enter, details above), continue up the gravel road to Potrero Nuevo and cross the bridge to join the trail on the south side of the river. The trail climbs gradually, clinging to the steep valley walls, and in

an easy day leads to the fascinating mineral formations at Baños Azules, which makes a good campsite. From here you can explore the upper valleys of the Río Colorado and Río Museo; mountaineers can continue east to 6,570m Volcán Tupungato. There are rustic hotsprings in the upper Tupungato valley, as well as excellent hiking/trekking routes in the Río Olivares valley.

Operators: 94 🐎 - 137 🐎

RAFTING AND KAYAKING IN THE CAJÓN
Río Maipo (III-V)

⏱varies

The Maipo is Santiago's bread-and-butter run, and one of the few rivers in central Chile that can be boated year round. During the spring *deshielo* (snowmelt), the Maipo is big-volume roller coaster of a river, with huge waves and holes and almost no eddies; the rest of the year it's considerably mellower. There are basically five main sections, each 2-3hrs, spread along about 40km of river. The upper section, from the powerplant at Los Queltehues to the confluence with the Río Volcán (where there is an unrunnable sieve) is steep, technical Class V. The lower sections, which are mostly class III-IV, are as follows: 1) From the confluence with the Yeso to the Class V drops at El Francés (scoutable from the road). 2) From the *cancha de futbol* to El Melocotón. 3) From El Melocotón to Parque Los Héroes, below San José de Maipo (this is the mellowest section). 4) From Parque los Héroes to below the confluence with the Río Colorado.

Operators: 10 - 49 (k) - 100 - 118 - 235 (k)

Río Yeso (IV-V)

⏱1-3h

An affluent of the upper Maipo, the Río Yeso is a long, continuous Class IV-V creek. Though most paddlers only run the last 4 or 5km, you could probably put in anywhere along the road to the Embalse el Yeso, and either take out at the San Gabriel bridge or continue on down to join the Maipo.

Río El Volcán (V-V+)

⏱3-4h

From the bridge at Baños Morales down to El Volcán, this is a steep, demanding Class V spring creek with several portages. Experts only.

ROCK AND ICE CLIMBING IN THE CAJÓN
El Manzano

The sandstone crags and boulders on the east side of the Estero Manzano provide for some excellent and extremely varied climbing within easy reach of Santiago. Standard access is via the *Zona de Picnic Estero El Manzano (the owner charges $2000/pp to enter)*, about 800m east of the El Manzano bridge.

The climbing is concentrated in three separate areas. PIEDRA ROMMEL is the easiest to access, consisting of a couple of large boulders along the stream, with steep bouldering and about 20 short sport routes ranging from steep pockets to easy jug hauls (rated 5.5-5.12). To get there, once inside the gate follow the signs to El Durazno and continue up the river past the picnic ground. LAS PALESTRAS feature longer, airier routes (about 40 of them ranging from 5.6 to 5.13) on bluffs high above the Maipo valley. To get there, head up the road as for Piedra Rommel, then turn right (east) on a trail along the irrigation canal, heading up when you see the cliffs above you. For longer routes, head for the TORRECILLAS, a massif of cliffs and towers looming to the east; the climbing here consists of about 20 6-8 pitch routes from 5.8 to 5.12. The bolts are runout and often quite old, and some small nuts and tricams are recommended. There are more routes around the north side of the towers. It takes about an hour to reach the base of the rock from the picnic area.

Operators: 31 - 49

San Gabriel

Though they don't look like much from below, the white granite crags north of the Carabineros post in San Gabriel offer some surprisingly good crack climbing; the classic here is Columbianos, a 10-pitch 5.9. Loose rock is a significant danger, so climb with caution. There are more granite cracks and sport routes (rated 5.8-5.11c) at Las Melosas, located 10km south of San Gabriel on the road to Los Queltehues.

Operators: 31 - 49

Placa Roja

Above the village of Lo Valdés, on the south side of the Río Volcán, a trail leads south to the base of the north arete of this unmistakable red pillar. The standard route consists of over 250m of exposed 3rd, 4th, and easy 5th class climbing on good but occasionally loose rock. Rapel anchors are usually in place but should be revised and possibly replaced.

The *Colgante* del Morado

The hanging glacier cascading off the SE face of Cerro El Morado offers ice climbers the opportunity to practice their skills year-round on vertical and even overhanging ice. To get there, follow the Río Morado upstream about 10km from Baños Morales; with 4WD you can usually drive most of the way. Even if you're not climbing, this makes for a rewarding overnight hike.

MOUNTAINEERING IN THE CAJÓN

Volcán Tupungato (6,550m)

The highest peak in Central Chile, Volcán Tupungato is an extinct volcano at the head of the Río Colorado valley. The approach to base camp at 3,320m Vega de los Flojos takes a long two days, with horse or mule support strongly recommended. From here, count on two days ferrying loads to Camp 1 at 4,800m, another day to Camp 2 at 5,600m, and another day for the summit push. Though there are no technical difficulties on the route, the length of the approach and extreme altitude make this an extremely challenging, committing, and rewarding ascent.

Operators: 31 - 199

Cerro Piuquencillo (4,047m)

Piuquencillo is the broad peak almost due east of Lagunillas, identifiable by its crown of stone pillars. Beginning at the ski area, the approach leads up the lift line and then east along the ridge to Punta Satler. From here the route to the peak is clear: follow the ridge over Morro Bayo and then up any of several prominent couloirs to the summit ridge (good camp at base of towers, 3,050m, 4hrs). The long but technically easy route is best in early springtime.

Mirador del Morado (3,883m)

At the north end of the Valle Morales (PN El Morado) the Mirador del Morado is virtually indistinguishable from its larger neighbor, Cerro Morado; not until you get well up into the valley can you see the col that separates them. From a base camp at Laguna San Francisco, the route to the Mirador climbs the right (east) side of the valley to the plateau below the peak and

traverses left to the Glaciar San Francisco; from here you must climb up and right to the col separating the Mirador from the south face of El Morado, and continue a further hour to the summit. Numerous crevasses make a rope essential on this route. Above the Mirador is a long 50° ice climb leading to the summit of El Morado (5,060m).

Cerro Puntiagudo (4,126m)

From a camp at the Baños de Colina (2,500m), follow the northern bank of the Río Colina to a ridge, cross over and continue east, following the north bank of the Estero de Caballos to fields at the base of the peak, with abundant marine fossils. The standard route climbs up the 50-60° slabs on the west face to the summit, in about 8 hours round-trip from the Baños.

Volcán San José (5,856m)
Cerro Marmolejo (6,100m)

Volcán San José is the hulking mass that dominates the view east from Lo Valdés. Its non-technical ascent begins in the La Engorda valley above Lo Valdés, on a trail that begins just after the bridge over the Estero Colina. From here, it's 4-5 hours to the refugio at Plantat (3,480m), and from here another day up a 40-degree couloir on the west flank to high camp at 4,520m. From here it's seven hours o/w to the summit crater. The SE peak is the highest; walk counterclockwise along the rim 1 hr from the SW peak to top out. Just north is 6,108m Cerro Marmolejo, the southern-most 6,000m peak in the world, of similar difficulty and length as San José, though with a longer approach. Both of these peaks also have immense ice cliffs on their upper slopes (above 4,000m), and make for excellent ski descents in springtime.

Operators: 13 - 31 - 199

Cerro Punta Negra (4,127m)

Punta Negra is the striking peak above the north end of the Embalse el Yeso. The 4-hour approach begins at the south end of the reservoir, and contours around the west bank to the Estero de los Picos Negros. There is a small tarn at 2,930m, which makes a good base camp. The route follows the major couloir on the south face to the summit ridge on 40-50° snow and ice, best in springtime. It's 4-6 hours from base camp to the summit, and you need to be down by midday. You need a rope for this route. Nearby Cerro Casa de Piedra offers more technical challenges, with mixed alpine routes up to 1,000m long.

The Aconcagua Valley

Draining the western slope of the highest mountain in the Americas, the Río Aconcagua flows through a fertile agricultural valley north of Santiago, separated from the capital by a chain of peaks known as the Cordón de Chacabuco. This is as far south as Diego de Almagro reached on his pioneering incursion into Chile in 1536.

International highway 60 runs the length of the valley, connecting the Chilean coast at Concón, at the mouth of the river, with the Argentine province of Mendoza. In the lower part of the valley (from Los Andes to the coast) you'll find agricultural service towns such as Quillota, noted for its production of chirimoyas and avocados. Closer to the mountains, the valley becomes narrower and more mountainous, and the soils and climate more apt for vineyards.

Tucked into the foothills of the Andes, the city of **LOS ANDES** is the largest in the valley, with a splendid climate and a lovely, active plaza. There is friendly lodging available at *Residencial Italiana*, and for views over the town you can climb (on foot or by car) to the top of Cerro La Virgen, which lies just east. Los Andes is also known for its ceramics; you can see artisans at work at *Cerámica Cala*, on the corner of Freire and Rancagua. The well-labeled **MUSEO ARQUEOLÓGICO** *(open Tue-Sun 1030-1300, 1500-1930)* is at the corner of Las Heras and Av. Santa Teresa. In the tributary valleys north of Los Andes are a couple of hotsprings, the Termas de Jahuel and Baños del Corazón . Also just north is the Río Putaendo Valley, traditional departure point for horsepacking trips across the Andes into Argentina, and the 8,000há privately-owned *Reserva Ecológica San Francisco de los Andes*, offering a wide variety of short adventure programs in the mountains above the town of San Esteban.

Termas de Jahuel

 ☎ (34)582320
🏠 hotel guests only

Visited by Charles Darwin in 1834, this hotsprings resort features a single large thermal pool, fed by a 20-22°C spring and available only to hotel guests.

Termas el Corazón

☎ (34)482852 🏠 NA
Family oriented resort near Los Andes with pools, modern spa and jacuzzi fed by a 21-25°C spring. Good restaurant, rooms with private pools.

RUTA DE LOS ANDES A MENDOZA

Reserva Ecológica San Francisco de Los Andes

☎ (34)488512
This 8,000há private park just north of Los Andes offers a variety of excursions on horseback, ranging from 1 day trips in the precordillera to 6-day crossings of the Andes. Open weekends and holidays only; call for reservations.

Across the Andes

🏇🥾9d ▢ This spectacular route crosses the Andes into Argentina north of Cerro Aconcagua, following the route travelled by José de San Martín's *Ejército de los Andes*. Beginning at the border post at Los Patos, the trail climbs the Río Rocin to the NE, crossing into Argentina at Paso Valle Hermoso (3,500m). From here the route drops down the Río Volcán to a refugio, then continues up the Río Los Patillos to the Paso la Honda (4,163m). End by following the Río Las Leñas out to the ski lodge at Manantiales; from here you may be able to hitch to Barreal, north of Uspallata, but if not it's a very long walk. There is another Cruce de los Andes further south, beginning at Los Queltehues in the Cajón del Maipo and ending at Laguna del Diamante in Argentina; allow 12 days for this route.
Operators: 10 🏇 - 17 - 49 🏇 - 137

About 20km east of Los Andes is the village of Río Colorado, where there are a couple of hosterías (*Hotel Refugio Río Colorado* and *Hostería La Gringa*), and shortly thereafter is Río Blanco, service town for the mine at Saladillo. From here to the border, the road winds along a series of spectacular gorges and into increasingly dramatic mountain scenery; past where the road leaves the Río Juncal, a series of 29 hairpin switchbacks climbs 680m up an immense glacial moraine, topping out in a huge Andean basin occupied by the pristine Laguna del Inca. On either side of the lake are the slopes of the Portillo Ski Resort 🛈.

Just past the ski resort, 63km from Los Andes, is the Chilean customs post Los Libertadores, and beyond this, at 3,185m, the Túnel Cristo Redentor crosses the Andes into Argentina. 21km past the tunnel, a dirt road to the left leads up the Horcón valley to Plaza de Mulas, departure point for Aconcagua expeditions, and another 4km down is the hotel at Puente del Inca. From here, it's another 175km of spectacular driving downvalley to Mendoza.

PORTILLO

Portillo Ski Resort

Owned and managed by a firm from the US, Portillo is the birthplace of skiing in South America and undoubtedly the most distinctive and efficiently run ski area in Chile. Several speed skiing records have been set here, and the World Championship held here in 1966 was the only one ever to take place in the Southern Hemisphere; you can really feel the history behind the place.

ACCOMMODATION
There is a surprising range of lodging options at Portillo, which otherwise has a reputation as one of Chile's spendiest ski areas. Top of the heap is the distinctive and elegant Hotel Portillo, while the Octagon and the Inca Lodge are more affordable options, though the bunk accommodations can be a little cramped.

RESTAURANTS
Most guests at Portillo will eat in the main dining room in the hotel. There is also a self-service cafeteria in the Inca Lodge, an on-mountain restaurant, Tío Bob's, at the top of the Garganta lift. For a cheaper alternative, try La Posada, an independent establishment across the highway from the ski area.

TRANSPORT
The resort provides guests with transport from Santiago. If traveling on your own, see The Aconcagua Valley for transport info, or contact Ski Total in Santiago (☎ 2460156, or 2466881).

Portillo's location is unbelievable, with lifts on both sides of the Laguna del Inca, an alpine lake just off the international highway to Mendoza. If you're only skiing for the day or the weekend, and can't afford to stay at the hotel, it's not as convenient as the areas right above Santiago, but it's worth the extra effort. The area is also noteworthy because of the special care they take with avalanches, hiring top-notch experts from the US to monitor snow conditions. All in all, terrain, snow quality, and world-class services (grooming, ski school, hotels and dining) make this a top recommendation for inclusive ski week trips.

PORTILLO

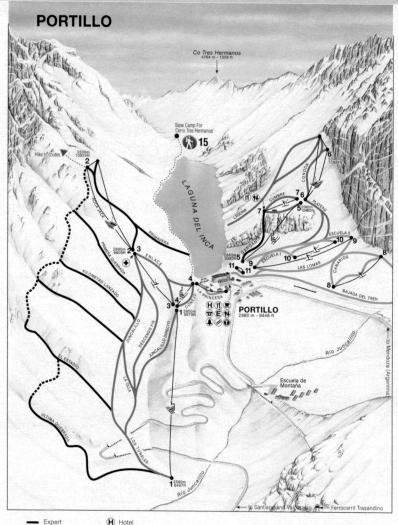

The north-south orientation of the valley makes gaging snow conditions simple. The first slopes to soften up in the morning are those near the Roca Jack lift, on the west side of the valley, while in the afternoon you'll want to move to the east side. The best intermediate runs are those like Juncalillo, which drops down the west side of the valley below the hotel, while advanced skiers will stick to the unique *va y vent* lifts on either side of the valley. On a powder day, it doesn't matter where you ski, for Portillo gets some of the lightest, driest snow in the Andes. It's all good.

Legend:

— Expert	(H) Hotel
— Dificult	(A) Ski School
— Intermediate	(II) Restaurant
— Easy	(A) Ski Patrol
— Free Skiing	(☎) Emergency Telephone
✗ Skating Rink	(⊤) Heliskiing
Chairlift	(M) Restrooms
Double Chair	(⊘) Ski Rental
Triple Chair	(T) Tickets
Quad Chair	(E) Car Park
Poma	(⊟) Cafeteria
T-Bar	(⊽) Paragliding

Expert and Backcountry Skiing

• For real steeps, you'll have to hike above the *va y vents* (on either side of the valley) or simply traverse north or south. If you traverse to the north (towards the lake), you'll either have to cut your run short or slog back out across or along the shore of the lake. Some of the best (and longest) shots are in the gullies above the Roca Jack lift.

Heliskiing

• An Alouette helicopter is available for trips to the following destinations:
- **Ojos del Agua**, 1,200m, US$132 pp.
- **Cerro Vermejo**, 1,000m, US$102 pp.
- **Valle Mardones**,1,200m, 2 runs
  US$300 pp.
- **Cerro La Parva**, 950m, US$132 pp.

• Helicopter capacity is three clients and one guide. Sightseeing flights and transfers to Santiago and Valle Nevado are also available.

To the Juncal Glacier

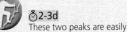

⇄ ⏱1-2d ⬜
Beginning at the bottom of the switchbacks below Portillo, head south on a gravel road that leads 6km up the Río Juncal valley. The route continues up the east bank of the river, crossing the Estero Navarro and climbing Estero Monos de Agua to the base of the Juncal Glacier, in the heart of the most heavily glaciated section of the Central Andes. In a 4WD vehicle it is possible to drive all the way up to the junction of the Río Juncal and the Río Mardones, a mere 3km from the glacier.
Operators: 10 🏇

Cerro Tres Hermanos (4,595m) ⬛
Cerro Alto la Posada (4,260m) ⬛

⏱2-3d
These two peaks are easily accessed from the Portillo ski area. At the north end of the Laguna del Inca, on the east (or right) side of the valley, are the three summits of Cerro

CERRO ACONCAGUA

Tres Hermanos; the approach skirts the west side of the lake to a base camp on the moraine at the base of the peak. From here, the route continues up the west face of the central peak, with exposed sections near the summit. The best conditions are in spring, when the peak makes a great ski descent. Due south of the ski area is the spectacular Alto la Posada, with its distinctive north-facing couloir. Access is from Juncal, where the switchbacks to the ski area begins. A five-hour approach leads to the base camp at the base of the 600m couloir, which ranges from 40-50°, with best conditions in early summer (Nov) due to its northern exposure. You need an alpine start and a rope to climb this peak.

Río Aconcagua

⏱6h
From Río Blanco to the bridge below Las Vizcachas, the Aconcagua is mostly class III and IV, with the exception of the powerful (and portageable) Class V-VI drops in the Salto del Soldado canyon. You can scout the drops from the railroad tunnel on the left. Note that there is also a small lowhead dam just below Río Blanco.

Cerro Aconcagua (6,959m)

⏱2-3w ⬜
The highest peak outside the Himalayas. The standard route, up the Northwest Ridge from Plaza de Mulas (base camp, 4,380m), is a non-technical walk-up, and the key to success is budgeting sufficient time to acclimatize, and coming prepared for the extreme cold. Most teams will establish three high camps en route to the summit. A more challenging alternative is the Polish Glacier route, which climbs steeply up the peak's a glacier on the northeast face beginning at Plaza Argentina, at the head of the Río Relinchos. Each member of a private expedition must pay a user fee in person to the Argentine *Dirección de Recursos Naturales Renovables* in Mendoza; costs are $120 in high season (Dec 15 - Feb 15th), US$80 in low season. Mules are available at Puente del Inca, just over the border on the road to Mendoza.
Operators: 10 - 13 - 17 - 31 - 137

Olmué and Parque Nacional La Campana

Midway between Santiago and Viña del Mar / Valparaíso, PN La Campana preserves 8,000há of wonderfully diverse mountain environments in the Coast Range, with excellent opportunities for hiking, biking, birdwatching and rock climbing. The centerpiece of the park is 1,900m Cerro La Campana, climbed in 1934 by Charles Darwin and one of the most-climbed peaks in Chile. Spring is the best time to visit the park, when flowering and bird activity is at its peak. Winter trips are also recommended – when there's too much snow to hike in the Andes, La Campana is a safe bet.

The park consists of three sectors, each with its own entrance. All three are connected by trails that converge at the Portezuelo Ocoa, in the center of the park.

The northern sector of the park, Ocoa, is home to one of the last remaining stands of the endemic Chilean Palm, . The sight of these weird, bulbous-trunked palms growing together with *quisco* cactus makes this sector absolutely spellbinding, but you need to bring water. Conaf administers a number of campsites, and there are several hiking trails, including the easy walk to La Cascada and the longer overnight hike south over the Portezuelo Ocoa.

The Granizo sector is accessed from the town of Olmué, at the eastern end of a narrow river valley with a rich, humid microclimate. Very popular with vacationing families, Olmué practically overflows with fruit and flowers, and there's a plethora of cabañas, hosterías, and restaurants to choose from. You can also rent horses or take a glider flight, and if you time it right you can catch the annual *Festival del Huaso* (Jan 17-19, Parque el Patagual). The surrounding hills provide plenty of hiking opportunities, not just limited to the national park.

Compared with Ocoa, the Granizo sector is relatively lush, with a lovely native sclyrophyllous forest that provides the park's best bird habitat and some shady campsites, with horses available for rent near the entrance. The ascent of Cerro La Campana (Sendero El Andinista) begins

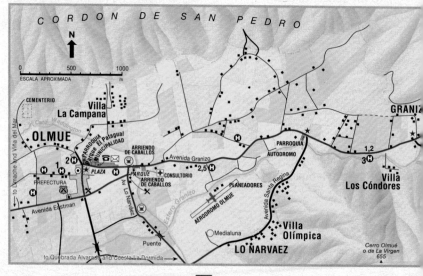

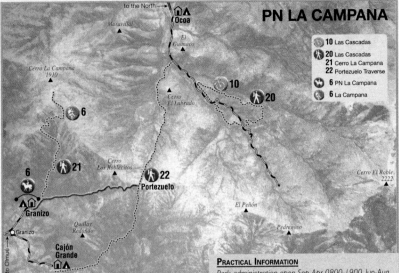

PN LA CAMPANA

- 10 Las Cascadas
- 20 Las Cascadas
- 21 Cerro La Campana
- 22 Portezuelo Traverse
- 6 PN La Campana
- 6 La Campana

here, as does the Sendero Los Peumos, which leads to the Portezuelo Ocoa. There is also a good granite rock climbing area below the summit of La Campana.

Also accessed from Olmué, the Cajón Grande sector has a campsite and a single trail through deciduous *roble* forest (fall foliage in April-May) to the Portezuelo Ocoa.

PRACTICAL INFORMATION

Park administration open Sep-Apr 0800-1900, Jun-Aug Sat, Sun, holidays 0800-1800, ☎ (33)441342. Entry adults $1000, children $500. There are no banks or ATMs in Olmué.

ACCOMMODATION

Conaf campgrounds at Ocoa, Granizo, and Cajón Grande, reservations via park administration (below). Abundant accommodation in Olmué, but few budget choices, reservations necessary on weekends and holidays.

TRANSPORT

Regular buses to Olmué from both Santiago and Viña del Mar. No public transport to Ocoa; you can have northbound buses from Santiago drop you off at the poorly marked turnoff before the bridge over the Aconcagua, but you'll have to walk 12 hot, dusty kilometers. Pullman Bus now offers revices from Santiago to Olmué via the dramatic gravel road over Cuesta La Dormida from Tiltil; if you are driving your own vehicle, you could easily combine this route with a visit to the native forests at Caleu.

Cerro La Campana

⟳ ⏱ 5-6h rt ▢

From Granizo, the Sendero Andinista trail begins with a gradual climb through sclyrophyllous forest and stands of roble. After crossing a mining road and a plaque commemorating Darwin's 1836 ascent, the trail steepens as it passes treeline. The upper trail along the ridge is excessively marked and the summit sadly spraypainted by thoughtless visitors, but the view from the summit, stretching from Aconcagua to the Pacific, more than makes up for it. Note that park rangers won't allow hikers to begin the ascent after midday.

Operators: 10 🐎 - 48 - 137 - 198

Portezuelo Traverse

 🏹 ⏱2d ▢

This two-day trip combines the Ocoa and Granizo sectors via Portezuelo Ocoa, which crosses the SE ridge of Cerro La Campana. As it is easier to find water (and public transport out) in Granizo, it is best to do this hike beginning in Ocoa. From the park entrance, follow Sendero El Amasijo through palm groves and up the Río Rabuco, setting up camp below the steep climb to the pass (14km). Once you reach the pass, you can continue down the Sendero Los Peumos to Granizo (5km), or down the Portezuelo Ocoa trail to the Cajón Grande Ranger station (7km).

Las Cascadas

 ⇄ ⏱2-3h ▢

This is the easiest of the trails in the park, suitable for biking as well as hiking. From the park entrance, the route follows a road 5km through stands of Chilean palms, after which a kilometer-long footpath on the left leads to a beautiful waterfall, an ideal lunchspot. The entire route is marked.

Horseback Riding in and around PN La Campana

 ⏱1d trips only

Horses are available for rent at a couple of stables near the hospital in Olmué, and at the park entrance in Granizo. In the park, you can make an excellent loop connecting the Cajón Grande sector with the trail to Cerro La Campana. There are also a number of options outside the park in the Olmué valley; ask locals for suggestions.

Rock Climbing on Cerro La Campana

 On the south face of Cerro La Campana, near the plaque commemorating Darwin's visit, you can't help but notice the easy top-roping routes on granite slabs, as someone has painted broad stripes up the rock face. Above are a couple of 2-3 pitch traditional crack routes in the 5.9-5.10 range, topping out near the summit. It's about an hour's walk from Granizo to the base of the routes.

SHORT ROAD TRIPS IN CENTRAL CHILE

● **Cultural Highlights of Central Chile**
⏱3d

A historic port, an abandoned whaling station, a poet's retreat, a 1920's beach resort, an artisan's village, a winery and a 16th-century hacienda – this trip is a whirlwind introduction to the culture and history of central Chile. From Santiago, principal stops include Valparaíso, Quintay, Isla Negra, Cartagena, Pomaire, Viña Undurraga, Calera de Tango, return to Santiago.
Operators: 70

● **The Best of the Coast and the Andes**
⏱5d

If we had to recommend one 5-day tour in central Chile, this would be it: you won't find diversity of landscapes like this anywhere. From Santiago, principal stops are Tiltil, Cuesta La Dormida, Olmué, PN La Campana, Concón, Horcón, Maitencillo, Zapallar, Catapilco, Los Andes, Portillo, Los Andes, return to Santiago.
Operators: 192

Valparaíso / Viña del Mar   *Pop. 577,827 (☎ city code 32)*

Together, Valparaíso and Viña del Mar constitute the second largest urban area in Chile, and are, respectively, the country's principal port and number one beach resort. The two cities are basically contiguous, but make odd bedfellows: Valparaíso practically overflowing with culture and history, Viña catering to a modern demand for flash and luxury.

Orientation

Viña and Valparaíso occupy the southern end of the Bahía de Valparaíso, 120km NW of Santiago; the trip from the capital, on one of the country's best highways, takes about an hour and a half. A coastal road, too narrow for the amount of traffic it receives, connects the two cities and continues north, providing access to a chain of beaches, dunes, and rocky headlands in a rapid process of development. The coast becomes less urban the further north you go; frequent urban transport extends as far north as Concón, with more sporadic buses continuing north to Quintero and Horcón. South of Valparaíso, the coast is steep and largely inaccessible.

GREATER VALPARAISO

VALPARAISO

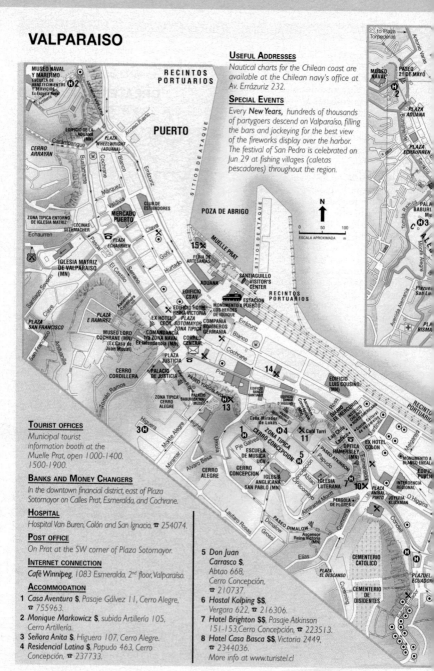

USEFUL ADDRESSES

Nautical charts for the Chilean coast are available at the Chilean navy's office at Av. Errázuriz 232.

SPECIAL EVENTS

Every *New Years,* hundreds of thousands of partygoers descend on Valparaíso, filling the bars and jockeying for the best view of the fireworks display over the harbor. The festival of San Pedro is celebrated on Jun 29 at fishing villages (caletas pescadores) throughout the region.

TOURIST OFFICES

Municipal tourist information booth at the Muelle Prat, open 1000-1400, 1500-1900.

BANKS AND MONEY CHANGERS

In the downtown financial district, east of Plaza Sotomayor on Calles Prat, Esmeralda, and Cochrane.

HOSPITAL

Hospital Van Buren, Colón and San Ignacio, ☎ 254074.

POST OFFICE

On Prat at the SW corner of Plaza Sotomayor.

INTERNET CONNECTION

Café Winnipeg, 1083 Esmeralda, 2nd floor, Valparaíso.

ACCOMMODATION

1 Casa Aventura $, Pasaje Gálvez 11, Cerro Alegre, ☎ 755963.

2 Monique Markowicz $, subida Artillería 105, Cerro Artillería.

3 Señora Anita $, Higuera 107, Cerro Alegre.

4 Residencial Latina $, Papudo 463, Cerro Concepción, ☎ 237733.

5 Don Juan Carrasco $, Abtao 668, Cerro Concepción, ☎ 210737.

6 Hostal Kolping $$, Vergara 622, ☎ 216306.

7 Hotel Brighton $$, Pasaje Atkinson 151-153, Cerro Concepción, ☎ 223513.

8 Hotel Casa Basca $$, Victoria 2449, ☎ 2344036.
More info at www.turistel.cl

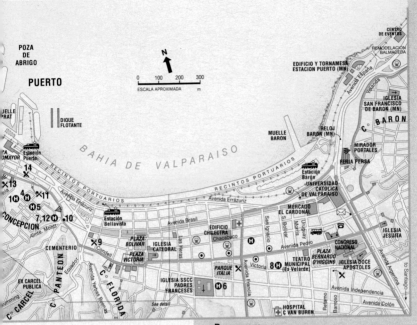

RESTAURANTS

9 Bambú, Pudeto 450. Inexpensive vegetarian meals, home of Valpo's Buddhist meditation group.

10 Cinzano, Plaza Aníbal Pinto. Local favorite for chorrillana and beers, live music.

11 Café Turri, at the top of Ascensor Concepción. Excellent views, lunch and dinner served.

12 Hotel Brighton, Paseo Atkinson, Cerro Concepción. Views, moderate prices, café menú.

13 La Colombina, off Paseo Yugoslavia, Cerro Concepción. Expensive dinner and moderate pub fare, highly recommended.

14 Bar Inglés, Cochrane 851 or Blanco 870. Dark wood, classic pub atmosphere, sandwiches, dominoes.

15 Bote Salvavidas, next to Muelle Prat. Seafood, touristy.

BARS AND NIGHTLIFE

Valparaíso is a great place to go out, especially for students. There are numerous bars on Calles Errázuriz and Blanco east of the Puerto (La Roca, La Cueva del Chivato and Puerto Bahía recommended). La Playa, on Cochrane just NW of the Plaza Sotamayor, is an old favorite.

AIRPORT, AIRLINE OFFICES, AIRPORT TRANSPORT

See the Viña del Mar entry, ⬆.

BUS STATION AND/OR OFFICES

Bus station at P. Montt 2800, across from the National Congress Building.

LOCAL TRANSPORT

See the Viña del Mar entry, ⬆.

RENT A CAR

Flota Verschae, Colón 2881 ☎ 227414.

VALPARAISO AS SEEN FROM PASEO 21 DE MAYO

VALPARAISO

Valparaíso must be visited, it cannot be explained. The city has too many faces, too many hidden corners; you have to explore it on foot to grasp its beauty. 'The only city where no one can get lost,' wrote Lukas, Valpo's famous cartoonist. 'When I see a bus full of tourists driving through the city, I realize with sorrow that they won't see anything. Valparaíso resides in the little things, in surprising discoveries, in unsuspected corners, in a thousand curious details.'

The Bahía de Valparaíso was first 'discovered' by Europeans in 1536, when Juan de Saavedra, a lieutenant on Diego de Almagro's exploratory expedition, met here with the tiny supply ship *Santiaguillo*; six years later, Pedro de Valdivia made Valparaíso Santiago's official port. Rather than being planned, the city grew organically, building out from the port, filling the narrow marine terrace – known as *El Plan* – and then spreading up into the steep *cerros* that hem the city in on all sides. Still, between Spanish restrictions on trade and the constant threat posed by earthquakes, fires, and marauding Dutch and English pirates, the city got a slow and halting start.

Not until after independence did things pick up. With traffic around Cape Horn and along the Pacific Coast booming and the port opened to trade, Valparaíso attracted a growing contingent of English, French, and German immigrants and entrepreneurs. Foreign money poured in, and the city became the financial and banking center of the country, financing mining operations in the north, sheep ranching in Patagonia, and railways and other urban infrastructure throughout the country. The narrow, cobblestones streets of El Plan were strung with the country's first electrical and telephone lines, the first electric trams, and the first urban gas lines. In 1883, the first of the emblematic funicular railways, known as *ascensores*, provided an elegant and functional link between the business district and the residential chaos spreading throughout Valparaíso's 41 *cerros*.

The boom in Valparaíso lasted until about 1914, when the opening of the Panama Canal took a big bite out of maritime traffic, and banks and other commercial institutions moved their headquarters to the capital. Today, the city is a little tarnished, a little gritty: it feels like a port. But it is also a major university center, home to artists, poets and immigrants, chock full of history, with the country's liveliest and most distinctive nightlife scene.

EL PLAN

Av. Argentina to the Subida Ecuador Av. Argentina runs almost due north-south through the widest part of *El Plan*, at the eastern edge of the city. The wide median running down the middle of the avenue fills up on Sat, Sun, and holidays with a sprawling flea market (*feria de las pulgas*) that is great for people-watching. On the corner of Av. Pedro Montt is the huge, authoritative-looking **Congreso Nacional**, home to Chile's legislative body since 1990, and somewhat of an eyesore. To the west of the congress building is Plaza O'Higgins, also site of an important *feria* on weekends and holidays, with more upscale antiques.

Av. Argentina is a good place to start a walking tour of *El Plan*. From here, you can head west along Av. Pedro Montt or any parallel street, through the city's modern commercial district, passing by a couple of active plazas, Parque Italia and Plaza Bolívar / Plaza Victoria. A block and a half west of Plaza Victoria, on Condell, is the **PALACIO LYON**, built in 1881, with over 50 rooms; inside is a natural history museum and an excellent art gallery. South of Palacio Lyon, near the end of Calle Huito, you'll find stairs and an ascensor providing access to Cerro Bellavista, described .

THE FINANCIAL AND PORT DISTRICT Plaza Sotomayor is the center of Valpo's historic port and financial district, and is good place to orient yourself. You can recognize it by the 1910 **EX-INTENDENCIA**, an imposing grey-and-white Victorian building on the SW side of the Plaza, with its back to the hills. Directly above, the spectacularly located **MUSEO DEL MAR LORD COCHRANE** , is reached by Ascensor Cordillera, at the north of Calle Serrano. South of the Ex-Intendencia is Ascensor El Peral, which provides access to Cerro Alegre, .

East of the Plaza, Calles Prat and Cochrane are the oldest and most traditional streets of Valpo's banking district. Until 1850, this sector barely existed: the waterfront began just north of Calle Prat, which itself was blocked at its eastern end by a rocky spur of Cerro Concepción. Over the course of years, landfill excavated from the hills gradually extended the width of *El Plan*, though the buildings erected on reclaimed land proved disastrously susceptible to the major earthquakes that have periodically leveled the city. Check out the Banco de Santiago and Banco O'Higgins buildings on Prat, and keep an eye out for electric buses imported from Germany, running on old trolley lines. To the south, stairs and funiculars lead to Cerro Alegre and Cerro Concepción, described .

To the NE of Plaza Sotomayor, past the Monumento Héroes de Iquique – where naval hero Arturo Prat's remains are buried – is the Muelle Prat (Prat pier). Here you'll find a replica of the *Santiaguillo*, a good view of the port and fishing boats, and a number of motor launches offering tours of the bay, including a crossing to Muelle Vergara in Viña.

NW of the Plaza Sotomayor, the street plan opens up again. Five blocks along Cochrane is Plaza Echaurren; just beyond is the Mercado Puerto, a large, open fish-and-vegetable market. Sanitation is a bit below par, but the interesting iron building and buzz of activity make it worth a stop (restaurants second floor). A couple of blocks inland from the Mercado is the Iglesia Matriz del Señor, the fourth church built on this site; the original 1559 church actually stood right on the waterfront.

Another two blocks brings you to Plaza Wheelwright and the 1854 Aduana (Customs House). Just to the right is the Ascensor Artillería, which climbs to the Mirador 21 de Mayo, described .

THE CERROS OF VALPARAISO

The trick to exploring the cerros of Valparaíso is to leave the car behind and just walk: it's literally impossible to get lost. You take a funicular railway up, wind along the hill, and look for a stairway, a passage, or another funicular down. Even if you could describe exactly what route to take (which you can't), it would take half the fun out of the experience.

Cerro Playa Ancha, Paseo 21 de Mayo Cerro Playa Ancha closes off the Bahía de Valparaíso to the south, protecting the port from prevailing SW winds. The most direct access is from the Plaza Aduana via the Ascensor Artillería, which brings you

PLAZA VICTORIA AS SEEN FROM THE CAMINO DE CINTURA

SPECIAL INTEREST TRIPS IN CHILE

CULTURE TRIPS · WINE TOURS · FAMILY HOLIDAYS
FLORA & FAUNA TRIPS · LUXURY NATURE TOURS
SALMON & TROUT FISHING · WALKING & HIKING · AIR TRIPS
BIKING · SEA KAYAKING · HORSERIDING · MOUNTAINEERING
MULTI-ACTIVITIES · SEA CRUISES · PRE & POST BUSINESS TOURS
CAMPING & TRIPS FOR TEENAGERS · TAILOR-MADE TRIPS

Latitud90

the sense of discovery

www.latitud90.com
info@latitud90.com

to Paseo 21 de Mayo, with a spectacular view over the port and the city. Behind the walkway is the **Museo Naval** (Naval Museum), the highlight of which is a display of items salvaged from the Esmeralda, Arturo Prat's famous ship, sunk off Iquique by the Peruvian ironclad Huáscar. Some of Valpo's most impressive turn-of-the-century homes are in the surrounding neighborhood.

Cerro Alegre, Cerro Concepción
These two interconnected cerros constitute the most picturesque part of Valparaíso, including the city's finest restaurants and small inns. In addition to a number of winding roads and stairways, two funicular railways provide access to this area.

Just south of the Ex-Intendencia, Ascensor Peral climbs Cerro Alegre to **Paseo Yugoslavo**, a pleasant tiled walkway where you'll find the **Palacio Baburizza**, an *art nouveau* mansion that houses the Museo de Bellas Artes de Valparaíso, closed for renovation at the time of writing. At the far end of the walkway is the entrance to the *La Colombiana* restaurant. From here, you can continue south (uphill) and east to **Paseo Gervasoni**, on Cerro Concepción.

Paseo Gervasoni is also accessed via Ascensor Concepción, the first of the funicular railways to grace Valparaíso. At the top of the ascensor is *Café Turri*, one of Valpo's finest restaurants, while at the east end of the walkway is the **Casa Mirador de Lukas**, with exhibits of drawings by Valparaíso cartoonist Renzo Pecchenino. Three blocks uphill from Café Turri on Calle Templeman is the nondescript **Iglesia Anglicana Saint Paul**, where splendid organ concerts are held every Sunday at 1230. From here, if you head back downhill on Calle Concepción, you'll come to Paseo Atkinson, at the east end of which is the *Hotel Brighton*, with a highly recommended restaurant.

Cerro Bellavista The principal attraction here is the **Museo de Cielo Abierto de Valparaíso**, a collection of outdoor murals painted by Chilean artists and students from the Universidad Católica. A simple walking tour of the 'museum' may be started at either end of Calle Aldunate, located south of the Plaza de La Victoria. If you don't care to walk uphill, you can take Ascensor Espíritu Santo, also located off Aldunate.

La Sebastiana The last of Pablo Neruda's three eclectic homes lies next to the Teatro Mauri, just off the Avenida Alemana (also known as the Camino de Cintura), which connects all of Valpo's cerros and makes for a good, dirt-cheap bus tour. Like his other homes, La Sebastiana is crammed with memorabilia brought back by Neruda from his world travels, but unlike the others you are allowed to wander freely within the house. To get to La Sebastiana, take bus Verde Mar D from Plazuela Ecuador or Verde Mar O from Av. Argentina.

MUSEUMS IN VALPARAISO

Museo Naval
Paseo 21 de Mayo, Cerro Playa Ancha. Excellent displays on Chilean naval history and implements.
Hours: Tue-Sat 1000-1800
Entrance: $500, children $200

Casa Mirador de Lukas
Paseo Gervasoni 448, Cerro Concepción. Home of Valparaíso's beloved cartoonist.
Hours: Tue-Sun 1030-1400, 1530-1900

Museo de Historia Natural
In the Palacio Lyon, Condell 1546.
Hours: Tue-Fri 1000-1300, 1400-1800, Sat 1000-2000, Sun, holidays 1000-1400
Entrance: $600, children $300

Museo del Mar Almirante Cochrane
Merlet 191, Cerro Cordillera. Access via Ascensor Cordillera. Maritime museum in an 1842 house, with the city's best view over *El Plan*.
Hours: Tue-Sat 1000-1800
Entrance: free

Galería Municipal de Arte
In the Palacio Lyon, Condell 1546.
Hours: Mon-Sat 1000-1700
Entrance: free

Museo La Sebastiana
Calle Ferrari 692.
Hours: Tue-Sun 1030-1430, 1530-1800
Entrance: $1500

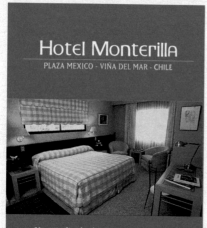
In 1855, the completion of the railway from Valparaíso made Viña that much more accessible to the port's increasingly affluent merchants and bankers. By 1872, several foreign entrepreneurs had rented properties along the railroad, where they constructed homes and gardens of a scale impossible in Valparaíso. By 1882, horse racing was all the rage at the Valparaíso Sporting Club, and Viña's first Gran Hotel attracted a steady flow of elite *Santiaguinos*. Ten years later, the lands north of the Marga Marga (along Calle Libertad) were subdivided and sold, and summer homes and permanent residences replaced the farm lands of the great hacienda. Viña has not stopped growing since.

Today, the exclusivity that marked Viña's early years has given way to the masses. Many of the sumptuous residences from the turn of the century have been replaced by modern condominiums and shopping complexes, and the city's narrow streets can become impossibly clogged during the summer high season. On a positive note, one of the city's principal shopping areas, Calle Valparaíso, has recently been converted into a pleasant pedestrian mall, giving new life to downtown Viña.

PALACIO CARRASCO (MN)

VIÑA DEL MAR

Viña del Mar, also known as the 'Garden City,' is a hugely popular beach resort just north of Valparaíso. The city occupies a relatively wide fluvial terrace on either side of the Estero Marga Marga, with residential neighborhoods climbing into the hills surrounding the town. The beachfront stretches for 3.5 kilometers, and has been transformed into a long boardwalk backed by high-rise condominiums owned by fat cats from the capital. During the summer, Chilean and Argentine tourists flock to Viña to take advantage of its beaches, its public gardens, casino, seafood restaurants and discotheques.

Viña is a young town, and in contrast to hard-working Valparaíso, its formation has always been linked to leisure and tourism. Through the Colonial era, Viña was comprised of two haciendas, one north and one south of the Estero Marga Marga. Between 1835 and 1840, Portuguese businessman Francisco Alvarez bought the two haciendas, and his wife installed herself in the Quinta Vergara, where she dedicated herself to her extensive gardens, the first of many in Viña.

QUINTA RIOJA (MN)

PALACIO VERGARA (MN)

VIÑA DEL MAR

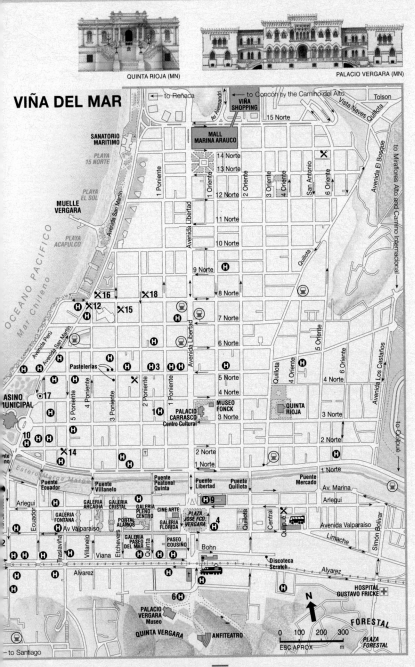

TOURIST OFFICES

Sernatur is at Valparaíso 507, 3rd floor, Mon-Fri only. Municipal tourist information booth at the NW corner of the Plaza Vergara (open 0900-1400, 1500-1900).

BANKS AND MONEY CHANGERS

On Calles Arlegui and Valparaíso, west of the Plaza Viña.

HOSPITAL

Hospital Gustavo Fricke, Alvarez 1532, ☎ 652246.

POST OFFICE

Valparaíso 846.

INTERNET CONNECTION

Ademn, 1 Norte 461, ☎ 695035.

ACCOMMODATION

1 **Residencial Helene Misch $,** *1 Poniente 239, ☎ 971565.*
2 **Residencial Blanchard $,** *Av. Valparaíso 82-A, ☎ 974949.*
3 **Residencial 555 $,** *5 Norte 555, ☎ 972240.*
4 **Hotel Español $$,** *Plaza Vergara 191, ☎ 685145.*
5 **Residencial Offenbacher Hof, $$,** *Balmaceda 102, ☎ 621483.*
6 **Hotel Quinta Vergara $$,** *Errázuriz 690, ☎ 685073.*
7 **Cap Ducal $$$,** *Marina 51, ☎ 626655.*
8 **Hotel Oceanic $$$,** *Camino Viña – Reñaca, ☎ 830006.*
9 **Hotel O'Higgins $$$,** *Plaza Vergara, ☎ 882016.*
10 **Hotel Monterilla $$,** *2 Norte 65, ☎ 976950*
11 **Club Presidente Roca Blanca Apartments $$,** *Iberia 390 (Cerro Castillo) ☎ 663333 (see ad inside front cover). More info at www.turistel.cl*

RESTAURANTS

12 **Diego Pizzas,** *San Martín and 8 Norte. Good pizza, close to the beach.*
13 **Cap Ducal,** *Av. Marina 51. Seafood, ocean views.*
14 **Barlovento,** *2 Norte 195. Distinctive, modernistic bar restaurant.*
15 **Mastrantonio, La Otra Cocina,** *3 Poniente 660 or 8 Norte 323. Italian food, homemade pasta, wild game.*
16 **Santa Fe,** *San Martín and 8 Norte. Fajitas and margaritas.*
17 **Bravissimo,** *Av. San Martín 302. Healthy lunch platters, juices, ice cream.*
18 **La Flor de Chile,** *8 Norte 601. Chilean food, daily menu, inexpensive.*

BARS AND NIGHTLIFE

Discotheques in Viña include Scratch, on Calle Bohn, and Kamikaze at Vicuña Mackenna 1106 in Reñaca.

FILM

Cine Arte, ☎ 680041on the west side of the Plaza Vergara, shows independent films.

AIRLINE OFFICES

LanChile, Ecuador 74, ☎ 251441. Ladeco, Ecuador 76, ☎ 979089. Aerocontinente, ☎ 6002092358.

BUS STATION AND/OR OFFICES

Bus station east of Plaza Vergara, at Valparaíso and Quilpué.

LOCAL TRANSPORT

BOAT

Tour boats cross the Bahía de Valparaíso between the Muelle Prat in Valpo. to the Muelle Vergara, on Playa Acapulco in Viña. The trip costs US$3, with regular departures every day in summertime, weekends and holidays only the rest of the year.

MICROS

Micros shuttle back and forth between Viña and Valparaíso all day, and most of the night; the trip takes about 15 min, as long as you avoid the late afternoon traffic (6-8pm). From Viña, you can take any micro with the word 'Puerto' on the sign; in the other direction look for 'Libertad.'

Many micros continue north as far as Reñaca, and a few continue on to Concón – pick these up in the Plaza Vergara or along Libertad. Again, look for 'Concón' on the sign; Sol de Pacífico micros with an 'X-Costa' sign follow the coastal road north. You can also catch Sol del Pacífico buses on Libertad that will take you directly to Quintero and Horcón, and occasionally to Zapallar and Papudo.

TRAIN

Commuter train service connects Viña and Valpo along the coast, and is a good alternative during peak traffic hours. In Valpo, the Estación Puerto is just east of Plaza Sotomayor; there are additional stops at Estación Bellavista and Muelle Barón. In Viña, the train stops at Estación Viña del Mar, on the south side of Plaza Sucre, and at Estación Miramar, at Viana and Agua Santa.

TAXIS COLECTIVOS

Taxis colectivos run the same routes as micros, only faster. For colectivos north from Viña, look on the east side of Plaza Sucre.

RENT A CAR

Flota Verschae, Libertad 1030 ☎ 971184.

SPECIAL EVENTS

Viña's wildly popular International Song Festival is held during the second week of February, in the Quinta Vergara.
The festival of San Pedro is celebrated on Jun 29 at fishing villages (caletas pescadores) throughout the region.

In-town Attractions

Plaza Vergara Just south of the Estero Marga Marga, the Plaza is the center of activity in Viña, and manages to impart something of the city's more exclusive years during the early 20th century. Along the south side of the plaza are horse-drawn carts, in which you can take a 30-minute tour of the city for about $6000.

Quinta Vergara Tucked into the hills south of the Plaza Vergara, the splendid gardens of the Quinta Vergara were begun by Dolores Alvarez and continued by her son Salvador, who sent back hundreds of exotic plants from his world travels. Following the catastrophic earthquake of 1906, Salvador's granddaughter Blanca Vergara contracted Italian architect Héctor Petri to build an elaborate Venetian palace, the **PALACIO**

VERGARA, now site of the MUSEO MUNICIPAL DE BELLAS ARTES. The impeccably maintained Quinta Vergara annually hosts Viña's international song festival every February, in the amphitheater in the SE corner of the park.

Palacio Carrasco Built by a French architect in 1912 for nitrate baron Emilio Carrasco, the Palacio Carrasco lies at Libertad and 3 Norte, a couple of blocks north of the Estero Marga Marga. There is a municipal library and cultural center inside, with periodic exhibitions. Behind the palace, on 4 Norte, is the MUSEO FONCK, with excellent displays on Chilean and Easter Island prehistory and anthropology, including an unequalled collection of books and maps on Easter Island; on the lawn outside is a *moai* statue from the island. Upstairs are displays on Chilean natural history, also worthwhile.

AERIAL VIEW OF CASTILLO WULFF (MN)

MUSEUM
Hours: *Tue-Sun 1000-1400, 1500-1800, $500.*
Entrance: *$300, children $100.*

Palacio Rioja Built by French architect Alfredo Azancot – who also built the Palacio Carrasco – the Palacio Rioja dates from 1906, and is another good remnant from Viña's *belle epoque*. The palace has been converted into a museum and there are periodic art film showings at the *Conservatorio de Música* inside. The Palacio Rioja is at the corner of 3 Norte and Calle Quillota, Viña's bustling cobblestoned commercial avenue, used since the colonial era to link Valparaíso with the Aconcagua valley.

Castillo Wulff This gothic castle, built in 1906 – again, in the aftermath of the earthquake – occupies a rocky promontory just south of the mouth of the Estero Marga Marga, on the coast road to Valpo. Above the castle is the upscale Cerro Castillo neighborhood, site of the presidential palace and a nice place for evening walks, with good views over the city.

Casino Viña's casino is just north of the mouth of the Estero Marga Marga, in a neatly manicured park. Formal wear is required for entrance to the *salón general*.
Hours: *Slots open at 1200, game rooms at 1800, closing at 0400-0500, earlier in winter.*
Entrance: *$3000 to enter game rooms.*

Laguna Sausalito, Sporting Club NE of downtown, Laguna Sausalito is a major watersports center, with water skiing and jetski rentals; in the surrounding area are 12 tennis courts, four swimming pools, a 25,000-seat stadium (Estadio Municipal), and a shooting range (Club de Tiro). Just south, along the Estero Marga Marga, is the hippodrome at the Valparaíso Sporting Club, site of an important derby held the first Sunday in February. No public transport; by taxi only.

Jardín Botánico Nacional On the north side of the Estero Marga Marga a few kilometers east of downtown, Chile's national botanical garden is situated in a narrow valley ringed by hills. With over 3,000 native and exotic plant species, the garden is administered by Conaf for scientific, educational, and reforestation purposes; among the current projects is a plan to reforest Easter Island with toromiro trees, extinct on the island. The Jardín Botánico also contains a remarkably complete collection of native Chilean cacti. Take micro #20 from Plaza de Viña to the end of the line, then get off and walk north across the bridge.

Beaches

The beaches right in town, Playa Acapulco, Playa 15 Norte, and Playa Los Marineros, are very popular in summer, but are better for sunbathing than swimming. There are far nicer beaches just north, easily accessed by public transportation; Reñaca is the closest ⬇.

Around Valparaíso and Viña del Mar   See map 🔼

See PN LA Campana (above) and The Coast from Viña to Papudo (below) for more recommended day trips.

Wineries

The chardonnay-producing vineyards of the Casablanca valley are 41km SE of Valparaíso and Viña, on Ruta 68 to Santiago, 🔲. Casablanca is easily accessed by bus from Viña or Valpo.

Scuba Diving on the Central Coast

 Viña and Valparaíso boast more dive outfits than any city in Chile apart from Santiago, and you can easily arrange logistics here for trips to Laguna Verde, Quintay, Zapallar, Papudo or Los Molles. Shipwrecks are the top attraction in the Bahía de Valparaíso itself; ask operators about excursions to *Las Locitas*, a sailboat sunk in front of Valpo's Playa Carvallo, the *Caupolicán* just off Playa San Mateo, and the *Indus* across from the Escuela Naval, and *El Caleuche* off Punta Gruesa in Viña del Mar.
Operators: 55 - 97 - 113

Laguna Verde

Just south of Valparaíso, the coast becomes steep and largely inaccessible. The one road leading due south is a wild one, leading through the outskirts of Playa Ancha (expansive views of the city), along precipitous coastal cliffs, and into the huge, half-moon bay of Laguna Verde. It's hard to believe this place is only 18km from the city, it has such an isolated, small-town feel; there's a campground, markets, fishing boats and a big white-sand beach. From here, if you have a bike or your own car, you can continue south on dirt roads (ask for directions, you have to cross private property) to Playa Las Docas, truly one of the most spectacular beaches in Chile. Bring a tent; you won't want to leave.

 Laguna Verde boasts two divable shipwrecks (the *Araucania* at 8m, and the Russian *Ecliptica*, near Punta Curamilla) and surprisingly a wild marine environment, with sea lion colonies and steep sea cliffs. You need a boat to dive here; arrange with operators in Viña.
Operators: 55

Quintay

Once the site of a major whaling station, the village of Quintay is now increasingly visited by urbanites from Santiago and Valparaíso. A golf course is being built near the lovely Playa Quintay, north of the village, where there is upmarket accommodation at the *Hostería Playa Grande*. Near the *caleta* itself – which remains the most distinctive part of the village – are modest restaurants and some low – to mid-range lodging. Accessed by bus from Santiago or Valparaíso, this is one of the best places in central Chile for scuba diving.

 There are two diveable shipwrecks in the Bahía Quintay the *Indus IV*, an immense (but badly deteriorated) whaling vessel, and a smaller but perfectly preserved freighter. The latter forms an artificial reef with a great variety of marine life; experienced divers can explore the interior of the engine room. Take special care with the current here.
Operators: 55

Horseback Riding in Ritoque

Beginning at a small working ranch in the foothills of the Coast Range, visitors can choose from a variety of highly recommended day and overnight trips, including the ascent of 728m Cerro Mauco (for expansive views of the Bahía de Valparaíso) and a more relaxed exploration of the vast dunes and wetland habitat extending to the north of the Río Aconcagua. All trips include a gourmet lunch.
Operators: 194

The Coast from Viña to Papudo   See map 🔼

This stretch of coast is hard to beat for accessibility and natural beauty alone. When you throw in the human element – an unusual mix of tiny fishing villages, hyped-up resorts, Mediterranean elegance and an earthy agricultural base to it all – you can see why this is the most visited section of coast in Chile.

Just 7km north of Viña, **Reñaca** is the site of the garden city's most prestigious and popular beach. Condos crowd the hillsides above the beachfront highway, and there

ACCOMMODATION

Great concentration of mid- to upper-range accommodations in Reñaca, also along the coastal road as far as Concón. Inexpensive lodging in Quintero and Horcón, more expensive in Maitencillo and Papudo, ritziest in Zapallar.

TRANSPORT

From Viña, via Buses Sol del Pacífico. From Santiago, via numerous companies.

are numerous bars, restaurants and discotheques. Reñaca gets absolutely packed during the summer months.

From Reñaca, most public transport heads inland direct to Concón, while a more scenic route continues north along the coast. There are beaches and more restaurants in Cochoa, at the foot of huge dunes; just beyond is a rocky promontory called Roca Oceánica (views, rock climbing), and beyond that **CALETA HIGUERILLAS**, with a fishing port, yacht club, and a major concentration of seafood restaurants.

Roca Oceánica / Conan

 On the coast road from Reñaca to Higuerillas, Roca Oceánica has a handfull of short, bolted sport routes and bouldering on granite crags right along the coast. There are a couple more toproping routes just north, on a crag (known locally as 'Conan') just south of the stone house Casa Cruz. Routes in the 5-8-5.11 range, damp with mist or heavy surf.

Windsurfing in Caleta Higuerillas

Open ocean sailing past the point; advanced sailors only.

Past a series of small, sheltered beaches good for swimming and bodyboarding, you come to **CONCÓN**. Built on a hillside above the large estuary at the mouth of the Río Aconcagua, Concón is another good place to stop for lunch or purchase seafood, and on weekends you can rent horses on the beach. Most public transport from Viña turns around here.

Past the Río Aconcagua, the immense Playa Ritoque stretches 11km to the north, backed by immense dunes; unfortunately, the beach is overrun by dirt bikes and other off-road vehicles. At the northern end of the beach is the village of Ritoque, and beyond

that the town of **QUINTERO** occupies the northern side of a granite peninsula, with tiny beaches set among the rocks on the northern and western shores.

Windsurfing in Quintero

 Ideal for speed sailing and slalom, with afternoon winds to 30 knots.

North of Quintero, skip the nasty refinery and power plant at Ventanas and head straight for **HORCÓN**, a cool little fishing village with a strong hippy influence. All along the beach you'll find lodging, restaurants, and artist and craft booths; seasonal lodging is available in cabañas around the point to the north. A couple of kilometers south is the idyllic beach at Cau Cau, while to the north are a series of nearly continuous beaches reaching almost all the way to Maitencillo. Nude sunbathing occasionally occurs in the remote enclaves at the extreme northern end of the beach. Camping is allowed along the beach, but sites are sometimes dirty, and in general Horcón gets awfully crowded on summer weekends.

Continuing north along the coast you'll soon pass the exclusive **MARBELLA COUNTRY CLUB**, which features a 27-hole golf course, tennis courts and other installations on a bluff overlooking the beach. Just past Marbella is **MAITENCILLO**, pleasant, slightly upscale vacation spot with a great string of beaches and the best selection of mid-range cabañas and hotels along this coast; a recommended option is *Cabañas Donde Julián*, at the south end of the beach.

Paragliding in Maitencillo

 There are two popular takeoff spots in this area. One is the well-maintained launch pad owned by Parapente Aventura, accessed by a signposted dirt road near the entrance to Marbella; from here you can either soar in the hills above the takeoff or fly out and land on the beach below. The other takeoff lies just off the coastal road from Maitencillo to Cachagua at the top of a 70m coastal cliff. Both of these sites feature similar conditions, with clean, relatively consistent winds straight off the Pacific.
Operators: 15 - 38 - 163 - 187

CACHAGUA, the next town north, is short on lodging but has a great beach as well, ideal for surfing, fishing, and beach sports;

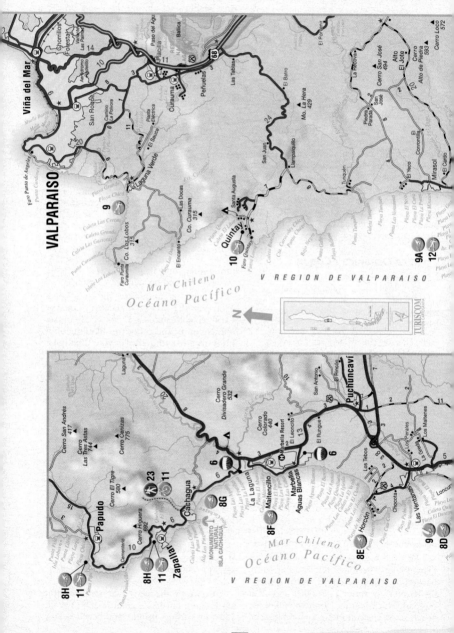

VALPARAISO

Viña del Mar

Chorrillos
Forestal
14
Recreo
Agua Santa
10
9
San Roque
Camino La Pólvora
11
Muelle Barón
Muelle Prat
20
Faro Punta de Angeles
Punta Carducci
Playa Grande
Playa Chica
9
El Sauce
Laguna Verde
Piedra Blanca
El Encanto
Las Docas
Co. Curauma 315
Co. Los Lobos 315
Punta Curaumilla
Faro Punta Curaumilla
Isleta Los Lobos
Caleta Las Cercas
Caleta Grande
Caleta Las Gaviotas

Paso del Agua
Ballica
Placilla
68
Curauma
Peñuelas
Las Tablas
Santa Augusta
Quintay
10
Faro Quintay

El Potenir
La Recova
Cerro San José 494
Cerro Alto de Piedra 583
Cerro Loco 572
Alto El Jote
San José
Piedra Parada
Cormonilla
El Yeco
Mirasol
El Cardo
Tunquén
El Barro
Mo. La Hera 429
San Juan
Lampaiquillo
24
7

9A 12

Bajo Negro
Caleta Blanca
Cta. Cerro Los Chicos
Punta Chica

V R E G I O N   D E   V A L P A R A I S O

Mar Chileno
Océano Pacífico

N

TURISCOM

Laguna
Cerro San Andrés 417
Cerro Tres Astas 744
Las Tres Astas
Cerro Cenizas 775
Cerro El Tigre 580
Papudo
Cerro Higuera 692
15
Zapallar
23 11
Cachagua
Cementerio
10
MONUMENTO NATURAL ISLA LA CACHAGUA
8H 11

Cerro Divisadero Grande 532
Cerro Colorado 440
Marbella Resort
El Leoncillo
La Laguna
6
6
8G
Maitencillo
Marbella
Aguas Blancas
8F

San Antonio
El Rungue
El Rincon
Puchuncaví
1
13
Los Corrales
Los Maitenes
La Greda
Los Telcos
2
3
5
11
3
6
Horcón
Chocota
Las Ventanas
Loncura
8E
9 8D
Caleta Quirilluca
Playa El Durazno

Mar Chileno
Océano Pacífico

V R E G I O N   D E   V A L P A R A I S O

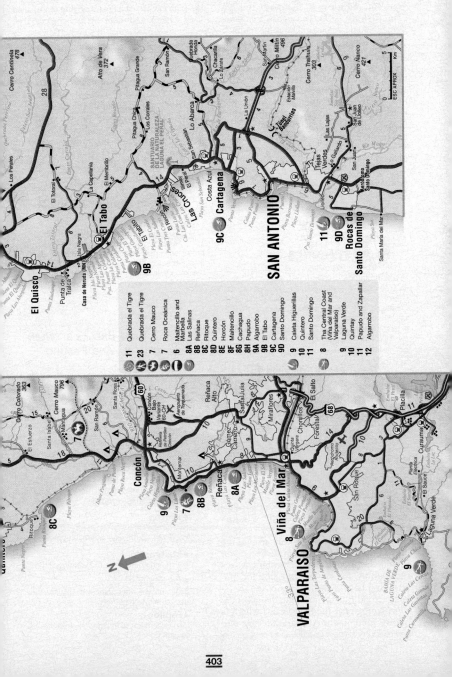

you can rent horses at the north end. Just 75m offshore is the ISLA DE LOS PINGÜINOS, home to some 2,000 Humboldt Penguins.

The village itself occupies a shady hillside above the north end of the beach; if you poke around a bit (and ask for directions) you'll soon find the long, winding staircase leading down to PLAYA LAS CUJAS, a tiny, sheltered half-moon beach that is truly one of the hidden gems along this stretch of coast. From the beach you can walk out towards the point to the south to check out the Isla de los Pingüinos and the giant mansions – complete with helipad – right across from it. Another worthwhile walk in Cachagua leads east from town into the Quebrada del Tigre.

Quebrada El Tigre

⟳ ⏱ 3-4h ▭

This mellow walk provides access to a surprisingly lush relict forest, similar to that of PN Fray Jorge. The normal trail begins near a stream which crosses the coastal road south of Cachagua; from here you simply walk up into the valley, following an obvious trail. If you wish to extend the trip, you can climb the north side of the valley and continue over the bare peaks to Zapallar or Papudo.

▶13.5km◀ ⏱ 4-5h ▣ ▭

Unlike the hiking route, the best route for bikes starts up a dirt road (close gate behind you) just north of the rodeo *medialuna* in Cachagua. From here it makes a big loop south, along the ridgetops surrounding the valley.

Continuing north you'll come upon the exclusive resort of ZAPALLAR, which dates from 1893 and retains every bit of its turn-of-the-century style and Mediterranean elegance. Large but tasteful homes lie hidden among the forests and exuberant gardens above the beach, accessed by winding streets and a footpath (known as *La Rambla*) that leads all the way around the north side of the bay. While here, you should check out the huge crashing waves south of town at Mar Bravo (good for sunsets), and have a meal at one of the excellent seafood restaurants along the beach. *El Chiringuito*, near the fisherman's wharf, is highly recommended. Another top-end choice for meals near Zapallar is *L'Ermitage*, off

the highway to Cachagua. Lodging in Zapallar is expensive, and there are few choices; reservations are essential in summertime.

10km north of Zapallar is PAPUDO, built on a hillside at the south end of a long beach. Like Zapallar, Papudo is heir to a long tradition as a vacation resort, as attested by a couple of cool early-twentieth-century homes near the waterfront. Today Papudo is considerably less charming than Zapallar, but is more active, with bars, discotheques and more lower-end accommodation. There is an excellent bar on the beach, el *Barco Rojo*, run by an *emigré* Frenchman

Diving in Papudo & Zapallar

The appeal of these neighboring resorts lies primarily in their calm, protected waters and elegant, relaxed surroundings. Either location makes a great for day trip or weekend dive retreat, wth easy beach entries. Zapallar is a preferred site for deep air diving.
Operators: 55 - 112

SURF BREAKS BETWEEN VIÑA AND PAPUDO

● **Las Salinas**
Inconsistent left point, needs west or NW swell.

● **Reñaca**
Beach breaks, best at high tide. One of the more crowded breaks along the central coast.

● **Ritoque**
Beach breaks at north end, best with north wind and mid- to high tide. Beach breaks on small days at Punta de Piedra, best at mid- to high tide.

● **Quintero**
Left point off west side of peninsula, long rides, sometimes crowded.

● **Horcón**
Beach breaks and a left point off Playa El Clarón, good with south wind and mid- to high tide.

● **Maitencillo**
Beach and point breaks on windless days.

● **Cachagua**
Beach breaks, right point with small swell, best at mid-to high tide.

● **Papudo**
Inconsistent left with big swell, best at mid-to high tide.

The Coast from Algarrobo to Santo Domingo *See map* 🔼

With a few exceptions, for most travelers the coast from Algarrobo to Santo Domingo lacks the appeal of the coast north of Viña.

ALGARROBO itself is extremely popular with vacationing families from the capital, and its beaches are quite nice; although, the town's extensive beachfront has been cluttered with an ever-expanding sea of condominiums. At the north end of town is a recommended seafood restaurant, *El Patito*.

 Algarrobo is the center of dive operations for the coast south of Valparaíso. The diving here is not particularly outstanding, but it's a fine place to take a course. Cinco Océanos has a dive shop in the Hotel Pacífico at Alessandri 1930, ☎ (35)481649 or 481040.

Windsurfing in Algarrobo

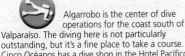 Winds to 20 knots in the bay, 30 knots in the open ocean beyond. Beach access.

South of Algarrobo is the rather uninteresting resort at **EL QUISCO**, and beyond that is **PUNTA DE TRALCA**, where you can check out the eight granite sculptures carved by French artists as a tribute to Pablo Neruda.

Climbing at Punta de Tralca

This granite promontory over the Pacific Ocean features about 10 relatively short crack and face climbing routes rated from 5.7 to 5.11. You'll need a sizeable rack just to set up a top rope, as bolts should not be trusted.

South of Punta de Tralca is **ISLA NEGRA**, site of Pablo Neruda's famous writer's retreat, which lies just down the hill from the main highway. Crowded with nautical memorabilia and collectibles, this eclectic beachside retreat was the favorite of Neruda's three houses. Guided tours are available in English and Spanish, and the rocky beach below the house – source of Neruda's inspiration in his later years – is great for beachcombing.

Hours: Open Dec 15 – Mar 11 / Tue-Sun 1000-2000, Mar 12 – Dec 14 / Tue-Fri 1000-1400, 1500-1830, Sat-Sun 100-1830).
Guided tours cost $1000 in Spanish, $2500 in English.

There is a recommended hosteria right near the museum, and cabañas in the surrounding area, though none are on the beach. Ask at the tourist information booth along the highway (at the turnoff to the museum) for lodging suggestions. Just south of Isla Negra, there is a great restaurant on the beach, *El Caleuche*.

On the northern outskirts of the port of San Antonio, **CARTAGENA** and **LAS CRUCES** are working-class resorts with lots of summertime energy and some lovely historic architecture dating from the early 20th century, when tourist trains connected these towns to Santiago. Though it is best not to visit this area during January and February, when the summer crowds can be rather oppressive, the rest of the year this is one of the most charismatic beach resorts on the Chilean coast. Aficionados of Chilean poetry can check out the house and tomb of Vicente Huidobro, set in hills to east of Cartagena's Playa Chica.

South of **SAN ANTONIO** – the port itself is best passed in a hurry – is **ROCAS DE SANTO DOMINGO**, a planned community near the mouth of the Río Maipo, with lots of green space, a country club and a very tranquil vibe. There are a couple of upscale hotels in town (which are also the only places to eat), and you can camp for free in the dunes south of town. The *Piedra del Sol* is Santo Domingo's traditional sunset spot.

Windsurfing in Santo Domingo

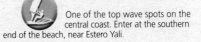 One of the top wave spots on the central coast. Enter at the southern end of the beach, near Estero Yali.

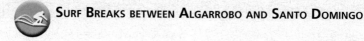

SURF BREAKS BETWEEN ALGARROBO AND SANTO DOMINGO

● **Algarrobo**
Left point over rocks, short rides, best at high tide.

● **El Tabo**
Beach breaks with medium to large swell and no wind.

● **Cartagena**
Beach breaks, left point at south end of beach.

● **Santo Domingo**
Beach breaks, best with high tide and no wind.

Rancagua
Pop. 179,638 (☎ city code 72)

Rancagua is an agricultural and mining service town in the Central Valley just south of Santiago. Like the capital, Rancagua occupies a narrow basin between high peaks of the Andes and Coast Range.

The town's relative fame dates from the 1814 *Desastre de Rancagua*, when Bernardo O'Higgins' revolutionary forces were besieged by the Spanish in the Plaza de Armas. Eventually, the the Spanish cut off the city's water supply, forcing *El Libertador* and his men to make a break for it. After a hasty escape to the east, the 300 survivors (out of an original force of 1500) crossed the Andes to meet up with San Martin's Army of the Andes near Mendoza.

Today, though Rancagua doesn't have so much to offer as an urban destination, it does provides good access to the mountains and a number of cultural attractions in the Central Valley. Each year in March, the city hosts Chile's National Rodeo Championships.

In-town Attractions

Plaza de los Héroes Interesting for its historical significance and unique design – take note of how the streets enter the Plaza in the center of each block, rather than at the corners. This was the site of the 1814 'Disaster of Rancagua.

Museo Regional de Rancagua In a traditional adobe building at the corner of Ibieta and Estado, three blocks south of the Plaza, this museum recreates the ambiance of a typical Chilean home from the 19th century, and features displays on colonial religious imagery and the Chilean independence movement. Across the street is the recently restored Casa de Pilar de Esquina, and a block south the Casa de Cultura, both of which date from the late-Colonial era.

Hours (Museum and Casa de Pilar de Esquina): Tue-Fri 1000-1800, Sat-Sun 0900-1300.
Entrance: $600, children and seniors $300

Around Rancagua

Centro de Ski Chapa Verde

Administered by a non-profit ski club comprised of some 400 families, Chapa Verde (60km NE of Rancagua) boasts a surprisingly modern infrastructure, thanks to low-interest loans from Codelco, the Chilean national copper company. The copper foundry at El Teniente is a nearby eyesore, but the skiing makes up for it.

Chapa Verde's biggest draw for in-bounds skiers is its immense skiable area: after a storm, the area boasts over 1,200há of open powder skiing, with almost no competition for first tracks. Expert and backcountry skiers should turn their attention to the recently opened Olla Blanca area, where there are short but very steep lines accessible via short walks from either side of the El Indio lift. Further afield, the options are limitless.

LODGING AND RESTAURANTS
Though there is no formal lodging at the area, with previous arrangements you may be able to rent one of the privately owned chalets at the base area; consult with administration for details (☎ (72)217651). There are reasonably priced restaurants at the base area and at mid-mountain, the latter owned by a French expat.

TRANSPORT
Buses depart from the Hipermercado Independencia parking lot at Av. Miguel Ramírez 665 at 0800 on weekends, 0900 during the week. Private vehicles are generally not allowed to make the ascent to the area.

RANCAGUA

El Teniente

Located 60km NE of Rancagua, El Teniente is the second largest copper deposit
in Chile, and the largest subterranean mine in
the world. Guided tours of the mine may be
arranged in Santiago.

Operators: 1

Termas de Cauquenes

☎ (72)297226 NA
Set in the foothills above the Río
Cachapoal, this is one of Chile's oldest and most
venerated spa hotels. The baths themselves consist
of some 24 private marble tubs with a temperature
ranging from 42-48°C, accessed via an elegant
sala de baños adorned with stained glass windows.
The grounds also include a colonial chapel, an
outdoor pool, and an acclaimed Swiss restaurant.

The Cachapoal Valley,
Lago Rapel

West of Rancagua, the paved road to
Lago Rapel leads along the north bank of
the Río Cachapoal, through the heart of rural Chilean *huaso* country. 5km west of
town is Viña Santa Mónica. Another
27km west is **DOÑIHUE**, home of Chile's most
acclaimed *chamanteros* (traditional poncho
weavers) and *guachucheros* (distillers of
aguardiente). At the town of Las Cabras, a
turnoff to the north leads to the Palmar de
Cocalán, one of two remaining major stands
of Chilean palms.

Lago Rapel is a 40km long artificial reservoir dating from 1968. Today it is a popular watersports center with vacationing families from Santiago, most of whom congregate in cabañas and camping complexes on the eastern extremes of the reservoir's two main branches. The lake is filled with sailboats, jetskis, waterski boats and the like; some complexes even have their own discotheques. Large portions of the shoreline have no road access. Transport by bus from Santiago or Rancagua.

Hacienda Los Lingues

☎ (2)2357604
This elegant and historic hacienda 37km south of Rancagua is also one of Chile's most prestigious horsebreeding farms, begun in 1760. Horse shows and riding around the vast grounds of the hacienda are part of the standard program for guests at Los Lingues. See 🄲 for details on this and other haciendas in central Chile.

Reserva Nacional Río Los Cipreses

This lovely 36,882há reserve protects the entirety of the immense Río Los Cipreses watershed, which stretches deep into the glaciated Andes southeast of Rancagua. Though it provides excellent opportunities for multi-day hiking, mountain biking, horseback riding and mountaineering trips, the reserve's difficult access makes it somewhat less than worthwhile for travellers on a tight schedule. On the other hand, for those with four or more days to spend, Los Cipreses is an excellent destination –as soon as you get past the trailhead, you are unlikely to see another soul.

Flora in the park ranges from native sclyrophyllous forests at lower elevations to subalpine stands of Andean Cypress. Parakeets, foxes and vizcachas are common in the park, and pumas and guanacos inhabit the remote interior. Interested parties should ask park rangers about petroglyphs located in the upper canyon, and about side hikes in general, most of which are unmarked.

The entrance to the park lies 16km beyond the Termas de Cauquenes, but be sure to arrive during daylight hours to avoid being locked out. The Conaf administration is in a lovely colonial *casa patronal* where you can check out a good 3D diorama of the park showing the major attractions. From here it's another 6km to the campground and trailhead at Ranchillos – the end of the road for vehicular traffic. On the left side of the road just before the campgound is a trailhead (Sendero Loros Tricahues) leading to parakeet nests in the cliffs above the river (best

observed in the morning and evening), and just beyond, on the right, is a short loop (Sendero Los Peumos) through native sclyrophyllous forests.

In order to fully enjoy the park, however, you'll need to continue upriver with camping gear. 6km up from Ranchillos (past a locked gate) is the old campground at Potrerillo de Maitenes, located above the confluence of the Río Los Cipreses and the Río Cachapoal. Beyond here, a full days' walk leads up-valley to Urriola, where there is a rustic *refugio* and further campsites set in a forest of cypress. With additional days to spend you can check out natural mineral springs (Agua de la Muerte and Agua de la Vida), high alpine lakes (Laguna de los Piuquenes), and the immense Glaciar Los Cipreses. Mountaineers will be lured further upvalley to 4,900m Volcán Palomo and the granite spires of the Cordón Granito.

Urrutia and the Upper Cipreses Valley

⟷ 🔲 ⏱2-3d rt, 4-5 to the glacier
From Ranchillos, follow the jeep track up the canyon to Potrerillos de Maitenes (6km), then continue up the Río Cipreses valley to Urriola (26km from Ranchillos), where there is a rustic refugio. Just upvalley from Urrutia are two mineral springs, Agua de la Muerte and Agua de la Vida, and a recommended sidehike leading up the Estero del Baul to the Laguna de los Piuquenes, a spectacular alpine lake. Otherwise, you can continue south another 12km or so to the base of the Glaciar Los Cipreses.

☎ (72)899015
Horses are not always available at Los Cipreses, so call with a couple of days' anticipation to make arrangements. Figure on about 4 days round trip to the Glaciar Los Cipreses, at the head of the valley.

San Fernando   *Pop. 42,684 (☎ city code 72)*

Capital of the Colchagua province, San Fernando is another Central Valley agricultural town, situated on the banks of the Río Tinguiririca. While you're in town you might check out the Casa de Lircunlauta, a typical 18th century hacienda whose original owner donated the lands for the foundation of the city.

> **BUS STATION AND/OR OFFICES**
> *Corner of Rancagua and Manso de Velasco.*

MUSEO DE COLCHAGUA, SANTA CRUZ

Around San Fernando

Termas del Flaco

 C **$500**

107km east of San Fernando, Termas del Flaco consists of a collection of simple but very pleasant concrete tubs filled with water up to 57°C. Numerous residenciales offer cheap accommodation near the springs, which are very popular during summer weekends; your best bet is to visit during the week. 500m past the carabineros post near the springs is a site called El Dino, with fossilized dinosaur tracks on a vertical cliff. Transport by regular buses from San Fernando (3 daily) and Rancagua (1 daily) in summer only.

Museo de Colchagua

Located in Santa Cruz, 41km west of San Fernando, this is the largest private museum in the country, created in 1994 in a traditional colonial house. It includes displays on paleontology, archaeology, and pre-Hispanic art, with a special focus on rural colonial artifacts and *huaso* culture. The *Fiesta de la Vendimia*, or grape-harvest festival, takes place every year in Santa Cruz near the beginning of March. Santa Cruz is also the starting point for the Ruta del Vino de Colchagua wine tour (below). Transport to Santa Cruz by regular bus from San Fernando.

Wineries

Six vineyards in the Colchagua valley have created the so-called Ruta del Vino de Colchagua, a guided circuit combining winery tours and tastings with historical and cultural context, including a visit to the Museo de Colchagua. Tours leave from Santa Cruz, **C**.

Chimbarongo

This otherwise unremarkable village 18km south of San Fernando, on the Panamerican Highway, is famous for its attractive, inexpensive wicker handicrafts and furniture. Transport via any southbound bus from San Fernando.

Hacienda El Huique

14km west of San Fernando, this is one of the best-preserved haciendas in the Central Valley – and one of few that's open to the public. See **C** for more details.

Hours: Wed-Sun 1100-1800 (to 1700 in winter).
Entrance: $1000, $500 children.

Río Tinguiririca

 ⏱5h

East of San Fernando on the road to the Termas del Flaco, the Tinguiririca is a glacially-fed class III-IV spring run, beginning at the confluence with the Río del Portillo and continuing down to Puente Negro.

Volcán Tiguiririca (4,280m)

 ⏱4d ▮

This remote volcano is the southernmost peak in Chile to top 4,000m. Access is from the end of the road up the Río Azufre, via a bridge to the left off the road to Termas del Flaco. The route, never greater than 40 degrees, switchbacks up the north bank of the Estero Piuquenes, and continues over higher ground to gain the Arroyo Fray Carlos, which it follows to the Baños de Azufre (thermal baths) at 3,300m, an obvious campsite. From here it's five hours to the broad summit.

The Coast from Pichilemu to Vichuquén

Located about 124km due west of San Fernando – or three-and-a-half hours from Santiago – **PICHILEMU** is the largest, hippest beach resort in south-central Chile. The town's origins date from the late 1800's, when local land baron Agustín Ross Edwards began to promote it as a port and vacation spot, linked to the capital by train. The town's principal attractions – the Palacio Ross, which housed the country's first casino, and the adjoining Parque Ross, with its elegant, manicured landscaping – date from Pichilemu's early 20th-century heyday.

Today, though most activity and services are still concentrated in the historic centro and the Playa Principal, Pichilemu

is best known for its surfing – especially that at **PUNTA DE LOBOS**, 6km south of downtown. A stark, treeless headland jutting into the Pacific, Punta de Lobos gives rise to one of the longest, most consistent left points on the continent. A French surfer owns the point, where he has established a surf camp and a *creperie*; even if you don't surf, this is a great place to hang out and watch the action (or the sunset), though it's much easier to find accommodation in town.

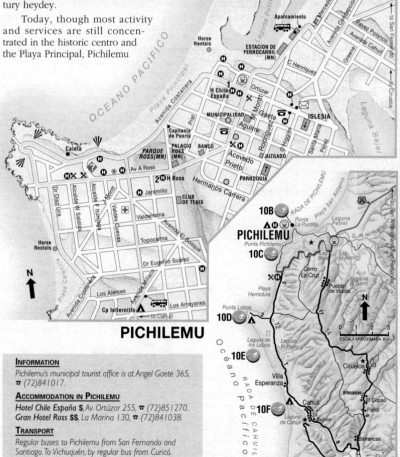

PICHILEMU

INFORMATION
Pichilemu's municipal tourist office is at Angel Gaete 365, ☎ (72)841017.

ACCOMMODATION IN PICHILEMU
Hotel Chile España **$**, Av. Ortúzar 255, ☎ (72)851270.
Gran Hotel Ross **$$**, La Marina 130, ☎ (72)841038.

TRANSPORT
Regular buses to Pichilemu from San Fernando and Santiago. To Vichuquén, by regular bus from Curicó.

South of Pichilemu, it's 12km on a gravel road to **CAHUIL**, located on the shores of a homonymous lake. A free ferry crosses the lake, beyond which it's another 22km to **BUCALEMU**, where you'll find basic accommodations, restaurants, and horses for rent at the south end of a long, black sand beach.

LAGO VICHUQUÉN, 37km south of Bucalemu via the coastal road, is a popular weekend getaway with upper-crust *Santiaguinos*. Like Laguna Aculeo, the lake is best known as a place for waterskiing, sailing and windsurfing, and lodging along the lakeshore is generally quite expensive. If you're on a budget, you might consider staying in Llico, a low-key village and windsurfing mecca at the north end of the lake. In addition to the beach, you can visit **RESERVA NACIONAL LAGUNA TORCA** *(Dec-Feb 0830-2000, Mar-Nov 0830-1715. Entrance $900, children $200)*, which protects wetland habitat for over 106 bird species, most notably the black-necked swan. Conaf operates an inexpensive campground within the reserve.

Most lodging on the lake itself is concentrated on the southern shore, in the sector

PALACIO AGUSTIN ROSS (MN), PICHILEMU

known as Aquelarre. Many of the upscale cabañas and campgrounds here offer motor boats, horses, and mountain bikes to guests and non-guests alike. For budget accommodation in this area, try the campground at Playa Paula. The town of **VICHUQUÉN** (to which you'll first arrive if coming from Curicó) is a worthwhile attraction in its own right; once the site of an Inca *mitimae* work colony, the town has preserved its traditional layout and colonial architecture. A local museum, the **MUSEO HISTÓRICO** *(Tue-Sun 1030-1330, 1530-1830. Entrance: $1000, children $500)*, features displays on local history and culture.

SURF BREAKS NEAR PICHILEMU

● **Puertecillo**
Long, beautiful lefts with medium swell and south wind. There also nice lefts just south at Punta Tuman and Topocalma.

● **Pichilemu**
Left point with medium swell and south wind, long rides.

● **Infiernillo**
Left point with medium swell just south of town, best with high tide and no wind.

● **Punta de Lobos**
The most famous wave in Chile. The entrance to this powerful, consistent left is via the rock ledges at the base of *Las Tetas*, the distinctive sea stacks out beyond the point. Best with south wind, waves up to 15', long rides.

● **Pancora**
Beach breaks with medium swell, best with north winds.

● **Cahuil**
Beach breaks with small-medium swell, best with north wind.

WINDSURFING NEAR NAVIDAD

● **La Boca**
On the river, light winds until 1300, good for beginners, then increasing to 30 knots. On the ocean, powerful beach break with onshore winds to 35 knots, experts only.

● **Matanzas**
Good wave sailing and jumping, winds from about 1100, advanced sailors only.

● **Pupuya**
Just south of Matanzas, another powerful beach break with onshore winds, good when waves are small in Matanzas. Strong currents north of the rivermouth.

● **Punta Topocalma**
Powerful beach break, offshore winds to 30 knots, advanced sailors only.

● **Pichilemu**
Winds from about 1400, usually 20 knots or less. Experts only.

● **Llico**
Winds from about 1400, up to 30 knots. Excellent for wavesailing, but with dangerously shallow water.

Curicó

Pop. 77,733 (☎ city code 75)

Like most towns in the Central Valley, Curicó is a service center for the surrounding farms and vineyards, and doesn't hold a lot for the visitor in the way of sightseeing. One of the town's highlights is undoubtedly the Plaza de Armas, with its sixty statuesque palm trees and a vivid carving of legendary Mapuche *toqui* Lautaro. An easy walk NE of town is Cerro Carlos Condell, with a public swimming pool and fine views over the city. Each year the municipality and surrounding vineyards sponsor the *Fiesta de la Vendimia* (grape-harvest festival) during the third week in March.

TOURIST OFFICES
Tourist kiosk in the Edificio Servicios Públicos, east of the Plaza de Armas. Open 0900-1830.

BANKS AND MONEY CHANGERS
Banks, ATMs on Calle Merced near the Plaza. Curi Cambio is at Merced 255, Of. 106, open Mon-Fri 0930-1330, 1530-1800.

HOSPITAL
On Chacabuco south of Av. San Martín, ☎ 310252.

POST OFFICE
Carmen 556 across from Plaza de Armas.

ACCOMMODATION
1 Hotel Prat $, Peña 427, ☎ 311069.

2 Residencial Rahue $, Peña 410, ☎ 312194.
3 Hotel Turismo $$, Carmen 727, ☎ 310823.
More info at www.turistel.cl

BUS STATION AND/OR OFFICES
Most companies at Av. Camilo Henríquez and Membrillar. Buses Lit and Tur-Bus are southeast of downtown, near the intersection of Manso de Velasco and the Panamerican. For buses to Lago Vichuquén, Molina and Radal / Siete Tazas, the Terminal de Buses Rurales is at the west end of Prat.

TRAIN STATION
Estación de Ferrocarriles is at the west end of Prat, ☎ 310028.

· Around Curicó

Wineries
Miguel Torres and Viña San Pedro are the major wineries in the area. The Miguel Torres bodega is just south of town, on the west side of the Panamerican Highway, while Viña San Pedro is just off the Panamerican on the road to Lontué . Local and intercity buses go right by the vineyards.

Los Queñes
This quiet mountain village is 51km east of Curicó, at the confluence of the Teno and Claro rivers. There is budget lodging and a campground in town, and beyond that, nothing but mountains. Transport via regular bus.

Río Teno
 ⏱4h
Beginning at a put-in below at the Class V+ drop at Piedra de la Mujer (70km from the Panamerican), the Teno is a Class III run ending at Los Queñes. There is also reportedly a more difficult upper run.
Operators: 100

Reserva Nacional Radal Siete Tazas
The entrance to the park at Radal is 50km SE of Curicó, via the town of Molina. See ⬆ for details.

Lago Vichuquén and Reserva Nacional Laguna Torca
Vichuquén is 110km from Curicó, transport by regular bus. See ⬆.

Río Lontué
⏱4h
The Lontué is a favorite with boaters from Santiago, as this is the first clearwater river on the way south – an indication of the lower elevations (and fewer glaciers) of this section of the Andes. In order to access the put-in, you must ask permission from the *fundos* on either side of the valley. Beginning at the confluence of the Río de los Patos and the Río Colorado, the Lontué starts as a beautiful, continuous Class III-IV that soon mellows to Class II-III.
Operators: 214

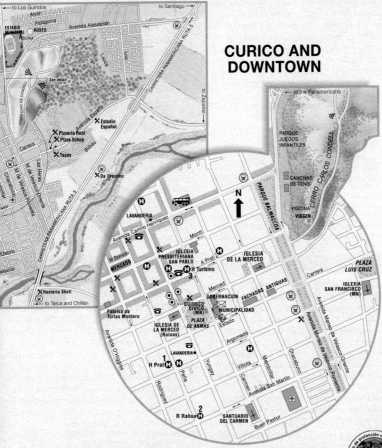

CURICO AND DOWNTOWN

Reserva Nacional Radal Siete Tazas

ACCOMMODATION

Free campgrounds at Radal and Parque Inglés, private campgrounds on the access road. Hotel in Parque Inglés.

TRANSPORT

By bus from Molina with Buses Hernández, Maipú 1723, with daily departures to Parque Inglés in January and February, weekends only the rest of the year

Situated in the Río Claro Valley SE of Curicó, Reserva Nacional Radal Siete Tazas is named for the so-called Seven Teacups, where the river has sculpted the basalt bedrock into a series of deep pools connected by waterfalls. Long renowned among kayakers and Chilean nature lovers, this 7,600há park is very popular on summer weekends, when

it fills up with vacationing families. Off-season and during the week, you'll have the park almost entirely to yourself.

The reserve's surprisingly lush forests combine elements of the Mediterranean flora of central Chile and the southern beech forests of the south, and a number of tree species with conservation problems are protected here. There are also a number of archaeological sites in the park (ask Conaf rangers for info), and Conaf runs a captive parakeet breeding program. There are a number of short hiking trails along the Siete Tazas, longer ones to Cerro El Fraile and Valle del Indio, and a multi-day excursion to RN Altos del Lircay.

The park entrance is at Radal, where there is a free campground that is sometimes left unpleasantly dirty. A better choice is to stay at the private campground at *Eco-Adventure Radal*, 1km before the entrance to the park, or else continue on to the campground at Parque Inglés, which is closest to the reserve's main attractions. In Parque Inglés there is also a Conaf information center, a private hosteria (the *Flor de Canela*), and horses for rent.

Río Claro

The put-in for this classic waterfall run is reached via an unmarked path about 500m up from the *mirador* (and takeout) in Parque Inglés. The first drop is about 8m while those that follow are somewhat smaller; all have big pools at the bottom. Above the Tazas is the more challenging and committing Veintidós

Saltitos (22 Waterfalls), which requires active scouting and a couple of portages – not recommended with high water. There is also a mellow, 2-3hr class II-III run below the Siete Tazas, beginning in Radal and continuing down to the slot canyon below the bridge known locally as 'Puente Pancho.'

Exploring in Radal Siete Tazas

Though the maintained trails here can't really compete with those at nearby parks (such as Altos de Lircay), you can hike over the course of 2-3 days, there are a few interesting options within the park, including the half-day ascent of Cerro El Fraile, which provides panoramic views over the surrounding valleys. Horses are available for rent (1 day trips only) near the park administration at Parque Inglés, and bikes are available at the *Radal Eco-Adventure* campground.

Operators: 89 - 214

Talca

Pop. 159,711 (☎ city code 71)

First founded in 1692, Talca had a rough start and had to be completely resurrected in a new location about fifty years later, this time on lands donated by the Augustine order. Many large hacienda owners built their 'city homes' here, and in 1818 Bernardo O'Higgins signed the Chilean Independence Act in Talca, further augmenting the town's prestige. Today, Talca is the capital of the region and an important agricultural service center. As a tourist attraction, it has more to offer than any other Central Valley town except Chillán.

The town occupies a flat plain between the Panamerican Highway and the Río Claro. Most streets have a number and a direction relative to the Plaza de Armas; note that *Oriente* means east, *Poniente* west. The train and bus station are on the east side of town, near the highway, while the main downtown area is between 3 Sur and Av. Bernardo O'Higgins.

In-town Attractions

Museo O'Higginiano y de Bellas Artes On the corner of 1 Norte and 2 Oriente, this 1762 home originally belonged to Portuguese businessman Juan Albano Pereira, Bernardo O'Higgins' tutor. The future 'liberator' of Chile lived here for six years during his childhood, and returned to sign the Chilean Independence Act here on February 2, 1818. The museum contains paintings by Chilean and foreign artists, and exhibits related to the independence era.

Hours: Tue-Fri 0915-1245, 1430-1845, Sat-Sun 1000-1245. Entrance: $500, children $250

Río Claro, Cerro La Virgen At the west end of Av. Bernardo O'Higgins you'll find a smattering of restaurants and boats for rent on the banks of the river. Across the river is a short climb to Cerro La Virgen, with a nice view over the city.

TALCA

Bus Station and/ or Offices
Main terminal at 2 Sur 1920, east of the railroad tracks. Tur-Bus and international buses are around the corner at 3 Sur 1960.

Train Station
Corner of 2 Sur and 11 Oriente (west end of 2 Sur). In addition to north-south service, a narrow-gauge train still runs to Constitución (departures daily 0730, returns Mon-Sat 1600, Sun 1500, 2.5hr trip).

Useful Addresses
Conaf is at 2 Poniente 1180, ☎ 233148.

Around Talca

Villa Cultural Huilquilemu

8km east of Talca, this well-preserved 19th-century hacienda now contains a religious art museum, modern sculptures and paintings, and displays of antique farming and winery equipment. There's a good restaurant and a wine-tasting boutique on the premises. Transport by regular bus.

Hours: Tue-Thu 1500-1830, Sat 1600-1830, Sun 1100-1400.
Entrance: $300, children $50

Wineries

There are 23 vineyards in the Río Maule valley, varying from giants like Concha y Toro to a number of small organic co-ops around Cauquenes. Transport to San Javier, the center of this region, via regular buses from Talca. See for details.

Vilches / Reserva Nacional Altos de Lircay

The park entrance is 67km east of Talca, transport by regular bus. See for details.

Complejo Turístico El Melado

31km east of Linares (84km SE of Talca), this is a pleasant destination resort with cabañas, a restaurant, swimming pools and other infrastructure set on a 40,000há property along the Estero El Melado. Excursions to the RN Los Bellotos and other destinations in the cordillera are organized here. See Alojamiento for contact info. No public transport.

Paso Pehuenche to Argentina

International Ruta 115 leads east from Talca, following the north bank of the Río Maule 178km to the Argentine border at 2,553m Paso Pehuenche. The road passes Lago Colbún, the country's largest artificial reservoir, and a couple of hotsprings (at km 3 and 15 above 'La Mina' before reaching the border). There's also good fishing and kayaking in the upper stretch of the river. The road, which provides access to San Rafael, Argentina, is open from December-April, depending on the weather. Buses from the international/Tur-Bus terminal provide summer-only service to Argentina.

In addition to the rustic baths along the Río Maule, there are commercial springs at Panimávida (73km from Talca) and Quinamá-vida (65km); transport by taxi colectivos and regular buses from Talca. Further south is the Termas de Catillo, accessed by bus and colectivo from Parral.

Río Ancoa

⏱3-4h

The Ancoa run begins at the Túnel Canal Melado, which carries water through the mountains from the Río Melado. From here down to that obvious diversion dam is an excellent class IV-V run. The Río Melado is also rafted commercially by the folks at the Centro Turístico El Melado.

Headwaters of the Achibueno

⚑ ⏱4-6d ▪

Southeast of Linares, the headwaters of the Río Achibueno offer a variety of wild, remote backpacking loops for experienced and independent trekkers. Destinations include Volcán Longaví to the south of the Achibueno, and the Las Animas and La Gloria valleys to the north. As there is no public transport to the trailhead at Aduana Pejerrey, these are difficult routes to access without a private vehicle or the help of an operator.

Operators: 99 🐎 - 214

The Coast from Constitución to Cobquecura

Set at the mouth of the Río Maule, the town of **Constitución** lies 61km SW of Talca. Directly south lies a dramatic coastline of black sand beaches and wild rock formations, but the town itself has been utterly ruined, permeated by the smell of the massive Celco cellulose plant. Still, there are three worthwhile reasons to visit: either to ride the narrow-gauge railway from Talca, to check out the traditional wooden boatshops along the Río Maule, or to continue south along the coast.

The coastal road is relatively industrial as well, passing through immense pine plantations en route to the towns of CHANCO (70km), PELLUHUE (81km), and CURANIPE (88km). Curanipe is probably the best place to stay, with a couple of reasonable hosterías, a protected campsite, and a couple of seafood restaurants near the beach. South of here, the road to COBQUECURA turns to gravel, and unless you have your own transport or want to hitch, you'll have to backtrack and return to the Panamericana via the city of

CAUQUENES. Along the way, you can check out the tiny RN LOS RUILES, created in order to protect the endemic ruil (*Nothofagus alessandri*), currently in danger of extinction.

Both Constitución and Cauquenes may be reached by regular bus from Talca, and local buses run all along the coastal route; see the Talca listing for details on rail service. Further south is Cobquecura, another quiet beach resort with a large sea lion colony (Piedra de la Lobería), accessed by regular bus from Chillán.

Punta Parrón

Good gentle waves, winds up to 18 knots.

Curanipe

Great waves, afternoon winds to 25 knots, easy entry.

Vilches and Parque Nacional Altos del Lircay

ACCOMMODATION
Hostería in Alto Vilches; backcountry camping in the park.

TRANSPORT
By regular buses from Talca; less frequent departures in winter.

Located in a microclimate valley 67km east of Talca, this 12,163há reserve features some lovely interconnected hiking trails through stands of native southern beech forest, with several excellent opportunities for extended walks into the high Andean valleys to the east. Six km past the village of **VILCHES ALTO**, the Conaf administration and *Centro de Información Ambiental* contains displays on the natural and human history of the park; nearby are the interesting *piedras tacitas* (Indian grinding mortars carved out of the rocks) and a short trail to the Mirador del Indio overlook. There is no formal campground in the park, but there are plenty of spots to camp for free, especially once you get into the backcountry. The large, cacaphonous Burrowing Parrot or tricahue nests in the cliffs above the Río Lircay.

El Ladrillero

The best views in the park are those from the top of El Ladrillero, a mountaintop platform formed of columnar basalt, 2,300m above sea level. El Ladrillero can be climbed from the Conaf administration in about 6-7hrs (rt) via the Laguna del Alto, or else made combined with the walk to El Refugio for an excellent two-day loop.

El Refugio and the Río Claro Overlook

From the Conaf administration, this well-marked trail leads east through roble forest above the Río Lircay. A campsite at El Refugio makes a good central location for exploring the park, while the entire hike to the viewpoint over the Río Claro and Volcán Descabezado Grande can be done in about 6hrs round-trip. Horses are usually available near the park administration.

Operators: 140 - 214

Volcán Descabezado Grande (3,830m)

⏱4-5d

From the Río Claro Overlook, head downstream to the Río Blanquillo (the next valley east), where you can set up your first camp. The trail then follows the Blanquillo upstream past some splendid natural hotsprings, with the volcano distinctly visible to the east. The slopes of the volcano are completely barren, consisting of an otherworldly expanse of white volcanic sand; if there is no snow on the mountain, you will have to bring all water with you to a second camp on the volcano's south face. From here the route continues through an obvious rock band to the immense, ice-filled summit crater, returning to the hotsprings the same day.

Operators: 214

Chillán   Pop. 145,759 (☎ city code 42)

First founded as a military fort in 1565, Chillán has been so routinely demolished by Indian raids and earthquakes that scarcely any buildings in the city are over 50 years old. As a consequence, Chillán is not a particularly historic city, though its wonderful open-air market and excellent access to the mountains makes it worth a visit.

In truth, modern Chillán is actually two towns, Chillán and Chillán Viejo. The old town, Chillán Viejo, was built on the modern site in 1751, after nearly two centuries of building and rebuilding the forts that marked the southernmost extent of Spanish dominion; beyond here, the Mapuches exer-

cised at least as much control as the conquistadors. In 1835, a major earthquake completely destroyed the city, leading to formation of modern Chillán. Some residents of Chillán Viejo could not or did not want to move, however, and so the two cities grew up side by side. In 1939, another devastating tremor shook the city to its foundations, destroying 90% of the buildings.

In-town Attractions

Escuela México Following the 1939 earthquake, Mexican president Lázaro Cárdenas donated this school to the city of Chillán. Before its inauguration, Mexican

TOURIST OFFICES

Sernatur: 18 de Septiembre 455, north of the plaza. Dec-Feb/Mon-Fri 0830-1930, Sat 0930-4000. Mar-Nov/ Mon-Fri 0830-1300, 1500-1845, Sat 0930-1400. **Municipal Tourist Office**: west side of the plaza. Open Jan-Feb 0930-1900, Mar-Dec 0930-1300, 1430-1815.

BANKS AND MONEY CHANGERS

Travelers' checks changed at Schüler Cambios, corner of Arauco and Av. Collín, open Mon-Fri 1000-1330, 1500-2000, Sat 1000-1800. Banks, ATMs on and around the Plaza.

HOSPITALS

Corner of Constitución and Av. Argentina, east of downtown, ☎ 208200.

LANGUAGE SCHOOLS

Interswop JB Turismo, Constitución 633, Of 03, ☎ 223526. Exchange programs, work-study.

POST OFFICE

North side of the Plaza.

INTERNET CONNECTION

Gateway, Av. Libertad 360.

ACCOMMODATION

1 **Hospedaje Sonia Segui** $, Itata 288, ☎ 214879.
2 **Hospedaje Su Casa** $, Cocharcas 555, ☎ 223931.
3 **Residencial 18** $, 18 de Septiembre 317, ☎ 211102.
4 **Hotel Libertador** $$, Av. Libertad 35, ☎ 223255.
5 **Hotel Quinchamali** $$, El Roble 634, ☎ 223381.
6 **Hotel Las Terrazas** $$$, Constitución 664, 5th floor, ☎ 227000.
More info at www.turistel.cl

RESTAURANTS

7 **Arco Iris**, El Roble 525. Vegetarian lunches.
8 **Café Paris**, Arauco 666. Real coffe, restaurant upstairs.
9 **Mercado**, north of the Feria. Fixed lunches, pushy waitresses.

AIRPORT

Aeropuerto Bernardo O'Higgins lies 7km east, on the road to Coihueco. Note that many flights operate in winter only.

AIRPORT TRANSPORT

Ladeco/Lanchile runs minibuses to the airport, consult for details. Radiotaxi La Plaza, ☎ 269333.

BUS STATION AND/OR OFFICES

The main station, Terminal María Teresa, is at the corner of Av. Ecuador and O'Higgins, on the road north to the Panamerican. The old Terminal de Buses Inter-Regionales is at the west end of Constitución.
Terminal de Buses Rurales is on Sargento Aldea between Maipón and Prat, a block east of the Feria de Chillán. Buses Loyola, with service to Termas de Chillán, is at 5 de Abril 594, east of the Plaza de Armas.

TRAIN STATION

West end of Libertad, ☎ 222424.

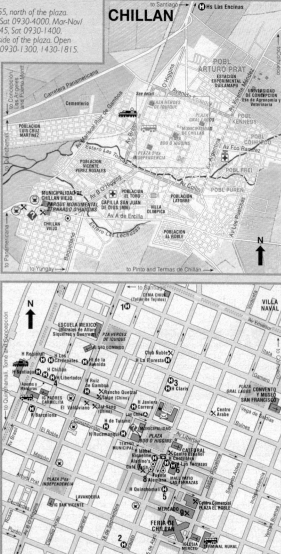

CHILLAN

muralists David Alfaro Siqueiros (a crony of Neruda's from his days as a Mexican consulate) and Xavier Guerrero painted the entryway and library. In the library, Siqueiros' *Muerte al Invasor* (Death to the Invader) is the school's *piece de resistance*, depicting scenes and characters from the conquest to the modern era; the north wall depicts the conquest in México, the south wall in Chile. Along the stairway to the library is Guerrero's *Hermanos Mexicanos* (Mexican Brothers).

On Av. Bernardo O'Higgins between Gamero and Vega de Saldías, the Escuela México is actually a functioning school, but you can go in and check out the murals.

Hours: Mon-Fri 1000-1300, 1500-1830, Sat 0900-1230
Entrance: free.

Feria de Chillán A few blocks southeast of the Plaza, Chillan's open-air market is the richest and most varied in the central region, with a mix of agricultural goods, dried fruit, baskets and ceramics, and handicrafts in leather, wood, and wicker.

Museo Franciscano Located in a convent on the corner of Sargento Aldea and Vega de Saldías, this religious museum depicts the history of the Franciscan order, committed evangelists of the Mapuche Indians since 1585.

Hours: Tue-Sun 1000-1300, 1600-1800
Entrance: $200, children $100

Parque Monumental Bernardo O'Higgins Conserves the foundations of O'Higgins first home, the tombs of his mother and sister, and a 60m mural depicting the life and achievements of *el Libertador*.

Hours: Dec-Mar 0800-2000, Apr-Nov 0800-1800

Around Chillán

San Fabián de Alico

72km NE of Chillán, sleepy, shady San Fabián de Alico is the biggest town in the Río Ñuble valley. Past the town, the road winds upvalley another 24km through a mixture of native forests and farmland, passing some excellent riverside campsites before coming to an end at the hanging bridge at La Punilla. Transport by regular bus from San Carlos, daily to La Punilla.

Río Ñuble

⏱4-6h
The Ñuble is a beautiful class III run (best during the spring *deshielo*), beginning at the hanging bridge at La Puntilla and continuing all the way to San Fabián de Alico. Scout for takeouts on the way up, as you'll probably want to take out before town.

The Upper Ñuble Valley

⏱5-6d
From the end of the road at La Punilla, continue across the bridge and up the Río Ñuble valley. The valley arcs to the south, through native forest and volcanic terrain on the back side of the Nevados de Chillán and Volcán Chillán; to make an excellent 5-6 day loop, climb to the head of the Río Las Minas valley and cross a pass to the SW, dropping into the Río

FERIA DE CHILLAN

Diguillín valley. From here, you can connect with the Aguas Calientes valley (where there are natural hotsprings), and end at the Termas de Chillán.
Operators: 92 🐎

Coihueco & Quinchamalí

Coihueco, 27km east of Chillán, is known for its wooden carvings in laurel (*Laurelia sempervirens*). You can find handmade ceramic figures in Quinchamalí, 31km west just off the road to Concepción. Transport by regular buses.

Hacienda San Agustín de Puñal

50km NW of Chillán, outside the town of Ninhue, this colonial hacienda has been preserved by the Chilean Navy as a museum in honor of Arturo Prat, naval hero from the Battle of Iquique. Prat was born here in 1848. Transport by regular bus from Chillán.

Las Trancas and the Termas de Chillán

TRANSPORT

By daily bus from Chillán as far as Las Trancas; from here consult at Turismo Rucahue or other hosterías for transport to the Termas. Termas de Chillán offers its guests transfers from Concepción or Chillán.

East of Chillán, a partially paved secondary road leads gradually up into the Andes, passing through classic Central Valley *campo* before eventually entering a lovely native montane forest. At km 67 on the road up the valley is the *Cueva de los Pincheira*, a cave that served as a hideout for a group of loyalist bandits in the years following independence; between men and captive women and children, the band reached some 2000 in number, and terrorized communities on both sides of the Andes before they were finally finished off in 1832. Today, you can have a picnic in their old digs.

Ten km further on is **LAS TRANCAS**, where you'll find an abundance of cabin complexes; recommended choices includes *Cabañas Rucahue, Parador Jamón, Pan y Vino*, and the HI hostel *Las Trancas*, while *Oliva* gets the nod for the valley's best pizza. Unless you can afford to stay up at the ski area, Las Trancas is the best place for skiers to stay in the valley. A signposted left leads from here up the Shangri-La valley towards the Nevado de Chillán range, home to the last huemules (Andean deer) known to survive in central Chile.

Another ten kilometers up the road, Termas de Chillán is a major ski and hotsprings resort situated in a lovely lenga forest at the base of Volcán Chillán. The presence of cacaphonous bright-green parakeets in the forest surrounding the hotel adds a surreal aspect to the whole scene, especially in winter. Buses Loyola (5 de Abril 594 in Chillán, ☎ 217878) runs daily buses as far as Las Trancas.

Termas de Chillán

Located in an area of transition between the semi-arid central region and the cooler, wetter climate of the south, Termas de Chillán gets top marks for snow conditions, weather, terrain and infrastructure. With tree skiing on the lower slopes, groomers leading from the peak to the base, seemingly endless off-piste terrain, an active volcano and a 5-star spa hotel at the base, this place is tough to beat.

Though it might be slow, Chillán's Don Otto lift is one of the best things about the mountain, taking you from the base of the area almost all the way to the summit. You can run laps on Don Otto all day, cruising on groomers – which typically stick to the gullies which crease the sides of the volcano, and are a bit narrow for some skiers' tastes – or heading south into vast off-piste terrain, described .

To the north (left as you're looking up the mountain) of Don Otto, a series of surface lifts provide access to 13km Tres Marías run, as well as other intermediate groomers and the steep lines off the ridge known as Elephant Rock (this area gets early sun).

LODGING / RESTAURANTS

There are two hotels at Termas de Chillán: the modern, luxurious Hotel Termas de Chillán and the older, more down-to-earth Hotel Pirigallo. Condominiums are also available at the base of the resort. There are restaurants in both hotels, a cafeteria at the base area, and a restaurant / discotheque at the 'Club House' between the two hotels. There's also a small minimarket in the condominium village.

Advanced skiers will inevitably be drawn to the off-piste terrain south of the Don Otto lift. To reach this area, traverse south (skier's left) from the top of the lift and drop down into the vast bowl, but remember to stay high and right as you reach the bottom, to avoid postholing out. The steepest lift-served terrain is on the west face of Cerro Pirigallo, accessed via a long, high traverse from the top of Don Otto. With sunny conditions, you must ski here early in the day to avoid wet slides – and look out for the gaping crevasses formed by steam escaping from the bowels of the volcano. You can smell the sulfur as you near the bottom of the bowl, and if you get the urge you can even stop for a bath at the ruins of an old hotel.

☎ (2)2331313, (42)223887
🏠 NA
Termas de Chillán features a top-notch spa hotel, with indoor and outdoor pools and jacuzzis from a source spring of 89°C. The spa also features hydrotherapy, relflexology, aromatherapy, and a dizzying array of other treatments – the perfect way to end a day of skiing. If you're not staying at the hotel, you may want to check out the thermal pool at Aguas Calientes, which is open to the public.

TERMAS DE CHILLAN

Volcán Chillán Nuevo
3122m - 10242ft

14

Nevados de Chillán

15

2700m 8858ft

LAS TRES MARIAS

LAS TRES MARIAS

EL VOLCAN

2400m 7874ft **6**

8

8 EL VOLCAN

TRAVERS

EL VOLCAN 2

CANDONGO 1

2125m 6971ft **6**

Elephant Rock

EL AGUILA

CAMINO

HOSPITAL

DON BENNO

5 3150m 7053ft

to Pirigallo Chutes

4 2500m 8202ft

EL HUEMUL

CONDOR 1

CONDOR 2

HUEMUL 2

EMBUDO

EL BURRO

LA MULA

PIRIGALLO

PIRIGALLO

PIRIGALLO

Estación Intermedia Torre 15

1830m 6004ft

2 1832m 6011ft

Parque de Aguas Termales

2 **2**

1800m 5902ft **4**

1720m 5643ft **5**

2 1800m 5902ft

BOSQUE

VUELTA EL EARRIL

BOSQUE NEVADO 2

PISTA 2

Snowmobile circuit

1600m **7**

Capilla

Club House cancha de tenis

minimarket

TERMAS DE CHILLAN 1600m 4615ft

9

to Chillán

— Expert	Chairlift	(H) Hotel	Restrooms
— Dificult	Double Chair	(A) Ski School	Ski Rental
— Intermediate	Triple Chair	(i) Restaurant	(T) Tickets
— Easy	Quad Chair	(+) Ski Patrol	(E) Car Park
— Free Skiing	Poma	Emergency Telephone	Cafeteria
Skating Rink	T-Bar	Heliskiing	Paragliding

Hiking around Termas de Chillán

⬥ ⏱varies 📖📖

There are many excellent options for day hikes and longer backpacking trips around the Termas de Chillán and Las Trancas. Closest to Las Trancas is the short, easy ascent of Mirador Curamanque, which provides panoramic views over the valley. In Shangri La there is an abandoned refugio and a spectacular day hike to the mountaintop Laguna del Huemul, as well as an easy trail leading past a couple of waterfalls (Cascada Valle las Trancas, Cascada Ruca-Pirén) to Puente Aserradero, located on the main road just above the Carabineros post. Most of the best hikes near the ski area are in the valleys just south, including the short walks to the waterfall at Grutas de los Pangues and the hotsprings at Valle Hermoso, both accessed from the second hairpin bend above Las Trancas. From here you can continue on to more hotsprings (Olla del Mote), fumaroles, and steam baths, looping east to rejoin the road near the public pools at Aguas Calientes.

Operators: 65 🐎 - 220 🐎

There are almost always horses available for hourly rental at the hotel (you don't have to be a guest). Furthermore, during the summer season there are 2 or 3 scheduled excursions a week, lasting about 4hrs and following the routes described above (consult for details). In Las Trancas you can rent horses for half-day trips from *Cabañas Las Añañucas*, ☎ (42)373665, at km 68 on the road to the ski area.

Across from the hotel on the south side of the valley are about 25 bolted sport climbing routes on volcanic crags, ranging from 5.5-5.12ª. You must ask permission at the hotel to climb here, as the crags are on private property.

Volcán Chillán (3,122m)

⏱1d ▧

If you begin at the top of the El Fresco lift (2,700m), it's only about a 2-3 hour hike to the top of the twin-peaks of Volcán Chillán, which means that fit skiers could easily make a trip to the summit into their ski day. If coming from the base, the easiest ascent is probably via Las Tres Marías.

Operators: 65 - 220

Nevados de Chillán (3,212m)

⏱2-3d ▧

The Nevados de Chillán can be accessed from 3 directions: from the ski area, the Shangri-La Valley (access via Las Trancas), or from San Fabián de Alico. This makes for great loop possibilities, and phenomenal backcountry skiing, with good lines on three separate faces. Note that the west face of Los Nevados is heavily glaciated, so it is a good idea to rope up beginning in early summer.

Operators: 65 - 220

Concepción

Pop. 326,784 (☎ city code 41)

Chile's second-largest city, Concepción is a major industrial center and university town that, despite its important historical significance, lies well off the average traveler's map. Still, the city holds a certain appeal for those interested in urban culture, nightlife, and the arts.

Pedro de Valdivia founded the original fort, in Penco, in 1550, and made the city into the political, military, and administrative capital of colonial Chile. The Spaniards skirmished constantly with the Mapuches, and after 1600, when the Indians rose up and regained control over the area south of the Biobío, the city became headquarters for the Ejército de la Frontera, one of two standing armies in all of Spanish America.

Meanwhile, repeated earthquakes and tidal waves took their toll on the Spaniard's adobe constructions; in 1751 one particularly disastrous tremor leveled the city entirely, prompting officials to abandon the original site and re-establish the city in its modern location. The cycle of natural disasters continued, however, and today there are very few historic constructions left standing in Concepción.

Relatively isolated from the rest of urban Chile, Concepción was an incubator for the independence movement in Chile, and in modern times the city has remained a hotbed of opposition and leftist politics. Above all, however, Concepción is an industry town, with a long history of coal extraction from the coast south, and a modern emphasis on the pulp, paper, and petrochemical industries. These industries – and others to follow – are to be the principal beneficiaries of cheap power produced by the hydropower dams in the upper Biobío watershed.

The city is located on the north bank of the Río Biobío, but there is no waterfront *per se*. Instead, the city center is laid out just north of Cerro Caracol; at the foot of the hill is the Parque Ecuador and the campus of the Universidad de Concepción. The port of Talcahuano lies to the north, separated from downtown by a sprawling industrial zone, while to the west two bridges span the Biobío, leading to Lota and *the Costa de Carbón* (below).

In-town Attractions

Galería de Historia Located in Parque Ecuador near the corner of Victor Lamas and Lincoyán, this excellent museum uses finely detailed dioramas and recordings to depict a variety of historical events and themes. The museum includes displays on Mapuche subsistence patterns and combat strategy, the original Spanish fort at Penco, and the 1939 earthquake.
Hours: Mon 1500-1830, Tue-Fri 1000-1330, 1500-1839, Sat-Sun 1000-1400, 1500-1900.
Entrance: free

Casa del Arte Across from the Plaza Perú on the campus of the Universidad de Concepción, this art museum displays a solid collection of paintings by Chilean artists, as well as Mexican muralist Jorge González Camarena's *La Presencia de América Latina*.
Hours: Tue-Fri 1000-1800, Sat 1000-1600, Sun 1000-1400

Museo de Historia Natural East of downtown, in the Plaza Acevedo near the corner of Roosevelt and Maipú, this museum contains photographs, Mapuche artifacts and other displays on the natural history of the region.
Hours: Tue-Sat 1000-1800, Sun 1500-1730.

Cerro Caracol, Cerro Alemán 256m Cerro Caracol can be climbed in about 15 minutes from Parque Ecuador, south of downtown. There's a good lookout over the city; if you wish you can continue on about the same distance to the top of the next peak south, Cerro Alemán.

Museo Huáscar Now anchored off the northern end of Talcahuano's port, the *Huáscar* was the world's second ironclad ship, built in Bikenhead, England in 1864 for the Peruvian navy. After having sunk Chilean war hero Arturo Prat's ship *Esmeralda* in the 1789

TOURIST OFFICES

Sernatur: NE side of the plaza, on Aníbal Pinto. Dec-Feb hours 0830-2000; Mar-Nov/Mon-Fri only, 0830-1300, 1500-1730.

BANKS AND MONEY CHANGERS

Banks, ATMs on the Plaza Independencia. For traveler's checks, Intercam is at Barros Arana 402, SW of the plaza.

HOSPITAL

San Martín and Av. Roosevelt, NE of downtown.

POST OFFICE

Corner of Colo Colo and O'Higgins.

INTERNET CONNECTION

Cyberc@fe, Caupolicán 553.

ACCOMMODATION

1 *Casa de Huéspedes* $, Rengo 855, ☎ 244152.
2 *Hotel Cecil* $, Barros Arana 9, ☎ 230677.
3 *Hotel Alonso de Ercilla* $$, Colo Colo 334, ☎ 227984.
4 *Hotel Della Cruz* $$, Aníbal Pinto 240, ☎ 240016.
5 *Hotel El Araucano* $$$, Caupolicán 21, ☎ 230606.
6 *Hotel Alborada*, $$$, Barros Arana 457, ☎ 242144.
7 *Hotel Club Presidente Concepción* $$$, Av. Pedro de Valdivia 721, ☎ 339090 **(see ad inside front cover)**. More info at www.turistel.cl

RESTAURANTS

8 *Barrio Estación:* The area around the train station and Plaza España concentrates a number of theme pubs and restaurants. Choices here include El Medio Toro, Av. Prat 594 (pizza), Mezcal, Prat 532 (Mexican), and El Bárbara, Freire 82-A (Chilean cuisine, live music).
9 *Le Chateau*, Colo Colo 340. French cuisine, spendy.
10 *El Rancho de Julio*, Barros Arana 337. Argentine-style steak house.
11 *Casino Alemán*, In the firestation, next door to the Museo de Historia. Good fixed lunches.
12 *L'Angelo*, Rengo 494. Sandwiches, beer, coffee, nice atmosphere.

AIRPORT

Aeropuerto Carriel Sur is 5km NW of downtown, on the road to Talcahuano.

AIRLINE OFFICES

LanChile, Barros Arana 600, ☎ 229138.
Ladeco, O'Higgins 533, ☎ 248824.

AIRPORT TRANSPORT

Minibuses (US$3) leave from Ladeco offices, or call for pickup: Turismo Ritz (☎ 237637), Airport Express (☎ 236444), Pedro Fuentes (☎ 313626). Radio Taxis (US$8): Radiotaxi Biobío, ☎ 380292.

BUS STATION AND/OR OFFICES

Terminal de Buses Puchacay is NW of town, off the highway to Chillán at Tegualda 860. Most buses use this terminal, and many have offices in town, NE of the plaza. Tur-Bus has its own terminal ('Chillancito') at Camilo Henríquez 2565, at the northeast end of Bulnes. Micros and colectivos provide frequent service to both bus stations. For the Coast del Carbón to the south, try the following companies: *Buses los Alces:* Arturo Prat 699 *Buses J Ewert*, Arturo Prat 535.

RENT A CAR

Avis, Chacabuco 726 ☎ 235837.
Budget, Chacabuco 175 ☎ 212438.
Full Fama's, O'Higgins 1154 ☎ 242385.
Retablo Rent a Car, Chaitén 8469 ☎ 410258.

TRAIN

West end of Arturo Prat. Tickets are also available at Aníbal Pinto 478, Local 3.

CONCEPCION

Battle of Iquique, the ship was captured later that same year by the Chilean navy. You must leave your passport at the gate and take a boat out to visit this wonderfully maintained vessel. Photography is allowed, but do not take photos of other Chilean naval vessels. Transport from Concepción via micros marked 'Base Naval'.

Hours: Tue-Sun 0930-1200, 1330-1800

Museo de Hualpén East of Concepción proper, on the north bank of the Biobío, this park and museum were dedicated to the city by Pedro del Río Zañartu, a wealthy businessman, whaler, farmer, nitrate baron and writer. Between 1880 and 1900, Pedro del Río traveled four times around the world, and his collection of art and artifacts displays his far-ranging interests. The house itself dates from 1885, with a central patio and glassed outdoor corridors, and the surrounding park is adorned with sculptures and winding paths. Public transport by city bus to Hualpencillo, then walk or hitch; the surrounding area is super-industrial and if you don't have a car, may not be worth it.

Hours: Tue-Sun 1000-1300, 1400-1900 (2000 in summer)

The Coast north of Concepción

TRANSPORT
Buses Línea Azul from Concepción runs as far north as Dichato.

The coast north of Concepción concentrates the city's most popular beaches. 14km north is **PENCO**, where you can check out the ruins of the 1687 La Planchada fort on the waterfront. Just beyond is the fishing village of Lirquén, locally renowned for its excellent seafood restaurants. To the north the road continues through pine plantations, passing by the Punta de Parra, a private beach to which entrance is charged, where there is a restaurant and cabins for rent. Next up is **TOMÉ** (km 34), a textile and lumber town; the best beach here is Playa El Morro, north of the rocky point past the port, with moderately priced lodging. Playa Cocholque, 4km north of town, is a better option if you want to get away from the crowds.

At km 51 is **DICHATO**, the most popular beach resort along this stretch, with lots of lodging and dining options and a free oceanic museum. Past Dichato are a few remote beaches, accessed by unsigned dirt roads; Playa Purda and Playa Merquiche are both recommended.

Dichato

Gentle waves, winds 18-23 knots, good for beginners.

The Costa del Carbón

TRANSPORT
Local buses run from Concepción as far south as Contulmo and Tirúa.

The coast south of the Río Biobío is Chile's major coal-producing area, and though the area is rather industrial there are some nice beaches and other attractions that make for good day trips.

Just across the bridge over the Biobío are two lakes, Laguna Chica San Pedro and Laguna Grande San Pedro, both recommended for swimming and watersports.

Laguna Grande San Pedro

South across the Biobío from downtown Concepción. Slalom sailing, winds 20-25 knots.

At km 30 is **CORONEL**, an important fishing and lumber port. At the south end of town is the popular Playa Blanca, with a free campground and restaurants.

At km 37 is **LOTA**, once center of Chile's coal industry; since the mines closed in April of 1997, the city has attempted to shift gears to tourism. The main attraction here is the **PARQUE DE LOTA** (open 1000-1800, and to 2000 from Nov-Mar. Entry $1600, children $1200), set on the peninsula north of the port. Designed by English landscaper Bartelet between 1862 and 1872 (and later continued by W. O'Reilly), the elegant park and its buildings were the brainchild of Isidora Goyenechea de Cousiño, wife of coal magnate Matías Cousiño – the park guides, dressed in period costumes, are known as 'Isidoras'.

The main house, begun in 1885, was destroyed during the 1960 earthquake, but the Museo de Lota, at the entrance to the park, has good displays on the coal industry and Lota's heyday. You can also take guided tours into the mines, which actually extend underneath the ocean floor.

Tours to 820m-deep Mina Chiflón del Diablo depart hourly from 1000-1700. Those to 1,500m Pique Carlos depart at 1000, 1200, 1400, and 1600.

At the far end of the península there is a lighthouse and good view over the bay.

From Lota's port, you can also catch a boat for the one-hour ride to Isla Santa María, a mellow fishing and agricultural community of about 3000, with beaches and campgrounds, hostels and good fishing, way off the tourist track.

Boats to Isla Santa María depart Tue and Sat at 1000, and return Mon and Fri at 0800; cost is $2400. Call ☎ (43)876068 or 885964 for details.

South of Lota, the paved road continues past Playa Laraquete (57km from Concepción), where you can camp for free on the beach. At 75km is the cellulose factory town of **ARAUCO**. West of here, the beaches at Caleta Llico and Punta Lavapie (107 and 118km, respectively, from Concepción) are sheltered by steep cliffs inhabited by hundreds of nesting birds.

The coast south of Arauco, traditionally inhabited by Lafquenche Indians, is now mostly owned by multinational lumber companies, and conflicts between the Indians and the *forestales* are quite common. The land rises steeply from the ocean to the peaks of the Cordillera de Nahuelbuta, where there are araucaria forests. **LEBU** (km 166 from Concepción) is a coal mining and fishing town, with big beaches and caves (Cuevas del Toro) to the north. Playa Morguila, 9km south, makes a good campsite.

143km from Concepción, **CAÑETE** was the site of important battles between the Spanish and the Mapuches. Pedro de Valdivia died in the fields beside the Río Cañete, and Mapuche cacique Caupolicán was gruesomely executed in the town's Plaza Caupolicán. 3km south is the **MUSEO MAPUCHE DE CAÑETE** *(open Mon-Sat 0930-1230 and 1400-1830, Sun 1430-1830)*, strangely housed in a concrete interpretation of the Mapuche *ruca*, but with a good collection of Mapuche jewelry, textile, musical instruments and other artifacts. There is a more authentic *ruca* behind the museum. If you have your own 4WD vehicle, you can head east from Cañete, through PN Nahuelbuta to Angol.

Further south, from the crossroads at Peleco a road leads east along the north shore of Lago Lanalhue to **MONUMENTO NACIONAL CONTULMO**, a 82há native forest reserve (camping is not permitted). The road south from Peleco continues past Lago Lleulleu to **QUIDICO**, the nicest place to stay along this stretch. This is a wild, exposed coastline, with high winds that make it a favorite with windsurfers.

Quidico

Powerful winds and the best left point in Chile.

Tirúa

A wave-sailing paradise, with winds from 25-40 knots and waves up to four meters.

Past the rather forlorn village of **TIRÚA**, the coastal road turns to gravel and continues on through pine plantations and Mapuche villages to Puerto Saavedra, passing a couple of remote beaches and a sea lion colony. About 50km offshore is **ISLA MOCHA**, an important anchorage for Spanish, English and Dutch explorers in the 16th and 17th centuries, now with just over 1,000 inhabitants. Four-person prop planes to the island depart from Cañete ($18,000 pp, ☎ (41)611179, 612290).

CAÑETE, MUSEO MAPUCHE

LOS ANGELES

TOURIST OFFICES

Municipal tourist office on south side of Plaza de Armas, on Caupolicán.

BANKS AND MONEY CHANGERS

ATM at Banco Santander, corner of Colón and Rengo. For travelers' checks, try Cultura Tours, Lautaro 164, east of the Plaza de Armas.

HOSPITAL

On Av. Ricardo Vicuña, east of Los Carrera (SE of downtown), ☎ 409720.

POST OFFICE

South side of the Plaza de Armas, on Caupolicán.

ACCOMMODATION

1 *Residencial Santa María $, Plaza de Armas.*
2 *Residencial Winser $, Colo Colo 335, ☎ 323782.*
3 *Hotel Mazzola $$, Lautaro 579, ☎ 321643.*
4 *Mariscal Alcázar $$, Lautaro 385, ☎ 311725.*
   El Rincón $, Panamericana Sur Km 494, ☎ 09-4415019.

AIRLINE OFFICES

LanChile-Ladeco, Lautaro 196, ☎ 323787.

BUS STATION AND/ OR OFFICES

Main inter-city terminal at Av. Sor Vicenta 2051, north of town, reached by micro or taxi colectivo on Villagrán. Most rural buses depart from Terminal Vega Techada, at the corner of Villagrán and Tucapel. Those to Antuco and PN Laguna del Laja depart from Terminal Santa Rosa, at the corner of Villagrán and Rengo.

Los Angeles

Pop. 94,716 (☎ city code 43)

Los Angeles dates from 1739, when it was established as a frontier post along the Mapuche-controlled Río Biobío. Its strategic location allowed the Spanish to defend both the banks of the river and the high passes to the east, home to the Pehuenche Indians.

Today, Los Angeles is an unremarkable forestry town whose greatest attraction continues to be its access to the mountains, namely Parque Nacional Laguna del Laja and the upper Biobío watershed. While you're in town you might check out the pleasant pedestrian malls on either side of the Estero Quilque.

PARQUE NACIONAL LAGUNA DEL LAJA

Around Los Angeles

Salto del Laja

This spectacular, horseshoe-shaped falls, nearly 50m high, is visible directly from the Panamerican Highway bridge over the Río Laja. There are a number of restaurants and lodging in the area, but apart from the waterfall this is just another place on the Panamericana. The Salto del Laja lies 27km north of Los Angeles, access by regular bus.

The Upper Biobío Watershed

Los Angeles provides the nearest access to the Pehuenche heartland of the Biobío valley. This is the area that will be most directly affected by the Ralco dam project. Regular buses from Santa Bárbara go as far as Trapatrapa and the Termas de Avellano. Recommended lodging in the valley at *Antukelen*, on the road to Ralco (☎ (43)326097). For access to the parks of the upper Biobío watershed, see the following chapter.

Maggi's Riding Stables

☎ (43) 371538
Located about 18km north of Los Angeles, near the El Rincón hospedaje, Maggi's offers classes and guided day trips through the *campo*. Owned by a Chilean / American couple.

Parque Nacional Laguna del Laja

This spectacularly desolate park protects some 13,200há of wild volcanic terrain along the south shore of the Laguna del Laja, just a few kilometers from the Argentine border. In addition to the lake itself – which was created spontaneously by a natural dam of lava and volcanic ash – attractions here include the perfect 2,985m cone of Volcán Antuco, a homespun ski area, views of the heavily glaciated Sierra Velluda, and hikes of varying lengths and difficulties. Flora within the park include the araucaria (found here at the northernmost limit of its range) and the Andean cypress.

Access to the park is from Los Angeles, via a road that is normally well maintained by Endesa, who operates several hydropower plants in the upper Laja watershed. Public transport, however, only goes as far as the town of El Abanico (85km from Los Angeles); from here, it's another 11km to the Conaf ranger station at **CHACAY**, where an entrance fee is collected. From Chacay, you can take a side hike to Saltos las Chilcas and El Torbellino, where the water from the lake spouts out of a sheer cliff, creating exuberant hanging gardens. The trail around the base of Volcán Antuco also begins near Chacay.

East of Chacay, a dirt road leads along the shore of the lake, passing the installations of Centro de Esquí Antuco (where lodging may be available) en route to the border station near Los Barros, at the southernmost end of the lake. Beyond here, travelers with their own vehicles can continue east across newly-opened Paso Pichachén into the Argentine province of Neuquén.

Area de Ski Antuco

From a pure skiing perspective, Antuco is the least worthwhile of the ski areas in central Chile. Its two surface lifts, reaching about a third of the way up the volcano, access mostly beginner and intermediate terrain, with snow conditions that normally turn soupy by midday, thanks to the area's northern exposure. Still, with expansive views of the Laguna del Laja and the Sierra Velluda to the east, Antuco may be worth a visit, especially if you are traveling with backcountry gear.

Río Laja

⏱2-3h
This steep, continuous Class V creek begins at El Torbellino, where crystaline water from the Laguna del Laja seeps out of a basalt cliff.

Around Volcán Antuco

⏱ ▭ ⏳ 2-3d rt,
4-5 to the glacier

Departing from Conaf's Guardería Chacay, this circumnavigation route heads due south, traversing around the bottom edge of a lava flow above the Estero Los Pangues before climbing to a 2,054m pass between the volcano and the Sierra Velluda to the SE. From here, the route continues east down the Estero El Aguado to the lake shore at Los Barros, where it intersects with the gravel road. To return, it's 23km back along the lakeshore to Chacay.

Volcán Antuco (2,965m)

⏳ 1d ▮

The ascent of Antuco normally begins at the ski area on the north side of the volcano, at 1,400m. From there, it's 4-5hrs to the summit, up slopes never steeper than 40 degrees. This is a classic ski descent, usually better earlier in the season than the volcanos further south. The view over the lake and the Sierra Velluda towards Chillán is awesome.

Angol Pop. 46,226 (☎ city code 45)

Founded in 1553 and destroyed and re-built on seven separate occasions, Angol played an important role in the Arauco war. The first church in La Araucanía, the Iglesia de Buenaventura, was built here in 1863, and some twenty years later the town sent off the last Chilean troops to march south against the Mapuche. Today, Angol's greatest attribute is its proximity to PN Nahuelbuta, and there are a couple of worthy in-town attractions for those with extra time on their hands. One is the Plaza de Armas – perhaps the prettiest and liveliest in southern Chile – and the other is the Centro Turístico El Vergel, located five km SE on Av. Bernardo O'Higgins. El Vergel features an interesting if somewhat random museum, a shady and relaxing garden, and Angol's finest place to stay, the *Hostería El Angol*.

ACCOMMODATION

Residencial Olimpia **$**, *Caupolicán 625,* ☎ *711162.*
Hostería El Angol **$$**, *in the Centro Turístico El Vergel,* ☎ *712103.*

TRANSPORT

Angol's long-distance Terminal de Buses is at the corner of Caupolicán and Chorillos. The Terminal de Buses Rurales (for buses to PN Nahuelbuta) is at the east end of Lautaro, three blocks east of the plaza.

Parque Nacional Nahuelbuta

ACCOMMODATION

Conaf campgrounds at Pehuenco and Cormallín.

TRANSPORT

Buses Angol from Angol to Vegas Blancas (7km from entrance), Sunday tours through park. If driving, 4WD is recommended in winter.

This 6,832há park is located high in the Cordillera de Nahuelbuta, an abrupt massif jutting high above the rest of the southern Coast Range. These peaks, up to 1,600m high, trap coastal rainfall to the tune of 1,000mm a year, creating a rare native forest ecosystem that combines Valdivian rainforest species with montane species, most notably the araucaria. The relative isolation of the park has furthermore transformed Nahuelbuta into a refuge for rare fauna such as the pudú deer and zorro chilote, and nearly all the classic Valdivian rainforest birds may be spotted here. These include the Slender-billed parakeet, White-throated hawk, Chilean tinamou, Patagonian tyrant, Des murs' wiretail, Ochre-flanked tapaculo, Chilean pigeon, and Magellanic woodpecker. The park administration is at PEHUENCO, 40km west of Angol.

There are only two short trails of note in the park, one leading from the visitor center to the overlook at Piedra El Aguila, the other leading north from a trailhead near the campground at Cormallín to the summit of Cerro Anay.

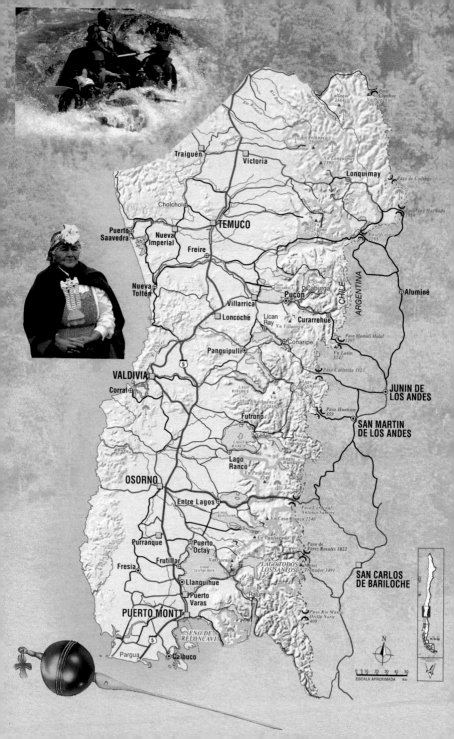

The South

La Araucanía and the Lake District

Land of volcanoes, of ancient forests and the indomitable Mapuche Indians, *el sur* – as it is known in Chile – pulls at the visitor with force that is quite nearly irresistible. What makes the south so attractive is not easy to pinpoint. Is it the warmth of the people, who invite strangers into their homes as if they were neighbors? Is it the flux and extravagance of the landscape? Is it the feeling that here people still remember that 'quality of life' is not just a question of numbers?

All these factors contribute to the singular appeal of southern Chile, as do the ease of transport, the quality of accommodations and other tourist services, and the wealth of options for active and adventurous travelers. Nowhere else in Chile – and perhaps even in South America – can you travel as safely and comfortably as you can in the south. This is the paradise of so-called 'soft adventure.'

Climb up or ski down a volcano. Raft a whitewater river. Hike up forgotten valleys to temperate rainforests and settlers' lands. Cast a dry fly to rainbows lurking in the shadows. Lounge on a black-sand beach, then share a meal and a drink with new friends. Learn about a living native culture. Soak away in a riverside hotspring, sleep in a cozy *hostería*, then get up and do it all over again. Southern Chile is one of those rare places where you really can have it all.

SOUTHERN CHILE: LA ARAUCANIA AND THE LAKE DISTRICT

GEOGRAPHY AND TOPOGRAPHY

The area described in this chapter extends from about 38°S to nearly 42°S. The northern limit is defined as those areas most easily accessed from Temuco, the so-called 'gateway' to the Lake District. The southern limits are the Canal de Chacao, which separates Chiloé from the continent, and the Río Puelo.

Chilean geographers tend to emphasize the prominence of the Central Valley, the geographic corridor separating the peaks of the Andes from those of the Coast Range. In this region, however, this division is not at all clear, for recent volcanism, glaciation, and fluvial geomorphism have fragmented the landscape into a wonderfully complex series of subranges, interconnected watersheds, and prominent river valleys extending from the Andes to the coast.

South of the abrupt peaks of the Cordillera de Nahuelbuta, the **Coast Range** is a gentle, densely forested range, crosscut by deep river valleys. In many places the range is indistinguishable from the sedimentary foothills that extend across the Central Valley west from the Andes. In the Canal de Chacao, the range disappears altogether below the Pacific, resurfacing just south on the *Gran Isla* of Chiloé.

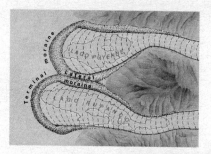

As mentioned above, the **Central Valley** would hardly feel like such if it weren't for the fact that most of the region's population is concentrated, as always, along the Panamerican highway. This pattern continues south all the way to Puerto Montt, where the Central Valley drops below sea level and the still wilder geography of Patagonia begins.

The Andes in this region are lower and broader than further north, and mountain passes to Argentina are consequently less exposed to the elements, permitting travelers to cross freely from one country to the other. Continuing a pattern begun further north, near Chillán, the highest peaks in this region are all volcanoes, arranged in a rough line west of the Argentine border. Dating mostly from the Pleistocene and the Holocene, these snowcapped and often glaciated volcanoes tower thousands of meters above the surrounding countryside. Near the southern limit of the region, around Cochamó and Puelo, granite batholiths have intruded among the volcanic peaks, forming a number of unique and singularly attractive granite domes.

Scattered along the eastern and western slopes of the Andes are over a dozen great **lakes** dating from the last round of glaciation, which ended about 10,000 years ago. Huge glaciers, flowing seaward from the peaks of the Andes, excavated great U-shaped valleys and pushed mountains of debris ahead of them; when temperatures began to rise and the glaciers receded, these mounds of debris were left as terminal moraines, behind which the water from the melting glaciers was trapped. This phenomenon is readily apparent in most of Chile's major lakes, where the west shore (the moraine) is relatively flat and regular, while to the east the lakes and their tributary rivers disappear into the mountains. In some places, such as Lago Lacar in Argentina, the terminal moraine was so high that water from the lake was actually pushed back across the Andes into Chile.

A few lakes are of more recent origin, owing their formation to 'plugs' of volcanic lava and ash that blocked the normal course of

Southern's Chile Volcanoes

LAVA IN VILLARRICA'S CRATER

As a group, southern Chile's volcanoes are the most active on the continent. Volcán Llaima, for example, has had four minor eruptions since 1994, while Volcán Villarrica has racked up a total of 61 registered eruptions since the 1600's. Climbers who ascend to Villarica's crater can observe the venting and small-scale lava flows that have continued persistently since the last major event in 1984. On the lower slopes of the volcano, you can also visit another volcanic phenomenon, the lava tube caves or *cuevas volcánicas*.

Further south, Volcán Puyehue erupted violently in 1960, triggered by a catastrophic earthquake that measured 8.9 on the Richter scale; today there are numerous fumaroles and hotsprings on the volcano's flanks. Though Volcán Osorno hasn't erupted since the mid-18th century (an event observed by Charles Darwin), fumaroles still occasionally appear on the volcano'e flanks. Nearby Volcán Calbuco has erupted twice in the past century, the last of which (1961) provoked a massive mudflow or *lahar* that actually reached the shore of Lago Llanquihue.

a river, creating a natural reservoir. These lakes – including Lago Pirihueico and Lago Todos los Santos – are the most dramatic of all, trapped deep within the Andes and flanked on either side by steep, glacially scoured cliffs.

CLIMATE AND BIOGEOGRAPHY

The climate in this region is temperate, similar in many respects to northern California and the US Pacific Northwest. From north to south, temperatures gradually drop, and rainfall increases, but wind and weather patterns from the west are strongly affected by local topography, creating a variety of different microclimates at a single latitude.

Huge quantities of **rainfall** are registered along the coast: 1,870mm a year in Valdivia, twice that of Seattle. Luckily, rain is mostly concentrated in the winter months. In this special environment of abundant rainfall and relatively constant year-round temperatures, a unique **forest environment** has evolved, known as the *Selva Valdiviana* or Valdivian Rainforest. This lowland forest is the most diverse in all of Chile and one of the most productive in the world, with a dense understory and a great variety of giant ferns and creeping vines.

Another product of this water-rich environment is the **alerce** (*Fitzroya cupressoides*), the world's second longest-lived tree, a relative of the sequoia, sacred *lahuén* to the Mapuches. Great forests of these majestic conifers once inhabited poorly drained lowlands and mountainous terrain throughout the southern Lake Region, Patagonian fjords and islands. Ruthlessly harvested and burned by European settlers, the alerce has been reduced to a few hastily organized preserves, and has been accorded the highest degree of protection possible under Chilean law.

East of the Coast Range, precipitation decreases significantly. During spells of high pressure, constant southern breezes sometimes bless the lakes with weeks on end of sunshine. Easterly winds known as *puelches* occasionally roar out of the Andes for two to three days at a time, carrying hot, dry air and assuring clear weather. During the winter, a heavy maritime influence keeps temperatures relatively high, and snowfall is rare at low elevations.

The forest in the inland valleys and foothills is less diverse than that of the coast, and with increasing elevation diversity continues to drop (the same effect occurs with increasing altitude). The dominant trees of this montane forest are of the genus *Nothofagus*, known collectively as **southern beech**. Lowland *Nothofagus* species are typically evergreen, while subalpine species are deciduous.

Inhabiting an extremely limited highlands range on both sides of the Andes, the magical-looking *pehuén* or **araucaria** tree (*Araucaria araucana*) forms pure stands or mixes with alpine *Nothofagus* species. Dating from the Jurassic era, supremely adapted to cold and snowy conditions, the araucaria is endemic to Chile and Argentina. See N for descriptions and illustrations of this and other notable species.

PREHISTORY

Southern Chile's prehistory is more poorly understood than that of areas to the north, due to a combination of factors. Increased rainfall tends to destroy material artifacts, dense forest grows over all and hides the past, and a lack of monumental constructions has discouraged archaeological glory-seekers. More importantly, the continued vitality and relevance of the Mapuche nation has concentrated studies on the south's ethnology, rather than its archaeology.

The archaeological dig at **Monte Verde**, near Puerto Montt, is a notable exception. This Paleo-Indian site is the earliest yet found in the Americas, dated at over 12,500 years of antiquity. Recent acceptance of Monte Verde's validity has radically transformed archaeologists' vision of the population of the Americas and called into question previous suppositions regarding the economy of these early Americans. See C for more information on Monte Verde and its profound impact on modern archaeology.

One thing Monte Verde proves is that the earliest inhabitants of the south were not exclusively hunters of big game. Instead, they probably made use of a wide variety of animals and plants, in a variety of ecological niches. Edible seaweed, sea lions, fish and shellfish abounded along the coast, while guanacos, huemules, and lesser fauna populated the forest and highlands. The dense rainforests yielded a cornucopia of edible and medicinal plants: the remains of 42 edible plants were found at Monte Verde, and the Mapuche Indians, thousands of years later, knew over 200 medicinal plants alone.

Artifacts from the Pitrén and El Vergel cultures (dating from around 1000 AD) provide the first evidence of ceramics and agricultural in the south. But the region's rich volcanic soils and abundant water supply eliminated the need for irrigation, terracing, or the marks of higher 'administration' that are often taken of signs of advanced native cultures. As it turned out, however, the 'failure' of southern Chile's Indians to adopt an intense, heirarchical agricultural economy saved them from the rapid conquest and servitude imposed upon native cultures throughout the Americas.

The relevance of the **Mapuche culture** goes far beyond the normally conceived sphere of anthropology. This apparently simple, mixed-economy society had no designs on an empire, and organization was mostly limited to the local level. Yet before Europe had even dreamed of America, the Mapuche language, *mapudungun*, had spread

Volcán Llaima
3060

Nevados de
Solipulli

Volcán Lanín
3807

Volcán
Quetrupillán

Volcán Villarrica
2847

The Andes as seen from Temuco

Alonso de Ercilla y Zúñiga

ESPAÑA A CHILE
ALONSO DE ERCILLA
E° 0.10 CORREO
+0.10 AEREO
CHILE

Alonso de Ercilla y Zúñiga had already visited most of the imperial domains of Charles V when he finally arrived in the New World in 1555. He was to remain eight years, seventeen months of which he spent in the south, fighting the Mapuches or *Araucanos*. Reports from his campaigns, which took him as far south as Chiloé, have him showing 'just courage and endurance' in his engagements with the Indians, though his career was not without its incidents: Ercilla was lucky to keep his head after being condemned to death by his commander, García Hurtado de Mendoza, following an altercation with fellow Spaniard.

Back in Spain in 1563, Ercilla set to writing down his experience, though he later claimed to have written it 'in the war itself and in the very steps and sites, writing many times on leather for lack of paper, and on scraps of letters, some so small that not six verses fit.' It took him six years to come out with the first version of the epic entitled *La Araucana*.

Based roughly on the Virgil's *Aeneid*, *La Araucana* features the Mapuche *toquis* Lautaro, Colo Colo, and Caupolicán in one of literature's classic representations of the

noble savage. Though Ercilla's Araucanos may not have been particularly human, they were certainly valiant, as noted in this excerpt:

They are of robust expression, beardless,
Their bodies grown to noble form,
Broad backs, powerful chests,
Strong limbs, stout nerves,
Agile, confident, and tireless,
Energetic, valiant and daring,
Hard workers and resistant
To mortal cold, hunger, and heat.

No foreign nation could claim
To have tread on its own terms upon
These liberated and independent people,
Nor any neighboring land ever dared
Move against them with swords uplifted:
They were ever free, indominable, feared,
Free of law and upstanding.

its influence throughout almost all of central and southern Chile, from the Río Aconcagua to Chiloé, from the coast to the pampa east of the Andes. Cultures with distinct origins and economies called themselves Mapuche ('people of the land,' *mapu*=land, *che*=people), while referring to other groups by the land which they inhabited. Thus the Picunche (people of the north), Pehuenche (people of the *pehuén* or araucaria tree), Puelche (people of the east), the Lafkenche (people of the coast), Tehuelche (people of the pampa), and the Huilliche (people of the south).

The Incas respectfully referred to all the mapudungun-speaking groups as 'aucas' or 'purumaucas.' In Central Chile, they found the Picunches – relatively sedentary compared to their brothers in the south – to be tolerant of *mitimae* colonists and other trappings of Tawantinsuyo. Further south this was not the case, and by all appearances, the Incas left southern Chile in peace, intimidated by the fierce, independent Mapuche warriors known as *toquis*. The Río Maule is generally accepted as the southern limit of Inca influence in Chile.

Volcán Llaima 3060
Nevados de Solipulli
Volcán Villarrica 2847
Volcán Lanín 3807
Bajos de Calafquén
Volcán Choshuenco 2415

View from cuesta Lastarria on the Panamericana

CONTACT

The Indians of the Mapuche heartland undoubtedly got notice of the arrival and activities of Pedro de Valdivia and his troops in the Santiago basin. Valdivia spent eight years

■ See pg 6 for photo credit

MACHIS WITH KULTRUN

MACHIS IN
HEALING RITUAL

building his colony in Central Chile before turning his attention to the greener fields of the south around 1550, founding eight fortified cities south of the **Río Biobío**, including Villarrica, Valdivia, Osorno, La Imperial, and Castro. The Spanish burned clearings and planted wheat around the forts, and through the latter half of the 16th century, Spain's most important settlements and agricultural holdings were concentrated south of the Biobío, while military and administrative power was concentrated in **Concepción**.

These new holdings were precarious at best. The initial terror provoked by the armored, mounted conquistadors soon gave way to open warfare, and Mapuche victories such as that of the 1553 Battle of Tucapel soon proved that the invaders could be beaten. In 1599, a general **Mapuche uprising**, sparked by the 'Disaster of Curalaba' near modern-day Angol, forced the Spanish to abandon all holdings between the Biobío and Chiloé.

The Spanish, whose power was virtually unchallenged in the greater part of the New World, were loathe to give up this paradise of rich soils and plentiful labor. During the early part of the 17th century, Jesuit priest Luis de Valdivia, acting with the King's support, tried to woo the Mapuches with politics, abolishing the *encomienda* labor system, requiring that the Indians be recompensed for their labor. Meanwhile, however, the Spanish were busy creating a standing army along the Biobío – the only such army in Spanish America apart from that of Mexico's *provincias internas*. Soon, this army began incursions into Mapuche territory, seeking to procure slaves for sale in the north.

The Mapuches, in response, evacuated the lands between the Río Biobío and the Río Toltén, seeking refuge further south. Making use of the landscape and their superior numbers, Mapuche war parties ambushed Spanish troops on their way south, inflicting grave losses and producing a level of respect granted few native cultures by their would-be conquerors. By 1640, the Spanish colony had begun to realize the ineffectiveness of the military campaign, and resorted to a series of parliaments and peace discussions with Mapuche leaders.

Meanwhile, however, another European seafaring nation was making its presence

Volcán Osorno
2652
Volcán Puntiagudo
2490
Volcán Puyehue
2111
Cerro Tronador
3460
Volcán Calbuco
2015

View across Lago Llanquihue

Bernardo Eunon Philippi and Vicente Pérez Rosales

What enticed all those 19th century Germans to pack up their lives and ship out for a piece of wilderness in southern Chile? Mostly it was a couple of adventurous and charismatic individuals, one German, one Chilean.

The first was **Bernardo Eunon Philippi (1)**, who first set foot on Chilean soil in the 1830's while sailing around the continent on a German merchant vessel. Impressed with the potential of the untamed south, he jumped ship and began a series of explorations, beginning in the Lago Llanquihue region and later continuing south to Chiloé and the Chonos archipelago. He wrote numerous reports and flyers based on his travels for publication in Germany, singing the praises of the Chilean landscape and its inhabitants. By 1946 Philippi had purchased a *fundo* in Valdivia and induced nine other families to help him homestead, including his brother Rudolfo

Amando, a notable scientist and explorer in his own right.

Having planted the seed at home, Philippi turned over the nuts and bolts of colonization to a jack-of-all-trades Chilean, **Vicente Pérez Rosales (2)**. Pérez Rosales' background could not have been more colorful: educated in Paris, abandoned in Rio while sailing with Englishman Lord Spencer, veteran of numerous enterprises including an *aguardiente* still and years of smuggling cattle between Chile and Argentina, Pérez Rosales had just returned from the California gold rush when he was charged with carrying on Philippi's labors. While Philippi headed south to oversee Chilean colonization in southern Patagonia – a labor that cost him his life at the hands of the Tehuelche Indians – Vicente Pérez Rosales was busy outfitting the thousands of Germans who arrived to make new lives in Valdivia, Puerto Montt, and Puerto Varas.

---

abundantly clear along the southern Chilean coast: **Holland**. With 60% of the planet's maritime fleet and a big headstart in cartography, the Dutch were a serious threat to the Spanish, with whom they had been at war since 1568. Moreover, the Dutch were on friendly terms with the Mapuches, whom they referred to as 'Chileans'; after sacking Castro and Carelmapu in 1643, Dutch admiral Enrique Brouwer carried 500 Mapuches north to Valdivia, helping them to escape Spanish dominion on Chiloé. Brouwer's attempt to establish a Dutch colony and strategic alliance with the Mapuches was foiled in 1645, when the Spanish refounded the city of Valdivia and established still-standing forts at nearby Corral, Niebla, and Isla Mancera.

For over a century, this tiny enclave was the only Spanish holding between the Biobío and Chiloé.

LA FRONTERA AND BEYOND

Today, it is hard to imagine a war zone in this landscape of idyllic farms, tranquil lakes and forested valleys. Yet the effects of the so-called **Arauco War** upon the culture of southern Chile and the Patagonian pampa cannot be overstated. Just over a hundred years ago, the greater portion of this territory was an independent Native American nation.

On the Spanish side, the maintenance of a standing army supplanted the demand for horses, leather, and other provisions already required by the mines in Perú and

Volcán Yate 2111   Volcán Apagado 1210   Cerros de Riñihue   Volcán Corcovado 2300

View of the Seno de Reloncaví from Chamisa, near Puerto Montt

Orelie Antoine I

Born of a humble French family, Orelie Antoine de Tounens, like many youths in the early 19th century, became enamored of travel tales and the legends of far-off America. But Orelie Antoine, as he would later be known, was different. He had a plan: to reunite the republics of Spanish America, or at least a portion thereof, under a constitutional monarchy. In other words, Orelie Antoine wanted to be king.

EL REY de la ARAUCANIA
por VICTOR DOMINGO SILVA

ZIG-ZAG

No slouch, he set off aboard ship and arrived in Valparaíso in 1858, realizing immediately that the busy central region was no place to set up a kingdom. To the south, however, the so-called 'Pacification of the Araucanía' was in full swing, as the Argentine and Chilean governments attempted to bring to heel the vast Indian-controlled region between the Río Biobío and the Strait of Magellan. Here Orelie Antoine saw his chance.

For two years, the would-be king busied himself learning Spanish, making contacts through his fellow masons and writing proclamations, decrees, even a constitution. He grew his hair and beard and began to sport a woolen Mapuche poncho, and in 1860 headed south, encouraged by the support of Mapuche *cacique* Quilapán, who had sworn to resist the Chileans to the death. Other Indian leaders, facing increasing pressure from the north and with nothing to lose, also gave their approval to the new monarchy, inciting Orelie, together with two fellow Frenchmen (who served as his cabinet) to make it official. He declared himself king, wrote personally to Chilean president Manuel Montt, and published various decrees in Valparaíso's *Mercurio* and other newspapers.

Little did Orelie suspect that his fortune was about to change. In 1862, back among his subjects, he was betrayed and captured by Chilean troops, who took him to prison in Los Angeles, for later transfer to the insane asylum in Santiago. If not for the intervention of the French consulate, Orelie Antoine's story would have ended there and then.

Instead, the deposed monarch was shipped back to France, where he set to restoring his kingdom. He set up court in Paris, minted coins, and solicited support far and wide, to the extent that the Chilean embassy had to ask the French government to intervene. Four times Orelie Antoine returned to the Araucanía, and four times he was thwarted. To the time of his death, in 1878, he continued to consider himself king.

Today, the Kingdom of Araucanía and Patagonia lives on, its court exiled in Paris. The current monarch, Prince Philippe D'Araucanie, maintains contact with Mapuche leaders and has spoken on their behalf before a United Nations Working Group on Indigenous People. Together with the North American Araucanian Royalist Society, the Kingdom continues to support the cultural integrity and autonomy of the Mapuche Nation.

Bolivia. *La Frontera* was very real and frighteningly close, for the Spanish had to worry not only about the Mapuches to the south, but also about Pehuenche warring parties descending west from the Andes. As a group, the Indians were feared and loathed, but also respected, as demonstrated by Alonso de Ercilla's *La Araucana*, a seminal depiction of the 'noble savage'. Meanwhile, the concentration of the Indian population in the southern region led to a lesser degree of *mestizaje* in Spanish Chile than in other parts of the Spanish empire – hence the more 'European' appearance of the Chilean populace.

The Mapuches, for their part, found their culture under siege together with their land. Demonstrating the resourcefulness that had elevated their culture and language to regional dominance, the Mapuches borrowed from the Spanish everything they considered useful, from apples and wheat, to silver jewelry, to livestock. The Mapuches proved able horsemen, which aided them in battle, produced greater group mobility, and precipitated the eventual migration – first of the language, then of the people themselves – into the Argentine *pampa*.

In the course of two centuries of continual warfare, the elusive Mapuche social organization proved its worth. In times of war, diverse clans fell under the leadership of a single *toqui*, facilitating strategy and logistics, and when a parliament was arranged with the Spanish, these *toquis* were authorized to make peace through whatever means they found necessary. Once peace was established, however, the authority of the *toqui* dissolved, and each clan went about its business and protected its own interests.

Beginning around 1740, the Spanish began to experience greater success in their attempts to incorporate La Araucanía into greater Chile. The tireless work of the Jesuits gradually softened Mapuche resistance to the Spanish presence, and by the early 19th century the Spanish had resurrected Osorno and secured the coastal road to Chiloé.

'PACIFICATION' AND COLONIZATION

With independence, pressure on the Mapuche homeland increased. Beginning in 1850, Bernardo Eunon Philippi and his partner Vicente Pérez Rosales loosed a tide of **German immigrants** upon the Valdivia and Lago Llanquihue regions, and in the 1880's, landless Chilean soldiers from the War of the Pacific flocked south to join the land rush.

Under the combination of demographic pressure and military pressure exerted by the Chilean and Argentine governments, the Mapuches were in dire straits. It was in this context that Orelie Antoine I arrived in southern Chile, where he proclaimed himself 'King of the Araucanía' and was welcomed by Mapuche leaders, who must have considered the rule of the eccentric Frenchman far preferable to that of newly independent Chile. By 1882, however, Orelie Antoine I was just a memory, and the Mapuches had been forced to cede land and sovereignty, and to accept property notions based on familial, rather than communal, rights.

Settlement on Lago Llanquihue

Puerto Octay
Centinela
Quilanto
Puerto Chico
BAHÍA COX
Los Bajos
Playa Maqui
Río Blanco
LAGO LLANQUIHUE
Frutillar
Punta Larga
Punta Lavas
Puerto Domeyko
Punta Oriente
Los Riscos
Ensenada
Puerto Phillippi
Punta Los Ingleses
Punta Christie
Punta del Molino
Puerto Rosales
Puerto Varas
Punta Cabras
La Fábrica
La Laja

	1852 - 1853
	1854 - 1855
	1856 - 1857
	1860 - 1870
	1870 - 1880

With the definitive incorporation of La Araucanía, the distribution and clearing of lands was swift and ruthless. By the end of the 19th century, 32,000 immigrants had arrived to occupy lands in La Araucanía, and another 5-6000 had set up shop in the Lake District. These independent settlers represented a unique demographic force, independent of the traditional landowner/inquilino relationship that characterized Central Chile.

THE TWENTIETH CENTURY

Today, the region encompassed in this chapter is composed of two administrative regions, La Araucanía and the Lake Region. **La Araucanía** remains the heart of Mapuche culture, and is home to the majority of Chile's 300,000 speakers of *mapudungun*, many of whom continue to live a traditional subsistence lifestyle; confusion regarding the titles to traditional Mapuche lands continues to generate conflicts between natives and the lumber companies that have bought up a great portion of the region's coastal forests. The **Lake Region**, and especially Valdivia and the Lago Llanquihue area, proudly display their European (mostly German) heritage, but for the most part this heritage is limited to architecture and family names. Few people speak German now.

The principal economic activities in the region are cattle, dairy, wheat, forestry, and the extraction of shellfish and seaweed from the coast. Tourism plays a growing role in the economy, providing a more sustainable alternative to an economy traditionally based on the exploitation of non-value-added natural resources. It remains to be seen how private philanthropy, education and grassroots activism can combine to raise awareness and save southern Chile's priceless forests and create a sustainable future.

Temuco

Pop. 210,587 (☎ city code 45)

Set in the broad Río Cautín basin, Temuco is the capital and commercial center of the *La Araucanía* province, and one of the fastest-growing cities in the south. Its high-rise buildings and bustling commercial district are modern manifestations of a regional importance that the valley has enjoyed for centuries: this is the very heart of Mapuche land and culture, surrounded by fertile farmland and providing rapid access to the coast and mountain valleys.

Modern Temuco was founded in 1881, during the final stages of the so-called 'Pacification' of *La Araucanía*. Once the Chilean state began the process of redistributing Mapuche lands, the city grew by leaps and bounds: by 1894 over 7000 Chilean and foreign immigrants had arrived in the area, and by 1896 rail connections to Santiago were up and running. From a traveler's perspective, Temuco is an important transportation link with a few worthwhile attractions, especially for those interested in Mapuche culture.

In-town Attractions

Mercado Municipal Temuco's municipal market, on the corner of Portales and Aldunate, is a good place to look for Mapuche handicrafts in wood, leather, ceramics, wool and silver, but finding quality goods requires a good eye and a little patience. This is also a good place to get a cheap bite to eat.
Hours: Mon-Sat 0800-1900, Sun 0830-1400

Feria Libre Four blocks east of the Mercado Municipal, on Barros Arana across from the train station, this sprawling outdoor market overflows with fruits, vegetables, and crafts brought directly from surrounding Mapuche villages. Use tact when bartering or taking photos.

Monumento Natural Cerro Ñielol

Cerro Ñielol is the prominent hill overlooking the city to the north. Though its protected status is due to the presence of the Copihue, Chile's national flower (*Lapageria rosea*, blooms Mar-July), Cerro Ñielol

---

TEMUCO

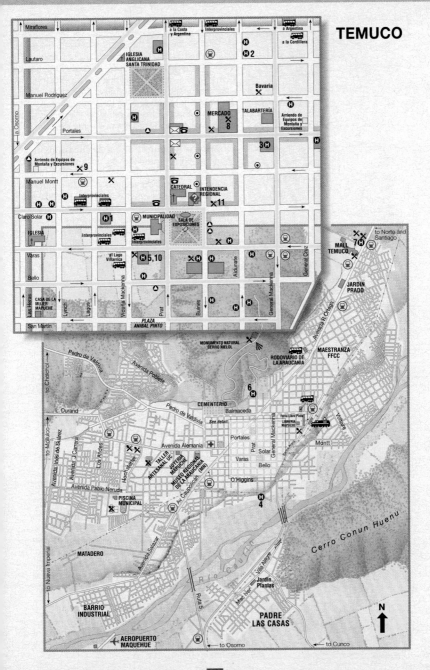

THE COAST FROM TIRUA TO MEHUIN

is best known in Chile as the site where the Mapuche leaders ceded their land, for once and for all, to the Minister of the Interior. In truth, the treaty was signed at the Chilean fort on the river, two blocks from the Plaza, but in 1956, the 'Friends of Cerro Ñielol' started circulating the myth that it was signed near the top of the hill at La Patagua, in order to promote and protect the park. An easy walk from the center, Cerro Ñielol makes for nice, shaded walking with excellent views over the city.

Hours: 0830-1900

Museo Regional de La Araucanía On Av. Alemania west of downtown, this quality regional museum focuses on the Mapuche nation before, during and after the 'Pacification' of *La Araucanía*. The crafts, historical photos, and other displays are labeled in Spanish only, but include one of the country's finest collections of Mapuche silver jewelry. Micro #1 and colectivo #11 from Av. Manuel Montt will drop you off at the museum.

Hours: Apr-Nov Tue-Sat 0900-1800, Sun 1000-1300. Dec-Mar Mon-Sat 0900-1900, Sun 1000-1300.

Around Temuco

Cholchol

29km NW of Temuco, Cholchol is a Mapuche village with a couple of demonstrative *rucas* in the center of town. This is a poor area where tradition lives on in the face of adversity, so take pains to demonstrate your respect and be sure to ask permission to take photos. Access by bus from Temuco's Terminal de Buses Rurales.

Parque Nacional Tolhuaca, Reserva Nacional Malalcahuello-Nalcas

Laguna Malleco (in RN Tolhuaca) is 127km NE of Temuco via Curacautín. Malalcahuello is 114km from Temuco, also via Curacautín. Access by bus from the Terminal de Buses Rurales. See 📖.

Parque Nacional Conguillío

Centro de Ski Las Araucarias is 82km east of Temuco. Lago Conguillío is 124km east of Temuco via Curacautín, 119km via Melipeuco. The ski area provides transport to Las Araucarias. Transport to Curacautín by bus from the Terminal de Buses Rurales. See 📖.

The Upper Biobío Watershed

Lonquimay is 139km NE of Temuco, via Curacautín. Access by bus from the Terminal de Buses Rurales to Lonquimay, and from there by local bus to Icalma. See 📖.

The Coast from Puerto Saavedra to Valdivia

This abrupt coastline is largely populated by Lafquenche Indians, who live from the recollection of the elongate edible seaweed known as *cochayuyo*. However, most of the land is in the hands of large lumber companies, and the hills are now covered with Monterrey pine instead of Valdivian Rainforest. Conflicts between the natives and the lumber companies are common.

ACCOMMODATION

Campgrounds, hospedajes at Balneario Maule (Puerto Saavedra), Boca Budi, and between Queule and Mehuín; hospedaje in Nueva Tolten. Hosterías, hotels in Boca Budi and Mehuín.

TRANSPORT

To Puerto Saavedra, by bus from the Terminal de Buses Rurales in Temuco. From here, rural buses as far south as Boca Budi only. To Mehuín, by rural bus from San José de la Mariquina.

Near the mouth of the Río Imperial, **PUERTO SAAVEDRA** provides transportation links north towards Tirúa (described in the Central Chile chapter under Concepción) and south to the enormous, exposed beach at **BOCA BUDI**. Inland of Boca Budi is the brackish Lago Budi, home to some 134 species of birds; a ferry crosses the outlet river to Isla Huapi, where local Mapuche families operate the *Centro Turístico Etnico de Puaucho*, an ethnic tourism project. Boats crossing the lake also depart from the ferry crossing.

South of here, the route continues further inland via Nueva Toltén to the beaches at Queule, Playa Cheuque, Pichicullín, and Mehuín. There is a sea lion colony near Queule, while the beach at **MEHUÍN** stands out for its dramatic sea stacks. All of these beaches have campgrounds and a passable variety of accommodation.

Parque Nacional Tolhuaca   See map

PRACTICAL INFORMATION / ACCOMMODATION

Conaf ranger station, campground at the SE corner of Laguna Malleco. Hotel, cabañas, camping at the Termas de Tolhuaca; cheaper at Hostal Suizandino, 27km east of Curacautín.

TRANSPORT

No public transport directly to the park. Buses from Victoria to San Gregorio, 20km west of Laguna Malleco. Taxi colectivos from Curacautín to Termas de Tolhuaca, 10km from Laguna Malleco via a 4WD road. For information on road conditions, contact Carabineros in Curacautín or Victoria.

Set in the forested precordillera along the north shore of the Río Malleco, this relatively small (6,374há) park contains some of the finest hiking in the northern Araucanía, and its relatively difficult access keeps the park uncrowded even when nearby Parque Nacional Conguillío is bursting at the seams. With its abundant araucaria forests, scattered lakes, waterfalls and overlooks, Tolhuaca easily merits a few days' visit, especially for those traveling with bikes or their own vehicles.

If driving, the easiest access is direct from the Panamericana via a gravel road leading east from Inspector Fernández, a tiny village just north of Victoria. Otherwise, public transport will get you closer if you head for Curacautín and catch a *colectivo* to the **TERMAS DE TOLHUACA**, though the road from here to the park is apt for 4WD vehicles only. Either way, you'll want to head to the park administration and campground at **INALAUFQUÉN**, located at the SE corner of

Laguna Malleco, a shallow, marshy lake teeming with birdlife. This makes a good base from which to explore the park.

Termas de Tolhuaca

 ☎ (45)881211 🏠thermal pool $6,000, tubs $3,000
This century-old hotspring resort on the edge of PN Tolhuaca features natural pools along the river, a large common pool, individual tubs, mud baths, massage and respiratory treatments. There is a hotel, cabañas and a campground on the premises, and horses are available for rent. The springwater emerges from a steam-filled cave upstream of the pools, which have an average temp of 30-35°C.

Short hikes in PN Tolhuaca

✧ ⌚1-2d
From the administration, a well-trodden trail leads around to the northern side of the lake, where trails branch north to the Prados de Mesacura and Lagunillas, each a full-day hike. For an easier walk, continue west along the shore of the lake to the Salto del Malleco, a spectacular 50m waterfall. The park's best overnight hike leads east along the Río Malleco and up to Laguna Verde, a tiny alpine lake set at 1,300m in the eastern portion of the park. This trail may also be accessed from a trailhead located 5km west of the Termas de Tolhuaca on the park access road.

Volcán Tolhuaca (2,806m)

⏱ 5-7h rt ▮

From a camp on the shore of Laguna Blanca (accessed via a gravel road branching north from the village of La Sombra, 6km east of Curacautín), climb to the saddle between Tolhuaca and Volcán Lonquimay. From there, continue up the volcano's east face, following a line to the right of some obvious cliffs. Beware of crevasses in the snow-filled inactive crater. This is a relatively easy but nonetheless infrequent ascent.

Curacautín

See map 📍

Curacautín may well claim the prize for having more one-way streets than any other town its size in Chile, which is strange considering the utter lack of traffic. Perhaps – one has to imagine – city planners foresee a brighter future for Curacautín, which provides direct access to a wonderful array of parks, hotsprings, volcanoes, and hiking and biking routes.

Recommended lodging in town includes the *Hotel Turismo* and *Hospedaje Tolosa*, and just east of town on the road to Lonquimay are two dramatic waterfalls, the Salto del Indio (14km) and the Salto de la Princesa (22km). Curacautín's Terminal de Buses is at the corner of Yungay and Rodríguez, on the main highway to Lonquimay.

Termas de Manzanar

☎ (45)881200 🏠 $2,000, private tubs $3,000

Located 18km east of Curacautín, this hotsprings hotel features a common pool and private indoor tubs along the Río Cautín, with a spring temp. of 48°C.

Reserva Nacional Malalcahuello-Nalcas

See map 📍

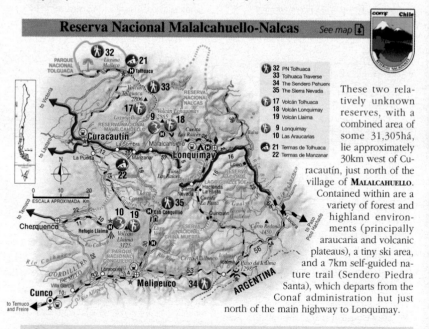

🥾 32	PN Tolhuaca
33	Tolhuaca Traverse
34	The Sendero Pehuenche
35	The Sierra Nevada
🥾 17	Volcán Tolhuaca
18	Volcán Lonquimay
19	Volcán Llaima
🏠 9	Lonquimay
10	Las Araucarias
♨ 21	Termas de Tolhuaca
22	Termas de Manzanar

These two relatively unknown reserves, with a combined area of some 31,305há, lie approximately 30km west of Curacautín, just north of the village of **MALALCAHUELLO**. Contained within are a variety of forest and highland environments (principally araucaria and volcanic plateaus), a tiny ski area, and a 7km self-guided nature trail (Sendero Piedra Santa), which departs from the Conaf administration hut just north of the main highway to Lonquimay.

Just a few kilometers east of the administration, a gravel road branches off to the north, providing access to the Centro de Ski Lonquimay (4km, take the left fork) and the spectacular Cuesta Las Raíces (26km to Lonquimay, take the right fork). The road to the ski area continues north past Crater Navidad (which erupted in 1988) and down into the Upper Biobío watershed.

Tolhuaca Traverse

🥾 ⏱3-5d ▢
This remote traverse connects the town of Malalcahuello with the Termas de Tolhuaca. Best done from south to north (concluding at the Termas), the route leads along the southern flank of Volcán Lonquimay to Laguna Blanca, over a pass to the NE, and from there along the north flank of Volcán Tolhuaca to the Termas. Careful routefinding is required in the

latter part of this unmarked route; ask in Malalcahuello for guides (Pepe Córdoba recommended) and/or horses.

Centro de Esquí Lonquimay

The 'resort' itself at Lonquimay is nothing to get excited about: basically it consists of a couple of surface lifts that whisk skiers up for a whopping 200m of vertical. If you're a true beginner, you can have a fine time here, but otherwise you're better off forgetting about the lifts altogether, putting your skis on your pack, and heading for the summit. The south face of Lonquimay, accessed by a near-continuous ridge from the top of the lifts, leads directly to the 2,865m summit crater and provides a solid 1,400m of 35-45° skiing. All told, the route takes about 5-7 hrs round-trip. Below the lifts, near the limit of a pure araucaria forest, is a charming, friendly refugio that sells hot meals.
Operators: 193 - 207

The Upper Biobío Watershed *See map* 🔳

The upper Biobío watershed is the most traditional indigenous culture area in southern Chile. Here, in a complex of remote valleys tucked away to the east of the Andes, live the last intact communities of Pehuenche Indians. Today, the Pehuenche homelands and way of life are seriously threatened by hydroelectric development on the Biobío.

If you have your own transportation, you can access the upper Biobío any of several ways. If using public transport, however, your only choice is to come via Curacautín and the TÚNEL LAS RAÍCES, which at over four and a half kilometers is the longest tunnel in South America. Once through the tunnel, you'll begin the descent into the broad, open Biobío valley. At approximately 50km from Curacautín is a gravel road on the right leading to LAGUNA GALLETUÉ and LAGUNA ICALMA, the former of which is considered the source of the

Biobío. There are campgrounds and simple accommodations on the south shores of both lakes, which may be accessed by infrequent rural buses from Lonquimay. Laguna Icalma is the starting point for the nascent Sendero Pehuenche ecotourism project.

LONQUIMAY, 63km east of Curacautín via Túnel Las Raíces, is the largest town in the Alto Biobío, and contains the best selection of lodging in the region; *Hotel de Turismo* and *Hostería El Pehuén* are both recommended choices. From here you can continue SE to the border post at Liucura (41km) and on to PASO PINO HACHADO (63km) and the Argentine province of Neuquén. Note that most international buses fill up in Temuco, so it may be necessary to purchase tickets in advance.

The Sendero Pehuenche

🥾 ⏱5-7d ▢
Leading through traditional Pehuenche Indian lands from Laguna Icalma to Reigolil, this route is currently being developed as one of precious few true eco-tourism projects in Chile. Consult with Hosteria Ecole for details on this and other native-guided treks.
Operators: 90

Multi-Day Bike Tours in Southern Chile

a) ▶215km◀ ⏱6d P D ☐
Lautaro (0km) – Curacautín (54km) – Lago Conguillío (40km) – Melipueco (30km) – Cunco (32km) – Temuco (59km)

b) ▶310km◀ ⏱8d P D ☐
Lautaro (0km) – Curacautín (54km) – Lonquimay (via Cuesta Las Raíces 59km) – Laguna Galletué (38km) – Laguna Icalma (15km) – Melipueco (53km) – Cunco (32km) – Temuco (59km).

c) ▶332km◀ ⏱9d P D ☐
Lautaro (0km) – Curacautín (54km) – Lonquimay (via Cuesta Las Raíces 59km) – Liucura (41km) – Laguna Icalma (34km) – Melipueco (53km) – Cunco (32km) – Temuco (59km).
Operators: 164

2. Around Pucón
See pg. 454 for details.

3. The Siete Lagos
▶131km◀ ⏱4-5d P D ☐

This is among the steepest, most challenging multi-day rides in this book, with bad roads and several serious passes. This means slow going (and probably lots of walking), but the scenery is truly spectacular in this lush, remote corner of the Lake District. The route is described in a clockwise fashion from Lican Ray, though numerous options are possible, including crossings to Argentina from Liquine or Puerto Fuy, and direct access from Pucón via PN Villarrica (above).

Lican Ray (0km) – Coñaripe (21km) – Liquiñe (28km) – Lago Neltume (21km) – Choshuenco (13km) – Panguipulli (48km).

4. Around Lago Llanquihue
▶152km◀ ⏱4d P D ☐

This route circles the largest lake in the Lake District, passing through the remote lava fields and forests at the foot of Volcán Osorno, and concluding with the rolling countryside and German-founded villages of Puerto Octay and Frutillar. To avoid traffic, opt for the dirt roads along the lakeside instead of the main highways.

Puerto Varas (0) - Ensenada (46km) - Las Cascadas (22km) - Puerto Octay (22km) - Frutillar (36km) - Puerto Varas (26km).
Operators: 101 - 164 - 205

5. Volcán Osorno Downhill
See pg. 489 for details.

1. The northern Araucanía
▶215-330km◀ ⏱6-10d P D ☐

Typically overlooked by travelers bent on Pucón and the Lake District, this traditional Mapuche/Pehuenche culture area is makes for excellent multi-day loops on roads with relatively little traffic. The paved route through from Lautaro to Curacautín and Lonquimay is the principal axis; from here you can choose from 3 separate gravel roads leading south either through PN Conguillío or (for a longer route) the Alto Biobío, returning via Melipueco.

6. The Estuario de Reloncaví
▶203km◀ ⏱5d P D ▪

This spectacular loop begins along the shores of Lago Llanquihue and continues south along the steep Estuario de Reloncaví fjord. From the village of Puelo, a new road along the south shore of the fjord leads to Caleta Puelche, from which point ferries cross the mouth of the fjord north to La Arena and the road to Puerto Montt. Long-haul riders can continue south down the Carretera Austral towards Hornopirén.

Puerto Varas (0) – Ensenada (46) – Ralún (33km) – Cochamó (15km) – Puelo (29.5km) – Caleta Puelche (35km) – La Arena (ferry) – Puerto Montt (45km).

Operators: 205

> **Bike Rentals:**
> • Villarrica
>   La Torre Suiza ☎ 411213
> • Pucón
>   Operators: 12 - 172 - 222
> • Puerto Varas
>   Operator: 26

OVERLANDS AND CIRCUITS IN SOUTHERN CHILE

1. Backroads tour of La Araucanía
⏱4-6d

Our top choice for road trips in the south. In 4-5 days you can see the whole of the Araucanía district without even coming near the Panamericana. The route indicated is for normal passenger vehicles, but with high clearance / 4WD you can also check out the protected areas in the Upper Biobío watershed, take the seldom-traveled back entrance to Pucón (via Lago Colico and Reigolil), or continue south to the Siete Lagos via the spectacular (and nearly impassable) road through Palguín and PN Villarrica. An even better option would be an integrated loop through Argentina, via Paso Pino Hachado and/or Paso Mamuil Malal.

Operators: 93 - 152

2. The Siete Lagos
⏱2-3d

Bad roads, steep passes, and some of the lushest, least-visited landscapes in the Lake District. Traveling in your own vehicle will allow you to stop off at the Salto de Huilo Huilo or head up to Volcán Choshuenco. If you take the ferry across Lago Pirihueico to Paso Hua Hum, you can continue into the Argentine Seven Lakes district and loop back into Chile via another pass.

3. Osorno to Bariloche
⏱1d

This entirely paved international highway shows you a classic cross-section of the Andes, from the lush farmlands around Lago Puyehue, through the evergreen and deciduous forests of PN Puyehue, over the Andes and down into the cypress forests of Argentina's PN Nahuel Huapi, near Bariloche. With your own vehicle, you can easily stretch this trip to 3-4 days or more, camping in the parks on either side of the pass. This is an ideal route in winter, as it connects some of the best ski areas in southern Chile and Argentina.

4. Around Lago Llanquihue
⏱2d

No problems with navigation here - just keep the lake on one side and you can't get lost. The route is paved for all but a 22km section between Ensenada and Las Cascadas, where it passes through lava flows and native forests; otherwise the landscape consists mostly rolling farmland with plenty of lodging, camping, beaches and fishing streams. This makes for a great, inexpensive 2-3 day trip from Puerto Montt, with stops at attractions ranging from the Saltos de Petrohué and Volcán Osorno (make the detour to La Burbuja for views), to the charming Germanesque villages of Puerto Octay and Frutillar.

Operators: 192 - 201

5. The Estuario de Reloncaví
⏱3-4d

This route either makes a wonderfully varied loop or a highly scenic alternative to the northernmost portion of the Carretera Austral. Great fishing and access to some of the finest hiking in the Lake Region puts this route near the very top of our list – it's like a quick glimpse of Patagonia. Most of this road is dirt, but passable in a normal vehicle, and the ferry across the mouth of the Estuario de Reloncaví provides continuous service throughout the day. Ensenada, Ralún, and Cochamó are the best places to stay along this loop.

> Operators offering integrated circuits in the Chilean and Argentine Lake Districts:
> Operators: 10 - 84

Parque Nacional Conguillío

See map 🔼

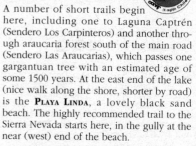

PRACTICAL INFORMATION
Slide shows, lectures, information on flora and fauna, etc, at Conaf's Centro de Información Ambiental on south shore of Laguna Conguillío. For information on road conditions, contact Carabineros in Curacautín or Melipeuco.

TRANSPORT
Summer-only buses from Curacautín to Laguna Captrén; otherwise by taxi from Curacautín or Melipeuco. No public transport directly to sector Los Paraguas, though frequent buses from Temuco go to Cherquenco, 17km west of the ski area.

ACCOMMODATION
Lodging on the west side of the volcano at Centro de Ski Las Araucarias, or at nearby cabañas. Several Conaf campgrounds along south shore of Lago Conguillío, with hot showers, reservations recommended in season. Cabañas in the park at Los Ñirres and La Baita; outside the park at Río Colorado, on the road from Curacautín, as well as in Curacautín and Melipeuco (Hostería Hue Telen recommended). Backcountry camping is not allowed in the park.

Conguillío has long been recognized by Chileans as one of the most spectacular, diverse and representative parks in the south, but many foreign tourists bypass the area in their haste to get to Pucón or Puerto Varas. The park protects 60,800há of rapidly evolving volcanic terrain, alpine lakes, and ancient southern beech and araucaria forests – in any season, a majestic, almost unreal landscape.

3,125m Volcán Llaima dominates the park and divides it in terms of access. On the west side is CENTRO DE SKI LAS ARAUCARIAS (also known as Los Paraguas), with a variety of lodging set in a sector of pure araucaria forest. There is also excellent nearby accommodation at *Cabañas El Gringo*, whose German owner organizes orienteering competitions, horseback riding, mountain biking, and visits to ice caves on the upper slopes of the volcano.

To the north and east of the volcano is a broad volcanic plateau, which may be divided into northern and southern sectors, each comprising a separate watershed.

The northern sector of the park centers around LAGO CONGUILLÍO and LAGUNA CAPTRÉN, which are drained by the north-flowing Río Captrén. The northern entrance to the park is at Laguna Captrén, where there is a campground and trailhead for the trek around the volcano to Las Araucarias. Six km east is Lago Conguillío, where you'll find the park administration, an excellent environmental information center, and some overpriced lakeside cabañas and campgrounds (there are also a limited number of backpacker sites).

A number of short trails begin here, including one to Laguna Captrén (Sendero Los Carpinteros) and another through araucaria forest south of the main road (Sendero Las Araucarias), which passes one gargantuan tree with an estimated age of some 1500 years. At the east end of the lake (nice walk along the shore, shorter by road) is the **PLAYA LINDA**, a lovely black sand beach. The highly recommended trail to the Sierra Nevada starts here, in the gully at the near (west) end of the beach.

In the southern sector of the park, Lago Verde and Lago Arco Iris are drained by the Río Quetruleufu, an affluent of the Río Allipén. This is an awe-inspiring wasteland, heavily modified by Llaima's frequent eruptions: Laguna Arco Iris was formed by a lava dam in 1994, and the park road runs right between the lava fields and the forest that was saved by a hair. At Lago Verde, there is a short trail leads to the beach at La Ensenada, and near the southern entrance to the park is another trail leading to the Salto Truful Truful, a thundering waterfall in a canyon with vivid geological strata. Believe it or not, the waterfall has been run in a kayak.

Centro de Esquí Las Araucarias

Lift infrastructure at Las Araucarias is currently limited to two poma lifts accessing 300m of vertical, but plans are under way to install two new chairlifts, bringing uphill capacity up to speed with the area's impressive lodging capacity of nearly 400 beds. In fact, Las Araucarias probably boasts the best variety of on-mountain accommodation of any area in the south, with furnished 6-person apartments for rent and a very affordable shared-bath refugio (for which you'll need your own sleeping bag).

The lift-served terrain is appropriate mostly for beginning and intermediate skiers. Expert skiers will want to tackle Llaima's summit 🔼.

Volcán Llaima (3,125m)

⏱ 5-7h rt ▯ ▮

One of the classic backcountry ski descents in the region. The standard route begins at the ski area on the west side, while a longer ascent (10hrs rt) may be made from the east side of the peak; consult at *La Baita* for details.

Operators: 131 - 207

The Sierra Nevada

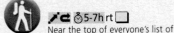

⏱ 5-7h rt ☐

Near the top of everyone's list of short hikes in the Araucania, the Sierra Nevada trail departs from Playa Linda, at the SE corner of Lago Conguillío. The trail climbs the steep ridge above the lake through magnificent stands of coigüe, entering a pure araucaria forest near treeline, with otherworldly views of Volcán Llaima. From here, you can continue up towards the glaciated peaks of the Sierra Nevada, or trend north and cross the Sierra Nevada to the Termas de Río Blanco for a challenging, unmarked 2-3 day trip, involving a short glacier crossing. Camping is prohibited in the backcountry.

Operators: 131 🐎 - 152 - 193

Villarrica

Pop. 22,608 (☎ city code 45)

Villarrica's regular grid of streets lies on the SW shore of Lago Villarrica, just south of the Río Toltén. The town is popular with vacationing Chileans, many of whom stock up here while staying at one of the many lakeside cabañas and campgrounds along the road east to Pucón. Most foreign travelers skip Villarrica altogether and head straight for Pucón.

Though you'd hardly guess it, the town dates from 1552, when Gerónimo de Alderete founded a fort here to facilitate the exploitation of gold placer mines in the Andes and secure a route across the Andes to the *pampa*. Some 600 Spaniards were living here in 1598, when the fort was laid siege by the Mapuches; for three years, the Spanish held out while their numbers gradually but surely declined, through starvation and incorporation into the surrounding Mapuche community. By 1602, only 11 men and 13 women remained in the last Spanish fort standing between the Biobío and Castro.

Over 280 years later, in 1883, the last Parliament between Mapuche *toquis* and the Chilean government was held here, and the following day – as the Mapuches were relegated to *reducciones* in the hinterlands – the city was refounded and land distributed to settlers. It wasn't long before tourists began to arrive from the north, traveling by train to Freire and continuing to Villarrica by horseback. By 1933 the train arrived directly to the lakeshore, and steamships provided regular service to the new hotels in Pucón.

In-town Attractions

The Waterfront Though the beaches are much nicer in Pucón and along the Villarrica-Pucón road, you can rent boats at the *muelle* (pier) off General Körner or at the east end of José Manuel Balmaceda, where locals offers float/fishing trips down the Río Toltén.

Mapuche Museum On the east side of Pedro de Valdivia between Julio Zegers and Aviador Acevedo.

Hours: Museum open Dec-Mar/ Mon-Sat 0900-1300, 1800-2200, Sun 1800-2200. Apr-Nov /Mon-Fri 0900-1300, 1500-1900.

TOURIST OFFICES

Oficina Municipal de Turismo, near the corner of Pedro de Valdivia and Aviador Acevedo.

BANKS AND MONEY CHANGERS

ATMs, banks, money changers on Av. Pedro de Valdivia.

HOSPITAL

Corner of San Martín and Manuel Antonio Matta, ☎ 411169.

POST OFFICE

Corner of Urrutia and Anfión Muñoz.

INTERNET CONNECTION

La Torre Suiza, Fco. Bilbao 969.

ACCOMMODATION

1 Residencial Villanueva $, Pedro de Valdivia 678, ☎ 411392.
2 La Torre Suiza $, Francisco Bilbao 969, ☎ 411213.

3 Hostería Rayhuén $$, Pedro Montt 668, ☎ 411452.
4 Hostería Dieggo's $$, Alderete 709, ☎ 411370.
5 Hostería de La Colina $$$, Presidente Ríos 1177, ☎ 411503.
6 Hostería Kiel $$$, Körner 153, ☎ 411631.
7 Hostería Huequimey $$$, Letelier 1030-B, ☎ 411462.
More info at www.turistel.cl

CAMPING

8 Many cabañas and camprounds along the Villarrica-Pucón road, closest are Los Castaños and Dulac, both 2km east.

RESTAURANTS

9 The Travellers, Letelier 753. Friendly, daily happy hours.
10 Café Bar 2001, Henríquez 379. Sandwiches, sweets.
11 El Rey del Marisco, Letelier 1030. Seafood.

BUS STATION AND/OR OFFICES

Tur-Bus and Buses Jac are right acros the street from each other at the corner of Bulnes and Anfión Muñoz.
For buses to Argentina, Buses San Martín is at Anfión Muñoz 634.

SHOPPING

Villarrica is a good place to pick up Mapuche crafts, most notably silverwork and carvings in raulí. Try the feria artesanal at the west end of Gerónimo de Alderete, and at the Muestra Cultural Mapuche, at the corner of Pedro de Valdivia and Julio Zegers. There are also a number of shops east of here on General Körner. If you walk around the downtown area you will find a bunch of smaller artisan's markets, but the selection is pretty similar all over.

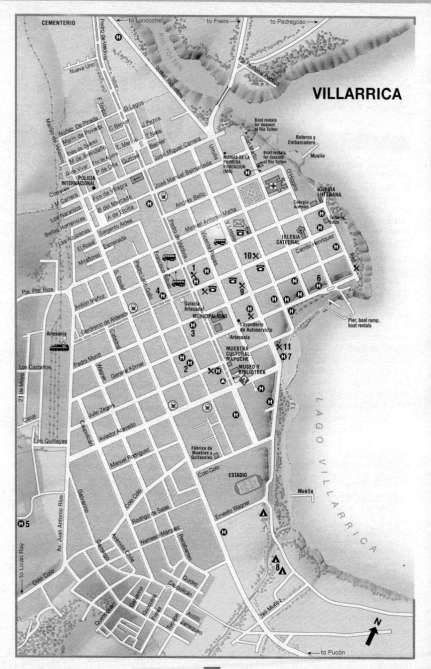

CEMENTERIO

to Loncoche →   ← to Freire →   ← to Pedregoso →

RIO TOLTEN

VILLARRICA

Pedro de Valdivia

Nueva Uno

Mariño de Velasco

F. Tábago

Núñez De Pineda

Marín de Poveda

D Lagos

C Becker

J Pezoa

Inas de Suárez

T Ness

Mi de Avendaño

Becker

S. de Vivar

Fco de Aguirre

S. Merino

Sguttner

F. de Oña

José Miguel Carrera

POLICIA INTERNACIONAL

Claveles

J M Carrera

Fco de Villagra

José Manuel Balmaceda

Los Naranjos

B. del Mercado

Bellas, Hortensias

A de Ercilla

Andrés Bello

Las Azucenas

Sargento Aldea

I. J.

El Rosal

Esmeralda

MiraFlores

S Epulef

Pedro León Gallo

Francisco

Antión Muñoz

Pje. Pte. Ríos

Gerónimo de Alderete

Catedral

Artesanía

Pedro Montt

Wagner

General Körner

Los Castaños

Julio Zegers

Chapulican

21 de Mayo

Aviador Acevedo

Qanal

Los Quillayes

Manuel Rodríguez

Colo Colo

H 5

Av. Juan Antonio Ríos

Galvarino

Garbanzo

Chapulican

Colo Colo

Rodrigo de Salas

Avenida Chile

Nemesio Márquez

Recabarren

to Lican Ray →

Quebeqkem

Guacolda

Fresia

Huinca

Antifil

Quidez

Caupolicán

Ianequeo

RIO TOLTEN

Pje. Peatonal Futrono

Boat rentals for descent of Río Tolten

Boteros y Embarcadero

Muelle

San Martín

Urrutia

RUINAS DE LA PRIMERA FUNDACION (MN)

Boat rentals for descent of Río Tolten

O'Higgins

Colegio Alemán

IGLESIA LUTERANA

Tintorería Suiza

Camilo Henríquez

Prat

IGLESIA CATEDRAL

Manuel Antonio Matta

Vicente Reyes

V. Letelier

10 ✕

1 ✕

4

9 ✕

6

Galería Artesanal

MUNICIPALIDAD

3

Lavandería de Autoservicio

Artesanía

Pier, boat ramp, boat rentals

MUESTRA CULTURAL MAPUCHE

11 ✕

H 7

MUSEO Y BIBLIOTECA

2 ✕

Fábrica de Muebles y Quitasoles

Colo Colo

ESTADIO

Muelle

Ernesto Wagner

8

Yali Muñoz

L A G O V I L L A R R I C A

N

to Pucón →

Around Villarrica

The South Shore of Lago Villarrica

The 25km paved route along the south shore of Lago Villarrica is crammed with cabañas, campgrounds, hosterías and private homes. If you want to camp, you're probably better off right in Pucón, but if you're looking for a waterfront cabaña this is probably your best choice; recommended option include *Altos del Lago* (14 km from Villarrica) and the more upscale *Almoni del Lago* (19km). . If you do stay here, you'll probably want to have access to a car or bike, though in a pinch you can get by with the frequent *micros* (daytime only) that run between Villarrica and Pucón.

Parque Nacional Villarrica

The entrance to sector Rucapillán is 33km east of Villarrica. Transport to the park by tour only (more easily arranged in Pucón), 🔁.

The Siete Lagos

Lican Ray is 30km south. Transport by regular bus, 🔁.

Pucón

Pop. 8,023 (☎ city code 45)

Set between the lower slopes of Volcán Villarrica and the beaches of Lago Villarrica, Pucón is a unique phenomenon among towns in southern Chile. Or perhaps more accurately, it is a place where several different phenomena have converged, for the town is at once the epicenter of southern Chile's real estate boom, the top summer vacation spot for Santiago's newly-rich *cuicos*, a focal point of the national and international environmental community, and one of the most diverse, spectacular, and increasingly chaotic adventure travel destinations anywhere. Most visitors feel strongly about it, one way or another.

The town was 'settled' by Chilean troops in 1883, soon after the refoundation of Villarrica. A fort on the site of the modern plaza served to secure Chilean sovereignty over the mountain passes to east, particularly Paso Mamuil Malal, today the site of a major pass to Argentina. The Mapuche Indians, whose tongue-twister names grace all the local landforms, were granted lands in the spectacular Quelhue hills that dominate the eastern horizon, and further afield in Palguín and Curarrehue.

In the early 20th century, artists and intellectuals from Santiago began to frequent Pucón, starting the town on the path to tourism. In 1923 the town had its first hotel, and by 1934, the Gran Hotel Pucón – complete with a golf course – had established Pucón's primacy in the south. The real boom, however, has come only in the last 10 years or so. These days, what in winter is a sleepy town of 8,000 swells during the summer months (February in particular) to a hive of 70,000 Chilean and foreign tourists.

Luckily, you have plenty of options; if you want, you can mix with the crowds on the beach, in the bars and the discotheques, or you can go to bed early and blaze out of town every morning for a new destination. With two national parks, one private reserve, a handful of volcanoes and more hotsprings than you can count in the surrounding area, there's no reason that you have to see *anybody*. Most folks find a happy medium, make new friends and end up staying longer than they'd planned. The shoulder seasons (Oct-Dec and Mar-Apr) are especially good times to visit, with great weather and a more relaxed atmosphere. It should be further noted that no guidebook could possibly keep up with the rapid-fire appearance (and disappearance) of adventure travel outfits and other services in Pucón.

In-town Attractions

La Península Currently owned by a private condominium development and golf course, La Península is a tongue of lava from an old eruption of Volcán Villarrica. Unfortunately (some would say illegally) public access to La Península is not allowed, but the shoreline is public domain. From the west end of the Playa Grande, you can walk out along the shore for great views and swimming off the rocks.

Playa Grande Pucón's black-sand beach extends 4km east from La Península to the Río Pucón Delta (described below). Composed of relatively coarse black volcanic sand, the beach is the focus of in-town activity during the summer months. There are

TOURIST OFFICES
Private **Cámara de Turismo** near the west entrance to town, at Calle Brasil and Caupolicán.
Conaf is next to the post office at the corner of Gerónimo de Alderete and Fresia.

BANKS AND MONEY CHANGERS
ATMs in the Eltit grocery store on O'Higgins, at the corner of Gerónimo de Alderete and Lincoyán, and several other locations. Casas de cambio on O'Higgins, but rates are not good. Many tour operators and hotels also accept dollars.

HOSPITAL
On Uruguay between Fresia and Ansorena, ☎ 441177.

LANGUAGE SCHOOLS
Spanish programs, with or without lodging, available through **Hostería Ecole** and **La Casita** (see Accommodation listings for contact info).

POST OFFICE
Corner of Fresia and Alderete.

INTERNET CONNECTION
Brinck House, Ansorena 243.
La Casita, Palguín 555.
Café Trancura, Palguín and O'Higgins.

ACCOMMODATION
1 *Hostería Ecole* $, General Urrutia 592, ☎ 441675.
2 *Hospedaje La Casita* $, Palguín 555, ☎ 442712.
3 *Hospedaje Sonia* $, Lincoyán 485, ☎ 441269.
4 *La Tetera* $, General Urrutia 580, ☎ 441462.
5 *Hotel Gudenschwager* $$, P. de Valdivia 12, ☎ 441156.
6 *Hotel Araucarias* $$, Caupolicán 243, ☎ 441286.
7 *Gran Hotel Pucón* $$$, Holzapfel 190, ☎ 441001.
8 *Hotel Antumalal* $$$, Camino Villarrica-Pucón, ☎ 441013.
9 *Hotel del Lago* $$$, Ansorena 23, ☎ 441873.
Cabañas Altos del Lago $$$, Km 14 Camino Villarrica-Pucón, ☎fax 450022 - 450261.
More info at www.turistel.cl

CAMPING
10 *La Poza*, off Costanera Roberto Geiss, ☎ 441435. Shady sites, popular, close to town.
11 *Nature*, at the east end of O'Higgins, ☎ 443081. Israeli-run, excursions.

RESTAURANTS
12 *Hostería Ecole*, General Urrutia 592. Vegetarian food, good breakfast, real coffee.
13 *Trancura Express*, corner of O'Higgins and Palguín. Fast food, large portions.
14 *La Tetera*, General Urrutia 580. Best breakfast in town.
15 *El Turista*, corner of Fresia and Alderete. Breakfast, desserts, chocolate.
16 *La Marmita de Pericles*, corner of Urrutia and Fresia. Fondue, raclette, expensive.
17 *Como Pizza*, west end of Holzapfel. Quiet location, good pizza.
18 *Cambalache*, O'Higgins 480. Parrilladas, all-you-can-eat salad bar.
19 *Trawen Deli*, O'Higgins 311. Vegetarian food, Kunstmann on tap.
20 *Empanadas Lleu Lleu*, on General Urrutia between Arauco and Palguín. Serious empanadas.

BARS
Bar del Pelao, corner of O'Higgins and Arauco.
Bar Bazul, Lincoyán between Urrutia and Alderete.
Mama's & Topa's, corner of O'Higgins and Arauco.

DISCOTHEQUES
Several discos east of town on the road to Caburgua, access by regular taxi colectivos. *Brahma* is the only one open year-round, while the current in-town favorite is *Living*, at the corner of Colo Colo and O'Higgins.

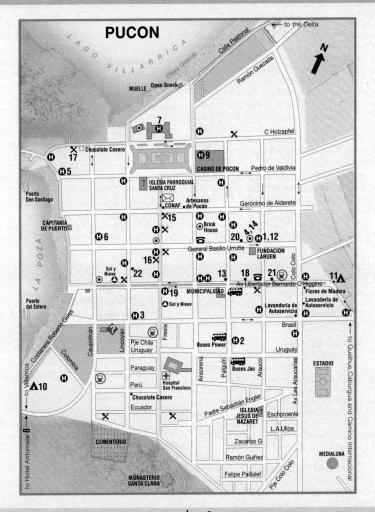

PUCON

AIRPORT

Pucón's newly improved airport, 5km east of town on the road to Caburgua.

AIRPORT TRANSPORT
Radio Taxi El Volcán, ☎ 441009.

AIRLINE OFFICES
LanChile-Ladeco, General Urrutia 102, ☎ 443516.
Aerocontinente, ☎ 6002092358.

BUS STATION AND/OR OFFICES
No central bus station.
Tur-Bus is 2km west of town, on the road to Caburgua.
Buses Jac has its terminal on Palguín, three blocks south of O'Higgins.

SHOPPING

Mapuche handicrafts are available at Artesanos de Pucón, on Alderete next to the post office. For books on flora, fauna, and local culture, as well as locally produced natural products, try Hostería Ecole. For fishing gear, try El Pescador Don Ele, on Gen. Urrutia between Ansorena and Fresia.

USEFUL ADDRESSES

For information on volunteer opportunities, local environmental issues, and visits to Cañi reserve, contact the Fundación Lahuén at General Urrutia 477, ☎ 441660. *Other sources of this type of information include Hostería Ecole and the Consejo Ecológico, located in the Municipality building at the SW corner of the Plaza.*

beach volleyball courts, rowboats and wind-surfers for rent, and though they were closed at the time of writing, most years there are also a couple of wildly popular open-air bars. Concerts and other events are occasionally held here at night. Unfortunately, the water at the west end of the beach (closest to town) is rather contaminated, thanks to Pucón's vastly insufficient waste-treatment system, but that doesn't stop people from swimming. If you walk a bit down the beach, you'll find fewer people and cleaner water.

La Poza This protected inlet lies due west of town, and is separated from the Playa Grande by La Península. Sheltered from winds off the lake, this is where most summer folks keep their boats, and in season you can rent kayaks and rowboats for a relaxing paddle. Past the south end of the beach is Pucón's best (and most popular) campground, *Camping La Poza*.

The Delta The mouth of the Río Pucón, 4km north of town along the Playa Grande, is an extensive wetland habitat that was quite nearly eclipsed by real estate development. The local *Consejo Ecológico* has proposed to have the Delta – essential for water quality as well as wildlife habitat – transformed into protected green area, known as *Parque Pucón*. The biking and hiking trails winding through the Delta forest are the most accessible in Pucón; ask at *Hostería Ecole* for details and maps.

Casino Pucón's casino was inaugurated in 1998, together with the top-of-the-line Hotel del Lago. Gaming rooms are open every day, and entrance is free.

Around Pucón

See Parque Nacional Villarrica, Parque Nacional Huerquehue, Curarrehue and the Upper Trancura Valley, and the El Cañi Nature Sanctuary for more recommended destinations and activities around Pucón.

Río La Plata

Set in the steep, forested Quelhue hills above the eastern shore of Lago Villarrica, the Río La Plata valley makes for an excellent half-day escape from Pucón. Hiking trails lead up the valley along the stream, which abounds with deep swimming holes and natural waterslides. To get there (by tour or bike), cross the Pasarela Quelhue and take a left at the first crossroads.

Ojos del Caburgua

Set in a lush forest to the NE of Pucón, Ojos del Caburgua marks the spot where the waters of Lago Caburgua (which has no superficial outlet at most levels) bubble up out of the earth to give rise to lovely pools, waterfalls, and a cold, crystalline stream. A nominal fee is charged at the entrance, and you can camp in the fields near the stream. There are also several other waterfalls in this area of lush native forest, as well as a couple of German-style hosterías and teahouses, the *Landhaus San Sebastián* and the *Salto del Carileufú*. There is no public transport to the site, which lies 15km from Pucón; [↕].

Lago Caburgua

Lago Caburgua occupies an oblong, glacially-formed basin to the NE of Pucón, and because the lake's outlet is subterranean, it is typically several degrees warmer than Lago Villarrica.

In and around the village of Caburgua, 25km from Pucón at the south end of the lake, there are a variety of campgrounds, hosterías, and cabañas. Directly in front of Caburgua is the Playa Negra, and 3km north along the west shore of the lake is Playa Blanca, also with a variety of lodging, boats for rent, and a recommended campground, *Vergara Hermanos*. A trail along the shore connects the two beaches. If you are driving or on a bike, from Caburgua you can continue NE along the lakeshore, cross a pass to Paillaco, and from there go on to PN Huerquehue and/or the Río Liucura valley. Buses run regularly between Pucón and Caburgua.

At the northern end of the lake, accessed via Curarrehue and Reigolil, is another Playa Negra –this one with coarse black sand, a nearby campground, and unbelievable views across the lake towards Volcán Villarrica. There is no public transport to the north shore of the lake.

The Upper Palguín

The primary attractions of the upper Palguín valley are a series of dramatic waterfalls, a hotsprings resort, and the Quetrupillán sector of PN Villarrica (described below). Access is via a signposted turnoff, 20km east of Pucón on the international highway. Just beyond the turnoff, in Palguín Bajo, the *Kila Leufu* working farm offers homestyle accommodation and excursions in the area.

Once you leave the paved highway behind, the road begins to climb, gradually at first and then steeply, through a lovely native forest; from time to time the Río Palguín appears on the left, and in a couple of spots there are trails leading down to hidden waterfalls. 27km from Pucón is the Salto Palguín, the only one visible from the road, and another 3km up, the road levels out and passes a turnoff on the left to the 70m Salto La China, where there is a nice campground and an interesting rustic hydropower plant. Shortly thereafter is the entrance to the Salto El León, which is somewhat higher but carries less water than La China. Entrance is charged at both Salto La China and Salto El León.

At 30km from Pucón is the Termas de Palguín hotel, and at 37km is the entrance to the PN Villarrica. There is no public transport to the Upper Palguín.

14A Ojos del Caburgua Loop
14B Lago Caburgua-
Río Liucura Loop
14C The Río Trancura Loop
14D Alto Palguín Chinay
14E Correntoso

36 Around Volcán Villarrica
37 Villarrica Traverse
38 Andean Lakes Hike
39 Pampas del Quinchol

15A Rancho de Caballos
15B Caballos de Bacher-Alm
15C Turismo Huepill

20 Volcán Villarrica
21 Volcán Lanín

12 Cerro Las Peinetas

10 Villarrica-Pucón

13A Lower Trancura (III)
13B Upper Trancura (IV)
13C Liucura (II-III)
13D Palguín
14 The Puesco Run (V)
15 Río Maichín (IV+)

23 Termas de Palguín
24 The Río Liucura Valley
25 Termas de Calafquén
26 Termas de Pangui
27 Termas de San Sebastián
28 Termas de San Luis
and Menetué

AROUND PUCON

Termas de Palguín

 ☎ (45)441968 🏠 $4,000, children $2,500

The hotel at this resort, located near the Quetrupillán sector of PN Villarrica, has recently been rebuilt after a 1998 fire. Installations include a large common pool and individual indoor tubs, with water temperatures from 35-46°C.

The Río Liucura Valley

A major affluent of the Río Trancura, the cold, clear-flowing Liucura is a local favorite among fishermen and kayakers. Access to the lower stretches of the river is via the Pasarela Quelhue (hanging bridge) about 4km east of Pucón; from here, a lovely, winding dirt road leads through farmland and forests along the north bank to the Ojos del Caburgua (above). Ideal for biking, this road offers are great views of the lake and volcano.

The upper stretch of the Liucura Valley is accessed by a dirt track (look for signs to Huife) branching off the right side of the road to Caburgua just before the Liucura bridge, 14km from Pucón. Just past the hamlet of San Pedro is a turnoff on the right that follows the Río Coilaco upvalley to Laguna San Jorge and Quira Quira, where there is a trail to an araucaria forest in the Cordón Cañi. At 20km is the native tree nursery and operations base for the Cañi Nature Sanctuary (described below), and shortly afterwards is Huepil, where the working farm at *Huife Chico* offers lodging as part of its 'agro-tourism' programs.

At 25km is the Tres Esquinas crossroads. The road to the left (north) leads to Paillaco, PN Huerquehue (described below), and across a pass to Caburgua. The road to the right continues up the Liucura valley to the Termas de Quimey-Co (29km), the Termas de Huife (33km), and the Termas Los Pozones (km 36).

Buses Liucura, at the corner of Urrutia and Ansorena in Pucón, runs daily buses to the upper Liucura, and many local agencies offer tours.

Hotsprings in the Río Liucura Valley

 🏠 C🛁

The Río Liucura valley boasts three separate hotsprings with facilities for all tastes.

Closest to Pucón, the Termas de Quimey-Co ($3,500; ☎ (45)441903) has a hosteria and campground, riverside pools (water temp 68°C), a mud bath and restaurant. Next up is Termas de Huife ($6,500; ☎ (45)441222), the first spa-hotel in the region, designed for families, with upscale lodging and two 38-40°C outdoor pools. Near the head of the valley, Termas Los Pozones ($4,000) is the local favorite, with spectacular, super-hot stone pools right on the edge of the river. Best of all, Los Pozones is open all night.

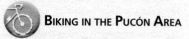

BIKING IN THE PUCÓN AREA

● Ojos del Caburgua Loop
▶30km◀ ⏱1d P D ☐

From Pucón (0km) head east on the paved road towards Caburgua, crossing the bridge over the Río Liucura and turning left at the dirt road next to the 'El Cristo' cross (18km). The road leads past Ojos del Caburgua and other signposted waterfalls and swimming holes, and continues west along the Río Liucura to the Pasarela Quelhue (hanging bridge, 8km). From here, it's 2km to the paved highway and another 2km to Pucón.

● Lago Caburgua - Río Liucura Loop
▶60km◀ ⏱1-2d P D ☐

From Pucón (0km) head east on the paved road towards Caburgua, taking the second major right after the Río Liucura bridge, which climbs 10km to Paillaco. From here you can climb the steep switchbacks to Lago Tinquilco and Parque Nacional Huerquehue (5km) or continue south to an intersection with the road up the upper Liucura (4km). Finish by turning left to the hotsprings of the upper Liucura valley (4 to 10km) or returning downvalley to Pucón (26km).

● The Río Trancura Loop
▶61km◀ ⏱1d P D ☐

Head east from Pucón (0km) on the road to Caburgua. After the bridge over the Río Trancura (11km), turn right on the signposted route towards the Termas de Menetué. The gravel road climbs gradually up the Río Trancura valley, passing the Termas de Menetué (18km) and continuing past the Termas de San Luis (6km); there are good picnicking and swimming spots all along the route. From Termas de San Luis, cross the bridge over the Trancura to rejoin the international highway and return to Pucón (26km). Several other hanging bridges cross the Trancura further down, so shorter loops are also possible.

● Alto Palguín / Chinay
▶60km◀rt to the Termas
⏱1-2d P D ☐

This is either a challenging out-and-back route, or the beginning of a longer tour through the Siete Lagos (below). From Pucón (0km), head east on the international highway, turning right at the signposted turnoff to Alto Palguín (20km). From here the road climbs steeply into the highlands, leveling out somewhat at the Salto La China (8km). There are campsites at each of the waterfalls here, and a hotel just above at the Termas de Palguín (4km), but if you really get an early start you might be able to make the Conaf campsite at Chinay (17km). Beyond Chinay the road worsens and steepens, climbing into ancient araucaria forest on the pass itself. From here it's either back to Pucón or over the pass to Coñaripe and the even wilder Siete Lagos (27km, see [↱]).

● Correntoso
▶varies◀ ⏱1d **P** **D** ▭

Accessed via a dirt road (marked 'Aguas Calientes') branching right off the camino internacional just before the Río Turbio bridge (7km from Pucón), the Correntoso valley offers solitary riding and wide-open views in the stark volcanic landscape to the NE of Volcán Villarrica. Once off the highway, the road climbs 5km to a bridge over the Río Correntoso, and from here you can either turn right up the Correntoso or else continue straight on to explore the Río Turbio valley to the east. For a very long day, you might be able to hike up from the top of Correntoso to the base of a glacier on the volcano. There is water all along the route.

Fishing in the Pucón Area

Fishermen in the Pucón area should key upon clear-flowing streams such as the Liucura, the Palguín, and the Maichin; the Río Trancura is cloudier and generally overfished in all but its uppermost stretches. For big fish (including the occasional salmon up to 6 kilos), you might try a float trip on the Río Toltén, which drains Lago Villarrica; boats are usually available on the waterfront in Villarrica. Highland lakes such as Laguna San Jorge and Lago Huife in the Río Liucura valley, Laguna del León near the Termas de San Luis, Lago Hualalafquén near Reigolil, and Lago Quilleihue (and others) in PN Villarrica present another option for catch-and-release fishermen.

Operators: 119 - 145

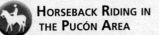 HORSEBACK RIDING IN THE PUCÓN AREA

● Rancho de Caballos
☎ 09-4457676

From their base right next to the Salto El León in the upper Palguín valley, this German-run outfitter offers trips ranging from 3hrs to 9 days, most in the Quetrupillán and Puesco sectors of PN Villarrica.

● Caballos de Bacher-Alm
☎ 09-8750425

German-run horsepacking and 'packdonkey' treks in the spectacular, wide-open Los Nevados valley to the northeast of Volcán Villarrica.

● Turismo Huepil
☎ 09-4534212

Widely regarded as one of the best choice for horseback trips in the south, with excellent instruction and horses, and a first-class *asado*. Trips range from 1-3 days, mostly in the Cañi range east of Pucón.

RAFTING AND KAYAKING IN THE PUCÓN AREA

Operators: 12 - 49 (k) - 172 - 189 - 207 (k) 222 - 234 (k)

● Lower Trancura (III)
⏱1.5h

Chile's most popular rafting run begins above the Puente Metreñehue and ends below the hanging bridge (Pasarela Quelhue). The run is easy Class III, with big waves at *El Pescador* during high water.

● Upper Trancura (IV)
⏱1.5h

Pucon's staple class IV run is almost totally drop-pool, which means that though the drops are relatively big, they're also pretty safe. The real fun begins at the 3rd drop, El Salto Feo, which is immediately followed by a portage around the Mariman waterfall. Right after the portage, a long, technical last rapid (La Ultima Sonrisa) raises the stakes a bit, and after this comes a long, continuous runout to the finish. Aks operators about full-day trips combining the upper and the lower Trancura.

● Liucura (II-III)
⏱1-2h

In winter, when the Trancura is too big to run commercially, rafting companies switch to the crystal-clear Liucura, a northern tributary. The rest of the year, the Liucura makes for the perfect beginning kayaking or ducky run, and boasts one the most consistent play holes in the area. The put-in is most easily reached via the dirt road from the Pasarela Quelhue to the Ojos del Caburgua, and you can take out either at the pasarela or at the commercial takeout for the Lower Trancura, or even – for the full trip – paddle out to the lake and then back to the beach in Pucón.

● Palguín (IV-V)
⏱2h

There are three Class V sections on the Palguín. The first, beginning at the Salto de Palguín waterfall and continuing to the first bridge downstream, is the quintessential waterfall run, featuring 4 drops up to 25 feet and a portage around a horrendous-looking 60-foot double-drop. The rarely-run middle section features bigger, more complicated waterfalls up to 60 feet high – well beyond most paddlers' abilities. The lower section (hard to identify from the road) features relatively continuous creeky rapids with a couple of lovely basalt waterfalls, including one nicknamed 'the automatic boof.' Below here is portage around a complicated drop with a deadly undercut cave at the bottom. The run ends at another bridge, this one accessed via a turnoff marked 'Playa Anzuelo' on the drive upvalley.

Rock Climbing in the Pucón Area

Though Pucón is still far from being a climbers' mecca, in recent years a number of remarkably diverse crags have turned up in the surrounding area. During the summer, there is a climbing wall in town behind the *Artesanos de Pucón* handicraft mall, while the closest climbing on real rock is on the short cliffs on the west side of La Península; there are similar crags in the Río Correntoso valley. For a longer trip, sign up for guided ascents of Cerro San Francisco, the largest of the impressive 'Machu Picchu' towers just NE of the volcano; the route features over 800m of climbing and steep scrambling. Finally, for alpine challenges, experienced climbers might turn their attention to Cerro Las Peinetas, a collection of imposing spires on the Argentine border near Puesco.
Operators: 207

Canyoning in the Pucón Area

With such an abundance of waterfalls in the surrounding area, it makes sense that canyoning would start to catch on in Pucón. Two highly worthwhile trips currently offered include the free rappel of the 84m Salto Claro and the more involved descent of 'Magic Falls,' a slot canyon in the upper Trancura valley near Puesco. No previous experience is necessary for these trips.
Operators: 207

Parque Nacional Villarrica

See map 🔼

ACCOMMODATION
Conaf campgrounds at Chinay and Puesco; mountain refugio on the Argentine side of Volcán Lanín.

TRANSPORT
No public transport to Villarrica or Quetrupillán sectors; access by taxi or tour only. To Puesco, by bus from Pucón with Buses Jac.

PN Villarrica extends from the Villarrica volcano roughly SE to the Argentine border, protecting 61,000 wonderfully diverse hectares of southern beech and araucaria forest, three volcanoes, and a broad expanse of high volcanic plateau. The park is divided into three sectors, each with its own access and characteristics. Ambitious hikers can link all three sectors in a single traverse.

The **RUCAPILLÁN** sector of the park recalls the ancestral Mapuche name for Volcán Villarrica (*ruca*=house, *pillán*=sacred). Rapidly accessed from Pucón (via the *camino al volcán*), with a ski area and the popular *Cuevas Volcánicas* (volcanic caves), this is the most frequently visited sector of the park. Volcano ascents typically begin at the base of the ski area, and a recommended hike departing from here circumnavigates the volcano to connect with the Quetrupil-

lán sector. The caves, 5km off the main access road via a signposted turnoff, are 1,200m long and over 200m deep; geological information is provided, and the trail into the caves is lit by electric lights.

Accessed via the road to the Upper Palguín, the **QUETRUPILLÁN** sector is named for the lowest of PN Villarrica's three volcanoes. There is a Conaf ranger station and campground at Chinay, 27km from the turnoff on the *camino internacional*; a signposted trail leads east from here to Laguna Azul and the Villarrica Traverse. (The Villarrica Traverse is more often begun from the end of the road through 'Paraíso Escondido,' a housing development accessed via a signposted turnoff on the left above the Termas de Palguín.) If you continue up the road past the guardería, you'll eventually come to some trailheads on the right (in the midst of an araucaria forest) leading up to the glacier on the east side of Volcán Villarrica. The road over the pass and down to Coñaripe is in exceedingly poor shape, which keeps traffic down and makes this a great route – though brutally steep – for mountain biking.

Termas de Calafquén

 C NA

On the south side of the pass (4WD only) between Pucón and Coñaripe is a small, informal installation of rustic indoor and outdoor tubs. This makes a great campsite if biking over the pass.

The **PUESCO** sector is the easternmost of the three, lying right along the Argentine border, where it delimits with Argentina's PN Lanín. The sheer, glaciated peak of Volcán Lanín, the highest volcano in La Araucanía, dominates this sector of the park, though ascents are generally made from the Argentine side, where a couple of mountain *refugios* simplify access. Like the Rucapillán and Quetrupillán sectors, Puesco protects mainly volcanic plateau, southern beech and pure araucaria forest, as well as a scattering of tiny, seldom-visited alpine lakes.

The entrance to this sector of the park is at the Puesco border post, 63km from Pucón. There is a nice campsite in a coigüe forest just east of the highway; if you're not planning on crossing into Argentina, you must leave your passport here with customs officials for the duration of your stay in the park. Past the border post, the road continues to climb towards the border, passing a trail on the right (ask Conaf rangers for directions) leading up the Río Puesco valley towards Laguna Abutardas and the Quetrupillán sector. 9km up the road is Laguna Quilleihué – a true spectacle with fall foliage – and at the far end of the lake you'll find a trail, also on the right, leading south to Laguna Perdida and Laguna Plato. 2km past Laguna Quilelhué, where the road flattens out on a high araucaria plateau, a couple of roads on the right lead to still more pristine lakes (Laguna Huenfuica and Laguna Verde) on NW slopes of Volcán Lanín. This is great area for mountain biking, and the starting point for the *Ruta Chilena* up the north side of Volcán Lanín.

To the north of the border post at Puesco, another narrow sector of PN Villarrica protects a long ridge along the Argentine border, including the unmistakable spires of Cerro Las Peinetas.

Around Volcán Villarrica

 3d

Beginning at the base of the ski area and finishing at the Chinay campground, this incredibly scenic route contours around the western and southern slopes of Volcán Villarrica, winding through lava fields and high lenga and araucaria forest. Each day of the trek is progressively harder, with the final day involving steep ups and downs and somewhat complicated routefinding. From Chinay (ideal third camp), you can walk down the road 3hrs to the Termas de Palguín, where you can arrange transport back to Pucón.

Villarrica Traverse

 3-5d

The best multi-day hike in the Pucón area, this route can be completed by strong parties in three days, though more are recommended. The route begins at the very end of the road past the Paraíso Escondido parcelation (between the Termas de Palguín and Chinay), climbing up the Estero Mocho and over the west flank of Volcán Quetrupillán to Laguna Azul. From here, the trail trends east across an expansive volcanic plateau (marked by cairns and stakes), past Laguna Blanca to Laguna Abutardas, at the headwaters of the Río Puesco. The trail then veers north to join the international highway just above Puesco.

Operators: 176 - 207

Volcán Villarrica (2,860m)

 5-7h rt

Villarrica's intensely active summit crater inevitably beckons nearly every visitor to Pucón. Smoking by day and glowing an eerie red by night, *el volcan* dominates the horizon – and it's right there, ready to be climbed.

Villarrica's magnetic attraction and ease of ascent make it easily the most frequently climbed peak in Chile, and during the summer high season, as many as 200 people may be on the summit at once. Out of season, of course, it's another story.

The standard route begins at the ski area and follows the lifts up to the cavernous concrete 'capilla,' built years ago to house a lift that never came to fruition; you can save the first hour or so of walking by paying a small fee to ride the chairlift. From La Capilla, the route trends right (west) to the saddle above the 'roca negra,' then continues up the rocky shoulder to the summit crater, where you may be able to spot the lava bubbling up out of the depths of the earth. Gas masks or lemon-soaked rags are recommended to counteract the nauseous effects of the volcano's sulphurous gases.

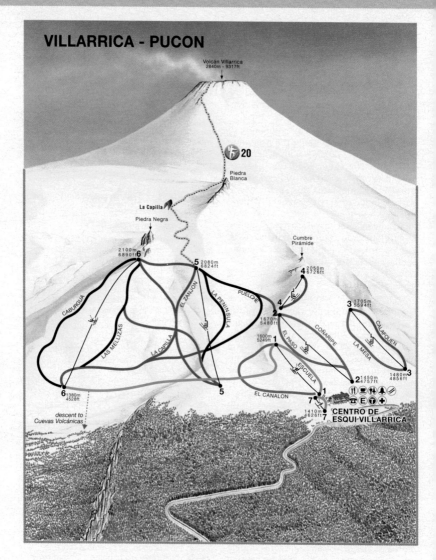

VILLARRICA - PUCON

Volcán Villarrica
2840m - 9317ft

20

Piedra
Blanca

La Capilla
Piedra Negra

2100m
6890ft 6

5 2080m
6824ft

Cumbre
Pirámide

4 2050m
6726ft

PUELCHE

CABURGUA

LAS MELLIZAS

EL ZANJON

LA PENINSULA

LA CAPILLA

4

3 1705m
5594ft

1670m
5480ft

CONARIPE

CALAFQUEN

LA MESA

1600m
5249ft 1

EL PASO

6 1380m
4528ft

descent to
Cuevas Volcánicas

5

ESCUELA

EL CANALON

2 1450m
4757ft

1480m
4856ft 3

7

1410m
626ft 7

1

CENTRO DE
ESQUI VILLARRICA

━━ Expert	🚡 Chairlift	Ⓗ Hotel	🚻 Restrooms
━━ Dificult	🚡 Double Chair	🔺 Ski School	⊘ Ski Rental
━━ Intermediate	🚡 Triple Chair	🍴 Restaurant	Ⓣ Tickets
━━ Easy	🚡 Quad Chair	✚ Ski Patrol	Ⓔ Car Park
━━ Free Skiing	🚡 Poma	☎ Emergency Telephone	⊚ Cafeteria
⅄ Skating Rink	🚡 T-Bar	⊕ Heliskiing	⊙ Paragliding

460

In spring (usually until late Nov), Villarrica makes an excellent ski or snowboard descent, with 45-50° pitches near the summit, but remember to stay close to the ascent route to avoid crevasses. You can also ascend the volcano over the course of two days via the more scenic and remote Correntoso route.

Operators: 12 - 29 - 172 - 189 - 207 - 222

Centro de Ski Villarrica - Pucón

Set on the north side of Volcán Villarrica, this area boasts the best lift infrastructure and steepest lift-served terrain in the south, and the location simply cannot be beat. The area is owned by the Gran Hotel Pucón and features a modern base facility with a restaurant, rentals and ski school – not quite at the same level as the areas above Santiago, but close.

Directly above the lodge, the slopes on Cerro Pirámide are appropriate mostly for beginning and intermediate skiers, while advanced skiers will prefer the terrain off the #5 chair, with the steepest skiing lying in the upper reaches of the basin directly west of the lift, accessed by a high traverse. This area can also be reached by heading east (skier's right) off the #4 chair, but you must skirt the impassable cliff bands at the top. The #6 lift almost never runs, but motivated skiers can access this terrain by doing a rising traverse east from the top of the #5 lift. Deep gullies and natural halfpipes separate most of the

groomed trails, providing some ideal snowboarding terrain. Expert skiers will inevitably be drawn to the ski mountaineering descent from the crater of the volcano, with pitches up to 45°. Pucón is also the only place in Chile where you can rent randonee equipment.

During the winter, weather here is pretty much hit or miss. Ice storms and wind can shut down the area for days or even weeks at a time, but after the clouds clear, you can sometimes ski way down the hill to the east of the lodge, through the woods to rejoin the road below. Because it is higher than the other areas, Villarrica stays open much later in the year, usually closing in late October.

Volcán Lanín (3,747m)

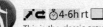

🕙2-3d ▮

This imposing border peak – the highest in the Lake District – is generally climbed from Argentina. From the customs post and ranger station near Lago Tromén, the route climbs a small wash and then a prominent ridge, the Espina del Pescado (fish bone) to two basic refugios. 7-10hrs rt should be allowed for climb from here to the summit, with no water on the route. In springtime it is also possible to ascend from Puesco via the Ruta Chilena, which climbs the steep, non-glaciated north face. This also makes an excellent ski mountaineering descent.

Operators: 207

Parque Nacional Huerquehue

Pronounced *where-kay-way*, this 12,500há park protects a compact, densely forested massif to the east of Lago Caburgua, 33km from Pucón. Road access is via a series of steep switchbacks above the village of Paillaco, though experienced hikers may also access the park via the *Centro Termal San Sebastián* (formerly *Termas Río Blanco*) to the north.

The centerpiece of the park is a clear, oblong mountain lake, Lago Tinquilco. Park administration is on the east side of the lake, together some nice walk-in campsites; the trail to Cerro Quinchol begins here. At the north end of the lake are more privately-run campgrounds (*Camping Fanor Castillo* and *Camping Tante*

Hilde recommended) and an excellent hostería, the *Refugio Tinquilco*. Past the hostería are trailheads for the Cascada Nido de Aguila and the ever-popular Andean lakes hike, 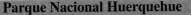.

Andean Lakes Hike

🗡🔁 🕙4-6h rt ▭

This is the classic araucaria hike near Pucón. The trail begins at the north end of Lago Tinquilco, switchbacking through a forest of coigüe and mañío with magnificent views of Volcán Villarrica. After a climb of 1.5-2hrs the trail reaches a high basin with five lakes amid pure stands of araucarias. A short loop takes you by Lago Chico, Toro, and Verde; from the latter you can veer left (west) to climb 1,621m Cerro Comulo, or head along the right (east) side of the lake to Lago Los Patos and Lago Huerquehue (you can also loop back east to Lago Toro). For overnight trips, from Lago Huerquehue you can continue north past Laguna Abutardas to the Mirador Renahue, and then either descend the Estero Las Mercedes (north) to the Termas de Río Blanco, or head west down the Estero Renahue to the shore of Lago Caburgua. From here, you can either head north along the lakeshore to Río Blanco and Playa Negra or head back south to Caburgua. Note that crisscrossing cowpaths in the upper Río Blanco valley make careful routefinding essential on this part of the route. The inicial part of the route is equally recommended for snowshoeing trips in winter (consult at *Hostería Ecole*).

Operators: 137 - 172 - 189 - 222

Pampas del Quinchol

⇄ ⏱ 3-4h rt ▭

Departing from a signposted trailhead about 300m past the Conaf guardería, this well-marked route begins with a series of switchbacks up the steep hillside east of Lago Tinquilco. After about an hour and a half, the trail emerges from the forest into an open pampa consisting of coarse bunch grasses (*coironales*) and scattered araucarias; from here, you can head SW about 15 minutes to the summit of 1,463m Cerro Quinchol. Return via the same route.

El Cañi Nature Reserve

PRACTICAL INFORMATION
The Fundación Lahuén manages visits in the reserve; contact them at Hostería Ecole for transport and guided visits.

Located in a pristine highland basin in the heart of the Cordon Cañi (between the Liucura and Coilaco valleys), the 400há Cañi is Chile's first private nature reserve. The reserve was purchased in 1990, using funds raised in the US by Ancient Forest International, and a year later administration was turned over to the newly-created Lahuén Foundation. The following years brought the construction of a *refugio* near the town of Pichares, a native tree nursery funded by the Fondo de las Américas, and the implementation of native-guided nature tours. All in all, the Cañi is more than just a reserve: it is a prime example of how a forest can bring people and ideas together.

There are a number of ways to access the ancient araucaria forests and 18 small lakes of the Cañi reserve, but because trails are not marked, all visitors must go with a guide the first time. The most common access is from the base area east of Pichares, where you can pick up field guides and homemade granola for your hike. From here it's about two hours of steep climbing to the Laguna Seca, where you get your first glimpse of the araucarias. The rest of the lakes are just above, with trails leading among them and to peaks such as the Mirador Tres Picos (1,550m) and Cerro Redondo (1,500m). The park can also be reached directly from Pichares via the trail past Piedra Santa, or from the south via Coilaco Alto. The Cordón Cañi continues to the east of the park, with more lakes and araucaria forests that can be accessed from Huepil and Quira Quira.

Curarrehue and the Upper Trancura Valley

TRANSPORT AND ACCOMMODATION
Buses Jac in Pucón runs daily buses to Puesco, leaving Pucón at 1800 and departing Puesco at 0700. Basic lodging in Curarrehue, hostería near Puesco.

East of Pucón, international highway 119 follows the Río Trancura valley 76km to the Argentine border at Paso Mamuil Malal. The road is currently undergoing improvement and is slated to become the second paved highway between the Argentine and Chilean lake districts.

The *camino internacional*, as it is called, splits off the Pucón-Caburgua road some 7km east of Pucón, just past the bridge over the Río Turbio. At km 18 is the turnoff to Palguín, and at km 25 is the vil-

lage of Catripulli, where you can buy excellent, inexpensive carvings in *raulí*. Keep your eyes open on the left for bridges across the Río Trancura; if you wish you can cross and loop back along the north side of the river, visiting the Termas de Menetué or San Luis.

35km from Pucón is a signposted turnoff on the left to the Termas de Panqui, and shortly beyond is the town of Curarrehue, set on a bluff above the confluence of the Río Trancura and the Río Maichín. There are basic hospedajes, restaurants, and markets in town, including an excellent bakery on the NW side of the plaza. From here a dirt road branches north up the Río Maichín valley to Reigolil and Playa Negra, at the north end of Lago Caburgua.

Termas de Panqui

 ☎ (45)442039 ^C $5,000

One of the finest commercial springs in all of Chile, the Termas de Panqui are located 15km north of Curarrehue via a signposted gravel road ideal for mountain biking. Installations include three pools of varying temperature along the Río Panqui, a tasteful Asian-style 'mini-hotel,' 10 Sioux tipis, and a vegetarian restaurant. Massage, full moon celebrations, and a variety of New Age therapies are also offered at Panqui, and you can camp for free in the fields above the springs. Ask owner Daniel Little about the hike to Laguna Alicia in the araucaria forest above Panqui.

Centro Termal San Sebastián (Termas de Río Blanco)

 ☎ (45)341961 ^C free NA

Located in the Río Blanco valley at the north end of Lago Caburgua, these rustic springs feature a 50°C common pool, two cabins, a campground and a basic restaurant. Access is via Reigolil.

Termas de San Luis ☎ (45)411388

$5,000, private tub / sauna $3,000 extra.

Termas de Menetué ☎ (45)441877

$4,500, $6,000 w/ private tubs.

 Located in open country to the north of the Río Trancura (near Catripulli), these two hotspring resorts are specifically oriented towards families. Each has outdoor pools and lots of grass to play on, individual tubs, cabins and a restaurant. San Luis is slightly more upscale, and also has a sauna and indoor pool.

Above Curarrehue, the road steepens as it continues to climb up the Río Trancura valley. Some 15km past town on the right (east) side of the valley is the entrance to

Campamento Cóndor Blanco, a new age retreat center, and just beyond on the left is the *Casa de Té Trancura*, a riverside *hostería* with cabins for rent and a spectacular view of Cerro Las Peinetas across the river to the east. From here it's 4km to the customs station and the Puesco sector of PN Villarrica.

The Puesco Run (V)

 ⏱1h

The uppermost runnable section of the Río Trancura only flows in winter and spring or during a hard rain. Continuous blind drops in a steep canyon with abundant strainers make this one experts-only. The run begins at the Puesco border station and ends at the unmistakable blue church about 10km downvalley.

Río Maichín (IV⁺)

 ⏱2-3h

One of the most beautiful runs in the Pucón area, the Maichín flows through a deep, inaccessible canyon NE of Curarrehue. At most levels there is a portage around a drop with a nasty undercut. The Maichín usually runs in winter and spring or following a hard rain; access is via the road from Curarrehue to Reigolil.

Cerro Las Peinetas

 These dramatic spires on the Argentine border near Curarrehue offer a variety of alpine routes with phenomenal top-out possibilities. This is adventure climbing with loose rock and no fixed gear whatsoever, so assume nothing; most of the spires have never seen an ascent. Even if you don't care to climb, the steep hike to the base of the towers is recommended, affording views of Volcán Lanín and Lago Tromen across the border in Argentina's PN Lanín. Access is via private land across the bridge from the *Casa de Té Trancura* (ask permission to enter).

Operators: 207 - 234

The Siete Lagos
See map

See map

ACCOMMODATION

There is a great concentration of campgrounds, cabañas, hostería and other lodging along the north shore of Lago Calafquén (Lican Ray-Coñaripe). Other places with a selection are Panguipulli, Liquiñe, and Choshuenco; apart from this, you can find campgrounds and hostería-style lodging at the west end of Lago Riñihue, both near the town of Riñihue and at the

source of the Río San Pedro. Many locals will let you camp on their land, but be sure to ask for permission first.

TRANSPORT

Access to Lican Ray and Coñaripe by bus from Villarrica or Panguipulli; from here you can catch daily buses on to Liquiñe. Buses also run from Panguipulli to Choshuenco, Neltume, and Puerto Fuy. Access to Riñihue by bus from Los Lagos.

Tucked into a compact, convoluted mountain region to the east of Valdivia and the south of Villarrica and Pucón, the Seven Lakes district is like a little Patagonia: wild, seemingly remote and overwhelmingly rural, with spectacular landforms, washed-out roads and lots of privacy. All seven lakes are connected, and are ultimately drained by the Río San Pedro, at the west end of Lago Riñihue. In addition to being a top recommendation for challenging bike tours, this is a paradise for fishermen and whitewater kayakers.

Connected by a paved road to Villarrica, **LICAN RAY** is the most popular summer resort in the region, with a full range of accommodations and a couple of nice beaches with boats for rent. What the town is proudest of, however, is its claim to the world's largest outdoor barbecue, held every year during the first weekend in January. The rest of the year, you'll have to be content with the beaches and manicured gardens on the peninsula south of town. Recommended lodging in town includes *Hostería Inaltulafquén*, while some of the best camping is at *Cabañas y Camping Foresta*, east of town on the paved road to Coñaripe.

20km east, **COÑARIPE** is somewhat less popular than Lican Ray, but has most of the same services. Volcán Villarrica looms directly above the town, and at times major eruptions and landslides have destroyed significant parts of the village. From here a 4WD road leads past hotsprings and over a pass to Sector Quetrupillán of PN Villarrica, 🔼.

The pavement ends in Coñaripe. From here the most direct route to Panguipulli leads 35km west past tiny Lago Pullingue, but a more interesting route leads east over a high pass, *cuesta Los Añiques*, passing the Termas de Coñaripe and the marshy Lago Pellaifa en route to a signposted crossroads (23km). Straight on east is the verdant, apparently forgotten village of **LIQUIÑE**, with a wealth of hotsprings, hosterías and campgrounds, and past Liquiñe is the long, remote crossing over Paso Carirriñe, through Argentina's PN Lanín and on to Junín de los Andes.

Termas de Coñaripe

 ☎ (45)431407 🏠 $5,000, children $2,500

16km east of Coñaripe, this popular spa hotel features five hot pools (3 outdoor, one indoor, 1 jacuzzi, temp 39-42°) plus mud baths, a sauna, cabañas, tennis courts and a restaurant.

Hotsprings in Liquiñe

This small, remote Mapuche village is known for its local carvings in *rauli* and its abundant hotsprings. At the western entrance to town is the Termas de Río Liquiñe, (*$4,000pp*, ☎ *(63)317377)*, with a large 45° pool, jacuzzis, massage and local excursions. In town is the Termas de Liquiñe, (*$3,000pp*, ☎ *(63)311060)*, with a hosteria and cabins with private tubs. There are also a number of rustic, inexpensive springs in the valley, including some funny concrete tubs (entrance $1,500pp) in the field across the street from the Termas de Liquiñe and a lovely spring on a hill above the Río Liquiñe, reached via turnoff of the left (north) just before the bridge into town *(entrance $1,800pp)*. 8km east of town on the road to Argentina are the rustic Termas de Hipólito Muñoz *($1,500pp)*.

The road south from the aforementioned crossroads leads over another serious pass to the nearly virgin Lago Neltume (road-access camping) and on to another crossroads, 17km from the last. Here, the

SIETE LAGOS

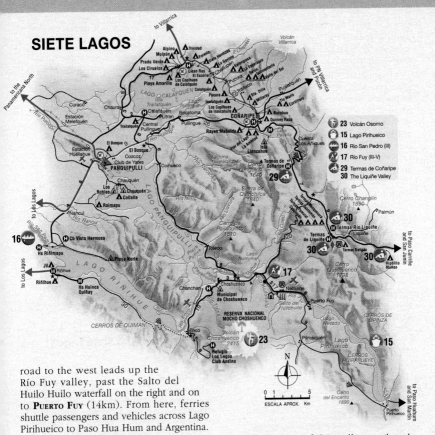

Map legend:
- 23 Volcán Osorno
- 15 Lago Pirihueico
- 16 Río San Pedro (III)
- 17 Río Fuy (III-V)
- 29 Termas de Coñaripe
- 30 The Liquiñe Valley

road to the west leads up the Río Fuy valley, past the Salto del Huilo Huilo waterfall on the right and on to **PUERTO FUY** (14km). From here, ferries shuttle passengers and vehicles across Lago Pirihueico to Paso Hua Hum and Argentina.

Across Lago Pirihueico (Transbordador Mariela)

⏱ 1.5h

Trapped deep in the Andes by lava flows, Lago Pirihueico is crossed twice a day by ferry (once on Sundays in winter), connecting the Chilean Siete Lagos district with Paso Hua Hum, San Martín de los Andes, and the Argentine Seven Lakes District. This is one of the finest and most affordable ways to cross the Andes, and is especially recommended for bikers.

East of the crossroads at Neltume, the road crosses a bridge over the Río Fuy before reaching another crossroads, at 4km. The road north leads along the steep north shore of Lago Panguipulli to Panguipulli (described below), while straight west past the crossroads is the tidy little village of

CHOSHUENCO, one of the mellowest 'beach towns' in the south. There is a fine *hostería* here (*Hostería Pumalhue*) and a campground on the beach. 19km south of Choshuenco is end-of-the-road **ENCO**, point of access for the remote, heavily glaciated Volcán Choshuenco, protected as a national reserve. There are a couple of refugios at the base of the mountain (including a very nice one belonging to the Universidad Austral in Valdivia), but neither is open to the public.

The road west from Enco, along the south shore of Lago Riñihue, has not been open for several years because of washed-out bridges. If you wish to access the village Riñihue or the Río San Pedro, you must do so from Panguipulli or Valdivia/Los Lagos. Those who make the trip will be rewarded by one of the least-visited corners of the Lake District. Services are limited to a couple of fine hosterías (*Hs. Riñimapu* and *Cabañas Vista Hermosa* north of the river, *Hs. Huinca Quiñay* near Riñihue) and simple campgrounds.

PANGUIPULLI is the largest town in the region, providing services to outlying communities and exporting their forest products. Situated on a hill overlooking the lake, with well-maintained farms in the surrounding countryside, the town prides itself on its rose bushes, celebrated the first week of every February in the *Semana de las Rosas*. Still, Panguipulli is more of a transportation link, information center and last-minute stock-up spot than an attraction in its own right. Just above town on Padre Sigfredo is a campground, *El Bosque*.

Río San Pedro (III)

⏱2d
The warm, crystal clear San Pedro flows out of the east end of Lago Riñihue, draining the entirety of the Siete Lagos region. Safe, big volume Class III rapids, unbelievable playspots, and camping on sand beaches makes this the classic two-day trip in the Lake District.

Operators: 207

Río Fuy (III-V)

⏱1d
There are three world-class sections on the beautiful, electric-blue Río Fuy. Beginning at Puerto Fuy (on Lago Pirihueico), the Upper Fuy starts as ledgy Class IV, then steepens through a series of classic Class V waterfalls, including one super-clean 30-footer (La Leona);

there is a takeout at a roadside pasture below the canyon. Below the Salto Huilo Huilo, the long, remote and committing Huilo Huilo gorge is only runnable with low water (and only then with extreme caution), consisting of consecutive Class IV and V drops with a couple of mandatory portages around waterfalls. The lower Fuy (Class III-IV) begins at a fish farm (piscicultura) above the Huilo Huilo bridge and continues to the next bridge downstream.

Volcán Choshuenco (2,415m)

⏱1d ⬛
Once a popular winter sports center, Volcán Choshuenco has since relapsed into obscurity, and is now among the least-visited peaks in the Lake District. In reality there are two peaks here: the rounded, lower-elevation Volcán Mocho and the steeper, more technically challenging Volcán Choshuenco. The ascent of either initiates at the (locked) *refugios* above the town of Enco, and starts by climbing the gentle northwest ridge, which provides splendid views of Lago Panguipulli and Lago Riñihue. The remote, glaciated south face of Choshuenco is a good choice for experienced parties seeking to practice their ice-climbing skills.

Fishing in the Siete Lagos

This relatively remote area provides some of the best fishing in the northern Lake District. Boats are available for rent on all the major lakes, and float trips may be arranged on the Río Llanquihue, the Río Enco, and the Río San Pedro. Smaller streams appropriate for wading include the Río Toledo and the Río Mañío (both affluents of Lago Panguipulli) the Río Liquiñe, the Río Pellaifa, and the Río Fuy. Consult at the *Municipalidad* in Panguipulli for local guides and boat rentals.

Operators: 117

Valdivia
Pop. 112,712 (☎ city code 63)

Riverside Valdivia is the most distinctive city in the south, replete with history and German architecture and alive with students and flowers.

Founded by Pedro de Valdivia in the 1550's during his initial 'conquest' of the south, the original Spanish settlement was destroyed – like so many others – during the Mapuche uprising in 1599. Forty years later, however, a failed attempt by the Dutch to establish a colony here in cooperation

with the Mapuches motivated the Spanish to reoccupy this strategic site at the confluence of the Río Calle Calle and the Río Cruces. In 1645, a massive Spanish expedition began laying the foundations for what would become one of the greatest fortifications in Spanish America, with multiple forts at the mouth of the Río Valdivia; the city itself was enclosed within a walled fortress. Throughout the remainder of the Colonial era Valdivia served as an essential link on the

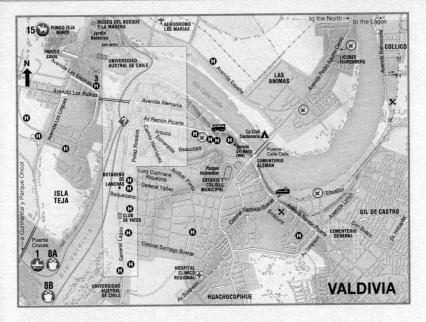

VALDIVIA

coastal road to Chiloé, and it remained one of the final royalist holdouts during the battles for independence. The forts and city were finally captured in 1820 by a force under the command of Lord Thomas Cochrane, founder of Chile's navy.

Beginning in the 1850's, a flood of German immigrants was loosed upon the city. Homesteaders soon seized upon the rich land being offered in the interior valleys, while merchants and professionals stayed in town, where their ingenuity and work ethic soon transformed Valdivia into the leading industrial center in the south, with breweries, shipyards, bronze foundries, and dozens of other businesses.

Valdivia's prosperity continued through the early 20th century, but on May 22, 1960, a massive earthquake – 8.9 on the Richter scale at its epicenter – brought the city to its knees, destroying the majority of the German-built buildings in town and causing the surrounding area to sink a full three meters. Valdivia's waterfront disappeared below the river, and thousands of hectares of surrounding farmland were converted, almost overnight, into wetlands.

Today Valdivia has been rebuilt, and the German influence, while no longer quite so obvious, continues to lend character to the city. The main downtown area is concentrated in triangular area bounded by a curve in the Río Calle Calle, while across the bridge to the west is Isla Teja, site of the Universidad Austral.

In-town Attractions

Feria Fluvial and the Muelle Schuster

Along the Río Valdivia waterfront just south of the bridge to Isla Teja, the Feria Fluvial is a colorful celebration of fresh seafood, fruits and vegetables, much of which arrives at the market by boat from the coast or interior valleys. Just south of the market is the Muelle Schuster, where motor launches offering tours on the local waterways are tied up (see ⊡ for listings).

Historic German Homes

The majority of German-built homes to have survived the 1960 earthquake are found on Calle General Lagos, the southern extension of Calle Yungay. Most of these homes date from the mid- to late-1800's. Of special note is the CENTRO CULTURAL EL AUSTRAL, in an 1870 house, with exhibitions of furniture

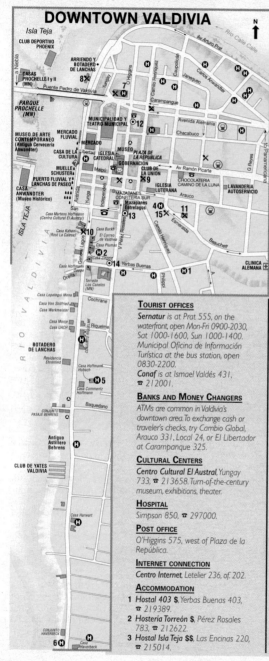

DOWNTOWN VALDIVIA

N

Isla Teja
CLUB DEPORTIVO PHOENIX
Río Calle Calle
Av. Arturo Prat
CASAS PROCHELLE I y II (MN)
ARRIENDO Y BOTADERO DE LANCHAS
8
Higgins
Yungay
Puente Pedro de Valdivia
Caupolicán
Carlos Anwandter
Janequeo
7
Camino Henríquez
Carampangue
PARQUE PROCHELLE (MN)
MUNICIPALIDAD Y TEATRO MUNICIPAL 12
Avenida Alemania
Chacabuco
MUSEO DE ARTE CONTEMPORANEO (Antigua Cervecería Anwandter)
MERCADO FLUVIAL
MERCADO
MUSEO
CASA DE LA CULTURA
Libertad
IGLESIA CATEDRAL
PLAZA DE LA REPUBLICA
GOBERNACION
MUELLE Y SCHUSTER
Maipú
CLUB DE LA UNION 9
Av Ramón Picarte
G Reyes
PUERTO FLUVIAL Y LANCHAS DE PASEO
Yunga
Independencia
IGLESIA LUTERANA
CHOCOLATERIA CAMINO DE LA LUNA
LAVANDERIA AUTOSERVICIO
CASA ANWANTER (Museo Histórico)
San
Alameda
MAZABANES CONFITERIA SUR
Arauco
Mazapanes Entrelagos
13
4 11
15
Esmeralda
Casa Martens Hoffmann (Centro Cultural El Austral)
Casa Burkh
10
Casa Kahen (Rest La Calesa)
El Correo de Valdivia
Gral Lagos
2
Casa Plumas
Beaucheff
Camino Henríquez
CLINICA ALEMANA
ISLA TEJA
Casa Hoffmann Nieto
Casa Zilleruelo
14
Yerbas Buenas
Orilla
Philippi
1
RIO VALDIVIA
Casa Lopetegui Mena
Cochrane
Casa Von Stülfried
Casa Werkmeister
Casa Monje
Casa UACH
Riquelme
BOTADERO DE LANCHAS
Casa Hoffmann Hubach
Residencia Ehrenfeld
5
Casa Commentz Hoffmann
Baquedano
CONJUNTO PASAJE BEHRENS
Antiguo Astillero Behrens
CLUB DE YATES VALDIVIA
Casa Harwart
Casa Hoffmann
HOSPITAL
CONJUNTO HAVERBECK
6
Casa Haverbeck

Tourist offices

Sernatur is at Prat 555, on the waterfront, open Mon-Fri 0900-2030, Sat 1000-1600, Sun 1000-1400. Municipal Oficina de Información Turística at the bus station, open 0830-2200.
Conaf is at Ismael Valdés 431, ☎ 212001.

Banks and Money Changers

ATMs are common in Valdivia's downtown area. To exchange cash or traveler's checks, try Cambio Global, Arauco 331, Local 24, or El Libertador at Carampangue 325.

Cultural Centers

Centro Cultural El Austral, Yungay 733, ☎ 213658. Turn-of-the-century museum, exhibitions, theater.

Hospital

Simpson 850, ☎ 297000.

Post Office

O'Higgins 575, west of Plaza de la República.

Internet connection

Centro Internet, Letelier 236, of. 202.

Accommodation

1 **Hostal 403 $**, Yerbas Buenas 403, ☎ 219389.
2 **Hosteria Torreón $**, Pérez Rosales 783, ☎ 212622.
3 **Hostal Isla Teja $$** Las Encinas 220, ☎ 215014.
4 **Hostal Esmeralda $$**, Esmeralda 651, ☎ 215659.
5 **Hotel Jardín del Rey $$**, General Lagos 1190, ☎ 218562.
6 **Hotel Naguilán $$$**, General Lagos 1927, ☎ 212851.
7 **Hotel Pedro de Valdivia $$$**, Carampangue 190, ☎ 212931.
HI Residencial Germania $, Picarte 873, ☎ 212405.
More info at www.turistel.cl

Restaurants

8 **Camino de Luna**, on a boat on the waterfront north of the bridge to Isla Teja. Expensive, varied menú.
9 **Club de la Union**, Camilo Henríquez 540. Traditional social club, seafood, bar.
10 **La Calesa**, Yungay 735. In old German house, good fixed lunches.
11 **New Orleans**, Esmeralda 682. Cajun food, movie theme
12 **Café Haussmann**, O'Higgins 394. Local favorite for steak tartar 'crudos.'
13 **Entrelagos**, Pérez Rosales 640. Café menu, deserts, coffee.
14 **Café de la Ultima Frontera**, corner of Pérez Rosales and Yerbas Buenas. Coffee, bookstore, art exhibits.
15 **Approach**, Esmeralda 675. Pizza.
Kuntsmann Brewery, SW of town on the road to Niebla. Microbrew, pub fare, brewery tours.

Airport

Aeropuerto Pichoy is 29km north of Valdivia.

Airline Offices

LanChile, Maipú 271, ☎ 258840.
Ladeco, Caupolicán 364 local 7, ☎ 213392.
Aerocontinente, ☎ 6002092358.

Airport Transport

Minibuses: Transfer Valdivia, ☎ 225533, US$5.
Radio Taxis: Radiotaxi Ríos del Sur, ☎ 219200.

Bus Station and/or offices

Bus Station at Anfión Muñoz 360, on the banks of the Río Calle Calle.

Rent a Car

Assef y Méndez ☎ 213205.
Autovald ☎ 212786.
Turismo Cochrane ☎ 212213.

Train Station

No direct rail service. For combination bus-rail service via Temuco, Ferrocarriles del Estado is at Ecuador 2000, ☎ 214571.

Shopping

Fruit, vegetables, seafood at the Feria Fluvial.
Locally-made chocolates at Chocolatería Entrelagos, Pérez Rosales 622, and Chocolatería de Luna, Picarte 417.

and decorative items from the era. Across the street is the **TORREÓN LOS CANELOS**, built in 1781 as part of the defensive wall that enclosed the city. There is another Spanish-built tower, the **TORREÓN DEL BARRO**, across town on Av. Picarte.

Museo Histórico y Arqueológico Mauricio ven de Maele Located in a historic German home on the Isla Teja waterfront, directly across from the Muelle Schuster, this fine museum features exhibits on Mapuche ethnography, the colonial era and German immigration. Just north in the old Cervecería Antwander building is the **MUSEO DE ARTE CONTEMPORÁNEO**, with temporary exhibitions of sculpture and painting.

Hours: Museo Histórico 15 Dec-15 Mar daily 1000-1300, 1400-2000, rest of the year Tue-Sun 1000-1300, 1400-1800. *Entrance:* $900, children $300. Museo Contemporáneo Tue-Sun 1000-1300, 1500-1800.

Universidad Austral Valdivia's shady, energetic university is located across from downtown on Isla Teja. North of the main campus is the **JARDÍN BOTÁNICO** (Botanical Garden), with labeled tree species and lovely paths and benches; the garden is open daily during daylight hours only. Occupying the entire northern end of the island is the Fundo Teja Norte, with longer trails along the river, a campground and picnic area. Parque Saval is another small park with two ponds and a picnic area.

Fundo Teja Norte

 ☎ (63)221956
With previous notice, you can arrange day trips on horseback in this large forest reserve, owned by the Universidad Austral and located within easy walking distance of downtown Valdivia.

Around Valdivia

Santuario de la Naturaleza Río Cruces

The Río Cruces ecosystem – one of only seven protected wetlands in Chile – was formed during the 1960 *terremoto*, when these lands sunk and were inundated. Over 119 species of birds have been observed in the sanctuary, of which 75% are thought to be resident species. Other notable fauna includes the endangered huillín, a fresh-water otter.

At the time of writing, efforts were underway to implement an ecotourism project with locals in the village of **PUNUCAPA**, set at the northern end of the sanctuary and renowned for its production of sparkling cider. Near Punucapa is the **CASTILLO DE SAN LUIS DE ALBA DE AMARGOS**, a 17th-century Spanish fort .

Paddling on the Río Cruces

The calm, protected wetlands of the Río Cruces make for ideal day trips in canoes or sea kayaks: your chances of spotting (and not disturbing) birds and other fauna are much better than aboard a noisy tour boat. Be sure to arrange these trips ahead of time.
Operators: 195 – 234

Niebla, Corral and Isla Mancera

About 20km west of Valdivia, this group of Spanish forts and coastal resort villages constitutes Valdivia's most popular nearby attraction.

If you are traveling on public transport, the easiest (and cheapest) way to get to the coast is by regular bus or taxi colectivo. Just past the steeply inclined bridge over the Río Cruces, the route passes the Kuntsmann brewery, and then parallels the Río Valdivia for the run to the coast. The town of NIEBLA (18km from Valdivia), set on a commanding headland above the mouth of the river, has a number of seafood restaurants and places to stay, as well as a Spanish fort, the **CASTILLO DE LA PURA Y LIMPIA CONCEPCIÓN DE MONTFORT DE LEMUS**; to the north, the coast is steep and rugged with scattered beaches and campgrounds, but no more formal lodging.

From the ramp below town, you can catch a 15min ferry or motor launch (frequent departures for cars and passengers) across the mouth of the river to ISLA MANCERA and CORRAL. There is another Spanish fort on Isla Mancera, the **CASTILLO DE SAN PEDRO DE ALCÁNTARA**, but the largest and best-preserved in the bay is the **CASTILLO SAN SEBASTIÁN DE LA CRUZ** in Corral. During summer there are daily re-enactments of Colonial life and defensive tactics. There are cabins and basic accommodations in Corral, which you can also reach directly by car from Valdivia.

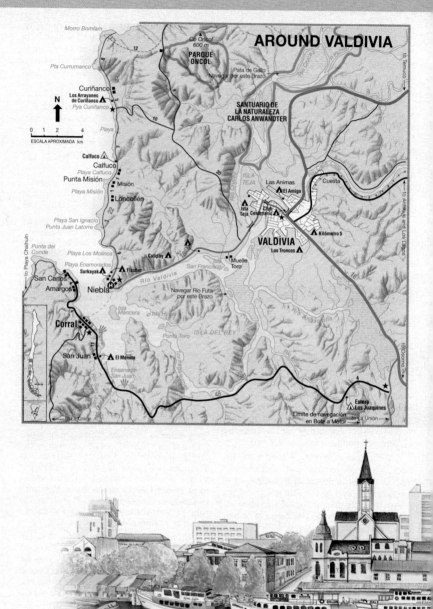

AROUND VALDIVIA

Morro Bomfam

Ce Oncol
600 m

PARQUE
ONCOL

Pta Currumanco

Pata de Gallo
Navegar por este Brazo

Curiñanco
Los Arrayanes
de Curiñanco
Pya Curiñanco

N

SANTUARIO DE
LA NATURALEZA
CARLOS ANWANDTER

0 1 2 4 km
ESCALA APROXIMADA

Playa

Calfuco
Playa Calfuco
Punta Misión
Misión
Playa Misión
Loncollén

Playa San Ignacio
Punta Juan Latorre

ISLA
TEJA

Las Animas
El Amigo

Cuesta

Isla
Teja
Club
Centenario

VALDIVIA
Los Troncos

Kilómetro 5

Punta del
Conde
Playa Los Molinos
Playa Enamorados
Surkayak
Fischer
San Carlos
Amargos
Niebla

Gutipay

San Francisco

Muelle
Toro

Río Valdivia

Navegar Río Futa
por este Brazo

Corral

Isla
Mancera

Isla Hygni

Punta Toro

ISLA DEL REY

San Juan
El Morrito

Ensenada
San Juan

Estero
Los Juaquines

Límite de navegación
en Bote a Motor

to La Unión

to La Unión

to Playa Chaihuín

to La Unión

to Temuco

to Antilhue and Los Lagos

to Osorno

MUELLE SCHUSTER

470

Boat Trips Around Valdivia

BOAT TOURS ON THE RÍO CRUCES

● **M/N Isla del Río**
⏱6h

The Isla del Río is one of the few boats on the Valdivia waterfront that offers regular tours of the Santuario de la Naturaleza Río Cruces. The complete trip through the reserve to the Spanish fort San Luis de Alba de Cruces departs in the early afternoon and costs *$14,000 pp* with meals.

● **Colico**
⏱1-6h

This 1907 German steam-powered vessel is the most distinctive craft on the Valdivia waterfront. Tours include the circumnavigation of Isla Teja (*$6500 pp*) and the Santuario de la Naturaleza Río Cruces (*$10,000 pp*).

BOAT TOURS ON THE RÍO VALDIVIA AND RÍO TORNAGALEONES

Valdivia's most popular boat trips descend the Río Valdivia to the coast, visiting the Spanish forts at Niebla, Corral, and Isla Mancera, and returning via the Río Tornagaleones. Trips typically include *once* (afternoon tea) and lunch, though passengers can choose which meals, if any, they wish to eat. Most tours depart around 1330.

● **Catamarán Extasis**
⏱6-7h - $17,000 pp with meals.

● **M/N Neptuno**
⏱5h - $16,000 pp with meals, $9,000 w/o.

● **M/N Orión III**
⏱6h - $15,500 pp with meals.

● **M/N Reina Sofía**
⏱6h - $10,000 pp with meals.

● **M/N Calle Calle**
⏱6h - $14,000 pp with meals, $8,000 w/o.

● **Crucero Pollux**
⏱5h - $12,000 pp with meals.

● **L/M Bahía, Bahía II and Bahía Blanca**
⏱ One-hour tours around Isla Teja, departing every 30 min. $2,500 pp.

Monumento Natural Alerce Costero

This remote park in the Coast Range south of Valdivia protects one of few remaining coastal stands of alerce (*Fitzroya cupressoides*), including one tree with a diameter of 4.2 meters and an estimated age of over 3000 years. You can camp in the park; hiking options are limited. The park entrance is 89km south of Valdivia on dirt roads that may be nearly impassable with heavy rains. There is no public transport to the park.

■ See pg 6 for photo credit

Lago Ranco

See map

See map

ACCOMMODATION

Best range of accommodation in Futrono and Lago Ranco. Commercial campgrounds all around the lake, on Lago Maihue, and at the Termas de Chihuío. Up-market apart-hotel at Bahía Coique. Hostería-style accommodation in Llifén, on the road from Llifén to Lago Maihue and near the source of the Río Bueno at Puerto Nuevo.

TRANSPORT

Along the north shore, to Futrono and Llifén, by bus from Valdivia via Paillaco. Along the south shore to Lago Ranco and Riñinahue, by bus from Osorno or Valdivia via Río Bueno.

Long reknowned among Chilean fishermen and increasingly visited by wealthy *Santiaguinos*, Lago Ranco nonetheless remains relatively unknown to foreign tourists, most of whom pass it by in favor of the more famous attractions to the south. Like the rest of the lakes, the west shore is low and relatively level, formed by a glacial moraine, while the wilder eastern shore edges into the Andes.

On the northern shore, the town of **FUTRONO** is set back on a hillside with nice views over the lake; if you want to stay right on the lakeshore, you might try the recommended *Posada del Lago*. You can also catch a boat from here to visit **ISLA GUAPI**, home to a community of Huilliche Indians. The full moon in late January or early February is the cue for a community-wide council, called the *trapëmuwn*, and though there is no lodging on the island, you may be able to crash in the schoolhouse. Otherwise, the island makes an interesting day trip in summer. Use tact when taking photos.

Barcaza Guapi

⏱ **45min**

Departs from Futrono on Mon, Wed, Fri and Sat at 1700 ; in summer there may be two boats daily.

LAGO RANCO

🚶 **40C** Puyehue Traverse
🚢 **16** Isla Guapi
♨ **31** Termas de Chihuío

23km east, near the mouth of the Río Calcurrupe, is the town of **LLIFÉN**. There is a long chain of upscale lodging at the entrance to the town, beginning with *Hostería Huequecura* and ending at Llifen's port, where boats are available for rent. Llifén also has an excellent beach, Playa Bonita.

A dirt road leads east out of town, climbing into the Andes along the Río Calcurrupe. Along the way you'll pass the entrance to a top-notch fishing lodge, the *Río Cumilahue Lodge*, before reaching **LAGO MAIHUE**; access to the lakeshore is possible at Puerto Llolles, at the west end, and at La Barra and Playa Maqueo, at the east end. A narrow dirt road continues north and then west to the Termas de Chihuío.

BOSQUE QUILLIN ON LAGO RANCO

Termas de Chihuío

 C free NA

About 42km east of Llifén on a dirt road above Lago Maihue, these remote 82°C springs have been channeled into rustic wooden tubs in five tiny cabins.

South of Llifén, you must cross the Río Calcurrupe on a ferry to continue the lake circuit. The Salto de Nilahue, a double-drop waterfall 14km from Llifén, is worth a visit; nearby is the trailhead for the walk south into PN Puyehue (ask locals to help you find it). 7km east of the falls is a lakeside campground at Playa Arenales, while 7km SW on the main road is the village of **RIÑINAHUE**. Note the burnt-out forests and deposits of volcanic ash in this area, dating from recent eruptions of Volcán Carrán (in 1954 and 1979).

The road continues along the lakeshore to **LAGO RANCO** (47km from Llifén), where you'll find the normal range of low- to mid-range lodging and restaurants.

Fishing Around Lago Ranco

The eastern shore of Lago Ranco is blessed with a great concentration of fishable streams, including the Río Cumilahue, the only mandatory catch-and-release river in Chile (Chilean flyfishing pioneer Adrián Dufflocq has a lodge here). Llifén and Riñinahue generally attract substantial numbers of Chilean fishermen, but the deeper you venture into the cordillera, the less company you are likely to have.

Operators: 82

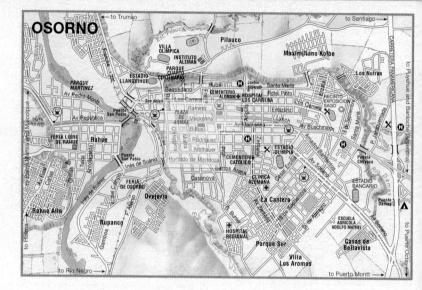

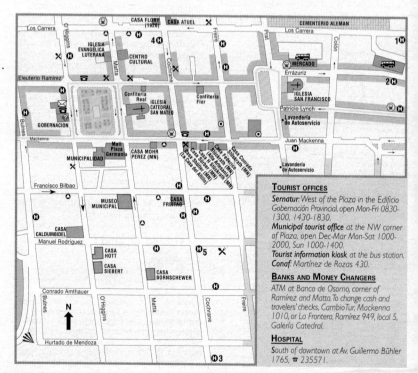

TOURIST OFFICES

Sernatur: West of the Plaza in the Edificio Gobernación Provincial, open Mon-Fri 0830-1300, 1430-1830.

Municipal tourist office at the NW corner of Plaza, open Dec-Mar Mon-Sat 1000-2000, Sun 1000-1400.

Tourist information kiosk at the bus station. *Conaf:* Martínez de Rozas 430.

BANKS AND MONEY CHANGERS

ATM at Banco de Osorno, corner of Ramírez and Matta. To change cash and travelers' checks, CambioTur, Mackenna 1010, or La Frontera, Ramírez 949, local 5, Galería Catedral.

HOSPITAL

South of downtown at Av. Guillermo Bühler 1765, ☎ 235571.

Osorno
Pop. 114,239 (☎ *city code 64*)

Osorno is an agricultural service center in the midst of Chile's major dairy region, founded in 1553 during the first wave of Spanish expansion in the south and destroyed 50 years later by the Mapuches. In 1792 the town was re-founded, and through the latter half of the 19th century the city received hundreds of European immigrants, most of them German.

The city center is compact, set on the east bank of the Río Rahue. From a traveler's perspective, Osorno is an important transport link but otherwise holds limited appeal.

In-town Attractions

Historic homes on Av. Mackenna On Av. Mackenna east of the plaza, six German-built homes from the 19th century have been declared National Monuments. In the Casa Schilling Buschman, on the corner of Bilbao, is the MUSEO Y ARCHIVO HISTÓRICO, with displays on local history and native culture. None of the other homes are open to visits, but they're worth a quick look to get an idea of what Osorno looked like 100 years ago.
Hours: Jan-Feb Mon-Fri 0900-1700, Sat-Sun 1100-1900, Mar-Dec Mon-Fri 0900-1700, Sat 1500-1800)

Agricultural Markets and Fairs

Those interested in rural culture (or just looking to stock up on vegetables) can visit the Feria Libre de Rahue, at the corner of Chillán and Concepción on the west side of the Río Rahue. Another spectacle is the daily livestock auction at the Feria de Osorno, on Inés de Suárez SW of downtown.

Around Osorno

The Coast

Accessed by a recently paved road, the coast around BAHÍA MANSA makes a good day trip for those looking for a break from the gringo trail. 2km south of Bahía Mansa is Maicolpué, with seafood restaurants and a couple of reasonable *hosterías*. North is Pucatrihue, also with a *hostería* set in a unique dune habitat with a small lagoon.

40km NW of Osorno, local Huilliche Indians in PILFUCO offer hiking and horseback riding in the ancient evergreen and alerce forests of the Coast Range. Access is via the town of Misión de San Juan de la Costa; for information, contact Matías Huenupán at ☎ (09) 8313948 or (09) 7736979. Transport via daily buses from the Feria de Rahue.

Down the Río Bueno

⏱5h
Departing from the *balseo* (ferry) near Trumao (leaves Wed 9 am, returns Thur 2 pm), a small steamship takes you 5hrs downriver through the Coast Range to the mouth of the Río Bueno. This is an excellent way to begin the three-day coastal hike to Valdivia, following the colonial route.

Those seeking more adrenaline can contact *River Jet* for trips aboard high-speed 310-hp jet boats, covering the entirety of the Río Bueno – from its source at Lago Ranco to its mouth at La Barra – in just over 45min. Similar trips are also offered on the Río Rahue and Lago Rupanco.

POST OFFICE
O'Higgins 645, west of the Plaza de Armas.

INTERNET CONNECTION
Satanca Pub, Patio Freire 542.

ACCOMMODATION
1 Residencial Sánchez **S**, *Los Carrera 1595,* ☎ *232560.*
2 Hospedaje Millantué **SS**, *Errázuriz 1339,* ☎ *242480.*
3 Hotel del Prado, *Cochrane 816,* ☎ *235020.*
More info at www.turistel.cl

RESTAURANTS
4 Los Troncos, *Cochrane 527. Pizza.*
5 Peter's Kneipe, *Manuel Rodríguez 1039. German food, expensive.*

AIRPORT
Aeropuerto Carlos Hott Siebert is 7km east of town.

AIRLINE OFFICES
LanChile, Eleuterio Ramírez 802, ☎ *314949.*
Ladeco, Juan Mackenna 1098, ☎ *234355.*

AIRPORT TRANSPORT
Radiotaxi: Radiotaxis Osorno, ☎ *317000.*

BUS STATION AND/OR OFFICES
The long-distance bus terminal is at Av. Errázuriz 1400.
Buses towards the mountains depart from the Mercado Municipal, 1 block west, while buses to the coast depart from the Feria Libre de Rahue, across the Río Rahue to the west.

TRAIN STATION
West of downtown, near the corner of Juan Mackenna and Portales.

Motorbike Tours

MotoAventura offers ⏱1-10d on- and off-road adventures in the Osorno and Lago Llanquihue region, using a fleet of 2001 Yamaha XT600's. Consult for details.

The North Shore of Lago Llanquihue

Puerto Octay is 54km SE of Osorno. Transport by regular bus, [↓].

Parque Nacional Puyehue

PRACTICAL INFORMATION

Access to the park is charged at Anticura, but not at Aguas Calientes, though vehicles are charged for the ascent of Volcán Casablanca. Park rangers at Anticura and Aguas Calientes are good sources of information on hikes and other activities.

ACCOMMODATION

Best range of accommodation in Entre Lagos and along the south shore of Lago Puyehue. Campground, cabañas, hostería at Aguas Calientes. Hotels at Termas de Puyehue and Antillanca. Rustic Conaf campground at Anticura. For backcountry hikers, there are a number of refugios inside the park.

TRANSPORT

To Entre Lagos, Aguas Calientes, and Anticura, by bus from the Terminal de Buses Rurales in Osorno.

This 107,000há park protects a variety of forest and montane environments, including huge tracts of evergreen temperate rainforest, alpine deciduous forest, and treeless

LAGO PUYEHUE

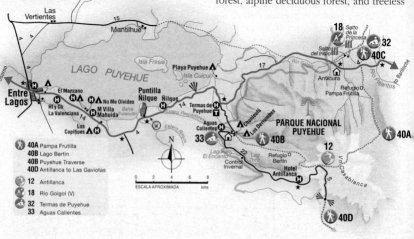

40A Pampa Frutilla
40B Lago Bertín
40B Puyehue Traverse
40D Antillanca to Las Gaviotas

12 Antillanca

18 Río Golgol (V)

32 Termas de Puyehue

33 Aguas Calientes

volcanic plateaus. There is a ski area, several hotsprings, excellent fishing and kayaking, and more diverse hiking options than almost any other park in the south. Nonetheless, the area is relatively neglected by travelers, most of whom simply pass through the park on paved route 215 to Bariloche. To the north, the park extends almost all the way to Riñinahue, on the southern shore of Lago Ranco, while to the south it joins with PN Vicente Pérez Rosales. The protected area here is enormous, especially when you consider the extent of Parque Nacional Nahuel Huapi, across the Argentine border to the east.

From Osorno, Route 215 runs through farmland along the south shore of Lago Puyehue, passing the sleepy lakeside village of **ENTRE LAGOS**, where there are a couple of fine places to stay on the lakefront, namely *Hostal Millaray* and *Hosp. Panorama*, the latter with a campsite. The route passes further campgrounds and cabaña complexes before reaching a Y in the road, 73km from Osorno.

The unpaved right (south) branch leads past the Termas de Puyehue hotsprings resort and continues to the **AGUAS CALIENTES** sector of the park. Here there is a popular thermal pool next to the river, plus cabins, a campground, and Conaf's *Centro de Información Ambiental*. Rangers here can provide information on several short walks through the surrounding rainforest, plus a longer excursion past Lago Bertín en route to Antillanca.

Termas de Puyehue

☎ (64)371382 🏠 $4,000
This massive wood and stone hotel features two large pools in a pleasant atrium, as well as mud and sulphur baths with an average temperature of 37°C. Excursions in the park and surrounding area may be arranged at the hotel.

Aguas Calientes

🏠 NA
This popular, accessible spring features a large cement pool along the river and 16 private indoor tubs. Well located at the entrance to PN Puyehue on the road to Antillanca; cabañas, hostería accommodation, and camping are all available.

Antillanca, the ski area, lies 18km further up from Aguas Calientes. There is hotel at the base of the ski area, which occupies the western flank of Volcán Casablanca. An access road (passable in an ordinary vehicle) leading to the summit of the volcano, where you can connect with trails leading north to Pampa Frutilla and Anticura. There is also an unmarked track leading south to the western shore of Lago Rupanco, from which point you can connect with trails through PN Vicente Pérez Rosales.

The paved left (north) branch continues through rainforest, crossing the Río Golgol twice en route to the Conaf ranger station at **ANTICURA**, 91km from Osorno. There is a Conaf campground and *Centro de Información Ambiental* here, and just upvalley are the trailheads for short walks to Salto La Princesa and Salto El Indio. Longer trails departing from here include the route to Pampa Frutilla (and Antillanca) and the Volcán Puyehue trail, which can be continued north to Riñinahue.

Route 215 continues east from Anticura, climbing into pure southern beech forest (spectacular fall foliage) en route to Argentina. Ask rangers in Anticura about a seldom-used trailhead on the left providing access to Lago Constancia and Lago Gris, located in the high volcanic plateau along the Argentine border.

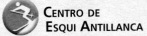

CENTRO DE ESQUI ANTILLANCA

Antillanca provides an ideal combination of modern infrastructure and the friendly, down-home atmosphere found in smaller resorts. Though a few more lifts and some steeper lift-served skiing would be nice, the clubhouse ambiance and ample backcountry make this one of the friendliest, most distinctive resorts in the south. For those on a ski tour in the south, Antillanca makes a logical stop for those heading across the border to the bigger, spendier resorts in Bariloche.

The resort is set on the SW slopes of Volcán Casablanca, an irregular, multi-coned peak that rises above the temperate rainforests of PN Puyehue. The only accommodation at the base of the mountain is the hotel, but there is also upscale accommodation available down the road at the Termas de Puyehue, moderately-priced cabins at Aguas Calientes, and budget lodging in Entre Lagos. Note that the road to the ski area is one-way: traffic goes up in the morning, down in the afternoon.

ANTILLANCA

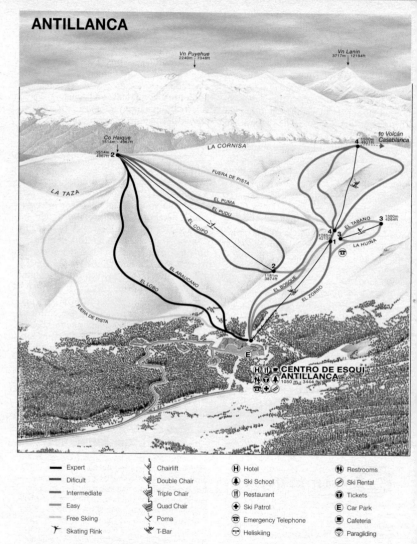

▬ Expert	⟋ Chairlift	Ⓗ Hotel	🛉 Restrooms
▬ Dificult	⟋ Double Chair	ⓐ Ski School	⊘ Ski Rental
▬ Intermediate	⟋ Triple Chair	ⓘ Restaurant	Ⓣ Tickets
▬ Easy	⟋ Quad Chair	✚ Ski Patrol	Ⓔ Car Park
▬ Free Skiing	⟋ Poma	☎ Emergency Telephone	Ⓒ Cafeteria
✈ Skating Rink	⟋ T-Bar	Ⓗ Heliskiing	Ⓥ Paragliding

The lifts begin in the lovely lenga forest that tapers off just above the hotel, providing access to trails that are mostly appropriate for beginning and intermediate skiers. Advanced skiers will end up running laps off the Haique T-bar, where there are good, steep, continuous pitches. If you are willing to hike for your turns, you can investigate the Taza Chica, an extinct crater west of the Haique lift, or ski off the main summit of the volcano, which may be reached by a 2-hour hike from the top of the #4 T-bar. Most of this off-piste terrain is relatively low angle, but the scenery in this intensely volcanic region makes up for the lack of steeps. Off to the north you can see the peak of Volcán Puyehue, which makes for a great overnight backcountry trip, especially in spring.

Antillanca's biggest drawback is its low elevation, which means that the area often walks the fine line between rain and snow. The snow here is always heavy, and sometimes it simply washes away. But if that happens, you can always just head for the hotsprings.

Río Golgol (V)

 🕐1d
Beginning below the Salto de la Princesa, the Golgol run drops steeply through the temperate rainforest of Parque Nacional Puyehue. There are five major waterfalls on the run, all with relatively complicated entries and Class V consequences. The run ends at the Salto del Indio, a seldom-run 40-footer. Experts only, to say the least.

TREKKING IN PARQUE NACIONAL PUYEHUE

● Pampa Frutilla
 🕐2-3d ▭
Heading south from Anticura, this trail follows an old 4WD road through the forest to a Conaf refugio in the foothills of Volcán Casablanca. From here, you can continue south over volcanic ridges to the ski area (and connect with the Antillanca - Las Gaviotas trail, below), hitch a ride back down the road, or follow the old track via Lago Bertín to Aguas Calientes.

● Lago Bertín
🗡🕐1-2d ▭
This easy rainforest/volcano hike begins in Aguas Calientes, leading east past a couple of trailheads to reach Lago Bertín (and the rather shoddy *Refugio Bertín*) after about 2hrs. From here the route climbs south past treeline onto the treeless flanks of Volcán Casablanca, ending after about 2hrs at Antillanca.

● Puyehue Traverse
🗡⮌🕐3-4d ▭
Beginning at El Caulle, a *fundo* near Anticura, this route climbs through dense forest to the open volcanic slopes of Volcán Puyehue, arriving at Refugio Puyehue in 4-6 hours. From here the route continues past the west flank of the volcano to a campsite at Los Baños, which makes a good base for exploring the geothermal fields on the NW flank of the volcano; in general, this entire area is geothermally active, and you'll find steam vents and geysers scattered all along the route. It's another two days from here out the Río Contrafuerte to Riñinahue (on the shore of Lago Ranco); otherwise, it's back out the way you came.

Operators: 215 🐎

● Antillanca to Las Gaviotas
🗡🕐1-2d ▭
This unmaintained trail leads south from the crater of Volcán Casablanca, dropping through extremely dense rainforest along the Estero Casablanca en route to the beach at Las Gaviotas, at the east end of Lago Rupanco. From here, you can walk out (trail on south shore) or hire a boat to the boat ramp at Puerto Rico ($15,000). An even better option is to do this route from south to north, as a continuation of the Termas El Callao route – but assume nothing about trail conditions.

Volcán Puyehue (2,240m)

 🕐2-3d ▭
From Refugio Puyehue, it's about 3 hours to the summit of the volcano, via a northward traverse followed by an ascent of the prominent ridge on the peaks' west side. The natural hotsprings at Los Baños sweetens the pot for this gentle walk-up, which also is a prime overnight destination for backcountry ski trips.

San Carlos de Bariloche (Argentina)

Better known simply as Bariloche, this immaculate tourist resort on the SE shore of Lago Nahuel Huapi is the *de facto* capital of the Argentine lake district. With its distinctly European feel, Bariloche is more urban – and much pricier – than its counterparts in Chile, and stays active year round, with quality ski areas and tons of hiking, boating, climbing and fishing in the summer season.

Bariloche has direct connections with Chile via two routes: paved Ruta 215 to Osorno, and the **CRUCE DE LOS LAGOS**, involving ferries across major Andean lakes including Lago Todos los Santos 🚶. It may also be reached by public transport via a couple of lesser-known but equally worthwhile passes to the north, **PASO HUAHUM** and **PASO MAMUIL MALAL**. To the south, Bariloche provides the easiest driving access to Futaleufú and other destinations along the Carretera Austral 🅐 overland.

With a bunch of mountaineering clubs and shops, Bariloche is also a great place to get informed and load up on (or get rid of) gear. Travelers with their own vehicles should be aware that fuel is very expensive in the lake region north of Bariloche, less so to the south.

LAGO NAHUEL HUAPI

LAGO RUPANCO

Lago Rupanco

Most of the southern shore of this remote, seldom-visited lake pertains to the immense **HACIENDA RUPANCO**, Chile's largest dairy farm, and by consequence there are really no towns at all. The hacienda itself offers upscale lodging and excursions, and there are a number of campgrounds and *hosterías* near the distinctively shaped Península El Islote; infrequent buses pass by here en route to the boat launch at **PUERTO RICO**.

Beyond here, the road continues along the increasingly rugged lakeshore, passing the *Puntiagudo Flyfishing Lodge*; soon thereafter the road narrows further to a horse trail, which continues all the way to **LAS GAVIOTAS**, the black sand beach at the far east end of the lake. From here, trails depart north to Volcán Casablanca (see PN Puyehue, 🚶), and south to Lago Todos los Santos (🚣). This area is largely wilderness, populated by a few rugged *campesinos*.

Fishing Around Lago Rupanco

A number of small, fishable streams drain into the remote southern and eastern shores of Lago Rupanco; the Río Nalcas may be accessed by road, while you need a boat to reach the more remote Río El Salto and Río Gaviotas. You also need a boat to fish the Río Rahue, which drains the lake to the west.
Operators: 32 - 159

The North and West Shores of Lago Llanquihue

The second largest lake in Chile, Lago Llanquihue could be considered the archetypal Lake District landscape, with the almost too-perfect cone of Volcán Osorno dominating the eastern horizon and quaint German-built villages and manicured farmland along the gentle western shores.

In 1842, when the Mapuche stronghold on the region began to ease and the lake was 'rediscovered' by Bernardo Philippi,

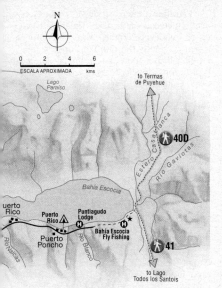

ACCOMMODATION

1 *Hospedaje Kaisersseehaus* **$**, Av. Philippi 1333, ☎ 421387.
2 *Hotel Ayacara* **$$$**, Av. Philippi 1215, ☎ 421550.
3 *Hotel Volcán Puntiagudo* **$$**, Camino Fundo Las Piedras, ☎ 421648.

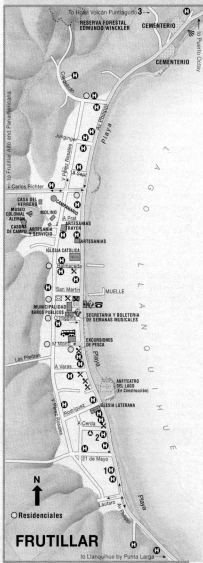

dense temperate rainforest covered the entire lakeshore. The area between Puerto Varas and Puerto Montt, to the south of the lake, entirely covered in ancient alerce forest. Beginning in 1852, however, German immigrants began to receive lands along the lakeshore, and by 1856 almost the entire lakefront was in private hands (with the exception of the wilder eastern shore around Ensenada).

The *colonos* burned and cleared the forests, exporting wood and importing supplies across the lake, while towns such as Puerto Octay, Frutillar, Llanquihue and Puerto Varas were built around a few strategically located

PRACTICAL INFORMATION

Tourist offices in Puerto Octay on the east side of the plaza, open Dec-Feb 0900-2100. In Frutillar, they're on Philippi between San Martín and O'Higgins, open Jan-Feb 1000-2100, rest of the year 1000-1800.

ACCOMMODATION

Greatest variety in Puerto Octay and Frutillar. In addition, there are many campgrounds, cabins and hostería-style accommodations along the roads circumscribing the lake.

TRANSPORT

Buses to Puerto Octay from Osorno, with afternoon connections to Las Cascadas (note: bus service does not continue south to Ensenada). Regular buses run between Puerto Octay and Frutillar Alto, with connections to Puerto Varas, Puerto Montt, other cities.

loading piers. Today, the architecture in these towns reflects the northern European roots of their founders, and though German is no longer spoken all that much, you can still count on finding freshly baked apple *kuchen* in most villages.

Built on rolling hills above the northwest corner of the lake, **PUERTO OCTAY** is the largest town on the north shore. It's biggest attraction is its museum on German settlement, the **MUSEO EL COLONO** *(Hours: Dec-Feb Mon-Sat 0930-1300,1500-1900, Sun 1100-1300,1500-1900)* at Independencia 591. Further displays of antique farm machinery may be visited south of town on the road to Península Centinela, where there is a historic hotel with a stunning view over the lake, the *Hotel Centinela*. There is also a campground on the waterfront and a couple of simple *residenciales* in town, while 2km north, the *Zapato Amarillo* guesthouse caters primarily to foreign travelers.

East of Puerto Octay there are two roads, one paved and the other (closer to the lake) gravel. The gravel road leads past Playa El Maitén (6km) and rejoins the paved road en route to **LAS CASCADAS**, just beyond the end of the pavement, 37km from Puerto Octay. There is a campground and *hostería* in Las Cascadas, as well as another black sand beach. South of here, the road narrows and public transport ends. The trip through old lava flows at the foot of Volcán Osorno to Ensenada is a popular bike route.

Two roads also lead south along the lake shore from Puerto Octay to Frutillar. The more direct paved route is about 25km long; the more scenic gravel road is about twice that, and passes by a couple of nice beaches en route, including the protected Playa Maqui (6km north of Frutillar), where there is a campground and basic lodging.

Frutillar is the most 'classic' of the German settlements on the lake. The town is set up on two levels: Frutillar Alto is the upper town, originally the railroad depot, while Frutillar Bajo is 4km east on the lakeshore. With a long, lovely beach backed by gardens, Frutillar Bajo looks straight out across the lake at Volcán Osorno, and has the best variety of lodging outside of Puerto Varas.

Near the north end of town on Arturo Prat, the **MUSEO COLONIAL ALEMÁN** *(Hours: 15 Dec-15 Mar daily 1000-1400, 1500-2000, rest of the year 1000-1400, 1500-1800. Entrance: $1.500, children $500)* reunites elements from the daily lives of second- and third-generation German immigrants. There is water-powered mill, a blacksmith's forge, a circular threshing mill known as a *campanario*, a well-preserved mansion and a good collection of household and farming implements.

Further north, in the hills at the north end of Caupolicán, is the 33há **RESERVA FORESTAL EDMUNDO WINKLER**, with a short trail through native forest and student guides in summer; this is a good place to look for help in identifying Valdivian Rainforest species.

During the last week in January, a variety of musical groups converge on Frutillar for the *Semanas Musicales de Frutillar*. The main concerts are held nightly in the Municipal Gymnasium, while mid-day concerts are held in local churches. Lodging should be reserved in advance for the Semanas Musicales, as should tickets for the major events, which run about US$10. A new theater in under construction at the time of writing.

South of Frutillar, it's 26km on the paved road to Puerto Varas (described 🔁). Those with their own transport might opt for the longer route along the shore of Punta Larga, where there are numerous campgrounds and cabañas.

Puerto Varas

Pop. 28,000 (☎ city code 65)

Situated on the SW shore of Lago Llanquihue, Puerto Varas ranks alongside Pucón as one of the most important destination cities in southern Chile, with an astounding variety of excursions, activities and natural attractions in the surrounding area. Since its beginnings in the mid-19th century, Puerto Varas' proximity to Puerto Montt has made it the largest settlement on the lake, and today the town preserves a host of German-built mansions, most dating from the arrival of rail service in 1912 🔁.

The center of town consists of about nine square blocks centered around the Plaza de Armas, with hills rising directly above to the north and west. A long waterfront connects the *centro* with the beach at Puerto Chico, where there is another cluster of lodging and restaurants. From Puerto Chico, a paved road leads east to Ensenada 🔁.

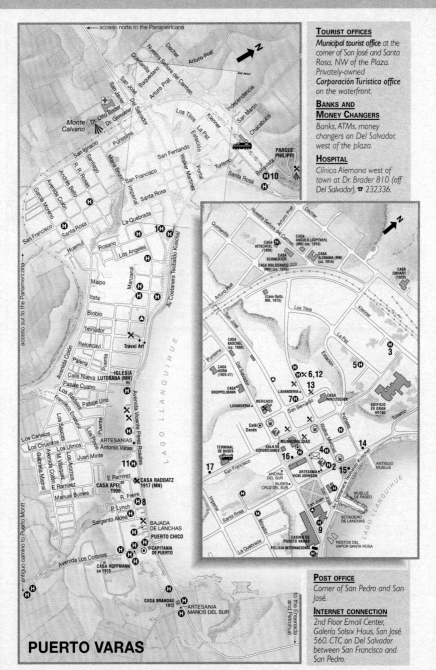

PUERTO VARAS

← acceso norte to the Panamericana

TOURIST OFFICES

Municipal tourist office at the corner of San José and Santa Rosa, NW of the Plaza. Privately-owned *Corporación Turística* office on the waterfront.

BANKS AND MONEY CHANGERS

Banks, ATMs, money changers on Del Salvador, west of the plaza.

HOSPITAL

Clínica Alemana west of town at Dr. Brader 810 (off Del Salvador), ☎ 232336.

POST OFFICE

Corner of San Pedro and San José.

INTERNET CONNECTION

2nd Floor Email Center, Galería Solsix Haus, San José 560. CTC on Del Salvador between San Francisco and San Pedro.

ACCOMMODATION

1 *Hospedaje Casa Azul $*, Mirador 18, ☎ 232904.

2 *Colores del Sur $*, Santa Rosa 318, ☎ 338588.

3 *Hospedaje Compass del Sur $*, Klenner 467, ☎ 232044.

4 *Hospedaje Ellenhaus $*, Walker Martínez 239, ☎ 233577.

5 *Hotel Westfalia $$*, La Paz 507, ☎ 235555.

6 *Hotel Merlín $$*, Martínez 584, ☎ 233105.

7 *Outsider $$*, San Bernardo 318, ☎ 232910.

8 *Hotel Los Tilos $$*, Pérez Rosales 1057, ☎ 233126.

9 *Hotel Colonos del Sur $$$*, Del Salvador 24, ☎ 233039.

10 *Hotel Cabañas del Lago $$$*, Klenner 195, ☎ 232291.

11 *Los Alerces Hotel y Cabañas $$$*, Pérez Rosales 281, ☎ 232070. More info at www.turistel.cl

RESTAURANTS

12 *Merlín*, Imperial 0605. Small, cozy, excellent ambience and food, expensive.

13 *La Olla*, San Bernando 240. Chilean food, hearty portions, inexpensive.

14 *Café Mediterráneo*, on the waterfront on the corner of Portales. Gourmet cuisine, lake views.

15 *Ravi's Casita de Kebabs*, in a stand near the waterfront north of the plaza. Falafel, giros, etc.

BARS AND ENTERTAINMENT

16 *El Barómetro*, San Pedro 418. Local favorite for drinks, Kuntsmann on tap.

17 *Pim's Pub*, on San Francisco near the bus station.

AIRPORTS

See Puerto Montt.

AIRLINE OFFICES

LanChile-Ladeco, Av. Gramado 560, ☎ 234799.
Aerocontinente, ☎ 6002092358.

AIRPORT TRANSPORT

Settur (☎ 251515) provides pick-up minibus service for $6000/pp.

BUS STATION AND/OR OFFICES

No central terminal. Inter-city bus offices are clustered in the commercial center west of the plaza.
Buses to Ensenada, Petrohué, Ralún, Cochamó, and the Río Puelo depart from the corner of Walker Martínez and San Bernardo. Regular buses to Llanquihue, Frutillar, and Pto. Montt can be caught on Calle Dsel Salvador or Calle San José.

RENT A CAR

TraviViajes, Camino Ensenada km 1, ☎ 233491.

SHOPPING

Vicki Johnson Fine Food and Gifts, Santa Rosa 318, for chocolates, homemade jams, and tasteful handicrafts and other items. Claudio Caro, San Pedro 422, for handicrafts, music, local products. Bianca Torres' handmade ceramics available at Tranco Expediciones.

CAMPING EQUIPMENT

A variety of articles are available at *Alsur*, *Trauco Expediciones*, and *Aquamotion* offices downtown.

while the original dirt road to Puerto Montt branches south, passing through the village of Alerce.

Puerto Varas is a great place to base yourself for explorations throughout the southern lake region, as it concentrates a great number of tour operators and the region's best variety of lodging. Mellower than Pucón, it is also just a great place to relax.

In-town Attractions

Historic houses Eight wooden mansions in Puerto Varas have been declared national monuments, and at least twelve others – most dating from the early 1900's – impart a measure of elegance to the city. Most are concentrated along the railroad line above the *centro* to the NW, but there are others along Del Salvador and Purísima, and in Puerto Chico (see for drawings). Puerto Varas' Iglesia Parroquial, at the corner of San Francisco and María Braun, is also worth a visit.

Parque Philippi Located within easy walking distance of downtown at the far end of Calle Decher, Parque Philippi is a pleasant forest preserve with a few trails and views over the lake and the town.

Around Puerto Varas

The North and West Shores of Lago Llanquihue

Frutillar is 26km north on a paved road. Transport by regular buses, [↑].

East to Ensenada and Parque Nacional Vicente Pérez Rosales

East of Puerto Varas, a paved road continues along the shore of the lake through fields and forests and past German built farmhouses and churches. 16km east is the the bridge at **La Poza**, a lovely lagoon surrounded by dense forest and almost completely hidden from the road; you can rent boats here and row out to Isla Loreley. At km 21 is the bridge over the Río Pescado, with a lovely wooden chapel just beyond on the right, and at km 35 is the bridge over the Río Blanco.

46km from Puerto Varas, **Ensenada** itself is little more than a crossroads, though its proximity to Parque Nacional Vicente Pérez Rosales has made it into something of a tourist hub; in the surrounding area there is an abundance of lodging (*YankeeWay Lodge* recommended for lodging and dinner) and a couple of lakeside campgrounds (*Caleta Trauco* recommended). From here, a dirt road branches north (left) towards Las Cascadas and **La Burbuja** (on Volcán Osorno), while the paved road continues east towards Petrohué (69km from Puerto Varas) and Ralún. Transport to all destinations (except La Burbuja) by regular bus.

The Estuario de Reloncaví

Ralún is 79km east of Puerto Varas, Cochamó is at km 94, and Puelo is at km 120. Transport by bus, [↕].

Navigation aboard the *Capitán Hasse*

⏱2-4h

This 65-foot wooden motorsailer, usually anchored off the Puerto Varas waterfront, runs a variety of luxury cruises in Lago Llanquihue, with daily departures in summer (weekends only off-season). Enjoy breakfast or sunset on board, or catch a launch out in the evening for on-board drinks in the piano bar. Consult for other programs and charters.

Down the Río Llico

⏱15min

Departing from Yerbas Buenas Bajo (approx. 40km SW of Fresia) motor launches available at the dock will take you on the 15-30 min. ride downriver to the remote beach at Llico Bajo. There is a hostería on the beach, and good fishing both along the river and in the tidal estuary.

Parque Los Volcanes

On the road to Ralún just east of the turnoff to Petrohué, this locally-run stable offers day trips on the northern flanks of Volcán Calbuco, with excellent views of Lago Llanquihue and Volcán Osorno. Ask about trips to the Salto El Angel and the Salto del Caliente waterfalls.

Operators: 8 - 18 - 91 - 101 - 190

Affluents of Lago Llanquihue

Thanks to its abundant population of resident trout and salmon, Lago Llanquihue is open for fishing two months before other bodies of water in the south. Traditionally, the Río Pescado has been the focus of so-called 'boca' (rivermouth) fishing on the lake, but overfishing has hurt the fishery. Still, on some days there is excellent (albeit crowded) streamer fishing here. Further east, the Río Blanco, Río Tepu, and Río Ensenada also have good fishing along their lower stretches and rivermouths, and numerous outfitters also offer trolling on the lake for monster salmon and lake trout. Other local highlights for fishermen include the immense Río Maullín, which drains the lake to the west, and the Río Petrohué and Río Puelo, both described below.

Operators: 2 - 11 - 109 - 183 - 190

Kayaking in and around Lago Llanquihue

Beginning paddlers can get a feel for the water by renting a sea kayak on the waterfront in Puerto Varas, and test their skills in La Poza, the protected lagoon east of town on the road to Ensenada. Lago Todos los Santos makes for wilder, more exposed paddling, but with a number of possibilities for spectacular multi-day trips, camping on beaches and exploring the long, fjord-like branches of the lake. (Be sure to take care with afternoon winds, as in many places the steep shores of the lake offer little or no refuge.) Other easy day trips in the Puerto Varas area include flatwater descents of the Río Maullín and the Río Petrohué from Huiñe Huiñe to Ralún. The later trip could then be combined with a trip on the Estuario de Reloncaví, [↓].

Operators: 26 - 45 - 234

Parque Nacional Vicente Pérez Rosales — *See map* [↓]

Created in 1926, this 253,780há park was Chile's first, and it continues to be its most popular. However, few visitors stray from the paved roads and major ferry routes, and in most parts of the backcountry you can still find all the solitude you could ask for.

The centerpiece of the park is LAGO TODOS LOS SANTOS, a marvelously steep-walled, serpentine, landlocked fjord that stretches over 36km from Petrohué, at the west end of the lake, to Peulla at the east end. 'Discovered' by Jesuit priests on

PRACTICAL INFORMATION / ACCOMMODATION

*Conaf Centro de Visitantes in Petrohué, camp-
ground, hotel in Petrohué. Campgrounds, residencial,
hotel in Peulla.*

TRANSPORT

*By bus to Petrohué from Puerto Varas and Puerto Montt.
Cruce de Lagos bus-boat trips link the park with
Bariloche* 🛥. *No public transport to La Burbuja. Motor
boats are available for transport on Lago Todos los
Santos, prices vary.*

All Saint's Day, 1670, Todos Los Santos dates
from the Holocene eruptions of Volcán
Osorno, which blocked the Río Petrohué
and diverted it from its accustomed course
to Lago Llanquihue. Today the Río Petrohué
flows out of the lake clear and blue in
Petrohué, cuts through a series of lava flows
(forming spectacular basalt waterfalls such
as the Saltos de Petrohué), and empties into
the ocean at Ralún.

Volcán Tronador towers above the east
side of the lake, cloaked in immense cascading glaciers, while to the north is the unmistakable Volcán Puntiagudo, with its peak
formed of an erosion-resistant volcanic plug.
In general, the landscape surrounding the
lake combines lowland temperate rainforest,
highland deciduous forest, vast lava fields,
remote settlers' outposts and dozens of
tributary rivers. The scale and majesty of this
park almost make it appear an invention.

VOLCÁN OSORNO has two separate access
roads. From Puerto Clocker on the north
shore of Lago Llanquihue, a dirt road climbs
20km to the old site of the Refugio La
Picada, which recently burned to the ground
and is tentatively slated for reconstruction
by the summer of 2001-2002 (for updates
contact *Chile Individuell*). La Picada may
also be accessed by trail from Petrohué via
the trail over Paso Desolación 🛥.

On the south slope of the volcano at an
elevation of 1,300m, the old ski area at LA
BURBUJA is accessed via Ensenada. Though the
lifts stopped functioning long ago, simple accommodation and meals are available at the
Refugio Teski Ski Club, with phenomenal
views over Lago Todos los Santos, Lago Llanquihue, and south to Volcán Calbuco. Local
operators offer easy walking trips on the
flanks of the volcano beginning at La Burbuja,
which is also the starting point for mountaineering ascents of Volcán Osorno; if you wish
you can camp for free below the Conaf ranger
station. At the time of writing, construction
had begun on a new charlift at La Burbuja.

The road from Ensenada to Lago Todos
los Santos follows the course of the Río
Petrohué. At 12km from Ensenada, on the

right, is the entrance to the **SALTOS DE
PETROHUÉ** *(Open Dec-Mar 0900-2000, Apr-Nov
0900-1800. Entrance $1000)*, a picture-perfect
basalt waterfall with Volcán Osorno looming
in the background, and at 23km the road
ends at the lakeside settlement of **PETROHUÉ**.
Here there is a first-class hotel (*Hotel
Petrohué*), a Conaf *Centro de Educación
Ambiental*, and trailheads leading north towards Paso Desolación and Playa Larga, a
lovely black-sand beach just half an hour
along the shore. Across the river to the
south are privately owned rustic campgrounds. Wooden motor launches are available at the dock to provide shuttle across
the river and also offer tours and transport
to the following destination:

● **Cayutué**
At the end of the first branch off the
south side of the lake, Cayutué is an agricultural settlement with an excellent fishing lodge, and provides access to tiny
Lago Cayutué and the two-day hike to
Ralún (see 🛥 The Estuario de Reloncaví).

● **El Rincón**
On the north side of the lake near the mouth
of the Río Sin Nombre, this lakeside trailhead
provides access to the Termas del Callao and the
three day route north to Lago Rupanco 🛥.

● **Río Blanco**
A long, narrow inlet on the south shore of the
lake, near Peulla. From the mouth of the river,
a trail east over Paso Vuriloche to Argentina 🛥.

● **Peulla**
At the extreme east end of the lake, Peulla
has a hotel, a *residencial*, and a couple of
campgrounds. There is a short trail to the
Cascada de los Novios, as well as a number of
possibilities for longer walks to Laguna
Margarita, up the Río Peulla to Volcán Tronador, or up the Río Negro to Volcán Casablanca.

The *Cruce de Lagos*

This is the most famous lake
crossing in the Andes, connecting
Puerto Montt and Puerto Varas with Bariloche, Argentina via a series of ferries and short bus trips. The route
begins in Petrohué aboard a 310-passenger catamaran, which crosses Todos los Santos to Peulla in just
under two hours. From here, it's a 27km drive across
the border to Puerto Frias, where another ferry takes
you across Lago Frías (20min). Another short bus
ride leads to Puerto Blest, where a 320-passenger
ferry crosses Lago Nahuel Huapi (approx 1.5hrs).
A final bus leg (25km) brings you into Bariloche. In
summer, the route may be done in a single day, with
lunch in Peulla. Longer packages are also available.

Operators: 79

Río Petrohué (III)

 🕐1d

Flowing out of the west end of Lago Todos los Santos, the Petrohué is one of the best commercial Class III runs in Chile – a rollicking big-volume joyride with turquoise green water and fantastic views of Volcán Osorno. The commercial put-in is on the route from Ensenada to Petrohué, and the takeout is at Huiñe Huiñe, on the road to Ralún. The harder upper section (appropriate for kayaks only) begins at Lago Todos los Santos and drops through a series of basalt rapids, including one class V (La Machina) at most levels. Keep an eye open for the portage around the Saltos de Petrohué (which, incidentally, have been run both on the right and the left). Below Huiñe Huiñe the Petrohué flattens out and makes for an excellent, highly scenic float trip 🔽.

Operators: 8 - 18 - 26 - 91 - 101 - 190 - 210 - 214 - 234 (k)

Fishing on the Río Petrohué

Departing from the the boat launch at Huiñe Huiñe and continuing for about 7 hours through an immense, roadless flatwater canyon to the coast at Ralún, the Río Petrohué is the classic float trip in the Puerto Varas region. The top attractions here include the December influx of powerful sea-run browns and a late-summer salmon run. Another local option is Lago Cayutué, a shallow, reedy lake just south of Lago Todos los Santos. Both the lake and the Río Cayutué (which drains it to the north) offer excellent dry-fly fishing, though access may be restricted; be sure to ask local landowners before crossing private property.

Operators: 2 - 11 - 18 - 26 - 51 - 86 - 91 - 109 - 190 - 201

Termas del Callao

 🚶‍♂️🔁 🕐2-3d
□ c 🏠 $4,000

This route begins at El Rincón, on the north shore of Lago Todos Los Santos. From there a well-marked trail climbs the valley of Río Sin Nombre 3-4hrs to the hotsprings, where you'll find two wooden tubs in a small riverside cabin, together with a simple *refugio*. This hike is frequently offered by operators in Puerto Varas, so in high season the refugio may not be available to solo hikers; if you bring a tent you can always camp in the fields along the stream, but note that you will still have to pay a small fee to the local caretaker for use of the springs. From here, most hikers return the way they came, though for a nice traverse you can continue north towards Laguna los Quetros, veering west before the lake and heading down to the beach at Las Gaviotas (on Lago Rupanco). Here you can walk or hire a boat out, or climb north to Antillanca (above).

Operators: 8 - 10 - 18 🐎 - 101 - 137 - 190

Paso Desolación

 🚶‍♂️🔁 🕐1d □

From Petrohué, an easy trail leads through forest along the lakeshore to Playa Larga, and from there traverses across the NE slopes of Volcán Osorno towards Refugio La Picada (due for reconstruction 2001-2002).

Operators: 8 - 103 - 199

Los Alerzales

🔁 🕐1d □

Beginning on the south shore of Lago Todos Los Santos about a 10min boat ride from Petrohué, this trail climbs the Río León to one of the only accessible alerce forests remaining in PN Vicente Pérez Rosales (there is another in the Río Manzano valley). This is a challenging full-day hike.

Operators: 101 - 190

Paso Vuriloche

 🕐3-4d □

This superb international hike begins at the mouth of the Río Blanco (SW of Peulla), and follows the river upvalley to La Junta, where there are rustic hotsprings (ask at the house nearby for permission to bathe or camp). The next day carries you on to the confluence with the Río del Norte, where there are more hotsprings and a view of the glacier on the south side of Tronador; from here, a final days' walk leads across Paso Vuriloche (just south of Volcán Tronador) and down to Pampa Linda, in the Argentina's Parque Nacional Nahuel Huapi. If attempting this unmarked route alone, be sure to consult with customs officials in advance.

Operators: 101

Volcán Osorno (2,652m)

🕐6-8h rt □

Much like Volcán Villarrica (near Pucón), Osorno's arresting form and proximity to Puerto Varas has made it one of the most frequently climbed peaks in the south.

Unlike Villarrica, however, the ascent is not such a breeze. The route begins at La Burbuja, and follows the old ski lifts up onto a gentle ridge that climbs to the NE. After about two hours you reach the base of the glacier, and from there the route leads up and left to the summit. The final 500m are quite steep (45-50°), and to reach the summit it is often necessary to climb a near-vertical cornice. All parties should rope for this section, as a fall into the deeply crevassed glacier below could have fatal consequences; many parties leave a fixed rope off the summit to descend.

The views from the summit cap simply defy description, and if you have time you can explore the unusual ice caves off the NE side of the crater. Climbers should be aware that the dense clouds that often cap Osorno's summit can move in with surprising swiftness.

Operators: 8 - 18 - 47 - 101 - 137 - 201

Monte Tronador (3,451m)

⏱2-3d ■
Tronador dominates the eastern end of Lago Todos los Santos, towering nearly a kilometer above nearby Volcán Osorno. The peak is usually climbed from the Argentine ranger station at Pampa Linda, 85km from Bariloche. Count on a full afternoon to hike the 22km to the *refugio* (1,850m), and another 7-10hrs rt from here to the summit, with a vertical gain of over 1,500m. It is also possible to climb Tronador from the Chilean side beginning either in Peulla or Casa Pangue, but the route involves a long bushwack through dense *selva* and tricky routefinding up the immense glaciers covering the peak.

Climbing in the Petrohué Valley

The only sport climbing area to speak of in the southern Lake District is located just off the road to Petrohué, a short distance above the Saltos de Petrohué. Consisting of a handpull of bolted and toproping routes on a short basalt cliff, the crag is located on the left side of the road (heading up) directly across from a major rapid known as 'La Machina.'

Operators: 101 - 190

Canyoning on the Río León

The Río León forms a steep, narrow canyon on the south shore of Lago Todos los Santos. During a typical five-hour trip, participants will be transported to the river outlet by boat, and from there will climb up fixed rope ladders and swim across pools to base of an 80m waterfall.

Operators: 8 - 18 - 190 - 201

Volcán Osorno Downhill

▶16km ⏱4h **D** ■
Local operators can provide bikes and shuttle service for the 1,200m white-knuckle descent from La Burbuja to Ensenada, a route which combines unbeatable panoramic views of Lago Llanquihue, the Petrohué valley and Volcán Calbuco with a healthy dose of self-administered adrenaline. The road is in good condition, and though it begins with steep switchbacks, it soon mellows to a more manageable pitch, and in general is an appropriate ride for most anyone.

Operators: 190 - 205

The Estuario de Reloncaví   See map ⬆

PRACTICAL INFORMATION
Ask at the municipalidad in Cochamó for an excellent map showing local hiking routes linking the Puelo and Cochamó valleys.

ACCOMMODATION
Campgrounds in Ralún, Cochamó, and on the west side of the fjord near Canutillar. Hospedajes in Ralún and Cochamó, cabañas in Ralún. Hostería-style accommodation at Campo Aventura south of Cochamó, and at fishing lodges on the Río Puelo.

TRANSPORT
Buses Fierro runs twice-daily buses from Puerto Montt/ Puerto Varas to Ralún, Cochamó, and Puelo.

Due east of Puerto Montt (but accessed via Puerto Varas), the Estuario de Relocaví is a huge, curving fjord that receives the crystal waters of the Río Petrohué at its northern extreme. Along the eastern side of the fiord, gravel roads carved into the rock walls provide access to remote fishing and farming communities, temperate rainforest and a mixture of volcanic peaks and granite valleys. Most of the west side of the fjord – formed by the steep peaks of Parque Nacional Alerce Andino – has no road.

At the mouth of the Río Petrohué, the town of **RALÚN** signals the end of the pavement, 79km from Puerto Varas. There is a broad range of lodging here, as well as boats for rent and hotsprings upriver on the east bank. Before the bridge, a dead-end road branches to the south, leading to Canutillar and Lago Chapo, on the west side of the fjord. Most of the lodging in the Ralún area is along this road.

Termas de Ralún

C 🔥 NA
These rustic springs on the lower Río Petrohué are often visited by floating and fishing trips; if arriving by road, look out for a sign reading 'Termas,' on the road just north of Ralún. In springtime, these springs may be covered by the river, and they are not always as clean as one would like. Use your judgement.

Along the main road, 15km past the Ralún bridge, is the village of **COCHAMÓ**, with a nice but modest selection of lodging and a

---

489

AROUND PUERTO VARAS TO PUERTO MONTT

15	Volcán Osorno
41	Termas del Callao
42	Paso Desolación
43	Los Alerzales
44	Paso Vuriloche
45	Ralún to Cayutué
46	Up the Cochamó Valley
47	Up the Puelo Valley
48	PN Alerce Andino
49	Reserva Nacional Llanquihue
17	Parque Los Volcanes
18	Up the Cochamó Valley
19	Up the Puelo Valley
23	Volcán Osorno
24	Monte Tronador
25	Volcán Calbuco
13	The Petrohué Valley
14	Canyoning on the Río León
15	Cochamó
10	The Cruce de Lagos
17	La Arena-Caleta Puelche
3	The Estuario de Reloncaví
19	Río Petrohué (III)
20	Río Cochamó (V)
34	Termas del Callao
35	Termas de Ralún

lovely Chiloé-style church near the waterfront. Note the huge flats that separate the town from the ocean at low tide; tides here can vary as much as 7m.

Three km further on is the mouth of the Río Cochamó. A dirt road on the left, before the bridge, provides trail access to the **LA JUNTA VALLEY** and the so-called 'Gaucho Trail'; just past the bridge is the entrance to Campo Aventura, a tasteful hostería offering horsepacking trips in the Cochamó valley. Beyond here, the road continues 25km along the shore of the estuary, passing numerous salmon farms before reaching the mouth of the Río Puelo; a new bridge (27km) crosses the river to the village of **PUELO**. Lodging is available here in local houses. From Puelo, a pickup truck regularly runs the 10km road east to **LAGO TAGUA TAGUA**, which in turn may be crossed by a daily motor launch departing around 1000. Near the far end of the lake is the exclusive *Río Puelo Lodge*, and from here, backcountry hikers can continue SE up-valley to Lago Puelo, in Argentina. Road construction is under way in the upper portion of the valley, so changes are sure to occur.

A recently completed road along the south shore of the Estuario de Reloncaví now connects Puelo with **CALETA PUELCHE**, southern terminal for the ferry from Caleta Arena. For Caleta Puelche and the Carretera Austral south, see the Patagonia chapter.

Río Cochamó (V)

⏱1-2d
The Cochamó is an incredibly
steep, continuous Class V granite creek,
appropriate for experts only and even then with
low water only. A 10km hike to the La Junta put-in
raises the stakes on this committing wilderness run.

Ralún to Cayutué

⏱5-7h
This relatively easy walk, occupied
by the Jesuits for their travels between Castro and
Bariloche, begins by climbing the Río Reloncaví
valley via a 4WD road beginning 3km east of the
Río Petrohué bridge. Where the road ends, a trail
continues on over Paso Cabeza de Vaca and down
to Lago Cayutué, then follows the west side of the
lake en route to the settlement of Cayutué. From
here, you may be able to hire a boat back to
Petrohué, though the surest way to avoid
backtracking is to do the walk in the opposite
direction, beginning by boat in Petrohué. Note
that camping is not allowed on the shore of Lago
Cayutué, and in general locals may be sensitive
about crossing private property between here and
Lago Todos los Santos.

Operators: 8 - 190

Up the Cochamó Valley

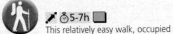

⏱3-6d
This perhaps the perhaps
the most spectacular and atypical hike in the Lake
District. From the bridge over the Río Cochamó,
the trail climbs about 10km – often through shin-
deep mud – up the north side of the valley to La
Junta, a U-shaped valley flanked on either side by
enormous granite domes. From here, you can
cross to the south side of the valley and check out
the waterfalls above the Campo Aventura *refugio*,
or else continue east, crossing the Río Traidor en
route to the Saltos de Cochamó (about an hour
from La Junta) and the ancient alerce forest at El
Arco (2-3hrs).

The route can then be continued east
through settlers' outposts to Lago Vidal Gormaz,
and from there either to Paso León
and Argentina or south down the
Río Manso to join the Río Puelo
⬆. *Campo Aventura* runs 4-day
horseback trips into the valley,
with stays in the hosteria at the
base of the route and their refugio
in La Junta. Longer trips (up to 9
days) up the 'Gaucho trail' to Lago
Vidal Gormaz and on to Argentina
may also be arranged.

Up the Puelo Valley

⏱4-5d
This route climbs
through the heart of the Andes along the
immense Río Puelo, beginning at the ocean and
ending in Argentina.

The hike really begins in the village of Puerto
Arena, at the east end of Lago Tagua Tagua (see
⬆ for transport). Just upvalley, the Río Manso
flows into the Puelo, and if you wish you can head
north up the Manso towards the Cochamó valley.
Otherwise, you continue on an obvious track the
Puelo, arriving after a full day's walk in the village
of Llanada Grande. Above here the trail leads on
past Lago Azul and Lago Las Rocas to Segundo
Corral, where there is an airstrip and a customs post.

If you wish to continue on to Argentina, you
can continue walking along the north shore of
Lago Interior to Paso El Bolsón, cross the border,
and then either walk out or hire a boat to take you
across Lago Puelo to El Bolsón. If you don't wish to
cross, you can catch a charter flight back to Puerto
Montt from Segundo Corral. Note that it is also
possible to hike south from the town of Puelo, up
the Río Puelo Chico and over a pass into Parque
Nacional Hornopirén. This trip is commonly offered
as a six-day horsepacking trip, with visits to local
settlers' homes in the spectacular countryside near
the head of the valley. Impending road construction will undoubtedly change the character of the
valley in the coming years.

Operators: 10 🐎 - 18 - 158

Climbing in Cochamó

Known (not unaccurately) as 'the
Yosemite of South America,' the
remote La Junta valley is surrounded by granite
domes up to 1,000m high. About 15 routes are
thought to have been completed to date, all
involving free and aid climbing (5.9-5.12, A4) on
the relatively accessible walls on the south side of
the valley. Note that access to the base of the cliffs
is complicated by dense temperate rainforest, and
that the rock is reported to be quite dirty due to
the heavy local precipitation.

Operators: 207

THE COASTAL ROAD FROM LA ARENA TO PUERTO MONTT

Paddling in the Estuario de Reloncaví

The Estuario de Reloncaví provides all the adventure of a paddling trip in the Patagonian fjords with somewhat simpler logistics and less exposure than those further south. An ideal traverse can be made between Ralún and Puelo in 2-3 days, depending on the weather; most of this route is fairly protected, and there is an access rod all along the east shore of the fjord in case you have to bail out. It is also possible to paddle all the way out to Caleta Arena, though the mouth of the fjord is quite exposed. This area is inhabited by home-steaders and mussel divers, and increasingly exploited by salmon farms.

Operators: 26 - 234

Fishing on the Río Puelo

The Río Puelo routinely produces some of the largest resident and sea-run trout in the Lake District. The lower section (below Lago Tagua Tagua) is more accessible and more frequently fished, and generally produces larger fish because of its proximity to the ocean. You need a boat with a powerful motor to really fish the lower Puelo.

Above Lago Tagua Tagua, the river is shallower, the fish somewhat smaller, and most of your fishing will be done from the bank. The Río Manso and the Río Traidor are among the Puelo's several fishable tributaries.

Operators: 11 - 109 - 179 - 229

Puerto Montt   *Pop. 110,139 (☎ city code 65)*

Set on the north shore of the Seno de Reloncaví, Puerto Montt is the capital of the lake region and its most important city. For travelers continuing south to Chiloé, the Carretera Austral, or by ferry to Puerto Natales, Puerto Montt is an unavoidable link, which explains the tremendous number of travel agencies, cyber-cafés, artisans' markets and seafood restaurants. Above all, however, Puerto Montt is a working port, a major exporter of wood chips, salmon and shellfish, and supply point for the far-flung inhabitants of the islands and fjords. Most overnight visitors prefer to stay in cleaner, quieter Puerto Varas.

Puerto Montt is relatively young – it wasn't until 1851 that a clearing was first hacked out of the forest to make way for the boatloads of German immigrants arriving to take ownership of lands around Lago Llanquihue, just north. Vicente Pérez Rosales, promoter of German immigration, inaugurated and named the port in 1853, and within a decade there were three tidy streets with wooden homes, mills, breweries and stores. Supplies arrived by ship and traveled overland to the pier in Puerto Varas, while forest products – principally alerce – traveled in the other direction.

The completion of the Santiago-Puerto Montt railroad line, in 1912, hastened the development of the port, making it the logical market for the products from the Chiloé archipelago, a role it continues to fulfill. The catastrophic earthquake of 1960, however, left hardly a single building standing. Today, Puerto Montt's downtown area is unremarkably modern, while the port of Angelmó retains the charm and character of the ageless islands to the south.

In-town Attractions

Museo Juan Pablo II Just east of the bus station, this regional museum (named in honor of Pope John Paul II's 1984 visit to Puerto Montt) features permanent and temporary exhibits on natural history, anthropology and archaeology, plus colonial maps, antique furniture, household and farm implements, displays on Chilote myth and architecture, and photos from turn-of-the-century Puerto Montt.
Hours: Jan-Feb daily 0900-1900, Mar-Dec daily 0900-1200, 1400-1800.
Entrance: $250, children $100.

Angelmó Puerto Montt's port district, Angelmó lies at the west end of the waterfront road, within easy walking distance of the *centro* and the bus station. The major passenger shipping companies have their offices and ports here, and both sides of the road are lined with shops packed with handicrafts from the Chiloé archipelago. At the end of the road on the left is a large *palafito*-style gallery of seafood eateries, while past the parking lot is the true heart of Angelmó: its local seafood and vegetable market. The road along the coast continues through an active port area to Chinquihue, eventually rejoining Ruta 5 south to Pargua and Chiloé. See [C] for local products to look out for in Angelmó.

Isla Tenglo Accessed by inexpensive launches from Angelmó *($200/pp)*, Isla Tenglo protects the port from southerly winds and provides a good viewpoint over the city, the Mirador Cruz de Tenglo. There are also relatively nice (if often dirty) beaches and a traditional restaurant on the island, *Los Galpones de Tenglo* (☎ 09-6953025, 09-4106619), serving daily lunches and *curanto en boyo* with previous notice.

Exploring the Seno de Reloncaví by Boat

Even if you only have a couple of hours to spend, it's easy to get out on the water and get a taste of maritime culture in Puerto Montt. If you have a group, you can inexpensively hire a local boat in Angelmó to take you around Isla Tenglo (for the short trip) or out to Isla Guar and Isla Maillén (for a full afternoon). A more organized option is to sign up for a day aboard the *Jonas*, a traditional vessel that carries passengers south on a two-hour cruise to Panitao, where they are greeted with a traditional curanto; afternoon options include horseback riding and sea kayaking, and there is a sauna and campground on site for those who wish to linger. Otherwise, transport is provided back to Puerto Montt.
Operators: 70

TOURIST OFFICES

Municipal tourist office in kiosk on Varas and O'Higgins, open Mon-Sat 0830-1330, 1400-1930, Sun 1000-1400.
Sernatur is above town in the Edificio Intendencia Regional, O'Higgins 480 2nd floor. Open Mon-Fri 0830-1300, 1330-1745.

BANKS AND MONEY CHANGERS

Banks, ATMs, casas de cambio in the downtown area between Urmeneta and the waterfront, west of the Plaza de Armas.

HOSPITAL

On Seminario near the corner of Décima Región, on the bluff above downtown, ☎ 261199.

POST OFFICE

Rancagua 126, one block west of the Plaza.

INTERNET CONNECTION

Travelers, Av. Angelmó 2458, ☎ 258555. Many cafes between the bus station and Angelmó.

ACCOMMODATION

1 *Hospedaje Casona Suiza* **S**, Independencia 231, ☎ 252640.
2 *Casa Perla* **S**, Trigal 312, ☎ 262104
3 *Hospedaje Rocco* **S**, Pudeto 233, -☎ 272897.

4 *Hotel Gamboa* **$$**, Pedro Montt 57, ☎ 252741.
5 *Residencial Millantú* **$$**, Illapel 146, ☎ 252758.
6 *Hostal Pacifico* **$$**, Juan José Mira 1088, ☎ 256229.
7 *Gran Hotel Don Luis* **$$$**, Urmeneta and Quillota, ☎ 590001.
8 *Viento Sur* **$$$**, Ejército 200, ☎ 258701.
9 *Hotel Vicente Pérez Rosales* **$$$**, Antonio Varas 447, ☎ 252571.
10 *Hotel Club Presidente Puerto Montt* **$$$**, Av. Diego Portales 664, ☎ 251666 **(see ad inside front cover)**. More info at www.turistel.cl

RESTAURANTS

11 Best value in the seafood stalls in *Caleta Angelmó.*
12 *Club Alemán,* San Felipe and A. Varas. Chilean food, Kunstmann on tap.
13 *Di Napoli,* Gallardo 119. Pizza.
14 *Balzac,* Urmeneta and Quillota. Seafood, expensive.
15 *Las Piratas,* in Angelmó across from the palafitos. French and chilean food, good wine list.
Fogón de Cotelé, in Pelluco. Excellent steaks, reservations required.

AIRPORTS

Aeropuerto El Tepual, 16km west of town.

AIRLINE OFFICES

Aeromet, A. Varas 215, ☎ 268960

LanChile-Ladeco, O'Higgins 167, ☎ 253315.
Aerocontinente, ☎ 6002092358.

FERRIES

Ferries depart Puerto Montt bound for Chaitén, Quellón, the fishing villages of the Palena coast, Puerto Chacabuco, Laguna San Rafael, and Puerto Natales.
Navimag (Alejandrina, Evangelistas, Puerto Edén): ☎ 253318.
Transmarchilay (Colono): ☎ 270416.
Catamaranes del Sur (high-speed catamaran to Chaitén): Diego Portales 510, ☎ 482308, 267533.

AIRPORT TRANSPORT

Frequent buses from the bus station to the airport.
Radio Taxi Venus, ☎ 256909.

BUS STATION AND/OR OFFICES

Bus station on the waterfront between downtown and Angelmó.

LOCAL TRANSPORT

Local motor launches run from Angelmó to Isla Tenglo.

RENT A CAR

Autovald ☎ 254306.
Avis ☎ 253307.
Budget ☎ 286277.
Full Fama's ☎ 258060.

PUERTO MONTT

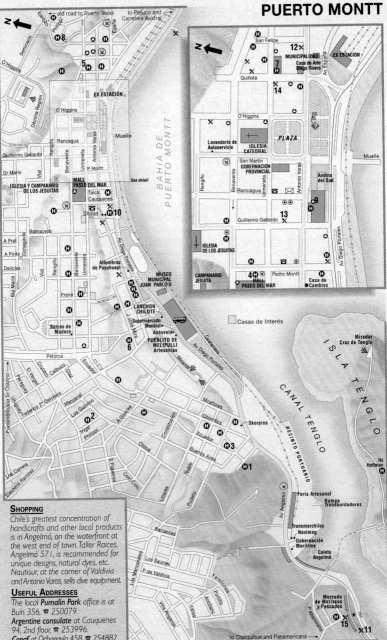

SHOPPING

Chile's greatest concentration of handicrafts and other local products is in Angelmó, on the waterfront at the west end of town. Taller Raíces, Angelmó 571, is recommended for unique designs, natural dyes, etc. Nautisur, at the corner of Valdivia and Antonio Varas, sells dive equipment.

USEFUL ADDRESSES

The local **Pumalín Park** office is at Buín 356, ☎ 250079.
Argentine consulate at Cauquenes 94, 2nd floor, ☎ 253996.
Conaf at Ochagavía 458, ☎ 254882

Around Puerto Montt

See entries above for The North and West Shores of Lago Llanquihue, Around Puerto Varas, Parque Nacional Vicente Pérez Rosales, the Estuario de Reloncaví and Chiloé (in the Patagonia chapter) for more attractions within easy reach of Puerto Montt.

Parque Lahuén Ñadi

This small reserve protects a tiny remnant of the extensive forests of alerces (*lahuén* in Mapuche) that once covered a great portion of the lowlands (or *ñadi*) between Puerto Montt and Puerto Varas. This makes a good stop for those headed out of town without having seen an alerce, as the park lies right off the access road to Aeropuerto Tepual. Public transport on airport buses from Puerto Montt's Terminal de Buses.

Calbuco

Connected to the mainland by a causeway, Calbuco is the principal town in a small chain of islands 111km SW of Puerto Montt. The town dates from 1602 (some 250 years before Puerto Montt), when it was founded by settlers escaping the Mapuche destruction of Osorno, and for the better part of 200 years was almost entirely isolated. Thus Calbuco – which flourished briefly during the alerce exportation boom of the mid-1800's – presents an architectural and cultural panorama very similar to that of the Chiloé archipelago, and makes a good substitute for travelers with time limitations.

While in town, you can check out the 400-year-old image of San Miguel Archangel, brought by the original settlers in 1602 and preserved in the recently reconstructed Iglesia Parroquial. 7km from Calbuco at the SW end of the island is the tiny village of Caicaén, with a chapel, a nice beach and good views over the surrounding islands. Contact Turismo Rural Insular (☎ (65)461300) for locally operated tours in the Calbuco archipelago.

Maullín and Carelmapu

Founded in 1790, Maullín is the principal port of the Río Maullín, which drains Lago Llanquihue. The buzz of activity on the town's waterfront reflects the importance of the river (and the town) in the daily lives of the farms and communities along the river and further out on the coast. There are modest restaurants and a residencial in town, and cabañas on the coast in Pangal, 5km north.

18km south of Maullín, the town of Carelmapu was founded by Spanish refugees heading south towards Chiloé after the 1602 destruction of Osorno. There are campgrounds, residenciales, and a couple of restaurants in town, and free camping around Playa Brava (3km west), an exposed beach with huge views and intense wind and surf. Each year on Feb 2nd, the *Fiesta de la Virgen de la Candelaria* attracts devout fishermen from throughout the Chiloé archipelago. Transport by regular bus from Puerto Montt.

South to the Carretera Austral

The ferry terminal at La Arena is 45km SE, and Hornopirén is at 99km (plus a 30-minute ferry). See the Patagonia chapter for details. Transport by buses Fierro, one departure in the morning, two in the afternoon.

Parque Nacional Alerce Andino

Set in the steep, glacially scoured peaks SE of Puerto Montt, this 39,255há park is rainy, rugged, and wild – precisely the reasons for which it preserves one of the most breathtaking old growth forests in the Lake District. This is the *selva valdiviana* in full splendor, with towering broadleaf evergreens, pure stands of alerces exceeding 3000 years of age, and abundant epiphytes, vines and tree ferns. Though the most impressive forests lie a considerable distance off the road, it is now feasible (with the use of canoes) to visit them in a single day, but you really need to stay for longer to get a feel for the park. Alerce Andino lies only about 40km from Puerto Montt, but the park sees relatively few visitors, especially compared to nearby hotspots such as PN Vicente Pérez Rosales.

The northern sector ot the park (Correntoso) has the best infrastructure and trails. To get there, turn left off coastal Ruta 7 (the Carretera Austral) just before the Río Chamisa, 9km east of Puerto Montt. 19km up is a signposted turnoff to Correntoso and the park entrance, while the road straight on provides access to Lago Chapo and the trailhead to RN Llanquihue and Volcán Calbuco.

CORRENTOSO is the end of the line for bus service to the park. 2km further up is a bridge over the Río Chamiza, where you can camp; from here it's another 12km walk along the road (or by trail,) to the privately run *Refugio Lahuén*, where there is another campground and bunk accommodation for up to 15 guests. Most of the park's best trails begin here, and the folks at the refugio rent canoes for the paddle across Lago Sargazo.

The more southerly **CHAICA** sector is accessed via a 7km dirt road up the Río Chaica valley, which branches north off Ruta 7 in the village of Lenca, 32km east of Puerto Montt. There is a Conaf ranger station at the entrance, as well as a six-site campground and a handful of young alerce trees; hiking trails are rather limited. Note that the gate at Chaica is open 0900-1700 only, so park outside if you think you may leave the park after closing hours.

Nearby the Chaica sector is the Alerce Mountain Lodge, a tasteful, elegant (and expensive) lodge is set in a 2,000há private park with ancient alerce forest and numerous lakes. It is accessed via a dirt road (signposted 'The Lodge') branching north out of the Chaica valley, just past Lenca. Guided day trips may be arranged in the reserve with previous notice.

Trekking in PN Alerce Andino

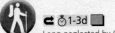

Long neglected by Conaf, the trails in Alerce Andino have recently come under the management of a private concessionaire, and today the park is one of the finest destinations in the southern Lake Region for fit, able hikers.

From the bridge over the Río Chamiza, a trailhead on the left provides access to the 5½ hr walk to Refugio Lahuén. Unfortunately, this hike does not pass through any alerces, and you might be better off sticking to the road and saving your energy for walks deeper within the park.

Two trails begin at Refugio Lahuén: the short (2hr) hike to the 'Radal de Alerces,' a humble stand of relatively young alerce trees, and the longer – but far more worthwhile – hike to Laguna Fría and the ancient alerces in the park's remote interior.

Like the Radal hike, the trail to Laguna Fría begins along the north shore of Laguna Sargazo. After about two hours, you'll reach the campsite at the eastern end of the lake, and from here it's another two hours to a 4-bed refugio on the western shore of Laguna Fría. In between the two lakes is an *alerzal* with trees exceeding 3500 years in age – far and away the highlight of the park. You can also begin this hike by crossing Laguna Sargazo from Refugio Lahuén by canoe, and finish by walking back out along the lakeshore.

In the Chaica sector, you can walk up the road from Guardería Río Chaica to Laguna Chaiquenes (4km), then continue on a trail another 4km to the south shore of Laguna Triángulo. At the time of writing, the trail linking Laguna Triángulo with Laguna Fría was so overgrown as to be practically nonexistent, so from here you'll have to return the way you came.

Operators: 6 - 7 - 91 - 205

Reserva Nacional Llanquihue (Volcán Calbuco)

This highly recommended trail leads up the south side of Volcán Calbuco through alerce forests and past impressive volcanic rock formations to a rustic *refugio* at treeline. The signposted entrance to the reserve is near Correntoso on the road to Lago Chapo, just before a bridge over the Río Blanco. 3km up, the road ends and a trail climbs steeply to the Conaf ranger station, where you must register; beyond here it's about an hour upvalley to some lovely basalt pools and waterfalls along the Río Blanco, and a total of three hours to the *refugio*. There are good campsites in the gully below the refugio (which leaks), and depending on conditions you may be able to continue up from here to the summit of the volcano (allow 4-5 hrs rt). By midsummer the route is usually a non-technical walkup, though some scrambling is required to reach the summit towers. Even if you don't continue up, the views from the *refugio* over the Seno de Reloncaví make this hike well worth the effort.

Operators: 6 - 8 - 201

Patagonia

In reality, Patagonia needs little introduction. Five centuries of unending exploration, of myths, legends, tragedies and triumphs have burned the image and aura of Patagonia deeply into our collective consciousness. Patagonia is the southernmost end of the American continent, the 'Uttermost Part of the Earth,' *Finis Terrae*. An untamed wildlands where the unrelenting wind, *La Escoba de Dios* – the Broom of God – roars out of the west leaving the earth barren and immaculate.

the myth, and to great extent the myth is valid: now as always, Patagonia is the scene of the some of the world's greatest adventures. But in this day and age, Patagonia is no longer *terra incognita,* and although blank spots still sprawl across the map, the greater portion of Patagonia is now accessible to the average tourist.

Patagonia is more than just Torres del Paine. As much as Torres del Paine deserves its worldwide acclaim, other regions in Patagonia – the wilderness of the Carretera Austral, for example, or the mystical island of Chiloé, or the seldom-visited expanses of Tierra del Fuego – are equally if not more impressive. And what all these regions have in common is a sense of authenticity, a sense that this is a place where adventure *still happens* – and that it will remain so for a long time to come. After all, this is Patagonia – and all myths arise for a reason.

PATAGONIA

GEOGRAPHY AND TOPOGRAPHY

Geographical definitions of Patagonia vary. In Argentina, Patagonia is usually defined as the area south of the Río Colorado, at about 37°S – an area characterized by the vast, arid steppe or *pampa* that descends gradually from the Andes to the Atlantic coast. In Chile, on the other hand, the term generally refers exclusively to the area south of Puerto Montt – considerably further south at 41.5°S – though the dividing line can be rather fuzzy. In this chapter, we consider the area south of the Río Puelo and the Canal de Chacao, including the island of Chiloé.

Patagonia's geography differs vastly from that of the rest of Chile. As the Andes continue their long trajectory south, the range migrates ever closer to the Pacific coast, where an increasingly hostile climate has produced a long series of glaciations that have modified the landscape to a degree matched in few places on earth. With glacial processes having affected the region almost continuously for the past 800,000 years, there are few geographical features in Patagonia whose form cannot be attributed to glacial sculpting or deposition.

In reality, this area consists of three separate geographical entities – the *Gran Isla* of Chiloé, Northern Patagonia (also refered to as the *Carretera Austral*), and the Southern Patagonian regions of Magallanes and Tierra del Fuego. As it is impossible to travel from one area to another without taking a boat, flying, or passing through Argentina, it could be said that the term Patagonia refers as much to an idea – or a state of mind – as it does to an actual geographical or cultural unity.

Big Feet ?

The name Patagonia is derived from the term *Patagon*, which Antonio Pigafetta, the Venetian chronicler who accompanied Magellan on his historic first trip around the globe, used to refer to the Tehuelche Indians the expedition encountered in San Julian. For years, popular opinion has maintained that Pigafetta chose this name because of the Indian's extraordinarily large footprints ('*pata*' is Latin for foot).

However, research conducted by Argentine María Rosa Lida (and later confirmed by Marcel Bataillon of France) appears to have definitively refuted this theory. As it turns out, the name *Patagon* first appeared in the 1512 novel *Primaleón*, a work that Magellan and Pigafetta are very likely to have read. The book makes several mentions of a wild '*gigante patagon*,' as well as an entire '*pueblo de patagones*,' which sounds suspiciously like Pigafetta's '*tierra de patagones*' – a denomination later shortened to the more sonorous Patagonia.

Chiloé

Chiloé is the second-largest island off the South American coast, after Tierra del Fuego. Essentially, the island is an extension of the **Coast Range**, which, having dipped briefly beneath the Canal de Chacao, forms a 180km spine down the central-western portion of the island. In the northern part of the island, the range is known as the *Cordil-*

Volcán Hualaique 1670   Volcán Hornopirén 1572   Volcán Huequi

Entrance to the Estuario de Reloncaví   Isla Llancahue

lera de Piuche, in the south as the *Cordillera de Pirulil*. Separating the two ranges is a glacial valley now occupied by a couple of lakes, Lago Huillinco and Lago Cucao.

West of the range, Chiloé's **Pacific coast** is wild and abrupt. Massive beaches and dunes alternate with rocky headlands, wetland habitat, and dense temperate rainforest. There are very few roads and few human inhabitants in the western sector of the island.

Chiloé's eastern shore is gentler, more sheltered, and more heavily modified by human hands. The 30-odd islands of the **Chiloé archipelago**, formed of erratic glacial deposits worn by the tides, have long been farmed by their *mestizo* inhabitants, while the rolling hills on either side of the Panamerican highway have been cleared only in the past hundred years or so. East of the island, the Golfo de Ancud and the Golfo de Corcovado – geomorphically considered extensions of the Central Valley – are relatively calm compared to the notoriously exposed Golfo de Penas, just south.

South of Chiloé, the Cordillera de la Costa reemerges from the Pacific to form the labyrinthine islands of the Guaitecas archipelago. Beyond the Taitao peninsula the range disappears below the ocean for good, and the Andes themselves become a coastal range.

Aisén and the Carretera Austral

Accessed by the 1000-plus kilometers of gravel highway known as the Carretera Austral, Northern Patagonia is characterized by vast **rainforests**, enormous **rivers and fjords**, and, towards the south, the increasingly conspicuous presence of **glaciers** in the high peaks of the Andes.

In the northernmost portion, between Puerto Montt and Chaitén, continental Chile is a narrow strip of mountains falling directly into the sea, deeply incised by major fjords. The severity of the landscape makes this the last and least-explored area in the country, with hundreds of thousands of hectares of virgin wildlands. Though the highest peaks in the range are **volcanoes** such as Yate (2,011m), Michimahuida (2,404m), Corcovado (2,300m) and Melimoyu (2,400m), many mountainous areas are composed of intrusive (granitic) formations.

From Chaitén south to Puerto Cisnes, Chile's continental territory widens. There is no sharply defined continental divide here; instead, glacial modeling has created beautiful Andean lakes and thundering rivers, such as the **Futaleufú**, that begin in Argentina and flow through Chile to the Pacific. Here the landscape is segmented into three strips: temperate rainforests and fjords along the coast, backed by high, precipitation-blocking ranges such as the heavily glaciated **Cordillera Queulat**, and beyond that a narrow strip of *pampa* along the border. Here precipitation declines abruptly and the landscape opens up for the long, gradual descent to the Atlantic.

Coihaique, the capital of the Aisén region, occupies a transitional zone between the coastal forests and the pampa. Though there are high peaks both east and west of the city, those to the west are directly exposed to the ceaseless, moisture-laden winds off the Pacific, and consequently receive far greater levels of precipitation. This pattern continues to the south, and from Coihaique to Villa O'Higgins almost all Chilean settlements are located to the east of the Andes, while to the west loom immense ice fields and glaciated massifs such as Monte San Valentín (4,058m), the highest peak in Patagonia. In general, the scale of this landscape is quite nearly overwhelming, characterized by immense lakes such as **Lago General Carrera** (the second-largest lake in South America), and the country's highest-volume rivers, the **Río Baker** and the Río Pascua. Volcán Hudson, which darkened the skies, covered the road and ruined agricul-

Pico Amunátegui

ance to Fiordo Reñihue

Volcán Michimahuida 2470

Chaitén

Volcán Corcovado 2300

View of The Andes from Chiloé

The Patagonian Ice Fields

Smothering the granite spires of the Patagonian Andes beneath ice up to a kilometer thick, the Patagonian Ice Fields or *Campos de Hielo* are among the most inhospitable and least-explored places on the planet. First visited by Alberto De Agostini, Federico Reichert, and Otto Nordenskjöld in 1920-1921, this area proved a logical next step for Himalayan explorers like Harold Tillman, who visited this region aboard his yacht 'Mischief' and made the first crossing of the Southern Ice Field in 1956. The hostile climate, long approaches, and sheer lack of information repeatedly stymied attempts to cross the Southern Ice Field longitudinally, a feat first accomplished by a team of Chileans in 1999.

TOPOGRAPHY AND RAINFALL (Northern Patagonian)

TOPOGRAPHY AND RAINFALL (Puerto Natales)

TOPOGRAPHY AND RAINFALL (Strait of Magellan)

tural lands in a major eruption in 1991, is the southernmost of Chile's major volcanoes. South of here, the range is dominated by the chiseled granite and metamorphic spires of the Patagonian Batholith.

Compared with the densely forested region north of Coihaique, the landscape around Lago General Carrera consists largely of open terrain with soaring, expansive views – a product both of the rainshadow effect and (more notably) the disastrous **wildfires** which, since 1940, have destroyed an estimated 1.2 million hectares of forest. Aside from the ferries which routinely ply the inside passage between Puerto Montt and Puerto Natales, few people ever get a first-hand view of the wild, glaciated coast, almost all of which is preserved in massive national parks.

South of Cochrane, the effects of the great fires tapers out, and the road again enters great forests of cypress and other Sub-Antarctic forest species. Beyond Villa O'Higgins – the southernmost town in the Aisén province – the unmapped Southern Patagonian Ice Field straddles the Andes, definitively blocking road passage south.

Magallanes and Tierra del Fuego

The geography of Southern Patagonia follows the pattern established in the southernmost Aisén province, in which the major peaks and ice fields of the Andes are found along the coast, while roads and other human manifestations are all located to the east, on the pampa. Where the Southern Patagonian Ice Fields tapers out near **Torres del Paine**, the Andes begin a sweeping curve towards the east, and the range becomes so thoroughly fragmented by glaciers, fjords, and ocean channels it is difficult (even on the map) to distinguish between islands and mainland. Here, on a long western peninsula off Tierra del Fuego, we find the frighteningly remote peaks of the **Cordillera Darwin**, from the flanks of which hundreds of glaciers cascade directly into the sea. South of here the range descends precipitously into the Drake Passage, which separates the continent from Antarctica. The rocky escarpments of **Cape Horn** constitute the Andes' southernmost expression.

The long series of ice ages which last peaked about 21,000-19,000 years before the present (ybp) scraped nearly all the existing

Junius Bird

In 1932, a doctoral studies dropout named Junius Bird arrived alone in Punta Arenas, led there by a newly discovered passion for high-latitude archaeology. No institution sponsored Bird's hunch, nor did he rely on anyone for logistical support. He simply caught a boat to Porvenir, hitched a ride to Ushuaia, *rowed* across the Beagle Channel to Isla Navarino, and stayed for three months, excavating.

In 1934 Bird was back, this time with his wife Peggy. Together they bought a 19-foot cutter in Puerto Montt, installed a new motor, and spent five months exploring in the southern archipelago. Afterwards, they bought an old Ford, spent the winter on Chiloé, and drove south in the springtime to initiate a long round of excavations at Cueva Fell, Cueva Pali Aike, and Cueva Sota, three of the most important Paleo-Indian sites yet discovered in the Americas. In the end, the couple sold the Ford and the cutter; when all was said and done, Bird calculated, the trip had cost them $65/month.

Later, Bird switched his focus north to the Atacama Desert, where he began to investigate the threshold between ceramic and pre-ceramic cultures, further refining the chronology originally proposed by Max Uhle. In 1957 – twenty-five years after his first visit to Patagonia – Bird was named curator of South American Archaeology for the American Museum of Natural History. Bird's Travels and Archaeology in Southern Chile provides an anecdotal account of his travels and excavations.

vegetation off the Patagonian mainland, carved the rocky spires of Torres del Paine, and gouged the massive channel now occupied by the **Strait of Magellan**. By about 14,000 ybp, the glaciers were in full recession, leaving immense moraines and glacial lakes in their wake, and the first Indian inhabitants of Tierra del Fuego are thought to have used the bridges formed by these moraines to cross to the Great Island around this time. By 8,000 ybp, the moraines (now known as the Primera and Segunda Angostura, or First and Second Narrows) had been worn away by tidal erosion, and Strait was converted into a full-fledged marine waterway.

Throughout the region – including Tierra del Fuego – the area east of the Andes is typically composed of rolling hills and grasslands, with scattered lakes and marshes and a mixture of glacial and volcanic formations.

CLIMATE AND BIOGEOGRAPHY

Patagonia's climate is a result of the near-constant westerly (varying from NW-SW) winds that roar in off the Pacific, loaded with precipitation. Though precipitation does decline during the summer months, winds generally increase, drawn by the large low-pressure zone that forms over the pampa as a product of increased solar radiation. At Isla Evangelistas (52°S), gale-force winds were recorded 80 days in one year.

Though they vary throughout the day and throughout the year (November and April-May are usually calmest), these winds can be considered a constant, and rain invariably approaches from the west. For this reason, a sharp **climatic and floral gradient** exists throughout the region, with the rainiest areas found on the coast and the driest to the east, past the Andes. For example, at around 45°S, the port of Puerto Aisén receives over 2,900mm of annual rainfall, while in Balmaceda – only about 100 km away, but east of the Andes – this figure drops to a mere 600mm. In more northerly areas, the flora of the coast is composed of dense evergreen **temperate rainforest**, which shifts gradually to deciduous forest on the western and high eastern slopes of the Andes, and finally gives way to the grasses and shrubs of the **pampa**. Further south, the coastal **Magallanic forest** is far less diverse, composed principally of coigüe, lenga, and ñirre – a formation quite similar to the highland forests further north. On Tierra del Fuego, sunlight in high summer reaches a maximum of over twenty hours a day.

PREHISTORY

The wide-open grasslands of the Patagonian pampa provided ideal hunting grounds for the earliest inhabitants of the American continent, who arrived in this area on the heals of the great megafauna that originally led them across the Bering Strait. **Paleolithic sites** in southern Patagonia, most notably those at Cueva Fell and Pali Aike, have been dated to 11,000 BP or earlier, while the earliest sites thus far identified on Tierra del Fuego have been dated to around 9,500 BP.

These early Patagonians were the precursors of a vast, long-lived **hunter-gatherer tradition** that extended over more than 2 million square kilometers in Uruguay, Paraguay, most of Argentina and Tierra del Fuego. These cultures – including the Tehuelche of the mainland pampa, the Selk'-nam of northern and central Tierra del Fuego, and the Huash of southeastern Tierra del Fuego – represent some of the few indigenous hunter-gatherer cultures in the world to have survived into the modern era. They are furthermore responsible for a magnificent repository of **rock paintings** concentrated in central Patagonia. With the exception of Chiloé, the Indians of Patagonia practiced no agriculture whatsoever, and apparently used no ceramics.

Occupation of the rugged Patagonian coast was somewhat later, with the first evidence of **canoe cultures** appearing some 5-6,000 BP. In Northern Patagonia and the Chiloé archipelago, the nomadic canoe tribes encountered by the first explorers were known as Chonos, while those further south were known as Alakalufes. The glaciated southern shore of Tierra del Fuego was inhabited by the Yamanas, another group of oceangoing nomads.

At the time of the Spanish conquest, the demographics of the **Chiloé archipelago** were in a process of transformation, as Mapuche-speaking Huilliches from the Lake Region began to push south into areas inhabited by the Chonos and Cunco Indians. This area was rapidly occupied by the Spanish, leading to the rapid transformation and degradation of native cultures, with the Chonos apparently disappearing around the end of the eighteenth century. Further south, however, contact with Europeans was sporadic and native cultures remained relatively intact until about a century later, when they too entered rapidly into decline.

COLONIAL HISTORY

With few exceptions, Spanish colonial influence in Patagonia was limited to Chiloé. Beginning in 1540, the island was

The Ciudad de los Césares

Much like *El Dorado*, this mythical city served as inspiration for dozens of Colonial-era explorations. The origins of the myth are thought to date from 1528, when members of Sebastian Caboto's expedition to the upper Río Paraná (in modern-day Paraguay) encountered a fellow Spaniard, living among the Indians, who hinted of great riches further inland. Reports by the Indians were less enthusiastic, and in the end Caboto chose to send one Francisco César to investigate.

César and his men were gone about a month and a half, and when they returned – as Caboto later told the Spanish court – they reported having seen a rich and well-kept Indian city. Later, colonial historians would claim that César had reached the Inca capital of Cuzco, some five years before Pizarro; more likely is that César made the city up (he was known as something of a braggart in his later days) and that Caboto, anxious to fund further explorations, willingly propagated the lie.

News of César's findings took root in the fertile soil of the colonial imagination. '*Lo del César*' (that of César) or '*la Gran Noticia del César*' (César's big news) came to signify the limits of the known, with the implication that somewhere beyond lay a yet-undiscovered Indian city. As Spanish knowledge and influence migrated south, the supposed location of the city migrated with it. One version had it that *los Césares* had been

founded by Inca warriors who had been fighting in the south at the time of the Spanish invasion of Cuzco, a frightening prospect that spurred Spanish authorities to redouble their efforts.

Over time, the myth evolved. At some point, '*lo del César*' left off being an Indian city, and was instead thought to be a city founded and peopled by white men. But from where? Documents dredged up from the depths of colonial history suggest that this portion of the myth originated in the Obispo de Placencia's disastrous 1540 expedition to the Strait of Magellan, in which one ship was wrecked, and its crew abandoned, on the northern shore of the Strait. Though nothing more is known of the ship's crew – who undoubtedly suffered a similar fate as the inhabitants of Sarmiento de Gamboa's *Puerto Hambre* – they were somehow credited with founding a burgeoning city somewhere in the vast wilderness of Patagonia.

visited by a number of Spanish expeditions, culminating in the foundation of **Santiago de Castro** in 1567. By the year 1600, there were about 200 Spanish settlers on the island, dedicated to the extraction of gold from the beach at Cucao and the exploitation of the island's ancient alerce and cypress forests – as usual, with the help of native labor.

The general Mapuche uprising of 1598, however, changed Chiloé's destiny forever. With the entirety of the Araucanía and the Lake District under Mapuche control, Chiloé was isolated from the rest of the colony, and directly dependent upon the Viceroyalty in Lima for communication with the world beyond. With luck, ships arrived once a year to the port of Chucao, trading desperately needed staple goods for the few items that could be produced on the island. Meanwhile, Dutch 'pirates' Sebastián de Cordes

and Enrique Brower continued to wage war on the Spanish crown's furthest-flung possessions, occupying and burning Castro on multiple occasions. Poverty was extreme, and in 1646 the Spanish colonists petitioned Lima for permission to abandon the island. Permission was denied.

The **Jesuit order** arrived in the Chiloé archipelago in 1608, liberated the local Indians from the *encomienda* system and began the evangelization and education of the local population in what they referred to as the world's *último rincón* – the furthest corner of Christianity. By 1717 the Jesuits had erected some 69 lovely wooden chapels in communities throughout the archipelago, a number that has grown to a present toll of over 150.

Under the watchful eye of the Jesuits, the native and Spanish inhabitants of Chiloé began a steady process of integration. In

Magellan and Pigafetta

Seasoned during years of service in the spice islands, crippled while battling the Moors in Morocco, **Ferdinand Magellan** finally reached the end of his rope with the Portuguese and demanded a raise, and when that was denied, he asked for permission to offer his services to another country. Magallanes had a hunch, and once relieved from obligations to Portugal, he approached the Spanish crown with an audacious plan: to sail around the globe, from east to west.

When the expedition finally set sail in September of 1519, it was an impressive if compact group, composed of five ships and 260 men. Leading the way was Magallanes, in the ship Trinidad. At his side was his *cronista*, Antonio Pigafetta.

Pigafetta was an astute, intelligent, and occasionally very imaginative writer. It is not hard to imagine how he might have felt some exaggeration was justified, considering the strangeness of his experiences. In Pigafetta's accounts we find the first mention of penguins and sea lions, previously unknown to Europeans; but we also hear of birds that kill whales, trees that give water, and women that are impregnated by the wind. Nowhere is this mixture of careful observation and wild exaggeration so patent as in Pigafetta's description of the expedition's first encounter with a Tehuelche native, to whom he referred as a 'Patagon':

> *'One day when we were least expecting it, a man of gigantic stature appeared before us. He was on the beach almost naked, singing and dancing all at once and throwing sand on his head.... Upon seeing us, he displayed great admiration, and lifted a finger above his head, undoubtedly to signify that he thought we had descended from the sky....*
>
> *This man was so tall that our heads barely reached his waist. He was well formed, with a wide, red-tinged face, eyes circled in yellow, and with two stains in the shape of a heart on his cheeks... His clothing, or rather his cape, was of sewn skins, of an animal that abounds in that country...'*

That Pigafetta and his chronicle survived at all is nearly a miracle in its own right. All in all, of the 260 men who started out on the voyage, only 18 actually made it back to Spain aboard the Victoria, the only ship to complete the voyage. Even Magellan – 'our mirror, our light, our sustenance and true guide,' in the words of Pigafetta – had been killed along the way while skirmishing with natives in the Philippines.

Pedro Sarmiento de Gamboa

A gifted navigator, learned in geography and astronomy, **Pedro Sarmiento de Gamboa** is the central figure in one of the most tragic – or perhaps pathetic – stories in the history of the conquest. After a series of sea voyages out of the port of Callao, Sarmiento was sent south to chase down Francis Drake, who had made his way through the Strait of Magellan and was wreaking havoc on Spanish settlements all along the unprotected Pacific coast. Though he was unable to catch the English buccaneer, Sarmiento did find his way back into the Strait, where the expedition was struck by a colossal storm, nearly wrecked and blown out into the Atlantic. Despite these difficulties, Sarmiento evidently concluded that the area could be inhabited and even defended.

When he next embarked from Spain, it was at the head of an enormous force of 23 boats and some 3000 crew and settlers. They too were decimated by storms and dissention, and by the time they arrived at Cabo Vírgenes, at the mouth of the Strait, their numbers had dropped to a mere five boats and 500 individuals. It got worse: four of the boats either mutinied and left or were simply blown out of the Strait (some sources are contradictory here), leaving Sarmiento alone with one boat. After founding two 'towns,' Nombre de Jesús and Rey Felipe, Sarmiento too was caught by a roaring westerly and forced to desert the colony.

The rest of the story only gets sadder. From a base in Brasil, he organized three rescue missions: two were sunk and one was taken prisoner by the English, Sarmiento included. After passing from English to French Huguenot hands, he finally made it back to Spain in 1890.

By then, all the colonists had long since perished. When Thomas Cavendish passed by the site in 1587, only eighteen of them remained – only one of which was brave enough to come aboard and be rescued. Cavendish himself renamed the settlement Port Famine, now on Chilean maps as Puerto Hambre.

conditions of extreme isolation and scarcity of resources, a unique material and spiritual culture evolved, most notably manifested in the island's **mythology**, handicrafts and endlessly inventive rural implements.

In contrast to Chiloé, the imposing fjords and dense rainforests of **Northern Patagonia** remained almost entirely unknown to the Spanish, which doubtlessly contributed to the widespread belief that here might well lie the fabulous *Ciudad de los Césares*. In 1544, Juan Bautista Pastene and Jerónimo de Alderete became the first Europeans to make tentative explorations in the region, as part of a general reconnaissance of the coast from Valparaíso to the Strait of Magellan. Francisco de Ulloa landed on the Península de Taitao in 1553, while Bartolomé Diez is credited with the discovery of Laguna San Rafael and its immense tidewater glacier. The first explorations of the interior were carried out by Jesuit priests from Chiloé, including Melchor Venegas, Mateo Esteban, and José García Alsué, and the first map of the region was produced by José de Moraleda in 1793, when he ascended the Río Aisén while searching for a passage to the Atlantic.

The experiences of early explorers in **Magallanes and Tierra del Fuego** reinforced the legendary status conferred on the region by Hernando de Magallanes' pioneering 1520 voyage through the Strait. The Strait itself was harrowing and unpredictable – early crossings, battling the consistent westerly winds, took between 17

The *Mision Circulante*

The Circulating Mission was the glue that the Jesuits used to hold together the far-flung communities of the Chiloé archipelago, most of which were too small to have their own clergy. Each September 17th, two missionaries set sail from Castro with three portable altars and the effigies of several saints to be used in religious processions; throughout the entire summer, the pair traveled from one community to another, giving sermons, conducting weddings and baptisms, hearing confession and doling out penance. Each visit lasted three days, after which boats would come to get them from the next village on the itinerary.

IGLESIA DE VILLIPULLI

and 219 days – as was the prospect of permanent habitation, as proved by the disastrous fate of Pedro Sarmiento de Gamboa's 1584 attempt to establish a Spanish colony in the Strait.

After Dutch mariner Willem Cornelius Schouten pioneered the route around Cape Horn, the Strait was abandoned by sailors until the steamship era. Contact with the natives was limited to brief encounters, some friendly, some not: Pedro Sarmiento de Gamboa's men tried to kidnap some of the Selk'nam during a welcome feast in 1579, and in 1598 Oliver van Noort's landing party was attacked by about 40 Tehuelches, leaving three or four wounded. In retaliation, the Dutch killed all the male warriors and took several boys and girls captive. But the real drama between the Europeans and the natives of Tierra del Fuego was yet to come.

INDEPENDENCE

Chiloé

Despite having been virtually abandoned for over two centuries by the Spanish crown, the inhabitants of Chiloé – known as Chilotes – did not participate in the independence movement. Instead, some 20% of the island's male population actually fought with

PATAGONIAN CACIQUES (CHIEFS)

Hans Steffen and Augusto Grosse

German historian and geographer **Hans Steffen Hoffman** (1865-1937) **(1)** arrived in Chile in 1889 as a professor at the Universidad de Chile's teacher's college. However, he soon found a more adventurous calling: when both Chile and Argentina sent survey teams to map the Andes, Steffen was contracted for a series of voyages in the almost entirely unexplored Palena and Aisén regions. Between 1893 and 1903, Steffen explored the watersheds of the Puelo, Manso, Palena, Cisnes, Aisén, Baker and Pascua rivers, and was a principal witness in the British-arbitrated treaty between Chile and Argentina. Steffen produced over two dozen written works, from geographic reports of his expeditions, to exploratory history and historiography, including diatribes on topics ranging from the biography of Christopher Columbus to the origins of the myth of the Ciudad de los Césares.

Nearly fifty years after Steffen's first explorations, however, the area now traversed by the Carretera Austral remained unpopulated, and its potential for use largely unknown. Upon this scenario happened another German, **Juan**

Augusto Grosse (2). Trained in agriculture, Grosse struck off into the wilderness and helped found the seaside village of Puyuhuapi in 1934, and was later contracted by the Chilean Ministry of Public Works to evaluate road-building and settlement opportunities throughout Aisén. Traveling preferentially with *campesinos* from Chiloé, Grosse put together over a dozen extended expeditions, on foot and horseback, by sea and through dense rainforest, from Futaleufú to the Northern Patagonian Ice Field – braving the worst of climates with the most rudimentary of equipment.

the royalists, repelling attacks by Chilean nationalists Lord Cochrane and Ramón Freire. Only in 1826 – eight years after Chilean independence was declared – were the forts at Ancud finally taken, followed four days later by the fall of the Spanish at Callao (Perú), thus ridding the continent of the last bastions of colonial power.

As throughout Chile, independence brought increased trade to the island of Chiloé, though its products remained the same. Whaling ships from the South Pacific stopped off for provisions, and as railroads spread throughout the continent, Chiloé's forests supplied the ties. The towns of Quemchi, Dalcahue, Chonchi and Quellón arose in response to these increased exports, the most important of which was the rot-resistant alerce, which once proliferated on the main island and is still the only wood that Chilotes will use for shingles. Only in 1912, when the railroad between Castro and Ancud was completed, the interior of the island was finally cleared and

occupied, creating the patchwork of agricultural lands that now lines both sides of the Panamerican highway.

Despite these steps towards modernity, the lack of a market for Chiloé's principal agricultural product, the potato, has created a historical shortage of work on the island. For this reason, the Chilotes have become great travelers, shipping south to work the sheep *estancias* of southern Patagonia, north to the nitrate *oficinas*, or east to homestead in the wilds of Aisén and Palena. Universally recognized for their work ethic and good humor, Chilotes formed the core of many exploratory expeditions in the high Andes and Patagonia. The legacy of the Jesuit priests lives on in education as well as religion, and the island consistently boasts the highest literacy rate in the country.

Today, the rapid growth of the salmon industry is changing centuries-old subsistence patterns in the archipelago, and the summer homes of rich *Santiaguinos* have begun to spring throughout the countryside.

Plans to build a bridge across the Canal de Chacao will doubtlessly speed the process of change in Chiloé – a prospect welcomed, for better or worse, by the majority of Chilotes.

Northern Patagonia: Palena and Aisén

The post-independence history of Northern Patagonia is largely a history of exploration, as settlement and industry in the region are quite recent phenomena. As recently as 1902, when border disputes with Argentina were settled with arbitration by the king of England, there were as few as 200 inhabitants in the whole of the Aisén region.

Unknown sealers and foresters were the first to explore this wild coast, but it was only via the late 19th-century expeditions of Enrique Simpson that the Chilean government began to get hints of what lay to the south. In 1869, Englishman George Musters spent a year exploring the pampa in the company of the Tehuelche natives, inspiring a series of Argentine expeditions culminating in the 'discovery' of Lago O'Higgins, Lago General Carrera, and the upper reaches of the Futaleufú, Palena, and Cisnes rivers, among others. Welsh immigrants established the first settlements in this region, also via Argentina.

Still, vast expanses of Chilean territory remained completely unexplored, prompting the Chilean government to contract German geographer Hans Steffen for a long series of expeditions. Steffen was later followed by fellow Germans Augusto Grosse and Dr. Federico Reichert, who pioneered routes in Northern and Southern Patagonian Ice Fields, including the first attempts at Monte San Valentín.

Steffen and Grosse's exploration's were absolutely pragmatic: the intent was to settle, and beginning in 1903 huge **land grants** totaling over a million hectares were awarded to the cattle and sheep ranchers already established in the Magallanes region to the south. These concessions were later reduced to encourage homesteading, which was regulated by the state beginning in 1937; tragically, one of the requirements of the homestead act was that lands had be cleared, and in the following years an estimated 1.2 million hectares of forest went up

Jemmy Button

Europe's first glimpse of the Fuegian Indians came in 1826, when Captain **Robert Fitzroy** arrived in England with four Yamana youths abducted in retribution for a lost whaling boat. One of the Indians, named 'Boat Memory' by Fitzroy's crew, died of smallpox immediately upon arrival, while 20-year old 'York Minster,' 14-year-old 'Jemmy Button,' and 9-year-old 'Fuegia Basket' became figures of some reknown among the British. In The Uttermost Part of the Earth, Lucas Bridges reports that Queen Adelaide took quite a liking to little Fuegia Basket, placing her own lace cap upon the bewildered child's head and even giving her a bit of cash for her dowry.

JEMMY BUTTON IN ENGLAND...

In 1832, the three youths boarded the *HMS Beagle* for long trip back across the Atlantic. Among their companions on the trip was none other than Charles Darwin, who after interrogating the trio concluded that in their natural state the Fuegians were cannibals, and that their vocabulary consisted of only 100 words. (Tomas Bridges, Lucas' father and one of the first white settlers on Tierra del Fuego, later assembled a 32,000 word dictionary of the Selk'nam tongue.)

Upon being left off at the island, the three Fuegians soon reverted to the age old manners and customs of their people, though Jemmy Button – who apparently became something of a dandy during his stint in England – had not yet finished with the whites. When missionaries arrived at the Yamana settlement of Wullaia, Jemmy and company allowed them to build their mission and then turned on them in the midst of the very first service. Mission cook Alfred Cole, who escaped by rowing to the far side of the cove, later reported having seen all eight missionaries brutally massacred with stones and clubs.

...AND BACK HOME IN TIERRA DEL FUEGO

EXPLORATION AND SETTLEMENT

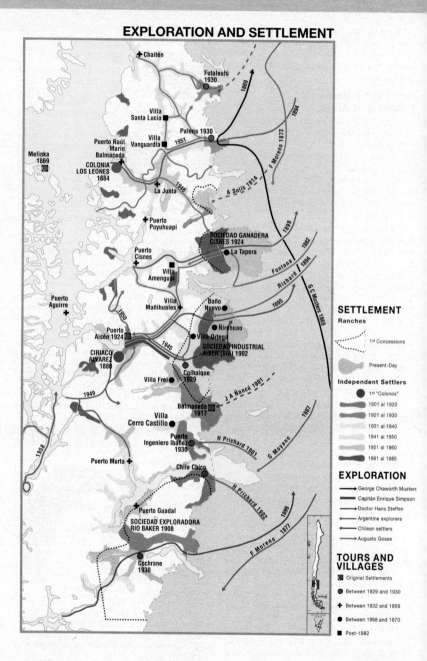

Settlement of the Magallanes Province, 1878-1905

Source: Historia de La Región Magallánica, Mateo Martinic.

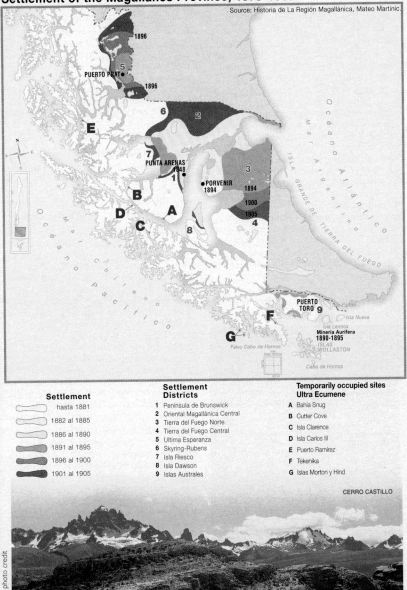

1896

5

PUERTO PRAT●

1896

6

2

E

7

PUNTA ARENAS
1848

1

●PORVENIR
1894

3

1894

1900

1905

B

D

C

A

8

4

ISLA GRANDE DE TIERRA DEL FUEGO

Océano Atlántico

Mar Argentino

Océano Pacífico

Mar Chileno

PUERTO TORO

9

Isla Nueva

Isla Lennox

Minería Aurífera
1890-1895

ISLAS WOLLASTON

F

G

Falso Cabo de Hornos

Cabo de Hornos

Settlement

	hasta 1881
	1882 al 1885
	1886 al 1890
	1891 al 1895
	1896 al 1900
	1901 al 1905

Settlement Districts

1 Península de Brunswick
2 Oriental Magallánica Central
3 Tierra del Fuego Norte
4 Tierra del Fuego Central
5 Ultima Esperanza
6 Skyring-Rubens
7 Isla Riesco
8 Isla Dawson
9 Islas Australes

Temporarily occupied sites
Ultra Ecumene

A Bahía Snug
B Cutter Cove
C Isla Clarence
D Isla Carlos III
E Puerto Ramírez
F Tekenika
G Islas Morton y Hind

CERRO CASTILLO

in flames. The harbor at Puerto Aisén filled so quickly with sediment from the burnt, eroding forests of the Río Simpson valley that port services soon had to be transferred to Puerto Chacabuco.

By 1960, the town of Coihaique had been around for nearly forty years, Chaitén a shaky thirty. Work on the first roads had been underway for about twenty years, and horse paths led nearly everywhere, just as they do today. Aerodromes appeared near towns and *estancias*, and new lands were expropriated from the large landowners and redistributed. Beginning in the mid 1970's, this campaign to populate the wilds of Northern Patagonia was embraced by Augusto Pinochet, who invested over US$300 million in the construction of the **Carretera Austral**, a thousand-kilometer gravel 'highway' uniting the region from Puerto Montt to Villa O'Higgins. First inaugurated in 1988, the main axis of the Carretera Austral was finally completed in 1999, though several new branches are in the planning or construction phase.

Today, Northern Patagonia remains a frontier. The temperate rainforests of the coast and the ice fields of the south remain

WATERFALLS IN PUMALIN PARK

as pristine and unknown as any on earth: a vast wilderness with a few scrappy settlements clinging to its shores. The patterns and people of these remote ports, mountain villages and four-days-out homesteads are as elemental and as fascinating as the landscape itself. Fishing, livestock, and forestry continue to be the biggest money makers in a region with more potential tourism growth than any other in Chile, while private initiatives such as Douglas Tompkin's **Pumalín Park** suggest a path to a more sustainable future for Palena and Aisén.

Southern Patagonia: Magallanes and Tierra del Fuego

If the 'discovery' and earliest explorations of Southern Patagonia are shrouded in myth, the last two hundred years of history have been surprisingly well documented.

Chile established its first settlement in the region in 1853, prompted by a flurry of foreign activity in the Strait: in addition to the explorations of the *HMS Beagle*, the English had recently occupied the Falkland Islands, and even the French had mounted an exploratory mission or two. The settlement, named Fuerte Bulnes, was soon transferred to **Punta Arenas** and transformed into a penal colony. The local atmosphere was ruthless and violent, as renegade sealers murdered the Indians and one another in the tempestuous archipelago, while clashes with the Tehuelche Indians were common on the pampa to the north and east of the city. Only the Selk'nam of central Tierra del Fuego avoided serious contact with the whites.

In 1867, the Chilean government began offering cheap leases on grazing land in Patagonia, and in 1868 Punta Arenas – no longer a penal colony – was made a free port, a status it still enjoys. The city grew rapidly, and with the rise in wool prices, the Menéndez, Braun, and Nogueira families, among others, began to accumulate wealth and land. When the leased lands were sold at public auction in 1902, the larger, more successful landowners were able to leverage financing from Valparaíso, with the result that some 1,600,000 hectares were sold to a mere 29 buyers.

Now the industry went through the roof: from 1885-1907 the population of

Martin Gusinde

"All their property is limited to what is absolutely essential. As such, there is so little that a demanding, civilized human being marvels at such perfected self-sufficiency."

Much of what is known today about the native cultures of Tierra del Fuego is derived from ethnological observations carried out by Salesian priest Martin Gusinde during the four trips he made to the region between 1918 and 1924. Gusinde's definitive three-volume *Die Feuerland-Indianer* (The Fuegian Indians) makes for highly entertaining reading, with meticulous, insightful and compassionate descriptions of the customs, economy, and worldview of the Selk'nam, Yamana, and Alakaluf people on the very eve of their cultural extinction.

Between 1918 and 1922, Gusinde focused largely upon the Yamana water nomads, and managed to record a great portion of that culture's incredibly rich oral storytelling tradition. He had similar success with the Selk'nam, with whom he lived for nearly four months, during which time he was able to witness and photograph the last *Hain* initiation ceremony thought to have taken place on the island (See [c]). By the time Gusinde reached the Alakaluf, however, the tribe had already been reduced to a group of only eighty individuals, and their oral tradition had been all but forgotten.

Martin Gusinde
Expedición a
Tierra del Fuego

Magallanes grew by a factor of eight, while the number of sheep grew by a factor of 42, to over 2 million. With the California and Yukon gold rushes in full effect, maritime traffic in the Strait soared, and the discovery of placer gold on the south shore of Tierra del Fuego enticed Yugoslav, Italian, and Spanish prospectors to join the many Scots already working the lonely **estancias**. Meanwhile, the fortunes of the great landowners continued to build, and Punta Arenas – a third of whose inhabitants were foreign-born – was transformed by the construction of magnificent private mansions and institutional buildings.

By and by, the sheep ranchers came to realize that the lands in the center and eastern portions of Tierra del Fuego actually had a milder, more productive climate than those north of the Strait. Beginning about 1880 the whites began to invade the island, and the Selk'nam – who began to prey on the sheep that were steadily replacing the island's guanaco herds – were systematically shot by farm administrators, prospectors, even 'professional killers' hired by the *estancias*. The Indians sought refuge in the homes of the Bridges family, or were transferred voluntarily or by force to Salesian missions, but these often became breeding grounds for the European diseases against which the Indians had no defenses.

In the space of just over 20 years, the population of the Selk'nam and neighboring Huash was reduced from some 3,500-4000 individuals (as estimated by Martin Gusinde, see above) to less than 500. At present there are no remaining full-blooded Indians on the island.

In the twentieth century, the Magallanes province has continued its halting, stop-and-go progress. In 1918, the opening of the Panama Canal took a huge bite out of maritime traffic through the Strait, and a steady decline in wool prices reduced the local importance of the *estancias*, though the region still concentrates some 45% of Chile's sheep. Since 1950, the extraction of oil and natural gas from Tierra del Fuego and the east end of the Strait has grown to become the major industry in the region. Tourism is growing steadily, but is generally concentrated in Puerto Natales and Ushuaia (Argentina), traditional departure point for ships headed south to Antarctica. The spread of tourism into the magnificent forested ranges of southern Tierra del Fuego could provide a sensible alternative to native wood-chip forestry projects such as that proposed by the US-based Trillium corporation.

CHILOE

Chiloé's draw for travelers is quite different from that of other parts of Patagonia. Although the Coast Range and Pacific Coast remain in a state of raw, entangled wilderness, what brings most visitors to Chiloé is the island's rural culture, gastronomy, handicrafts and architecture – in short, the people of the island and the manifestations of their long history of isolation and rugged subsistence. While these are most easily observed in tourist-oriented centers such as Ancud and Castro, Chilote life follows more traditional patterns in the smaller, more remote villages and islands of the archipelago. With over a dozen daily buses connecting Ancud and Castro directly with Puerto Montt, Chiloé is far and away the most accessible portion of Chilean Patagonia. If coming from mainland Patagonia, you can catch a ferry to Quellón from Chaitén, Puerto Cisnes, Puerto Chacabuco, or any of the tiny, isolated fishing villages along the Aisén coast.

Every summer, Chilean students flock to Chiloé to travel on the cheap, hitchhiking and sleeping on beaches or with local families. A growing 'agrotourism' network, sponsored by national and international development organizations, provides a more structured opportunity to 'go local' in Chiloé. Contact the Fundación Con Todos in Ancud (☎ (65)622604, contodos@entelchile.net) for details.

Ancud
Pop. 23,148 (☎ city code 65)

Set on the east shore of the Golfo de Quetalmahue, Ancud was founded in 1767 as a military fort intended to protect Spanish maritime traffic and possessions along the southern Chilean coast. Political and military power was transferred here from Castro, and with forts in town and across the bay at Agüi, Ancud became one of the best-defended ports in Chile. This was the last settlement in Chile to fly the Spanish flag.

Following independence, Ancud retained its administrative and commercial hegemony over the rest of the island. Whalers set for the Antarctic Sea stopped in here for provisions, and when the Alerce harvest began in earnest in the late 19th-century, Ancud became a major lumber port. Throughout the twentieth century, however, Ancud has been overtaken by more centrally-located Castro.

Perhaps for this reason, while Castro is increasingly urban and touristy, Ancud retains its quaint, fishing-village ambiance.

With a top-notch museum, excellent lodging and seafood, a long, attractive waterfront and a wealth of excursions in the surrounding area, Ancud is the ideal spot to base an exploration of northern Chiloé.

In-town Attractions

Museo Regional Aurelio Bórquez Canobra At the SW corner of the plaza, this excellent museum presents local artifacts and displays on the history, ethnography, natural history and art of the Chiloé archipelago. There are representations of Chilote mythological characters, Chilote churches, traditional farming and household implements, and a life-size reproduction of the schooner *Ancud*, which sailed south in 1843 to found Fuerte Bulnes, Chile's first settlement on the Strait of Magellan. The museum also has its own restaurant, which serves a traditional *curanto* on weekends.

Fuerte San Antonio North of the port at the end of Calle Cochrane, the remains of Fuerte Antonio consist of little more than a stone foundation, but there are excellent views across the bay towards Fuerte Agüi. Behind the fort is Ancud's finest place to stay, *Hostería Ancud*.

Mirador Cerro Huaihuén East of downtown, this overlook provides sweeping views over the Golfo de Quetalmahue and the Río Pudeto estuary. A walk here could easily be combined with a visit to the traditional wooden boatyards on the riverbank near the entrance to town.

ANCUD'S MUSEO REGIONAL

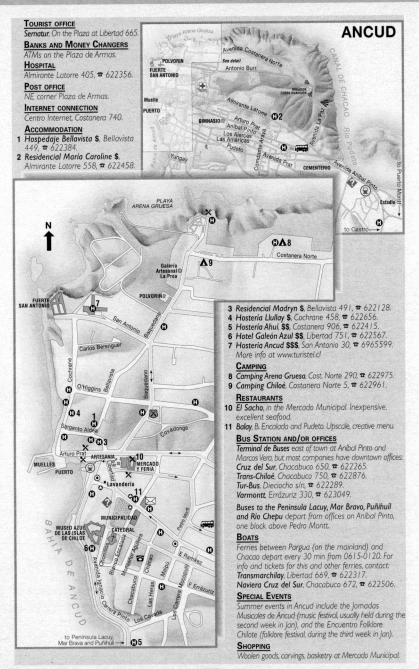

ANCUD

TOURIST OFFICE
Sernatur, On the Plaza at Libertad 665.

BANKS AND MONEY CHANGERS
ATMs on the Plaza de Armas.

HOSPITAL
Almirante Latorre 405, ☎ *622356.*

POST OFFICE
NE corner Plaza de Armas.

INTERNET CONNECTION
Centro Internet, Costanera 740.

ACCOMMODATION
1 *Hospedaje Bellavista* $, *Bellavista 449,* ☎ *622384.*
2 *Residencial María Caroline* $, *Almirante Latorre 558,* ☎ *622458.*

3 *Residencial Madryn* $, *Bellavista 491,* ☎ *622128.*
4 *Hostería Llullay* $, *Cochrane 458,* ☎ *622656.*
5 *Hostería Ahui.* $$, *Costanera 906,* ☎ *622415.*
6 *Hotel Galeón Azul* $$, *Libertad 751,* ☎ *622567.*
7 *Hostería Ancud* $$$, *San Antonio 30,* ☎ *6965599.*
   More info at www.turistel.cl

CAMPING
8 *Camping Arena Gruesa,* Cost. Norte 290, ☎ *622975.*
9 *Camping Chiloé,* Costanera Norte 5, ☎ *622961.*

RESTAURANTS
10 *El Sacho,* in the Mercado Municipal. Inexpensive, excellent seafood.
11 *Balay,* B. Encalada and Pudeto. Upscale, creative menu.

BUS STATION AND/OR OFFICES
Terminal de Buses east of town at Aníbal Pinto and Marcos Vera, but most companies have downtown offices:
Cruz del Sur, Chacabuco 650, ☎ *622265.*
Trans-Chiloé, Chacabuco 750, ☎ *622876.*
Tur-Bus, Dieciocho s/n, ☎ *622289.*
Varmontt, Errázuriz 330, ☎ *623049.*

Buses to the Peninsula Lacuy, Mar Bravo, Puñihuil and Río Chepu depart from offices on Aníbal Pinto, one block above Pedro Montt.

BOATS
Ferries between Pargua (on the mainland) and Chacao depart every 30 min from 0615-0120. For info and tickets for this and other ferries, contact:
Transmarchilay, Libertad 669, ☎ *622317.*
Naviera Cruz del Sur, Chacabuco 672, ☎ *622506.*

SPECIAL EVENTS
Summer events in Ancud include the Jornadas Musicales de Ancud (music festival, usually held during the second week in Jan), and the Encuentro Folklore Chilote (folklore festival, during the third week in Jan).

SHOPPING
Woolen goods, carvings, basketry at Mercado Municipal.

CHILOE

16A The Brujo Coast
16B Isla Quinchao
16C Isla Lemuy
50 Walking in Duatao
51 Río Chepu, Ahuenco and the Río Lar
52 Cucao to the Río Anay
20 Cucao to the Río Anay
4 The Chiloé Archipelago

ESCALA APROXIMADA   Km
0   10   20   30

Around Ancud

West of Ancud

The northwestern corner of Chiloé features some of the most dramatic coastal scenery on the island. On the PENÍNSULA LACUY, which closes off the Golfo de Quetalmahue to the north and west, you can visit FARO CORONA, an exposed lighthouse set on a point jutting out in the Canal de Chacao; further east are the remains of FUERTE AGÜI. One of the last Spanish-held forts in South America, Fuerte Agüi may be reached on foot (1km walk from the end of the road) or else by sea aboard the locally-moored *Cahuella*.

Southwest of Ancud is a wild coastline with immense beaches, rocky headlands, sea stacks and storm-battered offshore islands. The top attraction here is PINGÜINERA PUÑIHUIL, a group of islands that serve as breeding habitat for Magallanic and Humboldt penguins. Visits to the penguin colony are regulated by the non-profit Fundación Otway, which charges *$3000/pp* for the boat ride out the island, including chest waders (wading out through the breakers to board the zodiac is quite an experience). You can also here ask about a trail leading south to a nearby sea lion colony. Daily buses run from Ancud to both Península Lacuy and Puñihuil, but departure times are rather inconvenient; if you go with a guided tour, you can combine a visit to Puñihuil with a walk on the beach at MAR BRAVA or further south in Duatao.

Walking in Duatao

c⟷ ⏱3h ▢
South of the Península Almanao, Duatao's rugged seacliffs, scattered islands and old-growth forests reveal a side of Chiloé that is witnessed by precious few visitors. This walk perfectly complements a visit to Puñihuil, but there is no public transport; access by tour only.
Operators: 25 🐎

East of Ancud

27km east of Ancud, via a paved highway, is the terminal port at Chacao. A more scenic route follows a dirt track along the coast (submerged during high tide) via Caulín, where you can pick up locally cultivated oysters at *Ostras Caulín*. The dirt road from Caulín to Chacao is also worth checking out, especially if you're traveling by bike (see 🛈 for more suggestions on bike tours in Chiloé). Regular buses run from Ancud to Chacao, continuing on across the channel by ferry and then on to Puerto Montt.

Río Chepu, Ahuenco, and the Río Lar

c⟷ ⏱2-3d ▢
This highly recommended coastal hike into the Chepu sector of PN Chiloé begins in the rather dismal little settlement of Puerto Anguay, 38km SW of Ancud. From here, you must hire a boat ($7,500 o/w) for the 30-minute ride down the Río Chepu to a trailhead on the left (south) bank of the river. The trail leads initially through farmland before emerging onto a broad, beautiful beach, and then continues from the end of the beach up and over scrubby headlands. About three hours south from Chepu is the beach at Ahuenco, where Chilean environmentalists have purchased a large tract of forest and dune habitat for conservation purposes; there is a campground near the caretaker's hut, and visits may be arranged to the penguin colony on an island just off the beach. From Ahuenco it's another 2hr walk past immense beaches to the Conaf *refugio* near the Río Lar, and about the same from there to the mouth of the Río Refugio. Transport to Puerto Anguay by regular bus from Ancud.

Fishing on the Río Chepu

Converted into a vast wetlands by the devastating earthquake of 1960, the Río Chepu offers good trout fishing in its upper stretches and trolling for saltwater species near the rivermouth. Boats and guides are available at the *Refugio de Caza y Pesca* (☎ (65)622612) near the bridge in Puerto Anguay.
Operators: 25 🐎

Quemchi and the coastal route south

For those heading south towards Castro, the gravel roads along the east coast of the island provide an excellent alternative to the paved, largely generic Panamerican Highway (Ruta 5). Most of this section of coast was cleared and settled only in the late 19th century by Scottish, German, French, Belgian and Spanish immigrants. Today it is classic Chiloé countryside, with great views (on clear days) across the Golfo de Corcovado towards the Andes.

The major settlement along this stretch, and the only one accessed by a paved road, is **QUEMCHI**, 63km from Ancud by the inland route. There are basic accommodations here, and good camping at the north end of the beach; 5km north of town in Tubildad is a bed and breakfast owned by Sr. Juan Dougnac, one of the most highly recommended participants in Chiloé's agrotourism program. Just south is **ISLA AUCAR**, a tiny island in a protected bay, accessed by a decrepit walking bridge. At low tide you can wade out to the island and check out its lovely wooden chapel.

About 18km south of Quemchi is the turnoff on the left for the 7km road to **QUICAVÍ**, notorious in Chiloé mythology as the site of a hidden witches' cave. Wooden walkways lead along the shore, permitting passage between seaside homes at high tide. Quicaví's unusually large church is also worth a look.

Another 12km past the Quicaví turnoff is **TENAÚN**, located on an exposed point with views of the Islas Chauques to the east. Tenaún's colorfully painted chapel is one of the most unusual in the archipelago. From here, it's 33km along a rutted country road to Dalcahue.

TRANSPORT / ACCOMMODATION

Five buses a day from Ancud to Quemchi. Daily buses Castro-Quicaví via Tenaun. Basic accommodation in Quemchi and with local family in Tubildad.

Dalcahue and the Northern Archipelago

See map

PRACTICAL INFORMATION

Dalcahue's oficina de Información Turística is next to the post office and taxis stand on Ramón Freire. In Achao, it's at the corner of Serrano and Ricardo Jara.

ACCOMMODATION

Hosterías and hospedajes in Dalcahue, Curaco de Vélez, Achao, and Mechuque.

TRANSPORT

Frequent buses and taxis colectivos connect Dalcahue with Castro. Transportes Arriagada (at the bus stations in Castro and Dalcahue) provides service to Achao. The 5-min ferry between Dalcahue and Isla Quinchao runs 0700-2230 every day; pedestrians ride for free.
Boats to the Islas Chauques and Butachauques (Mechuque, etc) depart several times a week from the dock near the Feria Artesanal in Dalcahue. Consult with locals for details.
Boats to the Islas Quenac and Chaulinec depart from Achao on Monday and Fridays; consult in the Capitanía del Puerto for details.

Just NE of Castro, the village of Dalcahue is the site of Chiloé finest handicrafts market and gateway to some of the most traditional sectors of the archipelago. For those staying in Castro, this area makes for a fine day trip that could just as easily be stretched into a week.

The action in **DALCAHUE** (pop. 3,000) is concentrated along the waterfront, where dozens of colorfully painted boats lay at anchor or loll on their sides awaiting the rising tide. Here you'll find Dalcahue's market sector, which comes alive every Sunday with vendors arrived from the outlying islands. Woolen goods, baskets, smoked salmon, abundant produce, and blocks of more modern, commercial kitsch crowd the streets, especially in high season; for a traditional *curanto en hoyo* or a lamb *asado*, try *Restaurant Fogón Playa* on Manuel Rodríguez near the plaza.

The rest of the week, the waterfront lapses into a much mellower rhythm. Just up the hill, Dalcahue's 1858 church (declared a national monument) is worth a visit, as is the humble Museo Histórico Etnográfico, located in the *Centro Cultural* just east of the market square. Just west, the fishermen's pier stays active all week, with motor launches departing for and arriving from the Islas Chauques and Butachauques.

At the west end of town is a ramp for the short ferry *(free for pedestrians, $1500 autos)* to **ISLA QUINCHAO**, the most accessible of the islands in the archipelago. Once across the channel, head south 9km on the main island road to the village of **CURACO DE VÉLEZ**, which looks west towards Dalcahue. The surprising architectural resplendence in this tiny burg of 470 inhabitants dates from a mid-18th-century lumber boom. From the plaza, follow the road south along the waterfront, looking for signs that say 'Ostras': halfway down the beach is an open-air restaurant with huge, cheap, locally cultivated oysters.

At the far south end of the island (26km past Curaco de Vélez) is the town of **ACHAO**, administrative center for Isla Quinchao and the outlying islands ever since the Jesuits established a mission here in 1743. As is so often the case in Chiloé, Achao's pier is the center of activity in town, thanks to the constant flux of islanders traveling to and from the islands. Achao's best restaurants are found near the pier.

The plaza, meanwhile, is set back from the waterfront, several blocks east of Serrano. On the south side of the plaza is the **Iglesia Santa María de Achao**, Chiloé's oldest and perhaps most beautiful church, begun in 1730 by the Jesuits but not finished until after their expulsion from Spanish America in 1767. Originally, the church was built with no metal pieces at all, using wooden pegs instead of nails. On the north side of the plaza is the recommended *Hostal Plaza*.

The outlying islands in the northern part of the Chiloé archipelago are broken down into two groups. The **Islas Chauques**, accessed by frequent launches (*lanchas de recorrido*) from Dalcahue, is comprised of a maze of larger and smaller islands, many of which are linked at low tide by sand bars. This is an area of protected channels and tiny villages that makes for ideal sea kayaking and cruises. The only services to speak of are in the picturesque island community of **Mechuque**, where you'll find basic markets and a recommended *hostería* run by Mario Ojeda, located on the north side of the bridge in the 'center' of town.

The **Islas Quenac** consist of six islands, generally accessed from Achao. Isla Caguache is the site of Chiloé's largest religious festival, while Isla Linlin is known for its production of woolen goods and Isla Llingua for its baskets. Visits to the islands aboard local boats may be arranged in Achao.

Sea kayaking in the Chiloé Archipelago

Sheltered from westerly breezes and inhabited by communities of subsistence fishermen and farmers, the islands of the Chiloé archipelago make for excellent 3-5 day 'soft adventure' trips, with lodging in hosterías and plenty of opportunity for cultural interaction. The area most frequented by paddlers is the Canal Dalcahue, where there is a sea kayak center, complete with wood-fired jacuzzi; an ideal day trip combines a visit to the Sunday craft fair in Dalcahue with a crossing to the charming church in San Javier, across the channel on Isla Quinchao. Day trips are also run out of Chonchi, just south, but the most attractive area for paddling is found among the charming, protected Chauques and Butachauques island groups. Independent paddlers can seek accommodation with local families or camp wild, though you should always ask landowners for permission.

Operators: 10 - 128

Castro

Pop. 20,634 (☎ city code 65)

Founded in 1567, Castro is the third oldest continuously inhabited city in Chile, though a long history of earthquakes and pillaging English and Dutch corsairs – who found here the most isolated and helpless of Spanish outposts – have left not a single construction from the colonial era.

Near the close of the Colonial era, the Spanish transfered military and administrative power from Castro to the more strategic port of Ancud. Not until 1912, when the Ancud-Castro railroad was completed, did the town regain importance as a service center and point of export for the outlying communities. Today it is once again the most important city in Chiloé.

The city sits atop a headland that protrudes into the Fiordo de Castro. The downtown commercial area centers around the Plaza de Armas, while the main waterfront area, with its large handicrafts market and numerous restaurants, is down the hill to the SE.

CASTRO

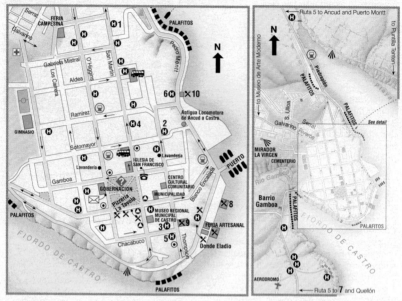

TOURIST OFFICES

Private tourist office on the Plaza de Armas.
Conaf: Gamboa 424, ☎ 632289.

BANKS AND MONEY CHANGERS

ATMs on and around the plaza.
For money exchange, Julio Barrientos, Chacabuco 286.

HOSPITAL

Freire 852, ☎ 632444.

POST OFFICE

West side of the Plaza de Armas.

INTERNET CONNECTION

Gamboa 447, 2nd Floor.

ACCOMMODATION

1 Hospedaje Mansilla $, San Martín 879B.
2 Hospedaje Mirador $, Barros Arana 127.
3 Hostal Kolping $$, Chacabuco 217, ☎ 633273.
4 Hostal Quelcun $$, San Martín 581, ☎ 632396.
5 Hostería de Castro $$$, Cahacabuco 202, ☎ 632301.
6 Hotel Unicornio Azul $$$, Pedro Montt 228, ☎ 632359.
More info at www.turistel.cl

CAMPING

Several campgrounds about 4-5 km south of town:
7 Camping Santa Elba, ☎ 638178.
7 Camping El Chilote, ☎ 636537.
7 Camping Llicaldad, ☎ 635080.

RESTAURANTS

8 Restaurant Palafito, Lillo 30. Traditional chilote cuisine, waterfront setting.
9 Restaurant Sacho, Thompson 213. Highly recommended, views from upstairs dining room.
10 Octavio, Pedro Montt 261. Traditional menu, pleasant atmosphere.

BUS STATION AND/OR OFFICES

The Terminal Cruz del Sur is at the corner of San Martín and Sotomayor. The Terminal de Buses Rurales is at the corner of San Martín and Aldea.

USEFUL ADDRESSES

Transmarchilay, Thompson 273, ☎ 635691.

SPECIAL EVENTS

During Jan and Feb, Castro is the site of a nearly continuous series of events showcasing local gastronomy, music, handicrafts and other trappings of Chilote culture. The biggest of these include **Nercon y sus Tradiciones** (held during the last weekend in Jan, south of town in Nercón), the **Maja Chilota** (cider pressing, held during the second week in Feb in Llau Llao), the **Festival Costumbrista Chilote** (held during the third week in Feb in the Parque Municipal), and the **Peña Folclórica Coche Molina** (music festival, held during the second or third week in Feb). There are also many similar festivals on the islands of the archipelago (consult with local tourist offices for details).

SHOPPING

Wide selection of Chiloé handicrafts at the waterfront market, also on the plaza during peak season.
For books, **Libros Chiloé** is at Blanco Encalada 202. For unique gifts, T-shirts, music, etc, try **Años Luz** on the east side of the plaza.

In-town Attractions

Iglesia San Francisco de Castro Probably the most visited church in Chiloé, this is also the least representative of the island's traditional wooden architecture. Built from 1910-1912 (almost two hundred years after the church at Achao was begun), this immense Neogothic wooden church nonetheless stands as one of the Castro's must-see attractions. Be sure to visit the luminous, recently refinished natural wood interior.

Locomotora Ancud-Castro North of the waterfront handicraft market at the corner of Sotomayor and the Costanera, this is the original steam engine from the Ancud-Castro railway, opened in 1912 and abandoned after the 1960 earthquake.

Palafitos The most-photographed palafitos (stilt houses) in Chiloé are located along Castro's waterfront both north and south of town.

Museo Regional de Castro On Esmeralda south of the plaza, this small museum contains exhibits on Chiloé history, mythology and ethnology, but can't compete with the museum in Ancud. There are, however, interesting photos from the 1960 *terremoto*.
Hours: Summer Mon-Sat 0930-2000; Sun 1030-1300 hrs. Winter Mon-Sat 0930-1300 and 1500 to 1830; Sun 1030-1300 hrs.
Entrance: with donation.

CIDER PRESS ON DISPLAY IN CASTRO

Museo de Arte Moderno de Castro 3km up the hill NW of town (via Galvarino Riveros), this independent contemporary art museum features permanent and temporary collections by Chilote artists. Just north of the museum is Castro's Parque Municipal, site of the annual *Festival Costumbrista*.
Hours: Jan and Feb, Mon-Sun 1000-1800. Nov, Dic and Mar 1100-1400 hrs. Closed Apr to Oct.
Entrance: free

Feria Artesanal On the waterfront SE of downtown. Extensive variety of woolen goods, baskets, etc.

Around Castro See map 🔼

Dalcahue and the Northern Archipelago

Dalcahue is 20km NE of Castro, Curaco de Vélez 27km, Achao 46km. Transport to Dalcahue by hourly bus or colectivo from Castro, with less frequent connections to Achao, 🔼.

Parque Nacional Chiloé

Cucao is 58km west of Castro, transport by regular bus from Castro, 🔼 (only one a day off-season).

Chonchi and Isla Lemuy

While not a major attraction itself, the town of CHONCHI (pop. 2,898) makes a pleasant, lower-key base for explorations in Chiloé's central culture area. The main areas of interest are concentrated along the waterfront,

where you'll find good seafood restaurants and the town's best lodging; recommendations include *Hotel Huidín*, *Esmeralda by the Sea* and *El Antiguo Chalet*. Calle Centenario climbs steeply from the waterfront, passing the 1859 Iglesia de San Carlos en route to rejoining the Panamerican Highway.

ISLA LEMUY may be accessed directly by bus from Castro or Chonchi, by motor launch from the Chonchi's port, or by ferry from Puerto Huinchas, located just south of town. Public transport on the island is limited, but with a bike or a car (or hitching) you can explore the many villages scattered around the perimeter of the island. The villages of Detif and Aldachildo, the latter with well-preserved church, are especially recommended.

TRANSPORT
Ferries from Puerto Huinchas to Chulchuy depart Mon-Sat every 30 min from 0800-2100; every hour Sun and holidays.

Parque Nacional Chiloé

ACCOMMODATION

Numerous hospedajes and private campgrounds on either side of the footbridge in Cucao. Conaf campground near visitor center. Private campgrounds (may be crowded in season) at Lago Huelde, reached by signposted path east of main road. Wild camping and refugios along the beach north.

TRANSPORT

Regular buses Castro – Cucao (only one a day off season).

Chiloé's only protected area is comprised of three different sectors along the wild Pacific coast of the island, with a total area of 43,057há. The area includes an interesting mix of dune habitat, endless white-sand beaches, and a variety of wetland and forest habitats, as well as a significant population of resident Huilliche Indians. Most of the inland portions of the park have no access whatsoever, which is likely responsible for the survival of notable endemic mammals such as the Chilote fox and the *pudu* deer.

The northernmost sector, CHEPU, is accessed from Ancud [🛈]. The middle sector, ABTAO, is accessible on foot only, via a road leading west off the Panamerican Highway from Puente Puchagrán, 10km north of Castro. From here, it's 17km to the end of the dirt road, and then another 18km hike across the Coast Range to the mouth of the Río Abtao. There is one refugio about halfway along the route, and another (in poor condition) on the coast.

Access to the more frequently visited CUCAO sector is via Castro on a dusty dirt road that runs alongside Lago Huillinco and Lago Cucao to the beachfront town of Cucao. There are a number of restaurants and inexpensive hospedajes in town, mostly clustered around the walking bridge that leads across the Río Cucao to the park.

Across the bridge, there are several restaurants and mediocre campsites run by private concessionaires; much nicer are the Conaf cabañas and campgrounds, located near the Centro de Información Ambiental. From here, there are two short, marked hiking trails: Las Dunas de Cucao, which leads through dunes to Cucao's splendid beach, and El Tepual, an interpretative trail on walkways through dense stands of tepu (*Tepualia stipularis*). This entire area, known as Chanquín, is very popular with beachgoers in summertime.

For more solitude, follow the dirt road north along the beach from Cucao. A signposted turnoff on the right heads inland to LAGO HUELDE, where there are a couple of locally-run campsites in the midst of Huilliche settlements. A trail from Lago Huelde heads back south through forested and deforested hills to connect with the El Tepual trail. It is also possible to hike from Cucao to a sea lion colony on the precipitous coast to the south of the park.

Cucao to the Río Anay

This is the standard trek in PN Chiloé, with easy access and unique coastal scenery. Beginning in Cucao, a dirt track heads north along the coast and eventually peters out on the beach. Continue up the beach until it itself ends, then look for a trail branching inland, over the top of Punta Chaiquil and back down to a basic refugio at the mouth of the Río Cole Cole. From here it's an easy day hike (8km o/w) to the refugio at the mouth of the Río Anay. Cucao is also a great place for horseback riding, and horses are readily available near the park entrance in season; out of season you may have to ask around.

CHILOE

Quellón

Pop. 7545 (☎ city code 65)

Quellón is the southern terminus of the Panamerican Highway and an important port for ferries headed east and south to continental Patagonia.

Unlike the other towns described above, Quellón did not figure into Chiloé's colonial history. In 1743, the Jesuits installed a community of Caucahue Indians on the nearby island of Cailén for their eventual conversion; the priests called this region 'the world's southernmost enclave of Christianity.' Not until the early 20th century was Quellón formerly founded and some of the surrounding islands inhabited, mostly by European settlers. Meanwhile, massive timber exploitation largely stripped the remote Cordillera de Pirulil to the east, leaving the town, after a brief boom, right back where it had started. This late-blooming history explains Quellón's lack of historic architecture.

As always in Chiloé, Quellón's waterfront is the center of activity. There are numerous dining and lodging options all along the Costanera Pedro Montt to the east of the ferry terminal, and traditional Chiloé handicrafts available in shops lining Calle Gómez García, the main drag directly above the ferry ramp.

In-town Attractions

Museo Inchin Cuivi Ant Located on Calle Ladrilleros on the way out of town to the north, this small museum's displays of traditional Chilote farm and household implements serve as an informative and aesthetic lesson in appropriate technology.

Around Quellón

Chaiguao

Just 5km east of Quellón is this modest village and, just beyond, a long beach excellent for camping. On Sundays during the summertime, residents offer traditional meals and handicrafts in the village.

TOURIST OFFICES
Corner of Gómez García and Santos Vargas, above the ferry ramp (summer only).

BANKS AND MONEY CHANGERS
Banco del Estado, corner of Freire and Ladrilleros. Poor rates.

HOSPITALS AND MEDICAL SERVICES
Dr. Ahués 305, ☎ 681443.

POST OFFICE
Corner of 21 de Mayo and Ladrilleros.

ACCOMMODATION
1 Hotel La Pincoya $, La Paz 64, ☎ 681285.
2 Hotel Golfo Corcovado $$, Santos Vargas 680, ☎ 681528.

CAMPING
Campgrounds near the beach on Punta Lapa, SW of town.

BUS STATION AND/OR OFFICES
Frequent service to Castro and Puerto Montt. Cruz del Sur and Transchiloé are on Aguirre Cerda half a block up from the waterfront.

BOATS
Ferries depart Quellón bound for Chaitén, Puerto Chacabuco, and the scattered fishing villages of the Palena coast.
Transmarchilay (Pincoya) Pedro Montt 457, ☎ 681331.
Navimag (Alejandrina): Angelmó 2187, Puerto Montt, ☎ (65) 253318.

QUELLON

PALENA, AISEN AND THE CARRETERA AUSTRAL

With the possible exception of southern Tierra del Fuego, this is the wildest part of Chile. The towns are young, public transport is infrequent, and services are few and far between. To get here, you must either fly, take a ferry, or drive through Argentina. See the atlas road at the back of this guide.

Perhaps for this reason, countless travelers miss out altogether on the Carretera Austral, bypassing the region on their hell-bent pilgrimage to Torres del Paine or sticking with the creature comforts of the Lake District. Meanwhile, the

rivers, glaciers, fjords and vast archipelago of Palena and Aisén remain as remote, pristine, and spectacular as ever.

In all reality – and considering the rewards – it's not that hard to get here. Regular flights connect Puerto Montt with Chaitén and Coihaique, ferries connect Chaitén, Puerto Aisén, and Puerto Chacabuco with Puerto Montt and Quellón, and there are no fewer than ten separate passes connecting the Carretera Austral with Argentine Ruta 40. Though you'll always be better off with your own vehicle, there exist plenty of options for travelers of all budgets.

Caleta Puelche - Hornopirén   See map 🔼

See map 🔼

ACCOMMODATION
Camping, hotels, hospedajes, cabins in Hornopirén; campgrounds in the national park and in Pichanco. On the road to the national park is the Río Salvaje fishing lodge.

TRANSPORT
Bus tickets and pickup at Supermercado Oelckers, on the plaza. To Puerto Montt, two early morning buses, one early afternoon; from Puerto Montt, the reverse. Buy tickets in advance to be sure of a seat.

FERRIES
Transmarchilay's Tehuelche runs frequently between La Arena and Caleta Puelche from 0800-2100 daily throughout the year; the trip lasts 30 min.
The Mailén runs once a day from Hornopirén to Caleta Gonzalo during Jan and Feb only, departing Hornopirén 1500, departing Caleta Gonzalo 0900. No ferry service the rest of the year.

USEFUL ADDRESSES
Conaf is south of the plaza on Diego Portales, ☎ 217297.
The Pumalín Park office in Hornopirén is at I. Carrera Pinto 388, ☎ 217256.

This is the northernmost section of the Carretera Austral, a near-wilderness of coastal rainforest and recently-cleared homesteads. Most visitors here will hustle through on their way south towards Pumalín Park and Chaitén, but as the ferry south from Hornopirén only operates during the very peak of summer, even these hurried visits are relatively rare. The rest of the year, the stoic, rain-battered locals and salmon farmers are the only folks here.

CALETA PUELCHE is the southern terminus of the short ferry across the mouth of the Estuario de Reloncaví from La Arena (9 ferries a day, from 0800-2100). You can also reach Caleta Puelche via a new road along the south shore of the Estuario from Puelo. See the Southern Chile chapter for details on the area north of La Arena.

South of Caleta Puelche, the Carretera Austral winds 48km south through forest and past ragged homesteads en route to Hornopirén. A longer, rougher coastal road branches off the main route in Contao, rejoining the Carretera in Hualaihue.

HORNOPIRÉN is the northern terminus of the 5hr ferry to Caleta Gonzalo. Operating once a day in Jan and Feb only, it often fills up well in advance, and since it's not possible to make reservations, many travelers end up staying longer in Hornopirén than they had anticipated. If you do wind up staying in town, you can camp along the Río Negro below the bridge east of town. Otherwise there are numerous places to stay around the plaza, including the recommended *Hotel Hornopirén* and a couple of cabaña complexes down the hill from the plaza. Right next to the ferry terminal is a friendly *hospedaje* and restaurant serving delicious *salmón a la mantequilla*.

Protecting the mountain environments to the east are the 48,232 protected hectares of **PARQUE NACIONAL HORNOPIRÉN**. Created in 1988, the park consists of extensive alerce forests, glacial valleys, lakes and high peaks, but the severity of the topography makes for limited access. At present, there is a campsite on the Río Blanco, 11km from town, and another on the west shore of Lago General Pinto Concha. From here there is a short trail along the shore of the lake and a longer one – difficult and unmarked –. to Lago Inexplorado, in Pumalín Park. Plans are underway to continue improving services in the park and further integrate it with Pumalín. Consult with Conaf in Hornopirén for transport to the park, and with the Pumalín foundation for updated information on campsites and a proposed visitors' center along the road to **PICHANCO**, 35km south.

Cruises and sea kayaking trips in the Quintupeu, Cahuelmó, and Comau fjords often begin in Hornopirén. South of the port is Isla Llancahué and the Termas de Llancahué.

Termas de Llancahué

☎ 09-6538345
C $9,000,
children $4,000

Outdoor pool and personal tubs in a small bath house on the shore of Isla Llancahué, accessible by boat from Hornopirén. There is also a restaurant and modest hosteria, and at low tide you can swim in the warm sea water where the 50°C water seeps out around the catchment. Call ahead to arrange for boat transport from Hornopirén.

Fishing Around Hornopirén

Close to town, the Río Negro and Río Blanco are both attractive freestone rivers but are somewhat overfished because of ease of access. They're worth fishing if you happen to be caught in town waiting for a ferrry, but otherwise can't compare with other rivers in the region. Further south on the road to Pichanco, the Río Cholgo sees considerably less traffic.

Operators: 180

53A	Inexplorado	26	Volcán Michimahuida
53B	Laguna Abascal		
53C	Up the Río Vodudahue	20	Hornopirén-Caleta Gonzalo
53D	Across the Península Huequi		
53E	Lago Reñihue	5	The Northern Patagonian Fjords
53F	Sendero Cascadas		
53G	Sendero Tronador	36	Volcán Osorno
53H	Sendero Los Alerces	37	Monte Tronador
53I	Sendero Cascadas Escondidas	38	Monte Tronador
53J	Volcán Michimahuida Trail		

PUMALIN PARK

Pumalín Park   See map

INFORMATION / ACCOMMODATION

Information center, cabins, campground at Caleta Gonzalo, many other campsites throughout the park. Remote cabin in the Reñihue valley.

TRANSPORT

During Jan and Feb, access to Caleta Gonzalo from Hornopirén by ferry and from Chaitén by daily bus. No public transport the rest of the year.

In 1991 Douglas Tompkins, the founder of Esprit. The North Face, and the US-based Foundation for Deep Ecology, purchased his first 17,000há of temperate evergreen rainforest on the Reñihue fjord in the northern Palena province. He then set about purchasing adjoining properties, usually buying though intermediaries to keep unwanted attention to a minimum. When it was discovered that Tompkin's properties had grown to a total of nearly 300,000há (and effectively divided the country in half), Chileans were enraged. Tompkins was vilified in the national press, accused of everything from sabotaging Chilean forestry and salmon exports to compromising national security.

Despite these fears and a general lack of understanding regarding Tompkins' intentions, the Pumalín Park project has grown, fleshed out, and finally gained widespread acceptance. As Pumalín's own informational brochure reads:

'These properties are destined to become a Nature Sanctuary, a special designation of the Chilean state, granting it additional environmental and non-development protection. The Conservation Land Trust (a U.S. environmental organization) will donate these protected lands to the Fundación Pumalín (a Chilean foundation), for their administration and continual development as a type of National Park under private initiative.'

But Pumalín is intended to become more than a mere park. Instead, project organizers hope to fuse conservation and sustainability, combining the protection of forests and other resources with commercial and sustenance activities such as animal husbandry, cheese making, eco-tourism, bee-keeping and organic gardening. It can only be hoped that Pumalín Park will continue to develop and prosper along its sustainable path and will inspire other communities to follow suit.

The park consists of two large sectors separated by the 30,000há Huinay tract, now owned by Endesa, the Spanish-owned utilities company. Additionally, however, the Pumalín project has extended its sphere of influence to include Parque Nacional Hornopirén, with which it delimits to the north. As new trails, campsites, and combination farm/park stations are added yearly, the best advice for visitors to Pumalín is to contact the foundation either at home or in Chile for updated information on park infrastructure. In addition to land-based visits to Pumalín, a number of outfitters also offer cruises and sea kayak trips in the park's several fjords 🖪.

Most visitors to the park will either take the ferry south from Hornopirén to the visitor center at Caleta Gonzalo, or else arrive from the south (Chaitén) via the Carretera Austral. Nonetheless, in the interest of consistency, the park's features are described below from north to south.

South of Hornopirén, a gravel road leads 35km south to PICHANCO, where there is a Pumalín campsite. Beyond Pichanco, Fiordo Quintupeu incises deeply into the Andes, prohibiting further road-building. Travelers on the ferry from Hornopirén will not see any of this sector of the park, as the ferry route passes to the west of the islands that guard the entrance to the fjords.

Those traveling by boat, however, can explore the fascinating interiors of the QUINTUPEU, CAHUELMÓ, AND COMAU FJORDS. There are hotsprings, campsites, a sea lion colony and a short (but challenging) hiking trail in Cahuelmó, a campsite in the village of Huinay, and further hotsprings (the Termas de Porcelana) in the Comau fjord. At the south end of the Comau fjord is the village of VODUDAHUE, where there are plans to create further trails, campsites, and a farm/park station. Branching to the SE is a tributary fjord at the end of which is LEPTEPU, where there is an old ferry ramp, a staffed ranger station, and a campsite complete with a *quincho* for cooking and waiting out the rain. An abandoned section of the Carretera Austral leads south from here across the Península Huequi to the PILLÁN farm/park station and FIORDO LARGO, a tributary of FIORDO REÑIHUE. Further east (at the end of Fiordo Reñihue) is REÑIHUE, where you'll find a single family-sized cabaña, another farm/park station, and hiking/horseback trails up the valley to Lago Reñihue.

Sea Kayaking in the Northern Patagonian Fjords

Cutting deeply into the granite peaks of the coastal Andes, the Quintupeu, Cahuelmó, Comau and Reñihue fjords provide the most spectacular and accessible paddling experience in northern Patagonia. Numerous hotsprings, sea lion colonies, lush temperate rainforest and hundreds of cascading waterfalls form the background for these highly recommended 4-6 day trips, in which participants are given the unique opportunity to explore the fascinating and otherwise inaccessible estuaries at the end of the fjords. Tidal variations exceeding seven meters make careful trip planning essential in this area, and paddlers should also be advised that the abruptness of the landscape and intensity of the local climate makes this a somewhat exposed place to paddle. Most trips utilize a support boat.

Operators: 8 - 10

Fishing in the Northern and Central Patagonian Fjords

 Hidden at the eastern extremes of the great fjords are few tiny, remote tributary streams with wild and abundant trout populations, consisting primarily of rainbows in the 1-2 kilo range (a high percentage of which are escapees from the fish farms). You need an experienced guide, a support boat, and a zodiac to successfully fish these streams, as is the case throughout the maze of fjords and islands to the the south. Ask outfitters about trips to Isla Magdalena (near Puyuhuapi) and the Chonos and Guaitecas Archipelagos.

Operators: 11 - 25 - 80 - 86 - 147

Baños Cahuelmó

 ☎ (65)217256 **N** ⓣ $1,000
Natural hotsprings carved into calcareous rock, accessible only by boat at the east end of the Cahuelmó fjord. You now need reservations to visit or camp at these spectacular springs; contact Pumalín Park for details.

Termas de Porcelana

C ⓣ NA
More than just a spring, the Termas de Porcelana is actually more like a hot mountain stream, flowing through lush rainforest into the Comau fjord just north of Leptepu. These 42°C springs are now under private ownership and entrance fee is charged. Just north is another spring managed by the former owner, with a concrete tub just above the high water line.

On the south side of the fjord is CALETA GONZALO, the ferry terminal and operations center for Pumalín Park. The taste and charm with which the project has been executed is evident in the installations here: there is an information center and handicraft shop, a café with hot meals, fresh-baked bread, and other produce, and seven cozy wooden cabins with views of the fjord (reservations are required). Just up the road towards Chaitén is the entrance to the spotless *Camping Río Gonzalo*, accessed by a hanging bridge, and beyond the campground is the Río Gonzalo farm, where you can take a tour and possibly buy produce or lamb for an afternoon *asado*.

South along the road to Chaitén are a number of trailheads and walk-in campgrounds, and near the park's southern boundary there are roadside campsites, covered picnic areas, and short walks on the shores of LAGO NEGRO and LAGO BLANCO. Keep your eyes open for new installations along this road.

HIKING TRAILS IN PUMALÍN PARK

Though most of Pumalín's trails are clustered along the road from Caleta Gonzalo to Chaitén, there are also trails in the fjords (access by boat only) and a couple that are being developed in conjunction with Conaf, linking the park with PN Hornopirén.

● Inexplorado
⇄ NA
At the time of writing, this long, unmarked trail connecting PN Hornopirén and Parque Pumalín – and stretching from the coast far into the glaciated Andes – was still in the process of development. Consult with park offices for updates.

● Laguna Abascal
⇄ ▇
This wet, unmarked trail begins on the bank of a tiny tributary stream on the north side of the Cahuelmó estuary, about 2km up from the hotsprings. Almost impossible to find without a guide, the route leads through dense rainforest to a stunningly beautiful lake encircled by high peaks. Boat access only.

Operators: 10

● Up the Río Vodudahue
⇄ NA
Like the Inexplorado trail, the Vodudahue – Barcelo trail is currently in the process of development. Nonetheless, as settlers' trails lead along the entire length of the valley, it is still a possibility for experienced hikers. Again, consult for details.

● Across the Península Huequi
✎ ▇
This route follows an abandoned section of the Carretera Austral between the Fiordo Comau and the Fiordo Reñihue. There are campsites at either end of the trail and near the beekeeping station at Pillán, and a short sidehike to a mirador over the Reñihue fjord. Boat access only.

Operators: 8 - 25

• Lago Reñihue
⇄ ⏱5-6d ▢

Beginning in Caleta Gonzalo, this trail climbs the Río Reñihue valley 30km into the Andes, ending at Lago Reñihue. There is a cabaña near the mouth of the river and a couple of designated campsites along the route; ask in Caleta Gonzalo for guides and horses.

Operators: 8

• Sendero Cascadas
⇄ ⏱3h ▮

This short trail departs from Caleta Gonzalo and leads through dense rainforest to a 15m waterfall. Nearby is a trail to the small hydropower plant that provides energy for Caleta Gonzalo.

Operators: 8 - 68

• Sendero Tronador
⇄ ⏱4-5h rt ▢

From a trailhead on the road 12km south of Caleta Gonzalo, this relatively challenging route climbs to a hanging bridge over a spectacular gorge, continuing on to a mirador with great views of Volcán Michimahuida and ending at a campsite beside a pristine mountain lake.

Operators: 8 - 68

• Sendero Los Alerces
⟳ ▮

Just south of the Tronador trailhead, this easy trail loops through an ancient Alerce forest on lovely wooden walkways built of deadfall alerce. Tasteful wooden signs provide information on the natural history and perilous survival of these majestic trees.

Operators: 8 - 68

• Sendero Cascadas Escondidas
⇄ ⏱1.5-2h rt

From a roadside campground 14km south of Caleta Gonzalo, this easy hike leads over a hanging bridge and up to a series of three lush waterfalls.

Operators: 8 - 68

• Volcán Michimahuida Trail
↔ NA

At the time of writing, this route to a lookout over Volcán Michimahuida was still in the planning process, and may not be ready for a couple of years. Consult for updates.

Chaitén
Pop. 3,258 (☎ city code 65)

Chaitén is the capital of the Palena province and an extremely important transportation link, with regular air service from Puerto Montt, ferries to Puerto Montt and Quellón, and buses to most destinations as far south as Coihaique. This is also the best and cheapest place to stock up on groceries before continuing south.

The town was first established in the early 1900s, and in 1933 consisted of a grand total of only three houses. Over the years commerce gradually increased, as increasing numbers of settlers in the Futaleufú and Palena valleys descended to the coast to buy supplies. Today the town's economy appears to continue along the same lines, although in recent years Chaitén has begun to benefit from an increasing summer influx of tourists.

Though there's almost nothing at all to see in town, there's lots to do in the surrounding area, and the fishing is excellent (ask at American-run *Chaitur* for info). Still, most visitors will find Chaitén to be more of a stop-off point than a destination in itself.

Around Chaitén

Pumalín Park
Caleta Gonzalo is 56km north. Transport via Buses B&V, one or two daily Jan 1 – Mar 1 only, [↑].

Termas El Amarillo
32km SE of Chaitén, transport by tour, [↓].

Sea lion colonies
Half-day trip, consult with *Chaitur* for details.

BANKS AND MONEY CHANGERS
Banco del Estado (Libertad and O'Higgins) changes US cash and traveler's checks (poor rates). There is no ATM in town.

HOSPITAL
Off Carrera Pinto between Portales and Riveros.

POST OFFICE
North side of the plaza.

INTERNET CONNECTION
Entel, corner of Cerda and Libertad.

ACCOMMODATION
1 *Hospedaje Rita Gutiérrez $, Almirante Riveros and Prat,* ☎ 731502.
2 *Hospedaje El Triángulo $, Juan Todesco 2,* ☎ 731312.
3 *Hotel Mi Casa $$, Av. Norte 206,* ☎ 731285.
4 *Cabañas Tranqueras del Monte $$, Av. Norte s/n,* ☎ 731379.

CAMPING
Camping Los Arrayanes, 4km north of Chaitén, ☎ 731233

RESTAURANTS
5 *Hostería Corcovado, corner of Corcovado and Aguirre Cerda. Seafood, set lunches.*
6 *La Canasta de Agua, corner of Portales and Prat. Pub atmosphere.*
7 *Mi Casa, above town at Av. Norte 206. Home-cooked meals, recommended.*

AIRPORT
Ten minutes south of town, off the Carretera Austral. Airlines offer free transport to/from the strip.

AIRLINE OFFICE
Aeromet, Corcovado 243, ☎ 731844

BUS STATION AND/OR OFFICES
Main bus station and Chaitur office at the corner of O'Higgins and Portales. Chaitur can provide information on buses and tours to all nearby destinations.

FERRIES
Chaitén's ferry ramp is about a 10-minute walk north. Ferries depart from here bound for Quellón (5hrs), Puerto Montt (10-12hrs), Castro (2hrs by high-speed catamaran), Puerto Chacabuco, and the fishing

villages of the Palena coast.
Transmarchilay (Pincoya): Corcovado 226, ☎ 731272.
Navimag (Alejandrina): Juan Todesca 55, ☎ 731570.
Catamaranes del Sur: Juan Todesca 180 ☎ 731199.

USEFUL ADDRESSES
Pumalín Park project office at O'Higgins 62, ☎ 731341; *next door is the Puma Verde gift shop. Conaf is at O'Higgins 242.*

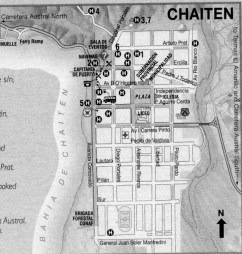

NAVIGATION IN THE NORTHERN PATAGONIAN FJORDS AND CHILOÉ ARCHIPELAGO

See the outfitter directory for contact information for the vessels listed here.
See pg. 540 for boats operating in Laguna San Rafael.

FERRIES & CRUISE SHIPS

1. Alejandrina (Navimag)
Ferry transporting passengers and vehicles between Puerto Montt and Chaitén year-round. Service between Chaitén and Quellón operates from Jan-Mar only.

2. Pincoya (Transmarchilay)
Ferry transporting vehicles and passengers along the Palena and northern Aisén coast, supplying a series of tiny fishing villages. From north to south, the route stops at the following ports: Puerto Montt, Chaitén, Quellón, Raúl Marín Balmaceda, Santo Domingo, Villa Melimoyu, Isla Gala, Puerto Cisnes, Puerto Aguirre, Puerto Chacabuco. Consult for departures.

3. Evangelistas (Navimag)
Ferry transporting passengers only between Puerto Montt and Puerto Chacabuco throughout the year, with service to Laguna San Rafael in Jan and Feb and on special events throughout the year. Regular Sat departures from Puerto Chacabuco, 5-day trip.

4. Colono (Transmarchilay)
Ferry transporting vehicles and passengers from Puerto Montt to Puerto Chacabuco throughout the year, with direct departures in summer only from Puerto Montt to Laguna San Rafael, leaving Puerto Montt on Fri afternoons at 1600. 24 hrs trip to Puerto Chacabuco; 5 days to Laguna San Rafael.

5. Catamaranes del Sur
70-passenger luxury catamaran running from Puerto Montt to Chaitén to Castro and vice versa. This is the fastest way to travel by water in northern Patagonia; the trip from Puerto Montt to Chaitén takes about 4hrs, while the trip from Chaitén to Castro takes only about 2hrs. From Sep-Mar Catamaranes del Sur also runs one-day trips from Puerto Chacabuco to Laguna San Rafael.

6. Skorpios I, II, & III
Luxury cruise ships with a respective capacity for 70,160, and 110 passengers. During July and August, Skorpios runs from Puerto Montt to Dalcahue, departing Sat and returning Sun; the rest of the year they operate principally in Laguna San Rafael (below). 2 days.

SAILBOATS AND MOTOR YACHTS

● Cahuella
⏱6-7d or by charter
This custom-built Chilote motor yacht based in Ancud offers luxurious accommodation for up to 8 passengers on special-interest trips in the Chiloé archipelago, in the fjords of northern Patagonia, Laguna San Rafael and other destinations. Trips can be combined with land tours and activities such as birdwatching and fishing.

● Crucero Bohemia
⏱6d or by charter
10-person motor yacht offering fixed departures to the islands and fjords of Northern Patagonia, departing Saturdays from Puerto Montt between 1030-1230. Also available for chartered fishing trips.

● Yate Arco Iris
17m, 6-person ketch available for chartered sailing and fishing trips in the islands and fjords.

● M/N Pamar
⏱6d
12-person motor yacht offering cruises and fly fishing trips in the fjords of northern Patagonia, the Chiloé Archipelago, and Laguna San Rafael.

For bare boat charters out Puerto Montt, contact:
Operator: 144

PUERTO MONTT
① ② ③
④ ⑤ ⑥
Dalcahue ⑥
Castro
⑤ ⑥
① ② ⑤
Chaitén
Quellón
① ②
Raúl Marín Balmaceda ②
Melinka ○
Villa Melimoyu ②
Isla Gala ② Termas de Puyuhuapi
Puerto Aguirre ② ⑥
② ③
④ ⑤ ⑥
Puerto Chacabuco
⑥
Termas de Quitralco
a Puerto Natales
Laguna San Rafael ③ ④ ⑤ ⑥

From Chaitén to Futaleufú

ACCOMMODATION

Campgrounds, cabañas and hosterías in El Amarillo, Puerto Cárdenas, Puerto Ramírez, Puerto Piedra, Espolón and Futaleufú, and scattered along the Futaleufú valley. To make reservations in Futaleufú, call the Futaleufú operator at ☎ (65)258633 or 258634 and ask to be connected.

TRANSPORT

Chaitur, on Manuel Rodríguez in Futaleufú, provides service to Chaitén. For transport to Argentina, contact Transporte Samuel Flores, Balmaceda 434. Fuel is scarce in Futaleufú, but is usually available on Balmaceda across the street from the school (or ask around).

South of Chaitén, the Carretera Austral leaves the coast and heads inland, paralleling the Río Yelcho up a glacial valley with waterfalls cascading off the peaks on either side. The road is paved for the first few kilometers, but soon turns to gravel; at 27km is the village of **EL AMARILLO**, where a turnoff on the left leads uphill to the Termas El Amarillo. At the intersection is the slightly tattered *Cabañas los Galpones del Volcán*, and from here on clear days there are excellent views of Volcán Michimahuida to the north.

Termas El Amarillo

C 🐦 **$2,000**

These charming, rustic springs lie just 5km off the Carretera Austral, in the midst of dense rainforest near the Río Michimahuida. There are several 50-60°C pools, a scorching mud bath, camping on-site, and some cozy cabañas for rent up the road.

46km from Chaitén is **LAGO YELCHO**, an immense lake ringed by high peaks. Just before the bridge over the lake outlet is Puerto Cárdenas, where you'll find the *Puerto Cárdenas Lodge*, departure point for fishing trips and lake cruises aboard the *Vapor Cristina*. As you cross the bridge over the Río Yelcho look out to the right, where you can see the milky-white glacial waters of a tributary stream mixing with the blue waters of the Yelcho.

At 54km is the entrance to *Yelcho de la Patagonia*, a hostería, campground, and fishing lodge on the lakeshore, and just beyond, on the right, is a signposted footpath ('Agua Mineral') leading 300m into the forest to a spring of sparkling water. On the right side of the road at km 60, just before the bridge over the Río Ventisquero, is the entrance on the right to another footpath,

this one to the Ventisquero Yelcho Chico. Buses from Chaitén can drop you off here, and you can camp for free at the trailhead.

Ventisquero Yelcho Chico

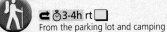 ⇄ 🕒 **3-4h** rt ☐

From the parking lot and camping area beside the Carretera Austral, an easy track leads up the Río Ventisquero into a broad glacial valley. Where the valley opens up, the trail drops onto the valley floor and continues through stands of immense *nalca* plants towards the Yelcho Chico glacier. Eventually, the river blocks passage along the valley floor, and the trail climbs steeply over scree on the north side of the valley to the base of the glacier.

Operators: 68

Continuing south, the road climbs steeply over 650m Cuesta Moraga before dropping down into the Río Frío valley. At km 81 is **VILLA SANTA LUCÍA**, a forlorn military outpost, where the road to Futaleufú and Palena branches off the Carretera to the east. (The Carretera Austral south of Villa Santa Lucía is described in La Junta and the Palena watershed, 🔲). This road almost immediately crests another pass to rejoin Lago Yelcho, this time at its southern end; before the road was built, supplies brought from the coast to Futaleufú and Palena were rowed up the Río Yelcho and across the lake, and then were transported further upvalley from here by horse. 105km from Chaitén is the turnoff to **PUERTO PIEDRA**, a small lakeside settlement near the mouth of the Río Futaleufú where you'll find boats for rent and cozy lodging at *Hostal Alexis*. From here you can look out at Isla Monita, site of a world-class fishing lodge.

At km 111 is **PUERTO RAMÍREZ**, a quiet, unremarkable village along the banks of the Río Malito, a tributary of the Futaleufú. There are several places to stay (*Hostería Verónica* recommended) as well as free camping along the river. Just past town you'll come across a Y in the road; the road on the right leads 64km SE on a good road to Palena 🔲.

The road to Futaleufú parallels the river, passing through spectacular burned-over countryside below huge cliffs. One of the first glimpses you get of the river is at the

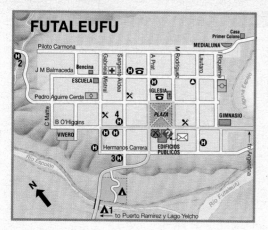

FUTALEUFU

ACCOMMODATION

1 *Camping La Vega $*, next to the bridge over the Espolón.
2 *Cabañas Río Espolón $$*, at the east end of Pedro Aguirre Cerda, anexo 216.
3 *Posada La Gringa $$*, Aldea and Carrera, anexo 260.
4 *Hostería Río Grande $$*, O'Higgins 397, anexo 320.

Casa Amarilla, a small yellow house on the right with a nearby campsite; apple and empanadas and cold beers are often available here for hungry boaters getting off the river. About a 120km from Chaitén is the Futaleufú bridge, known locally as 'the concrete bridge.' Above the bridge the road continues up-valley, now on the north side of the river.

As the road nears the upper portion of the valley, the forest begins to thin out, and farms, campgrounds, and outfitter's camps begin to appear along the roadside. Keep an eye out on the right for *Camping Cara del Indio*, a favorite among kayakers; a couple of kilometers further up you'll pass the turnoff to a hanging bridge known as the **PASARELA ZAPATA**, and beyond that on the right is the *Casa de Té*, a small hostería offering the coziest lodging in the valley. About 200m past here are turnoffs on the left and the right, the former leading to the upper Río Azul valley, the latter down to another *pasarela* over the Futaleufú. At km 139 from Chaitén is the bridge over the electric-blue **RÍO AZUL**.

At km 146, the road begins to wind along the shore of Lago Lonconao, and at km 152 is the turnoff on the left to **LAGO ESPOLÓN** (2km), a long, narrow lake with simple lodging, campsites, and boats for rent at its southern end. Another 6km past this turnoff, the road crosses the Río Espolón (good campground on the right before the bridge) and enters the town of Futaleufú.

Like many other mountain towns in northern Patagonia, **FUTALEUFÚ** was initially settled via Argentina. Only recently was the town linked by road to the coast, and today there is no pavement, groceries are scarce, and finding fuel can be almost impossible. However, in recent years Futaleufú has received an increasing amount of coverage in the international press, and today there is hardly a rafter or fishermen who has not heard of the place. How the town will respond to increasing tourist traffic – and to plans on the part of Endesa (the Spanish owned utility company) to dam the river – are yet-be-resolved issues that will weigh heavily in the future of this singularly beautiful region. At present, the only displays of the town's newfound status are a couple of upscale *hosterías*, a slick outfitter (*Futaleufú Adventure Center*), a better-than-average selection of restaurants, and increasingly conspicuous gangs of gringos decked out for the great outdoors.

If you stay in town, there are a number of options for excursions in the surrounding area. Closest to town, you can fish or paddle in the Río Espolón, or hike up the hill above Laguna Espejo (access past the rodeo *medialuna*) for a great view over the town. Just SE of town is another bridge over the Futaleufú, providing access to a dirt road that runs all along the south shore of the river, ideal for hiking and mountain biking.

East of Futaleufú along the road to Argentina, the landscape rapidly transforms into arid pampa. Just across the border, the towns of **TREVELÍN** and **ESQUEL** provide access to the Argentine National Park Los Alerces.

Rafting and Kayaking in Around the Futaleufú Valley

Operators: 35 - 49 - 88 - 105 (k) - 175 - 207

Few rivers in the world – if any – can match the Futaleufú for sheer power and beauty. Originating at a dam across the border in Argentina, the 'Futa' or 'Fu' flows anywhere from 6,000-30,000 cfs or more, with more gradient than most rivers half its size. Most outfitters on the Futaleufú (whose name translates as 'big river' in Mapudungún) operate out of a single base camp, running progressively more difficult sections as clients' abilities improve. All told, there are four major sections on the Futa, as well as a couple of runnable, lower-volume tributaries. Note that with high water, the difficulty of all these sections increases significantly.

● Infierno Canyon (V)
⏱6h

This is the longest and most challenging section on the river, with three major Class V's interspersed with long flatwater sections. First is the continuous Class IV-V mayhem of Infierno Canyon itself, followed by Zeta and Throne room, both of which can (and in many cases should) be easily portaged. The run normally ends at the *pasarela* near the Río Azul.

● The Terminator Section (IV-V)
⏱4h

Below the confluence with the Río Azul is a relatively long flatwater section leading into the long, complicated Terminator rapid. Below here, Kyber Pass and Himalaya boast some of the biggest waves on the river, and in general this run is noted for its phenomenal play spots. Takeout is at the Pasarela Zapata.

● Bridge to Bridge (IV)
⏱2-3h

The standard 'warm-up' run on the Futa features nonstop Class IV rapids and nothing particularly scary. The action starts just below the hanging bridge and continues through the intimidating (but eminently runnable) Pillow rapid; another highlight is the massive exploding wave at Mundaca, just below the Cara del Indio campground. The takeout is at the concrete bridge.

● Casa de Piedra (IV-V)
⏱2-3h

Below the concrete bridge is yet another highly worthwhile Class IV-V section. First up is the hole-studded Más o Menos, followed by a technical Class V easily identified by its namesake house-sized rock. Hot apple empanadas and cold beers are available at the Casa Amarilla, a popular campsite and the normal takeout to this section.

● The Lower Futaleufú (II-III)
⏱2-3h

Below the Casa Amarilla, the river shifts to Class II, with easily readable rapids and unintimidating play spots. This makes a good big-water warmup, and is also a popular float trip for fishermen, ending at Lago Yelcho.

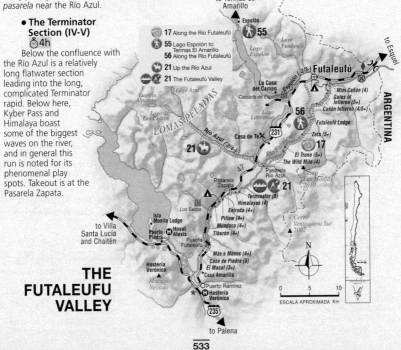

THE FUTALEUFÚ VALLEY

Futaleufu Lodge

• Small and intimate Flyfishing Lodge, bordering the Futaleufu river • Sonia and Jim Repine are your hosts • Ideal for couples • Only 4 clients per week • First class Chilean cuisine and the best Chilean wines • Flyfishing classes for beginners • Alternative programs for non fishing-guests such as sightseeing, horseback riding, trekking • Open from January to April

Casilla 1238 • Viña del Mar • Chile
Fax (56-32) 81 2659
soniad@entelchile.net • www.narksport.com

• Río Azul (III-IV)
🕐 1h

From the hanging bridge over the Río Azul to the confluence with the Futaleufú, this ledgy, medium-volume glacial stream makes for a good warmup or intermediate run, and is a logical put-in for the Terminator section.

• Río Espolón (II-III)
🕐 2-3h

Below the unrunnable Cascadas de Espolón, the Espolón mellows to Class II; the stretch from there to the Río Espolón bridge in the town of Futaleufú is the standard beginner's run in town. Below the bridge is a stretch of Class II-III water leading into the Infierno Canyon section on the Futa.

Lago Espolón to the Termas El Amarillo

 🖊 🕐 4-6d

Beginning at the remote north end of Lago Espolón (accessed by boat from the south end), this wet, unmarked track follows an abandoned road NW into the Río Michimahuida valley, ending on the road past the Termas El Amarillo. Consult with local settlers for route information.

Operators: 105

Along the Río Futaleufú

 🖊 🕐 1-3d

Dirt roads and trails lead all along the south bank of the Río Futaleufú, connecting a series of hanging bridges and allowing for hiking and mountain biking routes of varying lengths. One recommended route begins in the town of Futaleufú and follows the road SE towards Argentina for about 25 min (times given on foot), at which point a dirt track bears right to Puente Gelves. Beyond the bridge the road splits; take the right branch and continue over a pass, down through farmland, and along a precipitous track above Infierno Canyon to the lovely Las Escalas valley. Past a couple of stream crossings is another junction; the route on the right leads to another hanging bridge and back to the main road (for a long day trip), while the left branch continues downriver about 4hrs to the hanging bridge at the Río Azul (for an overnight). It is also possible to continue downriver from the Pasarela Río Azul to the Pasarela Zapata. Remember to ask permission before camping on private land.

Operators: 88 - 105

Volcán Michimahuida (2,404m)

 🕐 7-10d

This immense glaciated peak SE of Chaitén is usually climbed from the south, via an unmaintained trail up the Río Michimahuida from the town of Amarillo. A new trail off the Carretera Austral between Chaitén and Caleta Gonzalo may also provide a suitable approach to the volcano's east side. Count on at least a week for expeditions to Michimahuida.

Up the Río Azul

Consult at *Camping Cara del Indio* for details on the 3-day local-guided horsepacking trip up the Río Azul to a glacial cirque with five alpine lakes.

Fishing on the Río Futaleufú, Lago Yelcho & the Río Yelcho

From its source in Argentina to its terminus in Lago Yelcho, the Futaleufú boasts nearly 100km of prime trout waters in an idyllic mountain setting. The fishing on the Futa, on the Río Espolón, and on a plethora of nearby lakes is primarily for browns and rainbows in the 2-3 kilo range: not huge fish, but lots of them. Access to the upper stretches is complicated by the powerful rapids, and many areas are accessible only by raft; Jim Repine's *Futaleufú Lodge*, located in the Las Escalas valley, provides the best access to this area. The lower Futaleufú is wider, slower, and more accessible, and boats are available locally in Puerto Piedra; a more upscale option is to stay at the *Isla Monita Lodge*, located on a pristine island directly across from the rivermouth. Below the lake, the Río Yelcho flows another 35km or so to the Pacific, and receives a greater quantity of sea-run fish; excursions on the nearby Río Corcovado can be arranged in Puerto Cárdenas or Chaitén.

Operators: 68 - 105 - 125 - 238

Gelves Canyon

The Gelves Canyon drops a sheer 500m from its source in the granite peaks of the Andes to the east shore of Lago Espolón. Full- and half-day trips out of Futaleufú explore the canyon's numerous waterfalls and pools, with rappels of up to 45m.

Operators: 105

La Junta and the Palena Watershed

The next major river south of the Futaleufú, the Palena drains an immense watershed including a remarkable variety of environments, from the high, semi-arid pampa east of the Andes to the dense rainforest of the coastal lowlands.

The upper portion of the valley is accessed via gravel road leading SE from Puerto Ramírez, on the route from Chaitén to Futaleufú ⬆. The route climbs along the Río Malito, then crests a beautiful burnt-over pass and descends with wide-open views of the Río Palena.

64km from Puerto Ramírez, **PALENA** is a sleepy highland town that probably looks exactly like Futaleufú did before the gringos arrived. There are simple hospedajes, markets, and restaurants in town, but little else; the fishing is great, however, and from here in all directions there stretches a vast wilderness begging to be explored on foot, on horseback, or by raft or kayak.

Palena to Lago Verde

🚶 🧗↻ ⏱7-10d ▭

Locals in Palena can provide horses and guide services for the route south to Lago Palena, a binational lake that has been protected as a national park. From here,

experienced hikers with solid routefinding skills can continue south, down the Río Quinto to the town of Lago Verde. For a real epic, you could then keep heading south on horse along the east shore of the lake to finish in La Tapera, in the Río Cisnes Valley. This is a remote, unmarked track through virgen forest and remote homesteads.

Operators: 103 - 137

Río Palena (II)

⏱3d

Below the bridge just north of Palena, the Río Palena is one of the finest multi-day wilderness runs in the country, dropping through a remote, forested canyon, past white sand beaches and snowcapped peaks to La Junta, where it joins with the Río Rosselot. Below here, the river is more appropriate for sea kayaks.

The lower stretch of the Palena watershed (below the canyon) is accessed directly via the Carretera Austral. From Villa Santa Lucía, where the route to Futaleufu branches east, the Carretera continues south along the Río Frío, crossing to the west side of the river shortly before it joins with the Río Palena. 50km from Villa Santa Lucía the road crosses back over the Palena to the east side, and at km 70 is the bridge over the Río Rosselot, which drains **LAGO ROSSELOT** and the Río Figueroa valley. The views of the Palena valley and the surrounding peaks are incredible along this stretch.

On the far side of the bridge is the town of **LA JUNTA**. Here there is an excellent hostería, *Espacio y Tiempo*, as well as a host of cheaper lodging, restaurants, and markets. Though the town itself is rather drab, there's a lot to do in the surrounding area, and La Junta serves as a good base of operations.

Hostería Lodge Ensueño on the left, and continues up the Río Figueroa valley through dense rainforest to the village of **LAGO VERDE**, 73km from La Junta. Once owned by a single *estancia*, it is now a modest village at the north end of a stunning (but sadly deforested) lake. There is spectacular but exposed camping on the lakeshore south of town, while several kilometers to the north (through the *estancia*) there is a hanging bridge over the crystal clear Río Pico, which originates in Argentina and makes for great fishing. This is a transitional area between the temperate rainforest and the pampa that lies just over Paso Las Palmas – Lago Verde to the east, and so the weather is cooler but much sunnier than in La Junta.

Río Figueroa (III-V)

⏱2d
Flowing out of immense, chalk-green Lago Verde, the little-known Figueroa disappears into a series of whitewater and flatwater canyons. The upper sections are rated Class II-III, while the lower section is a dauntingly remote canyon with one major Class V, overhung by dense temperate rainforest.
Operators: 105

Fishing Around La Junta

There are literally dozens of unexplored rivers and lakes in this general area. The fishing on the Palena is best on the upper sections, above the confluence with the milky-blue Río Frío, but this section is accessible only by float trip or jet boat. The Figueroa may be fished in two sections. The first is upstream near the town of Lago Verde, where the river joins with the Río Pico; the lower section is accessible by boat from Lago Rosselot. Consult with local lodges or with locals in La Junta for boat rentals and excursions.
Operators: 11 - 41 - 188 - 190

Below La Junta, the Río Palena continues its lazy, winding course through the lowland forest. First explored in the 17th century by Italian Jesuit Nicolás Mascardi, who was searching for the Ciudad de los Césares, the immense lower Palena has always held an attraction for explorers and would-be colonizers: in 1871, Enrique Simpson tried and failed to establish a colony at the mouth of the river, and in the late 19th and early 20th century, the river was further explored by the expeditions of Hans Stephan and Augusto Grosse.

Today, there is a road leading 30km from La Junta down the south bank of the Río Palena; from here, you can arrange for boat transport down the river, past the imposing hulk of Volcán Melimoyu, to the port of Raúl Marín Balmaceda.

Down the Río Palena

⏱3h o/w
Motor launches bound for Raúl Marín Balmaceda depart every Thursday from km 30 on the road west from La Junta. For information on departure times or to arrange transport on other days, contact the Hotel Espacio Tiempo, ☎ (67)314141 in La Junta, or Alejandro Hechentleiner of Turismo Valle Palena, ☎ (67)681151 in Raúl Marín.

Paddlers can make the trip from La Junta to Raúl Marín Balmaceda in 2-3 days (depending on the wind), with one night at a splendid hotspring in the middle of the rainforest. The trip can be combined with the raft descent of the upper Palena (see above), or further extended to include the 5-8 day loop south around Volcán Melimoyu to the Termas de Puyuhuapi. Otherwise you can return to La Junta by motor launch, or head out by ferry.
Operators: 26 - 88 - 105

Set on a sandy tongue between the mouth of the Río Palena and the broad, protected Estero Pitipalena, **RAÚL MARÍN BALMACEDA** (pop. 300) has a restaurant, market, a telephone and a hostería, all rarities along this remote coast. Nearby, the *Casa del Rodrigo Parra* (☎ 681151) also offers hostería-style accommodation in a magical, isolated setting on the Estero Pitipalena; radio from town and a motor launch will come get you. Raúl Marín, as it is called, is also accessed via the ferry Pincoya, which calls upon this and several other, tinier settlements to the south. In the surrounding area is some of the wildest and most spectacular scenery along this section of coast, ideal for sailing, sea kayaking, and fly-fishing, but visitors should come prepared for rainy weather.

Puyuhuapi and Parque Nacional Queulat

South of La Junta, the Carretera Austral climbs gradually for 28km to **LAGO RISOPATRÓN**, a narrow, forested lake set within the northern confines of Parque Nacional Queulat. Near the north end of the lake is the entrance to *Cabañas El Pangue*, and further on is the Conaf guardería and campsite at **SECTOR ANGOSTURA**.

Laguna Los Pumas

 5-6h

From a trailhead located across the road from the ranger station at Sector Angostura, this trail climbs steeply to a 1,000m pass with excellent views of the Cordillera Queulat and the Puyuhuapi fjord. From here, it descends gently to a lovely highland lake, the Laguna Los Pumas.

At km 45 is **PUERTO PUYUHUAPI**, a quiet, pleasant village at the north end of the Canal Puyuhuapi, founded by German settlers during the 1930's. The town retains a great deal of its German character, and there is a full range of accommodation, restaurants, and provisions. To the west of the river that divides town, across from the gas station, you can check out the handmade rugs that have been produced in Puyuhuapi since 1945. There is a variety of budget lodging, and excellent mid-range accommodation at the *Casona de Puyuhuapi* (in the first home built in the bay) and the more central *Hostería Alemana*.

South of town, the road winds along the east shore of the Canal Puyuhuapi – look out for dolphins all along this stretch. 10km south of Puyuhuapi is the boat ramp for transfer across the fjord to the Termas de Puyuhuapi, Chile's top hotsprings resort. Shortly thereafter the road veers inland up the Río Ventisquero valley, crosses the river at km 20 and shortly thereafter passes the entrance to the **VENTISQUERO COLGANTE SECTOR** of Parque Nacional Queulat. This is the most spectacular and of-visited sector of the park, with a nice campground along the banks of the river and a number of hiking trails.

THE VENTISQUERO COLGANTE IN PN QUEULAT

Termas de Puyuhuapi

 ☎ (2)2256489, (67)325103
🏠 $12,000, children $5,000

This elegant wooden hotel complex on the west shore of the Fiordo Puyuhuapi is Chile's top hotsprings resort, with three outdoor pools on the Puyuhuapi fjord and a complete spa with indoor pool, jacuzzi, steam bath, massage and thalasso-therapy (algal treatments). Visits to the springs may be combined with all-inclusive tours aboard the *Patagonia Connection* catamaran to Laguna San Rafael, and a variety of activities are offered in the surrounding area, including sea kayaking, fly fishing on Isla Magdalena, and hiking in Parque Nacional Queulat.

Mirador Ventisquero Colgante

 3-4h rt

From the hanging bridge over the Río Ventisquero, this trail climbs the steep bluff to the north, leveling out near the top to reach a splendid lookout over the hanging glacier and the Laguna Los Témpanos. An easier option is to turn right directly after the bridge and walk up the riverbank about a kilometer to the shore of Laguna los Témpanos.

Operators: 98 - 103 - 167

Up the Río Ventisquero

 ⇄ ⏱5-6h rt ▯

Also in Sector Ventisquero, this longer trail climbs the Río Ventisquero Valley south into the heart of the glaciated Cordillera Queulat. Work continues on this hike, so ask the local rangers for an update before setting out.

Continuing south, the road hugs the shore of the Fiordo Queulat, passing the *Cabañas Fiordo Queulat* and shortly thereafter beginning the steep switchbacks of the **Cuesta Queulat Norte**. The route passes beneath overhanging ferns, creeping vines and countless waterfalls, and provides excellent views to the north of the heavily glaciated Cordillera Queulat. Keep your eyes open for the Salto Padre García waterfall, named for another Jesuit who wandered through this jungle in 1766 in search of the *Ciudad de los Césares*. At 87km, the road crests the pass and begins the descent in the Río Cisnes valley. There are a couple of worthwhile, signposted trails near the top of the pass.

Sendero Las Cascadas

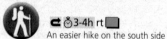 ⇄ ⏱3-4h rt ▯

An easier hike on the south side of the Portezuelo Queulat, on the way down into the Río Cisnes valley. A sign marks the trail, which leads through lush rainforest about 2km to a series of waterfalls on the Río Las Cascadas. The trail then climbs the riverbank to end at a glacial tarn surrounded by glaciers.

Puerto Cisnes and the Cisnes Valley

TRANSPORT

Regular buses connect Puerto Cisnes with Puyuhuapi and Coihaique, but there is no transport to La Tapera. Twice-weekly ferry service from Puerto Cisnes connects with Quellón, Raúl Marín Balmaceda, Puerto Chacabuco and isolated settlements along the coast.

On the south side of the Queulat range, 59km from Puyuhuapi, is the marked turnoff to Puerto Cisnes. As this is a dead-end road, most travelers continue south along the Carretera, but there are some excellent campsites along the Río Cisnes within a few km of the turnoff, and the road – blasted from the sheer rock walls of the Canal Puyuhuapi – is itself something of a spectacle. First settled in 1952, **Puerto Cisnes** (30km from the turnoff, pop. 2000) is the largest settlement between Chaitén and Coihaique. Here you'll find fuel, supplies, and a variety of restaurants serving fresh seafood. Recommended places to stay include *Hostería Gaucho* and *Cabañas Manzur*.

Beyond the Puerto Cisnes turnoff (km 0), the Carretera parallels the river for a short stretch. At 3km the road passes beneath the **Piedra del Gato**, an imposing mass of rock that crowds up against the river. This was the most costly part of the Carretera Austral, both in terms of money and human lives; you can still see remnants of the rope ladders that the demolitionists used to climb up and set charges. The road crosses a narrow gorge over the Cisnes at 22km, and shortly thereafter passes **Villa Amengual**, a not-so-prosperous service town for the settlers in the surrounding area, with basic restaurants and markets.

At km 30 is the turnoff to the upper Río Cisnes valley and **La Tapera**. The road to La Tapera rapidly rises along the south side of the valley, which soon narrows into a tight gorge. The change in landscape and climate is surprisingly abrupt, as the rainforest gives way to pampa grasslands and copses of deciduous forest. Almost the entire upper valley belongs to a single sheep *estancia*, one of the few that remains intact from the early days of settlement in the region; today there is a world-class fishing lodge here. Keep your eyes open on the left for a spectacular suspension bridge over the river. The town of La Tapera, 49km from the turnoff, has a market or two, but little else; beyond here it's 55km through the rolling pampa to the Argentine border.

3km south of the La Tapera turnoff, the Carretera Austral passes alongside Lago Las Torres, and at km 52 is **Villa Mañihuales**, with basic services but limited appeal. The forests of the entire Río Mañihuales valley were decimated by the great cycle of forest fires that began in 1940. Though this makes for fine, expansive views, most travelers will prefer to bolt south to Coihaique from this point. It's 140km to Coihaique from the La Tapera turnoff.

Río Cisnes (IV-V)

⏱2d (1 per section)

There are two runnable sections on the Río Cisnes. The upper canyon, visible but not scoutable from the road to La Tapera, is a Class IV-V expert kayakers run. The lower section (below Piedra del Gato) is also Class IV-V, but is also suitable for rafts. This is a stunningly beautiful, crystal clear river with outstanding fishing.

Operators: 105

Fishing the Río Cisnes

The prime dry-fly waters of the upper Cisnes run through the privately-owned *Estancia de los Ríos*, and access is generally restricted to guests at the lodge. The lower section – which receives impressive salmon runs in March and April – may be accessed sporadically from the road to Puerto Cisnes, but you need a boat to access most of the river. Consult in Puerto Cisnes for guided excursions on the lower Cisnes.

Operators: 86 - 188

Puerto Aisén & Puerto Chacabuco

ACCOMMODATION
Budget accommodation near the ferry terminal in Puerto Chacabuco and in 'downtown' Puerto Aisén. Upscale lodging in Puerto Chacabuco.

INTERNET CONNECTION
Cyber Ruca, Plaza de Armas, Puerto Aisén.

TRANSPORT
Buses: Frequent buses connect the two towns, and provide direct service from the ferry to Coihaique, 1.5 hrs east. Ferries: Ferries depart Puerto Chacabuco bound for Puerto Montt, Quellón, Chaitén, Laguna San Rafael and the fishing villages of the Palena coast. Transmarchilay (Colono, Pincoya, ☎ 351192), Navimag (Evangelistas, ☎ 351111), and Catamaranes del Sur (☎ 351112, 351115) all have offices in town.

At the east end of Seno Aisén, 83km by a paved highway from Coihaique, **PUERTO CHACABUCO** is a major ferry port with frequent connections to Puerto Cisnes, Quellón and Puerto Montt. Many cruises to Laguna San Rafael also depart from here, and there is fine lodging available at the *Hotel Loberías de Aisén*. The port dates only from the 1960's, when the original port at Puerto Aisén filled with silt after intentional wildfires burned tens of thousands of hectares in the Río Simpson valley.

Though its port is now apt only for smaller craft, **PUERTO AISÉN** remains the hub of the area, with a selection of hotels, restaurants, and markets. Fishing boats and *goletas* – available on an informal basis for cruises to Laguna San Rafael – drop anchor in Puerto Aguas Muertas or Puerto Palo, both just north of town. Those with their own transport might also want to explore the dirt roads that lead north (to Lago de los Palos) and south (up the Río Blanco to Lago Riesgo) from Puerto Aisén. The road to Coihaique leads through the Reserva Nacional Río Simpson, described below.

Parque Nacional Laguna San Rafael

TRANSPORT / ACCOMMODATION
Transport by boat or plane only. No formal accommodation in the park; expeditions are occasionally allowed to stay with Conaf in the old hotel.

Inaccessible by road, this 1,742,000-hectare national park and Unesco World Biosphere Reserve is easily one of the most famous spectacles in Chilean Patagonia. Though it's not easy or cheap to get to, it's well worth the trouble and expense.

The centerpiece of the park, **LAGUNA SAN RAFAEL**, lies at the south end of a long, narrow inside passage, the Estero Elefantes. To the west of the lake are the hills of the Península de Taitao, while to the east is Monte San Valentín and the immense Northern Patagonia Ice Fields, one arm of which – the **SAN RAFAEL GLACIER** – flows directly into the lake, calving off huge icebergs to the delight of visiting tourists. To the south of the lake is the narrow, relatively low Isthmus de Ofqui, through which the Chilean government once attempted to blast a shipping canal.

With previous arrangement, you can stay at the simple Conaf *refugio* in the park, though most visitors come for the day or stay aboard ship. There is only one maintained trail in the park, a 7km walk to an overlook above the glacier. Well-equipped

and experienced hikers, mountaineers and sea kayakers will find a wealth of challenging route opportunities in the surrounding area, but should be prepared for very inclement weather with scant possibilities for rescue.

If visiting aboard ship, be sure to inquire about shipping schedules and whether you'll be navigating by day or night. Though the lake and glacier are the most impressive parts of the trip, the traverse through the canals is far too pretty to sleep through.

BOATS OPERATING IN LAGUNA SAN RAFAEL

● Skorpios I, II, & III
Luxury cruise ships with fixed departures from Puerto Montt to Laguna San Rafael, departing Sat at 1100. These six-day trips include a visit to Skorpios' private hotsprings in the Quitralco fjord.

● Evangelistas (Navimag)
⏱5d
Ferry transporting passengers between Puerto Montt and Puerto Chacabuco throughout the year, with service to Laguna San Rafael in Jan and Feb and on special events throughout the year. Regular Sat departures from Puerto Chacabuco.

● Colono (Transmarchilay)
⏱24h to Puerto Chabuco;
⏱5d to Laguna San Rafael
Ferry transporting vehicles and passengers from Puerto Montt to Puerto Chacabuco throughout the year, with direct departures in summer only from Puerto Montt to Laguna San Rafael, leaving Puerto Montt on Fri afternoons at 1600.

● Cahuella
Luxury wooden motor yacht offering personalized trips to Laguna San Rafael, departing from Puerto Chacabuco or elsewhere by previous arrangements.

● Catamaranes del Sur
⏱1d
In addition to one-day tours from Puerto Chacabuco to Laguna San Rafael aboard the 70-passenger *Catamarán Iceberg Expedition*, Catamaranes del Sur also offers all inclusive 3-day, 2-night packages including all meals and lodging at the Hotel Loberías del Sur in Puerto Chacabuco. The trip itself departs at 0830 and returns at 2100.

● **Catamarán Patagonia Express**
⏱ 4-6d in high season
⏱ 1d in off season

High-speed catamaran with 70-passenger capacity, offering cruises from the Hotel Termas de Puyuhuapi to Puerto Chacabuco and the San Rafael glacier, as part of all-inclusive package tours. In the off-season, one-day tours are also available from Puerto Chacabuco (excluding the hotsprings), departing on Fri at 0900 and returning at 2100.

● **Lancha Patagonia**
by charter

12-person motor yacht based in Puerto Chacabuco, offering cruises to Laguna San Rafael and other destinations along the Aisén coast.

● **Lancha Ventisquero**
by charter

12-person motor yacht available for charter along the Aisén coast.

Scenic flights to Laguna San Rafael and the Northern Patagonian Ice Fields

From their base in Coihaique, Aerohein offers chartered flights in 5-person prop planes to Laguna San Rafael and other regional destinations. The full trip to Laguna San Rafael, including airport transfer, flight, motor launch to the lake, and the traditional whiskey served over glacier ice, costs around US$200/pp. You can also charter a plane on your own for US$250 (US$380 for bimotor) per hour of flight time, and US$50 per hour on the ground. The daily minimum is US$750 (or US$1140).

COIHAIQUE, THE RIO SIMPSON AND CERRO DIVISADERO

*See pg 6 for photo credit.

Coihaique   *Pop. 36,736 (☎ city code 67)*

Set below the towering slabs of Cerro Macay on a bluff between the Simpson and Coihaique rivers, Coihaique is the capital of the Aisén region and one of the cleanest and most prosperous cities in Chile. Founded in 1929 as a service center for local settlers, it is also one of the most confusing cities of its size anywhere, thanks to an unusual five-sided plaza. Finding your way around at first requires some careful navigating.

Coihaique's surroundings are what really sets the city apart. Within a couple of hours' drive are no fewer than four protected reserves, numberless lakes and blue-ribbon trout streams, waterfalls and a small ski area. As the town sits behind the westernmost ramparts of the Andes, the climate is relatively dry, intermediate between the coastal rainforests and the pampa.

For those traveling along the Carretera Austral, Coihaique will be a welcome change, a pocket of civilization where you can eat well, rest up, and prepare for coming adventures. For those arriving directly by boat (via Puerto Chacabuco) or plane (via Balmaceda), this is where the adventure begins.

In-town Attractions

Museo Regional de la Patagonia NE of the plaza at Baquedano 310, this museum features photographs of early 20th-century settlers in the Coihaique region.
Hours: Open Jan-Feb daily 0900-2100, Mar-Dec/Mon-Fri 0830-1300, 1430-1830.
Entrance: $400.

TERMAS DE PUYUHUAPI HOTEL & SPA

Located in an exclusive area of the exotic Chilea Patagonia, the TERMAS DE PUYUHUAPI HOTEL & SP emerges in complete harmony with the landscap surrounded by pristine nature. Its classy facilities provid the perfect conditions for an unforgettable sta The complete SPA and Thalassotherapy Center offer wide variety of treatments, using the benefits of th thermal waters and the marine environment, such a seaweed and sea water.

Termas de Puyuhuapi Hotel & Spa is a place reserve only for those who are looking for something differen

PATAGONIA EXPRESS

The San Rafael Glacier is an enormous mass of ic which flows from the high peaks of the Ande Mountains west towards the sea, into the San Rafae Lagoon, offering a wonderful spectacle.

Our programs include a full day excursion to enjoy th. beautiful experience by travelling through the patagoni fjords and channels on board the luxury PATAGONIA EXPRESS Catamaran.

Patagonia Connection
Termas de Puyuhuapi Hotel & Spa

Santiago: Fidel Oteiza 1921 of. 1006 • tel.: (56-2) 225 6489 • fax: (56-2) 274 8111
e-mail: info@patagoniaconnex.cl • www.patagoniaconnex.cl

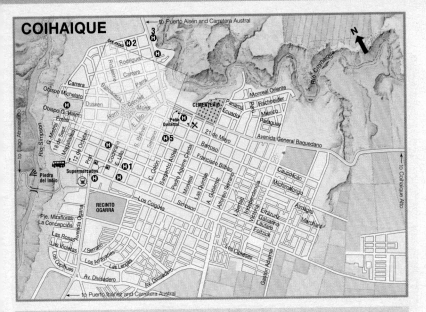

COIHAIQUE

TOURIST OFFICES

Sernatur, Bulnes 35, just off the Plaza.
Municipal tourist office at the Museo Regional de la Patagonia.

BANKS AND MONEY CHANGERS

ATMs in the commercial sector NE of the plaza (Calle Condell area). Cash and travelers' checks changed at Turismo Prado, 21 de Mayo 417.

HOSPITAL

West end of J.M. Carrera, ☎ 233172.

POST OFFICE

Cochrane 202, just off the Plaza de Armas.

INTERNET CONNECTION

Entel, Prat 340.

ACCOMMODATION

1 **Hospedaje Lautaro** $, Lautaro 269, ☎ 238116.
2 **Hospedaje Herminia Mansilla** $, 21 de Mayo 60, ☎ 231579.
3 **Unnamed hospedaje** $, Baquedano 20, ☎ 232520.
4 **Cabañas San Sebastián** $$, Freire 554, ☎ 231762.
5 **Hostal Austral** $$, Colón 203, ☎ 232522.

6 **Hotel Belisario Jara** $$$, Bilbao Jara 662, ☎ 234150.
HI Albergue Las Salamandras $, Carretera Teniente Vidal, 1.5km west of town on the road to the airport.
Cabañas Río Simpson $$, 3km north on the Río Simpson, ☎ 232183.
La Pasarela $$$, 2km north on the Río Simpson, ☎ 234520.
More info at www.turistel.cl

CAMPING

HI Albergue Las Salamandras (see 🛏️).
La Alborada, 2km north, next to the entrance to RN Coihaique.

RESTAURANTS

7 **Casino de Bomberos**, Parra 365. Fixed lunches, hearty portions.
8 **La Olla**, Prat 176. Regional specialties, cozy.
9 **Café Ricer**, Horn 48. Central location, popular.
La Pasarela, 2km north on the road to Puerto Aisén. Lodge atmosphere, reservations required.

BARS AND DISCOTHEQUES

10 **Bar West**, Magallanes and Bilbao. Homey western-theme pub.
11 **Piel Roja**, Moraleda between Parra and Condell. Coihaique's bumping nightspot.

AIRPORTS

Aeropuerto Teniente Vidal, 5km south, for regional flights
Aeropuerto Balmaceda, 1hr SE on the Argentine border, for larger aircraft.

AIRLINE OFFICES

LanChile, General Parra 402, ☎ 231188.
Aerotaxi Don Carlos, Subteniente Cruz 63, ☎ 231981.
Aerohein, Baquedano 500, ☎ 232772.
Línea Aérea San Rafael, 18 de Septiembre 469, ☎ 232048.

AIRPORT TRANSPORT

To Tte. Vidal, shared taxis from downtown, consult with airlines. To Balmaceda, by minibus or regular bus from the Coihaique bus station.

BUS STATION AND/OR OFFICES

Bus station at Lautaro and Magallanes, but most companies have other offices in town.
Taxi Bus Don Carlos, Cruz 63.
La Cascada, Bolívar 125.
Transaustral, Baquedano 1171.
Buses Litoral, Independence 5.
Buses Artetur, Baquedano 1347.
Colectivos Basoli, Puyuhuapi 061.
Colectivo Puerto Ibáñez, Presidente Ibáñez 30.

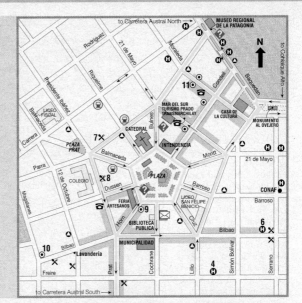

DOWNTOWN COIHAIQUE

RENT A CAR
Río Baker Rent a Car,
Aeropuerto Balmaceda
☎ *272163.*

FERRY TICKETS
Navimag, Presidente Ibáñez
347, ☎ *223306.*
Naviera El Colono, General
Parra 86, ☎ *231971.*

SHOPPING
Artisan's fair on the Plaza.
Fishing, camping supplies at
Ferretería Brautigam, on
Calle Horn one block from
the plaza.

USEFUL ADDRESSES
Conaf, Av. Ogaña 1060,
south of downtown.

Around Coihaique
See map 🔼

Reserva Nacional Coihaique

An hour and a half walk north of the city, this 2,150há reserve protects a group of small lakes set amid highland forest, with splendid views of the Simpson valley, Coihaique and the surrounding peaks. There are picnic areas and campsites at Laguna Verde and Casa Bruja, but no supplies of any sort. To reach the reserve, head north out of town on the Carretera Austral and take the steep, signposted dirt turnoff just beyond the bridge over the Río Coihaique. Access on foot or by taxi from Coihaique.

Reserva Nacional Río Simpson

West of Coihaique, this 41,160há reserve protects forest ecosytems on both sides of the Río Simpson valley. The road to Puerto Aisén runs right down the center of the reserve along the abrupt north bank of the river, providing access to two roadside waterfalls, the Salto Velo de la Novia (28km from Coihaique on the south side of the river), and the Cascada la Virgen (at km 36 on the north

side). Just beyond the last waterfall, also on the north side of the road, is Conaf's *Centro de Visitantes*, with exhibits on natural history. There are campsites at **RÍO CORRENTOSO**, 24km from Coihaique, and Camping San Sebastián, at km 32. Access via frequent buses Coihaique – Puerto Aisén.

🔁 ⏱3-4d ☐

From the bridge over the Río Correntoso, this trail leads north up the fire-scarred Correntoso valley, veering west up the Arroyo Catedral to a rustic refugio at the west end of Laguna Catedral. From here you can explore the glaciated peaks and forested valleys surrounding the craggy summit of Cerro Catedral.

Río Simpson (III)

Beginning above the town and continuing down through a canyon into the reserve, this is Coihaique's local run. The Simpson's abundant eddies and relatively low volume make it a good choice for beginning and intermediate boaters. Keep an eye out for fishermen, however.
Operators: 184

East of Coihaique

Travelers with bikes or private transportation can explore the high steppe and interconnected lakes to the east of Coihaique. A good loop can be made by heading south on the road to Balmaceda and taking the signposted left at km 15 towards the El Fraile ski area and **Lago Frío**, **Lago Pollux**, and **Lago Castor**, all of which have good trout fishing. Just past Lago Castor is a crossroads; to the east is Paso Triana to Argentina, while to the left a short road connects with the Coihaique – Coihaique Alto road. From here you can return to Coihaique or head east 4km to **Monumento Natural Dos Lagunas**, a 181há wetlands reserve with a Conaf visitor center, picnic area, and campsite. There is no public transport to this area.

AROUND COIHAIQUE

Centro de Esquí El Fraile

Run by Instituto Nacional de Deportes, Chile's national sports-promotion bureau, El Fraile is 29km southeast of Coihaique. Lifts and infrastructure are quite simple, with just one T-bar and one Poma lift, but the mountain boasts an impressive vertical of some 800m. The lower groomed section is appropriate for beginners, while the upper runs are mostly for advanced skiers, with some possibilities for tree skiing. Expert skiers can climb the ridge above the T-bar to access steeper terrain, including a couple of unskied bowls that feed back to the lifts at the base. Snow conditions here are typically very heavy, and occasionally the area is beset by rainfall, even in the dead of winter.

Lakes to the South

Set into the Andes just south of Coihaique is a subalpine ecosystem with five major lakes, countless rivers and waterfalls, and extensive southern beech forests. Roads are gravel and nearly all dead-end in the mountains; though there is no public transport, fishing trips around Coihaique commonly visit this area. Closest to Coihaique, **Lago Atravesado** is accessed via the bridge below the *Piedra de Indio*, though it remains to be seen what effects a recently approved hydropower plant will have on the area. Just south is **Lago Elizalde**, which has a campground and fishing lodge at its eastern end. Highly experienced backcountry hikers could conceivably hike from the south shore of **Lago Paloma** up the Río Turbio valley to join up with the Cerro Castillo Traverse .

Located in the heart of the Chilean Patagonia, Coyhaique

- Exclusive bedrooms with a view to the Andes Mountains
- Meals prepared by our chef on a wood-burning stove
- Fly-fishing (rainbow-brown trout)
- Walks
- Horseback riding
- Photography
- Agro-tourism
- Tourist excursions

☎ (56-67) 23 3273 - 09 871 6066
Fax (56-67) 23 3240
vmoya@entelchile.net

Fishing in the Coihaique Area

Coihaique is set in the midst of a tremendous variety of world-class rivers and lakes, served by the country's greatest concentration of fishing lodges and guide services. In general, the rivers here are more appropriate for dry fly fishing than those further north. The Río Simpson is the local standard, with excellent wading and drifting waters and trout in the 2-3 kilo range, though it's beginning to show signs of overfishing. North of town, the Río Nirehuao is a gin-clear dry-fly stream with abundant brown trout; grasshoppers are the favorite fly here, and the *Lodge Saltamontes* provides local accommodation and guides. Southwest of town are five lakes set in the eastern foothills of the Andes, with too many fishable tributary streams to mention. The *Hostería Lago Elizalde* and the *Río Paloma Lodge* are the top lodges in this area. Further east, in the drier transitional zone just below the pampa, American-run *Campo Chileno* provides access to Lago Frío, Lago Pollux, and Lago Castor, as well as an abundance of rivers and spring creeks. Finally, a number of outfitters organize boat expeditions to the fjords surrounding Puerto Aisén, with fishing conditions similar to those described in the Northern Patagonian Fjords 🔼.

Operators: 11 - 98 - 122 - 146 - 188

Coihaique to Puerto Ibáñez See map 🔼

See map 🔼

ACCOMMODATION
Hospedajes in Villa O'Higgins and Puerto Ibáñez.

TRANSPORT
To Villa O'Higgins from Coihaique via Taxi Bus Don Carlos or Radio Baker Taxi; to Puerto Ibáñez with Colectivo Puerto Ibáñez. Two ferries offer the 2 hr 15 min crossing of Lago General Carrera from Puerto Ibáñez to Chile Chico and vice versa. The Pilchero leaves Puerto Ibáñez Mon,-Fri at 0900, returning from Chile Chico at 1730. Saturdays it departs Puerto Ibáñez at 1000, returning on Sun at 1500. The Ferry Chalenco provides an identical service, but with different hours; consult for departure times.

South of Coihaique the Carretera Austral passes through a wide open landscape of rolling hills cleared of their forests during the devastating firest of the 1940's and 1950's. The road is paved for the first 41km at which point the road splits; the paved highway continues SE towards **BALMACEDA** (66km from Coihaique), while the Carretera veers to the west, climbing out of the Río Simpson valley into the Andes. On the right (north) side of the road at km 64 is Laguna Chiguay and the ranger station for **RESERVA NACIONAL CERRO CASTILLO**, a 179,550há reserve

that contains one of the finest short mountain hikes in Chile. Leave details with the ranger if attempting the hike, which begins 8km west at the road maintenance station at Las Horquetas Grandes, where the road diverges from the Río Blanco valley.

Cerro Castillo Traverse

 ⏱3-4d ⬜

From the road maintenance station at Las Horquetas Grandes, ford the stream and head NW up the Río Blanco valley, following the road past farmhouses and over a small shoulder into the valley of the Estero La Lima. The trail continues up this valley, entering an area of meandering cattle trails and logging roads, and passing a shallow lake on the left; if you continue west through the forest, you'll eventually come upon the wide glacial valley of the Río Turbio, which flows north to Lago Paloma (experienced trekkers could begin the trek there). From here, the route continues up-valley, climbing steeply up and left at the head of the valley to an obvious pass. On the other side of the pass, the route is harder to follow;

continue through the forest on the east side of the Estero el Bosque, fording the stream above the junction with a western branch. Below here, the river disappears into a narrow, impassable gorge (do not descend!), while the route continues west, crossing a couple of further tributaries en route to Laguna Cerro Castillo, at the base of the unmistakable glaciated peak. To finish, the route climbs over or around a flat peak, Morro Rojo, descending south on cattle trails to Villa Cerro Castillo. It is also possible to continue west and then north from Laguna Cerro Castillo to the Campamento Nuevo Zelandez, returning to Villa Cerro Castillo along the Río Ibáñez.
Operator: 103

Beyond Laguna Chiguay the road begins the steep climb to **PORTEZUELO IBÁÑEZ**, which was covered beneath a thick layer of volcanic ash following the 1991 eruption of Volcán Hudson. At 85km from Coihaique, the route begins the steep descent into the Río Ibáñez valley, with expansive views of Cerro Castillo and spectacular open country to the south.

At km 90 is a crossroads. The Carretera Austral proper leads right 8km to **VILLA CERRO CASTILLO**, where you'll find a very modest selection of lodging, markets and restaurants. Continuing west on the Carretera Austral takes you over the Río Ibáñez and around the west side of Lago General Carrera, described below.

Continuing straight south at the crossroads leads 31km through a wild lunar landscape of burnt-over canyons to the town of **RÍO IBÁÑEZ**, set on a semi-protected inlet on the north shore of Lago General Carrera. This windy, end-of-the-road village is the northern terminus for the 2.5hr ferry across the lake to **CHILE CHICO**. Those with bikes or a private vehicle can visit the thunderous Salto del Río Ibáñez waterfall, 6km from Puerto Ibáñez – keep an eye out for the

pumice stones floating in a pool below the falls. 29km south of town is **LEVICÁN**, a tiny hamlet on a peninsula that juts into the lake.

The West Shore of Lago General Carrera   See map 🔼

PRACTICAL INFORMATION
For boats from Puerto Tranquilo to the marble caves, contact Juan Carlos Garrido at Residencial Carretera Austral. For reservations in Coihaique, ☎ (67)231008.

ACCOMMODATION
Hospedajes, cabins in Bahía Murta, Río Tranquilo, Puerto Guadal and Puerto Bertrand. Upscale accommodation (lodges) in Puerto Guadal and Puerto Bertrand.

TRANSPORT
From Coihaique, by bus with Taxi Bus Don Carlos or Radio Baker Taxi.

West of Villa O'Higgins, the Carretera Austral enters ever more remote territory, with infrequent public transport and spectacular views of the Lago General Carrera and the Northern Patagonian Ice Fields. Self-reliant travelers, ideally with their own transport, will find phenomenal camping, fishing, and hiking all along this stretch. In recent years a number of upscale lodges have sprouted up along the lakeshore, opening this country up to travelers who are looking for a little more comfort.

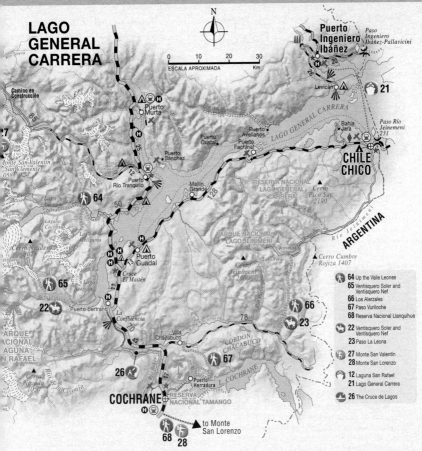

LAGO
GENERAL
CARRERA

N

0   10   20   30
ESCALA APROXIMADA   Km

Puerto
Ingeniero
Ibáñez

Paso
Ingeniero
Ibáñez-Pallavicini

Camino en
Construcción

Levicán

21

Puerto
Murta

Paso Río
Jeinemeni
231

Puerto
Cristal

Puerto
Avellanos

LAGO GENERAL CARRERA

Bahía
Jara

Puerto
Sánchez

Puerto
Fachinal

CHILE
CHICO

Monte San Valentín
4058

Paso
Frontana

Puerto
Río Tranquilo

64

Mallín
Grande

RESERVA NACIONAL
LAGO GENERAL
CARRERA

Cerro
Pico Sur
2190

ARGENTINA

128

Lago
Leopoldo

Laguna
Cochrane

Cerro Nevado
Sol

65

Lago
Bertrand

50

Puerto
Guadal

Cruce
El Maitén

PARQUE NACIONAL
LAGO JEINIMENI

Río Jeinimen

Cerro Cumbre
Rojiza 1407

22

Puerto Bertrand

La
Confluencia

42

Villa
Chacabuco

78

Cerro
Jeinimeni
2600

Cerro Verde

66

23

PARQUE
NACIONAL
LAGUNA
SAN RAFAEL

Cerro
Nevado
1050

Río Baker

CORDON
CHACABUCO

67

Río Cochrane

26

Puerto
Herradura

COCHRANE

RESERVA
NACIONAL TAMANGO

68   28

to Monte
San Lorenzo

64 Up the Valle Leones
65 Ventisquero Soler and
   Ventisquero Nef
66 Los Alerzales
67 Paso Vuriloche
68 Reserva Nacional Llanquihue

22 Ventisquero Soler and
   Ventisquero Nef
23 Paso La Leona

27 Monte San Valentín
28 Monte San Lorenzo

12 Laguna San Rafael
21 Lago General Carrera

26 The Cruce de Lagos

Just past the bridge over the Río Ibáñez, is the turnoff on the left to **Monumento Nacional Manos de Cerro Castillo** (2km). Protected beneath a rock outcrop, this collection of rock paintings pertains to the one of the oldest traditions of such art in the world, dating to some 10,000 ybp.

Beyond the turnoff, the road climbs into deforested hills with excellent views of the Río Ibáñez valley to the north. Now following the course of the Río Cajón, the route enters a dense forest, crosses a 600m pass, and descends into the Río Murta valley. Soon a branch of Lago General Carrera becomes visible; at the north end of this branch is the village of **Puerto Murta** (about 100km from Villa Cerro Castillo), with modest lodging, restaurants and markets.

The Carretera Austral does not pass through the village, but instead continues south along the lakeshore, arriving at km 130 in **Puerto Tranquilo**, also with modest services. Here a rough road leads west, up the Río Tranquilo valley to Lago Bayo, set on the northern fringe of the Northern Patagonian Ice Field. A horse trail (destined to become a road) continues past the lake and down the Río Exploradores to **Puerto Grosse**, a village on the Estero Elefantes north of Laguna San Rafael. Motorboats on the waterfront in Puerto Tranquilo will also take visitors on the half-hour trip to some unusual marble caves (see P). At 160km from Villa Cerro Castillo is the bridge over the Río Leones, where a poor road leads west, upriver towards Lago Leones and the surrounding lakes and glaciers.

Up the Valle Leones

 ↻ ⏱3d ▢

This demanding trek climbs the north bank of Río Leones valley to two spectacular lakes on the edge of the Northern Patagonian Ice Fields. The glaciers spilling off the ice cap calf directly into the lakes, filling them with floating icebergs or *témpanos*. The trip can be extended with a crossing of Lago Leones and an ascent of Mirador Leones. Just north, the Valle Exploradores is also worth exploring, despite continuing road construction.

Operators: 31

At km 175 is the bridge over the narrows between Lago General Carrera and Lago Bertrand, where there are a number of upmarket hosterías, including the recommended *Cabañas Mallín Colorado*, *La Pasarela 2*, and the *Bahía Escondida Lodge*, the latter located on Lago Bertrand and accessible only by boat.

Just beyond the bridge is **CRUCE EL MAITÉN**, the junction of the Carretera Austral and the road to Chile Chico, and 13km fur-

ther east is **PUERTO GUADAL**, a sleepy village with modest services and free camping along the waterfront to the east; the nearby *Hacienda Tres Lagos* and *Terra Luna* lodge run a variety of excursions in the surrounding area.

On the east shore of Lago Bertrand, 11km south of the Cruce El Maitén, is the town of **PUERTO BERTRAND**. This is a great place to stay while exploring the surrounding area, as there's a municipal campground here and a good variety of lodging; upscale options include the classy *Lodge Río Baker*.

The road to the south parallels the Río Baker, passing the *Patagonia Baker Lodge* at 3km. 14km south of town is a good view of the confluence of the Río Baker and the Río Nef, and beyond that, visible in the distance but accessible via a short trail, is the Salto del Río Baker waterfall. At 30km from Puerto Bertrand is the bridge over the Río Chacabuco, and shortly beyond is a road on the left that leads east up the Chacabuco valley and on to **PASO ROBALLO** and Argentina.

Río Baker (III-V+)

 ⏱1-5d

Flowing out of Lago General Carrera, the Baker is Chile's highest-volume river, with some 30,000-50,000 cfs of surging, aerated, tourquise-green whitewater. The standard run on the Baker begins at the lake and features 12km of big-water Class III, with a massive play hole about 5km down. Below here are three separate canyons appropriate only for advanced paddlers. The first is a 6km stretch of Class V and VI, beginning just below the confluence with the Río Nef. The second is a short Class III (but with Class V consequences) beginning upriver of the Pasarela Manzano on the road to the Maitén valley. The third canyon begins 1.5km below the second canyon, and runs 'crazed Class VI' (in the words of a local outfitter) for 10km to the confluence with the Río Chacabuco. Note that only a handful of world-class hairboaters have ever run these extremely powerful and potentially deadly canyons; commercial trips invariably portage them. It is also possible to continue down from the Balsa Cochrane for a spectacular 5-day wilderness float trip ending at Caleta Tortel, with a single portage around the Salton Baker waterfall.

Operators: 165

Hiking to the Ventisquero Soler and Ventisquero Neff

 ⇄ ⏱3d ◼

Beginning on the west shore of Lago Plomo (boat access only), this route climbs the Soler Valley and then veers north up the Río Cacho valley to the base of the Soler Glacier. You can also access the Ventisquero Neff from the same base camp, climbing the Soler Valley to its western extreme and then crossing a 300m pass to the south. Horse support can be a real blessing in this rugged country.

Operators: 31 - 165

Fishing Around Lago General Carrera and the Río Baker

Puerto Bertrand is the center of fishing activity in this wild, remote region near the end of the Carretera Austral. From here, you can arrange drift-boat trips on the Río Baker, trolling for huge lake trout on Lago General Carrera and Lago Cochrane, and sight-casting on the crystal-clear Río Cochrane. This area also receives occasional runs of coho and king salmon, and excursions can be arranged to the remote Villa O'Higgins region to the south (local guides are also available in Villa O'Higgins itself).

Operators: 11 - 31 - 138 - 165 - 166 - 208

Monte San Valentín (4,058m) and the Northern Patagonian Ice Fields

 ◼

The highest peak in Patagonia Monte San Valentín pierces the northern fringe of the Northern Patagonian Ice Fields, and receives some of the most consistently atrocious weather on the planet. Not until 1952 did San Valentín see its first ascent (by members of the Club Andino de Bariloche), and to the present day no more than a handful of climbers have successfully climbed the peak, despite its relatively low technical difficulty. Those hoping to summit should budget at least three weeks for the climb (most of which will doubtlessly be spent tent-bound or ferrying loads), but if you don't fix your sights on the summit, you can also get a feel for ice fields in a shorter trip. The standard access is via Parque Nacional Laguna San Rafael, but it is also possible (though difficult) to approach the peak via the Valle Exploradores. The more southerly portions of the ice fields may be accessed via the Valle Neff or the Valle Soler (above).

Operators: 13 - 31 - 165

THE BRIDGE OVER THE OUTLET OF LAGO GENERAL CARRERA

Chile Chico and RN Lago Jeinimeni

On the south shore of Lago General Carrera, just 9km from the Argentine border, CHILE CHICO lies to the east of the Andes in a relatively sunny climate on the edge of the pampa. The town lives from the mines along the lakeshore to the west, and from the production of its apple, pear, and cherry orchards. However, while the idea of sunny weather and fresh fruit may seem attractive, dusty, windblown Chile Chico is not much as towns go.

South of Chile Chico is an often-overlooked gem, the 161,100há PARQUE NACIONAL LAGO JEINIMENI. The road to the park parallels the Río Jeinimeni, climbing a series of broad, open plateaus and passing by a signposted turnoff to the rock paintings at CUEVA DE LAS MANOS. In summer, you may be able to spot flamingos in the Laguna de los Flamencos, 42km from Chile Chico, and at km 44 the road enters a forest of lenga and ñire. At 60km is the Conaf ranger station, and just beyond is Lago Jeinimeni, with a camping area and good fishing near the bridge over the outlet; the best camping is further on at the east end of Lago Verde. There are a number of good day hikes here for self-reliant hikers, including an easy walk up the Estero Gloria, climbs in the Cordón Gloria to the north of Lago Verde, and the walk up Valle Hermoso towards Lagos Ventisquero and Escondido. There is no public transport to the park.

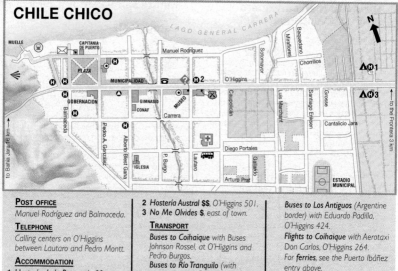

CHILE CHICO

POST OFFICE
Manuel Rodríguez and Balmaceda.

TELEPHONE
Calling centers on O'Higgins between Lautaro and Pedro Montt.

ACCOMMODATION
1 Hostería de la Patagonia $$, east of town, ☎ 411337.

2 Hostería Austral $$, O'Higgins 501.
3 No Me Olvides $, east of town.

TRANSPORT
Buses to Coihaique with Buses Johnson Rossel, at O'Higgins and Pedro Burgos.
Buses to Río Tranquilo (with connections to Coihaique) via Buses Don Orlando, at the Panadería La Espiga on O'Higgins.

Buses to Los Antiguos (Argentine border) with Eduardo Padilla, O'Higgins 424.
Flights to Coihaique with Aerotaxi Don Carlos, O'Higgins 264.
For ferries, see the Puerto Ibáñez entry above.

USEFUL ADDRESSES
Conaf is at Blest Gana 121.

Paso La Leona

Beginning at the south end of Lago Jeinimeni, this route leads south up the Estero San Antonio to Paso La Leona, and from there down the Estero La Leona to Estancia Entrada Baker in the Valle Chacabuco. Commonly offered as a 3-5 day horsepacking trip, this is a difficult route for independent trekkers because of lack of transport to (and from) the trailheads. An alternative route leads south from Valle Hermoso (at the west end of Lago Verde), over Portezuelo Avilés, and down the Río Avilés to the Valle Chacabuco.
Operators: 10 - 31 🐎 - 103 - 115

The road from Chile Chico west to Puerto Guadal and the Carretera Austral is a highly recommended, winding track through the high, treeless hills above the lake, with unbelievable views of the Northern Patagonian Ice Fields. Keep your eyes open for the bridge over the *Garganta del Diablo*, a narrow, vertical-walled slot canyon. There are no services at all along this road.

Cochrane   Pop. 2996 (☎ city code 67)

The last settlement of any size on the Carretera Austral, Cochrane (50km south of Puerto Bertrand) occupies a broad valley near the confluence of the Río Cochrane and the Río Baker. First visited in 1899 by the German geographer Hans Steffen, the valley was occupied beginning in 1908, when the Sociedad Exploradora Baker – administered by Lucas Bridges – began grazing sheep on 80,000há of federally owned land. In 1930, the Chilean government founded Cochrane in an attempt to concentrate services in an 'urban' setting, but as late as 1954 the town consisted of

little more than a school and a market. As settlement has continued in the region, however, Cochrane has become an essential part of the supply chain supporting *colonos* in Caleta Tortel, Villa O'Higgins, and beyond.

Travel services are surprisingly good in Cochrane, and the local options for fishing, trekking, horseback riding and mountaineering are nothing short of phenomenal. There is also a modest museum a block north of the plaza (open Mon-Fri 0830-1300, 1430-1800). Motorists heading south should note that this is the last place to fill up on gas.

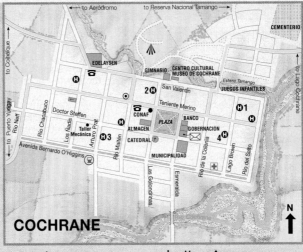

COCHRANE

POST AND TELECOMMUNICATIONS

POST OFFICE
SE corner of the plaza.

TELEPHONE
On Tte. Merina just west of the Plaza.

ACCOMMODATION

1 **Hotel Ultimo Paraíso** $$, Lago Brown 455, ☎ 522361.

2 **Hotel Wellmann**, Las Golondrinas 36, ☎ 522171.

3 **Residencial Sur Austral** $$, Prat 334, ☎ 522150.

4 **Hospedaje Paola** $, Lago Brown 150, ☎ 522215.

TRANSPORT

Buses: Services north with Taxi Bus Don Carlos (Prat 281), Buses Pudú (Tte. Merino and Río Maitén), and Radio Baker Taxi (Dr. Steffens 400).

Air: To Coihaique and Villa O'Higgins with Aerotaxi Don Carlos, Prat 281.

USEFUL ADDRESSES

Cochrane's hospital is at the corner of O'Higgins and Lago Brown.
Conaf is at the NW corner of the plaza.

Reserva Nacional Tamango

Located within walking of distance of Cochrane, this semi-arid forest reserve presents a variety of options for short hikes. 10km NE of town, at the end of a dirt road, is a Conaf ranger station and campsite on Laguna Tamango. From here you can make a day trip to 1,722m Cerro Tamango, or continue east to Laguna Elefantita, where there is also fine camping. For a short return you can follow the Arroyo Elefantita south to Lago Cochrane, where there is another Conaf campsite, then walk back out to town (4-5hrs from the campsite). Otherwise, from Laguna Elefantita you can continue north past Laguna Edita to the road through the Valle Chacabuco, from which point you can walk west to the Carretera Austral or head east to join up with the Paso La Leona trek, above.

Operators: 184

Monte San Lorenzo (3,660m)

First climbed in 1943 by a team led by Italian missionary and photographer Alberto D'Agostini, Monte San Lorenzo is an immense glaciated peak (the 2nd highest in Patagonia) located on the Argentine border SE of Cochrane. The ascent of the peak itself is a 7-10 day expedition requiring solid glacier travel and ice climbing skills, while the remote valleys at the base of the peak make for spectacular 3-7 day trekking routes appropriate for most anyone. The standard approach is up the Río Tranquilo valley, accessed via a dirt road branching east off the Carretera Austral near Laguna Esmeralda, about 4km south of Cochrane.

Operators: 31

CALETA TORTEL

South to Villa O'Higgins

PRACTICAL INFORMATION
Satellite telephone in Villa O'Higgins, uses prepaid cards.

ACCOMMODATION
Hospedajes in Tortel and Villa O'Higgins.

TRANSPORT
Bus transport from Cochrane with Transporte Los Ñadis, one departure weekly, $8000. By air from Cochrane to Villa O,Higgins and Tortel with Aerotaxi Don Carlos. The Barcaza General Carrera (often delayed) provides service across the Fiordo Mitchell from Puerto Yungay to Río Bravo.

South of Cochrane, the Carretera Austral winds through an ever wilder landscape of forests, lakes, and immense glacially-fed rivers. This is the quintessential one-way road into the wilderness.

103km south of Cochrane, on the right, is **RÍO VAGABUNDO**, the departure point for motor launches down the Río Baker to **CALETA TORTEL**. Originally founded to facilitate the exportation of the Guaitecas Cypress, Tortel – whose streets consist entirely of wooden walkways – occupies a spectacular position at the mouth of the Río Baker, in a protected harbor nestled in between the Northern and Southern Patagonian Ice Fields. Meals and lodging are offered in local homes, and you can camp for free on a wooden platform along the shore.

125km south of Cochrane is the rather desolate village of **PUERTO YUNGAY**, where you can catch the one-hour ferry across the Fiordo Mitchell to Río Bravo. From here, the very last leg of the Carretera Austral leads south another 102km to **VILLA O'HIGGINS**. Set on the banks of the Río Mayer at the northernmost extreme of Lago O'Higgins, the town dates only from 1966, when the Chilean armed forces set up camp here in an effort to establish Chilean sovereignty over the Laguna del Desierto region, some 60km

south. Until the completion of the Carretera Austral in 1999, the village suffered from unimaginable isolation, with air service frequently suspended by inclement weather; the trip to Cochrane by horse took up to seven days.

Today, Villa O'Higgins makes a good showing for itself: there are two hospedajes, a couple of restaurants, and a satellite telephone in town, and the nearby **RESERVA NACIONAL SHOEN** boasts a campground and a number of hiking trails.

Down the Río Baker

 1-2h downriver, 2-5h upriver, depending on the craft

Service from the boat launch at Río Vagabundo (103km south of Cochrane) to Caleta Tortel is provided by 25-person launches on Tue and Sun (3hrs downriver, 5hrs upriver), and by faster, flat-bottomed speed boats (*chatas*) on Thursdays (1hr 15min each way). Consult in Cochrane for prices and buses to the boat ramp. Once you're in Tortel, you can hire launches to visit the Ventisquero Jorge Montt (9hrs rt in regular launch, 3hrs in chata), Ventisquero Steffens (5hrs or 2hrs rt), or Isla de los Muertos (3hrs or 1hr rt). Caleta Tortel may also be reached by a 5-day float trip from Puerto Bertrand, 🔼 .
Operators: 31 - 165

Exploring Lago O'Higgins

varies

From the boat launch at Bahía Bahamonde, 7km south of Villa O'Higgins, motor launches can provide transport to wildly remote destinations such as the Ventisquero Chico, Ventisquero O'Higgins, Brazo Poniente, and Bahía Bajo Esperanza. Unfortunately, local fuel prices and the lack of demand make these 7-10hr trips prohibitively expensive.

THE VILLAGE OF PUERTO EDEN

SOUTHERN PATAGONIA

MAGALLANES AND TIERRA DEL FUEGO

This part of Chilean territory is essentially an island, cut off from the rest of the country by the imposing mass of the Southern Patagonian Ice Fields, which encapsulates the range to the north of Torres del Paine. Most travelers arrive by plane in Punta Arenas or by boat in Puerto Natales, although it is also possible to get here by bus or car by driving through Argentina. See the road atlas at the back of this guide.

Contrary to most travelers' images of Patagonia, most of the territory here is not mountainous. Instead, the high

peaks of the Andes run right along the coast, where they block the majority of the rain – and snow-bearing winds that come roaring off the Pacific. To the south the range curves, like a protecting arm, around the south shore of Tierra del Fuego, creating a labyrinth of glaciated fjords and islands, and producing a vast windswept pampa in the rainshadow to the east. As this pampa is far and away the most hospitable part of Magallanes, it is here that most Chilean settlements are found.

The Coastal Route South to Magallanes

Aboard the Puerto Edén (Navimag)

⏱4d

Two Navimag ferries, the *Puerto Edén* and the newly inaugurated *Magallanes*, offer year-round transport for 185 passengers (plus vehicles and cargo) between Puerto Montt and Puerto Natales. The 4-day, all-inclusive trip is offered 5 times a month from Nov to April and 4 times a month from Dec-Mar. Lodging varies from basic bunks to private cabins, with corresponding variations in price, beginning at a low of US$130 during high season. Travelers who are prone to seasickness should avoid eating before the ship enters the Golfo de Penas, a tumultuously exposed 5hr crossing just south of Puerto Chacabuco. An hour south of the narrow Angostura Inglesa, the ship calls upon the tiny fishing village of Puerto Edén, founded in the 1930's as a safety net for prop planes plying the route between Puerto Montt and Punta Arenas. As the only settlement in hundreds of kilometers of coastline, Puerto Edén

soon attracted a population of Kaweskar Indians, and today the town is home to the last surviving members of this nomadic hunter gatherer culture.

Continuing on its way south from Puerto Edén, the ferry squeezes through the 40m wide Paso Kirke, which gaurds the entrance to Golfo Almirante Montt and the port of Puerto Natales.

Glaciar Pío XI

⏱5-8d

This hike accesses one of the wildest and least-explored areas in all Patagonia. Beginning in Puerto Edén, the route begins with a boat crossing of the Canal Messier to the west coast of the Exmouth Península. From here, it's two days' walk through rainforest to the east coast of the península, where you need another boat to cross to the far shore of Bahía Elizabeth. Finally, it's an easy day's walk to base of the immense glacier, which spills off the Southern Patagonian Ice Fields directly into the ocean. Make arrangements ahead of time in order to coordinate with the ferry schedule.
Operators: 227

Puerto Natales   *Pop. 15,116 (☎ city code 61)*

Located on the east shore of Seno Ultima Esperanza, Puerto Natales is the southern terminus of the ferry from Puerto Montt and an operations base for travelers heading to Torres del Paine and other nearby destinations. The wealth of restaurants, lodging, and adventure travel outfitters in this middle-of-nowhere town reflect the enormous growth in tourism that has occurred here over the past decade.

This area was first explored in the 16th century by Spanish navigators Sarmiento de Gamboa and Juan Ladrilleros, who entered Seno Ultima Esperanza in search of the

western entrance to the Strait of Magellan. It wasn't until near 1900, however, that intensive explorations in the area were begun, largely in response to ongoing border disputes with Argentina. Expeditions such as that of German ship captain Hermann Eberhard and Norwegian polar explorer Otto Nordenskjöld mapped the area around the turn of the century and determined its potential for sheep ranching, and by 1905 the Chilean state had distributed massive swaths of pampa along the border. (One of the major *estancias* formed at this time included the entirety of Parque Nacional

Torres del Paine.) Puerto Natales itself was founded in 1911, and four years later a massive processing plant, *Frigorífico Bories*, began to export the meat and wool produced on the local *estancias*. With the decline of wool in the 20th-century, many Puerto Natales residents have switched gears to tourism, or else have been forced to cross the border to work the coal mines in El Turbio.

Despite the excellent views across the Seno Ultima Esperanza towards the Cordillera Riesco, there is very little activity on Puerto Natales' waterfront. Instead, the pole of activity in town is concentrated in a compact, roughly triangular area in the NW corner of town.

In-town Attractions

Museo Municipal At Bulnes 285, south of downtown, this small museum contains exhibits on local archaeology and ethnology, and historic photos of early settlement and life on the *estancias*.
Hours: Mon-Fri 0830-1230, 1430-1800, Sat-Sun 1500-1800.

PUERTO NATALES

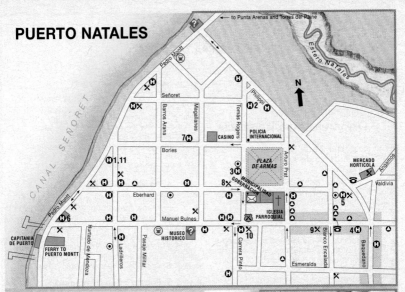

See detail

TOURIST OFFICES
Sernatur, Phillippi and Pedro Montt.

BANKS AND MONEY CHANGERS
ATMs at Bulnes 544 and nearby at the corner of Blanco Encalada and Bulnes. Many casas de cambia downtown.

HOSPITAL
O'Higgins and Carrera Pinto, ☎ *411583.*

POST OFFICE
South side of the Plaza de Armas.

INTERNET CONNECTION
Rincón de Tata, Prat 236.

ACCOMMODATION
1 *Concepto Indigo $, Ladrilleros 105,* ☎ *410678.*
2 *Hospedaje Cecilia $, Tomás Rogers 54,* ☎ *411797.*
3 *Patagonia Adventure $, Tomás Rogers 179,* ☎ *411028.*
4 *Hostal Lady Florence Dixie $$, M. Bulnes 659,* ☎ *411158.*
5 *Hostal Melissa $$, Blanco Encalada 258,* ☎ *411944.*
6 *Hotel Costaustralis $$$, Av. Pedro Montt 262,* ☎ *412000.*
7 *Hotel Martín Gusinde $$$, Bories 278,* ☎ *412770,* ☎ *225986.*

RESTAURANTS
8 *La Ultima Esperanza, Eberhard 354. Seafood, popular*
9 *La Tranquera, Manuel Bulnes 579. Draft beer, Chilean food.*
10 *El Cristal, Manuel Bulnes 439. For big portions on a budget*
11 *Concepto Indigo, Ladrilleros 105. Coffee, café menu.*

AIRPORTS
Puerto Natales' airport is used for charter flights only. Punta Arenas' airport is 230km to the south.

AIRLINE OFFICES
LanChile-Ladeco, Tomás Rogers 78, ☎ *411236.*
Aerocontinente, ☎ *6002092358.*

AIRPORT TRANSPORT
By taxi only to the Puerto Natales airport. Regular buses to Punta Arenas will drop passengers at the Punta Arenas airport.

BUS STATION AND/OR OFFICES
No central bus terminal.
Buses Fernández, Eberhard 555.
Bus Sur, Baquedano 534.
Austral Bus, Baquedano 384.
Servitur, Prat 353.
Buses JB, Bulnes 370.

RENT A CAR
Emsa, Bulnes 632 ☎ *410775.*

FERRIES
Navimag is at the corner of Bulnes and Pedro Montt, near the ferry terminal.

USEFUL ADDRESSES
Conaf is at Carrera Pinto 566.
Camping gear is available for rent at Casa Cecilia, Tomás Rogers 54, Path@gone, Eberhard 595, and Onas Patagonia, Blanco Encalada 599.

GLACIER CRUISES AND FERRIES IN MAGALLANES AND TIERRA DEL FUEGO

See the outfitter directory for contact information for the vessels listed here.

BOATS WITH FIXED DEPARTURES AND ITINERARIES

1. Cutter 21 de Mayo and the Alberto de Agostini
⏱ 1d

Twin motor yachts with respective capacity for 70 and 50 passengers, offering tours of Seno Ultima Esperanza to the Balmaceda and Serrano glaciers. You can also arrange to be dropped off at the *Monte Balmaceda Resort*, or combine the trip with a zodiac ride up the Río Serrano to *Camping Río Serrano* Torres del Paine (this can also be done in the opposite direction). Boats leave Puerto Natales daily at 0800, and zodiacs generally head downstream from *Camping Río Serrano* at about the same time.

2. Catamarán Hielos Patagónicos
⏱ 1d

This luxury high-speed catamarán offers the Seno Ultima Esperanza itinerary described above, with connections via zodiac to *Hostería Cabañas del Paine*, on the south shore of the Río Serrano. The boat departs daily from Oct-Mar at 0800. This boat also offers occasional 10-hour tours through the Canal Valdés and Paso Kirke to Fiordo de las Montañas.

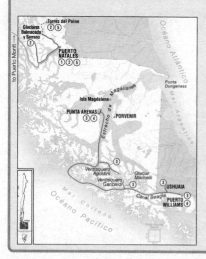

3. Terra Australis
⏱ 3-7d

Luxury cruise ship for 108 passengers, offering singular cruises through the glaciers and labyrinthine fjords of Tierra del Fuego, with naturalist-guided visits to the Beagle Canal, the Garibaldi and Agostini fjords, Ushuaia, Puerto Williams, Fuerte Bulnes and Isla Magdalena. Departures from Oct-Apr, every Sat from Punta Arenas, and every Wed from Ushuaia.

4. Barcaza Crux Australis
⏱ 38h

Passenger ferry providing 38-hour service from Punta Arenas to Puerto Williams, with four departures monthly from the Tres Puentes ferry terminal, usually departing Tue at 1900. The ship may also stop at Caleta Yendegaia on the south shore of Tierra del Fuego. Consult in Punta Arenas for precise departure details and prices.

5. Puerto Edén (Navimag)
See pg. 555.

CHARTERED SAILBOATS AND MOTOR YACHTS

• Callas, Ksar and Yagan III
⏱ 8d

Sailboats for four and six passengers, respectively, departing Ushuaia for destinations throughout the fjords and islands, including Tierra del Fuego.

• Foam
⏱ 3-12d

Six-passenger motorsailer offering a wide gamut of programs in Seno Almirantazgo, Fiordo Agostini, Skyring Sound and the Beagle Channel, often combined with sea kayaking.

• Victory Yacht Cruises
⏱ 1-4 weeks

From a base in Puerto Williams, Victory offers a variety of cruises in the Beagle Channel, Cape Horn, South Georgia Islands and the Antarctic Península. Victory's fleet includes special steel and aluminum-hulled boats for Antarctica expeditions.

• Yate Santa María
⏱ 1-4 weeks

15m steel-hulled Hydra sloop with capacity for six passengers, offering all-inclusive sailing trips out of Puerto Williams. Destinations include the fjords and archipelagos of Tierra del Fuego, Isla Navarino, Cape Horn and the Antarctic Península.

Around Puerto Natales

Cueva del Milodón

26km north of Puerto Natales, this Conaf-administrated site features an immense cave, some 30m high, 70m wide and 200 deep. Near the mouth of the cave is a life-size fiberglass reproduction of the prehistoric milodon or ground sloth (*Mylodón darwini*), remnants of which were found here in 1896 by German Hermann Eberhard, one of the first settlers in the area. The remarkably well-preserved state of the fur, bones, and excrement found by Eberhard prompted a hasty series of internationally-sponsored searches for a living milodon. A classic rendition of the milodon story appears in Bruce Chatwin's *In Patagonia*.

There is no public transport to the site, though buses to Torres del Paine can drop you off at the turnoff, 7km from the entrance.

Destinations in Argentina

Río Gallegos, on the Atlantic coast, is 296km from Puerto Natales via Río Turbio. Calafate is 289km north. Regular buses connect Puerto Natales with both destinations, and one-day tours to the Moreno glacier near Calafate may be arranged in town.

CUEVA DEL MILODON (MN)

Parque Nacional Bernardo O'Higgins

This 3,500,000há reserve is one of several enormous national parks along the west coast of Aisén and Magallanes, which together comprise more than 80% of all the protected landmass in Chile. Access is by boat only; 🚤. A luxury hotel, the *Monte Balmaceda Resort*, offers lodging and a variety of excursions from their base near the Balmaceda glacier.

Parque Nacional Torres del Paine

PRACTICAL INFORMATION
Entrance to the park costs $2500 for Chileans, US$10 for foreigners.

ACCOMMODATION
Abundant accommodation in the park, ranging from the 5-star Hotel Explora, to hosterías at Laguna Amarga, Las Torres, Lago Pehoé, Lago Grey, Laguna Verde, and near the park administration. Backcountry refugios (about US$15/pp) run by Andescape include Refugio, Pehoé, Refugio Grey and Refugio Dickson; Fantástico Sur runs the Refugio Chileno, the Refugio Los Cuernos, and the Refugio Las Torres. There are campgrounds (about US$3) near all the refugios and at numerous other backcountry sites.

TRANSPORT
Regular buses connect the park with Puerto Natales. These buses follow a route past Guardería Laguna Amarga to the Conaf administration and back. Van service is also available within the park, from Laguna Amarga to Hostería Las Torres. You can also access the park by zodiac up the Río Serrano.

Torres del Paine is Chile's most famous tourist attraction, and with good reason. No other park in South America can boast the

same combination of breathtaking landscapes, abundant wildlife, comfortable accommodation and services, and opportunities for remote backcountry hiking and serious mountaineering ascents. As a consequence, during the peak summer months Torres can get a bit crowded, but in the shoulder seasons it is pleasantly empty, and even during January and February you can still find plenty of solitude in the backcountry.

Formerly part of a huge *estancia*, the 242,242há park was donated to the Chilean state in 1959, and in 1978 it was designated a Unesco World Biosphere Reserve. Geographically, Torres occupies a unique location just south and east of the Southern Patagonian Ice Fields, in an area of transition between the evergreen and deciduous beech forests of the coast and the scrub and grasslands of the pampa to the east. The immense mass of the ice fields creates its own microclimate, shrouding the peaks to the

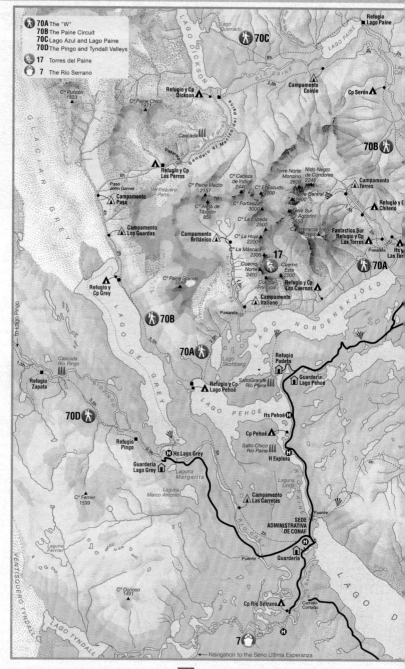

70A The "W"
70B The Paine Circuit
70C Lago Azul and Lago Paine
70D The Pingo and Tyndall Valleys

17 Torres del Paine

7 The Río Serrano

TORRES DEL PAINE

west in dense clouds and often obscuring views of the Paine Massif the centerpiece of the park – for weeks on end. Surprisingly, however, precipitation in the park is a mere 700mm/year. Winds pose the park's major climatic challenge, with gusts regular exceedingly 120km/hour during the summer months.

Wildlife in the park includes some 25 species of mammals, most notably guanacos, pumas, and two species of foxes. There are also over 115 species of resident and migratory bird species in the park, including a variety of raptors, flamingos, numerous ducks, coots, geese and other waterfowl, and the ñandú or avestruz (south american ostrich). Most wildlife is concentrated in the more benign, open grasslands and scrub of the park's eastern sectors.

Geologically, the dramatic soaring *torres* (towers) and *cuernos* (horns) of the Paine Massif are composed of a granite intrusion (the Patagonian Batholith) underlying a previously dated layer of metamorphic rock, primarily biotite and olivine. With several major glaciers cascading off the ice field into the park, Torres del Paine is an awe-inspiring demonstration of the metamorphic power of glacial sculpting.

Backcountry hiking is the most popular activity in the park, and there exist numerous options for treks up to ten days in length. Less hard-core travelers will find a wealth of comfortable accommodation in the park, and the major hiking routes may even be done without camping equipment, lodging each night in well-equipped backcountry refugios. These refugios also have restaurants and sell basic supplies to those who wind up short on food.

Backcountry campers should be aware of the persistent problem with rats at many campsites. Take care to hang your food away from your site and to minimize leaving food scraps around camp. Backcountry camping is only permitted at authorized sites, and solo backcountry hiking is not permitted.

Park entrances, lodging, trailheads and other landmarks are as follows:

Guardería Laguna Amarga

This is the main entrance to the park, and most backpackers heading out on the Paine circuit get off the bus and hike from here to Hostería Las Torres their first night; the road and footpath to LAGUNA AZUL and LAGO PAINE also begin here. Nearly tame foxes may often be spotted around the *guardería*. Nearby there is a free campsite and two places to stay, the upscale *Hostería*

Turis Goic (and the more basic *Refugio Laguna Amarga*. Buses through the park continue to *Guardería Lago Pehoé* and van service is available from here to Hostería Las Torres, for those who don't wish to walk.

Hostería Las Torres

Located 7km NW of Guardería Laguna Amarga, this is a good place to stay for those planning to hike up the **Valle Ascencio** to the Torres del Paine overlook. There are nice paid campsites in the pastures on either side of the road to the east of the hostería, and a small store in case you get caught short of supplies.

Past the hostería to the west is the trailhead for the Valle Ascencio. About 2hrs up is the *Refugio Chileno*, where you can camp; another 1.5hrs up is *Campamento Torres*, set in a lovely forest at the base of the final scramble to the *Mirador Las Torres*. You can also walk west from Hostería Las Torres along the base of the Paine Massif towards the **Valle Francés** and *Refugio Lago Pehoé*, a trekking route described below as 'the W.'

Portería Sarmiento

On the north side of Lago Sarmiento, this is an alternative entrance to the park. A short trail connects Portería Sarmiento with Guardería Laguna Amarga, just north.

Guardería Lago Pehoé

20km west of Laguna Amarga on the NE corner of Lago Pehoé, this ranger station marks the turnoff to *Refugio Pudeto*, departure point for motor launches heading across the lake to *Refugio Lago Pehoé* ⬙. Just past the refugio is the dramatic **Salto Grande**, a waterfall on the Río Paine, and from here another short trail leads north to an overlook over Lago Nordenskjöld and the Paine Massif. Just south along the main road is *Hostería Pehoé* (☎ *(61)411390)*, on

a tiny island accessed by a wooden footbridge, and beyond that (29km from Laguna Amarga) is the 5-star *Hotel Explora* (☎ *(61)411224)*. With its unusual design and unbeatable views across the lake, this is the most luxurious accommodation in the park. Right next to the hotel is another waterfall, the **Salto Chico**.

Conaf Administration Center

End of the line for bus service from Puerto Natales, the administration center is where you'll find Conaf's *Centro de Informaciones Ambientales*, with interesting exhibits on the geology, flora, and fauna of the park. Nearby is the *Posada Río Serrano* (☎ *(61)410684)*, with a restaurant and bar, and the simple Conaf-run *Refugio Lago Toro*. Roads from here lead to *Guardería Lago Grey* and south to *Camping Río Serrano* (which can also be reached by zodiac from Puerto Natales, ⬙). A trail off the east side of the road to Lago Grey leads north through open country along the Río Grey to *Refugio Lago Pehoé*.

Refugio Lago Pehoé

This popular refugio and campground on the NW side of Lago Pehoé provides access to two of the most popular hikes in the park. The first is the **Valle Francés**, a glacial valley just west of the dark grey spires of the Cuernos del Paine; 2.5hrs up at the base of the valley is *Campamento Italiano*, and another 1.5hrs up is *Campamento Británico*. The other trail leads north towards **Lago Grey**, reaching *Refugio and Campamento Grey* after about 3.5hrs on foot.

Refugio and Campamento Grey

Accessible only on foot or by boat from Guardería Lago Grey ⬙, this refugio and campsite provide the nearest access to **Glacier Grey**, which spills directly off the ice fields into the lake, calving off icebergs which are then blown east by the relentless westerly winds. North of here, a trail continues along the slopes above the glacier, passing Campamento Los Guardas and Campamento Paso en route to **Paso John Gardner**, the major pass on the Torres del Paine circuit.

PARQUE NACIONAL TORRES DEL PAINE

Guardería Lago Grey

Located at the south end of Lago Grey, this Conaf ranger station is the departure point for boats across the lake to the glacier and to *Refugio and Campamento Grey*, . There is also a trail leading up the remote **Río Pingo** valley to **Lago Pingo**, passing two rustic *refugios* en route. Lodging is available nearby at *Hostería Lago Grey*.

Guardería y Refugio Laguna Verde

In the southern sector of the park, between Lago Sarmiento and Lago del Toro, the ranger station and the *Hostería Mirador del Paine* nearby may be accessed by car from the access road from Puerto Natales or by trail from the bridge over the Río Paine (just north of the park administration).

LAGO PEHOE

Next, retrace your steps to the plain below the massif and traverse west along the north shore of Lago Nordenskjold, past the Refugio Los Cuernos en route to a junction with the trail up the Valle Francés; just up from the trail junction is the Campamento Italiano, while further up near the head of valley is Campamento Británico, both of which are exceedingly popular in high season. The view from the top of the valley, with the wildly sculpted *cuernos* towering above you, is incomparable. After returning down the Valle Francés to Refugio Pehoé, you can head NW to the Refugio Grey to check out the glacier, take a boat out across the lake to Refugio Pudeto, or walk out to the park administration.

TREKKING AND HORSEPACKING IN TORRES DEL PAINE

Operators: 10 - 13 - 16 - 21 -27 - 31 - 35 - 49 - 102 - 137 - 169 - 205 - 211 - 225 - 226

What truly sets Torres del Paine apart from other parks in Chile is its network of hiking trails, and you could easily spend two weeks or more here without ever retracing your steps. Signage and trail maintenance is quite good, and in truth the hardest part of organizing a hiking trip here is deciding which walks to rule out.

It is also possible to explore the park by horse. Numerous operators offer trips from 1-12 days, most of these in cooperation with Baqueano Zamora, the only licenced horse concessionaire in Torres del Paine. These trips are available with any combination of lodging, from camping and *refugios* to lodging in an elegant *hosteria* or historic *estancia*. It is also possible to rent horses by the day, always with the accompaniment of a local *baqueano* (horseman); consult at the park administration or Hostería Las Torres.

● The «W»
🕐 4-5d ▢

Named for the shape it inscribes upon the south side of the Paine Massif, this is the most popular multi-day trek in Torres del Paine. Beginning at Laguna Amarga (you can also easily do this hike in the opposite direction), follow the road in to Hostería Torres, and from there continue up the Valle Ascencio; the refugio and campgrounds within the valley itself make for a good first camp. The highlight in the Valle Ascencio is the *mirador* above Campamento Torres, which provides jaw-dropping views of the granite towers that give the park its name.

● The Paine Circuit
🕐 6-7d ▢

This classic Torres del Paine trek leads around the backside of the massif, through wild, open country between the Torres and the Southern Patagonian Ice Field. The route is commonly done counterclockwise from Laguna Amarga, but either direction is feasible, and you can easily combine the circuit with ascents of the Río Ascencio and/or the Valle Francés.

From Laguna Amarga, the route passes over high ground to the east of the Paine Massif, reaching the Campamento Seron after 4-5hrs; another 3 hrs leads to Campamento Coirón, and a further 2.5hrs takes you to Refugio Dickson, set on an exposed point at the south end of Lago Dickson. You can also take a day off at one of these sites to climb the gentle peaks on the backside of the massif.

From Dickson, the route climbs the Río de los Perros into a high, glaciated valley, arriving at Campamento Los Perros in about 4-5hrs. This is the last place to camp before tackling Paso John Gardner, the highest point on the circuit, so keep an eye on the weather. From the top of the pass (4hrs from Campamento Los Perros) you get stellar views of the immense Glacier Grey in the valley below you. The trail then drops steeply into the forest above the glacier to Campamento Paso. From here it's another 5-6hr walk to Refugio Grey, though there is another informal campsite about halfway along. From Refugio Grey it's a 3-4hr walk out to Refugio Pehoé, the end of the circuit.

● Lago Azul and Lago Paine
⏱3-4d rt

This less frequently traveled route also leads into the remote northern sector of park, scribing an arc to the east of that taken by the Paine Circuit. Beginning at Guardería Laguna Amarga, the route passes through level pampa en route to Refugio Laguna Azul (3.5hrs), at which point it veers west and continues along the north side of the Río Paine to Refugio Lago Paine (4hrs). It is also possible to bypass Refugio Laguna Azul and head straight for Refugio Lago Paine. If you wish to combine this route with the Paine Circuit, consult with rangers beforehand to see if boats are available to cross the Río Paine. Otherwise, you'll have to return the way you came.

● The Pingo and Tyndall Valleys
⏱2d rt

From Guardería Grey at the south end of the lake (not to be confused with Refugio Grey, at the north end), a trail heads up the Río Pingo valley, 8 hours to Lago Pingo. This is probably the least-visited sector of the park, and one of its most spectacular, with the Glaciar Zapata calving directly into the lake. From here you'll have to return the way you came, as Conaf now discourages hikers from attempting the circuit south via Lago Tyndall.

Río Serrano

From its source at Lago Toro, the Río Serrano follows a serpentine course south past the Tyndall, Geike, Serrano and Balmaceda glaciers en route to Seno Ultima Esperanza. In sea kayaks, you can descend the river over the course of two days as an extension to your visit to Torres del Paine; in a zodiac, the trip from the mouth of the

river (near the Monte Balmaceda Resort) to the campground on the Río Serrano takes about 2¹/₂ hrs.
Operators: 28 - 35 (sk) - 169 (sk) - 225 (sk)

Climbing in Torres del Paine

Operators: 13 - 35

The first ascent in the Torres Massif dates from 1937, when Germans Stefan Zuck and Hans Teuful climbed Cerro Paine Chico, a 1971m peak just north of Paso John Gardner. It wasn't until the 1960's, however, that the towering granite walls and *torres* themselves began to enter the realm of the possible, and the first aid routes were established on the Torre Norte (1958), the Torres Central and Sur (1963), and Cerro Catedral (1971). Since that moment – as climbing techniques developed in the Alps and Yosemite Valley began to be utilized in remote alpine ranges around the globe – Torres del Paine has remained one of the world's premier testing grounds for extreme alpine climbers.

The rock here is of superb quality, and the walls generally upwards of a kilometer in height. The true challenge of climbing here is that posed by the ferocious wind and relentless storms that can envelop the towers for weeks on end, leaving them encrusted with meters of frozen rime. Most parties budget on at least a month at the climbers' camps established in the upper portions of the glacial valleys draining the south side of the massif. Guided climbs in the park generally ascend the Monzino route on the Torre Norte (5.10a), or the Cuerno Este (5.6-5.10, depending on the route). Note that foreign climbers must pay a climbers' fee of US$100 pp to Conaf, and must also solicit permission in advance from *Fronteras y Límites* (see the general mountaineering chapter for details).

CUERNOS DEL PAINE

Punta Arenas — *Pop. 113,000 (☎ city code 61)*

Poised between the eastern foothills of the Andes, the Strait of Magellan, and the vast grasslands of the pampa, Punta Arenas is the southernmost city of its size in the world. Perhaps in response to their city's overwhelming isolation, the past and present inhabitants of Punta Arenas have labored to make their city a beacon of culture and civilization – something which comes as a pleasant surprise for most visitors.

The original Chilean settlement of the Strait was at Fuerte Bulnes, 56km to the south, but the site was so nearly uninhabitable that after five years the settlement was transferred here, to a site English mariners had named 'Sandy Point.' Originally a penal colony, the settlement was prone to violent confrontations such as M.J. Cambiaso's bloody mutiny in 1851. Rough-hewn whale and seal hunters provisioned their ships here before heading to the outer isles, adding to the carnage.

But near the end of the 19th century, a number of factors combined to catapult Punta Arenas from a bloody outpost to a bustling and increasingly cosmopolitan port. Between 1865 and 1875, the population grew from 200 to 1000, and by 1885 had doubled again; one-third of these were foreign-born. In 1868 Punta Arenas was declared a free port (a status it still enjoys), and as great sheep *estancias* grew up in the surrounding pampa, a lucky few built ever-greater fortunes, and elegant constructions brightened the drab façade of the city. The discovery of gold on Tierra del Fuego drew even more immigrants – largely Yugoslavians, Italians, and Spaniards, and from 1885-1907 traffic in the Strait increased from 300 to over 1900 ships a year.

Like all booms, that of Punta Arenas had to subside. The fall of wool prices, the end of the whaling trade, and the opening of the Panama Canal all combined to lay the city low in the early 20th century. Luckily, the subsequent discovery of local oil deposits gave the economy a much-needed boost, and today the city continues to live largely from its role as a service provider for the petroleum and fishing industries, as well as from trade in the duty-free *Zona Franca*.

PUNTA ARENAS

TOURIST OFFICES
Sernatur, Waldo Seguel 689, just west of the plaza.

BANKS AND MONEY CHANGERS
ATMs around the plaza and throughout the downtown area. Many casas de cambio on Lautaro Navarro.

HOSPITAL
Angamos and Arauco, NW of downtown, ☎ 244040.

POST OFFICE
One block north of the Plaza at Bories 911.

INTERNET CONNECTION
CTC, O'Higgins 1099.
Austrointernet, Boris 687, 2nd floor, Of. 3.
Hostal El Bosque, O'Higgins 424.

ACCOMMODATION
1 *HI Residencial Sonia Kuscevic* $, Pasaje Darwin 175, ☎ 248543.
2 *Backpacker's Paradise* $, Ignacio Carrera Pinto 1022, ☎ 222554.
3 *Huala* $, Maipú 851, ☎ 244244.

4 *Hostal El Bosque* **$$**, O'Higgins 424, ☎ 221764.

5 *Hostal de la Avenida* **$$**, Av. Colón 534, ☎ 247532.

6 *Hotel Plaza*, **$$**, José Nogueira 1116, ☎ 248613.

7 *Hotel José Nogueira* **$$$**, Bories 959, ☎ 248840.

8 *Hotel Finis Terrae* **$$$**, Av. Colón 766, ☎ 228200. More info at www.turistel.cl

RESTAURANTS

9 *El Mercado*, Mejicana 617, 2nd floor. Excellent, inexpensive seafood.

10 *Pérgola*, in the Hotel José Nogueira at Bories 959. Expensive, elegant, also good for drinks.

11 *Centro Español*, Plaza Muñoz Gamero 771. Old-school ambience, views over the Plaza.

12 *El Mesón del Calvo*, Jorge Montt 687. Expensive, famous for regional specialties.

13 *El Coral*, José Menéndez 848. Spanish cuisine, seafood, reasonably priced.

AIRPORTS

Aeropuerto Carlos Ibáñez del Campo, 20km north of town.

AIRLINE OFFICES

Aerovías DAP, ☎ 223340.
LanChile, Lautaro Navarro 999, ☎ 241232.
Ladeco, Lautaro Navarro 1155, ☎ 241100.

AIRPORT TRANSPORT

Austral Bus minibuses depart from the plaza; consult with travel agents or airlines for other arrangements. *Radiotaxi Patagonia*, ☎ 229330.

BUS STATION AND /OR OFFICES

No central bus terminal. *Austral Bus* and *Buses Ghisoni* offer service to Puerto Montt (24-hr trip).
Buses Fernández, A. Sanhueza 745.
Bus Sur, Magallanes and Colón.
Austral Bus, José Menéndez 565.
Buses Ghisoni, Lautaro Navarro 971.
Buses Pingüino, Armando Sanhueza 745.
Buses Pacheco, Av. Colón 900.
Transport Los Carlos, Magallanes 974.

RENT A CAR

Budget, O'Higgins 964 ☎ 241696.
Emsa, Roca 1044 ☎ 241182.

PUNTA ARENAS DOWNTOWN

BOATS/FERRIES

The terminal for ferries to Porvenir and Puerto Williams is at Tres Puentes, north of town past the Zona Franca. See below for ferries and cruise ships heading south to Tierra del Fuego and Isla Navarino. The Barcaza Melinka transports vehicles and passengers between Tres Puentes and Bahía Chilota on Tierra del Fuego. 1 departure daily, duration 2 hrs, leaving Punta Arenas in the morning, returning in the afternoon. This same boat also provides service to the penguin colony on Isla Magdalena from Dec to Feb, with afternoon departures on Tue, Thu, and Sat. *Navimag*, Av. Independencia 830. *Barcaza Crux Australis*, Av. Bulnes 05075, ☎ (61)218100. *Transbordador Austral Broom*, Av. Bulnes 05075.

SHOPPING

Duty-free electronic goods, film, leather goods and many other items may be purchased at the Zona Franca, north of town on the road to Puerto Natales. Access by frequent colectivos from downtown.

USEFUL ADDRESSES

Conaf, José Menéndez 1147.

With its wealth of historic architecture and first-class museums, Punta Arenas is worth a detained visit for those interested in history and culture at the end of the world. The city itself is rather spread out, but taxi *colectivos* go to most worthwhile sights.

In-town Attractions

Plaza Muñóz Gamero Centered around a bronze statue of Ferdinand Magellan (donated to the city in 1920 by José Menéndez), Punta Arenas' central plaza concentrates many of the city's most important historical buildings. The most important of these is the **PALACIO SARA BRAUN** (at the NW corner of the plaza), built between 1894 and 1905 by French architect Numa Mayer for the widow of sheep baron José Nogueira. The palace has been converted into an elegant hotel and restaurant, the *Hotel José Nogueira*.
Hours: Tue-Sat 1100-1300, 1800-2000.
Entrance: costs US$2.

Casa Braun-Menéndez Just north of the plaza on Calle Hernando de Magallanes, is the house built in 1905 for Mauricio Braun and Josefina Menéndez Behety, heirs to the two most powerful families in Punta Arenas. The house has been converted into a fine museum, the **MUSEO REGIONAL DE MAGALLANES**, with well-preserved rooms filled with imported furniture and other trappings of the turn-of-the-century boom in wool exports. Other exhibits include historic photos of Punta Arenas and the settlement of southern Patagonia and Tierra del Fuego.
Hours: Tue-Fri 1100-1700, Sat, Sun, holidays 1100-1400

Museo Naval y Marítimo Two blocks east of the plaza at Pedro Montt 989, this museum depicts the highlights of Chilean maritime history in the far south, with scale models of warships and a display on the 1916 expedition to rescue the crew of Ernest Shackleton's ship *Endurance*.

Museo Regional Salesiano Maggiorino Borgatello Seven blocks north of the plaza on Av. Manuel Bulnes, this excellent museum features extensive exhibits on the natural history and ethnography of southern Patagonia and Tierra de Fuego. The artifacts and photos are largely the work of the hardy Salesian priests who set up missions in the region beginning in the mid-19th century, when mounting pressure from the great sheep *estancias* first began to threaten the lifestyle of the region's resident Selk'nam, Haush, Tehuelche, Alakalufe, and Yamana Indians. There is also a life-sized replica of the Cueva de las Manos, an important rock art site located near Chile Chico, in northern Patagonia.
Hours: Daily 1000-1200, 1500-1800.

Cementerio Municipal Further north on Av. Manuel Bulnes, Punta Arenas' carefully landscaped cemetery provides an interesting post-mortem glimpse of the lives and aspirations of the inhabitants of this unlikely end-of-the-world boom town. Note the statue in honor of the Fuegian Indians, the simple graves of European immigrants, and the pretentious mausoleums erected by Sara Braun and José Menéndez. The Neoclassical gate to the cemetery was donated by Sara Braun on the condition that it be closed after she passed through, and never open again.

Instituto de la Patagonia North of town, across from the Zona Franca, this scientific and cultural research institute also contains an open-air *Museo del Recuerdo*, with horse-drawn carts, farm machinery, a replica of Fuerte Bulnes, and a few buildings brought from a nearby *estancia*.
Hours: Mon-Fri 0830-1130, 1500-1800, Sat 0830-1300

Charley Milward's House Fans of Bruce Chatwin's *In Patagonia* might want to check out the house occupied by Chatwin's relative Charley Milward, at España 959, between José Menéndez and Waldo Seguel. Ernest Shackleton lodged here in 1914 while planning the rescue of the crew of the *Endurance* after the ship was crushed by pack ice in Antarctica.

Mirador Cerro La Cruz At the west end of Fagnano, four blocks west of the Plaza, a series of steps leads up to this lookout over the city and the Strait of Magellan.

PALACIO SARA BRAUN (MN)

PALACIO BRAUN MENENDEZ (MN)

EDIFICIO DE LA GOBERNACION

CASA COMERCIAL J. MENENDEZ

Around Punta Arenas

Reserva Forestal Magallanes and Cerro Mirador

Nine kilometers west of Punta Arenas, this small deciduous forest preserve is a popular picnic area for local families. In the southern portion of the reserve is Cerro Mirador, a small, homespun ski area with trails entirely below tree line – a rarity for ski areas in South America. Snow conditions are remarkably consistent, and at the base of the mountain are hiking trails where you can cross-country ski in winter (though finding equipment can be a challenge). Despite this area's reputation for high winds, winter is generally calmer, and on good days, from the summit, you can look out across the Strait of Magellan to Tierra del Fuego. Though there's only one chair, there are trails here for skiers of most abilities. The density of the forest makes off-piste skiing an impossibility.

Parque Nacional Pali Aike

Located 188km NE of Punta Arenas (off the road to Río Gallegos), this 5,000há national park protects a unique volcanic landscape with lava flows, extinct craters, and several caves, all set in the midst of the vast, windswept pampa. The centerpiece of the park is **Cueva Pali Aike**, where North American archaeologist Junius Bird discovered Paleo-Indian artifacts and remains of milodons, American horses and other extinct megafauna. The park's only trail to speak of is the 9km walk to **Laguna Ana**, while further west (ask about road conditions) is **Cueva Fell**, another Paleo-Indian site, with a splendid collection of cave paintings. There is no public transport to the site, and camping is not permitted.

Penguin Colonies

Two colonies of nesting Magallanic penguins may be visited as day trips out of Punta Arenas. Located about 50km NW of town, **Pingüinera Seno Otway** is the closest of the two; having once dropped to a total population of only 500 individuals, this site is a true success story in the effort to protect Chile's beleaguered penguin population, as the efforts of the Fundación Seno Otway have caused its numbers to rebound to some 4000 nesting pairs distributed along a 2km stretch of coast. The penguins are present from Sep-Mar, and nesting occurs from Dec-Feb. Mid-morning is the best time to visit.

The much larger colony on Isla Magdalena, protected as **Monumento Natural Los Pingüinos**, may be visited only by ship (see ferry listings in Punta Arenas). Nearly 200,000 nesting penguins congregate here in peak season. A trail on the island leads to a lighthouse with excellent views and a Conaf information center inside.

Puerto Hambre and Fuerte Bulnes

South along the coast from Punta Arenas, these two historical sites represent the first attempts to inhabit the shores of the Strait of Magellan. 53km south of Punta Arenas is **Puerto Hambre**, site of Pedro Sarmiento de Gamboa's ill-fated 1584 settlement, Rey Felipe. Little remains except the ruins of a church and a memorial plaque.

Another 5km south is **Fuerte Bulnes**, where you can check out a reconstruction of the first Chilean settlement in southern Patagonia, dating from 1843. Set strategically on a rocky bluff overlooking the Strait, the fort was soon abandoned in favor of Punta Arenas, where the climate was much more benign. Today a private concessionaire is working to restore the fort and add a gift shop, snack bar, and the so on. There is no public transport to either site, but tours are regularly arranged in Punta Arenas.

Estancias

125km NE of Punta Arenas on the route to Río Gallegos, **Estancia San Gregorio** is a representative if somewhat dilapidated example of turn-of-the-century rural architecture in Magallanes. Once the center of a 90,000há ranch owned by José Menéndez, the estancia's several main buildings are now owned by a cooperative and largely abandoned. Though not technically open to the public, visitors are free to wander around and take photos. Buses to Río Gallegos can drop you off at the site, but you may have to wait a long time for another to pass. Nearby accommodation includes the *Hotel Sanhueza* and, further east at the turn-off to Punta Delgada, the recommended *Hostería Tehuelche*.

LIGHTHOUSE OF ISLA MAGDALENA

In the other direction, 91km NW of Punta Arenas on a side road off the route to Puerto Natales, is the town of **Río Verde**, once the seat of another old *estancia*. 6km south of town is the ferry to **Isla Riesco**; lodging is available near the ferry at *Hostería Río Verde* and further south at *Estancia Olga Teresa*, a working ranch also offering lodging and meals. There is no public transport to Río Verde.

Other traditional estancias now offering lodging and meals to guests include the *Hostería Río Penitente* and *Estancia El Palenque* (both on the road to Puerto Natales), and the *Estancia Rosario* (on the Península Antonio Varas, access by motor launch).

Fishing in Southern Patagonia and Tierra del Fuego

This area boasts some of the finest sea-run brown and steelhead trout fishing in the world, and fish of 10 kilos or more are not unusual. Note that conditions here are different than elsewhere in Patagonia, as the wide-open country and ferocious winds make heavy equipment and a solid double-haul essential. Guided trips are generally offered on Isla Riesco to the NW of Punta Arenas, as well as on Lago Blanco, the Río Grande, and the remote Río Azopardo, all in southern Tierra del Fuego.
Operators: 28 - 35 - 114

Tierra del Fuego

ACCOMMODATION IN PORVENIR
*Hostal Patagonia **$$**, Jorge Schythe 230, ☎ 580088.*
*Hotel España **$$**, Croatia 698, ☎ 580160.*
*Residencial Colón **$**, Ríobo 198, ☎ 580593.*

TRANSPORT
Air: Aerovías DAP, Señoret 542, connects Porvenir with Punta Arenas and Puerto Williams.
Ferry: Transbordadora Broom runs service between Tres Puentes in Punta Arenas and Bahía Chilota, 7km north of Porvenir. The southern portion of the island (Caleta Yendegaia) may be reached aboard the Barcaza Crux Australis (see pg. 558).
Bus: Transporte Senkovic, Carlos Wood 489, connects Porvenir with Río Grande Wed and Sat 1400 (book in advance), with connections to Ushuaia. The same bus that makes the Río Grande run also provides transport to and from the ferry terminal. Travelers with their own vehicles can also cross the Strait at Punta Delgada, 135km from Punta Arenas; ferries depart every 1.5 hrs from 0830-2300.

Porvenir

The largest town in Chilean Tierra del Fuego, Porvenir was founded in 1883 as a police regiment during the Tierra del Fuego gold rush, and was originally populated by immigrants of English, Scottish, Croatian and Yugoslav descent, as can be observed in Porvenir's cemetery, located four blocks north of the plaza. Another local attraction is the **MUSEO REGIONAL** *(Mon-Fri 0900-1300, 1345-1700, also during Jan and Feb Sat-Sun 1100-1300, 1430-1600)*, at the corner of Valdivieso and Scythe, where you can check out old photos of the gold rush, archaeological displays on the Selk'nam Indians, and a somewhat random display on Chilean film. For a view over the bay and the town, follow the coast road south along the edge of the bay to the *mirador*. If you have a car, you might check out the three lakes north of town, which during winter are occasionally visited by Chilean flamingos.

Cerro Sombrero

The only other town of any size in Chilean Tierra del Fuego, Cerro Sombrero is a surprisingly prosperous little oil town with such amenities as a municipal greenhouse in the central plaza. Though there's almost nothing else to see, there is one place to stay, *Hostería Tunkulén*.

South to Lago Blanco and the Cordillera Darwin

To the south of the Bahía Inútil, the landscape of Tierra del Fuego gradually transforms from the rolling grasslands of the windswept pampa to a wilderness of ancient forests and lakes in the foothills of the Cordillera Darwin. Here, just over 200km south of Porvenir, is **LAGO BLANCO**, one of the few places in Chilean Tierra del Fuego to have anything resembling a tourist industry. There's not much –just a few cabañas and a couple of upmarket fishing lodges on an island in the lake– but the landscape and solitude are sublime. There's no public transport to this part of the island, so you'll have to rent a car. On the way south around the Bahía Inutil (Useless Bay), take the time to stop off and visit the eerie English cemetery in the village of Onaisin.

 Fishermen keen on landing one of Tierra del Fuego's legendary steelhead or sea-run browns can arrange for lodging and guides on Lago Blanco at the *Isla Victoria Lodge* or the *Tierra del Fuego Lodge*.

Even further south of Lago Blanco, at the eastern extreme of Almirantazgo Sound, the renovated estancia at Caleta María serves as a cozy retreat and operations base for fly-fishing on the Río Azopardo and 3-8 day horsepacking and hiking trips in a 40,000há private reserve set in the Cordillera Darwin between here and Estancia Yendegaia. You can access Caleta María on foot by plane only, while Estancia Yendegaia may be reached by the ferry *Crux Australis* (see ferry listings above).
Operators: 35 - 87 - 114

Paddling in the Fuegian Fjords

 Reaching like fingers through the glacier – and storm-scoured peaks of the Cordillera Darwin, the branching fjords of the Seno Almirantazgo and Fiordo D'Agostini provide the ultimate in remote high-latitude paddling. Countless tidewater glaciers and abundant marine fauna, including fur seals, sea lions, elephant seals, and Magallanic and Macaroni penguins form the background for these 3-15 sailing/sea kayaking trips. Participants should be aware that actual itineraries will depend entirely upon weather conditions – the formidable westerly gusts known as *williwaws* can keep boats pinned at harbor for days at a time.
Operators: 35 - 87 - 114 - 226

Monte Darwin (2,488m)
Monte Sarmiento (2,404m)

You want remote? Got it. Nasty weather? Check. Low success rate? OK. These two peaks in the Cordillera Darwin represent the ultimate challenge for those climbers who just can't get enough suffering. If you can manage the brutal logistics, the howling wind and freezing rain, you'll join the ranks of the notable few – Alberto D'Agostini, Eric Shipman, Walter Bonatti and Yvon Chouinard among them –to have tasted hard-won success in this terrifyingly remote and inhospitable mountain range.
Operators: 35

ISLAS WOLLASTON, CABO DE HORNOS

See pg 6 for photo credit

Tierra del Fuego (Argentine side)

The eastern portion of Tierra del Fuego belongs to Argentina. Most of the landscape here is wide-open pampa, and there's relatively little to see; most travelers bypass **Río Blanco** (240km west of Porvenir) and head directly to Ushuaia. Both towns may be accessed by bus from Porvenir or Río Gallegos, and Ushuaia may also be accessed by plane or boat from Punta Arenas or Puerto Williams.

Located 240km south of Río Blanco on a protected bay off the Canal Beagle, **Ushuaia** is the largest, most attractive, and most traveler-friendly town on Tierra del Fuego. Its setting is truly spectacular, with glaciated peaks soaring directly from the Bahía Ushuaia to heights over 1,500m, and a wide array of hiking, skiing, horseback riding, mountain biking, fishing and boat

tours are offered in the surrounding area, most notably in **Parque Nacional Tierra del Fuego**. Ushuaia is also the principal point of departure for cruises and flights to Antarctica. Note that reservations are a must for travelers planning to visit during the Jan-Feb high season.

AIRLINE OFFICES
Aerolíneas Argentinas, Roca 126.
Austral, Roca 126.
LADE, Galería Albatros at Av. San Martín 564.
Líneas Aéreas Kaikén, San Martín 857.

BUS STATION AND/OR OFFICES
Transportes Los Carlos, Roosa 85.
Transporte Pasarela, Fadul 40.

BOATS / FERRIES
To Puerto Williams on the Luciano Beta, consult with municipal tourist office for prices and departures.
For cruises through the Beagle Channel to Punta Arenas, see pg 558.

Isla Navarino / Puerto Williams

Directly across the Beagle Channel from Ushuaia, the Chilean naval settlement at Puerto Williams is the southernmost permanent settlement in the world. It's not much as towns go – just a collection of colorful, weather-battered houses perched between the ocean and the raw, rugged peaks beyond. Unless you're visiting just to say you've done it, the peaks and the ocean are the only real reasons to come: either to hike in the rugged Cordón de los Dientes range or to embark on a sailing trip south to Cape Horn.

While you're in town, you should check out the **Museo Martín Gusinde** (Apr-Sep/ Tue-Fri 1000-1300, 1500-1800, Sat-Sun 1500-1800, Oct-Mar/ Mon-Thu 0900-1300, 1500-1800, Sat-Sun 1500-1800), which contains displays on the Yamana, Selk'nam, and Kaweskar Indians, including a replica of the ritual huts used by the Selk'nam in this Hain initiation ceremonies. You may also want to go for a beer at the Club de Yates Micalvi, proudly considered the southernmost yacht club in the world.

From Puerto Williams you can head west to the Yamana cemetery in Caleta Mejillones or east to Villa Ukika, where the last surviving descendents of the Yamanas are attempting to recover their native language as they continue to work the frigid waters of the Beagle Channel.

ACCOMMODATION
Hostería Wala $$, west of town, ☎ 621114.
Residencial Onashaga $, corner of Uspashun and Nueva, ☎ 621081.

TRANSPORT
Ferries: The Barcaza Crux Australis ferry connects Puerto Williams with Punta Arenas three times monthly, while the Chilean Navy (Armada) provides more sporadic service. The Luciano Beta also provides sporadic service to between Puerto Williams and Ushuaia, consult in town for details.
Air: To Punta Arenas with Aerovías DAP Mon, Wed, Fri, book in advance, US$60. To Ushuaia, also with DAP, US$40.

The Cordón de los Dientes Circuit

 ⏱5d ▬

This is a remote, demanding circuit through the stunted beach forest, tundra, and peat bogs of the Cordón de los Dientes range south of Puerto Williams. The route begins by following a well-used track up Cerro Bandera, and from there passes by the Laguna El Salto and crosses a pass to Laguna de los Dientes. From here the route trends west, passing Lagunas Escondida, Hermosa, and Martillo before recrossing the range and descending the Arroyo Virginia to the coast. Wet, boggy trail conditions along the length of the route have been exacerbated by damage caused by imported beavers upon the slow-growing forests surrounding Isla Navarino's many lakes.

MULTI-DAY BIKE TOURS IN PATAGONIA

Operators: 31 - 164

Chiloé

Unfortunately, there are few good loops on Chiloé, as most of the best back roads head out to land's end and stop. Still, there's no better way to explore the rural communities on the island's sheltered east coast. The following suggested tours out of Castro are intended only as the most general of guides, as the real fun is in asking around and exploring side roads and tiny villages.

● The Brujo Coast
▶198km◀ ⏱5d **P** **D** ☐
Castro (0) - Dalcahue (20) - Teunaún (69) - Quicavi (20) - Quemchi (20) - Castro (69).

● Isla Quinchao
▶126km◀ ⏱2-3d rt **P** **D** ☐
Castro (0) - Dalcahue (20) - Curaco de Vélez (9) - Achao (17) - Chequian (17) - return.

● Isla Lemuy
▶120km◀ ⏱2-3d rt **P** **D** ☐
Castro (0) - Chonchi (22) - Puerto Huicha ferry (6) - Chulchuy - Puqueldón (9) - Detif (14) - return.

The Carretera Austral

● Puerto Montt to Coihaique
▶Approx.600km◀ ⏱15d min. **D** ☐
The northern portion of the Carretera Austral is a good test drive for those considering continuing south from Coihaique. Though it's definitely remote, here you have relatively closely-spaced villages and regular public transport, in case you decide to bail out. There are two major passes, 650m Portezuelo Moraga and 500m Portezuelo Queulat. Otherwise the route follows river valleys.

Puerto Montt (0) - La Arena ferry (45) - Caleta Puelche - Hornopirén ferry (61) - Caleta Gonzalo - Chaitén (60) - El Amarillo (27) - Puerto Cardenas (19) - Ventisquero Yelcho Chico (14) - Villa Santa Lucía (21) - La Junta (78) - Puerto Puyuhuapi (45) - PN Queulat (24) - Villa Amengual (65) - Villa Mañihuales (58) - Coihaique (77km).

● Around Lago General Carrera
▶Approx.500km◀ ⏱12d min. **P** **D** ■

This section of the Carretera Austral, with its numerous passes and widely spaced settlements, is for strong, experienced riders. The route described here has been chosen with the idea that long-distance cyclists will want to head across the border into Argentina (which you can do from Chile Chico) while folks who are not continuing on will want to return to Coihaique. Alternatively, you can continue south to Cochrane (70km from Cruce El Maitén) and return to Coihaique by plane or bus.

Coihaique (0) - Villa Cerro Castillo (98) - Bahía Murta turnoff (105) - Puerto Tranquilo (25) - Cruce Maiten (51) - Puerto Guadal (10) - Chile Chico ferry (112) - Puerto Ibáñez - Coihaique (90).

Magallanes and Tierra del Fuego

● Torres del Paine
▶127km◀ow ⏱10d w / side hikes
P **D** ■

Though most folks tend to concentrate on hiking in Torres del Paine, if you have a bike you can tour the entire park, doing day hikes or short overnights from trailheads along the way. This suggested circuit, done over the course of ten days, allows you to take in all the park's main attractions while traveling at your own pace, free from bus schedules. To shorten the route, just load your bike onto a bus from Puerto Natales and start the ride at the park entrance at Laguna Amarga, and when you're done, catch a bus back.

Puerto Natales (0) - Cerro Castillo (60) - Guardería Laguna Amarga (65) - Hostería and Camping Las Torres (7km, day hike to Valle Ascencio) - Guardería Pudeto (27km, boat across Lago Pehoé and day hike to Valle Francés) - Park Administration (12) - Hostería Lago Grey (18km, boat to Glacier Grey or day hike up Valle Pingo) - return (147km, buses available).

● Tierra del Fuego
▶Approx.750km◀ ⏱15d min. **P** **D** ■

For those that simply have to get to the end of the world, this is the trip. The straight-line approach would take you straight east (with the wind at your back) from Porvenir to San Sebastián, cutting the distance in half.

Porvenir (0) - Cameron (150) - Lago Blanco (121) - San Sebastián (156) - Río Grande (97) - Lago Fagnano (135) - Ushuaia (101).

OVERLANDS AND CIRCUITS IN PATAGONIA

● The Carretera Austral
⏱7d minimun

This is the classic road trip in Chile: 1,000km of sheer wilderness, endless forests, hanging glaciers and roads etched into the bedrock above rivers, lakes, and fjords. There are any number of ways to approach the Carretera Austral, utilizing ferries and crossing back forth across the Andes to the Argentine pampa and Ruta 40. One highly recommended option is to take the ferry south from Puerto Montt to Puerto Chacabuco and make your way back north over the course of a week or ten days.
Operators: 10 - 18 - 31 - 103 - 153

● Ruta 40
⏱5d minimun

Running parallel to the Carretera Austral but on the far side of the Andes, Argentina's most famous desert highway brings new meaning to the word desolate, stretching through nearly 1,400km of rolling pampa between Esquel and Río Gallegos. Along the way, the route passes by nearby PN Los Alerces and PN Los Glaciares (El Calafate), two of the most important destinations in Argentine Patagonia. The contrast between the pampa and the forests to the west of the Andes is truly awe-inspiring. The following companies incorporate the Ruta 40 into integrated overland routes linking Argentina with the Carretera Austral and/or Torres del Paine.
Operators: 10 - 28 - 169 - 205

● Tierra del Fuego
⏱3-5d

If you really want to see Tierra del Fuego, you need your own vehicle. Rent a car in Punta Arenas, send it across the Strait to Porvenir, and head south to Lago Blanco, one of several major lakes at the foot of the Darwin Range. Then head back north, loop east into Argentina and continue south along the coast to Ushuaia. Finally, head SW another 19km to Lapataia – the end of Ruta 3, as far south as the roads go.
Operators: 21 - 28 - 153 - 192

Eastern
Island

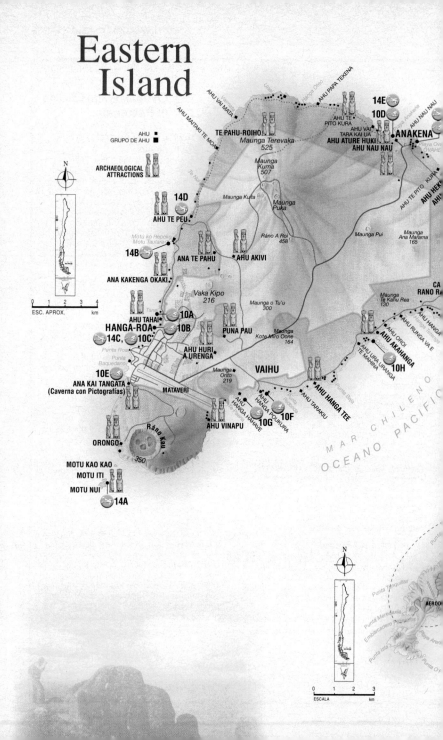

AHU ■
GRUPO DE AHU ■

ARCHAEOLOGICAL
ATTRACTIONS

N

ESC. APROX.
0 1 2 3 4
km

AHU VAI MATA

AHU MAITAKI TE MOA

TE PAHU-ROIHO
Maunga Terevaka
525

AHU PAPA TEKENA

14E
10D
AHU TE
PITO KURA
AHU VAI
TARA KAI UA
AHU ATURE HUKI
AHU NAU NAU
ANAKENA

Maunga Ohio

Uru

Maunga Oone

OVAHE

Maunga
Kuma
507

Te Nua

Maunga Kuta

AHU TE PEU
14D

Maunga
Puka

AHU TE PITO KURA

AHU HEK

AHI

Motu ko Hepoko
Motu Tautara

14B

ANA TE PAHU

AHU AKIVI

Ráno A Roi
458

Maunga Pui

Maunga
Ana Marama
165

ANA KAKENGA OKAKI

Vaka Kipo
216

Maunga o Tu'u
300

CA
RANO R

Maunga
Te Kahu Rea
130

AHU HANGA

AHU TAHAI
HANGA-ROA
14C, 10C
10A
10B

PUNA PAU

Maunga
Kote Miro Oone
164

AHU RUNGA VA E
AHU OROI
AHU AKAHANGA
10H

AHU HURI
A URENGA

AHU URA URANGA
TE MAHINA

Punta Roa
Punta
Baquedano

VAIHU

Maunga
Onito
219

AHU HANGA TEE

10E
ANA KAI TANGATA
(Caverna con Pictografías)

MATAVERI

Punta Baja

AHU TAFAKIU

AHU
HANGA NAHAVE
AHU VINAPU

AHU
HANGA POUKURA
10G
10F

M A R   C H I L E N O

O C E A N O   P A C I F I C

ORONGO
Ráno Kau
350

MOTU KAO KAO
MOTU ITI
MOTU NUI
14A

N

ESCALA
0 1 2 3
km

Punta Anguillas

Punta Merodaxia

Embarcadero

Punta Isla

AERODU

Chile's Pacific Islands

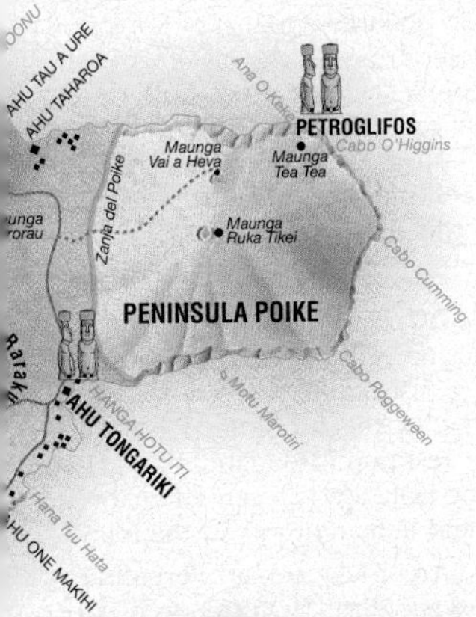

Juan Fernández Archipelago

AHU TAU A URE
AHU TAHAROA

PETROGLIFOS

Ana O Keke
Cabo O'Higgins

Maunga
Vai a Heva

Maunga
Tea Tea

Zanja del Poike

Maunga
Ruka Tikei

Cabo Cumming

PENINSULA POIKE

Cabo Roggeween

AHU TONGARIKI

Motu Marotiri

Hanga Hotu Iti

Hena Tuu Hata

AHU ONE MAKIHI

MAR CHILENO

Punta Norte
Punta Salinas

Cerro
Alto

Punta Inglés

CUEVA
DE-ROBINSON
CRUSOE
13B

QUEBRADA VAQUERÍA

Puerto Inglés

Punta San Carlos

Punta Suroeste

Cerro
Agudo
685

MIRADOR
DE SELKIRK

Bahía Cumberland

Punta Bacalao

Punta Pescadores

Islote Juanango

SAN JUAN
BAUTISTA

13E 13C

Cerro
Centinela
362

QUEBRADA VILLAGRA

QUEBRADA PIEDRA AGUDA

Travesía en Lancha
Robinson Aéreo

Cerro
Tres Puntas
482

Cerro
Damajuana
635

Piedra Francés

13A

CORBÓN ESCARPADO

PLAZOLETA
EL YUNQUE

Cerro
La Piña
REBAJE DE
LAPINA

Punta Bahí

EL CANOTE

Punta Blanca

Cerro
El Yunque
915

LOS
RAMPLONES

Punta Changos

Bahía Villagra

Punta Larga

Islote Vinilla

Punta Hueca

Travesía a Playa Arenal

Punta Hueso Ballena

Islote El Verdugo

Punta Blanca

OCEANO PACIFICO

CHILE'S PACIFIC ISLANDS

GEOGRAPHY AND TOPOGRAPHY

The Juan Fernández Archipelago

The Juan Fernández Archipelago consists of a group of three tiny islands located some 667km west of the South American continent at a latitude of 33° south – basically due west of Valparaíso. Geologically, the islands are extinct volcanoes originating along an east-west tending 'hot line' on the ocean floor, with a presumed age of some 3 million years. Today, everything about the archipelago's topography and ecology reflects this volcanic origin, this sudden appearance of land in the very midst of the great Pacific.

Isla Robinson Crusoe, also known as Isla Más a Tierra, is the closest to the continent, and is the only one with a permanent human population. Topographically, this 4,794há island may be divided into two sectors, east and west. The western sector basically consists of a long, narrow peninsular plateau – the only bit of level land on the island, which explains why the airport is located here. The eastern sector is incredibly abrupt, with steep coastal escarpments leading up to a complex series of knife-edge ridges that converge at peaks as high as 915m **Cerro Yungay**. Due to the difficulties created by this landscape, the interior of the island is entirely uninhabited and largely inaccessible. The only settlement on the island is **San Juan Bautista**, located along the northern shore of the island on the **Bahía Cumberland**, the best harbor in the archipelago. Bahía Cumberland is thought to be an ancient, eroded volcanic crater (caldera).

One kilometer west of Robinson Crusoe is tiny, insignificant **Isla Santa María** (221há), and another 180km west of that is **Isla Alejandro Selkirk**. Though its total area is approximately equivalent to that of Robinson Crusoe, Alejandro Selkirk rises to nearly twice the height, with Cerro Los Inocentes reaching a dizzying 1,650m above the sea level. Also known as Isla Más Afuera, Isla Alejandro Selkirk is entirely uninhabited aside from the seasonal camps set up by lobster fishermen from San Juan Bautista.

Easter Island

Easter Island is the world's most remote island, located 3,762km off the coast of South America and 1,900km east of tiny Pitcairn Island, the nearest populated land mass. This awe-inspiring isolation is a central factor in the natural and human history of the island.

Like the Archipelago Juan Fernández, Easter Island is entirely volcanic in origin, situated along another 'hot line' that extends east and west of the Pacific Meso-Dorsal rift (sea-floor spreading) zone. Beginning about 3 million years before the present (ybp), a huge volcanic cone rising 3,000m above the ocean floor first broke the surface of the Pacific. This original crater, now known as **Volcán Poike**, was followed by **Rano-Kau** (at about 2.5 million ybp), and finally by **Terevaka**, which is thought to have erupted as recently as 10,000-12,000 ybp. These three major craters now form the vertices of a 166 km^2 triangle, the interior of which has been filled in with deposits of lava and ash from about 70 smaller craters and vents. Surrounding the island is a submarine platform extending up to 60km out to sea, and beyond

BAHIA CUMBERLAND, ISLA ROBINSON CRUSOE

this platform, the ocean floor plunges to depths of over three kilometers.

Today all volcanic activity on the island has ceased, and the landscape is a relatively homogenous, undulant expanse of grassy hills, lava flows and extinct craters, the highest of which, Terevaka, rises 652m above sea level. Due to the porosity of the soil, there is no surface water on the island apart from that which collects in the major craters, and as a consequence the landscape shows no signs of fluvial erosion, in dire contrast to the Juan Fernández Archipelago. Extensive 'lava tube' caves abound along the coast and in the interior.

The coast, unprotected by coral reefs or significant harbors, consists primarily of abrupt cliffs and sea stacks. There are two **beaches** of white coral sand on the island (Anakena and Ovahe), both on the north shore. All the island's inhabitants live on the northwest coast in and around the village of **Hanga Roa**.

CLIMATE AND BIOGEOGRAPHY
Juan Fernández Archipelago

Climatically, the archipelago follows a similar regimen as Chile's central coast, with a long dry season (Sept-Apr) and a relatively brief, rainy winter. However, precipitation is more evenly distributed throughout the year, and is more abundant than on the coast, averaging a total of 956mm/year. Winds during summertime are usually from the south and SE, while in winter there are occasional westerlies.

The archipelago is situated to the west of the Humboldt Current, which sweeps north along the coast of continental Chile, forming a natural barrier to the migration of plants and animals from the continent. Those that did arrive (from South America or elsewhere) consequently developed evolutionary 'strategies' quite different from those they would have pursued in a more integrated, broadly competitive environment. As a result, the archipelago has developed a unique, **highly endemic biotic community**, generally divided into three ecosystems: the evergreen rainforest, the

evergreen heath, and the herbaceous steppe (See N for details). All told, 101 (or 70%) of the islands' 146 native plant species and 18% of its genera are endemic, while the islands' fauna includes three species of endemic birds. The archipelago's **marine ecosystem** is no less unique, as about 20% of fish species and 32% of algae species grow nowhere else on the planet. The endemic Juan Fernández spiny lobster (*Jasus frontalis*) is far and away the archipelago's most important economic resource.

Due to their long isolation and relatively small populations, these ecosystems are extremely vulnerable to outside forces, both human and natural. The endemic **Juan Fernández Fur seal**, for example, has only recently recovered after being hunted to near extinction during the 1800's. The fragrant sandalwood tree, harvested for the fabrication of scented oils, was last observed on the Isla Robinson Crusoe in 1908, and the endemic *chonta* palm is currently listed as an endangered species. Feral goats wreak havoc on native plants that evolved in the absence of grazing mammals, while the coatimundi or *coati*, imported in hopes of controlling the islands' rat population, has proven far more partial to native seabirds. Meanwhile, entire ecosystems are threatened by invasion by

THE TRAIL TO THE MIRADOR DE SELKIRK

more highly competitive exotic plant species, to the extent that over 40% of the plant species in the archipelago are non-natives.

In 1977, in recognition of archipelago's invaluable genetic patrimony, Unesco declared Juan Fernández a World Biosphere Reserve, and more recently the Dutch government has sponsored an intense environmental recovery project directed specifically towards eliminating non-native species. For more information on endemism and individual species, see .

Easter Island

Climatically as well as ethnographically, Easter Island is essentially Polynesian. The climate here is marine subtropical, which means that you can expect consistently warm weather and to-

tal precipitation adding up to about 1,100mm/year; summertime rains are typically short and violent, while in winter they tend to be longer and gentler. Winds typically blow from the east and SE during the austral summer and from the west, NW and SW during the winter season.

It is difficult to determine what Easter Island's ecosystem was like before the arrival of the first *homo sapiens*. Though research indicates that a sizable portion of the island was once covered in forests, the first westerners to visit the island reported seeing trees only in and around the islands' volcanic craters, the same places they are found to this day. In any case, today most of the island is covered by course grasses, and the only trees outside the craters are a few stands of introduced eucalyptus and palms, plus fruit trees including papaya, avocado, banana, guava, and pineapple. Still, some 34 species of native plants still survive on the island (compared to 60 exotic species), the most notable of which is the **toromiro** (*Sophora toromiro*). Prized by native artists and carvers for the quality of its wood, the toromiro disappeared entirely from the island in 1962, but has since been reintroduced in the crater of Rano Kau.

THE ARID WESTERN PLATEAU ON ISLA ROBINSON CRUSOE

The island's terrestrial fauna is so rare as to be almost nonexistent, and the only animals you're likely to see (besides a few seabirds) are domestics. The local **marine environment** demonstrates clear affinities with marine ecosystems in the tropical Indo-Pacific, with a couple of shallow-water coral reefs and a tropical fish population thought to be as much as 30% endemic. See for more.

HUMAN HISTORY

Juan Fernández Archipelago

As far as anyone knows, the Juan Fernández Archipelago was never inhabited or even visited by native South American cultures. Quite likely the first time human beings laid eyes on the islands was in 1574, when Portuguese mariner Juan Fernández, while plying the route between Callao and Valparaíso in the service of the Spanish crown, happened upon them when he steered west off the coast in order to avoid the incessant SW winds and the contrary Humboldt current. The route itself was a true innovation, but the Spanish made only halfhearted efforts to establish any sort of settlement in the archipelago. So for the next two centuries Juan Fernández (as it came to be called) remained an outpost of pirates, a gold mine for sealers, and a place for English privateers to hide out and relax, beyond the long-armed reach of the Spanish 'flotilla'.

Among these vessels was the *Cinque Ports*, which rounded the horn in 1704 as part of a British raiding expedition organized by famed buccaneer William Dampier. In September of that year the shipped stopped off on Juan Fernández to honor a most unusual request by one of its crew: Scotsman **Alexander Selkirk**, violently at odds with his captain, had demanded to be put ashore.

Armed with only the bare essentials on an island whose climate is far from tropical, Selkirk had his work cut out for him. At first, fearful of missing a passing ship, Selkirk stuck to the coast, where he collected shellfish and shot an odd sea lion. Eventually, however, he strayed inland, and found that the island abounded with food: turnips,

Juan Fernández Treasure Hunters

Given the archipelago's long history as a refuge for pirates and privateers, it seems unavoidable that somewhere on the island must lie a cache of hidden treasure. In 1998, American Bernard Kaiser arrived on the island with signed approval to begin excavations on the island, convinced that here lay Lord George Anson's US$10 billion stash of gold, silver, and precious gems, supposedly left during the 18th century. Though Kaiser's visit generated big headlines in Chile and hopeful anticipation on the island – which stood to receive some 30% of the total haul – no treasure was ever discovered.

parsley, watercress, parsnips and cabbage palm all grew wild on the island, lobsters abounded along the shore, and the feral goats left by the Spanish had become nothing short of a plague. These last formed the basis of Selkirk's food, shelter, and clothing.

After four and half years of solitude, Selkirk was finally picked up by the twin privateers *Duke* and *Duchess*, under the command of Captain Woodes Rogers and piloted by none other than Dampier. In his 1912 *A Voyage Around the World*, Woodes recalled Selkirk's predicament and salvation:

'He had with him his clothes and bedding, with a firelock, some powder, bullets and tobacco, a hatchet, a knife, a kettle, a Bible, some practical pieces, and his mathematical instruments and books. He diverted and provided for himself as well as he could, but for the first eight months had to bear up against melancholy, and the terror of being left alone in such a desolate place. He built two huts with pimento trees, covered them with long grass, and lined them with the skins of goats...........

'After he had conquered his melancholy, he diverted himself sometimes with cutting his name on trees, and of the time of his being left, and continuance there. He was at first much pestered with cats and rats that bred in great numbers from some of each species which had got ashore from ships that put in there for wood and water. The rats gnawed his feet and clothes whilst asleep, which obliged him to cherish the cats with his goats' flesh, by which so many of them became so tame, that they would lie about in hundreds, and soon delivered him from the rats. He likewise tamed some kids; to divert himself, would now and then sing and dance with them and his cats.....

'When his clothes were worn out he made himself a coat and a cap of goat skins, which he stitched together with little thongs of the same, that he cut with his knife. He had no other needle but a nail; and when his knife was worn to the back he made others, as well as he could, of some iron hoops that were left ashore, which he beat thin and ground upon stones. Having some linen cloth by him, he sewed him some shirts with a nail and, stitched them with the worsted of his old stockings, which he pulled out on purpose. He had his last shirt on when we found him on the island.'

Selkirk was enlisted as mate on the *Duke*, and for the next couple of years he made a fortune preying on Spanish ships, returning home in 1711 a wealthy man. There, the tale of his exploits made him something of a celebrity; first rendered in Richard Steele's 1713 *The Englishman*, Selkirk's story was later incorporated into Daniel Defoe's *Robinson Crusoe* – namesake of the archipelago's principal island.

Meanwhile, the Juan Fernández Archipelago continued on in its accustomed peace and obscurity. Thus it remained until the late 18th century, when

a dark shadow of change began to pass over the island, triggered by the growing **fur trade**. In 1683, William Dampier had commented on the abundance of the Juan Fernández fur seal:

'Seals swarm as thick about this island, as if they had no other place in the world to live in; for there is no Bay nor Rock that one can get ashore on, but is full of them...'

Little did Dampier realize the truth of his statement, for as an endemic species, the seals truly had no other place to live. They were essentially trapped, and brutally slaughtered: between 1797 and 1804 an estimated 3 million pelts were taken by North American vessels. By the end of the century they were considered extinct.

The archipelago's ambience was further injured by the establishment of a penal colony on Isla Robinson Crusoe. Though the idea was originally that of the Spanish, who exiled about 40 Chilean 'patriots' here after the 1814 'Disaster of Rancagua,' it was subsequently embraced by the founding fathers of the new republic. Not until 1877 was the settlement of San Juan Bautista permanently inhabited by civilians rather than felons and political prisoners.

Juan Fernández again stumbled into the spotlight during WWI, when the German cruiser *Dresden* was caught unawares by the English and sunk to the bottom of Bahía Cumberland. For the most part, however, the archipelago has remained wild, quiet and quite nearly forgotten in its isolation. The Chilean navy visits sporadically in order to provide Robinson Crusoe's 500 permanent residents with much-needed supplies, and aside from that the only people to visit the islands are biologists and conservation workers, a slow trickle of tourists, and the occasional international treasure-seeker.

ISLA R. CRUSOE,
CIRCA 1600

EASTER ISLAND

Prehistory

*'There is no other Polynesian is-
land whose past is so little known
as that of Easter Island.'*

-Alfred Metraux, *Ethnology of
Easter Island*

Easter Island is not only remote in a physical sense. It is also
remote in that its past has been summarily dislocated from the present,
lost in a confused tangle of
enigma, theory and myth. Despite
the abundant, almost overwhelming evidence, there exists no true authority and no
definitive version of the past. In the end, all
is speculation.

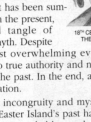

18TH CENTURY NATIVES, BY
THE ARTIST HODGES

The incongruity and mys-
tery of Easter Island's past has
led to a remarkable number
and array of theories, some
more credible than others.
Some theorists – it takes
all types – would have
us believe that the
island's great stone
monuments were cre-
ated by extraterrestrials,
while others imagine
that the island was
settled by refugees from
the lost continent of Mu.
Others, more highly per-
suasive, suggest that the
archaeological wonders
of Easter Island belong

RADIGUET'S ETCHING
OF 18TH CENTURY NATIVES

to the cultural tradition of the Andes, particularly that of the Tiawanaku and Tiwan-
tinsuyo (Inca) dynasties.

These theories to the contrary, most
scholars now agree that Easter Island was
populated from the west, by Polynesians. As
such, Easter Island culture may be considered the easternmost extension of an enormous Polynesian culture area stretching
across the entirety of the central and western Pacific. This theory is by no means new,
and has always been the most apparent, as
may be noted in the ever-astute Captain
James Cook's comments on the inhabitants
of Easter Island, which he visited in 1774:

*'In colour, features, and language they
bear such affinity to the people of the more
Western isles, that no one will doubt that they*

*have had the same origin. It is ex-
traordinary that the same nation
should have spread themselves over
all the isles in this vast ocean, from
New Zealand to this island, which is
almost one-fourth of the circumference of the globe.'*

Specifically, the first humans
to set foot on Easter Island are
thought to have arrived from
the Marquesas Islands, nearly
4,000km to the NW. Paddling
the sturdy seagoing canoes found
throughout Polynesia (though not
on Easter Island, where there are no trees of
appreciable size), they brought with them a
stock of plants and domestic animals from
their home island, among them sugarcane,
taro (a sort of tuber), plantains
and chickens. They were a stone
age society, with no use or
knowledge of metals or pottery, and they had arrived on
the world's most isolated
speck of land, which they
named *Te Pito o Te Henua*
– The Navel of the World.

From here, the his-
tory of the island re-
sides more in myth than in
any objective reconstruction.
Though Easter Island religion
has been entirely subsumed
by Christianity, the islanders'
oral history has survived
intact, and forms the basis for the modern
understanding of island chronology. Legends generally focus on three separate
events: the initial arrival of settlers led by
King Hotu Matu'a, the war between the
so-called **Long Ears** and **Short Ears** (ending in the death of the Long Ears), and the
more recent conflicts between the **Tuu** and
Hotu-iti clans.

As with many oral histories, each successive chapter appears in a number of different versions. Almost all, however, concur
in that the island was originally discovered
by a party of six men sent on a voyage of
discovery from an island known as Mare
Raenga. Katherine Routledge, who carried
out extensive interviews and excavations
during her visit to Easter Island in 1914, un-
earthed the following account of that voyage and the impetus behind it:

'Now there was on one of the islands a certain Haumaka, who had tattooed Hotu.... This man, Haumaka, had a dream, and during it his spirit went to a far country, and when he awoke he told six men, whose names are given, to go and seek for it; they were to look for a land where there were three islets and a big hole, also a long and beautiful road. So the six men went, each on a piece of wood, and they found the three islets, Moto Nui, Motu Iti, Motu Kao-Kao, and the big hole, which was the crater of Rano Kau. They landed on that part of the island and planted yams, and then walked around the island.'

Once scouted and planted with Polynesian crops, the island was ready for the arrival of Hotu Matu'a. With him the king brought his sister, Ava Reipua, along with a retinue of elders, priests, and warriors. This, according to orally recorded genealogies, was 57 generations of kings ago – or about 400 AD, the date commonly accepted for the initial settlement on the island. The myth also recounts how Hotu Matu'a divided the island among his sons, of whom the eldest, Atariki, was made Easter Island's second king. This initial division can be considered the basis of the territorial and patrolineal kinship groups that underlie Rapa Nui social structure.

THE TAPATAI RAPA NUI FESTIVAL

The next phase of Easter Island's discontinuous oral history, however, reflects a fundamental split in the structure established by Hotu Matu'a. Suddenly, the population appears divided into two groups, the 'Long Ears' (presumably a reference to the stretched earlobes noticed by early European visitors) and the 'Short Ears.' How did these two groups arise? And who is responsible for the construction of Easter Island's colossal stone monuments? Island lore gives the credit to the Long Ears, but it gives little clue as to their origin.

One explanation (that maintained by Thor Heyerdahl) is that the Long Ears arrived after the first settlers, but from the east – from the South American continent. Several native South American cultures are known to have undertaken lengthy oceangoing journeys on balsa rafts, reaching as far west as the Galapagos Islands, 1,000km off the coast of Ecuador. Such rafts could conceivably have reached Easter Island, borne onward by the constant easterly trade winds that blow all around the equator.

'While our own race still believed that the world ended at Gibraltar, there were other great navigators who knew better. In advance of their time, they plowed unknown seas in the immense watery void off the desolate west coast of South

FIRST CONTACTS WITH THE WEST, FROM THE ATLAS OF LAPEROUSE

America. Far out they found land. The loneliest little island in the world. They landed there, whetted their stone adzes, and set about one of the most remarkable engineering projects of ancient times. They did not build fortresses and castles, or dams and wharves. They made gigantic stone figures in man's likeness, as tall as houses and as heavy as boxcars, and they dragged them in great numbers across country and set them up erect on huge stone terraces all over the island.'

As attractive as Heyerdahl's theory may be – among other things, it provides an easy solution to the riddle of the *kumara* or sweet potato, a native South American plant that grew on the island before the arrival of the first European ships – it is not the most widely accepted. The presence of similar (if less impressive) monolithic carvings on the Marquesas and other western Pacific Islands, and the complete lack of concrete evidence (such as pottery shards) of a South American presence on the island, indicate that the monument builders of Easter Island were Polynesians.

MOAI HOA HAKA NANA,
BRITISH MUSEUM

In any case, the relatively peaceful and prosperous (if admittedly obsessive) constructive period of island history appears to have lasted over a thousand years, from about 700 AD to the late 1700's. During this time, some 245 **ahus** (ceremonial platforms) were erected along the coast, and a total of over 300 giant **moais** were carved from the Rano Raraku crater, transported across the island, and raised into a position of honor atop the ahus of each kinship group. By all appearances, artisans working for distinct kinship groups worked together peacefully in the quarries and collaborated in the labor-intensive transportation of the moai.

Such was the scene on Easter 1722, when Dutch mariner **Jacob Roggeveen** and his crew became the first Europeans to lay eyes on Rapa Nui. Though Roggeveen's account differs in

TOOLS USE IN THE
CARVING OF THE MOAIS

several fine points from that of crew member Carl Behrens, both suggest that *moai* worship was a central part of the islanders' religion.

The islanders were apparently unafraid of the ship and its crew. One man swam out and climbed aboard the ship; Roggeveen found him 'lively in mien, as well as pleasing in speech and gesture,' though he was appalled by this and other natives' propensity for theft. 'They were so daring,' he wrote in the ship's log, 'that they took the seamen's hats and caps from off their heads, and sprang overboard with the spoil.'

How many people inhabited the island at the time of Roggeveen's visit is impossible to determine. Roggeveen reported having seen 'a great number of natives,' but only two or three women. Behren apparently had a much different experience, reporting that the island women offered themselves freely to the sailors, a behavioral trait also observed in 1786 by French visitor La Perouse, who wrote that the women 'offered their favors to those who were willing to give them presents.'

The island was next visited by Europeans in 1770, this time by a Spanish expedition led by Don Felipe González de Haedo. Renaming it San Carlos, the expedition claimed the island in the name of the Spanish crown – a subtlety that was undoubtedly lost upon the islands' residents.

Captain James Cook dropped anchor briefly at Easter Island in 1774, during a three-year exploratory voyage intended to definitively affirm or deny the existence of a seventh continent over the South Pole. Though Cook himself only saw the area immediately surrounding Hanga Roa, he did send a small party to explore the island in hopes of restocking the expedition's supply of water, with dismal results:

'They saw not an animal of any sort, and but very few birds; nor indeed any

(1) Easter Island Archaeologists

THE MYSTERY OF EASTER ISLAND
Katherine Routledge

This rare book is back in print!

MYSTIC TRAVELLERS SERIES

The first serious archaeological excavations on Easter Island were those carried out by Englishwoman **Katherine Routledge (1)** in 1914. Routledge wrote a lively, entertaining narrative of the trip, The Mystery of Easter Island: the Story of an Expedition, but unfortunately the scientific data collected on the trip never made it to publication.

(2) Thor Heyerdahl's name remains synonymous with archaeological studies on the island, despite the fact that his theories postulating a South American origin for Easter Island stonework have gone out of vogue. Having already sailed halfway across the Pacific aboard the balsa raft Kon Tiki, Heyerdahl arrived in the island in 1955 at the head of an expedition sponsored by the king of Norway. The expedition spent the better part of

a year excavating at the base of the ahus, experimenting with methods of transporting and raising the moai, and eventually convincing the islanders to reveal the secret family caves whose existence had been concealed from island missionaries for nearly a century. Heyerdahl's Ahu Ahu and Reports of the Norwegian Archaeological Expedition to Easter Island and the East Pacific recount the expedition's findings.

William Mulloy (3), a North American archaeologist who first visited the island as part of the Heyerdahl expedition, later returned to the island and resumed excavations. Together with Chilean archaeologist **Gonzalo Figueroa**, Mulloy is responsible for the restoration of the Orongo ceremonial village and most of the other site restorations thus far realized on the island.

---

thing which can induce ships that are not in the utmost distress, to touch at this island.

'Here there is no safe anchorage; no wood or fuel; nor any fresh water worth taking on board. Nature has been exceedingly sparing of her favours to this spot.'

Cook and his party estimated the island's population at no more than six or seven hundred, of whom a full two-thirds appeared to be males:

'Tattowing, or puncturing the skin, is much used here. The men are marked from head to foot, with figures all nearly alike; only some give them one direction, and some another, as fancy leads... [they wear] nothing but a strip of cloth betwixt their legs, each end of which is fastened to a cord or belt they wear round the waist.'

Finally, though Cook commented favorably on the quality of Rapa Nui stonework, he did note – as visitors will today – that the ahus and moais appeared to belong to another age:

'[The ahus] are built, or rather faced, with hewn stones of a very large size; and the workmanship is not inferior to the best plain piece of masonry we have in England. They use no sort of cement; yet the joints are exceedingly close, and the stones mortised and tenanted one into another, in a very artful manner... yet had not all this care, pains, and sagacity, been able to preserve these curious structures from the ravages of all-devouring Time.'

In a word, construction had stopped. In the crater of Ranu Raraku, nearly 400 moais lay abandoned in varying stages of completion, surrounded by heaps of the basalt *tokis* that were used to sculpt them. Not only this, but something even more sinister was occurring, as Cook noted that several of the moais had been toppled from their ahus.

Moai Escoria Roja (Tahai)

Moai Ahu Vai (Tahai)

Moai Tuturi (Rano Raraku)

Warfare had broke out among the various kinship groups, the creative urge had been redirected towards the fabrication of obsidian weapons, and cannibalism had become an increasingly common practice among the warrior class that had superceded the islands' religious nobility.

What on earth had happened? Again, the initial clues reside in Rapa Nui's oral history, which tells of a horrible battle culminating in the near-genocide of the Long-ears. French ethnologist Alfred Metraux offers the following version of the story:

'The Long-ears said to the Short-ears: 'Come, let us carry stones to the seashore.' The Short-ears answered the Long-Ears: 'We do not want to carry away the stones on the ground, leave them for our food, for the [sweet potato] leaves, for the banana trees, for the sugar cane, to make them suffer and grow.' They left, they did not carry. They did not carry them away, they left them. They stayed. The Long-ears resented that the Short-ears did not help them in building the abu. They worked alone, because of that they were angry within at the Short-ears.

The Long-ears lived at Poike. They dug a long pit from Potu-te–rangi to Mahatua. When they finished digging that pit, they brought firewood, threw it down into the ditch, strewing the pit from one end to another.

A woman of the Short-ears had her house in Potu-te-rangi. The Short-ears did not know for whom the Long-ears were digging the pit and putting wood in it. The woman of the Short-ears of Potu-te-rangi had a husband of the Long-ears who told her: 'This pit that is being dug is for you, for the Short-ears.' Now that woman knew. She waited, at night, that woman of the Short-ears came and said to the people of the Short-ears: 'Look at my house, it is there you shall follow your path. Next day the Long-ears will light the oven for your corpses. When you get there, form yourselves into a line and tell everybody to join, to form a line, encircle the mountain of Poike. Commence killing, throw them in the pit, change the oven to your advantage, cook the Long-ears for yourselves.'

PICTOGRAPHS IN AN EASTER ISLAND CAVE

According to the legend, all but one of the Long Ears perished in the war, burned in the 'long pit' now known as **Iko's Trench**.

Modern researchers have offered a demographic and ecological explanation for the disintegration of Rapa Nui society. According to this theory, around the time of the first visits by Europeans, the island's population had begun to exceed its carrying capacity, resulting in an **ecological crisis**. Agriculture was already limited on the island by the scarcity of water, and excavations of pre-crisis garbage heaps indicate that pelagic fish such as bonito originally formed the bulk of the islanders' diet. But when the island's woody plants began to go extinct – as pollen samples taken from the marshy creaters suggest happpened right about the time of initial decay – the islanders were left without materials to construct the seagoing canoes they had used for centuries to fish the surrounding ocean. Most likely, the mythical battle between the Long Ears and the Short Ears was one of a protracted series of intertribal wars precipitated, in large part, by competition for resources.

Moai Ko Te Riku (Tahai)

Moai Ahu Tog / Moai Ahu Tongariki (hotu Iti)

Moai Paro (ahu Te Pito Kura)

Moai Rano Raraku (Terminal)

In any case, the age of construction was past, and one by one, the moai were pulled down from their platforms; by 1868, a visiting Russian doctor reported that not one remained standing. A new religion, known now as the **Birdman Cult**, began to dominate religious life on the island from its focal point in the ceremonial village of Orongo. And meanwhile, little by little, contact with the outside world became more continuous – with tragic results.

OCCIDENTAL CONTACT AND DECAY

In 1804, the American schooner *Nancy* visited Easter Island and kidnapped 12 men and 10 women, intending to take them to Isla Alejandro Selkirk, where they planned to set up a sealing station. Three days out to sea, they let the prisoners out onto the deck, and all of them immediately jumped overboard – intending, it may be presumed, to swim back to the island. After this, the islanders appear to have become rather hostile towards visiting ships, several of which were unable to land on the island at all.

Despite this increased vigilance, disaster struck in 1862, when the islanders were victimized by **slaving raids** of a much grander scale. A French prosecutor on the island of Papeete made the following observation of one raid, in which seven or eight ships participated:

'They spread themselves out while several members of the crew attracted the natives by showing them articles which excited their greed. When about 500 natives were gathered, the chief of the pirates gave the signal, which was a revolver shot. To this signal the men answered with a volley, and about ten natives fell never to rise again. The others, terrified, tried to

escape, running in all directions, some diving into the sea, others climbing the rocks; but about 200 were captured and firmly tied up. A witness says the captain of the Cora, Aiguirre, discovered two Indians in a cave trying to escape. As he could not convince them to come with him, he cruelly killed them. The 200 kidnapped natives were divided among the ships, which sailed some days later.'

All told, about a thousand islanders were taken to work the hideous guano mines in the Chincha Islands, off the coast of Perú – among them the island's king and the only remaining elders who could decipher the 'hieroglyphic' *rongo rongo* tablets. When the Bishop of Tahiti repeatedly complained to Peruvian authorities, the hundred-odd islanders who had survived the mines were shipped back to Rapa Nui, though only about 15 made it back alive; these, in turn, infected the remaining population with smallpox. The population of the island, which may have been as great as 10,000 at its peak, plummeted to no more than a couple of hundred individuals. As one 1867 visitor wrote, 'the mortality caused by misery and famine is increasing rapidly. The plantations have been plundered and they give scarcely any sweet potatoes, which these unhappy people eat half raw...'

Now intervention by Europeans was swift and intense. French Catholic Eugene Eyraud, having been once expelled from the island by its unhappy residents, returned in 1866 and proceeded with the business of conversion. Then in 1870, Frenchman **Jean Baptiste Dutroux-Bornier** purchased the island 'for a few bits of cloth,' imported a handful of sheep, established a compound at Mataveri, and began to wage an open war on the missionaries. A portion of the islanders

THE ANGAMOS, USED BY POLICARPO TORO IN HIS 1888 ANNEXATION THE ISLAND

(including, apparently, those of the Bird-man cult), sided with the French maniac, and the raids (and even shelling) continued until the missionaries finally evacuated. According to Metraux, all but 175 of the islanders eventually agreed to leave the island, and were shipped to a plantation in Tahiti.

The remaining islanders finally killed Dutroux in 1877, but freedom was short lived. Eleven years later, in 1888, Easter Island was annexed by the Chilean navy, and shortly thereafter fell under control of a sheep ranch owned by Scottish-owned **Williamson, Balfour and Company**. Their Compañia Explotadora de Isla de Pascua (Cedip) leased very nearly the entire island from the Chilean government, while the islanders remained confined to the village of Hanga Roa. As Alfred Metraux noted in 1940:

MAHUTE, TRADITIONAL DESIGNS PAINTED ON BARK

'The Williamson and Balfour Co. is the only real link the natives have with western civilization. It gives them work and the opportunity to buy the European articles and food they need... shearing is their only means of making money to acquire necessary goods.... Numerous conflicts have arisen between the natives and the company.... The most serious conflict occurred in 1914; the natives, encouraged by an old woman named Angata, killed a great many animals and claimed possession of the cattle and the land.'

In 1953, the Chilean government finally revoked the company's lease and placed the island under the control of the military. Only in the last quarter century have significant steps been taken to improve the lives of the islanders, but today education and social services are on a par with the rest of Chile, and an increasing amount of control has been ceded to the local government. As a major stopover point on flights from Tahiti to Santiago, the island is now connected to the rest of the world, and tourism has far overtaken ranching as the big winner in the local economy. In some islanders' eyes, however, the fact that the vast majority of the island has been declared a National Park and Unesco World Biosphere Reserve is simply another example of how the people of Rapa Nui continue to be denied self-determination and control of their island. Negotiations continue regarding the eventual transfer of National Park lands to island natives.

Regardless of who owns the land, however, the survival of Rapa Nui culture now seems assured (at least for the coming years), and Easter Island will always retain every ounce of its mysterious appeal. As researcher Katherine Routledge wrote in 1919:

'In Easter Island the past is the present, it is impossible to escape from it; the inhabitants of today are less real than the men who have gone; the shadows of the departed builders still possess the land.'

MIRADOR DE ORONGO, EASTER ISLAND

THE JUAN FERNANDEZ ARCHIPELAGO

GETTING TO THE ISLAND

Boat service to the island is sporadic and unreliable. A single private carrier, Naviera del Sur, is almost invariably booked by island residents, who are given priority. The Armada de Chile (Navy) has been known to carry tourists and islanders on the irregular provisioning ships that visit the island, but scheduling information is almost to come by, though you can try to obtain details before hand from the Armada in Valpraíso ☎ (32)252094, the trip typically lasts 36 hours; with bunk lodging and all meals the cost is about $24,000 p/p.

● Three *airlines* provide regular service to the island from Santiago. The flight, in 6-10 person prop-driven planes, lasts about 2-2.5 hrs and costs about $200,000, including boat transfers from the airport to San Juan Bautista.

● LASSA, Av. Larraín 7941 (in Aeródromo Tobalaba), ☎ (2)2735209, Fax (2)2734309. On demand from Oct-Apr, with daily departures in Jan and Feb. LASSA also runs the upscale Hostería Pangal.

● Servicio Aéreo Ejecutivo S.A.E., Apoquindo 7850, torre 3, local 4, ☎ (2)5314343, Fax (2)2293419. Regular departures Tue and Fri, and by demand.

● Transportes Aéreos Isla Robinson Crusoe 2-3 weekly departures or by demand from Apr-Oct. Daily departures Dec-Feb.

JUAN FERNÁNDEZ OPERATORS

ENDEMICA EXPEDICIONES offers scuba diving, trekking, horseback riding, and motorboat and sea kayak rental. LASSA offers similar services as part of their package tours including the flight from the mainland and lodging at El Pangal.

San Juan Bautista   Pop. 600 (☎ city code 32)

San Juan Bautista, the only settlement in the archipelago, is a tiny little fishing village on the west side of the Bahía Cumberland. There's not much to it: its streets are dirt, its buildings a ramshackle collection of wooden houses, and its inhabitants mellow and rather reticent. San Juan Bautista gives new meaning to the word relaxed.

Most of the families in the town live from lobster fishing. Each fine morning, the 40-odd boats anchored off the *muelle* motor out of the harbor, returning in the afternoon with their daily catch of *langosta*, which despite their professed abundance, don't come

particularly cheap. In winter, cod (*bacalao*) fishing provides supplementary income for some fishermen.

Behind the first couple rows of houses the hills rear up steeply, and the winding streets give way to narrow, slippery paths. Though there are basic services and a couple of interesting sights in the town, most visitors will soon feel the need to get out and explore. Most of the major trails are marked by Conaf, which manages every inch of the archipelago outside of San Juan Bautista. The best nearby place to swim is at El Palillo, at the south end of town.

TOURIST OFFICES
Information available at the Municipalidad, ☎ 701075, Fax 751047.
Conaf, Sendero El Pangal 130, ☎ 751022.

HOSPITAL
South of town near the Conaf office.

TRANSPORT
Transport to and from the airstrip is provided by the motor launch *Blanca Luz,* US$15, usually included in airfare; reservations at the Municipalidad. Boats are also available at the **Sindicato de Pescadores** (Fisherman's co-op).

TELEPHONE AND POST OFFICE
Next to the Municipalidad.

ACCOMODATION
1 **Residencial Villa Green $$,** Larraín Alcalde 246, ☎ 751044.
2 **Hostería Daniel Defoe $$,** Larraín Alcalde 449, ☎ 751075.
3 **Hostal Charpentier $$,** Ignacio Carrera Pinto 256, ☎ 751010.
4 **Hostería El Pangal, $$,** Caleta El Pangal, 3km south of San Juan Bautista by trail, or by motor launch from the muelle, ☎ (2)2734354.

CAMPING
Free camping in Plazoleta El Yunque and at Camping Lord Anson, near the Conaf office.

SPECIAL EVENTS
June 29, Fiesta de San Pedro.
Nov 22, Día de la Isla.

In-town Attractions

Cemetery and Lighthouse San Juan Bautista's cemetery is located near the shore at the north end of the village. Note the gravestones of the soldiers who perished on the German warship *Dresden*, which lies offshore at the bottom of Bahía Cumberland. Just past the cemetery is the lighthouse, from which point you can continue along the shore to the seacliffs of Punta San Carlos.

Fuerte Santa Bárbara Almost directly above the plaza, accessed via Subida Lo Castillo, this Spanish fort was built in 1749 to defend against marauding British privateers. Reconstructed in 1974, the fort contains seven 18th-century canyons.

Cueva de los Patriotas Just south of the Fuerte Santa Bárbara, this group of seven caves provided dank and embittered refuge to the forty-two revolutionary Chilean 'Patriots' exiled on the island after their defeat in the Disaster of Rancagua.

Around San Juan Bautista

The rugged, mountainous topography of Isla Robinson Crusoe has prohibited the building of roads anywhere outside San Juan Bautista, so if you want to see the rest of the island, you'll either have to walk or (in some cases) take a boat. Most of the trails on the island are steep and often quite slippery, so a moderate level of fitness and coordination is required. Most of the routes below may also be done on horseback.

● **Mirador de Selkirk**
During his four-year exile on the island, Alexander Selkirk climbed each day to this 550m overlook to scan the horizon for ships. The steep, 3km ascent from town takes about 90min, beginning at the uphill end of the Subida El Castillo and takes about 90 minutes, and on clear days rewards visitors with views across the entire island; in the distance to the west (train your eyes just right of Cerro Tres Puntas) you might be able to make out Isla Alejandro Selkirk. There are two commemorative plaques on the site, one left by officers of the HMS Topaze in 1868, the other left in 1983 by one of Selkirk's Scottish descendents.

EXPLORING THE ISLAND ON HORSEBACK

The trail continues west from the Mirador to the VALLE DE VILLAGRA, an agreeable camping spot (but without water); down the hill to the west there are some rocky pools ideal for swimming, known as LOS RAMPLONES. From here, a further 10km walk leads past the summit of CERRO TRES PUNTAS and the desolate-looking BAHÍA TIERRAS BLANCAS en route to the airport; all told, the hike takes about 6-7hrs. You can also continue on from the airport to PLAYA EL ARENAL, another good camping spot.

● Plazoleta El Yunque & El Camote

Also about 3km from the village, accessed via the continuation of Calle El Yunque, the Plazoleta El Yunque is a grassy clearing near the base of Cerro El Yunque, the island's tallest peak. The ruins on the site are from a homestead established by Hugo Weber, a survivor of the *Dresden* who lived in this spot for twelve years. Camping is free and there are picnic tables on the site. Fit hikers can consult with Conaf for information on the unmaintained trail to EL CAMOTE.

● Puerto Inglés

Located on the north shore of the island a 20-minute boat ride from San Juan Bautista, Puerto Inglés' principal attraction is a replica of the hut Selkirk lived in during his time on the island. There's also a beach and a campsite with nearby water, and a cave (La Cueva del Escorpión) long thought to contain the lost treasure of Spanish navigator Juan Ubilla y Echeverria. You can also get to Puerto Inglés via a steep, rugged 2-hour trail accessed from the top of Calle La Pólvora.

● Puerto Francés

Located near the east end of the island, a 15-minute boat ride from San Juan Bautista, Puerto Francés is the starting point of a nice day hike in Sector REBAJE DE LA PIÑA. The trail leads up through endemic *luma* forest to a mountain pass with spectacular views of the rugged southern coast of the island. It is also possible to walk back to town along the coast, passing over the summit of 362m CERRO CENTINELA, which provides panoramic views of Bahía Cumberland and San Juan Bautista. You can also climb Cerro Centinela directly from El Pangal.

● Isla Alejandro Selkirk *(Más Afuera)*

180km west of Isla Robinson Crusoe, Isla Alejandro Selkirk is so impossibly steep, rugged and remote that to this day it remains almost entirely uninhabited. Though tourists occasionally succeed in reaching the island with the help of locals, there exist no regular services or planned excursions to Alejandro Selkirk. Lobsterman from San Juan Bautista set up temporary encampments on the island during the summer fishing season.

DIVING IN THE JUAN FERNÁNDEZ ARCHIPELAGO

● El Cernícalo

Located in Bahía Tres Puntas on the north shore of the island, this is considered one of the best dive sites on the island, with a great variety of anemones, endemic black corals, and schools of amberjacks and pompanos. Average depth 25m.

● Quebrada Salsipuedes

This site NW of Bahía Cumberland is home to abundant actinia colonies and schools of jurel, pompanos and soldier fish. Other notable species include eels, Juan Fernández urchins, gobioids and scorpion fish. Depth 18m.

● El Adriático

Near Pangal, this easily accessible, relatively shallow (15m) area is a popular destination for night dives.

● La Lobera

Located in the arid western sector of the island near the airport (2hrs by boat from San Juan Bautista), Bahía Tierras Blancas is home to the island's only breeding colony of Juan Fernández Fur Seal. The seals are playful and unafraid, and will readily approach snorkelers.

● The *Dresden*

Sunk at a depth of 60m, this 118m German battleship may be visited by experienced deep-water divers only.

EASTER ISLAND

GETTING TO EASTER ISLAND

LanChile ☎ (2) 5262000 is the only airline offering service to Easter Island, with three flights a week from Santiago, continuing on to Tahiti and returning via the same route. Book well in advance for flights during the February peak season.

EASTER ISLAND OPERATORS

Chilean mainland operators offering all-inclusive packages to Easter Island include the following:
Operator: 10 - 31 - 49 - 164 - 192

Locally-owned operators include:
Operator: 4 - 5 - 19 - 126 - 129 - 150 - 160 - 177

Island dive centers:
Operator: 54 - 56

EXPLORING THE ISLAND ON FOOT, HORSEBACK, OR BY BIKE

Bikes are available for rent at a number of locales on Policarpo Toro. Prices area bout US$15 day. Many residenciales and private individuals rent horses, though quality varies widely. Consult in Sernatur for recommendations. Prices range from US$30-60 day.

As there is no 'public transport' per se on Easter Island, all visitors will have to decide what mode of transport they will use to explore the island. Though most visitors either rent vehicles or are shuttled about the island on group tours, motorized transport is not really necessary. Walking or riding a horse or mountain bike will not only provide you with exercise, but will also allow you to access sites not visited by most tourists. Remember that there is no potable surface water anywhere on the island, so you'll have to carry it with you.

The ceremonial village of **ORONGO** is among the island's easiest sites to visit on foot. The walk from Hanga Roa to Orongo takes about an hour, and you could easily make the round trip in half a day, though a full day will allow you explore the interior of the giant crater and even visit Ahu Vinapu, which lies about a 1.5hr walk (one way) south of town. **AHU TAHAI** and the **MUSEO ANTROPOLÓGICO** are also easy sites to visit on foot, lying about half an hour north of town.

In order to visit the sites north of Tahai, however, you might consider renting a horse or a bike. On foot, it's about a 3-4 hour walk north from Hanga Roa to **AHU TEPEU**, where the road ends. From here, you could continue up to the top of 652m **VOLCÁN TEREVAKA** (2hrs round trip) or continue along the coast to **ANAKENA** (4-5hrs), where you could camp or arrange transport back to town. The loop including Ahu Tepeu, **AHU AKIVI**, and the **PUNA PAO** crater would take about 7-8hrs round trip on foot.

The sites along the south coast are even more spread out, and there are more of them, so walking is not really recommended. If you were set on walking, you could get to **RANO RARAKU** from Hanga Roa in about 5-6hrs, not including visits to any of the archaeological sites.

Finally, the uninhabited, roadless **POIKE PENINSULA** makes a good destination for visitors looking for solitude. Though the archaeological sites on the peninsula are difficult to find on your own, you're unlikely to see another person.

AHU IN EASTER ISLAND

DIVING ON EASTER ISLAND

● Motu Kao Kao, Motu Iti, Motu Nui

These three islets off the western of the island feature some of the most dramatic underwater topography on the island. The towering Motu Kao Kao seastack, which rises over 180m above the seafloor, is probably the island's most-visited dive site. Calm conditions are essential for diving in this area.

● Motu Tuatara

This offshore stack north of Hanga Roa features a variety of interesting formations, including volcanic caverns and a underwater arch.

● Hanga Roa

The sandy, relative shallow and protected waters of Bahía Hanga Roa favor the development of large corals – ask operators to help you find an especially large example of *Porites lobata* known as *kare nui nui.*

● Tepeu

The main attraction here is 'La Pirámide,' a towering mountain of volcanic rock covered in coral and frequented by schools of tropical fish. North of here, the shallows at Omohi also attract an abundance of schooling fish.

● Ovahe, Anakena

Easter Island's only two beaches are ideal for snorkeling during the summer months. Further east, Bahía La Perouse is noted for its abundant coral formations.

EASTER ISLAND'S SURF BREAKS

● The North Coast

Easter Island's north coast typically works with waist – to head-high swell out of the NW. The most popular breaks are at Tahai, Matu Hava, and in Hanga Roa Bay. There are also breaks further east at Anakena and Ovahe.

● The South Coast

The south coast is the opposite, and needs big swell out of the south to go off. You'll find good lefts at Mata Veri Otai and Huevara, and good rights at Papa Tanga Roa and Akakanga. The latter wave works up to 18'.

Hanga Roa

Pop. 3000 (☎ city code 32)

Hanga Roa, Easter Island's only town, is a sprawling Polynesian/Chilean village in the southwest corner of the island. Nearly everyone on the island lives here, and the vast ma-jority of its inhabitants make their living either directly or indirectly from tourism; the town is packed with restaurants, hotels and family-run *pensiones*. Most of the action in town is centered around

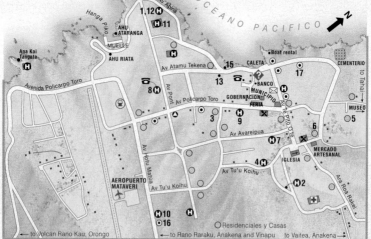

TOURIST OFFICES
Sernatur, across from the caleta,
☎ *223255.*
Conaf, Atamu Tekena s/n, ☎ *223236.*

BANKS AND MONEY CHANGERS
*Travellers' checks changed at the
Banco del Estado (poor rates) and
at the gas station on Hotu Matu'a.*

HOSPITALS AND MEDICAL SERVICES
East of the church,
☎ *100215, 100217.*

POST OFFICE
*Av. Te Pito O Te Henua, near
the caleta.*

TELEPHONE
Entel, across from the bank.

INTERNET CONNECTION
*Pacific Images, on Te Pito o Te
Henua across from the soccer field.*

ACCOMODATION
1 *Res Ana Rapu $, Av. Apina s/n,*
☎ *100540.*
2 *Res Martin y Anita $$, Simón Paoa
s/n,* ☎ *100593.*

3 *Res Pedro Atan $$, Av. Policarpo Toro
s/n,* ☎ *100329.*
4 *Res Sofia Gomero $$, Tu'u Koihu s/
n,* ☎ *100313.*
5 *Res. Tahai $$, Tahai-Pasaje Reimiro
s/n,* ☎ *100395.*
6 *Hotel Poike $$, Petero Atamu s/n,*
☎ *100286.*
7 *Hotel Chez Joseph $$, Av. Avareipua
s/n,* ☎ *100281.*
8 *Hotel Victoria $$$, Av. Pont s/n,*
☎ *100272.*
9 *Orongo Easter Hotel $$$, Av.
Policarpo Toro s/n,* ☎ *100294.*
10 *Hotel Manutara $$$, Av. Hotu
Matua s/n,* ☎ *100297.*
11 *Hotel Hanga Roa $$$, Av. Pont s/n,*
☎ *100299.*

CAMPING
12 *Residencial Ana Rapu, Av. Apina.
Camping at Conaf
ranger stations at Anakena
and Rano Raraku.*

RESTAURANTS
13 *Ki Tai, Av. Atamu Tekena s/n.
Beachside, good value.*

14 *La Taverne du Pecheur, in
the caleta. French-owned,
regular service.*
15 *Pea, Av. Atamu Tekena con Tu'u
Maheke. Renowned for fresh
tuna empanadas.*

DISCOTHEQUES
16 *Piriti, Av. Hotu Matu'a s/n.*
17 *Toroko, Atamu Tekena s/n.*

TRANSPORT
*While there is no public transport
per se on the island, countless
tour agencies and residenciales
offer tours, and about ten different
agencies rent jeeps (US$50/day)
and motorcycles (US$35/day).*

SPECIAL EVENTS
Tapatai Rapa Nui, 1st two weeks in Feb.

SHOPPING
*Handicraft market at
Aeropuerto Mataveri.
Street market Tues and Sat on
Policarpo Toro.
Hotu Matu'a's Favorite Shoppe,
Policarpo Toro s/n, for carvings.*

the waterfront (particularly the *caleta pescadores*) and the town's few paved streets, but some hotels are quite far off. Though most streets do have names, there are no street signs, and most people give directions by referring to well-known landmarks such as the *caleta*, the *municipalidad*, the church or the airport. There is another *caleta*, Hanga Piko, south of town.

Overlooking Caleta Hanga Roa is AHU TAUTIRA, a small ahu with two broken moai. Also worth a visit is Hanga Roa's small stone church, at the east end of Av. Te Pito O Te Henua. Inside the church are a number of interesting wooden carvings clearly illustrating the convergence of Catholicism and Rapa Nui culture, and during Sunday mass hymns are sung in the Rapa Nui language. Most locals of Rapa Nui ancestry speak *pascuense* at home.

Entrance to Parque Nacional Rapa Nui, which includes almost the entire perimeter of the island and all the archaeological sites, costs *$4000 pp.*

North of Hanga Roa

Ahu Tahai
A ten-minute walk north of Hanga Roa, this site was partially restored in 1968 by a team under the direction of American archaeologist William Mulloy. The first ahu, VAI URI, features five resurrected moai; at its base is a ceremonial plaza containing the remains of several *hare paenga*. The middle ahu is Tahai itself, with one moai without its topknot. The third, AHU KO TE RIKU, features one moai with an intact topknot. Just north is KIO'E, where there are two more ahus, each with one erect moai.

Museo Antropológico Sebastián Englert
Just north of Ahu Tahai, Easter Island's only museum is focused more on the ethnology of the Rapa Nui culture than upon archaeology. Especially noteworthy is the collection of early twentieth century photographs.
Hours: Tue-Sat 0930-1230, 1400-1730, Sat-Sun 0930-1230.
Entrance: $1000

MOAIS

Ahu Akapu

A lone ahu with one standing moai, north along the coast from Tahai.

Caverna dos Ventanas

About 3km north of Ahu Tahai are two offshore islets, **Motu ko Hepko** and **Motu Tautara**. Hidden in the cliff face directly opposite these islands (look for a cairn indicating the trail from above) is the entrance to a dark tunnel leading to a large, well-lit cave. Bring a flashlight.

Ahu Tepeu

Tepeu is a large, well-built ahu without any standing moai. To the northeast is a ceremonial plaza with several *hare paenga*. Road access north along the coast ends here, but in a long day you can walk along the coast to Anakena, circling Volcán Terevaka. There are a number of interesting ahus and petroglyph sites along the route, most notably at **Omohe** and **Ana Nga Heu**. Since there is no road access, this is one of the least-visited sections of the island.

Cueva de Te Pahu

South of Tepeu along the inland track, you'll see a conspicuous grove of greenery indicating the entrance to a large underground chamber. Like other such caves, this one has been transformed into a cool, protected Polynesian garden known as a *manavai*. From here you can walk down a 150-meter long lava tube tunnel to another *manavai*.

Ahu Akivi

This restored ahu with its seven standing moai appears to have been oriented astronomically. Like Tahai, it was restored by Mulloy in 1960.

Puna Pau

This small crater east of Hanga Roa was the island's topknot quarry. About 60 topknots, weighing up to 11 tons, were hewn from the soft red scoria of the crater and rolled across the island to be mounted atop standing moai. Twenty-five finished and unfinished *pukao* remain in the crater; many have petroglyphs carved on them.

South of Hanga Roa

Ana Kai Tangata

Half an hour's walk south along the coast from Hanga Roa is this large sea-cliff cave with red and white birds painted on the ceiling.

Orongo Ceremonial Village

Perched on the western rim of the Rano Kau crater, the Orongo Ceremonial Village was the ritual center of the Manutara or Birdman cult, thought to have arisen during the period of cultural decay and intertribal warfare following the extermination of the Long-ears. The ruins' position is overwhelming, with the immense crater (1.6km in diameter) on one side and towering coastal escarpments on the other; from here, the views over the ocean and the island are so expansive that the curvature of the earth is clearly perceptible.

Offshore are three islets, Motu Kau Kau, Motu Iti, and Motu Nui. The largest of the three, **Motu Nui** appears to have been used for the ritual seclusion of young initiates into the priesthood or other prestigious castes during the island's moai-building era. With the ascendance of the Birdman cult, however, Motu Nui assumed a new significance, as competitors annually besieged the islet in a quest to find the first egg of the manutara or Sooty tern, which formally nested there; the winner (or more likely his sponsor) became that year's birdman or

Tangata Manu. William Mulloy, who reconstructed about 50 of the ritual habitations here, described the birdman ceremony as follows:

'Departing at a signal, the contestants descended the cliffs by practicable routes and swam through shark-infested waters to the islet, sometimes with the assistance of elongate bundles of totora reeds called pora. They waited on the islet, sometimes for a number of days, until one contestant succeeded in obtaining an egg. He then called the name of his sponsor from the islet to a man awaiting the information in a cave in the cliff side below Orongo. Upon receiving the news, the sponsor had his head, eyebrows, and eyelashes shaved and his face painted red and black. He then descended to Mataveri in a procession by an established path and thence was conducted to the southwestern, exterior slope of the statue quarry volcano called Rano Raraku, where he remained in seclusion in a special house (hare paenga).....

'His isolation suggests that he was thought of as having considerable, perhaps dangerous, supernatural powers. One thing that, for obscure reasons, seems to have been associated with the investiture of a new bird-man, at least in historic times, was the apparent right of his kin to raid and plunder other groups....'

The existing structures at Orongo all face south and are constructed of flat basalt slabs. Rocks and statues around the site are carved with thousands of petroglyphs, most of them depicting images of Tangata Manu, Make Make (the creator god), and *komari* (vulva or fertility images). There is another concentration of petroglyphs at **VAI ATARE**, on the east side of the crater, but they are difficult to find without a guide.

Allow half a day to visit Orongo on foot from Hanga Roa. If you have more time to spend, you can walk down into the crater, which is filled with a large lake filled with totora reeds. Alternately, you can walk around to the south side of the crater rim (known as **KARIKARI**) where there is a steep path leading down to the shore. Adventurous souls may be able to arrange boat transport from Hanga Roa out to Motu Nui, where there are large caves decorated with painted Make Make faces and birdman images; an eight-passenger boat should cost around US$100.

Orito

Northeast of the airport, this small volcanic crater was prized by islanders for its hard black obsidian (volcanic glass), which was fashioned into a variety of weapons and utilitarian objects. The most notorious of these were the *mata'a* spearheads that began to proliferate in the late 1700's, as intertribal warfare raged across the island.

Ahu Vinapu

Located on the south coast near the end of the airport runway, this site features two ahus without any standing moai. Vinapu I has the island's finest stonework, and it is easy to see why Heyerdahl found its finely fitted masonry reminiscent of that of the Incas. He reckoned that it dated from the earliest period of construction on the island, and that the vastly inferior stonework of Vinapu II reflected a subsequent decline in building techniques. However, more recent carbon dating has indicated that Vinapu I is actually of more recent construction than Vinapu II, suggesting that these masonry techniques were developed on the island and not, as Heyerdahl argued, imported from South America. Also on the site is an atypical red stone moai with short legs, one of only two on the island displaying carved features below the waist.

The South Coast

Ahu Vaihu and Akahanga

These two large ahus (neither has any standing moai) are the first major sites you'll pass on your way east along the coastal road from Hanga Roa. Akahanga is the more interesting of the two, with several separate platforms and some petroglyphs carved into the facade of the main ahu. Legend has it that Hotu Matu'a is buried near here.

Ahu Hanga Tetenga

At the foot of this nearly demolished ahu lie two large moai, one of which is thought to be the largest ever moved.

Rano Raraku

Rano Raraku, the crater from which the moai were carved (also known as 'the nursery'), is unquestionably the island's most impressive site. Together with Tongariki (see 📖), it merits a full days' visit.

From the southern coast, a dirt track (the *camino del moai*) leads up the south slopes of the volcano, past dozens of finished moai abandoned while in the process of transport to their respective ahus. Above, the volcanic tuff of the upper slopes contains countless others in varying stages of completion. A trail leads up from the parking area to 'el Gigante,' the largest moai on the island, measuring over 20m in length. Further up is another giant statue left in the 'keel' stage, connected to the bedrock by a narrow spine of rock.

In the interior of the crater are another 20 statues or so, bringing the total at Rano Raraku to over 300 finished and unfinished moai. From the rim you can also check out the small, reedy lagoon in the center of the crater (the view from here is especially worthwhile at sunset). Finally, be sure to check out the anomalous kneeling statue known as the **Tuturi**, discovered by the Heyerdahl expedition.

Conaf runs a campground near the Rano Raraku ranger station.

Ahu Tongariki

Set just east of the towering cliffs of Rano Raraku, Tongariki is the largest and most impressive ahu on Easter Island. Almost completely destroyed by a 1960 tsunami (triggered by an earthquake that devastated southern Chile), the site has been completely restored, and today there are fifteen well-preserved moai atop the 200-meter long platform. Near the road is a solitary upright moai with a goatee.

Península Poike

At the extreme eastern end of the island is the roadless Península Poike, renowned in island myth as the final refuge of the Long-ears. This is one of the remotest parts of the island, and sees relatively few visitors.

Dividing the peninsula from the rest of the island is **Iko's Trench**, which the Long-ears are supposed to have dug and filled with wood as a last measure of defense against their enemies. Though researchers have found deep layers of ash and what appears to be evidence of intentional enlargement of this natural cleft, opinion remains divided regarding its actual origin and history.

Beyond the trench, at the far end of the peninsula, are a couple of interesting sites that are nearly impossible to find without a guide. These include the petroglyphs at **Papa ui hutu'u** and a secret cave known as **Ana o Keke**, in which young virgins were supposedly sequestered from the sun in order to bleach their sun. Ana o Keke may only be accessed via a dangerous scramble down the unstable coastal cliffs, and should not be attempted even if you can find a guide to take you there.

The Northeast Coast

Anakena

Easter Island's largest beach, Playa Anakena, is known in island lore as the landing place of king Hotu Matu'a. There is a pleasant grove of coconut palms here and a campsite run by Conaf, but you need to bring all supplies, including water. Nearby is one of the largest *hare paenga* on the island.

There are two restored ahus on the hillsides above the beach. **Ahu Ature Huki** features one moai, raised by islanders under the encouragement of Thor Heyerdahl. **Ahu Nau Nau** has seven erect moai in varying states of repair, four of them with topknots in place. Many have petroglyphs carved on their backs, and there are further carvings on the outer wall of the ahu.

Ovahe

Just east of Anakena, this idyllic pink sand beach gets its best sun during the morning hours. It is both more protected and less crowded than Playa Anakena, and there are caves to explore in the cliffs above the beach.

Ahu Te Pito Te Kura

East of Anakena on the hill overlooking the Bahía La Perouse, this ahu is best known for having once supported the largest moai ever erected. The 9.9-meter giant (known as **Paro**) and its topknot lie next to the ahu. The ahu's name derives from a round boulder down near the water that was supposedly brought to the island by Hotu Matu'a. Further east are **Ahu Ra'ai** (where there are some excellent petroglyphs) and **Ahu Hekii**.

Antarctica

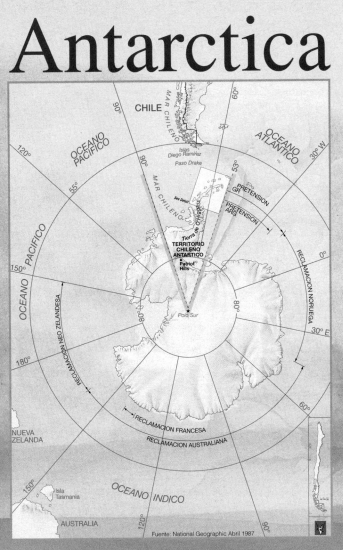

Fuente: National Geographic Abril 1987

Owned by no one and claimed by many, Antarctica is a frontier in every sense of the word. It is at once the most unusual of the seven continents, the last and least explored, the most hostile to human life, and perhaps most important to the future health of our planet. For travelers who feel they've seen it all, Antarctica stands alone – no other destination can compare. And for a human race that claims to know it all, the way we deal with Antarctica may be our greatest test of maturity yet.

ANTARCTICA

GEOGRAPHY AND TOPOGRAPHY

Antarctica has not always been the 'frozen continent.' Twice the size of Australia, the Antarctic landmass originally formed part of the Gondwana supercontinent, and was finally separated from the South American continent about twenty million years ago by the formation of the **DRAKE PASSAGE**, which connects the Atlantic and Pacific Oceans. Fossil remains of animals and plants that once lived on Antarctica (including now-extinct species of the genus *Araucaria*) attest to a warmer past, while evidence of Antarctic carbon deposits awakens the hopes of the world's petroleum multinationals.

With the migration of the continent to its current position, life on Antarctica changed. With the exception of the **ANTARCTIC PENINSULA**, the continent now lies entirely within the Antarctic circle, an imaginary line marking the furthest distance from the pole at which the sun does not rise above the horizon on the winter solstice (around June 21) or set on the summer solstice (around Dec. 21). South of the circle, the solar regimen becomes gradually more extreme, reaching its climax at the south pole, which experiences six months of unbroken solar daylight and six months of frigid winter night.

Covered by mass of ice up to four and half kilometers thick, Antarctica has an average elevation three times higher than any other on earth. Beneath the ice, its landmass may be divided into two regions: **EASTERN** or **GREATER ANTARCTICA**, which lies almost entirely above sea level, and **WESTERN** or **LESSER ANTARCTICA**, which if revealed would appear as an island archipelago. Antarctica's two major mountain ranges are the **ELLSWORTH RANGE** (which includes the 4,897m Vinson Massif, the continent's highest peak) and the **TRANSANTARCTIC RANGE**, which extends from the Antarctic Peninsula nearly 4,000km across the South Pole to the Ross Sea, and may be considered a southern extension of the Andes. Most scientific research stations are located on the Antarctic Peninsula and the **SOUTH SHETLAND** and **SOUTH ORKNEY** Islands.

Antarctica contains over 90% of the world's ice and 70% of global freshwater reserves. Pressing down mightily upon the continental landmass, this mass of ice forms immense *ice sheets* that flow slowly from the center of the continent (or *accumulation zone*) towards its edges (the *ablation zone*). Flowing through the ice sheets are faster-moving glaciers known as *ice streams*. When ice streams reach the end of the continent, they continue out over the surface of the ocean, forming floating *ice shelves*. These ice shelves currently cover 50% of the Antarctic coast, and make up over 10% of the continent's total area. In the past few years, however, many of these ice shelves have been melting at an alarming rate, and according to researchers, most of the major ice shelves on the Antarctic Peninsula have already reached a 'point of no return.' Though the melting of the ice shelves does not effect sea level, the effects of this melting on Antarctic ecosystems and global climate has yet to be determined.

Around the periphery of the Antarctic landmass, vast expanses of the Southern Ocean are covered by frozen seawater known as *pack* or *marine ice*. The area covered by pack ice varies from a low of three million square kilometers in March, the end of the austral summer, to a maximum of nearly twenty million square kilometers in September.

CLIMATE AND ECOLOGY

Antarctica is the coldest, the windiest, and the driest of the earth's continents. During the austral winter, temperatures in the interior average between -40° and -70°C (the world record for lowest recorded temperature, -89.6°C, was set here). Temperatures on the Antarctic Peninsula are much milder, averaging from -15° to -35°C in winter. During the summer, despite the long days, the extremely low angle of incidence and the reflective effect of the ice minimizes the warming effect. Summer temperatures average between -15° and -35°C in the interior, 0°C along the Peninsula.

The circulation and convergence of air and water around Antarctica have important effects on global climate and ocean circulation patterns. Throughout the year, both air and water move from west to east around the continent, causing the cold, carbon dioxide rich waters of the Southern Ocean to mix with the warmer waters of the Indian, Atlantic, and Pacific Oceans. In a similar fashion, frigid masses of air over the South Pole condense, drop to earth, and flow outwards (as a liquid might) towards the perimeter of the continent; known as *katabatic winds*, these powerful (up to 200 mph) and long-lasting winds are unique to Antarctica. Fog and snowstorms along the coast are often formed by the convergence of katabatic winds and warmer marine air.

During the winter, the circulation of air around the continent is concentrated in a *polar vortex* that creates lenticular clouds above the pole. Scientists believe that ice crystals within these clouds tend to trap chlorofluorocarbons (CFC's) present in the upper atmosphere; in springtime, with the increase in solar radiation and dissipation of the polar vortex, the CFC's are released, creating a massive hole in the ozone layer di-

The World's Last Carbon Sink

As most of us are now aware, the recent (and ongoing) destruction of the world's tropical rainforests has severely reduced our biosphere's ability to trap carbon dioxide and convert it to oxygen, exacerbating the continued buildup in greenhouse gases and their atmospheric warming effect. As cold ocean water is capable of retaining high concentrations of dissolved carbon dioxide, the Southern Ocean may be considered one of the world's last remaining carbon traps or 'sinks,' and the phytoplankton that inhabit these waters the last 'untouched' converters of CO_2. However, records released from the British Antarctic Survey in 1994 reveal that average temperature on the Antarctic Peninsula has increased by 2.5° C since 1947, and the extent of both annual sea ice and many ice shelves has been significantly reduced, suggesting that temperatures in the Southern Ocean are either already on the rise or soon will be. If this tendency continues, retention and conversion of CO_2 in the Southern Oceans can only decline, further compounding the global warming cycle.

rectly above the pole. By November, most of the CFC's have been released, allowing the ozone hole to make a partial recovery, though ultraviolet radiation remains dangerously strong throughout the summer.

Precipitation in the Antarctic interior averages only 120-140mm per year, a figure similar to that of many deserts, while that along the coast and the Antarctic Peninsula ranges from 400-1,000mm a year. A similar contrast is noted in Antarctic ecosystems: while life in the interior is limited to a few resilient plants and highly adapted invertebrates, the marine ecosystem of the South-

PATRIOT HILLS, DEEP IN THE ANTARCTIC INTERIOR

ern Ocean and the Antarctic Peninsula is one of the most productive on earth. However, as its health depends almost entirely upon that of one species (krill, *Euphasia superba*), this is also one of the world's most fragile ecosystems. See  for more information on Antarctica's unique and uniquely endangered marine environment.

DISCOVERY AND EXPLORATION

Though the existence of a final continent in the unexplored expanses of the Southern Ocean had long been debated by European scholars and navigators, it wasn't until 1772 that any real information was obtained. Unsurprisingly, it was none other that **CAPTAIN JAMES COOK** who first ventured into the iceberg-strewn waters south of the Antarctic Circle. In his ship's log, Cook reports having discovered a region of 'countries condemned to everlasting rigidity by nature, never to yield to the warmth of the sun, for whose wild and desolate aspect I find no words.'

In the wake of Cook's discoveries, sealing (and later whaling) vessels invaded the Southern Ocean for a 40-year free-for-all, until the uncontrolled slaughter led to the near-extinction of fur and elephant seals – and with it the virtual end of the industry. In order to protect prime

ROBERT FALCON SCOTT

ally-sponsored scientific expeditions made tentative explorations of the Antarctic interior, using sledging techniques developed in the Arctic. One of the first of these, Belgian **ADRIEN DE GERLACHE'S** 1897 expedition aboard the *Belgica*, was trapped in pack ice, forced to winter over, and beset by scurvy and some frighteningly intense cases of cabin fever. But the stage had been set, and in the coming years, some of the greatest explorers of the era trained their sights on the world's last great frontier. The Heroic Age of Antarctic exploration had begun.

In 1902, **OTTO NORDENSKJOLD'S** Swedish South Polar Expedition established a camp on the shore of the Antarctic Peninsula and spent the winter – this time intentionally. At the end of the following summer, however, as Nordenskjold was preparing his return north, his ship too was destroyed in the pack ice, forcing him and his men to spend another winter on the shore of Paulet Island, where they built a stone shelter that stands to this day. Meanwhile, the British-sponsored expedition aboard the *Discovery*, commanded by **ROBERT FALCON SCOTT** and including a headstrong Irish lieutenant named **ERNEST SHACKLETON**, was wintering over on the far side of the continent, on the shores of the Ross Sea. Other expeditions around this time include **W.S. BRUCE'S** Scottish National Antarctic Expedition (1902-04), and **J.B. CHARCOT'S** 1903-05 French expedition aboard the *Porquoi Pas?*

The famous race to the South Pole began to reach its peak in 1907, when Shackleton – now a formidable leader in his own right – mounted his own expedition aboard the *Nimrod*, armed with a prototype motorcar and a stable of Siberian ponies. Though they did succeed in reaching the magnetic South

ERNEST
SHACKLETON

hunting grounds, however, most sealers were unwilling to share information, and improving maps of Antarctica was a much slower and more difficult task than it might have been.

Still, in the first half of the 19th century, many important contributions were made to our understanding of Antarctic geography. From 1819-21, Russian mariner **FABIAN GOTTLIEB VON BELLINGSHAUSEN** circumnavigated the continent at high latitude, crossing the Arctic circle six times; in 1823, English whaler **JAMES WEDDELL** first sailed into the Weddell Sea; and from 1840-44, a British expedition under **JAMES ROSS** used fortified ships to break through the pack ice, pioneering the route to the Ross Ice Shelf and a mountainous region they named Victoria Land, (its twin volcanoes, Erebus and Terror, were named after the expedition's ships.) From a scientific point of view, however, the 1838-42 United States Exploring Expedition under **CHARLES WILKES** stands alone in this era for the rigor and breadth of its discoveries.

The late 19th century brought a new era of Antarctic exploration, as the first nation-

THE *FARM* EXPLORING THE BAHIA DE LAS BALLENAS

AERIAL VIEW OF THE PENINSULA FIDES

Pole, Shackleton and his men were turned back by deteriorating weather less than a hundred miles from the geographic pole. Then, two years later, in an atmosphere of secrecy and fierce nationalism, Scott and Norwegian explorer **ROALD AMUNDSON** embarked on simultaneous attempts to reach the pole, Amundson with a stock of rugged Greenland sled dogs, Scott relying on manpower alone.

On December 14, 1911 Amundson and his men became the first to stand atop the pole; one month later, when Scott's party finally arrived, they found the Norwegian flag flapping in the Antarctic wind. Disheartened, and in steadily worsening weather, they began the return journey they would never complete. Scott's journal, found beside his frozen body the following November, reflected the nationalist spirit of the era:

> '...but for my own sake I do not regret this journey, which has shown that Englishmen can endure hardships, help one another, and meet death with as great a fortitude as ever in the past. We took risks, we knew we took them; things have come out against us, and therefore we have no cause for complaint, but bow to the will of providence, determined still to do our best to the last...Had we lived, I should have had a tale to tell of the hardihood, endurance, and courage of my companions which would have stirred the heart of every Englishman. These rough notes and our dead bodies must tell the tale, but surely, surely, a great rich country like ours will see that those who are dependent on us are properly provided for.'

However, the most fantastic of all Antarctic adventure stories was still to come: Ernest Shackleton's 1914 Trans-Antarctic Ex-

pedition, a bold attempt to cross the continent from one coast to another, beginning at the almost completely unexplored Weddell Sea. Before the party ever touched land, Shackleton's *Endurance* was trapped in the pack ice, and for ten months, he and his crew stuck by their ship as it drifted with the ice over a thousand miles north, before finally being crushed. Then, the 28 crew members squeezed aboard two tiny open boats and made for tiny Elephant Island, from which point Shackleton and five men set out for the insanely perilous 800-mile crossing to South Georgia Island. Incredibly, they survived the boat voyage and the arduous crossing of the island to the Stromness whaling station. Finally, after being transported to Punta Arenas and making three aborted attempts to rescue the rest of the crew, Shackleton returned to Elephant Island

ROALD AMUNDSON

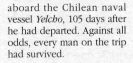

aboard the Chilean naval vessel *Yelcho*, 105 days after he had departed. Against all odds, every man on the trip had survived.

The final era of Antarctic exploration was led by US Naval pilot **RICHARD E. BYRD**, who in 1928 became the first to fly over the South Pole. The Heroic Age had given way to the Mechanized Age of Antarctic exploration.

ANTARCTICA TODAY

Today, the Antarctic continent is the only bit of land remaining on earth that does not 'belong' to anyone. All activity in Antarctica is currently governed by the **ANTARCTIC TREATY SYSTEM** (ATS), a singular assemblage of documents originally drafted in 1959, whose intent is to ensure that 'Antarctica shall continue for ever to be used exclusively for peaceful purposes and shall not become the scene or object of international discord.'

The ATS is currently adhered to by 44 member nations, 27 of which are involved in research projects in the frozen south, and seven of which actually claim a portion of Antarctica as their own. Though the ATS has put a freeze on all mineral exploration and discussion of ownership, it is not backed by any legal authority, and the effectiveness of the document is dependent upon the laws enacted by each member nation – a delicate situation, considering the fragility of the Antarctic environment.

ROALD AMUNDSON
IN EXPEDITION GEAR

TRAVELLING TO ANTARCTICA

The rapid growth of Antarctic tourism since the end of the Cold War has created myriad fears regarding its potential impact on these fragile ecosystems. In order to minimize this impact, all companies visiting Antarctica are required to adhere strictly to the protocols established by the Antarctic Treaty Organization, and all visitors should further adhere to the following guidelines, established by the International Association of Antarctic Tour Operators:

1. Maintain a safe distance from Antarctic animals. Do not attempt to touch or disturb them, and stay at least 15 feet (4.5m) away. If mammals or birds react to your presence, you are too close. Keep to the periphery of penguin and seabird nesting colonies; do not walk through nesting areas. Penguins have the right of way at all times; stop and wait for them to pass by. When approaching seals resting on a beach, walk inland and leave a path open to the sea for them. Fur seals deserve special precautions. They can move quickly and bite - remain at least 50 feet (15m) away at all times.

2. Do not collect or walk on plants. They are slow-growing and easily damaged.

3. Leave fossils and rocks where you find them.

4. Respect historic sites and the property and privacy of scientific stations.

5. Take your litter home with you. Leave nothing behind.

6. Antarctica can be a hazardous place. Avoid hidden dangers by keeping to established paths. Do not walk on undisturbed ground, large snowfields or sea ice. Stay with your group, stay alert and stay safe.

The majority of tours focus on the Antarctic Peninsula and the South Shetland islands, site of the continent's greatest concentration of scientific bases and research stations. Ushuaia is traditionally the last port of call for Antarctic cruise ships, while flights to Antarctica typically depart from Punta Arenas, and expedition sailboats may be booked out of Puerto Williams.

Navigation in Antarctica

The offering of nautical voyages to Antarctica is growing every year, and a simple internet search will provide the best overview of services. Boats range from small private yachts, to scientific vessels, to luxury cruise ships with a capacity of up to 500 passengers; trips booked in advance typically begin at about US$3500/pp for an 11-day cruise, to over US$12,000/pp for a month-long tour. Those with flexible schedules may also be possible to arrange less expensive trips on the spot in Ushuaia, depending upon availability. In any case, be sure to inquire carefully about ship personnel – any ship worth its salt should have at least a couple of specialists on hand to answer questions about the unique marine ecosystem of the Southern Ocean. Note that the following list of operators includes only those based out of Chile.

Operators: 230 - 236 - 237

Antarctic Flights

Flying to Antarctica is a good option for those without a week or more to spend aboard ship, or, alternately, for those set upon visiting the Antarctic interior. For the former, Aerovias DAP offers one – and two-day trips from their base in Punta Arenas to the Chilean scientific base at Villa Las Estrellas, on King George Island; the flights (aboard Twin Otter aircraft) last approximately 3-4hrs, and cost US$2500/pp for a one-day trip, US$3800/pp for an overnight, all included.

Located deep in the Antarctic interior at the base of the Ellsworth Mountains, **Patriot Hills** serves as base camp for ski traverses to the South Pole and mountaineering ascents of the Vinson Massif, the highest peak on the continent. The six-hour flight from Punta Arenas to Patriot Hills is made aboard a Hercules C-130 military plane, which lands upon a unique 'blue ice field' created by the scouring action of katabatic winds upon the surface of the ice cap. Currently, visits to Patriot Hills are arranged only through Adventure Network International (www.adventure-network.com), though plans are underway to open the Chilean base (nicknamed 'Blue Ice City') to civilian visitors.

Mount Vinson (4,897m)

First climbed in 1966, the Vinson Massif is most commonly targeted by climbers seeking to complete their tally of the coveted 'Seven Summits' – the highest peaks on each of the world's seven continents. The frigid weather poses the most significant challenge on this non-technical ascent, which typically takes a total of 7-10 days, including three high camps. Access to the Vinson base camp is by ski plane from Patriot Hills.

OUTFITTERS AND TOUR OPERATORS

INDEX

OUTFITTERS AND TOURS OPERATORS

Most guidebooks carry a similar disclaimer: prices change, places go out of business, new ones open up....

Chile is no exception to the rule – especially when you're talking about the fast-changing adventure travel industry. Over the course of four years, we've followed the dizzying (or dismal) trajectories of hundreds of operators of all sizes and orientations, and the best advice is to assume nothing.

This is not to say that there are no quality tour operators in Chile. To the contrary, many established operators and young startups offer their guests wonderful products and impeccable services. In many cases, tiny, family-run operations offer the best and most unique service of all – a sort of home-spun tourism that you won't find anywhere else.

In this directory we've included all the companies that have demonstrated dedicated market presence and a few latecomers whose services could not be excluded. We don't pretend to know every company or individual in Chile offering *turismo* of one variety or another, nor do we claim that the offering of adventure and special interest tours described in this book is completely exhaustive. Irregularities and omissions are unavoidable, and given the lack of industry standards, we've chosen not to rate the companies listed here. The assessment of competence remains a topic to be resolved between the operator and 'the client.' Best of luck.

1 **AcrossChile**
Av. Santa María 0172, Santiago
☎ (2) 7375131, fax (2) 7358406
info@acrosschile.com   www.acrosschile.com

2 **Adriazola Turismo Expediciones**
Santa Rosa 340, Puerto Varas
☎ (65) 233477, (09) 8886664, fax (65) 233477

3 **Aerotec**
Callao 2970 Of. 1011, Santiago
☎ (2) 2311645, fax (2) 2311645
aerotec@reuna.cl   www.chilnet.cl/aerotec

4 **Agencia de Turismo Manu Iti**
Tu'u Koihu s/n, Hanga Roa ☎ fax (32) 100313
hotelgomero@entelchile.net
http://ourworld.compuserve.com/homepages/hotelgomero

5 **Aku-Aku Turismo**
Tu'u Koihu s/n, Hanga Roa
☎ (2) 6332491, 6328173, ☎ fax (32) 100770
aku_aku@entelchile.net

6 **Alerce Andino Expediciones**
Pérez de Valenzuela 1098 Of. 69, Santiago
www.alerceandino.cl

7 **Alerce Mountain Lodge**
Casilla 411, Puerto Montt ☎ (65) 289969
smontt@telsur.cl

8 **Alsur Expediciones**
Del Salvador 100, Puerto Varas
☎ (65) 232300. fax (65) 232300
alsur@telsur.cl   www.puertovaras.com/alsur

9 **Altazor Skysports**
Serrano 145, Edificio Econorte, Of. 702, Iquique
☎ (57) 431382, 416208, fax (57) 431382, 416208
altazor@entelchile.net

10 **Altué Expediciones**
Encomenderos 83 Piso 2, Santiago
☎ (2) 2321103, 2332964, fax (2) 2336799
altué@netline.cl   www.altue.com

11 **Andean Rivers and Trails**
pablonegri@riosysenderos.com
www.riosysenderos.com

12 **Anden Sport Tours**
O'Higgins 535 A, Pucón
☎ (45) 441048, fax (45) 441236

13 **Andes Adventure Chile**
Gredos 7570, Santiago
☎ (2) 2111071, (09) 6295296, fax (2) 2111071
andes_adventure@entelchile.net www.andeschile.com

14 **Andescape Ltda.**
Eberhard 599, Puerto Natales
☎ (61) 412592, 412877, fax (61) 412592
andescape@chileaustral.com www.chileaustral.com/andescape

15 **Andes Flying School**
Fray Angelico 127, Santiago
☎ (2) 2101671, fax (2) 2011671
afschool@chilesat.net

16 **Andes Patagónicos**
Manuel Blanco Encalada 226, Puerto Natales
☎ (61) 411594, fax (61) 411594

17 **AndesTrek**
Av. Gabriel Dazarola 336, Villa Alemana
☎ (32) 956052, fax (32) 956052
andestrek@entelchile.net

18 **Aquamotion**
San Pedro 422, Puerto Varas
☎ (65) 232747, 235938, fax (65) 232747
aquamotn@telsur.cl   www.travelhouse.cl

19 **Archaeological Travel Service**
Av. Tu u Koihu, Hanga Roa
☎ (32) 100364, fax (32) 100284
archeots@rapanui.cl

20 **Area de Esqui Antuco**
O'Higgins 740, Concepción ☎ (41) 229054

21 **Arka Patagonia**
Magallanes 345, Punta Arenas
☎ (61) 248167, fax (61) 241504
turismo_arka@entelchile.net www.arkaoperadora.com

22 **Atacama Desert Expeditions**
Tocopilla 411, San Pedro de Atacama
☎ (55) 851045, 851145, fax (55) 851037
atacamadesert@adex.cl   www.adex.cl

23 **Atacama Inca Tour**
San Pedro de Atacama
☎ (55) 851062, 851034, fax (55) 851062
incatour@ctcreuna.cl

24 **Atmosfera 4**
Rosario Norte 90, Santiago
☎ (2) 2467922, 09) 8734386, fax (2) 2461545
contacto@atmosfera4.cl   www.atmosfera4.cl

25 **Austral Adventures**
Casilla 432, Ancud
☎ (65) 625977, fax (65) 625977
tours@austral-adventures.com www.austral-adventures.com

26 **Austral Exploraciones / Co-Kayak**
Casilla 896, San José 308 Piso 2, Puerto Varas
☎ (65) 346433, (09) 3105272
richard@whitewater.chile.ms

27 **Austro Hoteles**
Lautaro Navarro 1061, Pta. Arenas
☎ (61) 229920, 229512, fax (61) 229920, 229512
hgrey@ctcreuna.cl   www.chileaustral.com/grey

28 **Aventour Aventuras / Tierra del Fuego Lodge**
José Nogueira 1255, Punta Arenas
☎ (61) 220174, (61) 241197, fax (61) 243354
info@aventouraventura.com www.aventouraventuras.com

29 **Aventura Turismo**
12 Octubre 253, Coihaique
☎ (67) 234748, 238380, fax (67) 234748

30 **Aventurismo**
Casilla 134, Caldera ☎ (52) 316395
aventurismo@entelchile.net   www.aventurismo.cl

31 **Azimut 360**
General Salvo 159, Santiago
☎/fax (2) 2353085, (2) 2351519
azimut@terra.cl   www.azimut.cl
(or Caracoles s/n, San Pedro de Atacama
☎ (55) 851469, fax (55) 851469)

32 **Bahía Escocia Fly Fishing / Puntiagudo Lodge**
Casilla 1312, Osorno
☎ (09) 6434247, (64) 371515, 374731
desingklee@entelchile.net   www.bahiaescocia.co.cl

33 **Baqueano Zamora**
☎ (61) 412911, fax (61) 412911
baqueano@chileaustral.com www.chileaustral.com/baqueano

34 **Barcaza Crux Australis**
Av. Bulnes 05075, Punta Arenas
☎ (61) 218100, (61) 212126

35 **Bigfoot Patagonia**
Blanco Encalada 226-B, Puerto Natales
☎ (61) 414611, fax (61) 414276
explore@bigfootpatagonia.com
www.bigfootpatagonia.com

36 **Bio Bio Expeditions**
larsalvarez@compuserve.com   www.bbxrafting.com

37 **Birding Altoandino**
Correo Putre
☎ (58) 300013, fax (58) 222735
beknapton@hotmail.com www.birdingaltoandino.com

38 **Brisa Sur**
Cerro Colorado 5030 of. 513, Santiago
☎ (2) 3620565, fax (2) 3620566
brisa@usanet.cl

39 **Cabalgatas El Arrayán**
Los Refugios 17176, Santiago ☎ (2) 2183439

40 **Caballos de Bacher-Alm**
Casilla 92, Pucón ☎ (09) 8750425
pferdehans@hotmail.com

41 **Cabañas El Pangue**
☎ (67) 325128, 325211, fax (67) 325128, 325211
cpangue@entelchile.net

Cahuella
see Austral Adventures

42 **Callas Kzar and Yagan III**
see Transporte Maritimo Callas, Kzar and Yagan III

43 **Camping & Centro de Windsurf Los Alamos**
San Antonio 30, Santiago
☎ (2) 6393054, fax (2) 6393054

44 **Campo Chileno**
Casilla 265, Coihaique
domingo@campochileno.com www.campochileno.com

45 **Canoas Tours**
Rosario 1305, Puerto Varas ☎ (65) 233587

46 **Capitán Haase**
Walker Martínez 564, Puerto Varas
☎ (65) 235120, fax (65) 235166

47 **Carlos Whiting Expediciones**
☎ (09) 7771347
carloswhiting@tutopia.cl

48 **Casa Aventura**
Pasaje Galvez 11 cerro Alegre, Valparaíso
☎ (32) 755963, fax (32) 755963
casatun@ctcinternet.cl

49 **Cascada Expediciones**
Orrego Luco 040, Santiago
☎ (2) 2342274, 2327214, 2519223, fax (2) 2339768
info@cascada-expediciones.com
www.cascada-expediciones.com

Catamarán Hielos Patagónicos
see Turismo Hielos Patagónicos

50 **Catamaranes del Sur**
Isidora Goyenechea 3250 Of. 802, Santiago
☎ (2) 3337127, fax (2) 2329736
info@catamaranesdelsur.cl

51 **Cayutué Lodge**
☎ (65) 260627, fax (65) 233585
cayutue@entelchile.net   www.cayutue.com

52 **Centro de Buceo Ecosub**
Casilla 1296, Puerto Montt
☎ (65) 263939, fax (65) 250120
jeolivos@telsur.cl

53 **Centro de Buceo Magallanes**
ctorresd@entelchile.net

54 **Centro de Buceo Mike Rapu**
Caleta Hanga Roa s/n fax (32) 551055
mikerapudiving@entelchile.net

55 **Centro de Buceo Octopus**
Av. Libertad 1154 Casa C, Viña del Mar
☎ (32) 973857, fax (32) 973857
octopus@entelchile.net

56 **Centro de Buceo Orca**
Av. Pont s/n, Hanga Roa
☎ (32) 100375, fax (32) 100448
seemorca@entelchile.net   www.seemorca.co.cl

57 **Centro de Ski Chapa Verde**
Casilla 50 Correo 5, Rancagua
☎ (72) 217651, fax (72) 217651

58 **Centro de Ski Colorado Farellones**
Apoquindo 4900 Of. 47, Santiago
☎ (2) 2463344, fax (2) 2064078
colorado@ctcinternet.cl   www.elcoloradoski.cl

59 **Centro de Ski El Fraile**
Dussen 376, Coihaique
☎ (67) 231690, fax (67) 232970
digedercoyhaique@entelchile.net

60 **Centro de Ski La Parva**
La Concepción 266 Of. 301, Santiago
☎ (2) 2641466, fax (2) 2641569
www.laparva.cl

61 **Centro de Ski Lagunillas**
Municipalidad de San José de Maipo
☎ (2) 8611018, fax (2) 8611006

62 **Centro de Ski Las Araucarias**
Francisco Noguera 146, Santiago
☎ (2) 2349610, 2349611, fax (2) 2349608
publicidad@panamericanahoteles.cl
www.panamericanahoteles.cl

63 **Centro de Ski Lonquimay**
O'Higgins 796 Carrera 1115, Curacautín
☎ (45) 881166

64 **Centro de Ski Portillo**
Renato Sánchez 4270, Santiago
☎ (2) 2630606, 3617000, fax (2) 2630595
www.skiportillo.com

65 **Centro de Ski Termas de Chillán**
San Pío Décimo 2460 Of. 508, Santiago
☎ (2) 2331313, fax (2) 2315963
ventachi@termachillán.cl   www.skichillán.cl

66 **Centro Turístico y Deportivo Antillanca**
O'Higgins 1073, Osorno
☎ (64) 235114, fax (64) 238877
antillanca@telsur.cl

67 **Cerro Mirador / Club Andino de Punta Arenas**
Casilla 438, Punta Arenas
☎ (61) 241479, fax (61) 241479
capa-mag@ctcinternet.cl or cricco@cdmail.cl

68 **Chaitur**
Diego Portales 350, Chaitén
☎ (65) 731429, fax (65)731266
nchaitur@hotmail.com

69 **Chilean Travel Services**
Antonio Bellet 77 Of. 101, Santiago
☎ (2) 2510400, fax (2) 2510423
cts@ctsturismo.cl   www.ctsturismo.cl

70 **Chile Information Project**
Av. Santa Maria 227 Of. 12, Santiago
☎ (2) 7775649, fax (2) 7352267
anderson@chip.mic.cl   www.chip.cl

71 **Ciclomanía**
Huanhualí 900, La Serena
☎ (51) 210172, fax (51) 210172
http://usuarios.itn.cl/ciclomania   ciclomania@itn.cl

72 **Cinco Oceanos**
☎ (2) 2814145, (09) 8881126

73 **Civet**
Bolivar 684, Iquique ☎ (57) 428483, fax (57) 428483
civtcor@ctcinternet.cl

74 **Climbing Planet**
Av. Condell 703, Santiago
☎ (2) 634-6391, fax (2) 635-4516
climbingplanet@entelchile.net

75 **Complejo Turístico El Melado**
Av. 11 de Septiembre 2260 Local 100, Santiago
☎ (73) 211665, (2) 2334372, fax (73) 211665

76 **Cóndor Blanco**
☎ (2) 2080589, (09) 2229524
condorbl@chilesat.net   www.condorblanco.com

77 **Cosmo Andino Expediciones**
Caracoles s/n, San Pedro de Atacama
☎ (55) 851069, fax (55) 851156
cosmoandino@entelchile.net

78 **Cressi-Sub**
Av. Padre Hurtado 1549, Santiago ☎ (2) 2013766

79 **Cruce de Lagos**
marketing@crucedelagos.cl   www.crucedelagos.cl

80 **Crucero Bohemia**
Nautisur, Antonio Varas 949, Puerto Montt
☎ (65) 254675, fax (65) 256213

81 **Cruceros Australis**
El Bosque Norte 0440, Of. 1103, Santiago
☎ (2) 2035030, fax (2) 2035173
fruiztagle@australis.com   www.australis.com

82 **Cumilahue Lodge**
Casilla 2, Llifén ☎ (63) 481015, fax (63) 481015
adrian@anglingtours.com   www.anglingtours.com

Cutter 21 de Mayo
See Transporte Marítimo 21 de Mayo

83 **Desert Adventure**
Caracoles esq. Tocopilla, San Pedro de Atacama
☎ (55) 851067, fax (55) 851067
deserts@ctcinternet.cl
(or Antonio Varas 91 Local 209, Santiago
☎fax (2) 3660018, 3789730)

84 **Destination Management Chile**
Peumo 1185, Santiago
☎ (2) 3431334, fax (2) 3431393
dmcmana@dmcchile.cl   www.dmcchile.cl

85 **Diaguitas Tour**
Matta 510 of. 6 & /, La Serena
☎ (51) 214129, fax (51) 217265

86 **Dufflocq & Pumalino Angling Tours**
P.O. Box 558, Puerto Varas
☎ (65) 233585, fax (65) 233585
rioazul@chilesat.net   www.chilesat.net/estancia

87 **Dynevor Expeditions**
Casilla 171, Punta Arenas ☎ (61) 225888
dynevor@entelchile.net   www.sailingpatagonia.com

88 **Earth River Expeditions**
USA ☎ (914) 626-2665, fax (914) 626-4361
www.earthriver.com

89 **Eco-Adventure Radal**
Fundo Los Maitenes ☎ (2) 2442339, fax (2) 2442339
famclaussen@entelchile.net
www.geocities.com/famclaussen

90 **Ecolé - Adventures in the New World**
General Urrutia 592, Pucón ☎ (45) 441675
trek@ecole.cl   www.ecole-adventures.com

91 **EcoTravel**
Av. Costanera s/n, Puerto Varas
☎ (65) 233222, fax (65) 310644
ecotravel@entelchile.net

92 **Ecoturismo Puelche**
18 de Septiembre 373, Chillán
☎ (42) 224829, fax (42) 224829

93 **El Rincón**
Casilla 940, Los Angeles
☎ (09) 4415019, fax (43) 317168
elrincon@cvmail.cl

94 **Enbudelco**
Via Amarilla 9143, Santiago
☎ (2) 2426215, (09) 2217881, fax (2) 2426215
en_busca_del_condor@yahoo.com

95 Endémica Expediciones
San Juan Bautista, Isla Robinson Crusoe
☎ (32) 751077, 751023, (2) 3347841
endemica_exp@hotmail.com / endemica@ctcinternet.cl

96 Estancia Olga Teresa
Errázuriz 978, Apt. C, Punta Arenas
☎ (61) 311121, fax (61) 241310
olgateresa@chileanpatagonia.com

97 ET Divers
Concepción 479, Viña del Mar ☎ (32) 642684
etdivers@ctcreuna.cl

98 Expediciones Coihaique
Portales 195, Coihaique
☎ (67) 232300, fax (67) 232300
www.flyfishingexpedition.cl

99 Expediciones Cordillera
Manuel Rodríguez 712, Linares
☎ (73) 210240, fax (73) 219957

100 Expediciones Grado Diez
Las Urbinas 56, Santiago
☎ (2) 2344130, fax (2) 2344138

101 Expediciones Vicente Pérez Rosales
☎ (65)312524, (09) 6540567, fax (65)258042
contacto@petrohue.com

102 Explora Hotels
Américo Vespucio Sur 80, Piso 5, Santiago
☎ (2) 2066060, fax (2) 2284655
explora@entelchile.net
www.interknowledge.com/chile/explora

103 Exploraciones Lucas Bridges
Casilla 5, Coihaique ☎ (67) 233302, fax (67) 233302
www.aisen.cl

104 Fantástico Sur
Magallanes 960 Piso 2, Punta Arenas
☎ (61) 223442, (61) 226473, fax (61) 222641
birding@chileaustral.com   www.chilebirding.com

Foam
See Dynevor Expediciones

105 Futaleufú Adventure Center
USA 1-888-488-9082
office@kayakchile.com   www.kayakchile.com

106 GeoExpediciones
Camino al Volcán 07910, Las Vizcachas
☎ (2) 8424711
www.geoexpediciones.cl

107 Geotour
Baquedano 982 - Oficina 1, Iquique
☎ (57) 428984, fax (57) 428984
geotur@entelchile.net
(also Bolognesi 421, Arica
☎ (58) 253927, fax (58) 251675
geotour@entelchile.net)

108 Gran Hotel Pucón Resort & Club
Holzapfel 190, Pucón
☎ fax (45) 441001/ 002/ 003
ghp.guestservice@entelchile.net

109 Gray Fly Fishing
San Francisco 447, San José 192, Puerto Varas
☎ (65) 232136, (65)310734, fax (65) 232496
fishing@grayfly.com   http://grayfly.com

110 Hacienda Rupanco
Casilla 13-0, Osorno
☎ (64) 203000, fax (64) 203000, 203001

111 Hacienda Tres Lagos
Km 274 Carretera Austral Sur
☎ (67) 411323, fax (61) 411323
flyfishingchile@eurolatino.com.mx
www.flyfishing2000.com/haciendatreslagos

112 HI Divers
Av. Ossa 2259 B, Santiago
☎ (2) 2268746
hidiversrdc.net   http://fast.to/hidivers

113 Hostal Andino: Andisub Buceo
Viana 31, Viña del Mar
☎ (32) 690817, fax (32) 971996
http://fast.to/andisub

114 Hostal y Centro de Difusión Ecológico El Bosque
O'Higgins 424, Punta Arenas
☎ (65) 221764, fax (65) 224637
elbosque@patagonian.com

115 Hostería de La Patagonia
Camino Internacional Chacra 3-A, Chile Chico
☎ (67) 411337, 411965, fax (67) 411337, 411965

116 Hostería de Pesca Futaleufú Ltda.
Casilla 1238, Viña del Mar
☎ (32) 661840, fax (32) 812659
www.tbn-flyfishing.com

117 Hostería Riñimapu
Desagüe Lago Riñihue, Panguipulli
☎ fax (63) 311388   www.riñimapu.cl

118 Hot River
Camino al Volcán s/n, Melocotón ☎ (2) 8614230

119 Hotel Antumalal
km 2 camino Pucón - Villarica
☎ (45)441011, 441012, fax (45)441013
hotel@antumalal.com   www.antumalal.com

120 Hotel El Tatio
Caracoles 219, San Pedro de Atacama
☎ (55) 851092, 851263, 851264, fax (55) 851092
hoteleltatio@usa.net

121 Hotel Tulor
Domingo Atienza 523, San Pedro de Atacama
☎ (55) 851027, 851063

122 Hotelera Sudamericana
Av. Providencia 2331 Of. 602, Santiago
☎ (2) 3350579, 3350580, fax (2) 3350581
hotelsa@ctcinternet.cl   www.hotelsa.cl

123 Ingservtur
Matta 611, La Serena
☎ / fax (51) 220165
ingsvtur@ctcreuna.cl   www.cmet.net/ingsvtur

124 Intijalsu Tour
Prat 230, La Serena ☎ fax (51) 217945
intijalsu@entelchile.net   www.intijalsu.cv.cl

125 Isla Monita Lodge
Casilla 3390, Santiago
☎ (2) 2732198, fax (2) 2751898
www.islamonita.com

126 Isle de Paques Sejours
Av. Pont s/n, Hanga Roa ☎ (32) 100375, (32) 100448

127 Karanka Expeditions
Austral 05, Puerto Williams
☎ (61) 621043, fax (61) 621043
vademasi@ctcinternet.cl

128 Kayak Austral
☎ (65) 262104
kayakaustral@hotmail.com

129 Kia Koe Tour
Av. Policarpo Toro s/n, Hanga Roa ☎ (32) 100282

130 **Kila Leufu**
☎ (09) 7118064
margotex@yahoo.com

131 **La Baita**
PN Conguillío ☎ (45) 236037, fax (45) 264541
toy@chilesat.net

132 **La Herradura**
Tocopilla s/n, San Pedro de Atacama
☎ (55) 851087, fax (55) 851087

133 **LAN 4x4**
☎ (2) 7331345, (09) 8215824
lan4x4@ctcinternet.cl

134 **Lancha Ventisquero**
Presidente Ibáñez 202, Coihaique
☎ (67) 232234, fax (67) 232234

135 **LASSA**
Av. Larraín 7941, Aerodromo Tobalaba
☎ (2) 2735209, 2731458, fax (2) 2734309

136 **Latinorizons**
Bolognese 449, Arica
☎ (58) 250007, fax (58) 250007
latinor@entelchile.net   www.latinorizons.com

137 **Latitud 90**
Pedro de Valdivia 048 Of.31, Santiago
☎ (2) 2342430, fax (2) 2344036
info@latitud90.com   www.latitud90.com

138 **Lodge Río Baker**
Puerto Bertrand ☎ (67) 411499

139 **Lodge Saltamontes**
Casilla 565, Coihaique ☎ fax (67) 232779
info@theflyshop.com

140 **Los Patiperros**
Av. Chorrillos 1226 San javier
☎ (73) 322342, fax (73) 322342
lospatiperros@yahoo.com

141 **Los Quetros**
Alcalde Bertin 554, Osorno
☎ (64) 232781, 254195, fax (64) 232781
arcoiris@telsur.cl

142 **Maggi's Horse Stables**
P.O. Box 463, Los Angeles ☎ (43) 371538
bobbowden@entelchile.net

143 **Maricunga Expediciones**
Maipú 580-B, Copiapó
☎ (52) 210075, fax (52) 211191
www.exploreatacama.cl

144 **Marina del Sur**
Apartado Postal 13, Puerto Montt
☎ (65) 251958, 250815, fax (65) 251958
marinadelsur@yahoo.com

145 **Mario's Fishing Zone**
O'Higgins 590, Pucón ☎ (09) 8898624

146 **Mincho's Lodge**
☎ (67) 233240 - 09 8716066
vmoya@entelchile.net

147 **M/N Pamar**
Casilla 780, Puerto Varas
☎ (65) 234301, (09) 6448979, fax (65) 235888
rbourdel@entelchile.net   www.pamar.co.cl

148 **MotoAventura**
Casilla 1336, Osorno
☎ (64) 249121, fax (64) 249123
rbaum@entelchile.net   www.motoaventura.co.cl

149 **Motonave Isla del Río**
Puerto Fluvial, Valdivia ☎ (63) 225244

150 **Motu Tours**
Avareipua s/n, Hanga Roa ☎ fax (32) 100438
motutour@rapanui.cl

151 **Mountain Service**
Santa Magdalena 75 of. 306, Santiago
☎ (2) 2343439, fax (2) 2343438
mountainservice@entelchile.net www.mountainservice.cl

152 **Multi Tour**
Bulnes 307 Piso 2 Of. 202, Temuco
☎ (45) 237913, fax (45) 233536
cinopa@entelchile.net   www.chile-travel.com/

153 **Naturalis Expediciones**
☎ (2) 2143544, fax (2) 2143544
naturalis@terra.cl   www.naturalis.cl

154 **Nautisur**
Antonio Varas 949, Puerto Montt
☎ (65) 254675, fax (65) 256213
nautisur@telsur.cl

155 **Naviera del Sur**
21 de Mayo 1460, Punta Arenas
☎ (61) 674837, fax (61)248848

156 **Oceano Aventura**
Gabriella Mistral 57, Caldera ☎ (52) 315921

157 **Onas Patagonia**
Blanco Encalada 599, Casilla 78, Puerto Natales
☎ (61) 414349, fax (61) 412707
onas@chileaustral.com   www.chileaustral.com/onas

158 **Opentravel**
P.O. Box 1010, Puerto Montt
☎ (65) 260524, fax (65) 260524
opentravel@entelchile.net   www.opentravel.com.ar

159 **Osorno Chile Aventur**
Av. Zenteno 1203, Osorno
☎ (64) 238632, 255350, fax (64) 238632
eschmitt@entelchile.net www.osornoguia.co.cl/aventur

160 **Pacific Images**
Te Pito o Henua s/n, Hanga Roa
☎ fax (32) 100600
pacific_images@entelchile.net   www.osterinsel.net

161 **Palestra: El Gimnasio**
Av. Vitacura 5760, Santiago
☎ (2) 2182917, fax (2) 2191247

162 **Pangea Expediciones**
Casilla 332, San Pedro de Atacama
☎ (55) 851111, fax (55) 851111
pangeaexp@yahoo.com

163 **Parapente Aventura**
Casilla 19 Correo Maitencillo
☎ (32) 770019, (9) 3322426, fax (32) 770029
bengala@ctcinternet.cl   www.parapente-aventura.cl

164 **Pared Sur**
Juan Esteban Montero 5497, Santiago
☎ (2) 2073525, 2073160, fax (2) 2073159
paredsur@iactiva.cl   www.paredsur.cl

165 **Patagonia Adventure Expeditions**
☎ (67) 411330, Fax (67) 219894
riobaker@entelchile.net www.adventurepatagonia.com

166 **Patagonia Baker Lodge**
☎ (2) 2191097, (67) 411903

167 **Patagonia Connection**
Fidel Oteíza 1921 Of. 1006, Santiago
☎ (2) 2256489, fax (2) 2748111
info@patagoniaconnex.cl   www.patagoniaconnex.cl

168 **Patagonia Ice**
Casilla 76, Puerto Natales
☎ (61) 410630, fax (61) 410630, 411443

169 **Path@Gone**
Eberhard 595, Puerto Natales
☎ (61) 413291, fax (61) 413290
pathgone@chileaustral.com
www.chileaustral.com/pathgone

170 **Pietro 4WD**
Casilla 123, Iquique
☎ (09) 8490077, (57) 412943
plazaro@entelchile.net
www.geocities.com/pietro_malatesta

171 **Planeta Aventura**
Caracoles s/n, San Pedro de Atacama
☎ (55) 851023, 851173, fax (55) 851156
planeta@ctcreuna.cl

172 **Politour**
O'Higgins 635, Pucón
☎ (45) 441373, fax (45) 441373
turismo@politur.com   www.politur.com

173 **Powderquest Tours**
US ☎ (800) 5657158, (804) 2854961, (240) 2094312
info@powderquest.com   www.powderquest.com

174 **Puerto Viejo Lodge**
Casilla 74, Puerto Octay
☎ (64) 391244, fax (64) 391244

175 **Pura Vida Expediciones**
Lista de Correo, Futaleufu
puravidaexpediciones@hotmail.com
www.cuscoperu.com/puravida

176 **Rancho de Caballos**
Casilla 142, Pucón ☎ (45) 441575, fax (45) 441604

177 **Rapa Nui Travel**
Tu'u Koihu s/n, Hanga Roa ☎ (32) 100548, fax
rntravel@entelchile.net

178 **Río Paloma Lodge**
☎ (67) 231257

179 **Río Puelo Lodge**
Casilla 157 Correo 34, Puerto Montt
☎ (2) 9601001, fax (2) 9601002
merex@entelchile.net

180 **Río Salvaje Lodge**
☎ (65) 217201, fax (65) 217201

181 **River Jet**
M.A. Matta 595 Of. 1, Osorno
☎ (64) 203373, (09) 8830263, (09) 8830264
river-jet@entelchile.net

182 **Roberto Alegría**
Marañón 1126, Vallenar
☎ (51) 613865 - 613908, fax (51) 613908
roalol@entelchile.net

183 **Ruca Chalhuafe**
La Cascada El Salto, km 11, Camino Ensenada a Cascada
☎ fax (65) 233970, (02) 2222222
barrena@telsur.cl   www.rucachalhuafe.cl

184 **Salvaje Corazón**
Casilla 311, Coihaique ☎ (67) 211488
info@salvajecorazon.com   www.salvajecorazon.com

185 **San Bartolomé**
Balmaceda 417 of. 27, La Serena
☎ (51) 211670, fax (51) 221992
sanbartolome@entelchile.net

186 **San Francisco de los Andes**
Casilla 5-A, Los Andes
☎ (34)488513, (2) 2456163, fax (2) 2450662
sf@sf.cl   www.sf.cl

Skorpios
See Turismo Skorpios

187 **Sky Adventure**
☎ (2) 2192115, (09) 8882371
skyadv@rdc.cl   www.skyadventure.cl

188 **Sociedad Turismo Rucaray Ltda.**
Teniente Merino 668, Puerto Aisén
☎ (67) 332862, 332725, fax (67) 332725
rucaray@entelchile.net

189 **Sol y Nieve**
O'Higgins esq. Lincoyán, Pucón
☎ (45) 441070, fax (45) 441070
www.chile-travel.com/solnieve.htm

190 **Southern Chile Expeditions**
Casilla 197, Puerto Varas
☎ (65) 213030, fax 212031
www.southernchilexp.com

191 **Southern Cross Adventure**
José Miguel de la Barra 521 Dp.4E, Santiago
☎ fax (2) 6396591
adventure@scadventure.com   www.scadventure.com

192 **Sportstour Turismo Ltda.**
Moneda 970 Piso 14, Santiago
☎ (2) 5495200, fax (2) 6982981
mailbox@sportstour.cl   www.chilnet.cl/sportour

193 **Suizandina Lodge**
Casilla 44, Curacautín ☎ (09) 8849541
                                    www.suizandina.com

194 **SurAmerica Expediciones**
Punta de Piedra, camino Concón-Quintero
☎ (09) 8869482
suramerica@hotmail.com   www.suramerica.cl

195 **Sur Kayak**
☎ (2) 2072035, (09) 8296387
caguayo@ctcinternet.cl   www.surkayak.cl

196 **Surire Tour**
Baquedano 1035, Iquique
☎ (57) 411795, fax (57) 411795

197 **Surweste Yacht Charters**
Casilla 496, Viña del Mar
☎ (65) 293813, (09) 3315115, fax (65) 293813
leyenda@telsur.cl

Terra Australis
See Cruceros Australis

198 **Terracota Expediciones**
Agustinas 1547 Of. 705, Santiago ☎ (2) 6988121
natalia@terracotachile.cl

199 **Terra Incógnita**
Casilla 92 Correo 30, Santiago
☎ (2) 2028761, fax (2) 2028761
terrainc@entelchile.net

200 **Track-Aventura**
Las Lilas 6, Copiapó
☎ (52) 212714, (09) 4632196, fax (52) 212714

201 **Tranco Expediciones**
Puerto Varas ☎ fax(65) 311311
trancoaventura@yahoo.com   www.trancoexpediciones.cl

202 **Transbordadora Austral-Broom**
Av. Bulnes 05075, Punta Arenas
☎ (61) 218100, fax (61) 212126
tabsa@entelchile.net

203 **Transporte Marítimo Cutter 21 de Mayo**
Eberhard 554, Puerto Natales
☎ (61) 411978, fax (61) 411978
21demayo@chileaustral.com
www.chileaustral.com/21demayo

204 **Transporte Marítimo Callas, Ksar y Yagan III**
Juana Fadul 26, Ushuaia (Arg.)
☎ (54)901-33622, fax (54) 901-30707
allpat@satlink.com www.tierradelfuego.org/allpatagonia

205 **Travel Art**
Casilla 402, Puerto Varas
☎ (65) 232198, fax (65) 234818
info@travelart.cl   www.travelart.cl

206 **Travellers**
Casilla 854, Puerto Montt
☎ (65) 262099, fax (65) 258555
travlers@chilesat.net   www.travellers.cl

207 **Trawen Outdoor Center**
O'Higgins 311 Loc. 5, Pucón ☎ (45) 442024
trawen@entelchile.net   www.trawen.cl

208 **Turavent en Bahía Escondida**
Baquedano 103, Coihaique
☎ (61) 231872, fax (61) 231872

209 **Turismo Buenaventura**
Sotomayor 1959, Calama
☎ (55) 341882, fax (55) 341882
buenaventur@entelchile.net

210 **Turismo Cabo de Hornos**
Agustinas 814 Of. 706, Santiago
☎ (2) 6339119, fax (2) 6339119
cabo@chilesat.net

211 **Turismo Comapa**
Av. Independencia 830, Piso 2, Punta Arenas
☎ (61) 241322, 241437, 200200, fax (61) 225804
tcomapa@entelchile.net   www.comapa.com

212 **Turismo Corvatsch**
Antofagasta s/n, San Pedro de Atacama
☎ (55) 851101

213 **Turismo Ecuestre Huepil**
☎ (09) 4534212

214 **Turismo El Caminante Ltda.**
Casilla 143, Talca
☎ (71) 370097, fax 214226, (09) 4190625
casachueca@hotmail.com   .

215 **Turismo El Caulle**
Los Carrera 1145 Of. 15/19, Osorno
☎ (64) 233233, fax (64) 233233

216 **Turismo Hielos Patagónicos**
Boliviana 629, Punta Arenas
☎ (61) 220345, fax (61) 220345
lastorres@chileaustral.com
www.chileaustral.com/lastorres

217 **Turismo Los Canales**
Correo Puerto Raúl Marín Balmaceda
☎ (65) 681485, fax (65) 681485

218 **Turismo Ochoa**
Caracoles s/n, San Pedro de Atacama
☎ (55) 342479, fax 342479

219 **Turismo Pehuén**
Blanco 299, Castro
☎ (65) 635254, 632361, fax 635254
pehuentr@entelchile.net   www.pehuentour.com

220 **Turismo Rucahue**
Valle Las Trancas
☎ (42) 236162, fax (42) 236162

221 **Turismo Skorpios**
Augusto Leguía Norte 118, Santiago
☎ (2) 2311030, fax (2) 2322269
skorpios@tmm.cl   www.skorpios.cl

222 **Turismo Trancura**
O'Higgins 221-C, Pucón
☎ (45) 441189, fax (45) 441189
turismo@trancura.com   www.trancura.com

223 **Turismo Turavión**
Av. Apoquindo 3000, piso 3, Santiago
☎ (2) 3300860, fax (2) 3344435
turavion@entelchile.net

224 **Turismo Valle del Palena**
Correo Raúl Marín Balmaceda
☎ (65) 681151, fax (65) 681151

225 **Turismo Viento Sur**
Calle Fagnano 585, Puerto Natales
☎ (61) 225167, 226930, fax (61) 225167, 226930
vientosur@chileaustral.com   www.vientosur.com

226 **Turismo Yamana**
Casilla 556, Punta Arenas
☎ (61) 221130, fax (61) 240056
yamana@chileaustral.com www.chileaustral.com/yamana

227 **Turismo Yekchal**
Oficina Comercial Eberhard 564-A, Puerto Natales
☎ (61) 412530, 413591, fax (61) 412530, 413591
yekchal@entelchile.net www.patagoniayekchal.co.cl

228 **Valle Nevado**
Gertrudis Echeñique 441, Santiago
☎ (2) 2060027, fax (2) 2080695
info@vallenevado.com   www.vallenevado.com

229 **Victoria Tours**
Los Navegantes 1983, Santiago
☎ (2) 3343775, (2) 2328163
puelo@terra.net

230 **Victory Yacht Cruises**
Casilla 70, Puerto Williams
☎ (61) 621010, fax (61) 621008
victory@entelchile.net http://www.fcmr.com/victory

231 **Vicuña Tours**
Colón 650 Of. 133, Arica
☎ (58) 253773, fax (58) 253773

232 **Weche Ruka**
Comidad Juan Antonio Hueche, Sector Palihue,
Comuna Padre de las Casas, Temuco
☎ (45) 232793

233 **Windsurfing Chile**
Las Carmelitas 30, Santiago
☎ (2) 2156089, fax (2) 2115735

234 **Xalpen**
info@xalpen.com   www.xalpen.com

235 **Yak Expediciones**
Nocedal 7135, Santiago
☎ fax (2) 2270427
info@yakexpediciones.cl www.seakayaking-patagonia.com

Yate Arco Iris
See Turismo Los Quetros

236 **Yate Gondwana**
Correo Puerto Williams ☎ (61) 621177

237 **Yate Santa María**
Austral 200, Puerto Williams
☎ (61) 621017

238 **Yelcho La Patagonia**
Fundo Rucanpangue, Carretera Austral, Chaitén
☎ (65) 731337, fax (65) 731337
yelcho@chilnet.cl   www.yelcho.corp.cl

INDEX

ATLAS

GENERAL SYMBOLOGY

ROAD SURFACES

▬▬▬▬	Pavement
▬ ▬ ▬	Gravel Dirt
───────	Earth

ROAD CATEGORIES

▬▬▬▬	Highway
▬▬ ▬ ▬▬	Principal
▬ ▬ ▬	Primary
▬ ▬ ───	Secondary
░░░░░░░	Under Construction

SETTLEMENTS

IQUIQUE	Regional Capital
CALAMA	Provincial Capital
Caldera	Comunal Capital
La Herradura	City or Town
Quinchamali	Village
Puerto Yungay	Rural Settlement

CITY POPULATION

⬭	Over 10,000
⊙	5,001 to 10,000 inhab.
⊕	1,001 to 5,000 inhab.
o	less than 1,000 inhab.

BORDERS AND GEOGRAPHICAL AREAS

─ ─ ─	Internacional Border
────	Regional Border
▭▭▭	National Park Border
░░░░	Sal Flats
▨▨▨	Glaciers and Icefields

OTHER

⊶⊶⊷	Railroad
★ 14 ★	Distance between
Ⓕ	Fuel
🛡	Police
◆	Border control w/Policia International
◇	Border control w/out Policia International
🅿	Toll booth
◉-◉	Weigh station
✈	Airport
✗	Airfield
⛪	Parks and protected areas
▲	Major peak
⛷	Ski area
⫿⫿	Waterfall
⛺	Campground

ROAD MAPS

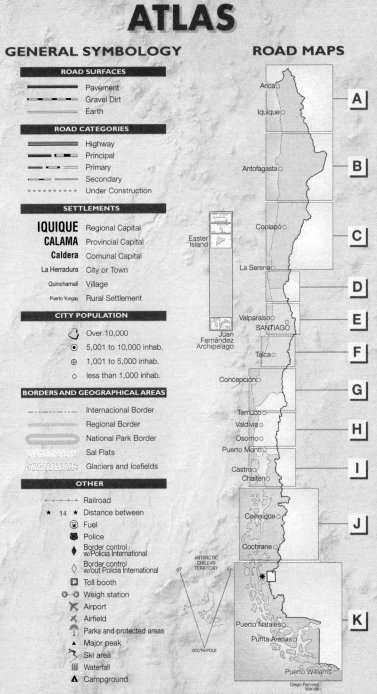

Arica ○ **A**

Iquique ○

Antofagasta ○ **B**

Copiapó ○ **C**

Easter Island

La Serena ○ **D**

Valparaíso ○ **E**
SANTIAGO ○

Juan Fernández Archipelago

Talca ○ **F**

Concepción ○ **G**

Temuco ○ **H**
Valdivia ○
Osorno ○
Puerto Montt ○ **I**

Castro ○
Chaitén ○

Coihaique ○ **J**

Cochrane ○

ANTARTIC CHILEAN TERRITORY

90° 53°

★

SOUTH POLE

Puerto Natales ○ **K**
Punta Arenas ○

Puerto Williams ○

Diego Ramírez Islands

★ "Agreement between Chile and Argentina to determine precise borders between Monte Fitz-Roy and Cerro Daudet". (Buenos Aires, Dec 16, 1998).

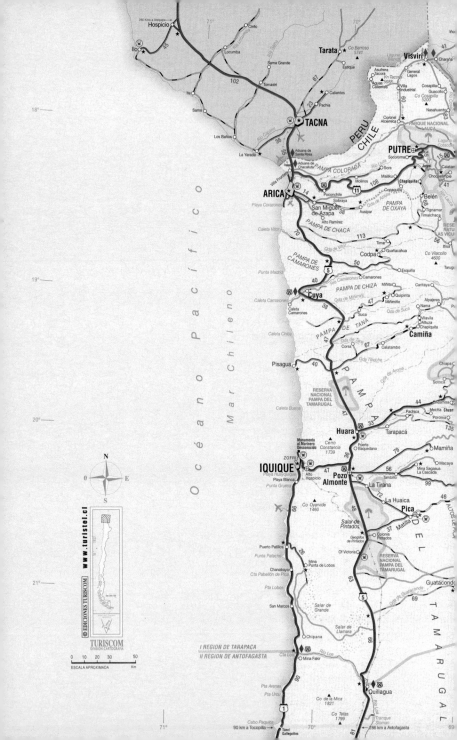

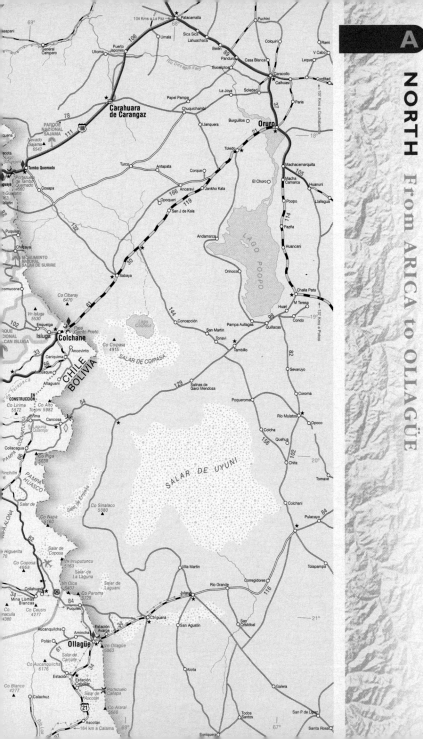

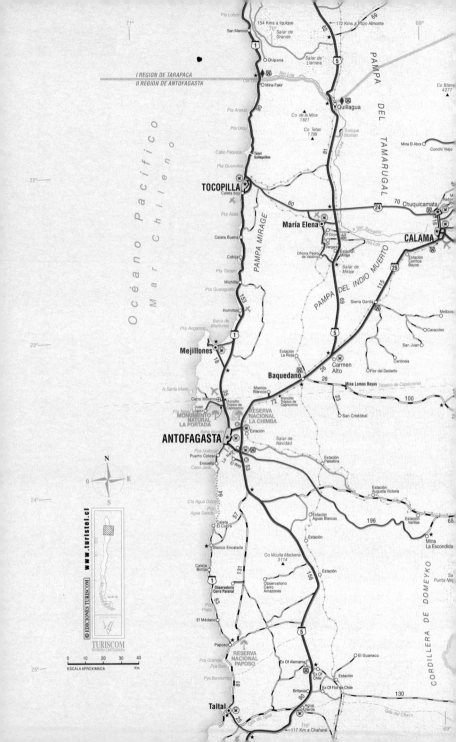

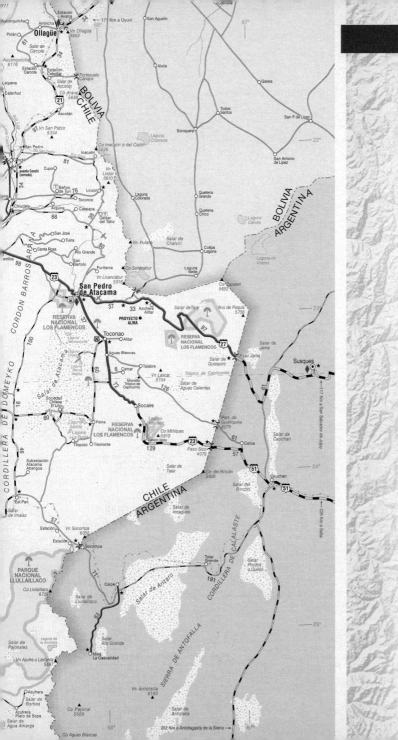

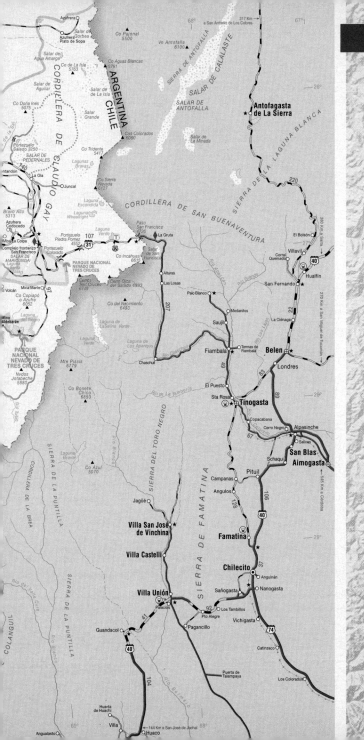

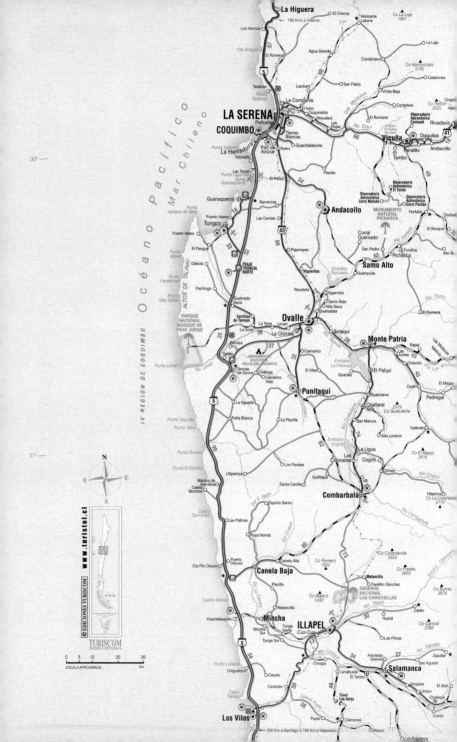

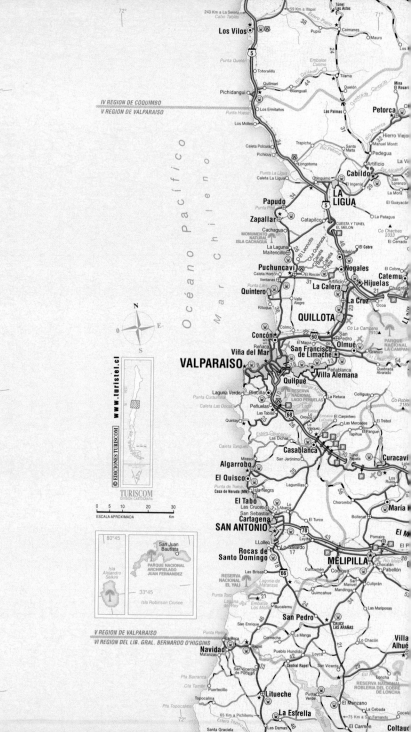

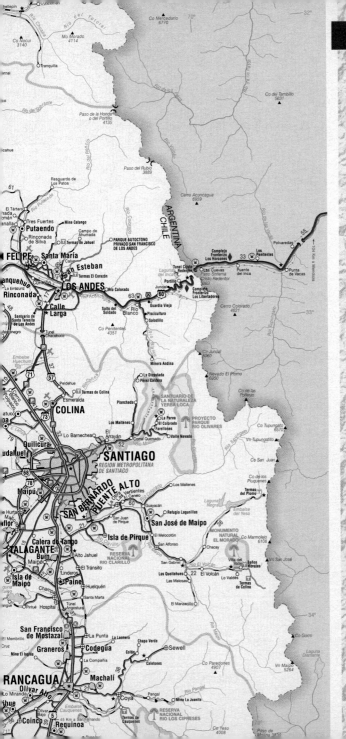

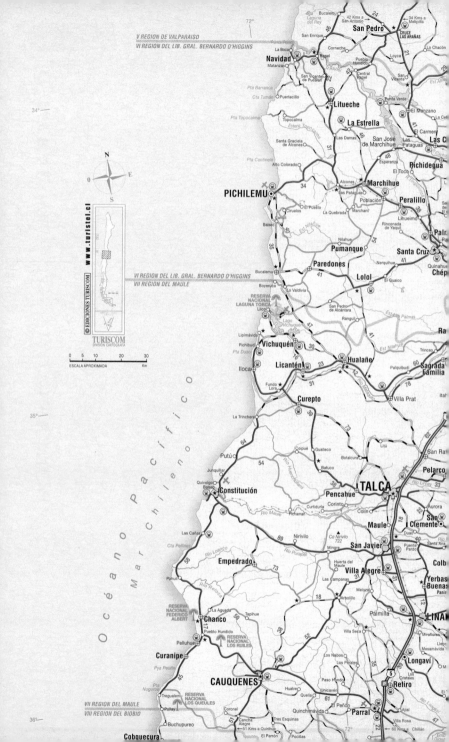

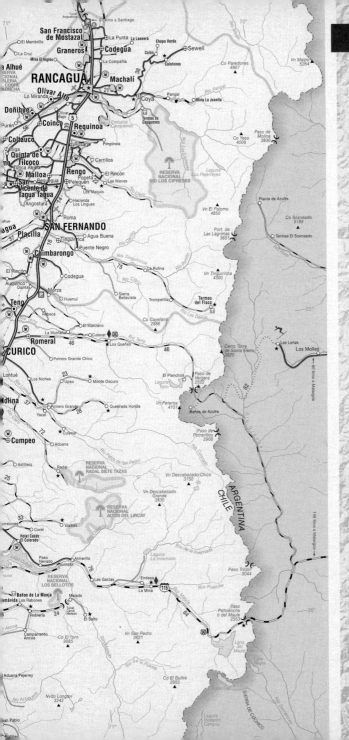

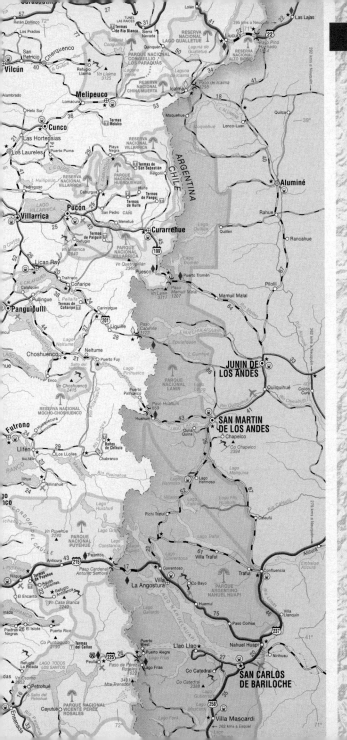

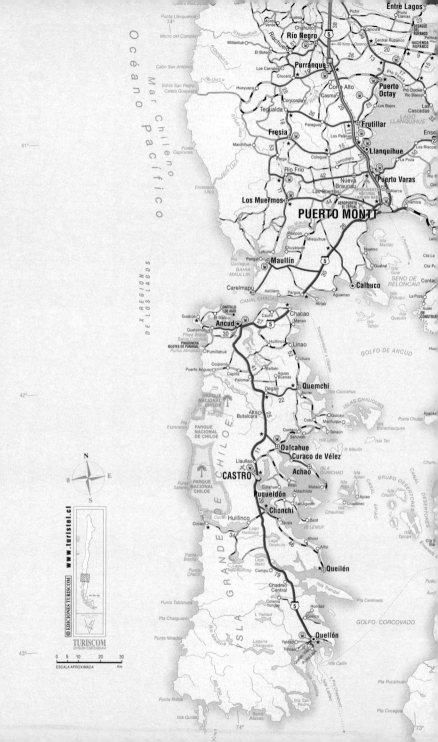

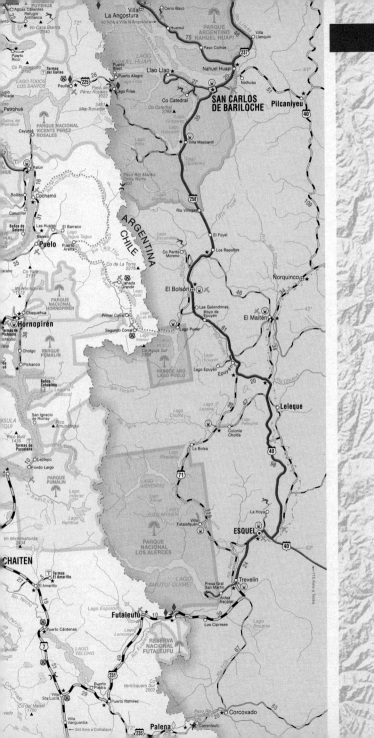

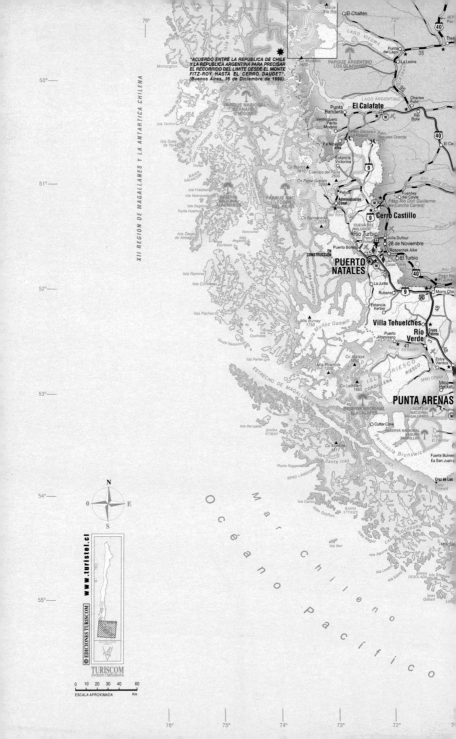